MATTHEW

A SHORTER COMMENTARY

MATTHEW

A SHORTER COMMENTARY

EDITED BY
DALE C. ALLISON, JR.

T & T CLARK INTERNATIONAL
A Continuum imprint
LONDON • NEW YORK

Copyright © 2004 T&T Clark International

A Continuum imprint

Published by T&T Clark International
The Tower Building, 11 York Road, London SE1 7NX
15 East 26th Street, Suite 1703, New York, NY 10010

www.tandtclark.com

British Library Cataloguing-in-Publication Data
A catalogue record for this book is available from the British Library

ISBN 05670 82393 (hardback)
05670 82490 (paperback)

Typeset by BookEns Ltd, Royston, Herts.
Printed on acid-free paper in Great Britain by Antony Rowe Ltd, Chippenham, Wilts.

CONTENTS

PREFACE

This book appears at the request of Geoffrey Green of T&T Clark, who invited me to prepare a shorter version of the three-volume International Critical Commentary on Matthew. It is intended to serve readers who find the larger commentary too involved or too difficult. The present work comments not on the Greek text but on my own English translation; it avoids most discussions of historicity and tradition-history; it offers far less documentation for its claims both about antiquity and scholarly opinion; and it abbreviates discussions of exegetical options and problems. Readers who wish for more details and for more arguments for positions taken herein will need to turn to the three volumes and the documentation offered there.

The longer commentary appeared in 1988, 1991, and 1997. Much relevant secondary literature has appeared since then, and I have also changed my mind about this and that. The present commentary, however, is not the place to introduce serious alterations. So this shorter work departs only on occasion from the longer one. Extensive revisions, corrections and additions will have to await a thorough revision of the longer commentary.

COMMENTARIES

Readers desiring to pursue further the study of Matthew may wish to consult the following English-language commentaries:

Allison, Dale C., Jr. *The Sermon on the Mount: Inspiring the Moral Imagination*. New York: Crossroads, 1999.

Betz, Hans Dieter. *The Sermon on the Mount: A Commentary on the Sermon on the Mount, including the Sermon on the Plain (Matthew 5:3–7:27 and Luke 6:20–49)*. Hermeneia. Minneapolis: Fortress, 1995.

Calvin, John. *A Harmony of the Gospels: Matthew, Mark, Luke*. 3 vols. Grand Rapids: Eerdmans, 1972.

Carter, W. *Matthew and the Margins: A Sociopolitical and Religious Reading*. Maryknoll: Orbis, 2000.

Chrysostom, John. *Homilies on the Gospel of Saint Matthew, in Nicene and Post-Nicene Fathers*, volume 10.

Clarke, Howard. *The Gospel of Matthew and Its Readers*. Bloomington/Indianapolis: Indiana University Press, 2003.

Davies, Margaret. *Matthew: Readings*. Sheffield: JSOT, 1992.

France, R. T. *Matthew*. Grand Rapids: Eerdmans, 1985.

Garland, David. *Reading Matthew*. New York: Crossroad, 1993.

Guelich, Robert. *The Sermon on the Mount: A Foundation for Understanding*. Waco: Word, 1982.

Gundry, Robert. *Matthew: A Commentary on his Literary and Theological Art*. 2nd edn. Grand Rapids: Eerdmans, 1994.

Hagner, Donald A. *Matthew*. 2 vols. Word Biblical Commentary 33A, B. Dallas: Word, 1993, 1996.

Hare, Douglas R. A. *Matthew. Interpretation*. Louisville: John Knox, 1993.

Harrington, D. *The Gospel of Matthew*. Sacra Pagina. Collegeville: Liturgical, 1991.

Keener, Craig S. *Commentary on the Gospel of Matthew*. Grand Rapids: Eerdmans, 1999.

Luz, Ulrich. *Matthew*. 2 vols. Minneapolis: Fortress, 1989, 2001.

Meier, J. P. *Matthew*. Wilmington: Michael Glazier, 1981.

Patte, Daniel. *The Gospel According to Matthew*. Philadelphia: Fortress, 1987.

Schweizer, E. *The Good News According to Matthew*. Atlanta: John Knox, 1975.

Senior, D. *Matthew*. Nashville: Abingdon, 1998.

Theophylact. *Matthew*. House Springs, MO: Chrysostom Press, 1993.

The commentaries of Davies, France, Garland, Hare, Harrington, Meier, Schweizer, and Senior are all easily accessible. Those of Carter, Gundry, Hagner, Keener, and Patte are more demanding.

Luz's scholarly commentary (which will be three volumes when it is completed in its English translation) is most valuable for its extensive materials on the history of the interpretation of Matthew. Clarke's more popular and often entertaining work also approaches Matthew from this angle.

Regarding the sermon on the mount, my own theological commentary carries forward the exegesis found herein. Betz is important and rewarding but much more difficult. Guelich's commentary remains a standard.

As for older commentaries, those of Chrysostom and Theophylact are good representatives of patristic and Byzantine work, and Calvin always repays reading.

INTRODUCTION

AUTHORSHIP

Eusebius, *H.E.* 3.39, attributes to Papias, a second-century Bishop of Hierapolis in Asia Minor, the earliest testimony to Matthew's authorship: 'Now Matthew made an ordered arrangement of the oracles in the Hebrew (or: Aramaic) language, and each one translated (or: interpreted) it as he was able.' These words and the traditional title, 'According to Matthew', presumably added in the first half of the second century, show that not long after it was written people attributed our Gospel to the disciple named in Mt 9.9; 10.3. Because the tradition is early, and because the apostle Matthew is a relatively unimportant figure in early Christian literature, the attestation still has its defenders.

Most, however, now doubt the tradition. (i) Papias and others after him consistently associate Matthean authorship with a Semitic original. Our Gospel, however, is not written in translation Greek. (ii) It is improbable that a Semitic document would have incorporated, as does Matthew, a Greek document (Mark) almost in its entirety; see below. (iii) Would an apostle who accompanied Jesus have used so little personal reminiscence but rather have followed Mark as closely as he has? (iv) Papias' tradition might have originally referred to one of Matthew's sources and then, when that source disappeared, have been connected with Matthew. It was common enough for a document to carry the name of the author of one of its sources.

These points are sufficiently strong that in the present commentary 'Matthew' will be used of the author without any claim to his apostolic identity. On one point, however, the tradition is correct: the author was a Jew. The Gospel has numerous Jewish features which cannot be attributed to tradition. These include the play on the Hebrew name of David in 1.2–17, OT texts seemingly translated from the Hebrew specifically for our Gospel (e.g. 2.18; 8.17; 12.18–21), concentrated focus on the synagogue (e.g. 6.1–18; 23.1–39), and affirmation of the abiding force of the Mosaic law (5.17–20). Matthew alone moreover records Jesus' prohibitions against mission outside Israel (10.5; 15.24), disparages Gentiles as such (5.47; 6.7), and shows concern that eschatological flight not occur on a Sabbath (24.20). These and other Jewish features have not been sprinkled here and there for good effect: they are an organic part of the whole and imply a Jewish-Christian author and audience.

DATE

The Gospel probably appeared between AD 70 and 100, most likely between 80 and 95.

(i) Although some scholars deny that the early apostolic Fathers betray certain knowledge of canonical Matthew, this is not a satisfactory judgement. Leaving aside the possibility that either the author of the Fourth Gospel (cf. Mt 10.24–5 with Jn 13.16) or the author of 1 Peter (cf. 1 Pet 2.12 with Mt 5.16, 1 Pet 3.14 with Mt 5.10) knew Matthew, both the writings of Ignatius of Antioch (d. c. AD 107) and the *Didache* (first half of the second century AD?) exhibit likely dependence upon the First Gospel. Further, Papias (see above), Polycarp (d. c. AD 156), the *Epistle of Barnabas* (ca. AD 135), and Justin Martyr (c. AD 100–165) all knew and used Matthew, which must accordingly have been in circulation by the year 100.

(ii) If, as seems likely, Matthew used Mark, and if Mark was, as current opinion holds, put together in the 60s or very shortly after the fall of Jerusalem, Matthew was composed sometime after AD 70.

(iii) In the middle of the parable of the great supper (22.1–10), the redactor has inserted this: 'The king was furious, and sending his troops he killed those murderers and burned their city' (22.7); contrast Lk 14.15–24; *Gos. Thom.* 64. This seems to be a clear reference to the destruction of Jerusalem in AD 70.

(iv) In 28.19 Jesus directs his disciples to baptize 'in the name of the Father, and of the Son, and of the Holy Spirit.' There are other trinitarian-type formulas in the NT, some even in Paul's letters (1 Cor 12.4–6; 2 Cor 13.14; Tit 3.4–6; 1 Pet 1.2; Jude 20–1). Nonetheless the loaded phrase, 'the name of the Father, and of the Son, and of the Holy Spirit', is, excepting possibly *Did.* 7, which in any case here depends upon Matthew, without true parallel in the first-century Christian literature. It involves a step towards later Trinitarian thought not taken in any other NT writing. One is, therefore, disinclined to place the document to which 28.19 belongs too many years before the beginning of the second century AD.

LOCAL ORIGIN

Modern scholarship has tended to place Matthew in Syria, especially in Antioch. The following points are among the reasons.

(i) Patristic tradition does not locate Matthew's composition in Italy or Greece or Asia Minor, that is, the West.

(ii) Peter's prominence harmonizes well with his undoubted status in Antioch (cf. Gal 2.11; church tradition makes him the first bishop there).

(iii) Antioch had a very large Jewish population. The city was, at the same time, the centre of the earliest Christian Gentile mission. This dual feature seems to be mirrored in Matthew, which breathes a Jewish atmosphere and yet looks upon the Gentile mission in a most favourable light.

(iv) The First Gospel probably has its first external attestation in the epistles of Ignatius, who was bishop of Antioch in the early second century. And when Ignatius writes of 'the gospel' (*Phil.* 5.1–2; 8.2), one may reasonably identify this with our Matthew.

Yet these and additional considerations do not add up to proof, and patristic tradition places neither our Gospel nor the apostle Matthew in Antioch. So other suggestions have been made: Jerusalem, Galilee, Alexandria, Caesarea Maritima, Phoenicia, or, more generally, east of the Jordan (on the basis of Mt 4.25 and 19.1, which may view Palestine as being on the other side of the Jordan). In a matter such as this, uncertainty is inevitable.

SOURCES

Serious study of the literary relationships among the gospels began in the latter half of the eighteenth century, and the time since then has seen an array of theories propounded. But, in the twentieth century, the majority of scholars came to accept one of two fundamental positions. According to most, Mark was a source for both Matthew and Luke. A minority has postulated the primacy of Matthew: both Mark and Luke knew and used the First Gospel. The first question, then, is to determine the direction of borrowing between Matthew and Mark. Assuming that the extensive overlaps in common material imply literary borrowing, did Matthew use Mark or did Mark use Matthew?

(i) Mark. Matthew's dependence upon Mark is indicated by several considerations. (a) The general direction of early Christology cannot be gainsaid. It was from the lesser to the greater. The passing of time incontrovertibly saw a development: there was an enhancing of feelings of reverence, an increase in Jesus' position and status. Hence, because Matthew possesses a higher Christology than Mark, and because he lacks certain details which make Jesus more human, presumption is against Matthean priority. Consider the following:

Texts in Mark but not Matthew where Jesus experiences emotion:

Mk	1.41:	'moved with anger' (or 'pity'; the text is doubtful)
	1.43:	'he sternly charged'
	3.5:	'he looked around him with anger, grieved'
	6.6:	'he marvelled'
	8.12:	'he sighed deeply in his spirit'
	10.14:	'he was indignant'
	10.21:	'he loved him'
	14.33:	'greatly distressed and troubled'

Texts in Mark but not Matthew where Jesus experiences inability or exhibits ignorance:

Mk	1.45:	'Jesus could no longer openly enter a town'
	5.9:	'what is your name?'
	5.30:	'who touched my garments?'
	6.5:	'he could do no mighty work there'
	6.38:	'how many loaves do you have?'
	6.48:	'he wanted to pass them by'
	7.24:	'he would not have anyone know it; but he could not be hid'
	8.12:	'why does this generation seek a sign?'
	8.23:	'do you see anything?'
	9.16:	'what are you discussing with them?'
	9.21:	'how long has he had this?'
	9.33:	'what were you discussing?'
	11.13:	'he went to see if he could find anything on it . . . he found nothing'
	14.14:	'where am I to eat?'

Other texts in Mark evidently omitted or altered out of reverence:

Mk	1.32–3:	Jesus healed 'many' becomes in Mt 8.16 'all'
	3.10:	Jesus healed 'many' becomes in Mt 12.15 'all'
	3.21:	'he is out of his mind' (omitted)
	10.18:	'why do you call me good?' becomes in Mt 19.17 'why do you ask me concerning the good?'
	14.58:	'I will destroy' becomes in Mt 26.61 'I am able to destroy'

One finds it perplexing to suppose that an early Christian writer with Matthew's text before him increased Jesus' ignorance and made him a much more emotional figure. But the reverse procedure is quite intelligible.

(b) Those who place Mark after Matthew tend to date the former towards the end of the first century or even in the first part of the second century. They also have little doubt that the author was a Gentile writing for Gentiles. How, then, do they account for the six Semitic expressions found in Mark but not in Matthew: *Boanerges* (3.17), *talitha koum* (5.41), *korban* (7.11), *Bartimeus* (10.46), *rabbouni* (10.51), and *abba* (14.36)? The magical papyri and books such as the Testament of Solomon (1st–3rd century AD) do, to be sure, reveal the possibility of Gentile interest in Semitic names; but are *Boanerges, korban,* and *Bartimeus* really words that would have survived for long in a non-Jewish environment? Related to this question is the problem of Mt 27.46 = Mk 15.34: 'My God, my God, why have you forsaken me?' Matthew has this either in Hebrew (at least the first three words) or in Aramaic; Mark has a different text, one in Aramaic. Now if Mark is prior to Matthew, this makes sense. The author of the First Gospel could read the Old Testament in Hebrew: so we can imagine him thus making the link with Elijah clearer (cf. 27.47). What is the alternative? One is forced to affirm that a Gentile Christian writing for Gentiles Christians somehow managed – and for what reason? – to change Hebrew words into Aramaic or Aramaic words into different Aramaic words. Is this credible?

(c) In Mk 6.17–29, Mark's version of the Baptist's martyrdom, all is in order. Herod, we are informed, feared and respected John, knowing him to be righteous and holy; and although the tetrarch had seized John and put him in prison (on account of Herodias, who had a grudge against the Baptist and wished him dead), Herod heard the prophet gladly. When, finally, the Baptist was beheaded, it was because Herodias had forced Herod to act against his will. Turning to Mt 14.3–12, we get a different picture. In this account Herod arrests John and wants to do away with him; but he cannot because he fears the crowd (14.5). Nothing is said of Herod's admiration for his prisoner. Yet when he is tricked by his sister-in-law into giving her John's head on a platter, Herod is said to grieve (14.9). Nothing has prepared for this remark on the tetrarch's emotion. Because Matthew fails to tell us about Herod's esteem for John, there is no place for grief. It seems to follow that Mt 14.9 betrays a knowledge of Mk 6.20. That is, having revised and abbreviated Mark's introduction but at the same time retained Mark's version of Herod's response to the beheading, Matthew unwittingly disturbs the coherence of Mk 6.17–29.

Matthew makes a second blunder in 14.3–12. In Mark the story of John's imprisonment and execution is told as a flashback. It is introduced with Herod's declaration, 'John, whom I beheaded, has been raised' (6.16); and after the story is finished the narrative jumps forward in time (cf. 6.30 with 6.13). In Matthew, however, the tale is introduced as a flashback but not so concluded. When John is buried, Jesus is told of it, and then he departs – all of which leads to the feeding of the five thousand (14.13–21). So Mt 14.1–12 begins retrospectively yet then flows smoothly into the narrative's present tense.

(d) In Mk 15.6–10, Pilate, who is aware of the machinations of the Jewish leaders, offers to release Jesus (he does not mention Barabbas). In Mt 27.15–18, by contrast, we find this: 'Pilate said to them, "Whom do you want me to release for you, Barabbas or Jesus who is called Christ?" For he knew that it was out of envy that they had delivered him up.' This makes little sense. 'For he knew' etc. does not explain why Pilate asked the question, 'Whom do you want me to release for you . . .?' In fact, 'For he knew' etc., offers a good reason for Pilate not to ask the crowd for their preference. But all is right in Mark. When Pilate asks, 'Do you want me to release for you the king of the Jews?', he does so because he perceives Jesus' innocence. It is only then that the crowd names Barabbas. In other words, Pilate offers the crowd no choice in Mark but rather seeks to set Jesus free; thus 'For he knew' etc., fits its context perfectly. Now how do we explain why Matthew has an illogical sequence, Mark a logical one? 'For he knew' etc. (Mk 15.10 = Mt 27.18) is in harmony with Mk 15.9 but not Mt 27.17; it also goes well with Mk 15.14 = Mt .27.23, where the governer asks, 'Why, for what evil has he done?' This is evidence for Markan originality. Mk 15.10 = Mt 27.18 and Mk 15.14 = Mt 27.23, being in both gospels, must belong to the original story; and because Mk 15.9 but not Mt 27.17 lines up with these two texts, Mark's account is shown to be more original. Matthew has again imperfectly assimilated Mark's narrative.

(e) Passages present in Mark but wholly absent from Matthew include: 3.20–1; 8.22–6; 9.38–40, 49–50; 11.16; and 14.51–2. If Mark used Matthew, the texts just cited would be Mark's additions. If Matthew used Mark, they would be Matthew's omissions. Which option is the more likely? Surely the latter. Mk 3.20–1 tells us that Jesus' family thought he was out of his mind. This is potentially embarrassing. So is 8.22–6, which tells us about a healing attempt that did not wholly succeed ('I see men but they look like trees, walking'): Jesus has to try again. Mk 9.38–40 attributes successful miracles to an individual outside of Jesus' circle, which could raise some awkward questions. As for 9.49–50 ('everyone will be salted by fire', followed by two non-sequiturs); 11.16 ('and he would not permit anyone to carry a vessel through the temple'); and 14.51–2 (the flight of the naked young man), these are among the most mysterious verses in all the gospels; their meaning has puzzled commentators. Omission by Matthew makes sense. Addition by Mark – who would on the theory of Matthean priority be responsible for dropping the miraculous birth of Jesus, the Sermon on the Mount, and the resurrection appearances – is much harder to fathom.

(ii) Q. If Mark was a source of Matthew, what was the source of the so-called double tradition, that is, the non-Markan material common to Matthew and Luke (about 230 verses)? There are four basic solutions: (a) Matthew and Luke had in common another source, a lost document customarily called 'Q'. (b) Matthew and Luke had in common several additional sources, some perhaps oral, some perhaps written. (c) Luke knew and used Matthew. (d) Matthew knew and used Luke.

Solutions (a) and (b) are the most probable, for sometimes it is Matthew who seems to preserve the more original form of a saying appearing in the double tradition, while at other times it is Luke. This is inexplicable if one evangelist is following the other. Further, with the exception of the words of John the Baptist and the temptation stories, Matthew and Luke do not agree in the placement of their common material into the Markan framework. Yet surely, if Matthew had used Luke or Luke had used Matthew, their agreement in this respect would be greater. Finally, if Luke drew upon the First Gospel it is remarkable that he betrays no knowledge of the obvious Matthean additions to Markan material (e.g. Mt 3.14–15; 9.13a; 12.5–7; 16.2b-3, 17–19; 19.9; 21.10–11; 26.52–4; 27.19, 24, 51b–53). In other words, Luke seems to have known Mark, not Mark as revised by Matthew.

This leaves options (a) and (b). The latter is unlikely to the extent that it postulates common oral tradition because such is unlikely to explain the word-for-word correspondence in the following passages:

Mt			Lk	
	3.7b–10	=		3.7b–9
	7.3–5	=		6.41–2
	7.7–11	=		11.9–13
	11.4–11	=		7.22–8
	11.21–23	=		10.13–5
	11.25–7	=		10.21–2
	23.37–8	=		13.34–5
	24.45–1	=		12.42b–6

Furthermore, Matthew and Luke share four common, large blocks of material:

I	*Sermon on the plain*	*Sermon on the Mount*
	Luke	Matthew
1	6.17, 20a	5.1–2
2	6.20b–3	5.3, 6, 4, 11–12
3	6.27–8	5.44
4	6.29	5.39–40
5	6.30	5.42
6	6.31	7.12
7	6.32–3	5.46–7
8	6.35b	5.45
9	6.36	5.48
10	6.37–8	7.1–2
11	6.41–2	7.3–5
12	6.43	7.18
13	6.44	7.16
14	6.46	7.21
15	6.47–9	7.24–7

II	*Missionary discourse*	*Missionary discourse*
	Luke	Matthew
1	10.2	9.37–8
2	10.3	10.16
3	10.4	10.9–10a
4	10.5	10.11–12
5	10.6	10.13
6	10.7	10.10b
7	10.9	10.7
8	10.12	10.15

III	*Polemic against leaders*	*Polemic against leaders*
	Luke	Matthew
1	11.39–41	23.25–6
2	11.42	23.23
3	11.43	23.6–7
4	11.44	23.27
5	11.45–6	23.4
6	11.47–8	23.29–30
7	11.49–51	23.34–6
8	11.52	23.13

IV	*Eschatological instruction*	*Eschatological instruction*
	Luke	Matthew
1	17.23	24.23
2	17.24	24.27

3	17.26–7	24.37–9a
4	17.30	24.39b
5	17.31	24.17–18
6	17.34–6	24.40–1
7	17.37	24.28

These four blocks appear in the same order in Matthew and Luke, and from them one may infer the existence of a document which contained a programmatic sermon towards its beginning, a missionary discourse and series of anti-Pharisaic denunciations towards its middle, and a collection of eschatological prophecies and warnings at its end.

(iii) M. If one subtracts from Matthew the material shared with Mark and Luke, the following matter is left:

1.1	The opening sentence
1.2–17	The genealogy
1.18–2.23	The infancy stories
3.14–15	John and Jesus
4.13–16	Jesus in Galilee
4.23–5	A summary report (cf. Mk 1.39; 6.6)
5.1–2	Jesus on the mountain (cf. Lk 6.17, 20a)
5.5	A beatitude
5.7	A beatitude
5.8	A beatitude
5.9	A beatitude
5.10	A beatitude
5.13a	'You are the salt of the earth'
5.14a	'You are the light of the world'
5.16	'Let your light so shine ...'
5.17	'I came not to abolish the law ...'
5.19	'Whoever then relaxes one of the least ...'
5.20	'Unless your righteousness ...'
5.21–4	On murder
5.27–8	On adultery
5.31–2	On divorce
5.33–7	On swearing
5.38–9a	On retaliation
5.41	On going the extra mile
5.43	On loving the neighbour
6.1	On righteousness before men
6.2–4	On almsgiving
6.5–6	On prayer
6.7–9a	The introduction to the Lord's Prayer
6.10b–c, 13b	Clauses in the Lord's Prayer

15.30–1	Jesus heals
16.2b-3	On signs (cf. Lk 12.54–6)
16.11b-12	The teaching of the Pharisees and Sadducees
16.17–19	Peter and the keys
16.22b	Peter speaks
17.6–7	The disciples at the Transfiguration
17.13	John and Elijah
17.24–7	The stater in the fish's mouth
18.3–4	As a little child (cf. Mk 10.15)
18.10	The angels of the little ones
18.14	One of these little ones
18.16–20	On the church
18.23–35	The unmerciful servant
19.1a	The conclusion of Mt 18
19.10–12	On eunuchs
20.1–16	Parable of the labourers in the vineyard
21.4–5	A fulfilment quotation
21.10–11	The entrance into Jerusalem (cf. Mk 11.11)
21.14	Crowds in the temple
21.15b–16	The Son of David
21.28–32	The parable of the two sons (cf. Lk 7.29–30)
21.43	The kingdom
21.44	The scribes and Pharisees (this is textually uncertain)
22.1–14	The parable of the marriage feast (cf. Lk 14.15–24)
22.33	The crowds
22.40	On the Law and the prophets
23.1–3	Moses' seat
23.5	On phylacteries
23.7b–10	On the one teacher
23.15–22	Woes
23.24	Blind guides
23.28	Outward appearance/inward state
23.32–3	Gehenna
24.10–12	On false prophets
24.20	Not on a sabbath
24.30a	The sign of the Son of man
25.1–13	The parable of the ten virgins
25.14–30	The parable of the talents (cf. Lk 19.11–27)
25.31–46	The last judgement
26.1	A transitional verse
26.44	A third prayer in Gethsemane

26.50	Jesus arrested
26.52–4	The sword
27.3–10	Judas
27.19	Pilate's wife
27.24–5	Pilate washes his hand
27.36	The guard
27.43	Words of mockery
27.51b–3	Signs and wonders
27.62–6	The guard at the tomb
28.2–4	An angelic appearance
28.9–10	Jesus appears (cf. Jn 20.14–18)
28.11–15	Soldiers bribed
28.16–20	Jesus' closing words

A great portion of the material found in neither Mark nor Luke is presumably redactional or partly redactional. Of the remaining non-redactional matter, all but 17.24–7 (the stater in the fish's mouth) falls into one of five categories. These are: (1) the infancy stories (1.18–2.23); (2) parables (13.24–30, 44–6, 47–50; 18.23–35; 20.1–16; 21.28–32; 22.1–14; 25.1–13, 14–30, 31–46); (3) isolated sayings (5.5, 7, 8, 9; 5.41; 7.6; 10.23; 11.28–30; 16.17–19); (4) three groups of sayings (5.21–4 + 27–8 + 33–7; 6.1–18; 23.1–3 + 5 + 7b-10 + 15–22); and, finally, (5) a few traditions about the passion and the resurrection (27.3–10, 19, 24–5, 51b-3, 62–6; 28.2–4, 9–10, 11–15).

It has, from time to time, been argued that, in addition to Mark and Q, Matthew also had at his disposal a third written document. Of late, however, conjectures on this matter have not had much of a following, and rightly so. There is no good reason to think of M as a unified composition.

If M is not to be equated with a particular document, the alternative is to employ the letter as a convenient symbol for a plurality of sources: for those sources behind Matthew – oral and/or written – which cannot be identified with Mark, Q, or Matthean redaction.

STORY, STRUCTURE, PLOT

Mt 1–4 opens with the title (1.1) and Jesus' genealogy (1.2–17). There follow infancy stories (1.18–25; 2.1–11, 12–23), the section on John the Baptist (3.1–17), and three additional paragraphs that directly prepare for the ministry (4.1–11, 12–17, 18–22). All of this material constitutes an extended introduction. We are told *who* Jesus was (1.1–18; 2.1, 4; 3.11, 17; 4.3, 6), *where* he was from (2.6), *how* he came into the world

(1.18–25), *why* he came into the world (1.21; 2.6), *when* he came into the world (1.17; 2.l), and *what* he proclaimed (4.17).

The Sermon on the Mount, the first major discourse, opens with a short narrative introduction (4.23–5.2) and closes with a short narrative conclusion (7.28–8.1). The discourse proper, 5.3–7.27, is also symmetrically centered. Blessings (5.3–12) are at the beginning, warnings (7.13–27) at the end. In between there are three major sections, each one primarily a compilation of imperatives: Jesus and the law (5.17–48), Jesus on the cult (6.1–18), and Jesus and social issues (6.19–7.12). The entirety may be set forth in this manner:

Introduction, 5.1–2
    Blessings, 5.3–12
        Law and prophets, 5.17–20
            Jesus and Torah, 5.21–48
            Almsgiving, Prayer, Fasting, 6.1–18
            Social issues, 6.19–7.11
        Law and prophets, 7.12
    Warnings, 7.13–27
Conclusion, 7.28–8.1

The sermon contains Jesus' demand for Israel.

If the Sermon on the Mount presents Jesus' words, Mt 8 and 9 recount his deeds. The chapters are largely a record of Jesus' acts, particularly his compassionate miracles, which fall neatly into three sets of three: 8.1–4, 5–13, 14–15 + 8.23–7, 28–34, 9.1–8 + 9.18–26, 27–31, 32–4. Jesus also speaks in this section, but the emphasis is upon his actions, what he does in and for Israel; cf. 8.16–17.

Having been informed of what Jesus said and did, in Mt 10, the second major discourse, we next learn what Jesus instructed his disciples, as extensions of himself, to say and do. The theme of imitation is prominent. The disciples are to proclaim what Jesus proclaimed (cf. 10.7 with 4.17) and do what Jesus did (cf. 10.8 with Mt 8–9 and 11.2–6). Disciples are like the teacher, servants like the master (10.24–5). Jesus is the first Christian missionary who calls others to his example.

The chapters on the words and deeds of Jesus and the words and deeds of the disciples are followed by 11–12. These record the response of 'this generation' to John and Jesus and the twelve. This is what the material on the Baptist (11.2–6, 7–15, 16–19) is all about, as well as the woes on Galilee (11.20–4) and the conflict stories in Mt 12 (1–8, 9–14, 22–37, 38–45). It all adds up to an indictment of the majority in Israel. The Messiah has been rejected. This, however, is unexpected. In Jewish eschatology God saves Israel in the latter days. Nothing prepares for the Messiah meeting opposition from his own people. Mt 13, the parable chapter, the third great discourse, is Matthew's attempt to attack this problem. It offers various explanations for the mixed response to the Messiah: there can be different responses to one message (13.1–23); the devil works in human hearts (13.24–30); and, if things are not right now, all will be made well in the end (13.31–3, 36–43, 47–50).

The fourth major narrative section, Mt 14–17, follows the parable chapter. The most memorable pericope is 16.13–20, where Jesus founds his church. This suits the larger context so well because after corporate Israel has, at least for the time being, failed to embrace its saviour, God must found a religious institution that will. That this is indeed the dominant theme of the section is hinted at not only by the ever-increasing focus upon the disciples as opposed to the crowds but also by Peter's being the rock upon which the church is built. For it is precisely in this section that he comes to the fore: see 14.28–33; 15.15; 16.13–20; and 17.24–7 – all insertions into Mark. Peter's emerging pre-eminence correlates with the emergence of the church.

All this is confirmed by Mt 18, the fourth major discourse. Usually styled the 'community' or 'ecclesiological' discourse, this chapter is especially addressed to the topic of Christian fraternal relations. How often should one forgive a brother? What is the procedure for excommunicating someone? These ecclesiastical questions are appropriate precisely at this point because Jesus has just established his church.

Having founded the new community and given it teaching, it remains for Jesus to go to Jerusalem, which is what happens in the next narrative section, Mt 19–23. The material is mostly from Mark, with the woes of 23 added. The bankruptcy of the Jewish leadership and the rejection of the Messiah are to the fore.

Before the passion narrative proper, however, Jesus, in Mt 24–5, speaks of the future of Israel and of the church. Here, in the fifth and last major discourse, we are taken beyond Mt 26–8 into the time beyond the narrative. The discourse foretells judgement upon Jerusalem and salvation through difficulty for the church.

Following chronological order, Matthew closes as Mark does (and Luke and John for that matter). The passion and resurrection constitute the conclusion.

The primary structure of the Gospel is, then, narrative (N) + discourse (D) + narrative (N) + discourse (D), etc., and the plot is determined by the major theme of each narrative section and each discourse:

THEOLOGY

Although there are aspects of a theology in Matthew they do not present themselves as coherent or systematic. Despite the book's theocentricity, a 'theology' of Matthew in our sense of the term is not really possible. Like the rabbinic corpus, Matthew contains much implicit theology but is primarily concerned not with doctrine or correctness of belief but with obedience.

Matthew was more tradent than theologian, more exegete and commentator than innovator. He was concerned above all to pass on the traditions – from the OT, Mark, Q, and M – he had received. His Gospel is less a statement of personal opinions than the expression of a traditional faith. He told his story more than authored it, or rather he retold his community's story to which he added commentary.

Matthew's genius was not that of theological invention. He was not a Paul or an Origen. To judge from his Gospel, the evangelist's religious convictions were traditional. Along with all the NT authors his God was the God of the OT, the God of Israel. In other words, his theology, in the proper sense of that word, was Jewish theology as transmitted to him by his Jewish education and the church. There was also nothing much original about his christology. All the christological titles found in his Gospel appear in other early Christian texts. Even his story of a virgin birth has its parallel in Luke. Matthew also contributed nothing new to soteriology. The Gospel says only that Jesus gave his life as a ransom for many and saved his people from their sins – convictions common enough in primitive Christianity.

One could, if the non-Markan material in 16:13–20 were thought redactional, make a case for a novel contribution to ecclesiology. But here the evidence again points to tradition. It is the same with Matthew's Deuteronomistic view of history, and with his eschatology.

The former reminds one of Q, and regarding the latter, while certain themes receive special accent, one can easily find parallels to every strand of Matthean eschatology: to Matthew's hope for a near end, to his 'realized eschatology', and to his use of apocalyptic expectation to tender encouragement, offer paraenesis, and explicate christology. Also in Matthew's moral teaching we find first of all tradition. The demand to love, the call to non-retaliation, and the imperative to imitate Christ were standard in the early church.

Even with regard to the law Matthew was no innovator. In some ways indeed he was at one with Paul on this matter: Gentiles did not have to become Jews in order to be saved; that is, they did not have to become circumcized and obey Moses. If it had been otherwise, Matthew could not have enthusiastically endorsed the Gentile mission in his conclusion, for by his time that mission was in most areas presumably free of the demand for circumcision. At the same time – here the harmony with Paul breaks down – Matthew believed that the Mosaic law was still in effect. This can only have meant that Matthew expected Jewish Christians to keep it. But this was also the position of Luke, who had no trouble passing on stories in which even the apostle of the Gentiles keeps the law. This idea, that Jewish Christians should keep the Torah while Gentiles need not, was, moreover, widespread, as appears from the decree reproduced in Acts 15. Whatever its precise origin, that decree was not Luke's invention; and it assumes that while Jewish Christians will observe the law, Gentiles need only follow a few general proscriptions. This position was probably the dominant one in first-century Christianity. Here too, then, Matthew swims in the mainstream.

GENRE AND MORAL INSTRUCTION

Prior to our century Matthew was, despite its many gaps and relative brevity, often referred to as a biography. Most twentieth-century scholars, however, rejected this view: the canonical gospels are not historical retrospectives but rather expressions of the earliest Christian proclamation. Yet recently there has been a change in the minds of at least some scholars, a reversion to the older view, to the idea that the Gospels are biographies – if the term is used not in its modern sense but in accord with ancient usage. The canonical gospels then qualify as a subtype of Graeco-Roman biography.

The truth is that Matthew is an omnibus of genres: apocalypse, community rule, catechism, cult aetiology, etc. Like the book of Job it is several things at once: it mixes genres. But included in that mixture is biography. There are indeed significant resemblances between the First Gospel and certain Hellenistic biographies; and despite its incompleteness as a biography in the modern sense, it is the partial record of a man's life, and so biographical.

The content of Matthew's faith partly explains why the First Gospel is biographical. The distinctiveness of Matthew's thinking over against that of his non-Christian Jewish contemporaries was the acceptance of Jesus as the centre of his religion: it was around him as a person that his theological thinking revolved. For Matthew, revelation belonged supremely to the life of the Son of God. The significance of this can be measured when Matthew's comparatively brief Gospel is set over against the literature of rabbinic Judaism. In rabbinic sources there are stories about rabbis, but no sustained lives such as we find in the Gospel of Matthew, report upon report of what Rabbi X or Rabbi Y purportedly said, but no biographies. Particular sages are seldom an organizing category or principle in rabbinic literature. So whereas rabbinic Judaism, with its subordination of the individual to the community and its focus upon the Torah instead of a particular human being, produced no religious biographies, the substance of Matthew's faith was neither a dogmatic system nor a legal code but a human being whose life was, in outline and in detail, uniquely significant and therefore demanding of record.

Matthew's biographical impulse also owes much to the circumstance that whenever social crisis results in fragmentation, as happened at the beginning of Christianity, so that the questioning of previous beliefs issues in the formation of a new social unit, new norms and authorities are inevitably generated. Such norms and authorities are always most persuasively presented when embodied in examples: new fashions must first be modelled. And in Matthew Jesus is the new exemplar. There is a multitude of obvious connections between Jesus' words and his deeds. If Jesus indirectly exhorts others to be meek (5.5), he himself is such (11.29; 21.5). If he enjoins mercy (5.7), he himself is merciful (9.27; 15.22; 20.30). If he congratulates those oppressed for God's cause (5.10), he himself suffers and dies innocently (27.23). Jesus further demands faithfulness to the law of Moses (5.17–20) and faithfully keeps that law during his ministry (8.4; 12.1–8, 9–14; 15.1–20). He recommends self-denial in the face of evil (5.39) and does not resist the evils done to him (26.67; 27.30). He calls for private prayer (6.6) and subsequently withdraws to a mountain to pray alone (14.23). Jesus advises his followers to use certain words in prayer ('your will be done', 6.10; 'do not bring us to the time of trial', 6.13), and he uses those words in Gethsemane (26.41–2). He rejects the service of mammon (6.19), and he lives without concern for money (8.20). He commands believers to carry crosses (16.24), and he does so himself, both figuratively and literally.

The evangelist's moral interest, apparent above all in the Sermon on the Mount, was well served by a story in which the crucial moral imperatives are imaginatively and convincingly incarnated. This the First Gospel supplies. To quote Clement of Alexandria, Matthew offers two types of teaching, 'that which assumes the form of counselling to obedience, and that which is presented in the form of example.' Jesus embodies his speech; he lives as he speaks and speaks as he lives.

PURPOSE AND SETTING IN JUDAISM

Following the revolt of AD 70 the Pharisees, or rather their descendants, emerged dominant. They set in motion a process which was to allow Judaism to continue and even thrive after defeat. Their leaders were concerned with the disunity of the Jewish people and with the attraction of movements from without, including Christianity. They accordingly promoted unity, began the process of collecting and standardizing their oral laws, sought to establish a standard calendar for the religious year, and tried to transfer to the synagogue rites previously performed in the temple itself. So in Matthew's time a highly self-conscious and probably aggressive rabbinism was asserting itself to reunite Israel. This involved defining itself in opposition to others, including Christians. It probably also involved activities Christians interpreted as persecution. Tolerance comes in times of self-confidence, and the period after the AD 70 destruction was not such a time for formative Judaism.

Matthew's mainly Jewish community had to come to terms with such a Judaism – a fact which helps to explain the great interest in the scribes and Pharisees. That community perceived itself as constituting or belonging to authentic Israel yet at the same time sought the expansion of Judaism beyond strictly Jewish confines through the Gentile Christian missions. Scholars disagree whether Matthew's community was still, as 23.5 implies, within Judaism or whether it had recently declared itself independent of its parent faith so that it had become a sect outside Judaism or, again, whether, having long been regarded as deviant by the Jewish community, it was in the process of deciding if it should leave while yet remaining under the authority of the local synagogue. Perhaps indeed not all Matthean Christians were in the same boat; maybe some still attended synagogue while others had already left.

Whatever the exact status of Matthew's community in relation to Judaism, his writing points to a process of differentiation which took place between his community and 'their synagogues'. Believers in Jesus may have preferred to refer to their own gatherings not as 'synagogue' but 'church'. Again, Christian leaders were not to be called 'rabbi', a term which in the Judaism of Matthew's day was presumably becoming an official title (23.7–8). Along with the differentiation went outright, polemical criticism; see especially Mt 23. The cohesion of the believers in Jesus was no doubt strengthened by such criticism: a common enemy unites the divided and insecure.

The establishment of group identity also involved legitimizing belief in Jesus over against Jewish criticism. Mt 28.15 is explicit about the existence of such criticism, which no doubt helps account for the formula quotations, the parallels between Jesus and Moses, and Jesus' endorsement of the Torah. One detects in all this a sort of apologetics. Christians claimed to be vindicated by antiquity, to have a lawgiver like Moses, and to keep Torah.

The need for group identity made the need for unity a paramount concern. This illuminates the emphasis in both the Sermon on the Mount and Mt 18 on forgiveness and reconciliation. Forgiveness up to seven times is advised in Luke, but 'seventy times (and) seven' in Matthew (18.22). Despite its often violent polemics, perhaps no other ancient document shows more sensitivity to the desperate need for love and peace to displace hate and vengeance. The tendency toward reconciliation appears also in Matthew's desire not to give away too much of his Jewish heritage but to bridge as sensitively as possible the gulf between Jewish and Gentile believers. He tried to preserve both the old and the new (8.17; 13.52). While calling for a mission to Gentiles, he also recognized Israel's special place (10.5–6; 15.21–8) and insisted on the demands for a righteousness even higher than that of the Pharisees. The proof of Matthew's ecumenical character is that both Jewish and Gentile Christians welcomed it as their own: it became the chief Gospel of both groups.

COMMENTARY

TITLE (1.1)

1 ¹Book of the genesis of Jesus the Christ, the son of David, the son of Abraham.

The three personal names that appear in 1.1 – Jesus Christ, David, Abraham (cf. 1.17) – also appear in 1.2–16, but in reverse order. So the very first verse offers a triad and the front half of a chiasmus:

   a. Jesus Christ (1.1b)
      b. David (1.1c)
         c. Abraham (1.1d)
         c. Abraham (1.2)
      b. David (1.6)
   a. Jesus Christ (1.16)

Book of the genesis is a literal translation of the Greek, *biblos geneseos*. The second word is usually translated 'genealogy' and so made the heading for 1.2–17. But the word can also mean 'birth' (as in 1.18) or 'origin' or 'beginning' and be taken as the introduction to 1.2–25 or 1.2–2.23 or 1.2–4.16. Yet another possibility is that 'genesis' is part of Matthew's title: the story of Jesus is a new creation. In accord with this last option, (i) *biblos* means 'book', and Matthew's opening phrase, *biblos geneseos*, is not a usual title for genealogies; (ii) in Gen 2.4 and 5.1, the only two places in the LXX to use *biblos geneseos*, the words are associated with more than genealogical materials; (iii) it was common in the prophetic, didactic, and apocalyptic writings of Judaism to open with an independent titular sentence announcing the content of the work: cf. Nah 1.1; Tob 1.1; Bar 1.1; *T. Job* 1.1; *Apoc. Abr.* title; 2 Esdr 1.1–3. So one may render 1.1 as 'Book of the new genesis wrought by Jesus Christ, son of David, son of Abraham' or some such. Yet even if 1.1 is not a title but has a more restricted reach, the first book of the Bible was already known by the title 'Genesis' before Matthew's time, and *biblos geneseos* occurs in Gen 2.4 and 5.1, so opening a book with that phrase echoes the first book of Moses. John's prologue, which introduces Jesus by recalling the creation story ('in the beginning'), supplies a parallel. So too Matthew's baptismal narrative, which depicts a new creation (see p. 47); cf. also 2 Cor 5.17; Gal 6.15.

Jesus the Christ. Although 'Christ' is already a personal name in most of the NT, in Matthew it still is a title, 'the Christ', 'the Messiah'; cf. 2.4; 16.16, 20; 22.42; 24.5, 23; 26.63, 68.

son of David was a standard messianic title for the rabbis, and a titular use may already be attested in the first century BC, in *Ps. Sol.* 17. Developing out of older expressions such as 'sprout of Jesse' (Isa 11.10) and 'shoot (of David)' (Jer 23.5; 33.15), 'Son of David' became the focus of a rich tradition; and, by the time of Jesus, the dominant, although not exclusive, Jewish expectation was that the messianic king would be a son of David. A deliverer was expected who would fulfil the promises made in 2 Sam 7. This largely accounts for the early Christian emphasis on the Davidic lineage of Jesus; cf. Rom 1.3.

son of Abraham. Cf. 3.9. 'Son of Abraham' was not a messianic title but an expression used either of one of Jewish blood (Lk 19.9; Jn 8; Acts 13.26) or of one worthy of father Abraham (4 Macc 6.17, 22; 18.23; Gal 3.7). Here, even though connexion with David is grammatically possible, the reference is to Jesus, and both meanings are appropriate.

God made a foundational covenant with Abraham, the 'father of fathers' (*T. Jacob* 7.22; see Gen 12, 15), and descent from him was the basis for membership in the people of God. Hence the significance for Matthew of Jesus being the son of Abraham: as the saviour of Israel, Jesus himself must be a true Israelite, a descendant of Abraham; cf. Jn 4.22; Heb 2.16–17. Beyond this, because the genealogy which follows 1.1 covers the period from Abraham to the Messiah, it is natural to think of Jesus as the culmination, the *telos*, of that history which began with the patriarch. But there is more. 'Son of Abraham', found only here in Matthew, probably also serves to announce the evangelist's interest in the salvation of the Gentiles. Abraham himself was a Gentile by birth, and in the OT it is promised that 'all the nations' will be blessed in him (Gen 12.3; 18.18 etc.). In older Jewish literature, Abraham was sometimes portrayed as 'the father of many nations' (Gen 17.5) or the first proselyte. When we come to Christianity, we find Paul representing Abraham as the true father of all who have faith, Jew and Gentile alike (Rom 4.1–25; Gal 3.6–29).

* * * * *

The 'Jesus Christ' of 1.1 is surrounded by three word pairs, 'book of genesis', 'son of David', and 'son of Abraham'. These give us the three major points of the title. 'Genesis' relates the story of Jesus to the primeval history. This means, according to the principle that the end will be like the beginning, that the gospel concerns eschatology: it recounts the fulfilment of the hope for a 'new creation'. 'Son of David' represents Jesus as the king of Israel, the rightful heir to the Davidic promises. This too pertains to eschatology: the Messiah has come. 'Son of Abraham' probably implies not only that Jesus is a true Israelite but also that, with his appearance, God's promise to the patriarch has been realized: all the nations of the earth have been blessed.

FROM ABRAHAM TO JESUS: THE DAVIDIC MESSIAH'S GENEALOGY (1.2–17)

[2]Abraham was the father of Isaac, and Isaac the father of Jacob, and Jacob the father of Judah and his brothers, [3]and Judah the father of Perez and Zerah by Tamar, and Perez the father of Hezron, and Hezron the father of Aram, [4]and Aram the father of Amminadab, and Amminadab the father of Nahshon, and Nahshon the father of Salmon, [5]and Salmon the father of Boaz by Rahab, and Boaz the father of Obed by Ruth, and Obed the father of Jesse, [6]and Jesse the father of King David.

And David was the father of Solomon by the wife of Uriah, [7]and Solomon the father of Rehoboam, and Rehoboam the father of Abijah, and Abijah the father of Asaph, [8]and Asaph the father of Jehoshaphat, and Jehoshaphat the father of Joram, and Joram the father of Uzziah,[9]and Uzziah the father of Jotham, and Jotham the father of Ahaz, and Ahaz the father of Hezekiah, [10]and Hezekiah the father of Manasseh, and Manasseh the father of Amos, and Amos the father of Josiah,[11]and Josiah the father of Jechoniah and his brothers, at the deportation to Babylon.

[12]And after the deportation to Babylon: Jechoniah was the father of Salathiel, and Salathiel the father of Zerubbabel, [13]and Zerubbabel the father of Abiud, and Abiud the father of Eliakim, and Eliakim the father of Azor, [14]and Azor the father of Zadok, and Zadok the father of Achim, and Achim the father of Eliud, [15]and Eliud the father of Eleazar, and Eleazar the father of Matthan, and Matthan the father of Jacob, [16]and Jacob the father of Joseph, the husband of Mary, of whom Jesus was born, who is called the Christ.

[17]So all the generations from Abraham to David were fourteen generations, and from David to the deportation to Babylon, fourteen

generations, and from the deportation to Babylon to the Messiah, fourteen generations.

Parallel: Lk 3.23–38

The most notable feature of 1.2–17, which cannot convincingly be harmonized with the geneology in Lk 3.23–38, is its carefully ordered structure. Fourteen generations fall (inclusively) between Abraham and David, between David and the Babylonian captivity, and – at least according to 1.17 – between the Babylonian captivity and Jesus. How does one account for and understand this triadic scheme, which is obviously artificial rather than historical?

Probably the most popular explanation among contemporary scholars sees a word play on David's name, which in Hebrew has three consonants, the numerical value of which amounts to fourteen: $d + w + d = 4 + 6 + 4 = 14$. So the suggestion is that the genealogy has 3×14 generations because David's name has three consonants whose sum is fourteen. It is not difficult to see why this particular solution has gained wide credence. Such word plays, known as *gematria*, were practised in both Jewish and Christian circles close to Matthew's time (note Rev 13.18), and the numerical interpretation of David's name can account for both the number three and the number fourteen. Furthermore, in this genealogy of 3×14 generations, the one name with three consonants and a value of fourteen is also placed in the fourteenth spot. When one adds that this name is mentioned immediately before the genealogy (1.1) and twice at its conclusion (1.17), and that it is honoured by the title, 'king', coincidence becomes effectively ruled out.

2. With this verse Matthew opens the first section of his genealogy, 1.2–6a, from Abraham to David. It is the sole section showing extensive agreement with Luke's genealogy; see Lk 3.31–4. In fact, there is only one significant difference: between Hezron and Amminadab Matthew has Aram, Luke Arni and Admin. The names in Mt 1.2–6 appear to be taken from the LXX, 1 Chr 1.28, 34; 2.1–15 (cf. Ruth 4.18–22).

Abraham. In view of the women listed in 1.2–16, the absence in 1.2 of Sarah as well as of Rebekah and Rachel is notable. The formula, 'A was the father of B', is used several times in 1 Chr 1–3, in Ruth 4.18–22, and elsewhere in biblical genealogies. Matthew, for the sake of parallelism and order, prefers to employ it exclusively, at least until 1.16.

Isaac. Isaac's birth was something of a miracle (Gen 17.15–21; 18.9–15; 21.1–7), so the first begetting in Matthew's genealogy has something in common with the last.

Jacob the father of Judah. Cf. Lk 3.33 and Heb 7.14 ('our Lord was descended from Judah'). The prophecy in Israel's testament (Gen 49) concerning Judah and his descendants came to be interpreted of the Messiah.

his brothers. The brothers of Judah appear in 1 Chr 2.1–2; but why has Matthew bothered to note them? Many commentators find here an implicit statement about God's selectivity and providential choice: of the several possible ancestors, Judah alone was chosen to propagate the royal line. Perhaps the most that can safely be said is this: 'Judah and his brothers' makes plain the character of 1.2–17: it is not just a genealogy but a résumé of salvation-history. Cf. the mention of the deportation in 1.11–12.

3. Cf. 1 Chr 2.3–9 and Ruth 4.12, 18–19.

Tamar was the wife of Er, Judah's eldest son, and probably a Canaanite. After Er died, Judah's other sons failed to fulfil the obligations of levirate marriage to raise up children for their brother, so Tamar deceived Judah, conceiving by him twins (Gen 38). Both *Jub.* 4.1–2 and *T. Jud.* 10.1–2 make Tamar an Aramean. She is mentioned nowhere else in the NT or in the earliest Christian literature.

Why add Tamar? The question cannot be raised without asking why Rahab, Ruth, and the wife of Uriah (Bathsheba) are likewise named. Women are not usually named in Jewish genealogies (cf. Lk 3.23–38), and although Tamar and Bathsheba appear in 1 Chr 1–3, the other two women do not, so Matthew's citation of four women signals some special interest.

It might be argued that the four women were sinners. Tamar seduced Judah. Rahab was a prostitute. Bathsheba committed adultery with David. Perhaps Ruth was also guilty of transgression, for Ruth 3.1–18 may imply that she enticed Boaz. Matthew's point would then be a demonstration of God's grace and power: God's purpose for the Davidic line was achieved despite human sin and failure (cf. 1 Cor 1.27–31). Against this, however, early Christian tradition held up Rahab as a model of faith and good works, as did Jewish tradition. Beyond this, 1.2–16 names several male figures whose sins were well-known (e.g., David and Manasseh), so the introduction of the women would hardly seem to be a fruitful way of furthering that theme.

There is probably more truth to the proposal, popular since Luther, that the women in 1.2–16 reflect an interest in the salvation of the Gentiles. Tamar, whether a Canaanite or an Aramean, was certainly a foreigner. Rahab was a Canaanite, Ruth a Moabite, and Bathsheba was (originally) the wife of Uriah, a Hittite. It is true that in some sources Tamar, Rahab, and Ruth are regarded as proselytes; but the knowledge that they were not Jews by birth was not thereby eliminated. Further, Matthew's concern to announce from the outset the inclusion of non-Jews in the church is clear from the story of the magi as well probably as from 1.1, where Jesus is 'son of Abraham'.

A third suggestion, to which a measure of assent can also be given, finds the common denominator of Tamar, Rahab, Ruth, and Bathsheba to be the nature of their marital unions. These, although irregular and even scandalous, eventuated, in God's providence, in the Messiah's coming. The union of Judah and Tamar was an 'abomination in Israel' (*T. Jud.* 12.8). Solomon was born because David his father took another man's wife. Ruth was a Moabite. And, although the Bible says nothing about Rahab's marriage to Salmon, she was both a Canaanite and a prostitute. So the occasion for calumny by outsiders was present in each instance. Yet any slanderer would in truth have been depreciating what God had chosen to bless. One can easily see how Matthew might have intended this to prefigure the situation of Mary.

Perez the father of Hezron. Hezron was the eponymous ancestor of a clan of Judah (Gen 46.12; Num 26.21; 1 Chr 4.1).

Hezron the father of Aram. In 1 Chr 2.9 MT the sons of Hezron are three: Jerahmeel, Ram, and Chelubai. The LXX adds a fourth, Aram, and makes him (not Ram) the father of Amminadab. At Ruth 4.19, the LXX has Arran for the son of Hezron. However one unravels the textual confusion, Matthew appears to have followed 1 Chr 2.9 LXX or a related tradition.

4. Cf. 1 Chr 2.10–11.

Aram the father of Amminadab. Amminadab was the father of Elisheba, Aaron's wife (Exod 6.23). Against the LXX and Matthew, Lk 3.33 makes Amminadab a son of the otherwise unknown Admin and a grandson of the otherwise unknown Arni.

Amminadab the father of Nahshon. Nahshon was the leader of the tribe of Judah (Num 1.7; 2.3; 7.12, 17; 10.14). 1 Chr 2.10 calls him 'prince of the sons of Judah'.

Nahshon the father of Salmon. Salmon occurs in the OT only in genealogies.

5. Cf. 1 Chr 2.11–2 and Ruth 4.21–2 LXX.

Salmon the father of Boaz. Boaz was the virtuous, righteous Bethlehemite who, according to the book of Ruth, took the Moabitess Ruth for his wife.

Rahab is the harlot of Jericho known from Josh 2 and 6. There is no parallel to the statement that Rahab married Salmon and mothered Boaz – which is not surprising since OT chronology separates Rahab and Salmon by almost 200 years. For the most part, Rahab receives a good report in both Jewish and Christian tradition, and the rabbis praised her as a proselyte, a prophetess, and one of the most beautiful women in the world.

Ruth is the Moabitess after whom the book of Ruth is named. Mt 1.5 contains the only NT reference to her, and she does not often put in an appearance in later Christian literature. Rabbinic tradition makes her a proselyte, the mother of kings, and an ancestress of the Messiah.

Obed the father of Jesse. David was known as the 'son of Jesse' (1 Sam 20.27, 30, etc.), and 'stump' or 'root' of Jesse has messianic meaning (Isa 11.1, 10; Rom 15.12). For Jesse in the OT see 1 Sam 16–17. He lived in Bethlehem.

6. Cf. 1 Chr 2.13–15; 3.4–5, 10; Ruth 4.22 LXX. This is the turning point between the first and second sections of the genealogy.

Jesse the father of King David. 'King David' is from the OT (2 Sam 6.12; 7.18; Prov. 1.1 etc.). 1.2–16 is a royal genealogy, and because he is the son of David the king, Jesus himself is royalty. The word 'king', however, must be carefully defined. Jesus is not a king who meets everyone's expectations. His kingship neither involves national sovereignty nor does it restore Israel to good political fortune. Jesus' kingdom is instead one which can be present even in the midst of Roman rule (see on 4.17). The Messiah's first task is to save his people from their sins (1.21), not deliver them from political bondage.

David was the father of Solomon. Luke traces Jesus' ancestry through another son of David, Nathan.

the wife of Uriah. Cf. 2 Sam 11.26; 12.10, 15. Uriah was a Hittite, so the expression, 'wife of Uriah', is better suited than the simple 'Bathsheba' for calling attention to Gentiles in Jesus' family tree; it could also evoke the sin of David, who had Uriah killed (2 Sam 11, 12). 1 Kgs 15.5 reads: 'David did what was right in the eyes of the Lord, and did not turn aside from anything that he commanded him all the days of his life, except in the matter of Uriah the Hittite.'

7. Cf. 1 Chr 3.10.

Solomon the father of Rehoboam. Rehoboam was the first king of Judah after the split of the northern and southern kingdoms. His mother was an Ammonitess, and the OT represents him as upholding pagan practices (1 Kgs 14.21–4; 2 Chr 12.13–14).

Rehoboam the father of Abijah. Abijah succeeded his father as king of Judah. Kings passes a negative judgement on him (1 Kgs 15.1–8), the writer of Chronicles a favourable verdict (2 Chr 13.1–22).

Abijah the father of Asaph. Matthew or his tradition probably confused the eponymous ancestor or founder of a guild of Levitic temple musicians (the 'sons of Asaph') to whom several Psalms were ascribed (50, 73–83; cf. 2 Chr 29.30; 35.15; Neh 12.46) with Asa the good king of Judah (1 Kgs 15.9–24).

8. Cf. 1 Chr 3.10-12.

Asaph the father of Jehoshaphat. Jehosaphat was the monarch whose achievements are praised in detail in 2 Chr 17–20.

Jehoshaphat the father of Joram. Joram, not to be confused with his namesake, the son of Ahab, was the wicked king whose reign of eight years is recounted in 2 Kgs 8.16–24 and 1 Chr 21.

Joram the father of Uzziah. This has the effect of striking out three kings between Joram and Uzziah or (if Uzziah is Ahaziah) between Ahaziah and Jotham. In order to maintain his 3×14 pattern, it seems that Matthew had to eliminate several kings from the monarchical section of his genealogy, and he may have decided to eliminate rulers who were associated with the cursed house of Ahab. Such omission of names from a genealogy for one purpose or another – including, apparently, brevity – was common practice.

9. Cf. 1 Chr 3.12–13.

Uzziah the father of Jotham, and Jotham the father of Ahaz, and Ahaz the father of Hezekiah. The OT portrays Hezekiah as an outstanding king who was faithful to Yahweh (2 Kgs 18–20; 1 Chr 29–32; Isa 36–9; Ecclus 49.4): 'there was none like unto him' (2 Kgs 18.5). Jotham also receives a favourable report (2 Kgs 15.32–8; 2 Chr 27). Ahaz, however, is thought of as an apostate (2 Kgs 16; 2 Chr 28). This entails that Matthew's concern must be something other than the listing of praiseworthy rulers.

10. Cf. 1 Chr 3.13–14.

Hezekiah the father of Manasseh. Manasseh was the most wicked king of Judah (2 Kgs 21.1–18; 2 Chr 33.1–9). It is, nevertheless, impossible to determine whether the evangelist would have thought of him as an unremittingly evil ruler or as one who finally came to repentance. Judaism held conflicting traditions on the point. There were legends about his repentance.

Manasseh the father of Amos. 'Amos' is Amon, who 'did what was evil in the sight of the Lord' (2 Kgs 21.19–26; 2 Chr 33.21–5).

Amos the father of Josiah. Josiah's lauded reign included commendable reforms and the discovery of the 'book of the law' (2 Kgs 22.1–23.30; 2 Chr 34–5).

11. The first tessaradecad, 1.2–6a, concluded with the appearance of King David and the inception of the monarchy; the second, 1.6b–11, concludes with a note of disaster, the deportation to Babylon.

Josiah the father of Jechoniah and his brothers. In 1 Chr 3.15–16, Josiah has four sons, the second being Jehoiachim, the father of

Jechoniah and Zedekiah. Why, then, does Matthew write, 'Josiah the father of Jechoniah and his brothers'? Again we may have deliberate omission in order to keep the 3 × 14 pattern.

at the deportation to Babylon. Cf. 1.12, 17. Although this is not developed in depth in first-century Judaism, the exile was not regarded as historical accident but instead interpreted in theological categories – God was punishing Israel for its sins or scattering Israel in order to make more proselytes or accomplishing some other wise purpose (cf. 2 Chr 36.15–21). Thus 'at the deportation to Babylon' should perhaps call to mind the hand of divine providence.

12. The genealogies of Luke and Matthew converge for Salathiel and Zerubbabel; but they disagree on the father of the former (Luke: Neri) and the son of the latter (Luke: Rhesa).

And after the deportation to Babylon. That the second major break point in Matthew's genealogy is the Babylonian captivity gives us a clue to the evangelist's eschatological orientation. The first break point is the establishment of the monarchy, while the culmination of the genealogy is Jesus Christ. Is not the reader to infer that the kingdom that was inaugurated with David and lost at the captivity is restored with the coming of Jesus, the Davidic Messiah?

Jechoniah was the father of Salathiel, and Salathiel the father of Zerubbabel. Zerubbabel, a descendant of David, was, after the exile, the Persian governor of Jerusalem. Messianic hopes came to rest upon him. In Haggai, he is the Lord's 'servant', his 'signet ring' (cf. Ecclus 49.11) and 'chosen' one (2.23). Zerubbabel's fate is unknown, but after him the Persians apparently did not choose governors from the Davidic line. 1 Chr 3.19 gives his descendants, but there is no Abiud among them.

13. This verse enters uncertain territory, for it is no longer possible to show that an OT genealogy is being copied. The names are just names: we know nothing about these people.

About five hundred years lie between Zerubbabel (who disappeared from history around 519 BC) and Joseph. For this period Matthew has only nine names, excluding Zerubbabel and Joseph (Luke has exactly twice as many: eighteen). Nothing could reveal more clearly the incomplete and inexact character of the evangelist's list of Jesus' ancestors.

15. Matthan the father of Jacob. In 1.16 Jacob (cf. 1.2; 8.11; 22.32) is the father of Joseph. In the OT too, of course, a Jacob begets a Joseph. Some would take this to be indicative of a Joseph typology in Mt 1–2. Joseph, the father of Jesus, is like the famous Joseph of old in that he (i) has a father named Jacob; (ii) goes down to Egypt; (iii) has dreams given to him about the future; (iv) is chaste and godly, and (v) is long-suffering and disinclined to shame others or exhibit their faults.

16. Unlike most OT genealogies, in which a genealogy's first name, the progenitor, is the key figure, in Matthew the final entry is the most important.

Jacob the father of Joseph. Joseph was a popular Jewish name. Leaving aside the apocryphal gospels, Jesus' father would be practically a faceless figure were it not for Mt 1–2. Nowhere else in the NT is he anything more than a bystander, the husband of Mary (Lk 1–2), or the father of Jesus (Jn 1.45; 6.42). Matthew, however, purports to tell us a few things about him: he was a Davidid, upright, a man of visions, and obedient to the Lord. The Gospel seems to go out of its way not to call Jesus the 'son' of Joseph or Joseph the 'father' of Jesus; and, at least in Mt 2, where Joseph is the guardian of 'the child and his mother', he avoids calling Mary the 'wife' of Joseph (note esp. 2.13–14, 20–1). The conjecture that Joseph might be the ultimate source for the material in Mt 1–2 is problematic given the likelihood – inferred from his absence from the public ministry – that he died at a time too early to pass on anything to believers in Jesus.

the husband of Mary. The four women named previously in the genealogy were introduced with the formula 'A was the father of B by C'. But we do not read that 'Joseph was the father of Jesus by Mary'. Mary's case stands by itself: it is an anomaly.

of whom was born. Mary now becomes the focus, Joseph being displaced. The 'divine passive' (absent in 1.2–1.6a) alludes to the activity of the Holy Spirit in Jesus' conception.

It may surprise that the genealogy is followed by a story which denies Joseph's participation in fathering Jesus. But Matthew has in mind legal, not physical, descent, that is, the transmission of legal heirship; and the idea of paternity on two levels – divine and human, with position in society being determined by the mother's husband – was familiar in the ancient near east.

17. So all the generations from Abraham to David were fourteen generations, and from David to the deportation to Babylon, fourteen generations, and from the deportation to Babylon to the Messiah, fourteen generations. From Abraham to David there are, in fact, fourteen generations, and from David to the deportation to Babylon, another fourteen; but from the deportation to the Christ there appear to be only thirteen generations. Numerous attempts have been made to explain this inconcinnity. None persuades. Perhaps it is best simply to ascribe a mathematical blunder to Matthew. Discrepancies between stated totals and actual totals are not uncommon in biblical and extra-biblical literature (cf. 1 Chr 3.22; Ezra 1.9–11; 2.2–64; Neh 7.7–66; 1 Esd 5.9–41).

* * * * *

(i) The biblical account of Noah (Gen 5–9) begins with a genealogy (5.1–31). Abraham's story (Gen 11–25) is likewise introduced by a genealogy (11.10–32). And the Chronicler prefaces his account of the kings of Judah with several genealogies. From this it appears that certain OT texts served Matthew as models for his compositional procedure, which fact in turn probably implies that the evangelist thought of his gospel as a continuation of the biblical history – and also, perhaps, that he conceived of his work as belonging to the same literary category as the scriptural cycles treating of OT figures.

(ii) The section offers proof of the title: Jesus is the son of Abraham and the Son of David. More particularly, because 'the heritage of the king is from son to son only' (Ecclus 45.25), and because Jesus is, through his father, a descendant of king David, in this respect he qualifies as the Davidic Messiah.

(iii) The genealogy implicitly reveals the identity and status of the church. Congregations which included both Jews and Gentiles could not find their identity in a shared racial heritage. They found it instead in their common Lord and saviour, who was with them when they gathered together (18.20). And since he was the Messiah, the Son of David and the son of Abraham, those who adhered to his words and participated in his destiny knew themselves to be heirs of the promises made to Abraham and David. In other words, the history of Jesus was his followers' history, his heritage their heritage. Despite its belonging to the rootless Hellenistic world of the first century, the church, by virtue of its union with Jesus, had a secure link with the remote past.

CONCEIVED OF THE HOLY SPIRIT, BORN OF A VIRGIN, IMPLANTED INTO THE LINE OF DAVID (1.18–25)

[18]**The birth of Jesus the Christ took place in this way. When his mother Mary had become engaged to Joseph, and before they had begun to live together, she was found to be with child of the Holy Spirit.** [19]**Her husband Joseph, being a righteous man and unwilling to expose her to public disgrace, determined to dismiss her quietly.** [20]**While he was contemplating this, behold, an angel of the Lord appeared to him in a dream, saying, 'Joseph, son of David, do not be afraid to take Mary as your wife; for the child conceived in her is of the Holy Spirit.** [21]**She will bear a son, and you will name him Jesus, for he will save his people from their sins'.** [22] **This all has happened in order to fulfil what had been spoken by the Lord through the prophet, saying,** [23]**'Behold, the virgin will conceive and bear a son, and they will call his name Emmanuel', which means, 'God is with us'.** [24]**When Joseph arose, he did as the angel of the Lord commanded**

him. He took her as his wife, [25] and he did not have marital relations with her until she had borne a son. And he called his name Jesus.

Parallels: Lk 2.1–7

If one compares 1.18–25 with the other two angelic appearances to Joseph (2.13–15; 2.19–21), a common pattern emerges:

A. note of circumstance (1.18–19; 2.13, 19)
B. appearance of the angel of the Lord in a dream (1.20; 2.13, 19)
C. command of the angel to Joseph (1.20; 2.13, 20)
D. explanation of command (1.20; 2.13, 20)
E. Joseph rises and obediently responds (1.24–5; 2.14–15, 21)

But 1.18–25 also exhibits features common to the angelic annunciation narratives in Gen 16 (Ishmael), Judg 13 (Samson), and Luke 1 (John the Baptist; Jesus):

A. description of circumstances (Gen 16.1–7; Judg 13.2; Lk 1.5–10; 1.26; Mt 1.18–20)
B. the angel of the Lord appears (Gen 16.7; Judg 13.3; Lk 1.11; 1.26–8; Mt 1.20)
C. angelic prophecy of birth, including child's future deeds (Gen 16.11–12; Judg 13.3–7; Lk 1.13–17; 1.30–3, 35–7; Mt 1.20–1)
D. account of the issue of things (Gen 16.13–16; Judg 13.19–25; Lk 1.18–25; 1.38; Mt 1.24–5).

18. The birth of Jesus the Christ took place in this way. Matthew is writing about the Son of David, and the events that follow take place in Bethlehem, the City of David, although this is not stated until 2.1. There are, in fact, no geographical notices at all in chapter 1 – this in striking contrast to chapter 2, where geography is a central theme.
When his mother Mary had become engaged to Joseph. To judge from the rabbinic sources, betrothal or engagement in ancient Judaism took place at a very early age, usually at twelve to twelve-and-a-half years. Following courtship and the completion of the marriage contract, the marriage was considered established: the woman had passed from her father's authority to that of her husband. But about a year typically passed before the woman moved from her parents' house to her husband's house. During that time, although the marriage was not yet consummated, the woman was 'wife' and she could become a widow or be punished for adultery. So betrothal was the legal equivalent of marriage, its cancellation divorce. This explains the situation of Joseph (cf. Lk 1.27). Even though he has not yet taken Mary, she is his wife (1.20, 24); and separation requires a certificate of divorce (1.19).

before they had begun to live together. This makes Matthew's major point, already hinted at in 1.16: Joseph is not the father.

she was found to be with child of the Holy Spirit. Cf. Lk 1.35. 'Of the Holy Spirit' (cf. 1.3, 5, 6, 16), a phrase which soon found its way into the creeds ('conceived of the Holy Spirit'), anticipates 1.20; it gives the reader knowledge the main character, Joseph, has not yet received.

19. a righteous man. Some have proposed that Joseph is 'righteous' in that he has mercy upon his betrothed: 'being a righteous man and (*therefore*) unwilling to expose her to public disgrace . . .'. The meaning of 'righteous' would then shade into that of 'compassion', and 'quietly' would be stressed. Still others, finding it difficult to suppose that Joseph suspected Mary of unfaithfulness, or finding it hard to think that Matthew so thought, take 'righteous' to imply reverential hesitation or awe: Joseph was afraid he would do wrong if he took Mary for his wife, for he might find himself interfering with God's plan. On this interpretation, Joseph already knows that Mary's pregnancy is of the Holy Spirit. But if this were so, we should expect to find Joseph in a quandary, at a loss concerning what action to pursue, not determined to divorce his betrothed. Moreover, the information divulged by the angel in 1.20 – Mary is with child of the Holy Spirit – is most readily viewed as revelatory; that is, Joseph does not yet know the true cause of his wife's conception. So it is better to endorse the view found already in Justin Martyr: 'Joseph, the husband of Mary, who at first wished to put away Mary his betrothed, since he supposed her to be pregnant by intercourse with a man, from fornication . . .'.

determined to dismiss her quietly. One of two options confronts Joseph. Either he can accuse his betrothed before the public authority and ask for a trial to determine whether she has been forcibly seized against her will or seduced with consent, or he can without further ado draw up a bill of divorce himself, without a trial, and call upon two or three witnesses to sign the document. The former course of action is represented by 'public disgrace'. The second course is represented by 'dismiss her quietly', the adverb indicating relative quiet, as opposed to the alternative.

In *LAB* 9, after Pharaoh commands the slaughter of all Hebrew children, the elders of the people conclude that no man should any longer come near his wife; cf. *Exod. Rab.* on 1.15, where even pregnant wives are divorced. After this decision is made, however, the pious Amram, reflecting on God's covenantal faithfulness, decides that he will go ahead and take a wife; and God blesses him. Amram foreshadows Joseph, who takes his wife despite difficult circumstances. See further below, p. 80.

20. The angelic revelation comes to Joseph in a dream. This shows us that the evangelist feels perfectly free to inform readers not just about objective events but also about what we must regard as subjective experiences. This is consistent with his stance as an omniscient narrator: his knowledge is not hindered by any circumstance. Thus Matthew informs us about a secret meeting between Herod and the magi (2.7) and about the latter's dream (2.12). He narrates an event at which only Jesus and Satan are present (4.1–11). He gives us the thoughts of the Pharisees (9.3) and the feelings of Herod (14.9). He tells us of Peter's fear (14.30) and of Jesus' hunger (21.18). He recounts the Pharisees' perceptions (21.45–6). He even knows the feelings and convictions of Jesus (9.36; 12.15; 13.58; 14.14).

While he was contemplating this, behold, an angel of the Lord appeared to him in a dream, saying. The 'angel of the Lord' is not, as in Gen 16; 21; 22; Exod 3; and Judg 6, a way of speaking of God; the angel is rather, in accordance with later Jewish thought, a being with its own identity. Apart from 28.2, 'angel of the Lord' is, in Matthew, confined to the infancy narratives (1.20, 24; 2.13, 19). In both 1–2 and 28 the angel is a messenger. Given the parallels shared by Mt 1.18–25; Gen 16; Judg 13; and Lk 1.5–23 (see above), it is certainly notable that an 'angel of the Lord' occurs also in Gen 16.7; Judg 13.3; and Lk 1.11.

The OT Joseph receives revelation in a dream (Gen 37.5–11). Maybe then the NT Joseph is meant to be like him. Yet the background is more plausibly to be found in the Moses legends, where the prophecies about the coming deliverer are given in dreams (e.g. *LAB* 9.10; Josephus, *Ant.* 2.212–17).

do not be afraid to take Mary as your wife. The quelling of human fear is a standard element in OT theophanies; it is also prevalent in intertestamental literature and the NT, where appearances of God are all but non-existent but appearances of angels common.

Mary, like her son Jesus, is a completely passive character throughout Mt 1–2. It is Joseph who does what needs to be done. This circumstance is partly to be explained by a christological interest: by his actions, Joseph, the Davidid, proves that he has made Jesus his own.

for the child conceived in her is of the Holy Spirit. This is the heart of the angelic message. Joseph now knows what readers know from 1.18: Mary has conceived miraculously by the Holy Spirit.

21. This prophecy of future greatness, which may be compared with those concerning Moses, Buddha, Confucius, Augustus, and many other religious heroes, exhibits a form common to birth annunciation narratives; see Gen 16.11; Gen 17.19; Isa 7.14; Lk 1.13, 31.

She will bear a son, and you will name him Jesus. Joseph, the son of David, is being instructed by the angel to name Jesus and thereby accept him as his own. Jesus will therefore himself be a Davidid. Cf. Isa 43.1: 'I have called you by name, you are mine.'

'As his name is so is he' (1 Sam 25.25; cf. Mt 16.17–18). 'Jesus' is the Greek for the Hebrew 'Joshua', which by popular etymology was related to the Hebrew verb 'to save' and to the Hebrew noun 'salvation'. Thus the saving character of Jesus (cf. 8.25; 9.21–2; 14.30; 27.42) is aptly evoked by his name.

for he will save his people from their sins. Whether 'his people' is Israel or the church, Jesus saves them 'from their sins'. This underlies the religious and moral – as opposed to political – character of the messianic deliverance. Liberation removes the wall of sin between God and the human race; nothing is said about freedom from the oppression of the governing powers. Beyond this, however, our verse is not very illuminating with regard to exactly *how* Jesus saves. The atoning death must be in view; but given the connexion in Matthew's world between sickness and sin (cf. 9.2), Jesus' healing ministry could also be thought of as having saved people from their sins. Furthermore, Jesus' revelatory imperatives and abiding presence (18.20; 28.20) are salvific in so far as they encourage and enable believers to obtain the 'better righteousness' (5.20). Perhaps, then, Jesus saves his people from their sins in a variety of ways.

The passion already comes into the picture, for it is at the crucifixion that Jesus pours out his lifeblood 'for the forgiveness of sins' (26.28). Thus the entire gospel is to be read in the light of its end. In addition, 1.21 makes clear from the outset that, notwithstanding Matthew's insistent demand for human righteousness, salvation is the gift of God. This fact will be reiterated in 20.28 and 26.28.

22. This verse contains the first of Matthew's formula quotations; see 2.5–6, 15, 17, 23; 4.14; 8.17; 12.17; 13.35; 21.4; 26.54, 56; 27.9.

It is difficult to decide whether Matthew intended the angel's speech to include 1.22–3. The parallel in 26.56 suggests that he did, as does the perfect tense, which well suits the point of view of one involved: 'this all has happened'. But the parallel in 21.4–5 as well as in other formula quotations, which are obviously to be read as editorial remarks, are against extending the quotation marks of 1.20–1 through 1.23.

what had been spoken by the Lord through the prophet, saying. For Matthew the prophets spoke of the latter days, that is, of the time of Jesus and his church.

23. At least two ends are served by the quotation of Isa 7.14. (i) It offers scriptural confirmation for the extraordinary history narrated in 1.18–25. Isaiah's words, which pertain to the house of David and speak of a virgin, are intended to show that Jesus' origin was according to the Scriptures. This is so important because it implicitly identifies and vindicates the church as the continuation of Israel. (ii) The mention of Emmanuel gives Matthew one more christological title with which to work. This is consonant with his desire to open his work by telling us *who* Jesus is. It also permits a sort of *inclusio*. For just as 1.23 speaks of Jesus as 'God *with us*', so the gospel ends with the promise, 'I am *with you* always . . .' (28.20).

Isa 7.14 was originally addressed to King Ahaz and perhaps prophesied the future coming of a Davidic king. Yet it is not certain that a royal person was in view. The force of the OT text could lie entirely with the name: 'Emmanuel' will be named because Yahweh will soon intervene for salvation and be with his people. However that may be, later Judaism apparently did not understand Isa 7.14 messianically; at least we have no positive evidence that it did. What Jewish traditions we do have connect the verse with Hezekiah. The application of Isa 7.14 to the Messiah may be peculiarly Christian.

Behold, the virgin will conceive and bear a son, and they will call his name Emmanuel. According to the MT, a 'young girl will conceive (or: 'is with child'; the tense is ambiguous) and will bear a son'. According to the LXX, 'a virgin will conceive and will bear a son'. The LXX probably means only that she who is now a virgin will later conceive and give birth: no miracle is involved. If the MT be understood similarly, then the OT does not clearly foresee an event like that in Matthew. This, along with the lack of pre-Christian evidence for a messianic interpretation of Isa 7.14, offers some reason for concluding that reflection on Isaiah's prophecy was not a sufficient cause of belief in the virginal conception of Jesus.

If Isa 7.14 does not of itself suffice to explain the Christian story of Jesus' origin, there is no agreement as to what might. The pagan parallels so often listed – such as the fertilization of the mothers of the Pharaohs by Amon, the begetting of Dionysus by Zeus, the supernatural origin of Romulus, son of Mars, the conception of Alexander the Great in the womb of his mother before the consummation of marriage, the fathering of Plato by Apollo – all of these are of contested worth for a couple of reasons. Conception without a male element in some form, parthenogenesis in the strict sense, does not seem to be attested. Beyond this, in narratives which breathe such a Jewish atmosphere as do Mt 1 and Lk 1–2, one prefers to seek for analogies in Judaism. Here too, however, the proposed parallels are of uncertain meaning. The possibility of impregnation by angels was believed in (cf. Gen 6.2 and the myth that Cain was literally engendered by Satan or an evil angel), but this notion can have had little to do with our canonical infancy narratives, at least in their present form. The bizarre story of the miraculous conception and birth of Melchizedek at the end of some mss. of *2 Enoch* (chapter 71), albeit intriguing, may be of relatively late origin; also, it neither has to do with a virgin nor does it mention a divine agent.

The best guess for a Jewish source is the possibility that there was a legend about Moses' virgin birth. The *Passover Haggadah* can be understood to interpret Exod. 2.25 ('God saw the people of Israel and God *knew*') in a sexual sense ('to know' can mean 'to have sexual intercourse with'), so that the conception of Moses is due to God's direct intervention. Further, already by the first century there was undoubtedly speculation about Moses' birth, because some believed that his mother, Jochebed, was exempt from the curse of Gen 3.16 and so had no birth pains. Beyond this, (i) rabbinic legend restored her virginity prior to her conception of Moses; (ii) tradition already by the first century equated the 'affliction' of Deut. 26:7 ('And he saw our affliction, and our distress, and our oppression') with sexual abstinence and so closely associated the time of Jochebed's impregnation with a time when men and women were not sleeping together (*LAB* 9); (iii) *Tg. Ps.-J.* on Exod. 2.2 has Moses born in the seventh month, and in Greek, Jewish, and Christian tradition, such an early birth is often a sign of miraculous origin; and (iv) *Exod. Rab.* 1.13 and 19 agree that Jochebed conceived before she remarried; and if anyone ever believed that and simultaneously believed (as many of the sources relate) that Amram divorced Jochebed in order to circumvent Pharaoh's decree, it would follow that Jochebed became pregnant between the time that her husband divorced and then remarried her, that is, during a temporary cessation of sexual relations. As explanation, only unlawful intercourse, of which there is no trace in the tradition, or supernatural intervention offer themselves for consideration. All of this is quite intriguing. But there are two problems, the first being that Jewish tradition is nowhere explicit about a virgin birth for Moses, and the second being that Josephus and Pseudo-Philo, our two richest first-century stories for Moses' birth, tell their tales in such a way as to exclude such.

None of the proposed parallels, either pagan or Jewish, seemingly accounts for the story we find in the NT. Because of this, some have considered the possibility of an historical catalyst. If, for instance, Mary did indeed, as both Matthew and Luke have it, conceive in advance of her marriage to Joseph, this potentially embarrassing fact might have been given a supernatural interpretation, with Isa 7.14 in mind. The story might also have arisen as a response to polemic about Jesus' origins. Or, if one is predisposed to find a genuine miracle in the birth of Jesus, appeal could be made to the idea of a 'family secret': Mary, who 'kept all these things, pondering them in her heart'

(Lk 2.19), could be the ultimate source of the account of Jesus' extraordinary entry into history. But this proposal raises difficult problems of its own, even apart from the question of the miraculous.

The doubtful character and meagre number of the extant sources and the limitations of historical research in general disallow a final verdict on the issue at hand. The origin of belief in the virginal conception and birth of Jesus remains unclarified. Yet, this being said, it should be plainly stated that the absence of any fully satisfactory mundane explanation is not to say that the historical evidence clearly confirms the miraculous conception of Jesus. The apparent silence of most of the NT, particularly Mark and John and Paul, the number of possible even though imperfect parallels in the history of religion, the fact that Mary and her family show no special understanding of Jesus during his ministry, and the non-historicity of so much in the infancy narratives all point rather strongly in one direction: affirmation of the virgin birth entangles one in difficult dilemmas. If the traditional belief is to be maintained, it will have to be on the basis of strictly theological considerations; historical reasoning offers little support.

God is with us. These words are from Isa 8.8 and translate the 'Emmanuel' of Isa 7.14. Either the evangelist is calling Jesus 'God' (cf. Jn 1.1–5; 20.28), or he is bringing out his significance as one in whom God's active presence, that is, the divine favour and blessing and aid have manifested themselves.

24. Joseph (i) rises and (ii) does as the angel of the Lord has commanded him; specifically, he (iii) takes Mary his wife (see on 1.20), does not have relations with her until she gives birth to a son, and calls the child's name Jesus. Cf. 21.6: the disciples (i) go and (ii) do as Jesus has commanded them; specifically, they (iii) bring the ass and the colt, put their garments upon them, and then Jesus sits thereon. These two sentences exhibit a form found in the OT. In Exod 7.10, for instance, Moses and Aaron (i) go before Pharaoh and his servants and (ii) do just as the Lord has commanded them; specifically, (iii) Aaron throws down his rod before Pharaoh and his servants and it becomes a dragon. Matthew, in employing the OT sentence form, wishes to show, first, Joseph's perfect obedience and, second, the complete fulfilment of the divine words spoken through the angel and through Scripture.

When Joseph arose, he did as the angel of the Lord commanded him. The biblical tradition has a habit of observing that visionaries arise or stand up after a divine encounter (e.g. Ezek 2.1–2; Dan 8.27; Lk 1.39).

25. and he did not have marital relations with her until she had borne a son. This retrospective observation does not necessarily imply that there were marital relations later on, for 'until' following a negative need not contain the idea of a limit which terminates the preceding action or state. At the same time, had Matthew held to Mary's perpetual virginity, he would almost certainly have chosen a less ambiguous expression – just as Luke would have avoided 'first-born son' (2.7).

And he called his name Jesus. The correlation between the angel's words in 1.21 and Joseph's obedience is thereby underlined; and, again, promise has become fulfilment.

* * * * *

(i) 1.18–25 is, like 1.1–17, introduction to the Gospel of Matthew, and that means introduction to Jesus. So here we have a piling-up of Christological facts. Jesus is the Christ, the Messiah (v. 18). He is conceived by the Holy Spirit (v. 18). He is the legal son of a Davidid (v. 20). He is the saviour of his people from their sins (v. 21). And he is 'Emmanuel', the presence of God in the world.

(ii) We cannot know whether Matthew thought of his infancy narrative as being solid, sober history. The issue admits of no straightforward resolution in part because of the lack of editorial comment, in part because Matthew's thoughts are not our thoughts: he could hardly have operated with our modern ideas of history and fiction. One nonetheless must wonder whether Matthew recognized the haggadic, indeed the poetic, character of his narrative. The rabbis were quite capable of making up stories when it suited their purposes, and the distinction between fact and edifying fiction is hardly a modern discovery. But, unfortunately, this is as far as we can go. Whether Matthew was persuaded that his infancy traditions, with their many parallels in the haggadic traditions about Moses, were more poetry than prose – how could one decide?

MAGI FROM THE EAST: GENTILES HONOUR THE NEW-BORN KING (2.1–12)

2 [1]**After Jesus was born in Bethlehem of Judea in the days of King Herod, magi from the East came to Jerusalem,** [2]**saying, 'Where is the one who has been born king of the Jews? For we have seen his star at its rising, and have come to pay him homage.'**
[3]**King Herod, upon hearing this, was frightened, and all Jerusalem with him.** [4]**And calling together all the chief priests and scribes of the people, he inquired of them where the Christ was to be born.** [5]**They said to him, 'In Bethlehem of Judea. For thus it has been written by the prophet,** [6]**"And you, O Bethlehem, in the land of Judah, are by no means least among the rulers of Judah; for from you will come a ruler who will shepherd my people Israel" '.**

⁷**Then Herod, secretly calling the magi, learned precisely from them the time when the star had appeared.**⁸**And sending them to Bethlehem he said, 'Go and search diligently for the child, and when you have found him, bring word to me, so that I also come and pay him homage.'**

⁹**Upon hearing the king, they went away. And behold, the star, which they had seen at its rising, went ahead of them, until it stopped over the place where the child was.** ¹⁰**Seeing that the star had stopped, they rejoiced exceedingly with great joy.**

¹¹**And upon entering the house, they saw the child with Mary his mother, and falling down they paid him homage; and opening their treasure chests, they offered him gifts, gold, frankincense, and myrrh.**

¹²**And having been warned in a dream not to return to Herod, they withdrew by another way for their own country.**

Parallels: none

Mt 1.1 opens the gospel by announcing that Jesus is the 'son of Abraham'. This means that Jesus brings salvation to the Gentiles, and 2.1–11 offers concrete illustration. In contradistinction to the leaders in Jerusalem, the magi, who are Gentiles, worship Jesus (the suggested link between the magi and Abraham is the stronger because, according to legend, the patriarch was a master of astrology and a teacher of eastern wise men).

1. 2.1–12 opens with the magi's arrival and ends with their departure.

After Jesus was born in Bethlehem of Judea. Cf. Jn 7.42: 'Does not the Scripture say that the Christ comes from the seed of David and from Bethlehem, the village where David was?' 'Bethlehem', where David was brought up and anointed king of Israel, was a Judean village located about five or six miles south-southwest of Jerusalem. Its important in the OT, where it is usually called 'the city of David', derives principally from its association with King David. Despite Mic 5.2; Mt 2.5; and Jn 7.42, it is uncertain to what degree Jewish opinion looked to Bethlehem as the Messiah's birthplace.

in the days of King Herod. Cf. Lk 1.5. Herod the Great, about whom we learn the most from Josephus, *Ant.* 14–18, probably died shortly before the Passover in 4 BC. So, according to Matthew (cf. 2.15, 19–20), Jesus must have been born shortly before this, perhaps between 7 and 4 BC. Matthew's concern, however, is not with chronology. Herod matters for two reasons. First, in his attempt to slaughter the Messiah, he is like the Pharaoh of Jewish tradition, who sought to kill the first redeemer, Moses. Second, although Herod could boast no royal genealogy, he was a king, and our evangelist is interested in contrasting his rule and kingdom with the rule and kingdom of Jesus the Davidic Messiah.

magi. *Magos* originally designated a member of a priestly caste of the Medes and Persians (Zoroastrians) who specialized in interpreting dreams. Later the word came to be used of those who possessed superior knowledge and ability, including astrologers, oriental sages, and soothsayers in general; it also became a label for all 'sorcerers' and 'magicians', and, finally, for 'quacks', 'deceivers', and 'seducers'.

from the East could call to mind: (i) Arabia, which is 'east' in the biblical tradition; Isa 60.6 associates gold and frankincense with Midian, Sheba, and Ephah; (ii) Babylon, which As. Mos. 3.13 calls the 'land of the east'; or (iii) Persia. A choice among these three alternatives is impossible, although if 2.11 alludes to Isa 60.6, one would be inclined to opt for Arabia, for that OT text speaks of Midian and Sheba; cf. also Ps 72.10. Whatever the solution, the undescribed and mysterious magi are representatives of the Gentile world; and while the Jewish leaders reject their Messiah, the Gentiles from outside the Land of Israel are anxious to greet him.

Magi and astrologers were widely regarded in the Graeco-Roman world as able to recognize the signs of the times, to foretell events of world importance, including the rise of kings. The dreams of King Astyages of Media (sixth century BC) were, according to Herodotus, taken by magi to mean that his grandson (Cyrus) would usurp the throne. And Persian magi allegedly prophesied on the night of Alexander's birth that one newly born would threaten all of Asia. The astrologer Publius Figulus purportedly cried out, when he learned the hour of the birth of Augustus, 'The ruler of the world is now born'. So Matthew's magi play a favourite, well-attested role, one they played often in the Graeco-Roman world. They are the mysterious foreigners who are able to recognize who it is that will be king – and in Mt 2 they testify to Jesus.

If the broad background to the story in Mt 2.1–12 is not peculiarly Jewish, the text also has a special background in the OT. In Num 22–4, the foreigner Balaam utters a prophecy about a star and a sceptre. This prophecy came in time to have messianic meaning, and it probably lies behind the star that Matthew's magi see. According to Num 23.7 LXX, Balaam was from the east, and Jewish tradition made him a *magos*, a prophet for the Gentiles, one of Pharaoh's advisers, and the father of Jannes and Jambres, themselves magi. When the evil king Balak tried to enlist Balaam in the cause against Israel, the seer turned around and prophesied the nation's future greatness and the coming of a magnificent ruler. This is rather close to Mt 2.1–12, where the cruel

Herod, in his attempt to destroy the king of Israel, employs foreign magi who in the event bring only honour to the new-born deliverer. So the magi are Balaam's successors, coming to witness the fulfilment of the OT oracle their predecessor uttered so long ago – 'A star will come forth out of Israel' (Num 24.17); 'He will rule many nations' (24.7 LXX). But the magi may be more than witnesses to the fulfilment of prophecy. They may, for Matthew, themselves fulfil OT promises, being 'those from Sheba who will come', who will bring to Jerusalem the wealth of nations, gold and silver, as the glory of the Lord rises upon her (Isa 60.3–6).

The very popular magi of later Christian tradition take us well beyond the Gospel. Matthew tells us neither that the magi were kings nor that they were three. Even greater problems are created by modern presentations – crèches and plays – which have the magi arrive in Bethlehem immediately after the birth of Jesus. In the First Gospel, the magi evidently come onto the scene only some time later – and they come not to a cave or a stable (as do the shepherds in Luke), but to the house of Mary and Joseph. Popular imagination, then, has taken many liberties with the canonical story.

came to Jerusalem. Matthew wishes to associate Herod with Jerusalem, for in his eyes many Jerusalemites share the king's malice and culpability (cf. 2.3–5). In addition, the opposition to Jesus is centred in the capital, for that is where the leaders are, and Matthew puts the heaviest blame on them, as will appear again and again in the passion narrative.

2. This is the only sentence the magi speak. Their general silence enhances the aura of mystery about them.

Where is the one who has been born king of the Jews? The query, 'where?', signals a leading theme of Mt 2. It is implicitly asked three times, and three different answers are given, each based upon Scripture. Where was the Messiah born? In Bethlehem of Judea, for so is it written of him, 'And you, O Bethlehem, in the land of Judah ...'. Where did the Messiah go after his birth? To Egypt and then back to Israel, for the word of the Lord through the prophet says, 'Out of Egypt have I called my son'. Where did the Messiah finally settle? In Nazareth, for as the word through the prophets has it, 'He will be called a Nazarene'. Scripture provides a messianic itinerary.

For we have seen his star. The testimony of the Scriptures (2.5) is supported by the testimony of nature. An intimate connexion between the natural world and the religious world of human beings is revealed; see further on 5.45; 6.26; 10.29; 27.51–3; and 28.2.

The story of the star and of the magi from the east seeking a king would not have been foreign to the ancients. According to both

Suetonius and Tacitus, at the turn of the era there was abroad the expectation of a world-ruler to come from Judea. And the hopes so elegantly expressed in Virgil's *Fourth Eclogue* probably reflect a general longing for a change in the times and the advent of a divine saviour. Furthermore, the association of astronomical phenomena with the appearance of a new king was common. Not only did ancient astrologers claim that the conjunction of certain constellations hailed the birth of a king, but, in Tacitus' words, 'the general belief is that a comet means a change of emperor'; so 'when a brilliant comet now appeared ... people speculated on Nero's successor as though Nero were already dethroned.' Eusebius wrote: 'In the case of ... remarkable and famous men we know that strange stars have appeared, what some call comets, or meteors, or tails of fire, or similar phenomena that are seen in connexion with great or unusual events.'

Mt 2 does not contain the First Gospel's only reference to astronomical phenomena. According to 24.29, the stars will fall from the heavens at the consummation. According to 27.45, the sun became darkened for three hours when Jesus was crucified. In both cases something terrible is involved: the judgement of the world and the torturing of Jesus. By way of contrast, the birth of Jesus is not something terrible. It is an occasion for joy (2.10) and thus accompanied neither by darkness nor falling stars but by a new star. A happy event on earth has as its correlate a good omen in the sky.

and have come to pay him homage. The custom of prostration before kings and high officials was universal in the ancient orient.

3. King Herod, upon hearing this, was frightened, and all Jerusalem with him. Herod thinks his throne to be in jeopardy. In this he is like Pharaoh, who, according to Josephus, 'feared' when he learned of Moses' birth.

While Jerusalem opposes Jesus in 2.1–12, Bethlehem is the place of his birth and Nazareth evidently becomes his home. Now Jerusalem was the centre of Jewish history and tradition, Bethlehem and Nazareth insignificant hamlets. Yet it is these last which welcome Jesus. One may see in all this a humbling of the exalted and the exalting of the humble. Herod, the Pharisees, the scribes, the chief priests, Pilate, Jerusalem – all are associated with power, all oppose Jesus, and all are rebuked by Matthew. In contrast, Bethlehem and Nazareth, the persecuted parents of Jesus, the twelve disciples – all are lowly, all receive Jesus, and all are exalted by Matthew. Often commentators have tended to overplay the Gentile/Jew contrast in Matthew and ignore altogether the powerful/powerless contrast. The result has sometimes been the unjustified discovery of anti-Judaism.

4. Our story offers a transmutation of a traditional motif – the superiority of the Jewish hero to foreign wise men. One thinks of Joseph's ability to interpret Pharaoh's dream when the Egyptian magicians and wise men could not (Gen 41), of the duels between Moses and Aaron and the sorcerers and wise men of Pharaoh (Exod 7–10), and of Daniel's success in revealing and interpreting Nebuchadnezzar's dream while the king's own enchanters are reduced to silence (Dan 2). The First Gospel too has a story in which foreigners must acknowledge the superiority of their Jewish counterparts. The magi do not know what is known by the chief priests and scribes, namely, where the Messiah should be born. They thus must seek enlightenment from the Jews. Beyond this, however, the traditional theme is turned on its head. For although the Jews excel in knowledge, they do not put their knowledge to its proper end; it is instead Gentiles who honour Jesus.

chief priests refers not to the present and past high priests alone but to an established college. It included the current high priest and his predecessors, the captain of the temple, the heads of the weekly courses, the directors of the daily courses, the temple overseers, and the temple treasurers. Matthew's association of this group with Herod may have been encouraged by his knowledge that the king personally selected several high priests. Because the 'chief priests' are found in the synoptic tradition above all in the passion narratives, their presence at the beginning of our gospel foreshadows their role at the end.

scribes were the 'teachers of the law', the 'lawyers' who interpreted the legal principles of the Torah, taught the people, and administered justice. They were Judaism's spiritual and intellectual leaders, its most prominent citizens. They lived chiefly in Judea, close to the capital; but there must also have been scribes in Galilee, even before AD 70. It is usual to identify the scribes as a professional class, not a party: thus some of the Pharisees were scribes, but not all scribes were Pharisees.

5. They said to him. There is no spokesman for the scribes; they speak instead as an impersonal unit.

by the prophet. The singular is used even though the citation is a conflation of sentences from two different books, Micah and 2 Samuel.

6. The quotation from 'And you' through 'ruler' is from Mic 5.2.

are by no means least among the rulers of Judah. 'By no means least' has no basis in the OT. Micah in fact remarks upon Bethlehem's insignificance. Matthew's denial can only mean that because the Messiah has come into the world at Bethlehem, he has brought the city greatness.

for from you will come a ruler. Jesus, not those Herod has gathered, should lead Israel.

who will shepherd my people Israel. This reproduces 2 Sam 5.2 = 1 Chr 11.2, save 'who will govern' replaces 'you will govern'. To a first-century Jew, reference to a ruler come forth to 'shepherd my people Israel' would have conjured up the eschatological expectation of the ingathering of the twelve tribes of Israel, an expectation apparently shared by Matthew (19.28). So Israel's blindness, it seems, is only for a season (see on 23.37–9). The alternative is to suppose that for Matthew the church of both Jew and Gentile had already come to supplant once and for all the place of Israel in salvation-history. Yet surely the OT promises of restoration prohibited this thought. Paul could, despite 1 Th 2.16, still hold out hope for Israel's final redemption (Rom 11); the same holds for Matthew.

7. Herod now inquires of the Gentile magi just as he inquired of the Jewish scribes. Putting together the information gathered from both, he can infer what has happened.

Then Herod, secretly calling the magi. The later (successful) attempt to do away with Jesus is also clandestine (26.3–5, 14–16, 47–50). Are we to suppose that just as Herod keeps his true devices from the magi, so too does he hide his machinations from the Jewish leaders, who are not privy to what the easterners divulge?

the time when the star had appeared matters because Herod must determine the age of the children to be slaughtered. The implicit assumption is probably that the initial appearance of the star coincided with the birth or conception of the child.

Although what the magi tell the king is not related, readers may infer that Herod cruelly chooses an excessively wide margin of safety when he determines to have every Bethlehem infant two years of age and under put to the sword.

8. and when you have found him, bring word to me, so that I also come and pay him homage. Herod's remark, 'so that I also come and pay him homage', which restates the magi's goal (2.2), is intended to deceive the magi and to put Herod on their side. Nothing could make plainer that the magi are free of complicity in the king's scheme: in order to comply, they must be tricked.

9. The magi go by themselves to find the new-born king. The Jewish scribes, if they know where he is, are not interested in going.

went ahead of them. The star, which has already appeared and disappeared, now reappears ('behold') and 'goes before' the magi, who must be travelling at night. This raises difficult questions. Why would one need supernatural guidance to make the six-mile trek from the capital to Bethlehem? And how could a heavenly light be said to go ahead of people, or stand over a precise place, seemingly a particular house?

It seems likely enough that Matthew, like so many commentators before Renaissance astronomy, understood the star to be animate and so an angel. Certainly modern attempts to identify it with a planetary conjunction, comet, or supernova are futile. The *Protevangelium of James* (21.3), Ephrem the Syrian, and Chrysostom all rightly recognize that the so-called star does not stay on high but moves as a guide and indeed comes to rest very near the infant Jesus. Matters become clear when we recall that the ancients generally believed stars to be animate beings, and that Jews in particular identified them with angels; cf. Job 38.7. So Theophylact and others must be right in identifying the magi's star with an angel. Cf. the angelic guide of the exodus (Exod 23.20, 23; 32.34).

Until it stopped over the place where the child was. Chrysostom: the star 'did not, remaining on high, point out the place, it being impossible for them [the magi] so to ascertain it; it rather came down and performed this office. For you know that a spot of such small dimensions, being only as much as a shed occupies, or rather as much as the body of a little infant takes up, could not possibly be marked out by a star. For by reasons of its immense height, it could not sufficiently distinguish so confined a spot, and reveal it to those desiring to see it.'

10. Seeing that the star had stopped, they rejoiced exceedingly with great joy. While Matthew's Gospel tends to be sombre, here joy breaks through; cf. Lk 1.14, 28; 2.10.

11. The first act of chapter 2 now comes to its climax. The goal of the magi's journey (stated in 2.2) has been obtained: 'and falling down they paid him homage'.

And upon entering the house. Cf. Lk 2.15–16. If 'the house' is the house of Jesus and his parents in Bethlehem, this would not harmonize with Luke's account, which explains that Jesus was laid in a feeding trough, 'because there was no room for them at the inn' (2.7).

they saw the child with Mary his mother. Until now the magi have gazed upon a star. Coming to Bethlehem, their eyes rest on what the guiding star has led to: Jesus. The phrase, 'the child with Mary his mother' recurs (with slight variations) in 2.13, 14, 20, 21. It serves three ends. (i) It puts Joseph out of the picture, thereby reinforcing the impact of 1.16–25: Jesus has no human father. (ii) 'The child and his mother' probably harks back to Exod 4.20, for Exod 4.19 is the basis for Mt 2.20, in which 'the child and his mother' appears again. The Moses typology is thereby furthered. (iii) Because 'the child' (see on 2.8–9) is named first, he is shown to be the focus of all the action. Even Mary is in the shadows, for she gains her identity only by being 'his mother'.

and falling down they paid him homage. Cf. 2.2. They fall down on their faces. This is perhaps noteworthy as there was a tendency in Judaism to think prostration proper only in the worship of God.

and opening their treasure chests. As the magi seem to know, earthly treasure is to be given up or given to God (2.11; 6.19). Only heavenly treasure matters (6.20–1; 19.21).

they offered him gifts. The three gifts symbolize loyalty and submission; but the magi are not – as the church Fathers taught – giving up the tools of their trade.

frankincense was an odoriferous gum resin from various trees and bushes which had a cultic usage in the ancient world. According to Exod 30.34–8, it was a prescribed ingredient of sacred incense. According to Lev 24.7, it was to be offered with the bread of the Presence. According to Lev 2.1–2, 14–6; 6.14–8, it was added to cereal offerings. In *b. Sanh.* 43a it is said to be an anodyne. Whether frankincense was cultivated in Palestine is debated and doubtful; that it was imported from Arabia is certain.

myrrh was a fragrant gum resin from trees particularly abundant in south Arabia and north Ethiopia. It had a variety of uses, being an element in perfumes, a component of holy anointing oil, and an ingredient in incense. It also served as a burial spice and, like frankincense, as an anodyne.

What is signified by the gold, frankincense, and myrrh? The most common interpretation in church history appears early: gold for Jesus as king, frankincense for Jesus as God, myrrh for Jesus as the one to die. But a better guess as to what the gifts mean is that the magi's worship and presentation are the first fruits of the eschatological pilgrimage of the nations and their submission to the one true God. The OT teaches that the great redemption will see the Gentiles come up to Zion, bringing gifts and offering right worship. Especially interesting in this regard is *Ps. Sol.* 17.31, according to which the heathen nations will come from the ends of the earth with gifts in hand to see the glory of the Son of David. *1 En.* 53.1 similarly foresees the time when all those dwelling on the earth and sea and islands will bring to the Righteous and Elect One, the Son of Man, gifts and presents and tokens of homage. Now undoubtedly both Isa 60 and Ps 72 would have been understood by Matthew and his readers in terms of the expected pilgrimage of the nations: and these two OT texts, although they are not explicitly cited, are probably echoed in Mt 2. Isa 60 contains these words: 'Arise, shine; for your light has come, and the glory of the Lord has risen upon you' (60.1); 'Nations shall come to your light, and kings to the brightness of your rising' (60.3); 'The wealth of nations shall come to you' (60.5); 'They shall bring gold and frankincense and proclaim the praise of the Lord' (60.6). And in Ps 72, which even a few modern interpreters have taken to be messianic, there is this: 'May the kings of Tarshish and of the isles render him tribute, may the kings of Sheba and Seba bring gifts' (72.10); 'May all kings fall down before him, all nations serve him' (72.11); 'Long may he live, may gold of Sheba be given to him' (72.15).

12. And having been warned in a dream not to return to Herod. Cf. Mt 27.19.

they withdrew by another way for their own country. Although we do not know when the magi left, we do know when they received their warning – at night, 'in a dream'. On this two points may be pertinent. (i) God spoke to Balaam in the night (Num 22.7–13, 19–20). (ii) According to some rabbinic sources, God speaks to the Gentiles only at night.

* * * * *

(i) 2.1–12 has the power to fascinate readers and to stay in the memory because it incorporates ever-popular and perennially pleasing characters and motifs: the mysterious magi from the east, the anomalous star coincident with the birth of a king, the threat to the life of an infant hero, the warning that comes in a dream. These are things to delight and enchant, to entertain and cause wonder.

(ii) In T. S. Eliot's poem, 'Journey of the Magi', the visitors from the east see, on their way to Bethlehem, 'three trees on the low sky', and 'six hands at an open door dicing for pieces of silver'. The three trees stand for the three crosses, while the men dicing for silver represent the soldiers casting lots for Jesus' garments and Judas' betrayal of his master for thirty pieces of silver. So at Jesus' birth his death is already anticipated. Matthew, one imagines, would have approved of Eliot's interpretation, for there are indeed connexions between Mt 2 and the passion narrative, such as the gathering of the Jewish leaders, the title, 'king of the Jews', and the decision of the ruling authority to do away with Jesus. Matthew wants the end foreshadowed in the beginning.

(iii) Leonardo da Vinci's *Adoration of the Magi* highlights an aspect of Matthew's text that other artists – and some exegetes – have missed: 2.1–12 has not only a foreground but also a background. In da Vinci's painting, behind the magi and Jesus and Mary there are buildings in ruin and horsemen at joust. The meaning is manifest. The world into which the Messiah comes is in chaos and decay; things need to be righted. This is also an element in Matthew's story. When Jesus is born, Jerusalem, instead of being overjoyed, is troubled at the news. And there is upon Israel's throne a wicked and illegitimate ruler. And innocent blood is about to be shed (cf. 2.13–23). In brief, the world is ill. It is no wonder that the first word of Jesus' public proclamation is, 'Repent!' (4.17).

THE MESSIAH'S FLIGHT AND RETURN (2.13–23)

[13]After they had departed, behold, an angel of the Lord appeared to Joseph in a dream, saying, 'Rise, take the child and his mother, and flee to Egypt, and remain there until I tell you; for Herod is about to search for the child, to destroy him.' [14]And rising he took the child and his mother by night, and departed to Egypt, [15]and he remained there until the death of Herod. This was to fulfil what had been spoken by the Lord through the prophet, saying, 'Out of Egypt have I called my son.'

[16]Then Herod, seeing that he had been tricked by the wise men, was exceedingly angry, and he sent and killed all the male children in and around Bethlehem who were two years old or under, according to the time that he had learned from the wise men. [17]Then was fulfilled what had been spoken through the prophet Jeremiah, [18]'A voice was heard in Ramah, wailing and loud lamentation, Rachel weeping for her children. She refused to be consoled, because they were not.'

[19]When Herod died, behold, an angel of the Lord appeared in a dream to Joseph in Egypt, [20]saying, 'Rise, take the child and his mother, and go to the land of Israel, for those seeking the life of the child have died.' [21]Then rising, he took the child and his mother and went to the land of Israel.

[22]But hearing that Archelaus ruled over Judea in place of his father Herod, he was afraid to go there. And after being warned in a dream, he withdrew to the district of Galilee. [23]And coming he dwelled in a town called Nazareth. Thus was fulfilled the word through the prophets, that 'He will be called a Nazorean'.

Parallels: none

A dramatic contrast is occasioned by the juxtaposition of 2.13–23 with the conclusion of 2.1–12. The reader is taken from a scene of prostration and gift-giving to a scene of danger and flight. The disparity between the magi's response to the child Messiah and that of Herod could hardly be more pronounced. While the foreigners worship Jesus, the king in Israel threatens his life. This circumstance reflects the extremes of possible responses to Jesus: one can either embrace him and his cause or react with anger or violence.

13. This verse has an almost perfect parallel in 2.19–20.

After they had departed, behold, an angel of the Lord appeared to

Joseph in a dream, saying. The magi were warned of Herod in a dream, but no angel appeared. That one appears to Joseph points to his importance.

Rise, take the child and his mother. Joseph is still the only active character in the family of Jesus.

and flee to Egypt. Almost as soon as he is born, the Son of man, who like Moses will grow up in Egypt, has no place to lay his head; cf. 8.20. Already he is the forerunner of his disciples, who will have to flee when the tribulation of the latter days falls upon them (10.23; 24.16); cf. 3.7; 23.33.

for Herod is about to search for the child, to destroy him. Cf. Exod 2.15.

14. Joseph obeys the angel's command to the letter: he rises, he takes, he goes, and he returns, just as instructed.

Matthew gives none of the details we might expect from other narrators, such as the route Joseph took to Egypt, or how long the family resided there, etc. The evangelist sticks to the barest essentials.

And rising he took the child and his mother by night, and departed to Egypt. In the passion narrative Jesus will declare that, if he willed it, more than twelve legions of angels would come to his aid: but the time has come for something else, the fulfilment of Scripture (26.53–4). In Mt 2, on the other hand, the time of the crucifixion lies far ahead, and Jesus must be saved for what is to come. This is why the angelic command to flee and Joseph's keeping Jesus safe from harm are for the moment necessary.

15. This verse anticipates 2.19–21: the stay in Egypt will be ended by Herod's death – just as Moses' stay in Midian was concluded when the king of Egypt died (Exod 4.19–20).

And he remained there until the death of Herod. Cf. Exod 4.19.

This was to fulfil what had been spoken by the Lord through the prophet, saying. See on 1.22. The following is a brief citation of Hos 11.1.

Out of Egypt have I called my son. The application of Hos 11.1 to Jesus seems gratuitous. In its original context the verse unambiguously refers to Israel: 'When Israel was a child I loved him, and out of Egypt have I called my son.' But three points may give us sympathy for Matthew's use of this OT Scripture. First, the evangelist was surely aware that 'Out of Egypt', etc. was originally spoken of Israel. He could not have been naïvely oblivious of the switch in referents when he applied Hos 11.1 to Jesus, not to the people. One can think this in part because, second, Christian tradition before Matthew had portrayed Jesus as repeating or recapitulating certain experiences of Israel; see 4.1–11. Third, in ancient Jewish sources concerned with eschatological matters, the redemption from Egypt often serves as a type for the messianic redemption, and the prospect of another exodus is held forth: before the consummation, the pattern of exodus/return will repeat itself; cf. Isa 40.3–4; Ezek 20.33–44; Hos 2.14–15. Given this expectation, it would have been no large step for Matthew to find it foreshadowed or realized in the life of Jesus.

16. The magi and the family of Jesus have left the stage and attention is now directed towards Herod, whose anger, inflamed by the magi's failure to cooperate, moves the king to act as Pharaoh once acted. The angel's prediction (2.13) comes to pass.

was exceedingly angry. The wise men were exceedingly joyous. Herod, because his plan has been frustrated, is exceedingly angry.

and he sent and killed all the male children in and around Bethlehem. Cf. Exod 2.15: Pharaoh sought to kill Moses. Note that the children to be slaughtered are all male children. In Matthew's mind there could be no thought of a female king. Recall also Exod 1.22, where 'every male born to the Hebrews' is, by Pharaoh's command, to be thrown into the Nile river.

17. Then was fulfilled what had been spoken through the prophet Jeremiah. Why the temporal 'then' instead of the expected, purposive 'in order that'? 'Then' also replaces 'in order that' in 27.9, where a quotation concludes the story of Judas' betrayal and hanging. Now both 2.17 and 27.9 introduce texts attached to stories in which evils are suffered because of opposition to Jesus. Matthew cannot attribute such evils directly to the hand of God. Rather, culpability lies with those who seek to do away with Jesus, and they bring judgement on themselves. So a distinction is implicitly drawn between what God foresees and permissively wills and what God actively wills and makes come to pass.

18. The clue to the meaning of v.18 may be found by looking at the context of Jer 31.15, the passage quoted here. The chapter as a whole is one of hope. It pictures in bright colours the joyous day on which the exiles will return to the land of Israel. That the chapter could be viewed as eschatological must be granted, especially in view of vv. 31–4, which foresee a new covenant and the dwelling of God with God's people. Certainly many early Christians thus understood the matter, for they applied the verses to the Messiah's advent and the consummation (Lk 22.20; Jn 6.45; etc.). Now if Matthew had read the chapter with the story of Jesus as he knew it in mind, a number of statements and expressions would have caught his attention. The one who returns to Israel is called a 'virgin' (vv. 4, 21) and 'my dear son . . . my darling child' (v. 20). In v. 9 God declares, 'I am a father to Israel, and Ephraim is my first-born.' Among those who return from exile is 'the woman with child' (v. 8). We further read that 'the Lord has saved his people' (v. 7), that 'your children shall come back to their own country' (v. 17), that God fixed 'the stars for light by night' (v. 35), that those who hunger and thirst will be filled (v. 25), and that God will establish a new covenant with his people (vv. 31–3). In view of all this, and given the typological equation of Jesus with Israel, the evangelist could readily have seen in Jeremiah's prophecy of Israel's return from the exile and of the new things promised for thereafter a transparent cipher or prototype for the Messiah's return to Israel and subsequent ministry: the words originally spoken of Israel are equally applicable to Israel's Messiah. It would then have been a small step to discover in v. 15 a reference to the slaughter of the infants of Bethlehem, for beyond the association made possible by the lamentation and weeping for children that are not, Ramah was near to Bethlehem, and Rachel's grave was thought by many to be in the city of David.

wailing and loud lamentation. Matthew's quotation reproduces the only gloomy verse in all of Jer 31: the chapter as a whole conveys joy and hopeful expectation. Indeed, the gist of 31.15 is immediately cancelled by the admonition not to weep and cry, for the lost children will return (v. 16). For this reason a number of scholars have suspected Matthew of hoping that his readers would take cognizance of the context of Jer 31.15 and recognize the implicit promise: exile is to be followed by return, sorrow is to be swallowed up by joy, for the oppression of the tyrant must be broken by God's victory.

19–20. The demise of Herod the Great introduces the concluding section of the infancy narrative, Jesus' return from exile to Egypt. The verses have their blueprint in the story of Moses:

Matthew	Exodus
2.19 But when Herod died, behold, an angel of the Lord appeared in a dream to Joseph in Egypt	4.19 After these many days the king of Egypt died (LXX only). The Lord said to Moses in Midian,
2.20 saying, 'Rise, take the child and his mother, and go to the land of Israel, for those seeking the life of the child have died.'	'Go back to Egypt, for all those seeking your child have died.'

2.21 Then rising, he took	4.20 Moses, taking
	his wife
the child	and his children,
and his mother	
	mounted them on asses
and went to	and returned to Egypt
the land of Israel.	(MT: 'the land of Egypt').

Particularly striking is the plural in Mt 2.20: 'those seeking . . . have died'. Herod is the only immediate antecedent. This might be explained as a 'rhetorical' or 'allusive' plural, with references to Herod's coactors in 2.3–4. But it is easier to believe that the language of Exod 4.19 has been retained without perfect grammatical adjustment, in order to make the parallel with the sentence from the story of Moses unmistakable.

When Herod died. Cf. Exod 4.19.When exactly Herod died is not stated, and the guesses of the commentators as to how long we should think of the family's stay lasting are just that – guesses.

21. Again the response of Joseph matches perfectly the angel's command.

22. But hearing that Archelaus ruled over Judea in place of his father Herod, he was afraid to go there. And after being warned in a dream, he withdrew to the district of Galilee. From whom Joseph is supposed to have learned of Archelaus we are not told. The situation, however, is similar to that recounted in 1.18–25. (i) Joseph learns a disquieting fact – in the one case that his wife is pregnant, in the other that Archelaus is king. (ii) Divine revelation intervenes to make plain the rightful course of action under the difficult circumstances.

If Joseph cannot take Mary and Jesus back to Judea, to the house in Bethlehem, this is because, presumably, the identity of the messianic child might somehow become known, and the response of Archelaus, Herod's son, would be like his father's – he would kill Jesus.

he was afraid to go there. In contrast to all that has gone before, human initiative now plays a role in Matthew's story.

23. The pressure on Jewish Christians to come up with a proof text for Jesus' having lived in Nazareth must have been considerable. The town was of little account and nothing in the OT or Jewish tradition prepared for its connexion with messianic events. To what extent non-Christian Jews turned Nazareth into a reproach we do not know; but early believers in Jesus certainly would have felt a difficulty (cf. Jn 1.46). Moreover, given the belief in the significance of Bethlehem and in Jesus' birth there, the prominence of Nazareth in the gospel tradition would have been all the more puzzling. Verse 23 is, then, an attempt to come to grips with a difficult fact.

And coming he dwelled in a town called Nazareth. The small, insignificant Nazareth (cf. Jn 1.46), an agricultural village about fifteen miles straight west of the southern tip of the Sea of Galilee, does not appear in the OT, Josephus, or the Talmuds. This led some earlier scholars to deny its existence. But *nsrt* turned up on a third- or fourth-century AD Jewish inscription of priestly courses found at Caesarea in 1962, and excavations on the traditional site have uncovered graves and objects from the first century.

Thus was fulfilled the word through the prophets, that. This introductory formula is marked by two peculiarities. Why is 'the word' not (as elsewhere) 'through the prophet' but rather 'through the prophets' (plural)? And why is the expected 'saying' displaced by 'that'? These two problems are almost certainly to be related to a third, namely, that 'he will be called a Nazarene' cannot be found in the OT. 'The prophet*s*' (cf. 26.26) probably alerts us to expect something other than the verbatim quotation of one particular Scripture: Matthew is not just reproducing an OT text. The displacement of 'saying' probably serves the same purpose.

In having no perfect OT parallel despite being prefaced by words which might be taken to indicate otherwise, 2.23 is not alone. Ezra 9.11–12 quotes a command purportedly delivered to the prophets, but no such command is found in the OT. In the NT, Jn 7.38; Rom 11.8; and Jas 4.5 attribute to Scripture sentences that at best paraphrase the substance of several OT passages.

He will be called a Nazorean. Even though grammatically awkward, the subject of this sentence appears to be Jesus, not Joseph. The words do not appear in the OT. Yet Matthew refers to 'the prophets' being fulfilled. Many explanations have been forwarded: the biblical text is Isa 11.1 (the branch [*neser*] from Jesse) or 42.6 or 49.6 or Jer 31.6–7 or Gen 49.26; or we should think of Nazareth as a humble place and so connect it with the contempt for Isaiah's suffering servant. It is more likely, however, that Matthew contains a word play. The LXX interchanges 'holy one of God' – an early Christian title for Jesus (Mk 1.24; Lk 4.34; Jn 6.69) – and 'Nazarite'; cf. Judg 13.7; 16.17. This matters because if we make that substitution in Isa 4.3 MT ('will be called holy'), the result is very near Mt 2.23.

In Acts 24.5, Christians are 'the sect of the Nazarenes', and in rabbinic writings Christians are *nosrim*, and we know of Jewish Christians who were called 'Nazoraeans'. Given the striking links between Matthean Christianity and Nazoraean Christianity as known through the fathers, as well as the fact that Syrian Christians commonly called themselves *nasraya*, it is quite possible that members of the Matthean community referred to themselves not as 'Christians' (a term missing from our Gospel) but as 'Nazoraeans'. Certainly that would have given 2.23 an even greater impact: Jesus' followers bear the name that he bore.

* * * * *

(i) There is in 2.13–23 a Jesus/Israel typology, a typology which will be taken up once again in chapters 3 and 4, where Jesus passes through the waters of baptism and then enters into the desert. In 2.15, for instance, the 'son' of Hos 11.1, originally Israel, becomes Jesus. And behind the quotation of Jer 31.15 in 2.18 there apparently lies, as argued, a typological equation of Jesus with Israel: in Jeremiah's prophecy of return for the exiles Matthew discerns a cipher for the Messiah's return to Israel. So if Jesus culminates Israel's history in chapter 1, in chapter 2 he repeats it. Jesus is not only the last redeemer who is like the first redeemer, Moses, he is not only the messianic king who is like the great king, David, but he is also like Israel in that he experiences exodus and exile and return; and Scriptures originally pertaining to Israel can be transferred to him.

(ii) At the end of Mt 1–2 one is left with the impression that, at least concerning salvation-history, human choice matters little. Rather does all come down to the divine will. The events and movements of 1.2–2.23 are determined by providence. There are, in Mt 1–2, five formula quotations, and these, taken together, seemingly imply that the unprecedented occurrences surrounding the Messiah's advent were 'determined' long before they happened. Moreover, to make sure that all goes according to plan, there is the angel of the Lord, who, when someone is not acting out the script, will intervene to put things right (1.20; 2.12). Our gospel's deterministic interpretation of history also seems manifest in the genealogy, in which we find the ancestral line of Jesus neatly divided into 3×14 generations, and in which the movement towards the Messiah appears inevitable. In short, then, one comes away from Matthew's first two chapters with the feeling that history is divinely run from first to last. At the same time, it must be said that the evangelist was nevertheless not naïvely persuaded that 'God's on his throne – all's right with the world'. In 2.16–18 there is a terrible tragedy, the massacre of the infants of Bethlehem; and Matthew, by substituting 'then' for 'in order that' in 2.17, betrays his reluctance to ascribe suffering or evil outcomes to the Lord God. Beyond this, there runs throughout Matthew's gospel a strong eschatological expectation – a sure sign of dissatisfaction with the world as it is. The conclusion, then, is that while history is, for our evangelist, the arena of God's mighty acts, it is also the arena of much else: there is darkness as well as light. God's will is not always done (cf. 6.10), and this will be true until the end of the age comes.

JOHN THE BAPTIST AND JESUS (3.1–17)

3 [1]**In those days John the Baptist appeared, preaching in the wilderness of Judea and saying,** [2]**'Repent, for the kingdom of heaven has come near.'** [3]**For this is the one who was spoken about by the prophet Isaiah, saying, 'The voice of one crying out in the wilderness: "Prepare the way of the Lord; make his paths straight".'** [4]**Now John wore clothing of camel's hair, and he had a leather belt around his waist, and his food was locusts and wild honey.** [5]**Then the people of Jerusalem and all Judea and all the region along the Jordan went out to him,** [6]**and they were baptized by him in the river Jordan, confessing their sins.**

[7]**But he, seeing many Pharisees and Sadducees coming for baptism, said to them, 'You brood of vipers! Who warned you to flee from the wrath to come?** [8]**Bear fruit worthy of repentance,** [9]**and do not presume to say to yourselves, "We have Abraham as our father"; for I say to you, God is able from these stones to raise up children to Abraham.** [10]**Even now the axe is laid at the root of the trees. So every tree that does not bear good fruit is cut down and thrown into the fire.** [11]**I baptize you with water for repentance, but the one who is coming after me is mightier than I, whose sandals I am not worthy to carry. He will baptize you with the Holy Spirit and with fire.** [12]**His winnowing fork is in his hand, and he will clear his threshing floor and will gather his wheat into the granary. But the chaff he will burn with unquenchable fire.'**

[13]**Then Jesus came from Galilee to the Jordan to John, to be baptized by him.** [14]**John would have prevented him, saying, 'I need to be baptized by you, and do you come to me?'** [15]**But answering Jesus said to him, 'Let it be so now; for thus is it proper for us to fulfil all righteousness.' Then he consented.** [16]**And when Jesus had been baptized, he came up from the water, and behold, the heavens were opened to him and he saw the Spirit of God descending like a dove and alighting on him.** [17]**And behold, a voice from heaven said, 'This is my Son, the beloved, in whom I am well pleased.'**

Parallels: Mk 1.2–11; Lk 3.1–22; Jn 1.19–34

John the Baptist Introduced (3.1–6)

Matthew now jumps over many years, passing from Jesus' infancy to his baptism. The intervening period is thus relatively unimportant and does not even merit an allusion. Perhaps Matthew, unlike Luke, inherited no stories about the boy Jesus. The omission might, however, be intentional, a part of Matthew's Moses typology, for Exod 2 similarly skips from Moses' infancy to adulthood.

1. John the Baptist is, in Matthew, distinguished by three chief characteristics. First, he is Jesus' forerunner, the messenger sent to prepare Israel for her encounter with the coming one (3.3, 11–12; 11.10); that is, he is Elijah (11.14; 17.11–13), whose task it is to ready God's people for the day of the Lord (Mal 4.5–6). Second, he is the subordinate of Jesus, his inferior. This subordination, which is particularly apparent in 3.11–12, 14 and 11.2–6, is implicit in John's ministry as forerunner, for it is his assigned task to point towards another (3.11–12). The origin of the theme is perhaps partly accounted for by the rivalry between Jesus' disciples and those of John. But of this rivalry there is no development in Matthew, and there is no significant polemic against the Baptist or his followers; see 9.14–17; 11.2–6; 14.12; contrast Jn 1. Indeed, side by side with the theme of subordination is – and this is the third major item in Matthew's portrait of the Baptist – a high degree of parallelism between John and Jesus; cf. Lk 1. The two men say similar things; cf. 3.2 with 4.17, 3.7 with 12.34 and 23.33, and 3.10 with 7.19. Both are introduced in similar fashion; cf. 3.1 with 3.13. Both are opposed by the Pharisees and Sadducees; cf. 3.7–10 with 12.34 and 23.33. Both appeal to the same generation to repent (11.16–19). Both act by the same authority, the authority of heaven (21.23–32). Both are taken by the people to be prophets (11.9; 14.5; 21.11, 26, 46). Both are rejected and executed as criminals (14.1–12; 26–7). And both are buried by their own disciples (14.12; 27.57–61). As prophets of the latter days, John and Jesus mirror each other.

preaching. Unlike Jesus and the disciples, John is not said to preach the gospel. Before Jesus, that cannot be done.

in the wilderness of Judea refers to the Judean wilderness in the lower Jordan valley, between the Judean plateau and the Dead Sea and lower Jordan river; further specification is lacking; contrast Jn 1.28; 3.23; 10.40.

The link between John and the wilderness is strong in early Christian tradition and must be regarded as first of all historical, whatever symbolic significance be attached to it. Some have thought that John the desert-dweller must have had some association with the Dead Sea community, and there are intriguing similarities between the Baptist and the Qumran sectaries (e.g. the prominence of ritual washings). These, however, prove less than has often been claimed, and the connexion with Qumran must remain only an inviting possibility. Perhaps we should see John's desert abode as indicative of three things, the first being his eschatological orientation, for a return to the desert was widely anticipated as one of the end-time events. Then, second, the wilderness, with its barren rocks and bleak landscape, would no doubt have been the appropriate spot in which to preach judgement – especially if Sodom and Gomorrah were in the vicinity. Third, given Matthew's identification of John with Elijah (17.10–13) and the Elijah-like traits given to the Baptist (see below), 'in the desert of Judea' just might be consonant with a desire to evoke memory of the Tishbite. Elijah found refuge in and wandered about the desert, and he was taken up in the fiery chariot near the Jordan (1 Kgs 17.3; 19.3–18; 2 Kgs 2.1–12).

2. The when ('in those days'), the what ('appeared ... preaching'), and the where ('in the wilderness of Judea') of John the Baptist were the subjects of v.1. Verse 2 continues by further unfolding the what ('Repent ...').

Repent, for the kingdom of heaven has come near are words also ascribed to Jesus in 4.17. In adopting Mk 1.4 and 15 for his summary of the Baptist's preaching, Matthew drops (i) 'the forgiveness of sins'; (ii) 'the gospel of God' and 'believe in the gospel'; and (iii) 'the time is fulfilled'. These phrases are in all likelihood omitted because of the feeling that they are more appropriately associated with the Christian Lord.

3. For this is the one who was spoken about by the prophet Isaiah, saying. Cf. 4.14; 8.17; 11.10 (also of John); 12.17.

The voice of one crying out in the wilderness: 'Prepare the way of the Lord; make his paths straight.' The quotation of Isa 40.3 agrees with the LXX, which takes 'in the desert' with 'the voice of one crying'. The MT has instead: 'make straight in the desert a highway for our God'. Isa 40.3 originally spoke to the exiles in Babylon, comforting them with the immediate prospect of return: the highway is even now being prepared for Yahweh, who will soon return to the Land with the people; cf. 40.11. In the gospels all is made new. The voice is not the voice of the Lord or the heavenly council or an unnamed herald, but of John the Baptist. The Lord is not Yahweh but Jesus. The exile is not in view but the time of the Messiah. Some precedent for this thorough reinterpretation which disregards original context can be found in the Dead Sea Scrolls. In 1QS 8.12–16, Isa 40.3 is programmatically applied to the community which prepares the way of the Lord by withdrawing into the wilderness to study Torah there.

4. After learning of the heart of John's message (3.2) and of his biblical role as the voice in the wilderness (3.3), we now read about his external appearance and habits; 3.5–6 will then tell us what John did. The point is not to satisfy simple curiosity or the historian's eye for detail. Rather, John's striking habits mark him off as a prophet, particularly as one like Elijah.

John wore clothing of camel's hair, and he had a leather belt around his waist. The garment of camel's hair is worn even today by Bedouin: it is rough desert clothing. On John it had special meaning. He was a noticeably ragged figure of striking, austere appearance, and his haircloth was a sign of his special status as a prophet. More than this, once the identification of John with Elijah was made, an eschatological motif must have been divined: Elijah the prophet has returned in the person of the Baptist. For according to the most plausible translation of 2 Kgs 1.8, Elijah 'wore a garment of haircloth'; and in 1 Kgs 19.13, 19 and 2 Kgs 2.8, 13–14 we read of his 'mantle'. The LXX translates this last with 'rough skin' or 'sheepskin'; and Tg. Ps.-J. to 2 Kgs 2.8 has 'coarse cloak'. The connexion with Elijah is all the more certain because, in addition to the common mantle, both John and the Tishbite had leather girdles around their waists; see 2 Kgs 1.8.

and his food was locusts and wild honey. Even today Bedouin and poorer inhabitants of Arabia, Africa, and Syria have been known to eat raw or roasted or boiled locusts and grasshoppers. There is no need to speculate that 'locusts' might mean something else, such as carob pods or dried fruit. Note also that in not worrying about what to eat or wear, John demonstrated the character of a disciple of Jesus (cf. 6.25–34; 10.10; 24.45).

5. The reason for John's appellation, 'the Baptist', is now recorded, and the meaning of his baptism is now explained.

Then the people of Jerusalem and all Judea and all the region along the Jordan went out to him. In the use of 'all' here it is usual to see a note of exaggeration reminiscent of the looseness with which the OT often employs 'all': John is being praised. Nevertheless, not only does Mk 11.27–33 presuppose knowledge of John in Jerusalem, but Josephus testifies to the Baptist's far-flung impact. And John's fame and influence are confirmed by his undoing at the hands of Antipas: an insignificant preacher would not have brought upon himself the death penalty. Historically, John was probably a sensation who drew large crowds.

Verses 5–6 should not be passed over in judging Matthew's attitude towards the Jewish people. If in 2.3 'all Jerusalem' is associated with the wicked Herod, and if in 27.25 'all the people' say, 'His blood be upon us and upon our children', in 3.5–6 'Jerusalem and all Judea and all the region about the Jordan' go out to John the Baptist and are baptized by him, confessing their sins. It is unfortunate that this last notice is usually left out of account in discussions of Matthew's view of Judaism. Mt 3.5–6 is instructive in several respects. (i) If 'all Israel' repents in 3.5–6, in 27.25 'all the people' proclaim their guilt. Clearly we cannot take Matthew's 'all' at face value. (ii) If there are verses which seem to dismiss the Jews, there are others which place them in a positive light. (iii) If the evangelist had believed that the Jewish people as a whole had rejected Jesus, how could he have written 3.5–6? Matthew seems to acknowledge that John and Jesus found a favourable reception among many Jews.

6. And they were baptized by him in the river Jordan. Apart from chapter 3, the verb, which in the active means 'to dip', 'to immerse', 'to plunge', occurs only in 28.19.

The antecedents of John's baptism have been much discussed. Resemblances have been observed with OT ablutions, with Jewish proselyte baptism, and with the washings of Qumran. And while some have argued that John's baptism should be seen as part of a much wider baptist movement in first-century Judaism, others have suggested that his action was more or less novel and based primarily upon certain OT texts. The truth probably lies in more than one solution. Perhaps, for instance, John was influenced by the sectaries at Qumran or other baptists, but made his own unique contribution through a novel reapplication of scriptural texts. In this regard Ps 51.6–9; Isa 4.4; 44.3; Jer 4.11–14; Ezek 36.25–7; and Zech 13.1 are worth considering. In any case, John's distinctiveness is clear. His baptism was directed towards the nation as a whole (contrast Qumran), administered once and for all (contrast OT ablutions), and was for Jews only (contrast proselyte baptism).

confessing their sins. The ineffectiveness of ritual without inward turning had long been emphasized by Jews. Matthew says no more than that those who came to John confessed their sins. He does not use the word 'forgiveness'; contrast Mk 1.4; Lk 3.3. 'Forgiveness' was apparently too central a feature of Jesus' work to be associated with another; cf. 1.23; 26.28.

John and the Jewish Leaders (3.7–12)

7. Pharisees. The Pharisees comprised a Jewish sect comparable with other Hellenistic philosophical schools. They prided themselves on their rigorous and accurate interpretation and keeping of the Law. And for them the Law consisted of the written plus the oral Torah, both of which they traced back to Moses on Sinai. In the gospels they are greatly concerned with purity laws, with Sabbath observances, and with agricultural taboos, and in all this at least the NT seems to be historically correct, for the rabbinic sources about the Pharisees paint a similar picture. They first appear on the stage of history during the second century BC, in the time of Jonathan, and they evidently emerged out of the non-priestly Hasidim known from 1 Maccabees. The name, 'Pharisee', probably derives from the Hebrew word for 'separatists', which was interpreted by the Pharisees in a positive sense, and by their opponents in a negative sense.

In Matthew the Pharisees are – more so than in Mark and Luke – the real opponents of Jesus, and this may reflect the fact that Matthew's Jewish contemporaries and opponents considered themselves heirs of the Pharisees, in which case our author would see his own enemies in those of Jesus. His words about them evince a special, living concern.

and Sadducees. The Sadducees were a priestly, aristocratic party whose locus was the temple in Jerusalem and whose influence on the populace was considerably less than that of the Pharisees. The origin of the name is uncertain. Most take it to derive from the personal name, 'Sadok', although which Sadok remains in dispute. Others trace it to *saddiq* = 'righteous'. The sect, which had its beginning some time after the Maccabean revolt, died out in AD 70, and we must reconstruct its convictions from secondary sources. Both the NT and Josephus report that the Sadducees denied the resurrection. Josephus adds that they rejected every idea of an after-life. Acts 23.8 has them also disbelieving in angels and spirits (which is difficult to accept at face value as angels appear in the OT from Genesis on; perhaps evil angels are meant, or perhaps the report arose from the Sadducees' repudiation of developed angelology). Josephus claims that they believed in Fate, not free will. The notion that the conservative Sadducees embraced as authoritative only the Pentateuch seems doubtful. Josephus is silent on the point, and the authority of the prophets was firmly established long before the group came into existence. The Sadducees did, however, deny the validity of the Pharisaic oral Torah.

You brood of vipers! Cf. 12.34 (of the Pharisees); 23.33 (of the scribes and Pharisees). The phrase stands over against the self-designation, 'children of Abraham'. The image is of vipers scurrying before dry scrub about to ignite.

Who warned you to flee from the wrath to come? Cf. 23.33, where Jesus takes up the Baptist's words (this adds again to the Jesus/John parallelism). The wrath is eschatological. It is unleashed when the great tribulation begins and culminates in the great assize (Lk 21.23; Rev 6.12–17; 16–17).

8. Bear fruit worthy of repentance. Cf. 7.16–20; 12.33. 'Fruit worthy of repentance' means 'fruit corresponding to (or befitting) repentance'; cf. Acts 26.20. John has already declared, 'repent' (3.2). Now substance is given to the injunction. The call to 'repentance' is uttered in view of the eschatological judgement looming on the horizon; and motivated by a fear of their own damnation (cf. Hos 3.5), people are called to be sorry for their transgressions and turn from them wholeheartedly – without delay. The Greek word literally means 'change of mind'; but it stands for a Hebrew word which means 'turn around', 'return', and a complete change in conduct, not just a change of opinion, is involved.

Repentance was a central concept in the Judaism of John's time, and the power of repentance was highly valued. Even the righteous had need of repentance. Indeed, it (paradoxically) characterized them. Wherein then lay John's distinctiveness? He evidently believed there to be two classes of people, the repentant and the non-repentant. Adopting a prophetic and pessimistic outlook, John saw his contemporaries headed for catastrophe and pleaded with them to make a radical and resolute break with the past. He declared that their salvation was not guaranteed by Abrahamic descent or any other circumstance save true repentance. His was not the opinion put forward in *m. Sanh.* 10.1, according to which only heretics, that is, those who repudiate the covenant, are condemned: 'all Israel has a place in the world to come'. Unlike some Jews, John did not think of repentance as primarily a daily affair which served to maintain one's status as a member of the covenant community. It instead signalled for him the transition from one group, the chaff facing the fire, to another group, the wheat for the granary.

9. and do not presume to say to yourselves. The thought is illusory.

We have Abraham as our father. To be born a Jew of a Jewish mother was to be born a member of the covenant community, and for many that was enough: Abrahamic descent was not only a necessary condition for salvation but a sufficient condition – unless one denounced the covenant or committed some other deed of apostasy and became a heretic. The Baptist held a different conception: salvation would come only to those who made a radical, one-time repentance. Abrahamic descent of itself guaranteed nothing. The merit of the fathers was insufficient. With this judgement the early church soon concurred (Jn 8.39; Rom 9.1–33), and the concept of 'sons of Abraham' accordingly came to include Gentiles (Rom 2.28–9; 4.12; Gal 3.16, 29; 4.21–31). We cannot say, however, whether John gave explicit teaching on non-Jews: only that, by his fulminating judgements on his contemporaries, his sceptical view of their favoured status before God, and his apparent diminution of the Torah as the standard of judgement, he placed a large question mark over the covenantal nomism of his day, and avowed that those born of Abraham were not by that fact alone members of the people of God.

for I say to you, God is able from these stones to raise up children to Abraham. The background for this picture is Isa 51.1–2: 'Look to the rock whence you were hewn and to the quarry whence you were digged. Look to Abraham your father and to Sarah who bore you. For when he was but one I called him and blessed him and I caused him to increase.' From Abraham, a lifeless rock (cf. Gen 17.17; 18.10–14; Rom 4.17), God had miraculously caused to be born Isaac and descendants as numerous as the stars of heaven. This, the Baptist declares, God can do again, which cuts the ground out from under those who would stand upon their physical sonship from Abraham.

Although we should probably not read a reference to the Gentiles into John's words if we are thinking of their first utterance, matters must be different for Matthew. Given his interest in the Gentile mission and the firm connexions between Abraham and the Gentiles in both Jewish and Christian tradition, 3.9 must for him imply criticism of the self-assurance of the Jews and the acceptance of non-Jewish Christians. From Matthew's perspective, God has in fact already raised up new offspring to Abraham: the Gentile Christians.

10. The imagery of verse 8 is picked up again.

Even now the axe is laid at the root of the trees. The line, whose content is similar to 3.12, expresses the imminence of the eschatological judgement. The choice of 'tree' is particularly apt because John is addressing the Pharisees and Sadducees, and leaders, as well as reputedly righteous people and scholars, were sometimes compared to trees (as in Judg 9.7–16; Ps 1.3; Jer 17.7–8 etc.).

So every tree that does not bear good fruit is cut down. In 7.19 Jesus repeats John's words verbatim (minus the 'so').

and thrown into the fire. Both as a concomitant of the final judgement and as an instrument of punishment of the dead, fire was a traditional eschatological prospect: Isa 66.24; Jdt 16.17; etc. For John, fire appears to have been the outstanding feature of the coming judgement; cf. 3.11–12. As for our evangelist, he is particularly fond of making fire a threat on the lips of Jesus: 5.22; 7.19; 13.40, 42, 50; 18.8, 9; 25.41. In 7.19 he even has Jesus repeat the words of the present verse. There, as here, the context has to do with false leaders and teachers, those most deserving of punishment.

11. 3.1–10 has informed us about the Baptist. Now the Baptist informs us about Jesus, making a christological statement (3.11–12). The context for the baptism (3.13–17) is the reader's knowledge of the two participants, John and Jesus.

I baptize you with water for repentance. Cf. Jn 1.26, 31, 33. 'For repentance' may be taken as meaning (i) baptism *effects* repentance or (ii) baptism *demands* or *summons* repentance. It is, however, better to endorse a more nuanced position: (iii) baptism presupposes and expresses repentance (cf. 3.7–10) while it also, through the action of God, issues in a true reformation.

but the one who is coming after me. On Jesus as the coming one see 11.3 and 23.39.

is mightier than I. Maybe our evangelist already has 12.29 in mind: Jesus has the strength to bind even the strong man, Satan; cf. Isa 49.25. Strength is in any case one of the pneumatic endowments of the shoot that shall come forth from Jesse in Isa 11.1–2, and in Isa 53.12 the suffering servant shares the spoil of the strong; also, in *1 En.* 49.3 the Elect One has a spirit of strength, and in *Ps. Sol.* 17.37 the Son of David is made mighty by God's Spirit. While 'the stronger one' may not have been a fixed title, strength was associated with messianic figures.

He will baptize you with the Holy Spirit and with fire. The OT contains numerous texts in which water, like fire, is a symbol of calamity (2 Sam 22.5; Ps 18.16; 32.6; 42.7 etc.) or an instrument of judgement (Gen 6.6; Hos 5.10). Further, as symbols of judgement, fire and water are closely linked in a number of Jewish sources: Ps 66.10–12; Isa 30.27–8; 43.2 etc. Of special importance is that, in apocalyptic literature and the Dead Sea Scrolls, fire and water are joined to become one symbol. In Dan 7.10; 1QH 3.29–36; *1 En.* 67.13 and elsewhere, we read of a river or flood of fire. Most of these texts have the last judgement in view: a stream of fire comes forth from God and consumes the wicked. The rabbis also spoke of the eschatological flood of fire. When John the Baptist warned of the coming one who would baptize with fire, he almost certainly had in view this fiery stream.

What then of the Spirit? It was sometimes associated with judgement (Isa 4.4; 40.24; 41.16; Jer 4.11–16; 23.19; 30.23; Ezek 13.11–13) or thought of as a purifying or cleansing element (1QS 4.21). Moreover, two passages in Isaiah reveal the possibilities for joining fire and spirit in prophecies about judgement. In Isa 30.27–8, the name of the Lord comes from afar, burning with anger and rising in thick smoke; his tongue is like a devouring fire; and his breath or spirit is like an overflowing stream reaching up to the neck to sift the nations with the sieve of destruction, and to place on the jaws of the people a bridle that leads astray. Isa 4.4 prophesies that the Lord will cleanse Zion and Jerusalem by a spirit of judgement and by a spirit of burning. Even more telling is 4 Ezra 13.8–11, in which a stream of fire and a flame of breath issue from the Messiah's mouth as judgement. Here is precisely the background requisite for interpreting John's talk of baptism in Spirit and in fire. Fire and Spirit are not two things but one – 'fiery breath'. At the boundary of the new age, all will pass through the fiery breath of God, a stream which will purify the righteous and destroy the unrighteous.

The influence of the Baptist's conception upon Jesus is almost certainly to be discerned in three different texts: Lk 12.49–51; Mk 10.35–40; and 9.49. In these Jesus interprets his own time as part and parcel of the eschatological tribulation; and he and his disciples will have to undergo the baptism of fire of which John spoke.

12. His winnowing fork is in his hand, and he will clear his threshing floor and will gather his wheat into the granary. But the chaff he will burn with unquenchable fire. Given its present context, the emphasis probably comes down not on the gathering of the wheat in the granary but on the burning of the chaff. Imminent judgement, not salvation, is the theme. Cf. the rabbinic parable in *Midr. Ps.* on 2.12: soon harvest will come and everyone will see and know for certain for whose sake the field was sown. In no time at all, with the coming of harvest, the straw is disposed of in the water, the chaff in the wind, and the weeds in flame, but the wheat is brought in for safe-keeping, and whoever handles it, kisses it. In the time to come, when the day of judgement arrives, the peoples of the earth will be dragged into the Valley of Hinnom, but Israel will remain.

The Baptism of Jesus (3.13–17)

The narrative foreshadows the transfiguration, as can be seen at a glance:

3.13–16/17.1–2	Setting
3.16/17.3	'and behold!'
3.16/17.3	Vision with Jesus at the centre
3.17/17.5	'and behold!'
3.17/17.5	Heavenly voice, mixing Ps 2.7 and Isa 42.1

13. Then Jesus came from Galilee to the Jordan to John, to be baptized by him. The parallel with 3.1 (where John the Baptist is introduced) is close. Jesus is like John.

14. John would have prevented him, saying. Because the verb, 'to prevent', appears in connexion with baptism in Acts 8.36; 10.47; 11.17 and elsewhere, it may have been part of early Christian baptismal ritual. When candidates were brought forward, enquiry was made as to whether the pre-conditions of baptism had really been met – 'What prevents?'

I need to be baptized by you. John has already detailed the superiority of the coming one; see v. 11. Implicitly he seems to identify this 'one' with Jesus – which makes his later doubt in 11.2–4 all the stranger.

15. This verse contains the first words uttered by Jesus in Matthew, and they are programmatic.

Thus is it proper for us to fulfil all righteousness. 'To fulfil' occurs sixteen times in Matthew, thirteen times in formula quotations or in verses where prophecy or the prophets are the subject (1.22; 2.15, 17, 23; 4.14; 5.17; 8.17; 12.17; 13.35; 21.4; 26.54, 56; 27.9). Of the remaining three instances, one is empty of theological meaning (13.48: a net is filled up) and another (23.32) probably has to do with an ironic fulfilment of prophecy ('Fill up, then, the measure of your fathers'). This leaves only 3.15, and it follows that all presumption is in favour of finding in it a reference to OT prophecy. This is seemingly confirmed by 3.17: the voice from heaven, drawing upon Ps 2.7 and Isa 42.1, makes plain that the baptism of Jesus brings to realization scriptural hopes. So when Jesus fulfils all righteousness, he is fulfiling Scripture. Although this interpretation leaves one free to interpret 'righteousness' in more than one way, it is best to think of moral effort or obedience to God's will: by fulfiling Scripture, John and Jesus are acting justly.

Then he consented. John, a model of discipleship, unhesitatingly obeys.

16. Jesus' emerging from the water and climbing the bank – which connects the heavenly vision and voice not with an action of John but with an action of Jesus – recalls at least two related images. (i) In Judaism creation was thought of as emergence from a watery chaos (Gen 1.3; Isa 43.16–20) – an important observation, since other creation motifs are also present in our story. (ii) Israel was adopted and became God's 'son' with the exodus from Egypt, at the crossing of the Red Sea, and the theme of a new exodus runs throughout Matthew 1–7.

the heavens were opened. The heavens open not only to signal the forthcoming of revelation but also to make it possible for the Spirit to descend. The text presupposes the mythopoeic cosmology common to the ancient near east: the sky is a solid firmament beyond which is the highest heaven, and beyond that is the abode of the gods or God.

And he saw the Spirit of God descending like a dove. Seemingly, and despite the singular form of the verb, 'he saw', at least two people, Jesus and John, are privy to the events recounted.

The appearance of the symbolic dove has occasioned much speculation. Ever since Tertullian it has often been connected with

Noah's dove: the former dove announced deliverance from the flood, the latter dove deliverance from sins; cf. 1 Pet 3.20–1. It is also possible to associate the dove with the new exodus motif, for in the *Mekilta* the Holy Spirit rests upon the people as they cross the Red Sea, and they are compared to a dove, and they are granted a vision. But the best guess relates the text to Gen 1.2, which involves the Spirit of God, water, and the imagery of a bird hovering. Further, in *b. Hag.* 15a the hovering of the Spirit over the face of the waters is represented more precisely as the hovering of a dove. The meaning is then once again that the last things are as the first: Jesus inaugurates a new creation. The correctness of this interpretation is seemingly confirmed by a Dead Sea Scroll fragment, 4Q521. In line 6 ('his Spirit will hover over the poor'), the language of Gen 1.2 characterizes the eschatological redemption: just as the Spirit once hovered over the face of the waters, so too, at the end, will the Spirit hover over the saints and strengthen them. This pre-Christian application of Gen 1.2 to the eschatological future has the Spirit hovering over human beings as opposed to lifeless material. The striking parallel with Matthew evidences a similar creative application of Gen 1.2.

And alighting on him. The significance of the vision of the Spirit is found in this phrase: the Spirit comes upon Jesus. This does not mean any sort of adoption, for already at his birth Jesus is of the Holy Spirit (1.18–25). It does, however, serve to reveal or confirm Jesus' already existing status and worthiness as the eschatological bearer of God's Spirit and therefore as the servant of the Lord; cf. 12.18. It also marks a turning point in salvation-history, for only after the Spirit comes does the Messiah's ministry begin (cf. Acts 10.38); and it sets Jesus in line with certain national leaders of the OT – Gideon (Judg 6.34), Samson (15.14), and Saul (1 Sam 10.6) – upon whom the Spirit came, as well as with the prophets.

17. A second witness, a heavenly voice, adds its testimony to that of the Spirit; cf. Rev 14.13.

A voice from heaven. Cf. 17.5. Heavenly voices occur frequently in old Jewish and Christian texts.

said. The following quotation, with its close parallel in 17.5, appears to be a conflation of Ps 2.7, a line from a royal psalm, and Isa 42.1, a line from a prophecy about the suffering servant.

my Son. The declaration of sonship does not reveal new truth to the readers. It only confirms and emphasizes with the voice of God the fact already expressed in 1.18–25 and 2.15. On the other hand, it may be significant that it is God who first openly proclaims by revelation Jesus as 'the Son of God'. This could explain the absence of 'Son of God' from 1.1, the gospel's title.

Here 'Son of God' refers firstly to Jesus' special relationship to God the Father; cf. 11.25–30. But one cannot give a simple or single definition to the title; its connotations vary. In 4.1–11, as in 2.15, it is, for example, associated with an Israel typology; and in 16.13–20 and 26.59–68 it is linked with Jesus' status as Davidic Messiah (cf. 2 Sam 7.14; perhaps this is so also in 3.17, for Psalm 2 is a royal psalm).

3.16–17, which was interpreted by later Christian theology as depicting the supreme manifestation of the Trinity, is only one of several NT baptismal texts in which the Father, Son, and Holy Spirit are present; see Mt 28.16–20; Jn 1.33–4; Acts 2.38–9; 10.38; 1 Cor 6.11; Tit 3.4–6; 1 Pet 1.2. Why the NT should contain so many triadic baptismal texts is far from obvious. But the ultimate cause could be the story of Jesus' baptism by John, in which God the Father speaks to the Son and the Holy Spirit comes upon him.

the beloved. Some have found in 'beloved Son' an Isaac typology; cf. Gen 22.2, 12, 26. But 'beloved' and 'son(s)' were commonly linked words, and as Isaiah's servant was known as 'beloved', and as Isa 42.1 has certainly influenced our text, any allusion to Isaac could only be secondary at best.

* * * * *

(i) The primary purpose of Mt 3.1–12 is to set the stage for Jesus' baptism. To this end the person and ministry of the Baptist are succinctly summarized. We have only a silhouette; John is no independent figure, but is viewed only from a Christian perspective. As the voice of Isa 40, as one like Elijah, as a baptizer, and as a preacher, John only prepares for Jesus. His words and deeds point away from himself to another.

(ii) The Baptist's division of his listeners into two categories, fruitful and unfruitful, wheat and chaff, gives us the first taste of a strong dualism that runs throughout Matthew. With the clarity characteristic of many moral visionaries, and despite his awareness of the need to qualify or to temper absolutes (cf. 5.32; 18.15–22), our evangelist often writes as though matters were black or white. There are good fish and bad fish (13.47–50). There are sheep and goats (25.31–46). There are those on the right hand and those on the left hand (25.31–46). There are wise men who build their houses upon rock and foolish men who build their houses upon sand (7.24–7). There are people for Jesus and people against him – and seemingly none in between (12.30). In all this the First Gospel exhibits an outlook reminiscent of the Dead Sea Scrolls and such ancient Jewish apocalypses as 4 Ezra and *2 Baruch*. For the Qumran covenanters and the apocalyptic seers, as for Matthew, it was the nearness of the eschatological assize, at which only two sentences, salvation and damnation, would be passed, that made the existing world appear to be composed solely of the sons of light on the one hand and the sons of darkness on the other.

(iii) Jesus is the one in whom God is pleased, that is, he is the servant of Isa 42.1. In that capacity he not only brings OT prophecy to fulfilment, receiving the Spirit (3.17; 12.18), taking up infirmities (8.17), and giving his life as a ransom for many (20.28): he is also the paradigm of the righteous sufferer. Thus he humbly accepts from God both the good portion and the portion of the chastized, and he meekly sides with the weak and powerless while being delivered into the hands of the mighty and powerful. Jesus came not to be served but to serve (20.28), and this idea presents itself at every turn. From this we learn that sonship largely consists in choosing to take up the ministry of the suffering servant.

THE BEGINNING OF THE MINISTRY (4.1–22)

4 [1]**Then Jesus was led up by the Spirit into the wilderness to be tempted by the devil.** [2]**And having fasted forty days and forty nights, afterward he was hungry.** [3]**And the tempter, coming to him, said to him, 'If you are the Son of God, command these stones to become loaves of bread.'** [4]**But answering he said, 'It is written, "One does not live by bread alone, but by every word that comes from the mouth of God".'** [5]**Then the devil took him to the holy city, and he set him on the pinnacle of the temple,** [6]**and he said to him, 'If you are the Son of God, throw yourself down; for it is written, "He will command his angels concerning you", and "On their hands they will bear you up, so that you will not dash your foot against a stone".'** [7]**Jesus said to him, 'Again it is written, "You will not put the Lord your God to the test".'** [8]**Again, the devil took him to a very high mountain, and he showed him all the kingdoms of the world and their glory;** [9]**and he said to him, 'All these I will give you, if you will fall down and worship me.'** [10]**Then Jesus said to him, 'Away with you, Satan! for it is written, "You will worship the Lord your God, and him only will you serve".'** [11]**Then the devil left him, and behold, angels came and served him.**

[12]**Hearing that John had been handed over, he withdrew to Galilee.** [13]**And leaving Nazareth he went and dwelled in Capernaum by the sea, in the territory of Zebulun and Naphtali,** [14]**so that what had been spoken through the prophet Isaiah might be fulfilled:** [15]**'Land of Zebulun, land of Naphtali, on the road by the sea, across the Jordan, Galilee of the Gentiles –** [16]**the people who sat in darkness have seen a great light, and for those who sat in the region and shadow of death light has dawned.'**

[17]**From that time Jesus began to proclaim, 'Repent, for the kingdom of heaven has come near.'**

[18]As he was walking by the Sea of Galilee, he saw two brothers – Simon, who is called Peter, and Andrew his brother, casting a net into the sea, for they were fishermen. [19]And he said to them, 'Follow me, and I will make you fishers of people.' [20]Immediately they left their nets and followed him. [21]And going on from there, he saw two other brothers – James the son of Zebedee and his brother John, in the boat with their father Zebedee, mending their nets; and he called them. [22]Immediately they left the boat and their father, and they followed him.

Parallels: Mk 1.12–20, 39; Lk 4.1–15, 44; 5.1–11; Jn 1.35–51; 4.1–6

The Temptation of Jesus (4.1–11)

In each temptation Jesus quotes from Deuteronomy, from Deut 8.3 in 4.4, from Deut 6.16 in 4.7, and from Deut 6.13 in 4.10. This is the key to the narrative: we have before us a haggadic tale which has issued forth from reflection on Deut 6–8. Jesus, the Son of God, is repeating the experience of Israel in the desert. Having passed through the waters of a new exodus at his baptism (cf. 1 Cor 10.1–5), he enters the desert to suffer a time of testing, his forty days of fasting being analogous to Israel's forty years of wandering. Like Israel, Jesus is tempted by hunger. And, like Israel, he is tempted to idolatry. Cf. Deut 8.2–3: 'And you shall remember all the way which the Lord your God has led you these *forty* years *in the wilderness*, that he might humble you, *testing you* to know what was in your heart, whether you would keep his commandments, or not. And he humbled you and let you *hunger* . . .'.

1–2. Then Jesus was led up by the Spirit into the wilderness. Although the exact location of the wilderness is not specified, the connexion with chapter 3 causes one to think of a place near John's activity, that is, the region around the Jordan. Yet the important fact is another: God's son Israel was tested in the desert after the exodus, and that history is being recapitulated.

to be tempted by the devil. In the OT, Satan is an accuser in the heavenly court, one of the sons of heaven, and he incites the deity to test people; see 1 Chr 21.1; Ps 109.6; Job 1–2; Zech 3.1–10. By the time we reach the NT there has been a metamorphosis. Satan, known by a variety of names, has become a demonic, wholly evil figure, bent on the destruction of Israel and every other good thing.

In the NT, 'the devil' is the same as 'Satan' (4.10; 12.26; 16.23) and Beelzebul (10.25; 12.24, 27). He is 'the enemy' (13.39), the 'evil one' (6.13), who is destined to be defeated and thrown with his angels into eternal fire (25.41). In tempting Jesus, he only acts as he does towards all (cf. 6.13; 26.41), even though a personal appearance is extra-ordinary. And because the Messiah has appeared and bound him (12.29), the devil and his host of evil demons, who seek nothing other than the destruction of humanity and its alienation from God (cf. 12.22 and 17.14–21), are subject to the name of Jesus (cf. 7.22; 10.1, 8).

Having fasted forty days and forty nights. The period of forty days is most often associated with hardship or affliction or punishment. The flood in Noah's day lasted that long (Gen 7.4, 12, 17; 8.6). So did the fasting of Moses (Exod 24.18; 34.28; Deut 9.9, 11, 25; 10.10) and the fasting of Elijah (1 Kgs 19.8). Forty days was the length of time Ezekiel lay on his right side, symbolizing the punishment of the house of Judah (Ezek 4.6). Jonah prophesied, 'Yet forty days and Nineveh will be destroyed' (Jon 3.4). Because, in the temptation narrative, a Jesus/Israel typology obtains, the most important consideration is this: Israel wandered for forty years in the desert. The forty days from the life of Jesus corresponds to the forty years during which Israel was tested in the desert; cf. Num 14.34 and Ezek 4.5–6, where a period of forty days symbolizes forty years.

3. And the tempter, coming to him, said to him. There developed over time in Judaism a tendency to view Satan rather than God as the source of temptation; cf. 2 Sam 24.1 against 1 Chr 21.2. And in Jas 1.13 we find this: 'God cannot be tempted by evil and he himself tempts no one.' In the NT in general God typically only 'tries' or 'tests', and that with hope for a good outcome; cf. 1 Th 2.4; 1 Tim 3.10; Heb 11.17. The devil typically 'tempts' with nothing but an evil end in view; cf. 1 Cor 7.5; 1 Th 3.5; Rev 2.10. As for Mt 4.1 and 3, the activity of the Spirit and the presence of Satan give the verb double connotation: Jesus is at the same time being 'tested' by God and 'tempted' by the devil.

If you are the Son of God. The reference is to the voice at the baptism, so the temptation may be to abandon the mission of the servant. At the same time, 'Son of God' is appropriate because it is the title Jesus shares with Israel (Exod 4.22–3; Deut 1.31; Hos 11.1).

these stones to become loaves of bread. Israel was hungry in the desert (Exod 16; Num 11). The devil now finds Jesus in a similar situation and wishes to make him anxious about his physical needs (cf. 6.34).

4. Although the experience of God's people of old – hunger in the desert – is being re-experienced by him, Jesus does not respond by murmuring. The Messiah does not command or complain or compel God.

But answering he said, 'It is written, "One does not live by bread alone, but by every word that comes from the mouth of God".' The quoted words are from Deut 8.3, which follows on from this: 'And you shall remember all the way which the Lord your God has led you these forty years in the wilderness, that he might humble you and test you to know whether you would keep his commandments or not' (8.2). Here are three elements of our gospel story: the number forty, the wilderness, and testing. Then, in 8.3, mention is made of hunger, and in 8.5 Israel is spoken of as a son, and in 8.9 we even find stones. Clearly an awareness of Deut 8.1–10 as a whole provides the presupposition for grasping the meaning of the devil's temptation and Jesus' response.

5–6. Then the devil took him to the holy city. Whether we are to think of a visionary experience or of a miraculous teleportation is unclear (cf. 2 Cor 12.2!), although 4.8 ('and he showed him all the kingdoms of the world') may argue for the former possibility. Origen found in Mt 4 prime proof of the folly of taking Scripture literally.

the pinnacle of the temple. Is this the pinnacle of the royal portico, south of the outer court, or a balcony in the temple wall, or perhaps the lintel of the temple gateway? However one resolves the issue, the temple was, in Jewish tradition, at the centre of Jerusalem, and Jerusalem, in turn, was thought of as being the centre of the world. So Jesus surveys the world from a raised point at its centre.

throw yourself down. Jesus responded to the first temptation by declaring his trust in God, and this is the point the devil now takes up: if you really trust God ...

'He will command his angels concerning you', and 'On their hands they will bear you up, so that you will not dash your foot against a stone.' This quotation is from Psalm 91.11–12. Whether or not the psalm was actually composed as an apotropaic prayer to ward off demons (as some have suggested), there is ample evidence that it came to be used as such. *b. Šeb.* 15b gives to it the title, 'A song against evil occurrences', and both ancient Jews and Christians used Psalm 91 as a talisman against evil spirits, while the LXX, Peshitta, and targum all translate 91.6 so that it refers explicitly to demons. No less importantly, Qumran's 11Q11 (11QapocrPs) is a collection of four apotropaic psalms, of which Psalm 91 is a member. Now if Matthew's readers also thought of Psalm 91 as apotropaic and recognized that the devil is quoting from it, there would be great irony: Satan would be quoting from a text that was used to drive away evil spirits. One might even find humour here: the devil is so incompetent that he seeks help from a text that is his enemy.

7. Just as he will in 26.53–4, Jesus rejects the proposal to call on angelic aid.

You will not put the Lord your God to the test. So Deut 6.16, which continues, 'just as you tested him at Massah'. The Hebrew in its entirety reads, 'You (plural) shall not put the Lord your God to the test, as you tested him at Massah.' In its original setting the verse refers to the time when Israel found fault with Moses because there was no water. The rebellious people put the Lord to the proof only to see water come forth from a rock struck by Moses (Exod 17.1–6; Num 20.2–13). The incident is recalled for a hortatory end in Ps 95.7–9: 'O that today you would hearken to his voice! Harden not your hearts as at Meribah, as on the day at Massah in the wilderness, when your fathers tested me and put me to the proof although they had seen my work'; cf. 1 Cor 10.9; Heb 3.7–4.13. The same hortatory application of the incident is presupposed in the text before us.

Deut 6.16 is cited not in order to dispute the truth of Ps 91.11–12. Jesus rather refutes the devil's erroneous application of a biblical text. One should indeed trust in God's providence, as Psalm 91 teaches; but this should not be taken as implying the propriety of putting God to the test.

8–9. to a very high mountain. The 'high mountain' seems to be the counterpart of the mountain in 28.16. Whereas Jesus, after his death and resurrection, will stand on a mountain and declare that he has received all authority in heaven and earth, here in the temptation narrative the devil takes him up to a mountain top and offers him the kingdoms of the world. Jesus must, of course, reject the devil's proposal. Only after the passion, and then only from the Father in heaven, can Jesus accept all authority. There is no getting around the crucifixion. The Scriptures must be fulfilled (26.54).

and he showed him. When the devil takes Jesus up a mountain and shows him all the kingdoms of the world, this seems to be a reminiscence of the story that Moses went to the top of Pisgah, looked in all directions, and saw the land he would not enter (Num. 27.12–14; Deut. 3.27; 32.48–52; 34.1–4). In both cases a supernatural figure (God or Satan) shows to a hero (Moses or Jesus) the entirety of a realm (all the land of Israel or all the kingdoms of the world), but the hero does not then enter or inherit that realm. In Matthew, moreover, all this takes place upon a very high mountain, which augments the parallelism. Further, the vocabulary reflects LXX Deut 34.1–4. The similarity is all the greater because if, in Deuteronomy, God shows Moses 'all the land, Gilead as far as Dan, all Naphtali, the land of Ephraim and Manasseh, all the land of Judah as far as the Western Sea, the Negeb, and the Plain, that is, the valley of Jericho the city of palm trees, as far as Zoar', the haggada greatly expanded this vision. *Sifre Deut.* 357 on 34:1–9 tells us that Moses was granted a vision of 'all the world', and *LAB* 19.10 also makes Moses' vision a universal one, which is what we have in Matthew.

all the kingdoms of the world. The notion that Satan has the authority to give Jesus the kingdoms of the world accords with the pessimism abroad in late antiquity. Satan was thought of as 'the god of this world' (2 Cor 4.4), 'the ruler of this world' (Jn 12.31; 14.30; 16.11). In Lk 4.6 the devil declares, 'I will give to you all this authority and glory, for it has been delivered to me and I give it to whom I will.' Nevertheless, as our gospel unfolds, we shall learn that Satan's position in the world has been dramatically lessened since the advent of the Son of God: the demonic hosts have been routed (12.22–30), and God has chosen to give Jesus authority over the earth (9.6–8; 10.1; 11.27; 28.16–20).

9. Having shown Jesus the kingdoms of this world and their glory, without a word the devil now speaks: all this is yours, if you will worship me. The subtlety of the earlier temptations is absent. Jesus is clearly being asked to break the first commandment of the decalogue. Note that what is evil is not the end – after all, as the Son of Ps 2, Jesus will inherit the nations and possess the ends of the earth. The problem is the means.

if you will fall down and worship me. In the wilderness Israel was guilty of idolatry, of bowing down before false gods (Exod 32).

10. Away with you, Satan! offers more than a verbal link with 16.21–3. In both places Jesus is choosing the path of duty: the end ordained by the Father is to be achieved by the manner ordained by the Father, namely, the cross. To reject the way of the cross is to be on the side of the devil.

You will worship the Lord your God, and him only will you serve. This quotes Deut 6.13, which in its original context pertains to idolatry and the incident with the golden calf.

11. and behold, angels came and served him. Cf. 1 Kgs 19.5–8, where Elijah is fed by an angel and then goes forty days without sustenance. We are probably to think of angel food, manna, and the point seems to be this: Jesus did not turn stones into bread. Nor did he force God to send angels. Instead he trusted the Father in heaven – and all his needs were met (cf. 6.25–34). As God once miraculously gave Israel manna in the desert, so now he feeds his Son – his Son who, unlike Adam, did not succumb to temptation and so received the food which the first man ate in paradise before the fall.

Jesus' First Preaching in Galilee (4.12–17)

On the literary level these verses signal the beginning of the public ministry, move Jesus from Nazareth to Capernaum, and introduce in summary fashion the content of his proclamation. On the theological level, they underline three recurring themes: the fulfilment of Scripture (4.14–16), the salvation of the Gentiles (4.15), and the announcement of the kingdom of God (4.17). This last calls the most attention to itself; 4.17 not only repeats words of the Baptist (3.2), but 'began to proclaim' connotes repetition: Jesus utters the words again and again. So 4.17 stands over the entire public ministry.

12. There is no real connexion with what has preceded.

Hearing that John had been handed over, he withdrew to Galilee. In accord with Matthew's chronological indifference, the span of time between the temptation and John's arrest is unspecified.

'Hand over', which is here used of John the Baptist, occurs often in the passion of Jesus. So the verb highlights the parallelism between the Messiah and his herald, the 'divine passive' showing John's sad end to be, like that of Jesus, the outcome of a divinely commissioned ministry.

Verse 12 has a close parallel not only in 2.22 but also in 14.13, where we are told that Jesus, upon hearing of John's demise, withdrew. In both 4.12 and 14.13 a turn of events in the life of John makes for a turn of events in the life of Jesus. When John is handed over, Jesus opens his public ministry in Galilee (4.12); and when John is finally put to death, it is the beginning of the end of Jesus' public ministry (14.13).

13. he went and dwelled in Capernaum. In writing that Jesus 'dwelled' in Capernaum, Matthew goes beyond Mark, although it can be argued that this is implicit in the Second Gospel. Luke says, simply, Jesus 'went down' to Capernaum (4.31). 'Capernaum' does not appear in the OT. In the NT it occurs only in the gospels. A small village in Jesus' day, it was located on the northwest shore of the Sea of Galilee, in the territory of Naphtali, about two miles west of the Jordan. Fishing, agriculture, and trading were undoubtedly its mainstays, and it was near the trade route that ran between Damascus and Ptolemais (Accho). Matthew tells of a custom station there (9.9–10; 17.24). Although the synagogue that modern archaeology has uncovered was built in the third or fourth century AD, it probably stands above the site of the first-century synagogue, which Lk 7.5 says was built by a Roman centurion.

by the sea, in the territory of Zebulun and Naphtali. The place names in 4.13 form a chiastic pattern with names in 4.15

```
 ⎧ a. Galilee                                                    ⎫
 ⎪   ⎧ b. by the sea                                       ⎫ Jesus
 ⎪   ⎪   ⎧ c. the territory of Zebulun and Naphtali ⎬
 ⎨   ⎪   ⎩ c. the land of Zebulun and the land of Naphtali ⎫
 ⎪   ⎩ b. towards the sea                                  ⎬ the OT
 ⎩ a. Galilee                                              ⎭
```

15–16. The function of these verses is to offer scriptural warrant for a geographical fact, Jesus' presence in Galilee. This recalls the similar function of the four redactional fulfilment texts in Mt 2, each of which is attached to a geographical place name.

In its original context the passage concerns a broken people who have suffered Assyrian attack and deportation (cf. 2 Kgs 15.29; 1 Chr 5.26); to them is promised deliverance: a son from the house of David will bring salvation (9.6–7). In Matthew the prophecy is taken up and applied to the ministry of the Messiah, whom the evangelist undoubtedly took to be the son of Isa 9.6–7. So there is a shift from literal destruction and political plight to moral and spiritual darkness.

Galilee of the Gentiles. The Messiah's work for the Gentiles has been foreshadowed. In 1.1, Jesus is the son of Abraham. In 2.1–17, there are Gentiles in the genealogy. In 2.1–11, non-Jews worship Jesus the infant. In chapter 3, John the Baptist proclaims God's ability to raise up new children to Abraham. Now Jesus himself goes to 'Galilee of the Gentiles' and there preaches the kingdom of heaven (v. 17).

17. Repent. Repentance is, in Matthew's gospel, less than a key theme. The noun 'repentance' occurs only twice (3.8, 11), both times on the lips not of Jesus but of John the Baptist. The verb, 'to repent', occurs five times. In 3.2, it is John who calls for repentance. Jesus himself speaks of repentance only four times: 4.17; 11.20; 11.21; and 12.41. To judge from these texts the evangelist has not introduced any change, fundamental or otherwise, into the concept of repentance. Perhaps this is to be explained by the fact that Matthew thought of repentance primarily as associated with entrance into the Christian community, in which case it would be applicable principally to outsiders and thus not prominent in a book addressed above all to believers.

for the kingdom of heaven has come near. Jesus proclaims what the Baptist and the twelve proclaim; cf. 3.2 and 10.7. The kingdom primarily signifies not the territory God rules or will rule – it is not just a place, like Shangri La – but God's eschatological activity as ruler. In its fullness, this rule is still unrealized, and its arrival in judgement will mark the end or transformation of the world, the restoration of an idyllic, paradisial state in which God's will will be perfectly realized. Yet it is even now establishing itself. In fact, it is entering the world through a complex of events, some of which have taken place (e.g. the Messiah's first advent; cf. 11.12; 12.28), some of which are taking place (e.g. 10.16–23), and some of which will take place in the near future (e.g. much of chapters 24 and 25).

Jesus Calls Four Disciples (4.18–22)

This pericope contains two parallel stories, 4.18–20 and 21–2. Both exhibit the same structure:

    (i)   The appearance of Jesus (vv. 18, 21)
    (ii) Remark on the disciples at work (vv. 18, 21)
    (iii) The call to discipleship (vv. 19, 21)
    (iv) The obedient response to the call (vv. 20, 22)

That this is a fixed and significant form appears from Mk 2.14, the story of Levi's call, which can be analysed thus:

    (i)   Jesus appears
    (ii) Levi is at work, sitting at the tax office
    (iii) Jesus calls Levi to follow him
    (iv) Levi obediently follows

The explanation for the common form is 1 Kgs 19.19–21, Elijah's call of Elisha, which can be set forth as follows:

    (i)   Elijah is travelling (v. 19)
    (ii) He finds Elisha, who is ploughing with oxen (v. 19)
    (iii) Elijah puts his mantle on Elisha and calls him to prophetic office (v. 19)
    (iv) Elisha asks to kiss his parents first and offers a sacrifice (vv. 20–1)
    (v) Elisha follows Elijah (v. 21)

The agreements between 1 Kgs 19.19–21 and the NT accounts are obvious. Just as obvious is an outstanding difference, namely, the request of Elisha to say farewell to parents and the sacrificial act. The difference is the more outstanding since, as opposed to what appears to have been the narrative's original intent, in the LXX and Josephus, Elijah grants Elisha permission to kiss his father and mother. In the NT, by way of contrast, family and possessions are forsaken on the spot: there is no parallel to 1 Kgs 19.20–1. Cf. Mt 8.21–2, where a disciple asks, 'Lord, let me first go and bury my father', and Jesus answers: 'Follow me, and leave the dead to bury their own dead.' While Elijah's call of Elisha was the OT model for the NT call stories, the model was modified under the memory of Jesus' radical demand. The Messiah required more of his disciples than Elijah required of Elisha.

    18. As he was walking by the Sea of Galilee. 'By the Sea of Galilee' picks up on 4.13 and 15. There is no note of time. The location is presumably near Capernaum; cf. 4.13.

    The so-called Sea of Galilee was also known by the names

Gennesaret, Tiberias, and Taricheae. It is actually an inland, fresh-water lake about thirteen miles long and eight miles wide at one point, not a sea as we think of such.

he saw two brothers. It is Jesus who sees Simon and Andrew, not Simon and Andrew who see Jesus; cf. Lk 5.2. The initiative lies with the master. He is choosing them, not they him. This again recalls the story of Elijah calling Elisha (1 Kgs 19.19–21), and contrasts with rabbinic practice, where the disciple chose his rabbi. Cf. Jn 15.16: 'You did not choose me, but I chose you ...'.

Simon, who is called Peter. For Peter's place in Matthew see on 16.13–20.

and Andrew his brother. Andrew is not a significant character in our gospel. According to Jn 1.35–49, he was from Bethsaida and was at one time a disciple of John the Baptist.

casting a net. The 'net' was a circular casting net. To its edges were tied stones which caused the net to sink rapidly, encompassing fish. When the net was lifted by a rope tied to the middle, the stones would be gathered together and keep the fish entrapped.

In 1 Kgs 19.19–21, the story of Elijah calling Elisha, the latter's engagement with his occupation is recorded: Elisha 'was ploughing'. Cf. Mk 2.14: Levi was 'sitting at the tax office'. By making Jesus' call come to one engaged in his livelihood, our text underscores the break with everyday affairs.

into the sea. Given the condensed narrative we cannot tell whether Peter and Andrew are supposed to be on shore or in a boat (cf. 4.21–2). Nets were thrown from both.

for they were fishermen. So Mark. Peter, Andrew, James, and John appear to have belonged to a fishing partnership which included Zebedee and a number of hired servants (Mk 1.16–20; Jn 21.1–3). If Lk 5.1–11 be accurate, they had at least two boats.

19. Having been informed as to what Jesus saw, we next learn what he said.

Follow me. Jesus' words, which contain no why, are not invitation but unconditional demand.

and I will make you fishers of people. The expression, 'fishers of people', occurs in the NT only here and in Mk 1.16. Maybe it had a negative ring to it, causing one to think of deceit or persuasion, of those who 'trap' people; cf. Jer 16.16. If so, the words would have been provocative or at least paradoxical, which would be characteristic for Jesus.

20. Immediately makes the disciples act according to the word of 8.22. When the authoritative call of Jesus comes, there is not even time to say farewell to one's father; contrast 1 Kgs 19.19–21.

they left their nets and followed him. In 1 Kgs 19.20 Elisha says to Elijah, 'I will follow you'. 'Left their nets' highlights the disciples' sacrificial obedience and radical commitment. Renouncing their old life, not even taking time to bring in nets (and boat?), they leave all and follow Jesus; cf. 19.27; also 6.25–34; 8.20; Lk 14.33. Their call is to homelessness. They are being ordered to deny self, to suffer the loss of their own lives and livelihood. Peter and Andrew no longer belong to kith and kin but to Jesus; cf. Mt 10.37 = Lk 14.26.

21. And going on from there leaves the impression that, after calling Peter and Andrew, Jesus walked along the shore a short distance until he encountered two more fishermen. This may just be a pictorial way of making one episode out of two incidents which were historically separate.

James the son of Zebedee. In Mark, James is named nine times (although never by himself; it is always 'Peter and James and John' or 'James and John'). A comparison of Mk 16.1 with Mt 27.56 seems to imply that Matthew believed that Zebedee was married to Salome. Interestingly enough, James the son of Zebedee and his brother are nowhere mentioned by name in the Fourth Gospel. In Jn 21.2, however, 'the sons of Zebedee' occurs in a list of disciples, and the two are fishing.

and his brother John. That James and John (the younger presumably) were with their father probably shows that they could not have been very old. Matthew even introduces their mother in 20.20.

in the boat. James and John, like Peter and Andrew and Elisha of old, are called to discipleship in the midst of their daily activity. They leave one occupation for another.

with their father Zebedee. This sets the stage for the next verse, where the sons leave their father. The theme is stressed because of Jesus' words in 8.22; 10.35–7; 19.29; and 23.9.

mending their nets. The mention of nets furthers the parallelism between 4.18–20 and 21–2. No symbolic significance is apparent, although commentators have often found here a sign of poverty: 'They were poor and as they were unable to buy new nets, they were stiching together their old ones' (Theophylact).

22. Immediately they left the boat and their father. James and John not only leave behind their means of livelihood but also give up personal, family ties. Perhaps the dissimilarity at this point with 4.20 – Peter and Andrew's parents do not come into the picture – betrays the knowledge that Peter did not forsake his family: as 1 Cor 9.5 states, he travelled with a wife; and as Mk 1.29–31 recounts, he lived with his mother-in-law.

* * * * *

(i) Jesus, as the personification or embodiment of obedient Israel, repeats the experience of the people of old: having passed through the waters, he enters the desert to suffer a time of testing; cf. Deut 8.2. Then he calls disciples (4.18–22), which begins the renewal of the people of God. Just as Israel was born in the first exodus, so is the church born in a second exodus. By repeating or recapitulating in his own person the exodus and the events thereafter, the Son of God brings a new people into being.

(ii) Satan and his evil legions appear not infrequently in Matthew. Whenever they do they always wear the faces of defeat. To illustrate: when the devil first appears and tempts Jesus, he is wholly ineffectual and in the end is vanquished. And when demons afflict suffering souls in Israel (as they do so often from chapter 4 on) they are readily cast out by the Son of God. And when Peter in 16.22 gives utterance to a word of Satan, he is rebuked and must fall into place behind his master. We have then in Matthew, as in early Christianity in general, recognition of the limitations of the powers of iniquity. These are strictly circumscribed, and they fail completely in the presence of the Son of God and those members of his community who are full of faith; cf. 17.14–21.

INTRODUCTION TO THE SERMON ON THE MOUNT
(4.23–5.2)

[23]And Jesus went about all Galilee, teaching in their synagogues and proclaiming the good news of the kingdom and healing every disease and every sickness among the people. [24]So his fame spread throughout all Syria, and they brought to him all the sick, those afflicted with various diseases and pains, demoniacs, epileptics, and paralytics, and he healed them. [25]And great crowds followed him from Galilee, the Decapolis, Jerusalem, Judea, and from beyond the Jordan.

5 [1]Seeing the crowds, he went up on the mountain, and when he sat down, his disciples came to him, [2]and he opened his mouth and taught them, saying ...

Parallels: Mk 3.7–13; Lk 6.17–20

Mt 4.23–5.2 is a literary unit which closes one door and opens another: it concludes Mt 3–4 and at the same time introduces Mt 5–7. It bears a close resemblance to the other introductions to major discourses; see below.

23. Cf. the almost identical 9.35. The two verses together create a sort of *inclusio*: between them Jesus first teaches (5–7) and then heals (8–9). Afterwards, in chapter 10, he instructs and sends out the disciples for mission. The logic behind the arrangement should not be missed. When Jesus instructs his missionaries, he is telling them to do exactly what he has done, for they too are to teach and to heal. This accounts for the parallelism between 4.17 and 10.6 as well as between 4.24 and 10.1:

4.17 Jesus preaches, 'The kingdom of heaven has drawn near'	10.7 The disciples preach, 'The kingdom of heaven has drawn near'
4.24 Jesus heals every disease and infirmity	10.1 The disciples are to heal every disease and every infirmity

Missionary activity is part of the *imitatio Christi*.

Mt 4.23 and the following two verses constitute the first of several such summaries, the others being 8.16–17; 9.35–8; 12.15–21; 14.13–14; 14.34–6; 15.29–31; 19.1–2; 21.14–16; cf. also 10.1, 5–8 and 11.2–6. Such summaries do not just sum up what has gone before or what will come after; they also supply narrative continuity, lengthen narrative time, expand the geographical setting, create a picture of movement (Jesus goes from here to there), highlight central themes, and tell us that the material in Matthew represents only a selection; cf. Jn 20.30; 21.25.

And Jesus went about all Galilee. Jesus, unlike the typical prophets of Israel and rabbis but not certain Hellenistic philosophers, is an itinerant wanderer; cf. 8.20; 23.15.

and proclaiming the good news of the kingdom. Cf. 4.17. The words could well evoke Isa 52.7 where, in a messianic passage, the LXX has both 'to preach good news' and 'to rule'.

and healing every disease and every sickness among the people. Cf. 10.1, where the disciples are likewise to heal every disease and every infirmity. The common language binds Jesus to his disciples; they do what he, the model missionary, does.

24. So his fame spread throughout all Syria. Only Jesus' fame goes out; he himself stays in Galilee. This accords with the biblical prophecy (4.14–16) and 10.5–6; 15.24.

and they brought to him. The subject is here unspecified. Are Galilean Jews in view (4.23)? Are those from Syria included? Are the crowds of 4.25 anticipated? Whatever the answer, the picture is of Jesus as the centre around which everything happens.

demoniacs, epileptics, and paralytics. The rare Greek word here translated by 'epileptics' literally means 'be moon-struck'. It seems to refer to epilepsy (cf. the description in Mt 17.15), which the ancients often supposed was caused by the moon.

and he healed them. Later the evangelist will tell us that Jesus' acts of corporal mercy fulfilled messianic expectation; see 8.16–17 and 11.2–6, both quoting Isaiah.

25. And great crowds followed him from Galilee. The crowds in Matthew serve several functions. First, they follow Jesus wherever he goes and thereby show him to be a charismatic figure, indeed a sensation (4.25; 8.1, 18; etc.). Second, as an audience they are open and receptive, for they respond to the Messiah with amazement, astonishment, and reverential fear (e.g. 9.8; 12.23; 15.31; 22.23). They in fact hold Jesus to be, like John the Baptist, a prophet (21.11, 46), and they bless him when he enters the holy city (21.9). Third, they are contrasted with the Pharisees (9.33–4; 15.1–10; 23.1). Jesus condemns the Jewish leaders, but he has compassion on the multitudes (9.36; 14.14; 15.32). Fourth, in 13.36 and 14.22–3 the crowd is clearly distinguished from the disciples, and there are places in Matthew where Jesus delivers esoteric teaching (e.g. 13.10–17, 36–52; 16.21–8; 24–5). The crowd, then, cannot represent the church. Finally, the crowd is implicated in Jesus' death: 26.47, 55; 27.20, 24. Yet one must be careful in interpreting this fact. The disciples likewise fail to follow Jesus when darkness comes. On the whole, the crowds seem more fickle than evil; they go wrong only because their leaders mislead them.

The crowds are more than neutral background, more than a Greek chorus. They are presented in a more or less positive light. Although they are not true followers of Jesus, they are also not in the same league with Jesus' opponents. The crowds fall somewhere in between. They are, above all, 'the lost sheep of the house of Israel'. They have not yet found faith in Jesus, but many of them hold him to be a prophet. If this is the extent of their faith, the blame lies with their leaders, Matthew's intellectual counterparts. Thus the appropriate attitude towards the multitudes is compassion, which is what Jesus displays. This probably implies that for Matthew the mission to Israel, despite Jewish opposition, is still open.

the Decapolis was a group of ten Hellenistic cities east of the Jordan (with the exception of Scythopolis) and south of the Sea of Galilee; it probably received its name sometime in the first century BC. It is mentioned only once in Matthew, twice in Mark (5.20; 7.31), and nowhere else in the OT or NT. The ten cities – Damascus, Philadelphia, Raphana, Scythopolis, Gadara, Hippos, Dion, Pella, Galasa, and Canatha, according to Pliny – were an administrative region within the Roman province of Syria.

5.1. he went up on the mountain. The impression created by this and the previous clause is that Jesus, having seen the crowds, goes up the mountain to get away from them; cf. Jn 6.3. Yet in view of 7.28–8.1, we must think of the crowds as overhearing the discourse. So there are two circles around Jesus, an inner circle (disciples) and an outer circle (the crowds).

Lk 6.17 has Jesus deliver the sermon on a plain. Against those who have harmonized Luke's plain with Matthew's mountain and argued that Jesus delivered his sermon on a flat ridge on the side of a mountain, it suffices to observe that the sick would hardly be carried up to such a place (see Lk 6.17–19) and that the 'coming down' of Lk 6.17 naturally involves leaving the mountain of 6.12. Calvin made the essential point long ago: the sermon is 'a brief summary of the doctrine of Christ ... collected out of his many and various discourses'.

It is common to view the mountain of 5.1 as a counterpart to Sinai. In Matthew Henry's words, 'Christ preached this sermon, which is an exposition of the law, upon a mountain, because upon a mountain the law was given.' Matthew's Greek recalls pentateuchal passages having to do with Moses (e.g. Exod 19.3, 12, 13), and Jewish tradition spoke of Moses *sitting* on Sinai. Moreover, other Moses typologies from antiquity have their Mosaic heroes sit on a mountain (e.g. 4 Ezra 14); *Mek.* on Exod 19.11 and 29.18 and other sources claim that Israel was healed at the foot of Sinai (cf. 4.23); and 8.1, the conclusion of the SM, is identical with Exod 34.29 LXX A, which recounts Moses' descent from Sinai.

his disciples came to him. Until this point, the word 'disciple' has not been used, and only four followers have been called (4.18–22). At this juncture, moreover, it is difficult indeed to identify the disciples with the twelve because at least one of them, Matthew the tax-collector (see 10.3), does not meet Jesus until 9.9. Who then are the disciples of 5.1? The author, one might argue, thought of the Sermon on the Mount as being addressed directly to the four disciples of 4.18–22. This, however, would be to read too much into the text. The problem of 5.1 simply warns us that our evangelist was not overly interested in informing readers as to who exactly was on the mountain when Jesus spoke. In 5.1, the unspecified disciples, who must be a group larger than the four of 4.18–22, are – and this is the key point – contrasted with the crowd and so represent the church. The Sermon on the Mount is spoken directly to Matthew's Christian readers.

and he opened his mouth and taught them, saying. The opening of the discourse is deliberate and solemn; cf. Job 3.1–2.

* * * * *

(i) Before Jesus utters his commands, the reader has been informed – by OT prophecy, by John the Baptist, by God, and by the devil – who he is: the Messiah, the Son of David, the Son of God; the fulfiler of prophecies, the bearer of the Spirit, the healer *par excellence*. This Jesus, therefore, by virtue of his identity, must speak with authority and make sovereign demands. The obligation to obey the commands of Mt 5–7 is grounded in Christology, in the person of Jesus. Matthew sets up his gospel so that one may first recognize Jesus' unique status and then heed his commandments.

(ii) Mt 4.23–5.2, which gives us in brief an overview of Jesus' ministry to Israel (he preached, he taught, he healed), introduces the Sermon on the Mount. It tells us that the disciples were not the only ones to hear Jesus. So did the crowds. What crowds? Those who were healed by Jesus; see 4.23–5. Before the crowds hear the Messiah's word they are the object of his compassion and healing. Having done nothing, nothing at all, they are benefited. So grace comes before task, succour before demand, healing before imperative. The first act of the Messiah is not the imposition of his commandments but the giving of himself. 'When he has finished the miracles and healed their bodies, then he heals their souls as well' (Theophylact). Today's command presupposes yesterday's gift.

(iii) The gospel opens with events recalling the birth and childhood of Moses. Then there is Jesus' baptism, which parallels Israel's passing through the waters. There follows next the temptation, in which Jesus re-experiences the desert temptations recounted in Deuteronomy. Finally, there is 4.23–5.2, where Jesus, like Moses, sits on the mountain of revelation. In other words, every major event in Mt 1–5 apparently has its counterpart in the events surrounding Israel's exodus from Egypt. Moreover, the order of the events in Matthew lines up with the chronological order of events in the Pentateuch:

Exodus	slaughter of infants	return of hero	passage through water	temptation	mountain of lawgiving
Matthew	slaughter of infants	return of hero	passage through water	temptation	mountain of lawgiving

The typology is extensive and consistently thought through. So when Jesus goes up on the mountain to utter the Sermon on the Mount, he is speaking as the mosaic Messiah and delivering messianic Torah.

THE BEATITUDES (5.3–12)

[3]'**Blessed are the poor in spirit, for theirs is the kingdom of heaven.** [4]**Blessed are those who mourn, for they will be comforted.** [5]**Blessed are the meek, for they will inherit the earth.** [6]**Blessed are those who hunger**

and thirst for righteousness, for they will be filled. ⁷Blessed are the merciful, for they will receive mercy. ⁸Blessed are the pure in heart, for they will see God. ⁹Blessed are the peacemakers, for they will be called the sons of God. ¹⁰Blessed are those who are persecuted for righteousness' sake, for theirs is the kingdom of heaven. ¹¹Blessed are you when people revile you and persecute you and utter all kinds of evil against you falsely on my account. ¹²Rejoice and be glad, for great is your reward in heaven, for thus did they persecute the prophets who were before you.'

Parallels: Lk 6.20–3

Matthew's beatitudes are first of all eschatological blessings; that is, they are first of all promise and consolation. The first half of each beatitude depicts the community's present; the second half foretells the community's future; and the juxtaposition of the two radically different situations permits the trials of everyday life to be muted by contemplation of the world to come. This hardly excludes the implicit moral demand: one is certainly called to become what the beatitudes praise. But 5.3–12 does not offer formal imperatives; like the eschatological blessings in 13.16; Rev 19.9; and 22.14, it offers hope, and indeed functions as a practical theodicy. Although there is no explanation of evil, the imagination, through contemplation of God's future, engenders hope and makes the present tolerable.

Because Isa 61.1, 2, and 7 speak of good news for the poor (cf. Mt 5.3), comforting all who mourn (cf. Mt 5.4), and of inheriting the earth (cf. Mt 5.5), Matthew's beatitudes make an implicit christological claim: they are uttered by the anointed one of Isa 61. The Spirit of the Lord is upon Jesus; he has been anointed to bring good tidings to the poor, to bind up the brokenhearted, to proclaim liberty to the captives, to comfort those who mourn; cf. Lk 4.18–19 and the messianic application of Isa 61 in 4Q521.

There is nothing formally remarkable about Matthew's beatitudes. The form, 'blessed' + subject + 'for', is attested elsewhere (e.g. Gen 30.13), as is the eschatological orientation (cf. Dan 12.12), the grouping together of several beatitudes (cf. 4Q525 2), and the third person plural address (cf. Tob 13.14). Mt 5.3–12 rather distinguishes itself by (i) its scriptural background in Isa 61, which makes an implicit christological claim (which becomes explicit in 11.2–6) and (ii) the illustration of its virtues in the life of Jesus; for mourning see 26.36–46, for meekness 11.29; 21.5, for righteousness 3.15; 27.19, for mercy 9.27; 15.22; 17.15; 20.30–3, for persecution and reproach the passion narrative in its entirety.

3. This beatitude, like most of the others, reverses ordinary values. Although few in the ancient world would have opposed mercy or peacemaking, it was obviously no good thing to mourn. Nor did 'poor' or 'meek' or 'thirst' or 'hunger' have better connotations then than now, and in no time or place do normal people wish to be persecuted or reviled. So in 5.3–12 Jesus takes up words with negative connotations and associates them with the saints. Chrysostom saw the truth: 'What could be newer than these injunctions wherein the very things which all others avoid, these he declares to be desirable? I mean being poor, mourning, persecution, and evil reputation ... And hearing things so grievous and galling, so contrary to the accustomed ways of human beings, the multitudes were astonished.'

Blessed is the opposite of 'woe', as in 'Woe to you, Capernaum' (11.23). The Greek word (*makarios*) is a way of expressing a good fortune which, because it is known, brings joy. 'Fortunate are the poor in spirit' would be as accurate a translation as 'Blessed are the poor in spirit' or 'Happy are the poor in spirit'.

are the poor in spirit, for theirs is the kingdom of heaven. 'Blessed are the poor in spirit' (cf. 1QM 14.7) means much the same as 'blessed are the meek', and 'for theirs is the kingdom of heaven' is another way of saying 'they will inherit the earth'; cf. Ps 37.11. Both beatitudes are about eschatological reversal. Those who are without power or status and who depend upon God will be given the kingdom of heaven and inherit the earth when things are turned upside down at the last judgement. As it says in *b. Pesah.* 50a, 'those who are on top here are at the bottom there, and those who are at the bottom here are on the top there.'

As in v. 10, 'for theirs is the kingdom of heaven' is in the present tense. But given the future tense in the other beatitudes, we should probably explain vv. 3 and 10 as expressions of certainty: the surety of the saints' possession of the kingdom is underlined by use of a proleptic present. Greek can use a present tense to indicate a circumstance which, although it has not yet occurred, is regarded as so certain that it is spoken as having already happened. The very last line in Matthew's beatitudes – 'for great is your reward in heaven, for thus did they persecute the prophets who were before you' – illustrates the point nicely. Although reward is yet to be bestowed, its secure reality is here conveyed through a present tense.

4. those who mourn are not, against Augustine, sorry for their sins so much as they are aggrieved that while now the wicked prosper, the saints do not, and God has yet to right the situation. Cf. Isa 61.2: 'to proclaim the year of the Lord's favour, and the day of vengeance of our God: to comfort all who mourn.' Here Israel is oppressed at the hands of her heathen captors; her cities are in ruins; her people know shame and dishonour. So God's own are on the bottom, their enemies on top. Mourning is heard because the righteous suffer, the wicked prosper. It is the same in Matthew. The kingdom has not yet fully come. The saints are reviled and persecuted (5.10–12). The meek have not yet inherited the earth (5.5). The righteous still have enemies (5.43–8) who misuse them (5.38–42). In short, God's will is not yet done on earth as it is in heaven (6.10), and that can only mean mourning for God's people.

5. This verse follows v. 3 in several early authorities; there is a good chance this was the original sequence. If so, maybe 5.5, which is a quotation from LXX Ps 37.1, was added at some point to clarify 5.3. It does offer a roughly synonymous sentence and so is an accurate exposition of 5.3.

Blessed are the meek. The 'meek' are the 'poor in spirit', that is, the humble whose avoidance of hubris corresponds to their powerlessness in the eyes of the world; cf. the situation of Jesus in 11.29 (Jesus is kind) and 21.5 (Jesus enters Jerusalem not on a war horse but on a donkey).

will inherit the earth means that the meek will possess 'the kingdom of heaven'. The ideal future state was often conceived of as possession of the land of Israel or of the entire earth.

6. Righteousness that is hungered and thirsted for is neither justification nor eschatological vindication but the right conduct that God requires; cf. 5.10. Seemingly implied is the notion that the saints are not as a matter of fact righteous; rather, righteousness is always the goal which lies ahead.

7. Blessed are the merciful. Matthew has a great deal to say about the virtue of mercy, which is typically the external manifestation of an internal feeling of compassion for the unfortunate. It is a fundamental demand (9.13; 12.7), on a par in importance with love and faith (23.23). Jesus himself enjoins it (18.21–35), even when the word itself does not appear (25.31–46). And he himself embodies it (9.27–31; 15.21–8; 17.14–18; 20.29–34). In 25.31–46 it appears to be the criterion for salvation at the final judgement, and 18.23–35 teaches that those who do not show mercy cannot receive it from God.

for they will receive mercy. Chrysostom helpfully commented that despite the reciprocal formulation in our verse, there is here no 'equal recompense', for human mercy and divine mercy are not on the same level: 'as wide as is the interval between wickedness and goodness, so far is the one of these removed from the other.'

8. the pure in heart (cf. Ps 24.3–4) are those with harmony between inward thought and outward deed; such purity involves a singleness of intention, that intention being the doing of God's will. So 'purity of heart' presumably has to do with what Augustine called a 'simple heart', one undivided in allegiance and so rightly directed. The 'pure in heart' are given over wholly to the will of God. As Kierkegaard famously put it, purity of heart is to will one thing.

they will see God. Seeing God could be understood as a literal vision of God's body (as in *Ps. Clem. Hom.* 17.7), a literal vision of the glorified Christ (cf. 17.1–8; Jn 14.9), a spiritual or mental apprehension (cf. 'I see the point'), an indirect perception through unspecified effects of God, or an apprehension of the image of God in the perfected saints (so much Eastern Orthodox tradition). The text unfortunately does not decide the point. One can say, however, that the beatific vision is here eschatological: nothing is said of the possibility of seeing God in the present life. One day the saints will enjoy what the angels, according to 18.10, even now experience.

9. Blessed are the peacemakers. Exegetical history provides a slew of possibilities for what it means to be a peacemaker. Pacifists have thought it refers to the healing and prevention of political and military conflicts. Others – including the majority of critical exegetes today – have thought more in terms of personal relationships: one should make strenuous efforts to be reconciled to others both within and without the community. Still others have thought in terms of making peace with God (cf. Col 1.20), and especially of missionaries, who bring others to faith. Given Matthew's keen interest in the subject of reconciliation (18.21–35), especially within the Sermon on the Mount itself (5.21–6; 6.14–15), one suspects that the interpretation which puts the emphasis upon interpersonal relationships (cf. Prov 10.10; Mk 9.50) comes closest to the authorial intention.

for they will be called the sons of God. The precise connection between this promise and peacemaking is unclear. One possibility is that Jewish liturgical language is in the background. The Palestinian recension of the prayer of the eighteen benedictions ends with: 'Blessed are You, O Lord, the maker of peace'. Verse 9 may well assume, against the background of a well-known liturgical line, that God makes peace, from which it follows that others who make peace are like God and so God's children. However that may be, our text is illuminated by 5.44–5, where God's children are like God in being good to all, even enemies.

10. The verse looks like it has been pieced together from the other beatitudes. 'Persecuted' anticipates the 'persecute you' in the following verse. 'Righteousness' is the object of hunger and thirst in 5.6. And 'for theirs is the kingdom of heaven' is also the conclusion in v. 3.

for theirs is the kingdom of heaven. See the comment on 5.3.

11–12. This is the longest by far of the beatitudes, and its form is irregular; note especially the shift from third person to second person. Here Matthew follows the literary convention of making the final line in a series different and longer than its predecessors. The effect is twofold: to signal that the end of the series is near and to put emphasis upon that which is given extra attention. Mt 1.2–16; 10.40–2; 23.13–36; and Lk 6.37–8 offer additional examples.

Blessed are you when people revile you and persecute you and utter all kinds of evil against you falsely on my account. In Matthew, it is above all Jesus who is spoken evil of and reviled. People say that he blasphemes (9.2; 26.65) and acts unlawfully on the Sabbath (12.1–14). The Pharisees accuse him of consorting with sinners (9.11) and of casting out demons by the power of Satan (9.34; 12.24). Crowds laugh at him (9.24) and mock him (27.30, 38–44). Others call him Beelzebul (10:25) and accuse him of being a glutton and drunkard (11.19).

for thus did they persecute the prophets who were before you. The effect of this is to draw readers into the sacred history of Israel.

* * * * *

(i) The beatitudes promise that the kingdom of God will bring eschatological comfort, a permanent inheritance, true satisfaction, the vision of God, and unprecedented intimacy with God. Clearly the coming of the kingdom will mean the fullness of the divine reality within human experience, and it is rightly considered the *summum bonum* of both the Sermon on the Mount and Matthew as a whole. No other subject, then, could more fittingly lead off Matthew's first and most important discourse.

(ii) In so far as the promises connected with the kingdom bring consolation and comfort, they function as a practical theodicy. The beatitudes hardly explain evil or human suffering. They do, however, lessen pain and anguish by putting into perspective the difficulties of the present. This happens through an exercise of the imagination. Eschatological promises for those on the bottom reveal that all is not what it seems to be. That is, the truth, like the kingdom, is hidden. Only the future, with its rewards and punishments, will bring to light the true condition of the world and those in it; cf. 25.31–46. Those who use the eye of the mind in order to foresee and live for the future promised by the beatitudes will, with their faith, possess a secret vision and hope that makes powerlessness and suffering bearable.

(iii) Origen saw that Jesus himself illustrates the beatitudes: 'All the beatitudes that Jesus uttered in the Gospel, he confirms by his example, exemplifying what he taught. So he says, "Blessed are the meek" and again of himself, "Learn of me, for I am meek". He says,

"Blessed are the peacemakers", and who is such a peacemaker as my Lord Jesus, who is our peace, who did away with the enmity and destroyed it in his flesh? "Blessed are those who are persecuted for righteousness' sake" – no one so endured persecution for righteousness' sake as the Lord Jesus, who was crucified for our sins. So the Lord displayed all the beatitudes in himself. Thus having said "Blessed are those who weep", he himself wept over Jerusalem, to lay the foundation of this beatitude also.'

THE SALT AND LIGHT OF THE WORLD (5.13–16)

13'You are the salt of the earth. But if salt has lost its flavour, with what can its saltness be restored? It is no longer good for anything except to be thrown out and trampled under foot by people.
14'You are the light of the world. A city set on a hill cannot be hid. 15Nor do they light a lamp and put it under the bushel basket, but on the lampstand, and it gives light to all in the house. 16In the same way, let your light shine before people, so that they may see your good works and give glory to your Father in heaven.'

Parallels: Mk 4.21; 9.50; Lk 8.16; 11.33; 14.34–5

The parables about salt, light, and lamp are the general heading for 5.17–7.12. They together offer a summary description of those who live the Sermon on the Mount. It is no longer the Torah or the temple or Jerusalem or Israel that is the salt or light of the world (cf. Isa 60.1–3; Bar 4:2), but the church.

13. You are the salt of the earth. Given the various uses for salt in the ancient world – it was, among other things, an element in sacrifices, a purifier, a condiment, a preservative – and its several symbolic associations – a sign of purity, of necessity, of loyalty, of peace, of good speech, of wisdom – it is quite impossible to decide what one characteristic is to the fore in 5.13. While it would make sense, for instance, to affirm that the disciples are the world's wisdom, it would also be reasonable to think that the pure in heart purify the world, or that they are willing to sacrifice themselves. But the ambiguity matches the function, for 5.13 is part of the introduction to 5.17–7.12, which covers a host of topics. Salt should not be limited to any one referent. The disciples have several characteristic qualities without which they would cease to be what they are and instead become useless. 'You are the salt of the earth' is parallel to 'You are the light of the world', and the light is associated with good deeds in general.

But if salt has lost its flavour, with what can its saltness be restored?
Luther: 'salt is not salt for itself, it cannot salt itself.' So it is with the
disciples: what they are, they are for the world, not for themselves.

**It is no longer good for anything except to be thrown out and trampled
under foot by people.** The good can become bad; there is no guarantee
of privileged status.

14. You are the light of the world. The saints are the locus of God's
activity in the world. If God, who is light and gives off light (Job 29.2–3;
2 Cor 4.6; etc.), shines through Jesus (4.16; 17.1–8), this is also true of
the saints; they are windows through which the divine light enters the
world.

A city set on a hill cannot be hid. The city is not Zion or the new
Jerusalem. The verse is understandable if any city is meant; and the
parallel v. 15 confirms this: any lamp would fit the bill.

15. Purpose should dictate action. A disciple is called precisely to do
the good deeds Jesus demands.

**Nor do they light a lamp and put it under the bushel basket, but on the
lampstand, and it gives light to all in the house.** Putting a light under a
vessel puts it out.

**16. In the same way, let your light shine before people, so that they
may see your good works and give glory to your Father in heaven.** In
6.1–18, drawing attention to oneself is false piety. So such cannot be
true piety here. If we are to interpret Matthew by Matthew, here the
thought must be that the disciples, who find their lives by losing them,
shine by becoming invisible; the divine light passes through
transparencies.

* * * * *

The summary description of the disciples as salt and light, a description
which fits those who live as 5.21–7.12 details, has the whole world as its
backdrop. So the Gentile mission is presupposed. The followers of
Jesus are the salt and light for all, Jew and Gentile the world over.
Matthew's universalism is once more apparent. No less apparent is the
evangelist's exalted estimation of the ecclesia's role in the religious life
of humanity. If the church does in fact consist of those who are the salt
of the earth and the light of the world, then the church must be the
primary locus of God's activity in and for all people. 'What the soul is
in a body, this the Christians are in the world' (Diognetus).

JESUS AND THE LAW (5.17–20)

[17]'**Do not think that I have come to abolish the law or the prophets. I
have come not to abolish but to fulfil.** [18]**For amen I say to you, until**

heaven and earth pass away, not one letter, not one stroke of a letter, will pass from the law until all is accomplished. [19]Therefore, whoever breaks one of the least of these commandments and teaches others to do the same will be called least in the kingdom of heaven. But whoever does them and teaches them will be called great in the kingdom of heaven. [20]For I say to you, unless your righteousness exceeds that of the scribes and Pharisees, you will never enter the kingdom of heaven.'

Parallel: Lk 6.17

Mt 5.17–20 is primarily an anticipation of objections. As the preamble to vv. 21–48, it is intended to prevent readers from making two errors. First, it plainly states that the subsequent paragraphs are not to be interpreted, as they so often have been, as 'antitheses' that, in two or three instances, set aside the Torah. Instead Jesus upholds the law, so that between him and Moses there is no real conflict. Second, and despite the concord with the law, v. 20 tells us that what Jesus requires of his followers surpasses what has traditionally been regarded as the requirements of the Torah. So although there is continuity with the past, the Messiah also brings something new, and it does not surprise when vv. 21–48 go beyond the letter of the law to demand even more.

17. not to abolish but to fulfil. What is the meaning of 'fulfil'? Perhaps most of the suggestions can be fairly placed somewhere among the following: (i) 'Fulfil' really means 'add': Jesus' imperatives go beyond and so add to those in the OT. (ii) The meaning is 'do' or 'execute' or even 'obey': Jesus follows and performs the law perfectly. (iii) Jesus fulfils the law by bringing it to perfection with a new law of his own. (iv) Jesus enables others to keep the Torah. (v) Jesus reduces everything to love, which is the fulfiling of the law. (vi) The fulfilment is eschatological: Jesus does not abolish the Torah but, on the contrary, fulfils its prophecies.

In a case such as this certainty cannot be obtained. Wisdom should, moreover, recognize that some of these meanings do not exclude others, so that some combination of them could be correct. Indeed, there may be some truth in each of the proposals. If, however, one were forced to select a single explanation, (vi) seems best. Not only does Matthew usually use 'fulfil' with reference to prophetic fulfilment (1.22; 4.14; 12.17 etc.), but our sentence refers to the prophets as well as the law. So Jesus' new teaching brings to realization that which the Torah prophesied. And that realization does not set the law and prophets aside. Fulfilment rather confirms the Torah's truth.

18. This reinforces and clarifies 5.17: Jesus, instead of abolishing the law and prophets, fulfils them, and this is consistent with their lasting until the new creation comes.

until heaven and earth pass away, not one letter, not one stroke of a letter, will pass from the law until all is accomplished. One may have difficulty reconciling this view of things with Paul (did Matthew believe that Jewish Christians but not Gentile Christians should observe the Mosaic commandments?). But Matthew's view of things seems manifest. Nothing in our Gospel calls the law into real question. On the contrary, Matthew's Jesus tells the Pharisees that they should practise justice and mercy and faith without neglecting the minor matters of the law (23.23–4).

19. Despite many, this is a statement about the law, not a statement about Jesus' commands.

Therefore, whoever breaks one of the least of these commandments and teaches others to do the same will be called least in the kingdom of heaven. But whoever does them and teaches them will be called great in the kingdom of heaven. This elaborates upon v. 18 in a way reminiscent of how the latter elaborates upon v. 17: if all of the law remains in force, then all of the law must be obeyed. So whoever relaxes even one of the least of the Mosaic commandments and teaches others to do so will 'be called least in the kingdom of heaven', whereas those who do and teach them will be called great. Whether 'be called least' means exclusion from heaven or a low rank therein is unclear.

20. This verse is the warning that vv. 21–48 will demand the extraordinary.

For I say to you, unless your righteousness exceeds that of the scribes and Pharisees, you will never enter the kingdom of heaven. This takes up the theme of being in the kingdom, implies that one must do at least what the scribes and Pharisees do, and explicitly states that one must do even more: namely, obey the demands of Jesus, which are to follow.

* * * * *

(i) In denying the suspicion that Jesus abolishes the Torah, these verses look forward, not backward, for no such suspicion could arise from what has gone before. Verses 17–20 introduce 5.21–48 and declare that the so-called 'antitheses' are not such: Matthew's Jesus does not set believers free from the law. (Alternative interpretations of 5.17–20 are typically motivated by a desire to bring Matthew closer to Paul; but the NT appears to have more than one judgement on the status of the Torah, and we should first read Matthew on its own terms.)

(ii) Verse 17–20 not only rebuts in advance a wrong interpretation of 5.21–48 but also supplies a clue for the right interpretation. Verse

20, in announcing that the righteousness of disciples must exceed that of the Jewish leaders, anticipates that Jesus' words in the subsequent paragraphs will require even more than the Torah itself requires. The tension between Jesus' teaching and the Mosaic law is not that those who accept the former will transgress the latter; rather it is that they will achieve far more than they would if the Torah were their only guide.

THE BETTER RIGHTEOUSNESS (5.21–48)

[21]'You have heard that it was said to those of old, "You will not murder"; and "whoever murders will be liable to judgement." [22]But I say to you that if you are angry with a brother, you will be liable to judgement; and if you insult a brother, you will be liable to the council; and if you say, "You fool," you will be liable to the Gehenna of fire. [23]If then you are offering your gift on the altar, and there remember that your brother has something against you, [24]leave your gift there before the altar and go. First be reconciled to your brother, and then come and offer your gift. [25]Make friends quickly with your accuser while you are going with him to court, lest your accuser hand you over to the judge, and the judge to the guard, and you be thrown into prison. [26]Amen I say to you, you will never get out until you have paid the last penny.

[27]'You have heard that it was said, "You will not commit adultery." [28]But I say to you that everyone who looks at a woman in order to lust after her has already committed adultery with her in his heart. [29]If your right eye causes you to sin, tear it out and throw it away. It is better for you to lose one of your members than for your whole body to be thrown into Gehenna. [30]And if your right hand causes you to sin, cut it off and throw it away. It is better for you to lose one of your members than for your whole body to go into Gehenna.

[31]'It was also said, "Whoever divorces his wife, let him give her a certificate of divorce." [32]But I say to you that everyone who divorces his wife, except on the ground of unchastity, causes her to commit adultery; and whoever marries a divorced woman commits adultery.

[33]'Again, you have heard that it was said to those of old, "You will not swear falsely, but perform the vows you have made to the Lord." [34]But I say to you, Do not swear at all, either by heaven, for it is the throne of God, [35]or by the earth, for it is his footstool, or by Jerusalem, for it is the city of the great King. [36]And do not swear by your head, for you cannot make one hair white or black. [37]Let your "Yes" be "Yes" and your "No" be "No". Anything more than this comes from the evil one.

[38]'You have heard that it was said, "An eye for an eye and a tooth for a tooth." [39]But I say to you, Do not resist an evildoer. Whoever strikes

you on the right cheek, turn to him the other also. ⁴⁰And to the one who wants to sue you and to take your coat, allow him to take your cloak as well. ⁴¹And whoever compels you to go one mile, go with him two. ⁴²To the one who asks from you, give, and the one wanting to borrow from you, do not refuse.

⁴³'You have heard that it was said, "You will love your neighbour and hate your enemy." ⁴⁴But I say to you, Love your enemies, and pray for those who persecute you, ⁴⁵so that you may be sons of your Father in heaven. For he makes his sun rise on the evil and on the good, and sends rain on the just and on the unjust. ⁴⁶For if you love those who love you, what reward do you have? Do not even the toll-collectors do the same? ⁴⁷And if you greet only your brothers, what more are you doing (than others)? Do not even the Gentiles do the same? ⁴⁸Be perfect, then, even as your heavenly Father is perfect.'

Parallels: Mt 18.8–10;19.9; Mk 9.43–8; 10.11–12; Lk 6.27–36; 12.57–9; 16.18; 1 Cor 7.10–11; Jas 5.12

The section falls into two triads. 5.21–6 + 27–30 + 31–2 constitute one subsection, 5.33–7 + 38–42 + 43–8 another:

First triadic set:

'You have heard that it was said to
those of old'   (full formula)
    Citation of Scripture (Exod 20.13;
    Deut 5.17)
        'But I say to you that'
'You have heard that it was said'   (abbreviated formula)
    Citation of Scripture (Exod 20.14;
    5.18)
        'But I say to you that'
'It was also said'   (abbreviated formula)
    Citation of Scripture (Deut 24.1–4)
        'But I say to you that'

Second triadic set:

'Again,
    you have heard that it was said to
    those of old'   (full formula)
        Citation of Scripture (Lev 19.2)
            'But I say to you' + imperative
    'You have heard that it was said'   (abbreviated formula)
        Citation of Scripture (Exod 21.24;

Lev 24.20; Deut 19.21)
　'But I say to you' + imperative
'You have heard that it was said'　　　(abbreviated formula)
　Citation of Scripture (Lev 19.18)
　　'But I say to you' + imperative

Although the paragraphs have generated many conflicting inter-pretations, four propositions seem more probable than not. First, 5.21–48 does not set Jesus' words over against Jewish interpretations of the Mosaic law; rather there is contrast with the Bible itself. 'You have heard that it was said to those of old' refers to Sinai. Second, although Jesus' words are contrasted with the Torah, the two are not contradictory; cf. 5.17–20. Certainly those who obey 5.21–48 will not find themselves breaking any Jewish law. Third, 5.21–48 is not Jesus' interpretation of the law. The declaration that remarriage is adultery, for example, is set forth as a new teaching grounded not in exegesis but in Jesus' authority. Fourth, the six paragraphs illustrate, through concrete examples, what sort of attitude and behaviour Jesus requires and how his demands surpass those of the Torah without contra-dicting the Torah.

Many have complained that the teaching of 5.21–48 is impractical. As Dostoevsky's Grand Inquisitor says, Jesus 'judged humanity too highly', for 'it was created weaker and lower than Christ thought'. But the sermon, which is so poetical, dramatic, and pictorial, offers not a set of rules (the ruling on divorce is the only possible exception), but rather seeks to instil a moral vision. Literal (mis)interpretation accordingly leads to absurdities. The text, which implies that God demands a radical obedience which cannot be casuistically formulated, functions more like a story than a legal code. Its primary purpose is to instil principles and qualities through a vivid inspiration of the moral imagination. What one comes away with is not a grossly incomplete set of irrevocable statutes or bloodless abstractions but an unjaded impression of a challenging moral ideal. That ideal may ever be beyond grasp, but that is what enables it ever to beckon its adherents forward.

Anger and Murder (5.21–6)

21. You have heard that it was said to those of old, 'You will not murder'; and 'whoever murders will be liable to judgement.' Jesus first quotes Moses and one of the commandments (Exod 20.13; Deut 5.17) and then summarizes what the Pentateuch says elsewhere, that the one who commits murder will be put to death (e.g. Exod 21.12; Lev 24.17).

22–3. These two verses in all likelihood allude to the story of Cain (which is also alluded to in 18.22 and mentioned in 23.35). To readers steeped in Jewish tradition, the mention of murder in conjunction with hating one's brother could readily have called to mind Genesis 4, particularly as the enmity between Cain and Abel grew out of God's rejection of Cain's sacrificial gift, and the offering of a gift is the situation described in 5.23–4. It was traditional to use the story of Genesis 4 to illustrate how anger can lead to murder. Wisd 10.3 tells the story of Cain this way: 'But when an unrighteous man departed from her [Wisdom] in anger, he perished because in rage he slew his brother.' After referring to Cain, 'who was from the evil one and murdered his brother', 1 Jn 3.15 goes on to say that 'all who hate a brother or sister are murderers'. Cyprian offered these comments on our passage: 'One who comes to the Sacrifice with a quarrel he [Jesus] calls back from the altar and commands him first to be reconciled with his brother and then, when he is at peace, to return and offer his gift to God. For neither had God respect for Cain's offering, for he could not have God at peace with him, who through envy and discord was not at peace with his brother.'

But I say to you that if you are angry with a brother, you will be liable to judgement. Cf. 1 Jn 3.15 ('All who hate a brother or sister are murderers'); *Derek Erez Rabba* 57b ('He who hates his neighbour is among the shedders of blood'). The striking equation shifts attention from the outward act to the inward state (cf. 5.27–30) and makes anger and harsh words grievous sins to be exorcized at all costs. Anger is not just perilous because 'anger leads to murder' (*Did.* 3.2): anger – the companion of hate, which is the opposite of love – is in and of itself dangerous and deserving of condemnation. It is insufficient to refrain from the act of murder, for the latter is simply the symptom of something else. The source of murder must be uprooted; anger must be eradicated. As Gregory of Nyssa put it, 'One can divide wickedness under two headings, one concerned with works, the other with thoughts. The former, the iniquity which shows itself in works, he [God] has punished through the old law. Now, however, he has given the law regarding the other forms of sin, which punishes not so much the evil deed itself, as guards against even the beginning of it.'

Although human experience teaches the dangers of anger, so that wisdom the world over warns against it (cf. Ps 4.4; Prov 14.29; 16.32), Jesus here seems to go further. He does not say that one should not be angry for the wrong reason. Nor does he imply that there might be some good reason for being angry with another. He seemingly prohibits the emotion altogether. Where is the allowance for justified anger? One way of countering this objection is to argue that the prohibition (perhaps hyperbole?) was never intended to cover all circumstances, to prohibit anger for every reason. The OT, which Jesus upholds (5.17–20), allows righteous anger and depicts heroes and God as angry; cf. Exod 4.14; 32.19; Ps 4.4; Jer 6.11 etc. Further, other early Christian texts allow anger (e.g. Eph 4.26), and Jesus himself gets angry in the Gospels; cf. Mk 1.41 v.l.; 3.5; and the overturning of tables in the temple. He also contradicts a literal reading when he calls others 'fool' (23.17). Some exegetes nonetheless find here a literal, blanket prohibition.

and if you insult a brother, you will be liable to the council. 'Council' substitutes for 'judgement' in the previous clause and can mean either 'the high council', the Sanhedrin in Jerusalem, or a local court as in 10.17. Given, however, the clauses on either side, perhaps the sense is eschatological: offenders 'will be liable to the council of the holy apostles when they sit to judge the twelve tribes' (Theophylact).

and if you say, 'You fool', you will be liable to the Gehenna of fire. Contrast 23.17.

24. leave your gift there before the altar and go. First be reconciled to your brother, and then come and offer your gift. Verses 23–4 and 25–6 are both illustrations of the self-discipline of reconciliation, which is the antidote to anger. That is, the things that are condemned in 5.22 – anger and insults – are in vv. 23–6 overcome by the offender making peace with the offended. So what is envisaged is not isolated individuals seeking to subdue their passions but disciples going about the often awkward task of trying to right perceived wrongs. Perhaps in this Matthew's Jesus is counselling the mean between repression and expression, between ignoring anger and venting it. Verses 21–6, which assume that anger does not have power over individuals unless they consent, say that anger is not to be hidden or disregarded. Nor should one foolishly act upon its impulses. Anger should instead be dealt with – by becoming the opportunity for repairing broken relationships.

26. you will never get out until you have paid the last penny was one of the classical proof texts for the doctrine of purgatory. This is bad exegesis, as the Reformers had little difficulty showing.

Adultery and Lust (5.27–30)

Jesus' prohibition of wrongful desire and its equation with adultery do not contradict the biblical injunctions against adultery (Exod 20.14; Deut 5.18), for Jesus himself speaks against this sin (5.32; 15.19; 19.9). Rather does he pass beyond the decalogue to require more: 5.27–30 at once upholds and supplements the law. Jesus upholds the Torah because, as Augustine had it, 'The one who does not commit adultery in the heart much more easily guards against committing adultery in actual fact. So he who gave the later precept confirmed the earlier; for he came not to destroy the law, but to fulfil it.' Jesus supplements the law because, while he approves the old law which condemns the external act as evil, he declares that no less evil is the intention that brings it forth.

27. You have heard that it was said, 'You will not commit adultery.' Cf. Exod 20.14; Deut 5.18.

28. But I say to you that everyone who looks at a woman in order to lust after her has already committed adultery with her in his heart. Matthew's construction ('in order to lust') implies that the sin lies not in the entrance of a thought but in letting it incite wrongful passion. Jesus is not indicting the involuntary arrival of sexual desire. He is instead telling followers that they are responsible creatures who have a choice in what they do with their natural drives. The body need not be the master. Luther got it right: 'It is impossible to keep the devil from shooting evil thoughts and lusts into your heart. But see to it that you do not let such arrows stick there and take root, but tear them out and throw them away.'

The hyperbolic, moral equation of wrongful desire with adultery was not Jesus' innovation. In the *Testament of Issachar*, the patriarch, at the end of his life, boasts, 'I have not had intercourse with any woman other than my wife, nor was I promiscuous by lustful look' (7.2). In the *Mekilta* of R. Simeon we read that one should not commit adultery 'either with the eye or with the heart' (111). And R. Simeon ben Lakish is recorded to have said, 'Even he who visualizes himself in the act of adultery is called an adulterer' (*Leviticus Rab.* 23.12).

29–30. By telling followers to pluck out their eyes and cut off their hands Jesus makes plain the difficulty of what he is asking.

If your right eye causes you to sin, tear it out and throw it away. The vivid demand for personal sacrifice, which reappears in 18.8–9, is hyperbolic: it underscores the seriousness of the sin. This is not about literal amputation. Matthew's Jesus knows as well as Paul that the problem is not the body as such but the sin that dwells in it (Rom 7.17, 20); cf. Mt 15.17–18. The believer 'amputates the passions of the soul without touching the body' (Origen).

It is better for you to lose one of your members than for your whole body to be thrown into Gehenna. We should not (despite Jn 20.20, 25) visualize a mutilated resurrected body. The bizarre images, which arouse the imagination and enhance memory, instead underline that one cannot disclaim responsibility by blaming the body. Actions are psychosomatic, and body and soul, being united, are judged as one accountable individual. On 'Gehenna' see on 7.19.

Divorce and Adultery (5.31–2)

If lust is like adultery, so too is divorce. Jesus summarizes Deut 24.1–4, where allowance is made for remarriage, and then goes on to say that (for a man) to divorce (a woman) except for 'unchastity' causes her (because she will remarry) to commit adultery. As it stands no explanation is offered; but 19.3–9 will offer such. The assumption is that monogamy must be upheld.

31. It was also said. This abbreviates the formula of vv. 21 and 27.

Whoever divorces his wife, let him give her a certificate of divorce. See Deut 24.1–4.

32. But I say to you that everyone who divorces his wife, except on the ground of unchastity. The meaning of 'unchastity' has been disputed. Most take it either to mean sexual unfaithfulness within marriage or incest. In favour of the latter, we can envisage a situation in which Gentiles entering the community were found to be, because of marriages made before conversion, in violation of the Levitical laws of incest (see Lev 17). But there is no patristic support for the equation of 'unchastity' with adultery, and in 1.18–25 Joseph, who determines to divorce his wife because of suspected adultery, is 'just' or 'righteous' – an odd comment if Jesus' ruling does not cover his case.

causes her to commit adultery, and whoever marries a divorced woman commits adultery. Erasmus and most Protestants have thought Matthew allows the innocent party to divorce and remarry in the event of 'unchastity'. But according to the almost universal patristic as well as Roman Catholic opinion, separation but not remarriage is permitted. Unfortunately the text does not admit of a definitive interpretation.

It has often been thought that Matthew's Jesus contradicts Moses in 5.31–2. But (i) the OT itself implies that divorce is a problem; cf. Deut 24.4; Mal 2.16 ('I [Yahweh] hate divorce'). Lev 21.7 and Ezek 44.22 prohibit priests from marrying divorcees, which suggests that divorce is at odds with holiness. (ii) The rabbinic school of Shammai interpreted Deut 24.1 as allowing divorce only for sexual unfaithfulness – the same teaching we find in Matthew. (iii) In 19.1–12 Jesus does not say that the teaching of Genesis is from God, and that in Deuteronomy from Moses. Rather, the instructions in Deut 24.1 were given because of Israel's moral petrification; that is, they were a 'concession' to the post-fallen state. Jesus distinguishes between a portion of the law that expresses God's original will for humanity on the one hand and, on the other, another portion in which divine instruction is a response to human failure. The OT *permits* but does not *command* divorce.

The history of the interpretation of our passage is instructive. Roman Catholic tradition, like the canons of the Church of England, has generally allowed separation but not divorce (although exceptions have been granted for cases of non-consummation and for one of two non-Christians converting to Catholicism). Marriage has been thought legally indissoluble, at least until one partner dies. The Church has and does, however, issue annulments. In these cases it is said that there was no real marriage in the first place.

Eastern Orthodox tradition has permitted divorce for many reasons, including mental illness, leprosy, and abortion. While recognizing one marriage as the norm, it has also allowed remarriage (although usually only one's first marriage is blessed in a eucharistic service; later marriages have been, until recent times, only civil affairs). Indeed, Orthodox tradition even has a few saints who remarried (e.g. the twelfth- and thirteenth-century Georgian Queen Tamar). Jesus' prohibition of divorce except for unchastity has not been interpreted as an inviolate law but a statement of the human ideal, which sinful humanity often does not live up to. So the church condescends, through its exercise of pastoral 'economy', to human weakness. At the same time, it has traditionally demanded penance (usually involving abstinence from communion for a year or more) upon entrance into a second wedding.

Protestants have tended to follow one of three courses. Most have traditionally agreed with Erasmus, who argued that Jesus allows divorce for adultery; and further that if adultery has occurred, then remarriage can take place. A minority has differed only on the subject of remarriage: even when adultery has occurred, there can be no remarriage. Recently, however, more and more Protestants seem to share the view of the Eastern Orthodox: Jesus' ruling should not be construed in a juridical or legalistic fashion.

On Oaths (5.33–7)

The Tanak permits oaths in everyday speech provided they are neither false nor irreverent. For Jesus, however, oaths are not needed (cf. Jas 5.12); for the presupposition behind the oath is that there are two types of statements, one of which demands commitment (the oath), and one of which does not (the statement without an oath). Jesus enjoins invariable commitment to every statement, making the oath superfluous.

33. You will not swear falsely, but perform the vows you have made to the Lord summarizes the teaching found in Exod 20.7; Lev 19.12; Num 30.3–15, and elsewhere. Perhaps Ps 50.14 in particular is in mind.

34–6. Do not swear at all. Despite the reservation shown to oaths in some Jewish sources (e.g. Ecclus 23.9; Philo, *De Dec*. 84; Josephus, *Bell*. 2.135; *m. Dem*. 2.3), one wonders whether Jesus' command is to be understood literally as forbidding all oaths (Tolstoy went so far as to affirm that Jesus' words require the abolition of courts). Perhaps indeed the situation envisaged is not swearing in court but swearing in everyday speech. However that may be, early Christian literature does not show much aversion to swearing (e.g. Gal 1.20; Rev 10.6), and our gospel itself seems to presuppose the validity of certain oaths (23.16–22). Further, the reduction of speech to 'yes' and 'no' in v. 37 is obviously hyperbole.

either by heaven, for it is the throne of God, or by the earth, for it is his footstool, or by Jerusalem, for it is the city of the great King. And do not swear by your head, for you cannot make one hair white or black. In the *Mishnah*, oaths by heaven, by earth, and by one's own head are all viewed as not binding by at least some authorities (e.g. *m. Ned*. 1.3). This may explain their appearance here. If it was claimed by some that oaths by heaven or earth or Jerusalem or one's head were, because not binding, not covered by Jesus' prohibition, 5.34–6 counters by linking heaven and earth and Jerusalem to God, thereby making all oaths binding and so voiding any casuistic attempt to circumvent 5.34a.

37. Let your 'Yes' be 'Yes' and your 'No' be 'No' means Let your yes be true and your no be true: or perhaps, Let your yes be only yes – not yes and an oath – and let your no be no – not no and an oath.

Anything more than this comes from the evil one. For examples in Matthew itself of oaths that entrap their speakers see 14.1–12 (Herod) and 26.69–75 (Peter).

Turn the Other Cheek (5.38–42)

Verses 38–42 are not a repudiation of Moses. While in the Pentateuch the *lex talionis* belongs to the judiciary process, this is not the sphere of application in Matthew. Jesus does not overthrow the principle of equivalent compensation on an institutional level – that question is just not addressed – but declares it illegitimate for his followers to apply it to their private disputes. The several brief scenes vividly represent the demand for an unselfish temperament, for naked humility and a will to suffer the loss of one's personal rights: evil should be requited with good.

38. You have heard that it was said. This abbreviates the formula in v. 33.

An eye for an eye and a tooth for a tooth. This is a citation of the law of reciprocation in Exod 21.24; Lev 24.20; and Deut 19.21.

39. The teaching on non-retaliation, although it goes against human instinct, does have its parallels. There is a rabbinic passage which declares, 'Our rabbis taught: Those who are insulted but do not insult, hear themselves reviled without answering, act through love and rejoice in suffering, of them Scripture says, "But they who love him are as the sun when he goes forth in his might"' (*b. Šabb.* 88b). Plutarch tells the story of how Pericles accepted in silence for an entire day a hooligan's abuse and reviling and, afterward, when darkness fell, commanded his servants to take a torch and escort the man home (*Pericl.* 5). Texts such as these – and there are others – show that, despite the recurrent protest that turning the other cheek is impractical, Jesus' teaching on non-retaliation is not isolated wisdom. Indeed, Graeco-Roman literature shows a developing tendency to speak against revenge (although this is usually based upon the desire for tranquility and command of the passions).

Do not resist an evildoer is the general principle that is then followed by four illustrations: disciples are: (i) personally insulted; (ii) taken to court; (iii) impressed to do a soldier's bidding; (iv) asked to help one in need of funds.

Whoever strikes you on the right cheek, turn to him the other also. Cf. Isa 50.9 and Lam 3.30. Striking the cheek with open hand is a gross insult; that it is the right cheek makes plain that the reference is to the backhanded insult.

If Jesus speaks of eschewing violence and not resisting evil, of being slapped, of having one's clothes taken, and of being compelled to serve the Romans, the conclusion to his own life makes his words concrete: he eschews violence (26.51–4); he does not resist evil (26.36–56; 27.12–14); he is struck (26.67); he has his garments taken (27.28, 35); and his cross is carried by one requisitioned by Roman order (27.32). Here then we meet two themes found throughout Matthew: (i) the congruence between word and deed, speech and action – an idea so important for Hellenistic philosophy – and (ii) Jesus' status as moral exemplar, which requires an 'imitation' of Christ. Furthermore, Jesus is in Matthew the suffering servant of Isaiah, and the language of Isa 50.6–9 has coloured 5.38–42.

40. And to the one who wants to sue you and to take your coat, allow him to take your cloak as well. Jewish males typically wore two garments, an inner garment (a shirt or tunic worn next to the skin) and an outer garment (a robe or cloak). Because, according to Exod 22.26–7 and Deut 24.12–13, one's outer cloak – which was also used as a sleeping blanket or coverlet – could not be taken away by another in pledge for any length of time, Jesus' hearers are being asked to give up their lawful rights. That the literal observation of such a rule might

land one in prison for nudity is an argument that we have here an
arresting illustration of a principle, not a rigid statute.

41. As with vv. 39–40 and 42, no motive is given for acting in the
peculiar manner Jesus desires. We are not told, for instance, that
turning the other cheek will save the wicked. This means that the
question of whether or not the world will be transformed by such
action is just not addressed.

And whoever compels you to go one mile, go with him two. Cf. 27.32.
We are probably to imagine a situation in which civilians are
compelled by Roman soldiers to do their bidding and carry their
equipment.

42. To the one who asks from you, give. This does not fit the context
well, which is about revenge and love of enemies.

and the one wanting to borrow from you, do not refuse. This is
synonymous with the previous line.

Love Your Enemy (5.43–8)

The material on love of one's enemy, as the last of the six paragraphs
introduced by 5.17–20, is climactic. It contains the most important and
surely most difficult commands.

43. You will love your neighbour. Jesus begins by quoting Lev 19.18,
which he shall again quote in 19.19 and 22.39.

hate your enemy is not found in the OT. There are, however, related
sentiments – as is only to be expected, for the maxim accurately
describes ordinary human behaviour. See 2 Chr 19.2; Ps 5.5; 139.21;
and the story of Elisha calling down bears upon young taunters in 2
Kgs 2.23–5. But the closest parallels occur in the Dead Sea Scrolls. In
1QS 1.10 the members of the sect are to 'hate all the sons of darkness',
and Josephus, *Bell.* 2.139, tells us that the Essenes swore 'to hate
always the unjust'.

44. But I say to you. Despite the antithetical formulation, Jesus does
not contradict Lev 19.18 but rather goes beyond it. The Pentateuch
understands 'neighbour' as 'fellow Israelite'. This allows one to
confine love to one's own kind, or even to define neighbour in
opposition to enemy. Jesus, however, gives 'neighbour' its broadest
definition (cf. Lk 10.29–37).

Love your enemies, and pray for those who persecute you. The
context equates enemies with those who persecute the faithful. This
means those enemies are not just one's personal opponents but God's
opponents. Further, 'love' is clarified by what follows: one must pray
for enemies, do good to them, and greet them. Jesus is not speaking of
an emotion but of actions which benefit enemies.

Although the succinct, arresting, and memorable imperative, 'Love your enemies', appears to be the distinctive invention of Jesus' own mind, it has parallels. Already an ancient Babylonian document contains this advice: 'Do no evil to your opponents; recompense with good the one who does evil to you; let justice be done to your enemy.' Epictetus instructs Cynics that if they should find themselves flogged as an ass, then they must love the one who flogs them. According to Seneca, 'If you are imitating the gods, you say, "then bestow benefits also upon the ungrateful, for the sun rises also upon the wicked, and the sea lies open to pirates ...".' For the close rabbinic parallel in *b. Šabb.* 88b see on v. 39.

45. so that you may be sons of your Father in heaven. For he makes his sun rise on the evil and on the good, and sends rain on the just and on the unjust. In loving the enemy the disciple is only imitating God, who causes the sun to shine and the rain to fall upon all, not just the righteous; cf. Ps 145.9 and Prov 29.13. God's generous actions break the rule of reciprocity and cost/benefit analysis. In accord with this, in 5.43–8, as in the preceding paragraph, God's kindness does not convert the wicked. On the contrary, God is good to them notwithstanding their continued unrighteousness. The same is true for the faithful disciple. Jesus does not say that kindness will end enmity or bring reconciliation. Although as a matter of experience this may happen from time to time, the text actually seems to presuppose just the opposite: despite the goodness God has brought to people through the creation, there are nonetheless wicked people. But the rain still comes down upon all, just as the sun still shines upon all. God's goodness can be without apparent effect. Similarly, Jesus asks disciples to act on principle without attention to the consequence. There is no hope of getting this for that, kindness for kindness. Nothing is said about breaking the cycle of revenge, or about bringing the enemy into the fold of faith.

47. And if you greet only your brothers, what more are you doing (than others)? Do not even the Gentiles do the same? The righteousness Jesus demands goes beyond that of scribes and Pharisees (v. 20), so it must likewise be greater than the righteousness of Gentiles.

48. Be perfect, then, even as your heavenly Father is perfect. This line belongs firstly to the unit that begins in v. 43, and the motif of imitating God takes one back to v. 45. At the same time, v. 48 is the fitting culmination of all of 5.21ff., for throughout the section Jesus asks for 'perfection', for something that cannot be surpassed. What more can be done about lust if it has been driven from one's heart? And who else is left to love after one has loved the enemy? Obviously 'Be perfect' is not a call to sinlessness; nor does the imperative posit two sorts of believers, the merely good on the one hand and the perfect on the other. Jesus' call to perfection is a call to completeness: there are things not to be left undone.

* * * * *

(i) Matthew's sermon is not an adequate or complete summation of Matthew's religion. It does not stand by itself but is rather part of a larger whole. So its demands are perverted when isolated from the grace and Christology which appear from Matthew in its entirety. The sermon is in the middle of a story about God's gracious overture to God's people through his Son. And read in its entirety it brings together gift and task, grace and law, benefit and demand.

(ii) 5.21-48 should not be read without 5.17-20. The law and the prophets are still in force. This proves fatal for interpretations of 5.21-48 that land one in fundamental conflict with the OT, which accepts armies, courts, and oaths as necessary; and it would seem to follow, on that interpretation, that 'Jesus Christ had retracted what had earlier been established by God his Father' (Calvin). In Matthew, the new and old hang together (9.17). So a literal-minded and legalistic observance cannot be, at least over the whole range of life, in accord with the Matthean intention. Tolstoy himself recognized that his interpretation of the Sermon on the Mount contradicts the OT, which is why he was so insistent that the new revelation replaces the old. He criticized the church for harmonizing the Sermon on the Mount with the revelation that was given before it. But here Eastern Orthodox, Roman Catholic, and Protestant have rightly been closer to the letter and spirit of Matthew's Gospel.

(iii) An inordinate desire to emphasize Jesus' uniqueness will lead to misinterpretation. The truth of Jesus' teaching cannot in any way depend upon its novelty. Verses 21-48 contain much which, if not exactly universal, is at least attested here and there in religious and philosophical texts from other times and places, with its links to the OT and Jewish tradition being especially close and numerous. So far from this being an embarrassment, – as though a brand new morality, an ethics *de novo*, would be desirable, – this is perhaps one answer to those who would accuse the Matthean Jesus of being an erratic boulder on humanity's moral landscape: and one reason for doubting that the Sermon is nothing more than an impossible ideal. His wisdom stands in significant continuity with much else that others have said and taught. Samuel Johnson was right when he wrote that we 'more often required to be reminded than informed' – and this is what 5.21-48 largely does.

(iv) Verses 21-48 give us insight into Matthew's understanding of ethical motivation. There is here an appeal to imitate God's benevolence and God's perfection (5.45, 48). There are also commands to do good lest one suffer eschatological retribution (5.22–6, 28–30) as well as appeals to reason, at least of a sort (5.34–6). Yet the overriding factor in 5.21–48 seems to be above all obedience to a sovereign lord ('I say to you'). This means that the 'righteousness' of v. 20 is in the first place submission to another. One should live Jesus' hard imperatives because the voice that utters them speaks with authority (7.29).

THE CHRISTIAN CULT: ALMSGIVING, PRAYER, FASTING (6.1–18)

6 [1]'Beware of practising your piety before other people in order to be seen by them, for then you have no reward from your Father in heaven.

[2]'So whenever you give alms, do not sound a trumpet before you, as the hypocrites do in the synagogues and in the streets, so that they may be praised by other people. Amen I say to you, they have their reward. [3]But when you give alms, do not let your left hand know what your right hand is doing, [4]so that your alms may be done in secret. And your Father who sees in secret will reward you.

[5]'And whenever you pray, do not be like the hypocrites, for they love to stand and pray in the synagogues and on the street corners, so that they may be seen by other people. Amen I say to you, they have their reward. [6]But whenever you pray, go into your room and shut the door and pray to your Father who is in secret, and your Father who sees in secret will reward you.

[7]'When you are praying, do not heap up empty phrases as the Gentiles do, for they think that they will be heard because of their many words. [8]Do not be like them, for your Father knows what you need before you ask him. [9]Pray then like this: Our Father in heaven, hallowed be your name. [10]Your kingdom come. Your will be done, on earth as it is in heaven. [11]Give us this day our daily bread. [12]And forgive us our debts, as we also have forgiven our debtors. [13]And do not bring us to the time of trial, but deliver us from the evil one.

[14]'For if you forgive other people their trespasses, your heavenly Father will also forgive you. [15]But if you do not forgive other people, neither will your Father forgive your trespasses.

[16]'And whenever you fast, do not look dismal, like the hypocrites, for they disfigure their faces so as to show others that they are fasting. Amen I say to you, they have their reward. [17]But when you fast, put oil on your head and wash your face, [18]so that your fasting may be seen not by other people but by your Father who is in secret, and your Father who sees in secret will reward you.'

Parallels: Mk 11.25–6; Lk 11.2–4

While the subject of 5.21–48 is Jesus and the Torah, in 6.1–8 the cult becomes the subject. The former has mostly to do with actions, the latter with intentions. Mt 6.1–18 is a sort of commentary on 5.21–48: having been told *what* to do, one now learns *how* to act.

The section consists of a general statement of principle which is elaborated upon in three subsequent paragraphs, the first on almsgiving, the second on prayer, the third on fasting. Each opens with a declaration of subject (vv. 2a, 5a, 16a), follows with a prohibition of wrong practice (vv. 2b, 5b, 16b), and concludes with instruction on proper practice (vv. 3–4, 6, 17–18).

1. This verse announces the major theme of the section: right-eousness is not to be done in order to be seen by others. Right deeds must come from right intention, which involves humility and self-forgetfulness.

Beware of practising your piety before other people in order to be seen by them, for then you have no reward from your Father in heaven. Cf. Rom 2.28–9: 'For a person is not a Jew who is one outwardly, nor is true circumcision something external and physical. Rather, a person is a Jew who is one inwardly, and real circumcision is a matter of the heart – it is spiritual and not literal. Such a person receives praise not from others but from God.' As 1 Sam 16.7 has it, 'the Lord does not see as mortals see; they look on the outward appearance, but the Lord looks on the heart.'

Almsgiving and Prayer (6.2–8)

Mt 6.2–4 concerns almsgiving, which perhaps is mentioned before prayer and fasting because it is, for obvious reasons, more difficult. It is in any case clear that Jesus does not call almsgiving itself into question, only its misuse for self-glorification. The problem is not whether but how, not the thing but the intent. The teaching is in line with those rabbinic texts that praise almsgiving but demand it be hidden. 'R. Eleazar said: One who gives charity in secret is greater than Moses our teacher' (*b. B. Bat.* 9b). The rabbis knew as well as Matthew that those who make their names great lose their names (*m. 'Abot* 1.13).

2. do not sound a trumpet before you is probably just a picturesque way of speaking against calling attention to oneself. But trumpets may sometimes have been blown when alms were asked for (cf. *b. Ber.* 6b), so it is just possible that some unknown custom is being protested. There may, moreover, be a pun on the 'sophar chests' which were set up in the temple and in the provinces. If the trumpet-shaped receptacles for alms could be made to resound when coins were thrown into them, perhaps our verse was originally a polemical barb at the practice.

3. do not let your left hand know what your right hand is doing. Some, remarking on the use even today in Arabic of the left hand to denote a close friend, think the exhortation is to hide one's good works from one's neighbours. Others think more literally: to use one hand is to be discreet, to use two is to call attention to oneself. But most commentators are probably correct to suppose that 6.3 is 'hyperbole of language' (Theodoret). It pictorially exhorts one not to think too highly of one's own almsgiving – which of course also implies leaving others in ignorance. One should not 'accept glory from one another' but instead 'seek the glory that comes from the one who alone is God' (Jn 5.44).

5. And whenever you pray may presuppose the three hours of prayer – morning, afternoon, and evening; cf. Acts 3.1; 10.30; *Did.* 8.3.

they love to stand and pray reflects the fact that Jews regularly prayed while standing; cf. 1 Sam 1.26; Neh 9.4; Jer 18.20; Mk 11.25; the Eighteen Benedictions is known as the 'Amidah', which is from the verb 'to stand'. Typically they bent their knees or prostrated themselves only on solemn occasions or during times of trouble (1 Kgs 8.54; Mt 26.39).

in the synagogues and on the street corners takes us indoors and outdoors, so that what is in view is prayer in every public place. Against a few of the old German Pietists, the point cannot be condemnation of public worship or public prayer as such. In 21.13 Jesus affirms the public temple as a place of prayer; and the OT, whose continuing force is declared in Mt 5.17–20, assumes the validity of public prayers.

6. go into your room and shut the door is not a mystical way of speaking of prayer within the heart (so Syrian tradition) but instead hyperbole, just a way of saying that prayer is not a performance for a human audience. Chrysostom rightly commented that one who went into an inner room to pray only after telling others about it would hardly win Jesus' approval. So once again we need to pass beyond the literal language to see the point. If the intent is right, then one can pray before others – as Jesus does in 11.25–30 (public thanksgiving); 14.19 (public blessing); 15.36 (public blessing); and 26.36–46 (Gethsemane; but contrast 14.23, where he prays alone). One should recall 18:19–20, where group prayer is presupposed, as well as the first person plurals of the Lord's Prayer: this is a communal prayer.

7–8. These verses directly introduce the Lord's Prayer. In contrast to 6.5–6, where Jewish misbehaviour is in view, they command Jesus' followers not to pray as the Gentiles. The effect is to suggest that the Christian way of prayer should rise above the errors of both Jewish and Gentile traditions.

When you are praying, do not heap up empty phrases as the Gentiles do, for they think that they will be heard because of their many words. Cf. Eccles 7.14 ('Do not prattle in the assembly of the elders, nor repeat yourself in your prayer'); *Mek.* on Exod 15.25 (the prayer of the righteous is 'short'); *b. Ber.* 61a ('One's words should always be few toward God'). The emperor Marcus Aurelius counselled people to pray in a 'simple and frank fashion' or not to pray at all (5.7).

The broad generalization that the Gentiles pray as they do because they believe that 'many words' will improve their chances of being heard probably refers not to time spent in prayer but to verbosity. At least in Gethsemane Jesus prays very few words, but the time involved seems considerable (26.36–46); cf. the behaviour of Hannah in 1 Sam 1.12.

8. your Father knows what you need before you ask him. Isa 65.24 promises (as part of an eschatological scenario) that 'Before they call I will answer, while they are yet speaking I will hear'. *Exod. Rab.* on 14.15 asserts that God knows what is in the heart before one speaks. One also thinks of Xenophon, *Mem.* 1.3.2: Socrates prayed simply, 'Give me that which is best for me', for he knew that the gods know what the good things are. The extreme brevity of the Lord's Prayer harmonizes with this sentiment.

The Lord's Prayer (6.9–13)

Formally, 6.1–18 exhibits much parallelism. The sections on almsgiving, prayer, and fasting all have the same outline:

1. Negative prohibition
   'Whenever you ... do not ...'
   'As the hypocrites do ...'
   'That they may be seen/glorified ...'
   'Amen I say to you they have their reward'

2. Positive injunction
   'But when you ...'
   Description of deed in secret
   'Your Father in secret'
   'Your Father will reward you'

The neat scheme is interrupted by 6.9–15, the section on the Lord's

Prayer, which, like the irregular last beatitude, therefore calls attention to itself.

Although Christian tradition has usually understood the Lord's Prayer, a model of brevity, as having to do with everyday needs, much is to be said for interpreting it as an eschatological prayer. Many have urged that 'hallowed be your name', 'your kingdom come', and 'your will be done' ask for God to usher in utopia; that the request for 'bread of the morrow' (NRSV margin) is a prayer for the bread of life or heavenly manna of the latter days; that 'forgive us our debts' is prayed in view of the coming judgement; and that 'do not bring us to the time of trial' refers to the messianic woes; cf. Rev 3.10.

Mt 6.1–18 has remarkably close parallels in 23.1–12. These include the following: (i) In both sections Jewish religious behaviour, cited first, serves as a foil for proper Christian behaviour; positive imperatives follow negative descriptions. (ii) The synagogue is in view (6.2, 5; 23.2–3). (iii) The chief sins are hypocrisy and piety for show. (4) 'To do/they do in order to be seen by others' (6.1; 23.5) appears. (v) 6.1 speaks of the 'Father in heaven', 23.9 of 'the heavenly Father'. (vi) 'But you' (6.3, 6, 17; 23.8) marks the transition from negative description to positive exhortation. Whether or not one explains these similarities as stemming from Matthew's editorial hand or instead from a source Matthew used, on a literary level the repetition makes for emphasis: it is the important things that are repeated. So if chapter 23 returns to the themes of 6.1–18, this can only drive home the gravity of what Jesus has to say about private piety.

It is a good guess that the Lord's Prayer took the place early on of the Shemoneh Esreh, the common daily prayer of Judaism. There are some parallels between the Shemoneh Esreh and the Lord's Prayer (e.g. requests for forgiveness, food, and eschatological fulfilment) as well as between the Lord's Prayer and abbreviations of the former (see esp. *b. Ber.* 29a). Moreover, the central portion of the Eighteen Benedictions, just like the Lord's Prayer, falls into two distinct parts (in the first half the petitions are for individuals, in the second half for the nation); and early Christian tradition instructs believers to say the Lord's Prayer three times a day (*Did.* 8.3) while standing (*Apost. const.* 7.24), which precisely parallels what the rabbis demanded for the Eighteen Benedictions.

9. In a way reminiscent of the decalogue and Mt 22.34–40, which first command duties to God and then duties to human beings, the first three petitions of the Lord's Prayer relate directly to God the Father or heavenly things, and the last three (which are sometimes said to pertain, in order, to the past, the present, and the future) to earthly necessities. Another way of putting this is that the first half offers expressions of piety, the latter half petitions in the proper sense.

Pray then like this could imply, despite the nearly universal practice of Christendom, that the Lord's Prayer is more an example of how to pray than a formula to be mechanically repeated. This view, which would help to explain the differences between the NT's two versions of the Lord's Prayer, was held by, among others, Isaac of Nineveh: 'If someone says that we should recite the prayer uttered by our Saviour in all our prayers using the same wording and keeping the exact order of the words, rather than their sense, such a person is very deficient in his understanding ... Our Lord did not teach us a particular sequence of words here; rather, the teaching he provided in this prayer consists in showing us what we should be focusing our minds on during the entire course of this life.' Origen labelled the Lord's Prayer a 'form' or 'outline' of prayer, and Tertullian suggested one add private petitions to it. Some rabbis objected to fixed prayers without extemporizing because they thought them potentially without sincerity.

Our Father. No prayer in the OT opens with this address, although the idea that God is the father of faithful Israel, his children, is certainly well attested; see esp. Isa 63.15–16; Jer 31.20; Hos 11.1–4. The *Mishnah*, however, does use the phrase, 'Our Father in heaven', and extrabiblical Jewish prayers do have invocations with 'Father'. Examples include 4Q372 1 16 ('My father and my God' as the opening address in an apocryphal prayer of Joseph); 4Q460 5 6 ('my father' in the conclusion of a prayer); Wisd 14.3 ('O Father' in the words of Solomon to God; cf. 2.16; 5.5). In the light of these parallels and others, it is unwise to insist that Jesus' use of 'abba' was unique.

The 'our' lays stress on a communal dimension; this is a prayer for the church. Within the immediate context, namely 6.1–18, the public character of the Lord's Prayer counterbalances the emphasis upon purely private piety in 6.1–8, 16–18 and so prevents the impression that all true piety is purely personal. One is reminded of the rabbi who reportedly was wont to pray not 'lead me in safety' but 'lead us in safety' (*b. Ber.* 29b-30a). Aquinas said that to pray 'our Father' is to express our love of our neighbour.

in heaven. We must reckon seriously with the possibility that the evangelist, as well as Jesus, understood the words spatially – although already the OT knows that God cannot be contained (1 Kgs 8.27; Isa 66.1). In any case, the effect of putting God in heaven is to underline that, for the present, although God is with the saints, yet God's rule is not fully effective in this world; there is a great gulf between the divine world and the human reality.

hallowed be your name. 'Name' is a reverential way of speaking of

God as revealed to human beings; perhaps the meaning is here close to our own 'reputation'. But Matthew may have thought more specifically in terms of the revealed name of power (Exod 3.13–15) which the Father shares with Jesus and the Spirit – 'the name of the Father and of the Son and of the Holy Spirit' (28.16–20); cf. Jn 17.11; Phil 2.9.

The passive construction probably has not human beings but God as the implicit subject: the Father is being called upon to act, as in Jn 12.28, 'Father, glorify your name'. This is a request for God to fulfil the eschatological promise of Ezek 36.23: 'I will sanctify my great name.' What is envisaged is God's universal rule, when God, because of the redemption of the saints and the restoration of paradise, will be fittingly honoured by both Israel and the nations.

'To hallow' or 'sanctify' God's name should be reckoned a traditional way of speaking (Isa 29.23); it denotes the opposite of 'to profane' the name (Lev 18.21; 22.32; Ezek 36.20). Cf. the earliest form of the Kaddish prayer, which was prayed in synagogues after the sermon:

> Exalted and hallowed be his great name
> > in the world which he created according to his will.
> May he let his kingdom rule
> > in your lifetime and in your days and in the lifetime
> > of the whole house of Israel, speedily and soon.
> Praised be his great name from eternity to eternity.
> And to this say: Amen.

The nearness of this to the beginning of the Lord's prayer is undeniable, so if it was already known in the first century (an uncertain issue) one would be inclined to suppose that it influenced the composition of the Lord's Prayer. But even if the Kaddish was not known before Matthew's time, its content shows us that the Lord's Prayer belongs to the Jewish tradition.

10. Your kingdom come is eschatological. While elsewhere in Matthew the kingdom has already entered the present, it still remains hidden (13.31–3); and its full manifestation – which will mean the hallowing of God's name and the doing of God's will on earth as in heaven – belongs only to the end of things (Dan 2.44). Ancient Jewish and Christian sources, however, preserve the conviction that prayer might hasten the coming of the kingdom (e.g. Lk 18.1–8; *b. B. Mes.* 85b). Is this the presupposition of our text? Certainly every other petition in the Lord's Prayer is uttered in the hope that the Father in heaven hears and answers.

Your will be done. This is a variant of the first two petitions. When God's name is hallowed and the kingdom has come, then God's will

will be done on earth as in heaven. In one sense then our line 'contains nothing new' (Calvin).

Even though 'your will be done' is to be given eschatological sense, its use by Jesus in Gethsemane shows that it can also have a broader meaning in accord with traditional expositions of our line. When Jesus negates his will before the will of his Father in heaven he illustrates that 'your will be done' is a comprehensive principle. Even though human beings may ask for specific things, in the end they must submit to the inscrutability of the divine will, whatever it may be.

on earth as it is in heaven. Cf. *b. Ber.* 17a: 'May it be your will ... to establish peace in the upper family and in the lower family'; also *b. Ber.* 29b: 'Do your will in heaven and give rest of spirit to those that fear you below.' Matthew's words can be interpreted in line with these Jewish prayers: both heaven and earth are spheres in which God's will is not yet done. If humans sin on earth, there are also 'spiritual forces of evil in the heavenly places' (Eph 6.12). Yet the more likely interpretation has it that heaven is here the standard for earth: what is now true of the former should become true of the latter. The church fathers typically thought of God's 'ministers that do his will' (Ps 103.21), the good angels.

11. daily bread is an unresolved puzzle. No modern discovery has put the lie to Origen's observation that 'daily' (*epiousios*) 'is not used by the Greeks, neither does it occur with the scholars, nor does it have a place in the language of the people. It seems to have been invented by the Evangelists.' It could mean (i) 'needful' or (ii) 'for the current day' or (iii) 'for the coming day'. The best choice may be (iii). Cf. the *Gospel of the Nazaraeans* according to Jerome: 'our bread of tomorrow give us this day.' Probably in the background is the story in Exodus 16, where Israel is given manna (called 'bread' in Num 21.5 and elsewhere) for the day to come; cf. Exod 16.5. But then what concretely is meant? Exegetical tradition offers several possibilities: what the body requires for the coming day; the Eucharist; spiritual sustenance in general; the preaching of the word of God; Jesus himself; the messianic banquet, specifically the heavenly manna or bread that God will give to the redeemed at the consummation (cf. Lk 14.15; Rev 2.17); or some combination of these. Given the eschatological outlook of the other petitions, one is inclined to accept the eschatological interpretation. But here, as Cyprian, Aquinas, and so many others have correctly seen, acceptance of one interpretation to the exclusion of the others would be foolish. A text can have multiple layers of meaning. The feedings of the five and four thousand, for instance, have several. Both Mt. 14.13–21 and 15.29–39 allude to the messianic banquet, the Last Supper, the story of Elisha in 2 Kgs 4.42–4, and the gift of the manna in the wilderness. It may be similar in the case of the Lord's Prayer, especially given the rich symbolism surrounding 'bread' in the biblical tradition. Certainly if one expects God to reward the faithful at the messianic banquet, both our Gospel and the rest of the Bible make it plain that God sustains them in every way, physically and spiritually, even now.

12. And forgive us our debts, as we also have forgiven our debtors. 'Debts' = 'sins'; cf. 6.14–15. The ubiquity of human sin is presupposed; cf. 7:11. That there is an eschatological dimension to this is obvious: elsewhere in Matthew forgiveness of sins is something to come at the last judgement (5.23–5; 18:23–35). For parallels see Ecclus 28.2 ('Forgive your neighbour the wrong done and then your sins will be pardoned when you pray'); Col 3.13; *m. Yoma* 8.9 (the Day of Atonement effects atonement only if one has forgiven others); *b. Šabb.* 151b ('The one who is merciful to others, mercy is shown to that one by Heaven, while the one not merciful to others, mercy is not shown to that one by Heaven').

God does not bestow grace in an antinomian fashion but rather demands actions in accord with mercy received. The point is made plainly in the parable in 18.23–35, which concludes with the lesson that God's mercy will be withdrawn 'if you do not forgive your brother from the heart'. Cf. *t. B. Qam.* 9.30: 'As often as you are merciful, the All-merciful has pity on you'. One should, however, not press the tense of 'have forgiven', as if God must wait to forgive until human beings have forgiven others. Our line is not a precise statement of theology but paraenesis, moral exhortation, and 18.23–35 teaches that God's mercy is the prior fact.

13. There was originally no doxology, although we would expect one in a Jewish prayer. This lack was made up by later liturgical insertions into the manuscript tradition, whence the well known closing, 'For yours is the kingdom and the power and the glory forever. Amen'; cf. 1 Chr 29.11.

And do not bring us to the time of trial asks, like many Jewish prayers, that God not let the faithful fall victim to 'temptation' or 'the time of trial'. The latter translation assumes that the eschatological birth pangs or messianic woes (cf. 24.8; Rev 3.10) are primarily in view: one hopes not to succumb to apostasy in the latter days. But since in the synoptic tradition and elsewhere in early Christian literature the great tribulation has already entered the present (cf. 10.34–6; Mk 13.3–23; 1 Cor 7.26; 2 Thess 2.7; Rev 7.9–17), there is no antithesis between eschatology and everyday life. All temptation belongs to the latter days.

but deliver us from the evil one. The jarring 'but' (*alla*) marks the close of the whole prayer, which ends with a sort of antithetical *inclusio*: the prayer commences with 'Father' and concludes with 'the evil one'. The Greek (*ho poneros*) can also mean 'from evil'. For the neuter see Lk 6.45 and Rom 12.9, for the masculine Jn 17.15; Eph 6.16; and 2 Thess 3.3. Unfortunately one cannot come to a firm decision on this matter. In Matthew *ho poneros* is sometimes masculine (13.19, 38), sometimes neuter (5.39; 12.35).

14. The Lord's Prayer is followed by two verses on forgiveness; these elaborate upon the fifth petition, recall 5.21–6, and anticipate 18.23–35. A similar sequence – prayer/forgiveness – appears in Mk 11.23–5 and Lk 17.3–6. There appears to have been a traditional connexion between prayer and forgiveness: prayer is not efficacious unless the members of the community are reconciled to each other.

Fasting (6.16–18)

This section probably has in view voluntary private fasting (as in Dan 9.3; Mt 4.2; Mk 2.18; Lk 18.12), something that provided special opportunity to call attention to oneself, not prescribed public fasting (as for the Day of Atonement).

16. And whenever you fast, do not be of sad countenance, like the hypocrites, for they disfigure their faces so as to show others that they are fasting. Fasting was often accompanied by external signs, such as sackcloth, ashes, and the rending of clothing (note Dan 9.3; Jon 3.5; Jth 8.5). So here Jesus can speak of those who look sad – is the meaning 'go unwashed' or 'cover (themselves) with ashes'? – in the attempt to proclaim to onlookers that they are fasting.

17. The general principle is clear: the inner state should not be advertised by artificial signs, for humility demands secrecy, and the goal of fasting is not enhanced reputation. The actual application, which covers not only fasting but all piety, is left to the reader.

put oil on your head and wash your face. Most find here a reference to everyday hygiene, so that the meaning is this: when fasting you should look just like you do normally. Cf. *T. Jos.* 3.4: 'For these seven years I fasted, and yet seemed to the Egyptians like someone who was living luxuriously, for those who fast for the sake of God receive graciousness of countenance.' Perhaps, however, we should follow Theophylact, who took the words to signify a special occasion of gladness. Anointing the head with oil was sometimes a sign of rejoicing (as in Ps 23.5 and 104.15), so our text might be suggesting that one even mislead others: one pretends to rejoice in the middle of the affliction of fasting. Such deception for the sake of humility became common among Christian ascetics.

18. so that your fasting may be seen not by other people. On the surface this means that one should hide one's fasting from everyone. But William Law observed that a husband or wife can hardly fast without the rest of the family knowing it. His conclusion was this: 'the privacy of fasting does not suppose such a privacy as excludes everybody from knowing it, but such a privacy as does not seek to be known abroad.' This is the sort of ad hoc, interpretative clarification that a text as dense and figurative and brief as the Sermon on the Mount constantly requires.

GOD AND MAMMON (6.19–34)

[19]'Do not store up for yourselves treasures on earth, where moth and rust consume and where thieves break in and steal, [20]but store up for yourselves treasures in heaven, where neither moth nor rust consumes, and where thieves do not break in and steal. [21]For where your treasure is, there will your heart be also.

[22]'The eye is the lamp of the body. So, if your eye is sound, your whole body will be full of light. [23]But if your eye is evil, all your whole body will be dark. If, then, the light that is in you is darkness, how great is the darkness!

[24]'No one can serve two masters. For he either will hate the one and love the other, or he will be devoted to the one and despise the other. You cannot serve God and mammon.

[25]'Therefore I say to you, do not worry about your life, what you will eat or what you will drink, or about your body, what you will wear. Is not life more than food, and the body more than clothing? [26]Consider the birds of the air, that they neither sow nor reap nor gather into barns, and yet your heavenly Father feeds them. Are you not of more value than they? [27]And is any of you by worrying able to add a single hour to his span of life? [28]And why do you worry about clothing? Consider the lilies of the field, how they grow. They neither toil nor spin, [29]yet I say to you, even Solomon in all his glory was not clothed like one of these. [30]But if God so clothes the grass of the field, which is alive today and tomorrow is thrown into the oven, will he not much more clothe you – O you of little faith? [31]Therefore do not worry, saying, "What will we eat?" or "What will we drink?" or "What will we wear?" [32]For all these things the Gentiles seek. For your heavenly Father knows that you need all these things. [33]But seek first the kingdom of God and his righteousness, and all these things will be added to you as well. [34]So do not worry about tomorrow, for tomorrow will bring worries of its own. Today's trouble is enough for today.'

Parallels: Lk 11.34–6; 12.22–34; 16.13

Having given teaching *vis-à-vis* Torah (5.17–48) and issued commandments concerning almsgiving, prayer, and fasting (6.1–18), Matthew's
Jesus next addresses social issues (6.19–7.12). The instruction falls into
two sections. The first, 6.19–34, teaches that one should disregard
mammon (6.19–24) and that the one who does this can rely upon the
heavenly Father's care (6.25–34). The second is about not judging
others (7.1–6) and, again, about the heavenly Father's care (7.7–11).
The entire section ends with the golden rule (7.12).

The three small paragraphs in 6.19–24 and the long paragraph in
6.25–34 are structurally similar, as can be seen at a glance:

thesis statement or introduction		22a	24a, 25	
two (supporting) observations in antithetical or compound parallelism	19–20	22b–23b	24b–c	26, 28–30
concluding remark(s)	21	23c–d	24d	32–34

The formal parallelism helps underline the unity of theme. There is,
nonetheless, a transition between vv. 24 and 25. The first three units all
function as imperatives. The last functions less to add new demands
than to comfort those who choose to live under the Sermon on the
Mount's harsh demands.

Treasure on the Earth (6.19–21)

19. Wealth is not a sign of divine favor.

Do not store up for yourselves treasures on earth enjoins not doing
what everyone does naturally.

where moth and rust consume and where thieves break in and steal.
Cf. Jas 5.2–3, which may allude to our saying. All the things people
typically strive for stand under the sentence, 'heaven and earth will
pass away' (24.35; cf. 5.18).

20. The second reason (given in perfect antithetical parallelism) for
not storing up treasures on the earth passes beyond common sense and
appeals to eschatological doctrine: one's efforts are better put into
storing up treasure in heaven, in a realm that is not touched by time,
chance, and decay; cf. 5.2.

but store up for yourselves treasures in heaven does not specify what is meant by 'treasure in heaven', but the beatitudes have already expanded upon that concept in detail. Readers also do not here learn *how* to lay up treasures in heaven. This too, however, is plain from the rest of the Sermon. Good deeds make for reward in the afterlife. One may perhaps think especially of the teaching about alms or giving to others (6.2–4). One gains by giving away.

21. For where your treasure is links itself by catchword to the previous line.

there will your heart be also. Just as deeds reveal intentions, so one's treasure tells the tale of what one is really all about.

The Eye Is the Lamp of the Body (6.22–3)

22. The eye is the lamp of the body does not set forth a novel idea. It is simply a statement of the common pre-modern understanding of vision. Cf. the variant in *Gos. Thom.* 24, where the 'light within a man of light' dispels darkness and 'lights the whole world'. The picture is one of light going out. For us the eye is a window: as a transparent medium it lets light in. We do not think of the eye as a lamp, that is, as its own light source. It was different in antiquity. Not only Greek philosophers believed the eye to have its own light: so did the general populace. The same generalization holds for ancient Jewish texts, which speak of 'the light of the [or: my] eyes' (Ps 38.11; Prov 15.30; Tob 10.5; Bar 3.14). So when the eye is compared with the sun (Bar 2.18; Ecclus 23.19) or with torches (Dan 10.2–9 LXX) or, as in our saying, with lamps (cf. Zech 4.1–10; *2 En.* 42.1; *b. Šabb.* 151b), we should think of the belief that 'rays shine through the eyes and touch whatever they see' (Augustine).

So, if your eye is sound, your whole body will be full of light means not that a good eye illuminates the body's interior. Rather, when an eye is sound, this shows there is light within; cf. the logic and structure of 12.28, where the 'if' clause names the consequence of the 'then' clause. A good eye is the proof of inner light, for the condition of the former is the existence of the latter. Inner light makes eyes shine.

23. But if your eye is evil, all your whole body will be dark. Although one can read this on a physiological level, 'evil eye' belongs to the ethical vocabulary of Judaism. It expresses the antithesis of generosity: selfishness, covetousness, an evil and envious disposition, hatred of others; cf. Deut 15.9; Prov 22.9; Tob 2.10. The locution is used again in Mt 20.15.

If, then, the light that is in you is darkness, how great is the darkness! This recalls Jewish laments or prophecies of judgement: Job 3.4 ('let that day be darkness'); 10.24 (in the land of death 'light is like darkness'); Zeph 1.15 ('a day of darkness and gloom'); 1QH 5.32 ('the light of my countenance is darkened to deep darkness'). The listener is called to self-examination. Am I filled with light or with darkness? Has my spirit become darkened? And how do I know one way or the other? Is my eye good, or is it bad?

Once one sees that our saying is a sort of riddle that can be read on two different levels, either as a statement about vision or about moral principles, it becomes obvious that 'if your eye is sound' has double meaning. It refers not only to the physical eye but also to moral intention. In Judaism, 'good eye' meant generosity; cf. Prov 22.9; *m. 'Abot* 2.13. So 6.22–3, read on its deeper level, says that just as a good eye, a proper disposition towards others, is an effect of the light within, so similarly is a bad eye, that is, a selfish, ungenerous, miserly spirit, the companion of inner darkness. One's moral disposition correlates with an inner darkness or light within.

It should now be obvious why 6.22–3 is in its present context. On either side are sayings about money: about not treasuring up treasure on the earth (6.19–21) and about serving God instead of mammon (= money). Verses 22–3 is also about money, or rather about what one does with it. The person with a sound eye is the one who, through generosity, thereby serves God instead of mammon and stores up treasure in heaven. The person with an unsound eye is the one who, because of selfishness, thereby serves mammon instead of God and stores up treasure only on the earth.

Serving Two Masters (6.24)

Verse 24 has the same structure as 6.22–3. Both are quatrains that consist of a thesis statement followed by two expository sentences in antithetical parallelism, followed by the conclusion or application. But the formal similarity is less important than the thematic connection, just noted. The sound eye, interpreted as generosity, serves God. The unsound eye, interpreted as selfishness, serves mammon.

24. No one can serve two masters. For he either will hate the one and love the other, or he will be devoted to the one and despise the other. 'It is impossible for love of the world to coexist with the love of God' (Philo).

You cannot serve God and mammon. 'Mammon' is a Semitic loanword meaning 'money' or 'possessions'. Whether or not it already had pejorative connotations in Jesus' time is unclear. Perhaps the tradition transliterated instead of translating because it functioned like the name of an idol.

The Heavenly Father's Care (6.25–34)

Those who do not store up treasure on the earth (6.19–21), who are generous with what they have (6.22–3), and who serve God instead of mammon (6.24) are inviting anxiety. For life in the world demands that we have and use things. Jesus inveighs against such anxiety; cf. 10.19. That sincere religious commitment might create anxiety was also recognized by the rabbis. In *Mek.* on Exod 16.4 Rabbi Simeon ben Yohai says: 'How can a man be sitting and studying when he does not know where his food and drink will come from nor where he can get his clothes and coverings?' If it is true, as Hillel purportedly said, that 'the more possessions, the more care' (*m. 'Abot* 2.7), it can also be that the less possessions the more care. But recognition of God's providence and wisdom concerning temporal things should encourage a spiritual equanimity. 'Do not worry about anything' (Phil 4.6).

25. Is not life more than food, and the body more than clothing? The force of the rhetorical question is not perfectly clear. Augustine took Jesus to be reasoning theologically from the lesser to the greater: God, 'who gave us life will much more easily give us meat ... Similarly, you are to understand that he who gave the body will much more easily give raiment'; cf. 10.28–31 and 1 Pet 5.7: 'Cast all your anxieties upon him, for he cares for you.' But it is equally possible that we have here an admonition against excessive worry, which can wreck all else.

26. Consider the birds of the air, that they neither sow nor reap nor gather into barns, and yet your heavenly Father feeds them. Cf. Job 38.41 (God 'provides the raven its prey, when its young ones cry to God, and wander about for lack of food'); Ps 147.9 (God 'gives to the beasts their food, and to the young ravens which cry'); *m. Qidd.* 4.14 (wild animals and birds practise no craft yet are sustained without care). In the background is the rich biblical tradition that God feeds God's people – and not just through mundane, natural processes. There are the stories of Israel's wilderness wanderings, during which the people were sent manna and quail and given water. There is the OT Jubilee legislation, which calls Israel to depend upon Yahweh's catering hand during the Sabbath year fallow (Lev 25.18–24). There is 2 Kgs 4.42–4, which tells of God, through Elisha, multiplying bread. Our Gospel also contains the theme, for twice Jesus miraculously feeds crowds (14.13–21; 15.32–9).

27. This offers a second supporting argument for not being anxious, namely, that worrying accomplishes nothing.

28. Jesus' third supporting argument is reminiscent of 6.26:

6.26	6.28–30
Look at the birds	Consider the lilies
they do not sow/reap/gather	they do not toil/spin
the Father feeds them	God clothes the grass
Are you not of more value?	will he not much more?

6.28–30 says the same thing as 6.26 but with a different illustration. The repetition is, however, not redundancy. It rather adds force, which is required because the text is addressing an anxiety deeply rooted in human nature.

29. Solomon in all his glory was not clothed like one of these might slightly disparage Solomon's excessive splendour. David's son was remembered as one who 'exceedingly plumed himself upon his riches' (Clement of Alexandria), and 11.8 has sometimes been thought to depreciate the fancy robes of Herod's courtiers. By contrast, God clothed Adam and Eve with simple garments of skins (Gen 3.21); and the disciples of Jesus, who is greater than Solomon (12.42), have only coat and cloak (5.40).

30. O you of little faith? Cf. 8.26; 14.31; 16.8; 17.20. One wonders if 'little faith' was not traditionally tied to anxiety over earthly necessities, for *Tanhuma* Beshallah 117b has this: 'R. Elazar of Modi'im said: If one has food for the day but says, "What shall I eat tomorrow?", he is deficient in faith. R. Eliezer the Great said: He who has yet bread in his basket and says, "What shall I eat tomorrow?", belongs to those of little faith.'

32. For all these things the Gentiles seek. Readers may be reminded of 6.7–8, where the Gentiles vainly heap up empty phrases whereas Jesus' followers can say little because their Father knows their needs. Perhaps indeed the reader is supposed to go back to the Lord's Prayer and realize that the one who prays in faith for bread need not worry about food or drink.

33. But seek first the kingdom of God and his righteousness. Probably the thought is that the kingdom, which has already begun to manifest itself in Jesus and the church, can be entered not only in the future but in the here and now, and since entering the kingdom is synonymous with salvation, one should make it one's overriding concern. On this reading, striving for the kingdom means in practice the same thing as striving for righteousness, for this last does not mean God's eschatological vindication of the saints or divine justice but the conduct God requires to enter the kingdom. So to seek the kingdom is to seek righteousness, which is its precondition, and to seek righteousness is to seek the kingdom, to which it leads.

34. So do not worry about tomorrow, for tomorrow will bring worries

of its own. Today's trouble is enough for today. This addendum is drawn from the well of Ancient Near Eastern wisdom. 'Do not prepare for tomorrow before it is come; one knows not what evil may be in it' and 'Do not spend the night in fear of the morrow. At dawn what is the morrow like? One knows not what the morrow is like' are both found in old Egyptian sources. Prov 27.1 and the rabbinic corpus and still other sources offer similar sayings. But these typically sound pessimistic or stoical, and counteract worry by appealing to unelaborated common sense. In Matthew, however, the traditional proverb is, through its new context, given a fresh sense. With God one can be content with what is at hand, and anxiety for tomorrow is foolish because the compassionate Father in heaven is Lord of the future.

* * * * *

(i) Mt 6.19–24 contains three antitheses: earth/heaven (6.19–21), darkness/light (6.22–3), and mammon (= wealth)/God (6.24). The focus of the first antithesis is the heart ('where your treasure is, there your heart will be also'), the second the eye ('the eye is the lamp of the body'), the third service ('you cannot service God and wealth'). The determination of the heart to store up treasure in heaven or on the earth creates either inner light or darkness, while the resultant state of one's 'eye' (= intent) moves one to serve either God or mammon. So one's treasure tells the tale of one's heart; and the firm decision to serve God fills one with light and assures everlasting treasure while the service of mammon creates darkness and leads only to the vain grasping for treasures that will certainly perish.

(ii) Mt 6.25–34 shows that the task of serving God instead of mammon is not easy. For 6.25–34 functions to give assurance: it encourages believers to be free from worrying overmuch about earthly things. But what is so hard about 6.19–24? The section is an integral part of the Sermon on the Mount, in which disciples are exhorted to give to those who ask and to refrain from turning away those who would borrow; and those who live accordingly will have good cause to feel insecure. And it is to this situation that 6.25–34 offers a pastoral response. The section reproaches no one. It is an attempt to free the faithful from anxiety, so that, unfettered, they might serve the cause of Jesus with freedom.

(iii) The promise that God will care for disciples cannot exclude trial and tribulation. The one who was crucified does not guarantee comfort, prosperity, or health. He does not assert that the righteous will flourish, and he holds no numbing nepenthe for fortune's slings and arrows. On the contrary, the disciple can expect the buffeting of fortune and difficulty at every turn; cf. 5.10–12; 10.16–39; 24.9–13. What then is the point? Jesus promises that God will give to the disciples what is truly necessary for them if they are to accomplish their God-given tasks. There is a road, and it can be travelled. That is enough.

(iv) Mt 6.19–34 does not offer concrete counsel on what to do with wealth. The section rather calls one to be generous with what one has, to exercise faith in the Father in heaven, to serve God by turning a deaf ear to the smooth words of the harlot mammon. Matthew knew of itinerant missionaries who lived close to poverty (cf. 10.9–10) as well as of well-to-do Christians (cf. 27.57), and he recognized the place both of them had in the community. It was consequently not possible for him to do other than set forth general principles regarding earthly needs. Such general principles will then be lived differently depending upon the situation in which one finds oneself.

THE TREATMENT OF ONE'S NEIGHBOUR (7.1–12)

7 **[1]'Do not judge, so that you may not be judged. [2]For with the judgement you render will you be judged, and with the measure you measure will you be measured.**

[3]'Why do you see the splinter in your neighbour's eye, but do not notice the log in your own eye? [4]Or how can you say to your neighbour, "Let me take the splinter out of your eye", and behold, the log is in your own eye? [5]You hypocrite, first take the log out of your own eye, and then you will see clearly to take the splinter out of your neighbour's eye.

[6]'Do not give what is holy to dogs; and do not throw your pearls before swine, lest they trample them under foot and turn and maul you.

[7]'Ask, and it will be given to you; seek, and you will find; knock, and the door will be opened to you. [8]For everyone who asks receives, and everyone who seeks finds, and to the one knocking, it will be opened. [9]Or is there a person among you who, if his son asks for bread, will give to him a stone? [10]Or if he asks for a fish, will give him a snake? [11]If you then, who are evil, know how to give good gifts to your children, how much more will your Father in heaven give good things to those who ask him!

[12]'All then that you want others to do to you, thus also you do to them; for this is the law and the prophets.'

Parallels: Mk 4.24–5; Lk 6.31, 37–42; 11.9–13; Jn 16.42; 15.7

Do Not Judge (7.1–2)

In 7.1–12 we now turn from one social issue, what to do with and about mammon (6.19–34), to another, how to treat one's neighbour. **1. Do not judge, so that you may not be judged.** Cf. Rom 2.1; 14.10; 1 Cor 4.5; 5.12; Jas 4.11–12; 5.9; *1 Clem.* 13.2. Simple ethical judgements cannot be in view, and believers are not being instructed to refrain from critical thinking. There is also no reason to entertain Tolstoy's idea that here the state's judicial activities are proscribed: that would be a flat contradiction of the OT and so a flat contradiction of 5.17–20. Rather, 7.1–2 enjoins mercy, humility, and tolerance between individuals. These qualities are inconsistent with taking on a role reserved for the only capable judge, God; cf. 13.36–43, 47–50, where the sorting out of good and evil awaits the last judgement. 'Do not judge' means 'do not condemn', and so one could translate our saying: 'Do not condemn, so that you may not be condemned at the last judgement.'

2. with the measure you measure will you be measured occurs in numerous Jewish texts and was proverbial.

The Splinter and the Log (7.3–5)

The concrete 7.3–5 clarifies the abstract 7.1–2 and adds a new element, the theme of hypocrisy. The thought is very close to Rom 2.1: 'Therefore you have no excuse, whoever you are, when you judge others; for in passing judgement on another you condemn yourself, because you, the judge, are doing the very same things.' One also recalls the story of David and his anger upon hearing Nathan's parable about the rich man who had taken the poor man's little ewe lamb: the king did not realize that what made him angry in another was his own fault (2 Sam 12.1–5). Because human beings unhappily possess an inbred proclivity to mix ignorance of themselves with arrogance towards others, the call to recognize one's own faults is a commonplace of moral and religious traditions; cf. Jn 9.41; 1 Jn 1.8.

3. Why do you see the splinter in your neighbour's eye, but do not notice the log in your own eye? 'Splinter' (not 'mote') stands for small moral defects, 'log' for sizeable moral defects. The image is intended to be comedic. It may have been proverbial; cf. *b. B. Bat.* 15b: 'If the judge said to a person, "Take the splinter from between your teeth", he would retort, "Take the beam from between your eyes".' It is just as absurd as the picture of a camel going through the eye of a needle (19.24) or someone straining at gnats and swallowing a camel (23.24).

5. then you will see clearly to take the splinter out of your neighbour's eye. In v. 3 one simply sees (*blepein*). In v. 5 one sees clearly (*diablepein*). In the latter instance one sees in order to help. The stare to find fault becomes the genuinely friendly eye of a brother or sister who is a servant. Some commentators fail to discern in vv. 3–5 any instruction concerning fraternal correction. For them, the text prohibits judging altogether. But Matthew shows a special concern elsewhere for the proper procedures for dealing with sin in others; see 18.15–20, a passage which our evangelist thinks consistent with unlimited forgiveness (18.23–5); cf. Lev 19.17, where love and reproof of neighbour go together. Matthew, moreover, usually uses 'brother' to mean Christian 'brother', so it is natural to see here intraecclesiastical activity (so most of Christian exegetical tradition).

Pearls before Swine (7.6)

This verse has a very colourful history of influence that has consistently ignored its present literary context. Augustine argued, like many after him, that the verse instructs the faithful not to reveal important esoteric teaching to outsiders who will only fail to appreciate them. Evagrius thought in terms of spiritual masters dispensing only a little truth at a time to spiritual novices, Elchasai of sectarian teachings being trampled upon by the orthodox, Origen of temporarily abandoning for their own good lapsed Christians. The *Didache* found in 7.6 a rule prohibiting giving communion to the unbaptized. John of Damascus took 7.6 to prohibit the giving of communion to heretics; cf. the equation of 'dog' and 'pig' with heretic in 2 Pet 2.22. Some modern scholars, identifying the dogs with Gentiles (cf. 15.26–7), have found a prohibition against the Gentile mission (cf. 10.5–6). Others have posited a mistranslation from the Aramaic: Jesus originally said (in dependence upon Prov 11.22) not to put a ring or earring in the nose of a dog (although this hardly illuminates the saying as it stands in Matthew). Luther assumed that our text is an admonition about the necessity to limit the time and energy directed towards the hardhearted. The gospel goes out to all; but when it is not received the proclaimers must move on. One recent commentator has declined to interpret the logion in its Matthean context: the evangelist simply took it over from his source without imparting any meaning to it.

Against all these suggestions, 'Do not give to dogs what is holy' fits very nicely into its present setting. Mt 7.1–5 has commanded that there be not too much severity: 7.6 follows up by saying that there should not be too much laxity. That is, the text anticipates a problem and searches for a balance, for moral symmetry. The principles in 7.1–5 are not to be abused. They do not eliminate the use of critical faculties when it comes to sacred concerns. As 18.15–20 shows, it is sometimes necessary to deal with the faults of others. This interpretation admittedly remains general, and it is possible that Matthew had something more specific in mind. But the general point is clear: one must not be meekly charitable against all reason.

6. Do not give what is holy to dogs was originally a priestly rule about sacrificial meat; see *m. Tem.* 6:5; etc. Here it is applied metaphorically.

Seek and You Will Find (7.7–11)

Mt 7.7–11 is the twin of 6.24–34. Both follow an exhortation (6.19–21; 7.1–2), a parable on the eye (6.22–3; 7.3–5), and a second parable (6.24; 7.6), and both refer to the heavenly Father's care for his own. Both also argue from the lesser to the greater and offer encouragement for those bombarded by the hard instruction in the rest of the Sermon on the Mount (cf. the rhetoric of 10.16–23 and its function within the missionary discourse). Visually:

	Three Imperatives	
exhortation, 6.19–21		7.1–2, exhortation
parable on the eye, 6.22–3		7.3–5, parable on the eye
second parable, 6.24		7.6, second parable

	Encouragement	
the Father's care, 6.25–33		7.7–11, the Father's care

Verses 7–11 have been almost as pliable in the hands of interpreters as has 7.6. Augustine thought of one asking for the truth kept from the dogs and swine of 7.6 and of the strength to live in accord with that truth. Others have drawn a line back to vv. 1–5: the disciple prays for wisdom to take the mote out of another's eye. Still others have gone further back to the Lord's Prayer: 7.7–11 encourages those who pray the Lord's Prayer to know that their prayers will be heard. Some link 7.7–11 with the golden rule, which immediately follows: just as God gives us good things, so we should give good things to others. Some modern commentators see no connection with the surrounding material and accuse Matthew of creating a messy amalgam. Already Luther interpreted 7.7–11 as for all practical purposes an isolated admonition to pray.

But the key to understanding 7.7–11 is its parallelism with 6.25–34;

see above. The parallelism in form coincides with a parallel in function. Verses 7–11 are, like 6.25–34, intended to bring encouragement to those who stand under the harsh imperatives of the Sermon on the Mount: the heavenly Father cares for them.

7. This is the thesis of 7.7–11.

Ask, and it will be given to you; seek, and you will find; knock, and the door will be opened to you. 'Ask' (the key word of our section) refers to prayer, as do 'seek' and 'knock'; cf. Isa 55.6; Jer 29.13–14; *b. Meg.* 12b.

8. This is the justification of the thesis.

9–10. Two illustrations of the justification of the thesis.

Or is there a person among you who, if his son asks for bread, will give to him a stone? The picture of a child asking for bread from a father sends the attentive reader back to the Lord's Prayer. One also recalls that 6.25–6, 31–3 is about how God feeds the faithful.

11. The concluding inference.

who are evil. This aside takes for granted human corruption: all swirl about in the abyss of sin. Sinners persecute saints (5.10–12, 38–48). People kill (5.21), get angry (5.22–6), commit adultery (5.27), divorce their spouses to marry others (5.31), and take oaths because the lie is so prevalent (5.33). They use religion for their selfish glorification (6.1–18), occupy themselves with storing up earthly treasures (6.19–21), fail in generosity (6.22–3), serve mammon (6.25), foolishly worry about secondary matters (6.25–34), and pass judgement on others (7.1–5).

how much more will your Father in heaven give good things to those who ask him! These words contain the main point. Mt 7.7–11 is less a collection of yet more imperatives than it is a way of telling hard-pressed disciples to take heart. 'All good things' should not be restricted: it includes spiritual gifts as well as the food, drink, and clothing of 6.25–34 – everything that is necessary to fulfil Jesus' demands.

The Golden Rule (7.12)

The so-called 'golden rule' (which was well known to pre-Christian Jewish tradition) brings to a climax the central section of the Sermon on the Mount, 5.17–7.12.

12. All then that you want others to do to you, thus also you do to them. Interpreted within the Gospel as a whole this is not an expression of naïve egoism or of common sense or of 'natural law' (Theophylact). Context determines meaning, and the context here is the Sermon on the Mount, which demands an exceptional 'righteousness' (5.20) that includes within its purview even love of one's enemies (5.43–8). Verse 12 is not a formula for justice or making the world better, but rather a call to exceptional benevolence.

Despite the importance the golden rule receives from its literary function in Matthew, the formulation itself is not new. Rabbinic sources tell us the following story about the rabbi Hillel, a contemporary of Jesus: 'A certain heathen came before Shammai and said to him, "Make me a proselyte, on condition that you teach me the whole Torah while I stand on one foot." Thereupon he repulsed him with the builder's cubit which was in his hand. When he went before Hillel he said to him, "What is hateful to you, do not do to your neighbour: that is the whole Torah, while the rest is commentary on it; go and learn"' (b. Šabb. 31a). One can easily collect dozens of additional parallels, not just from Jewish (e.g. Tob 4.15; 2 En. 61.1–2) and Graeco-Roman sources (e.g. Herodotus 3.142; 7.136; Isocrates, *Nicocles* 61; Diogenes Laertius 5.21) but also from Buddhist, Confucian, and Islamic texts.

for this is the law and the prophets creates an *inclusio* within which Matthew has treated the law, the cult, and social issues. Mt 7.12 is then, in rabbinic fashion, a general rule which is not only the quintessence of the law and the prophets but also of the Sermon on the Mount. This does not mean that one can deduce all of the commandments from 7.12 (obviously a falsehood in any case). Nor does it mean that one can use the verse to determine the validity of differing commandments (5.17–20 says they are all valid). Rather is 7.12 a fundamental demand which states the true end of the Torah, which remains in force.

* * * *

If it is indeed correct to see 7.7–11 as the fraternal twin of 6.25–34, and if the two sections really are intended to encourage readers, then it is distortion to think of Matthew as a stern perfectionist. Rather does he have a pastor's heart. He is aware that the Sermon on the Mount sets forth a well-nigh unattainable ideal and that the disciples who take its imperatives seriously will know themselves to be inadequate for the task. Our evangelist knows all about the storm of anxiety and doubt that will be brought on by Jesus' overwhelming injunctions. This is why, in 6.25–34 and 7.7–11, the sky suddenly clears and the torrential onslaught passes. In these two places our sensitive author, anticipating the reader's perplexity, is moved to make manifest the goodness of God and to write reassuringly about seeking, asking, and knocking. So just as the whole sermon is set in the context of mercy and compassion (4.23–5.2), so within the sermon itself do these two divine qualities become conspicuous and shed their light on all about. In 6.25–34 and 7.7–11, the call to do God's will is interrupted while the good news of God's supportive grace sounds forth.

THREE WARNINGS AND THE CONCLUSION OF THE OPENING SERMON (7.13–29)

[13]'Enter through the narrow gate, because wide is the gate and easy the road that leads to destruction, and there are many who enter through it. [14]How narrow is the gate and hard the road that leads to life, and there are few who find it.

[15]'Beware of false prophets, who come to you in sheep's clothing but inwardly are ravenous wolves. [16]You will know them by their fruits. Are grapes gathered from thorns, or figs from thistles? [17]Thus every good tree makes good fruit, but the rotten tree makes bad fruit. [18]A good tree cannot bear bad fruit, nor can a rotten tree make good fruit. [19]Every tree that does not bear good fruit is cut down and thrown into the fire. [20]So then you will know them by their fruits.

[21]'Not everyone who says to me, "Lord, Lord", will enter the kingdom of heaven, but only the one who does the will of my Father in heaven. [22]On that day many will say to me, "Lord, Lord, did we not prophesy in your name, and cast out demons in your name, and do many mighty deeds in your name?" [23]Then I will declare to them, "I never knew you; go away from me, you evildoers."

[24]'Everyone then who hears these words of mine and does them will be like a wise man who built his house on the rock. [25]The rain fell and the floods came and the winds blew and beat on that house, but it did not fall, because it had been founded on the rock. [26]And everyone who hears these words of mine and does not do them will be like a foolish man who built his house on the sand. [27]And the rain fell and the floods came and the winds blew and beat against that house, and it fell. And great was its fall.'

[28]And it happened when Jesus had finished saying these things, the crowds were astounded at his teaching, [29]for he taught them as one having authority, and not as their scribes.

Parallels: Mk 1.21–2; Lk 4.32; 6.43–9; 7.1; 13.23–7

If the Sermon begins with blessings (5.3–12), it winds down with warnings: with the parable of the two ways (7.13–14), the parable of the two trees (7.15–23), and the parable of the two builders (7.24–7). The blessings offer consolation by speaking of rewards in the eschatological kingdom. The warnings gain their force by speaking of eschatological judgement. Behind all this lies an old Jewish tradition. In Deut 11.26–7, God speaks to Israel through Moses: 'I am setting before you today a blessing and a curse: the blessing, if you obey the commandments of the Lord your God that I am commanding you today; and the curse, if you do not obey the commandments of the Lord your God, but turn from the way that I am commanding you today.' These words inspired Jer 21.8 ('Thus says the Lord: See, I am setting before you the way of life and the way of death'), and from Jeremiah on the theme of the two ways became a fixed element of Jewish moral exhortation; see 1QS 3.13–4.26; *T. Asher* 1.3–5; *2 En.* 30.15; *b. Ber.* 28b etc. Mt 7.13ff. stands in this tradition.

The Two Ways (7.13–14)

Mt 7.13–14 has a summarizing character. It looks back over all the demands delivered thus far and says that the 'way of righteousness' (21.32), the 'way of God' (22.16) propounded therein is arduous.

13. Enter through the narrow gate has consistently reminded interpreters of the eye of the needle in 19.23. Both passages contain the image of a small opening and have to do with the difficulty of entering into life or the kingdom. Clement of Alexandria mixed the two texts when he wrote of 'the camel that passes through a strait and narrow way sooner than the rich man'. There is, however, nothing to indicate that Matthew himself linked the two verses.

Because of its context within the Sermon on the Mount, the gate of 7.13, which is the entrance to life, must be equated with Jesus himself (cf. Jn 10.9), or more precisely with his demands.

because wide is the gate and easy the road that leads to destruction, and there are many who enter through it expresses a common theme within the Jewish tradition as well as within the world's religions in general. Everywhere honesty confesses that vice is easy to succumb to and attractive: to sin is natural, to repent unnatural. 'The way of evil is broad and well supplied with travellers; would not all people take its easy course if there were nothing to fear?' (Tertullian).

14. How narrow is the gate and hard the road that leads to life. Many have sought to discover a coherent image in vv. 13–14. Some imagine travellers on a path who are approaching a city gate: the entrance comes after the journey. One might then compare the gates to the New Jerusalem in Rev 21.21. But in *Pilgrim's Progress*, John Bunyan (who placed the knocking of 7.7 at the gate of 7.13) depicted a gate at the beginning of a road. This accords with the order of presentation in Matthew. Still others have envisioned a passage or gate on a road. It may be best, however, to abandon such pictures because 'gate' and 'way' seem to function synonymously.

there are few who find it need not be a statement that the vast majority of humanity will perish in Gehenna, although such a view would not have been foreign to the first century; see *4 Ezra* 7.47–51; *2 Bar*. 48.43; *b. Sanh*. 97b. It is true that in 22.14 Jesus declares that 'Many are called, but few are chosen'; 8:11, however, speaks of 'many' coming from east and west for salvation, and 20.18 speaks of Jesus' death as a ransom for 'many'. So in some contexts 'many' are saved, in others 'many' are lost. This seeming inconsistency is best explained in terms of the Semitic habit of making hyperbolic declarations in hortative material. Cf. *m. Qidd*. 1.10: 'If a man performs a single commandment, it shall be well with him and he shall have length of days and shall inherit the land. But if he neglects a single commandment it shall be ill with him and he shall not have length of days and shall not inherit the land.' It is impossible to take these words literally. They are exhortation. One is to act as if the fulfilment of one commandment means everything. In a similar fashion, Mt 7.13–14 functions to move one to act as if only a very few will enter through the gates of paradise.

On False Prophets (7.15–23)

The connection with the two ways of 7.13–14 appears to be this: the false prophets prevent others from entering the narrow gate and from following the difficult path. Some have envisaged false prophets standing before the broad gate, beckoning all to enter in, and standing beside the easy path, spreading their errors.

The identity of the false prophets in this passage is unknown, although suggestions abound (e.g. Pharisees, antinomians, enthusiasts). The only thing that can be said with assurance is that the false prophets are Christians of some sort, for they call Jesus 'Lord' and perform miracles in his name. Beyond that we do not know their identity or whether Matthew's readers would have thought of particular individuals. This, however, allows the application to remain open for a variety of situations.

15. Beware of false prophets. Warnings against false prophets are found often in early Christian literature; note Mk 13.21–3; 2 Pet 2.1–22; 1 Jn 4.1–3. In most of these texts false prophets belong to the eschatological scenario: they are part of the great apostasy of the end time. Readers of Matthew are also encouraged to think in these terms, for when we meet again with false prophets and warnings about them Jesus is talking about the latter days; see 24.4–5, 10–12, 23–8.

16. You will know them by their fruits. Cf. v. 20. Because like produces like, because evil comes from evil, the outside will inevitably give away what is inside; cf. Ecclus 27.6; Jn 15.2–17; Gal 5.19–23; Jas 3.10–12; *b. Ber.* 48a. False face cannot hide false heart forever.

17. Thus every good tree makes good fruit, but the rotten tree makes bad fruit. The situation is the same as in 6.22–3, which correlates inner light with generosity and inner darkness with selfishness and so teaches that one's internal life can be perceived in one's external deeds.

18. A good tree cannot bear bad fruit, nor can a rotten tree make good fruit. Chrysostom: the text says 'not this, that for the wicked there is no way to change, or that the good cannot fall away, but that so long as one is living in wickedness, that individual will not be able to bear good fruit. For one who is evil may indeed become virtuous, but while continuing in wickedness one will not bear good fruit.' Augustine was also correct to observe that 'if by these two trees he had meant to represent the two [fixed] natures of the people referred to, he would never [in 12.33] have said, "make [the tree good]", for what person is there that can make a nature?'

19. Every tree that does not bear good fruit is cut down and thrown into the fire. This repeats a word of the Baptist (3.10) and so adds to the parallelism between John and Jesus. The fire passes beyond metaphor; it is obviously the unquenchable fire of Gehenna (3.12; 5.22; 13.42, 50; 18.8, 9; 25.41), a thing first met in Scripture in Isa 66.24. How literally Matthew or Jesus took this fire is hard to tell: our Gospel also associates eschatological punishment with darkness (8.12; 22.13; 25.30). One should further observe the tension between the description of Gehenna as eternal (18.18; 25.41) and the threat of annihilation in 7.13 (the road to 'destruction'). These sorts of incongruities hint that Matthew's language about eschatological punishments is just as figurative as his language about eschatological promises and should not be pressed for details. The Sermon's purpose is to exhort, not to offer a blueprint of future states.

20. So then you will know them by their fruits. Cf. v. 16.

21. Verses 21–3 build upon the allusion to eschatological punishment in 7.19 and offer a little picture of self-delusion at the last judgement. The subject shifts from the false prophets' deeds ('fruits') to their words ('many will say') and from recognition by others in the present ('you will know them') to their rejection by Jesus in the future ('I never knew you').

Not everyone who says to me, 'Lord, Lord', will enter the kingdom of heaven. The false prophets are hardly the victims of what Coleridge diagnosed as Hamlet's fatal flaw, namely, the futile ado of thinking and thinking without ever doing. On the contrary, those rejected by the eschatological Lord have performed apparently great things. They have prophesied, cast out demons, and done many mighty deeds. So what is the problem? The answer to this question unfortunately depends upon the answer to another, namely, Who are the false prophets?, and the answer to this we do not know.

22. did we not prophesy in your name, and cast out demons in your name, and do many mighty deeds in your name? The false prophets are not said to have fed the hungry or welcomed strangers or visited the sick, all rather mundane, unspectacular acts. One supposes they have not done so because these acts are, like almsgiving, prayer, and fasting in secret, things for which one gets no public notice. But Matthew's text demands just such mundane, unspectacular acts. Whereas from one point of view our Gospel demands the morally heroic, in another sense 'virtue is not far from us, nor is it without ourselves, but it is within us, and is easy if we are willing' (Anthony the Great). For Jesus does not require supernatural feats but simple charity. The former can be more easily counterfeited than the latter (cf. 24.24). Charity is accordingly the true test of faith. Judgement is not rendered according to spectacular manifestations or verbal confessions but according to the demands of love and the secret matters of the heart.

The Two Builders (7.24–7)

24. Everyone then who hears these words of mine and does them takes up the key verb (*poiein* – 'to do', 'to make') of our section, where it occurs nine times (in vv. 17–18, 21–2, 24–7). Its repetition indicates the goal of the discourse as well as the fact that this goal is easily missed. Throughout this section we are confronted with the problem of all moral and religious discourse: it is only discourse. Instruction and exhortation are not ends in themselves but means to an end, that being proper life in the world (cf. Jn 13.17; Rom 2.13; Jas 1.22). As Luther wrote, 'doctrine is good and a precious thing, but it is not being preached for the sake of being heard but for the sake of action and its application to life.' Unlike Socrates, who equated sin with ignorance, Matthew's Jesus knows that the problem is even more fundamental. People are 'evil' (7.11), fond of the easy path (7.13), anxious (6.25–34), and beset by temptations (6.13). Given this, our text must do its best to warn, to motivate readers through a terrifying parable. 'The fear of the Lord is the beginning of wisdom' (Prov 1.7).

will be like a wise man who built his house on the rock refers to basing one's life upon the words of Jesus' sermon, which means, in effect, doing the will of the Father in heaven: it is what 10.32–3 means by 'confessing' or 'acknowledging' Jesus. Here Catholic exegesis has something important to contribute to the typical Protestant expositions of our passage, which are so quick to add and insist that what really matters is faith. Our text, on the contrary, says that works truly matter, that authentic discipleship is ethics. One recalls the picture of the last judgement in 25.31–46, where the one criterion is how one has treated others.

25. The rain fell and the floods came and the winds blew and beat on that house does not represent the calamities and afflictions of everyday life. Throughout the Bible the storm often represents God's judgement (Gen 6–7; Isa 28.2 etc.). And so probably is it here: the one-time eschatological crisis and judgement – which will fall upon the world as did Noah's flood (24.37–9) – are in view. Only obedience to Jesus will save on the last day. If the church is founded upon the rock, against which the gates of Hades will not prevail (16.18), so in like manner will the individual standing upon the firm words of the Messiah endure the storms of the end times.

26. And everyone who hears these words of mine and does not do them will be like a foolish man who built his house on the sand. Foolish people do not build a different sort of house: their problem is the foundation, which is something other than the Sermon on the Mount. So outwardly the two houses will appear identical.

The word translated 'foolish man' is the same as that in 5.22, where Jesus condemns the person who calls another a 'fool'. The tension between the two verses reveals that the call not to insult does not involve blindness to moral differences; cf. the discussion of 7.6.

Conclusion of the Inaugural Sermon (7.28–9)

This conclusion shares much with 4.23–5.2 and so makes the beginning and end of the Sermon mirror each other. It is also similar to other lines that close chapters 10, 13, 18, and 24–5 and help one outline the entire book.

28. And it happened when Jesus had finished saying these things puts one in mind of a formula used in Deut 31.1, 24 and 32.45. It seems likely enough, given the clear allusions to Moses in 5.1–2 and 8.1, that 7.28–9 is one more piece of Matthew's Moses typology.

the crowds. The disciples are not mentioned.

were astounded at his teaching. Cf. Jn 7.46. One thinks not only of the authority of the speaker (v. 29) but also of the novelty, difficulty, and eschatological sanctions of his teachings.

29. for he taught them as one having authority, and not as their scribes. It is Jesus' teaching, not that of his disciples, which is contrasted with the teaching of the scribes. This is because Jesus and no one else is the source of the Christian halakah.

* * * * *

(i) Each one of Matthew's five major discourses (5–7, 10, 13, 18, 24–5) concludes with eschatological warnings and promises. In this way the text reflects the inevitable flow of history: the present is always being swallowed up by the future, which will someday bring eschatological judgement. Matthew knows that everything falls under the shadow of the conclusion, and that the issue of things determines their meaning.

(ii) Matthew recognizes that seemingly supernatural phenomena are not sure signs of saving faith. This is in line with the OT, in which the magicians of Egypt do wonders aplenty (Exod 7–8), as well as with the rest of the NT, which foretells that, in the latter days, evil figures will do spectacular works (Mt 24.23–8; 2 Thess 2.9–10; Rev 13.13–15). In 1 Cor 12–14, Paul puts tongues and other spectacular manifestations in their place by calling for decency and order in worship and by exalting love above everything else as the more excellent way. Matters are similar with Matthew. Our Gospel knows that the gifts of prophecy, exorcism, and other miracles, while they have an important role to play (witness the ministry of Jesus), are not of utmost import. In particular, they can distract from the one thing needful, which is obedience to the Messiah's words. Jesus calls for obedience to his Torah (5.17–48), sincere practice of the Christian cult (6.1–18), and a right attitude toward the things of this world (6.19–7.12). He beckons his followers to travel down a very difficult road (7.13–14), a road without the promise of fame and glory, a road which instead holds forth the prospect of persecution (5.10–12).

A TRIAD OF MIRACLE STORIES (8.1–22)

8 [1] **When Jesus came down from the mountain, great crowds followed him.** [2]**And behold, a leper came to him and knelt before him, saying, 'Lord, if you will, you can make me clean.'** [3]**And stretching out his hand, he touched him, saying, 'I will. Be made clean!' And immediately his leprosy was cleansed.** [4]**And Jesus said to him, 'See that you say nothing to anyone; but go, show yourself to the priest, and offer the gift that Moses commanded, as a testimony to them.'**

[5]**As he entered into Capernaum, a centurion came to him, beseeching him** [6]**and saying, 'Lord, my servant is lying at home paralysed, in terrible distress.'** [7]**And he said to him, 'Should I come and heal him?'** [8]**And answering the centurion said, 'Lord, I am not worthy to have you come**

under my roof; but only say the word, and my servant will be healed. [9]For I also am a man under authority, with soldiers under me; and I say to one, "Go", and he goes, and to another, "Come", and he comes, and to my slave, "Do this", and he does it.' [10]Hearing this, Jesus was amazed and said to those who followed him, 'Truly I say to you, not even in Israel have I found such faith. [11]I say to you, many will come from east and west and eat with Abraham and Isaac and Jacob in the kingdom of heaven, [12]while the heirs of the kingdom will be thrown into the outer darkness, where there will be weeping and gnashing of teeth.' [13]And Jesus said to the centurion, 'Go; let it be done for you according to your faith.' And the servant was healed in that hour.

[14]When Jesus came to Peter's house, he saw his mother-in-law lying in bed with a fever. [15]He touched her hand, and the fever left her, and she got up and served him. [16]That evening they brought to him many who were possessed with demons; and he cast out the spirits with a word, and cured all who were sick. [17]Thus was fulfilled the word through the prophet Isaiah, saying, 'He took our infirmities and bore our diseases.'

[18]Seeing great crowds around him, Jesus gave orders to go over to the other side. [19]And coming up a scribe said to him, 'Teacher, I will follow you wherever you go.' [20]And Jesus said to him, 'Foxes have holes, and birds of the air have nests; but the Son of Man has nowhere to lay his head.' [21]Another of his disciples said to him, 'Lord, first let me go and bury my father.' [22]But Jesus said to him, 'Follow me, and let the dead bury their own dead.'

Parallels: Mk 1.29–34, 40–5; Lk 4.38–41; 5:12–16; 7.1–10; 9.57–60; 13.28–4; Jn 4.46–54

The three miracle stories in vv. 1–4, 5–13, and 14–15 are followed by vv. 16–22, a summary statement and teaching on discipleship. This establishes a pattern repeated in 8.23–9.17 and 9.18–38, which also consist of three miracle stories plus added material. Pictorially:

1 – 2 – 3		1 – 2 – 3		1 – 2 – 3	
miracles	8.16–22	miracles	9.9–17	miracles	9.35–8
8.1–15		8.23–9.8		9.18–34	

A Leper Cleansed (8.1–4)

Leaving behind the formidable eschatological warnings of chapter 7, Jesus (at the foot of the mountain?) becomes once again a healer; cf. 4.23–5.

1. Jesus descends the mountain he ascended in 5.1, and he is followed by the crowds already mentioned in 4.25–5.1 and 7.28–9.

When Jesus came down from the mountain. This is almost identical to LXX A Exod 34.29, which recounts Moses' descent from Sinai (cf. also 19.14; 32.1, 15). So 8.1, like 5.1–2, sends thoughts back to Moses.

Great crowds followed him. This phrase also appeared immediately before the sermon, in 4.25. It makes an *inclusio* and provides the audience for 8.10–12.

2. And behold. The leper's name, his motivation, and the place and time of his encounter with Jesus are passed over in silence.

a leper came to him. The leprosy of the Bible is not to be identified with, or at least not exclusively with, what we know and refer to as 'leprosy', that is, Hansen's disease. In the Bible, 'leprosy' covers a variety of skin diseases, including the different forms of psoriasis and vitiligo. These diseases were associated with uncleanness and entailed exclusion from Jerusalem and other walled cities; social stigma was inevitable. Several texts reflect the notion that lepers were the living dead: Num 12.12; 2 Kgs 5.7; Job 18.13. Others attribute leprosy to demons. Popular imagination tends to think of lepers living together in colonies, and in this it could be correct. Although Lev 13.46 is not proof, the idea is attested in the targum on 2 Chr 26.21. Yet the Mishnah indicates lepers could sit (by themselves) in synagogue, and the NT and rabbinic literature show that lepers were not completely isolated from the rest of society. So if there were leper colonies or 'hospitals', they were not prisons; their inhabitants were evidently free to come and go as they pleased.

There are, in the OT, two stories about lepers being healed. The first is in Num 12, the tale of Miriam's seven-day leprosy. The other appears in 2 Kgs 5.1–14, Elisha's healing of Naaman. Of particular interest is the second, which makes the ability to heal a leper the sign of a prophet (2 Kgs 5.8). Given the early church's belief that Jesus was an eschatological prophet, it could well be that our story was once interpreted as evidence for Jesus' status as such. Cf. 11.5: the cleansing of lepers is listed as one of the signs of messianic fulfilment.

Lord, if you will, you can make me clean. Instead of crying, 'unclean, unclean' (Lev 13.45–6), the leper asks for help. He is not only full of faith but also seems to have some insight into Jesus' power and status, for as Chrysostom wrote: 'For neither did he (the leper) say, "If you request it of God", nor "If you pray", but "If you will, you can make me clean". Nor did he say, "Lord, cleanse me", but (he) leaves all to him, and makes his recovery depend on him, and testifies that all authority is his.'

3. And stretching out his hand, he touched him, saying. When Jesus touches the man, leprosy does not spread to the healer; rather, healing power goes forth to conquer the disease.

And immediately his leprosy was cleansed. Jesus does not here use any magical word or formula. 'Be clean' works by itself.

4. Jesus tells the man to show himself to the priest. Eusebius' words are apt: 'Nor could our Lord have said to the leper, "Go show yourself to the priest and offer the gift which Moses commanded" ... if he did not consider it right for the legal observances to be carried out there as in a holy place worthy of God.' Here Jesus brings his avowal in 5.17–20 to life.

See that you say nothing to anyone. Cf. 9.30; 12.16.

But go, show yourself to the priest. Cf. Lev 13.49. Jesus tells the leper to go to the priest for three reasons, one implicit, the other two explicit. (i) Implicit is the need to be pronounced clean by a priest: without a priest's word of approval, reintegration into Jewish society would be impossible. (ii) Explicit is the need to fulfil a cultic requirement. The law must be obeyed. Note *m. Neg.* 3.1: 'Only a priest may declare them [lepers] unclean or clean'. (iii) Also explicit is the desire to provide a 'witness' or 'testimony' (see below).

and offer the gift. In Lev 14.4 the offering for leprosy is two clean birds, cedarwood, scarlet stuff, and hyssop; in Lev 14.10 two male lambs without blemish, one ewe lamb, a cereal offering, and one log of oil.

that Moses commanded. The reference is to Lev 13.49.

As a testimony to them recurs in 10.18 and 24.14. If it has negative sense – 'As a testimony against them', namely, the priests – this would harmonize with Matthew's penchant for criticizing the Jewish leaders in particular. The point would be that if the priests recognize the leper's recovery, then they cannot persist in their unbelief in Jesus without incriminating themselves. If, however, the phrase is given positive sense, maybe Jesus is showing the priest or the people in general that he keeps the law ('a testimony to them that I uphold the Torah'). Or maybe he is making it possible for the leper to re-enter society ('a testimony to them that the outcast has been made whole'). Then again, the expression may be self-referential: 'As a testimony to them that I have done this great work.'

The Centurion's Servant (8.5–13)

Mt 8.5–13, which consists primarily not of description but dialogue, typifies where Matthew's interest so often is: in what Jesus has to say.

5. The scene is an odd one. A Roman – reminiscent of the pious Gentiles who occasionally cross the pages of the OT: Abimelech (Gen 20–1), Rahab (Josh 2), Ruth (Ruth 1–4), Naaman (2 Kgs 5) – is asking for help from a Jew; a commander is playing the part of a supplicant.

As he entered into Capernaum. On Capernaum see on 4.13 and 8.14.

a centurion came to him, beseeching him. A Roman centurion was the officer in charge of a Roman 'century', that is, 100 foot soldiers. He was often an ordinary soldier of a legion who had been promoted, although the post was also held by magistrates or lower members of the equestrian order. His responsibilities were vast and included field command and the supervision of capital penalties. It is possible, however, that our character is not a member of the Roman army but a military official in Antipas' administration, which adopted Roman army terms for its own purposes. He could then be a Jew.

In the NT centurions are prominent. One is said to have built a synagogue (Lk 7.5). Another conducts Paul safely to Rome (Acts 27.1), while yet another stands near Jesus at the crucifixion and confesses him to be the Son of God (Mk 15.39). And when the centurion Cornelius is converted in Acts, Luke devotes an entire chapter (10) to the event. Whatever the reason, the favourable picture of the centurion painted in Mt 8.5–13 is typical of the NT. Roman centurions not only merit respect but are also pious. This is surprising given the hostility many first-century Jews felt towards the invincible Roman army.

If the centurion in 8.5–13 is a Gentile, then he, like the magi, foreshadows the successful evangelization of the nations (28.16–20). He is in any case a paradigm for the believer in so far as he exhibits true faith: the ear of his soul is open. The man trusts implicitly in Jesus' power and authority. This is why his faith is mentioned not once but twice: 8.10, 13.

7. And he said to him, 'Should I come and heal him?' Do Jesus' words show compliance or resistance? Is the proper translation: 'I will come and heal him' or 'Should I come and heal him?' Probably the latter. In the story of the Syro-Phoenician woman (15.21–8), which in so many ways is similar to 8.5–13, a Gentile's request for her daughter's healing is initially met with a negative response. Further, hesitation to help a Gentile would accord with Jesus' conviction that he has come only for the lost sheep of the house of Israel (10.6; 15.24).

8. If 8.7 be understood as a question and test, then the soldier now proves himself and clarifies his request: you need not even come into my house but need only say the word. If, however, 8.7 records Jesus' readiness to offer aid, 8.8 becomes a declaration either of surprise or gratitude: even though you are willing to enter my house, do not trouble yourself; just say the word. In either case, faith is the victor on the battlefield of the centurion's heart.

but only say the word, and my servant will be healed. Cf. Ps 107.20 ('He sent forth his word and healed them') and Mt 8.16 (Jesus 'cast out the spirits with a word').

9. This verse supplies the reason for the confidence conveyed in 8.8. The implicit logic is from the lesser to the greater: if the centurion, a man under authority, can command power with a word, how much more Jesus, who is under no earthly authority at all.

10. Hearing this, Jesus was amazed. It is rare for Matthew to record Jesus' emotional state.

Truly I say to you. When Jesus speaks not to the centurion but to the crowd, he is no longer addressing a Gentile but Jews. The switch in addressees adds poignancy. Jesus is speaking directly to those who, despite the revelation they treasure, have less faith than the pagan soldier.

not even in Israel have I found such faith. The fundamental importance of faith for Matthew is revealed by this, that in the only two places where Jesus grants a Gentile's request, it is because of his or her faith (8.5–13; 15.21–8). Although Jesus has come only for the lost sheep of Israel, the restriction is overcome when he meets genuine belief. Faith conquers the separation between Jew and Gentile.

11. Who are the many who come from east and west? Almost all ancient and modern exegetes assume that Gentiles are meant. This is very far from self-evident, whether one is thinking of Jesus or even of Matthew. Not only are Gentiles not explicitly named, but the apparent allusion to Ps 107.3 sends thoughts back to a passage about the return of Jewish exiles to the land. Furthermore, the phrase, 'east and west,' is, in Jewish texts, frequently associated with the return of diaspora Jews to their land. In this connexion the directions refer to Babylon and Egypt respectively, the two centres of the diaspora. At the same time, there appear to be no instances in which the phrase is used of the eschatological pilgrimage of the Gentiles. So perhaps we should understand 'in Israel' (v. 10) not in an ethnic fashion but – which certainly accords with his storyline, for Jesus does not go beyond the borders of Israel – in a geographical sense: 'in (the land of) Israel'. The point of 8.11–12 would then lie not in the salvation of the Gentiles as opposed to the damnation of all Jews, but in the salvation of the exiles as opposed to 'the sons of the kingdom', the wise and privileged who have lived in Israel and beheld the Messiah, and yet do not believe. On this reading, the many from east and west would serve primarily as a foil. All the emphasis would lie upon the miserable lot of those who have failed to welcome the Messiah.

and eat with Abraham and Isaac and Jacob in the kingdom of heaven. The mention of the patriarchs makes for a 'sharper sting' (Chrysostom). Although there are texts in which the faithful meet one or more of the patriarchs immediately after death, in 8.11 the resurrection and the messianic banquet are in view. The redeemed will mingle with the fathers of Israel at the great heavenly banquet. Are we to think of Abraham, Isaac, and Jacob as the hosts or the guests of honour?

12. while the heirs of the kingdom will be thrown into the outer darkness. Our author, like most of his Jewish and Christian contemporaries, imagined the place of perdition to be, despite its fire, dark, as being removed from God's light.

where there will be weeping and gnashing of teeth. Cf. 13.42, 50; 22.13; 24.51; 25.30; also Ps 112.10; Lam 2.16.

13. Go. Cf. 8.4, 32; 9.6 (all addressed by Jesus to people he has healed).

let it be done for you according to your faith. Cf. 9.29; 15.28. Whether we are to think of Jesus' assurance as involving some sort of 'clairvoyance' or as stemming from absolute faith in God or his own powers is left unsaid.

And the servant was healed in that hour. Cf. 9.22; 15.28; 17.18; Jn 4.53.

The Healing of Peter's Mother-in-Law (8.14–15)

The first part recounts the actions of Jesus, the second part the results of those actions:

8.14–15a	Jesus' actions
8.14a	He comes into the house
8.14b	He sees Peter's mother-in-law
8.15a	He touches her hand
8.15b–d	The result
8.15b	The fever leaves
8.15c	The woman rises
8.15d	The woman serves Jesus

14. This verse introduces as succinctly as possible the setting for a healing miracle.

Peter's house. Chrysostom speculates about Peter's 'mean hut' and declares that Jesus displayed humility entering it. However that may be, archaeologists may have located Peter's house in Capernaum. Less than 100 feet from what is left of Capernaum's magnificent ancient synagogue lie the remains of a fifth-century church with three concentric octagonal walls. This church in turn incorporates a fourth-century house church whose central hall was originally part of a house built in the first century BC. This original house, which appears to have been quite ordinary, seems to have become a public meeting place during the last half of the first century AD: the floor, walls, and ceiling of the central room were plastered at that time, and to judge from the pottery, the place was no longer the site of domestic activities. When one adds to this that the graffiti on the walls refer to Jesus as Christ and Lord, one suspects that archaeologists may have unearthed a first-century house church. The octagonal shape of the fifth-century structure indicates a venerated place, and we know that Christian pilgrims of the fourth and sixth centuries recorded having seen in Capernaum a church made out of Peter's house. There is a good chance, then, that sometime during the first century AD Peter's residence in Capernaum was turned into a Christian centre and that this church was eventually converted into the octagonal structure whose ruins now lie midway between the Jewish synagogue and the Sea of Galilee.

The scene of Jesus in a house with his disciples is very common in the synoptic tradition. One recalls that early Christian gatherings were held in homes (Rom 16.5; Col 4.15; 2 Jn 10; etc.). One accordingly wonders whether the stories of Jesus ministering and teaching in houses helped to legitimate the new location, the new ritual centre. Temple and synagogue no longer had a monopoly on holy space. The presence of Jesus made space sacred, and during his earthly ministry he chose to bless houses with his presence.

he saw his mother-in-law lying in bed with a fever. Obviously more than an innocuous symptom is meant. Perhaps we should think of malaria. We know independently from Paul that Peter was married (1 Cor 9.5).

15. He touched her hand. Cf. Acts 28.8, where Publius' father, sick with fever, is cured by Paul's touch.

and the fever left her. It is unclear whether we should think of the fever as caused by a demon and thus of the cure as an exorcism.

and she got up and served him. The demonstration confirms the miracle: the woman can do what she could not do before. 'Served him' means 'served him (at table)'. The motive is gratitude. Observe that nothing is said of any time needed for recovery. Not only is the fever gone, but full health and vigour have evidently been restored instantly.

The Sick Healed at Evening (8.16–17)

Mt 4.23–5 and 9.35–8 frame 5.1–9.34 and alert the reader that the five chapters concern what Jesus said and did. But the summary which occurs in 8.16f. mentions only Jesus' deeds. This implies that whereas the emphasis in 5–7 is upon things said, in 8–9 it is upon things done.

16. and he cast out the spirits with a word. The mention of 'word' helps bind together Jesus' teaching and his healing ministry.

17. Thus was fulfilled the word through the prophet Isaiah, saying.

See on 1.22. Isaiah is also mentioned in the formula quotations in 4.14 and 12.17; cf. 3.3.

He took our infirmities and bore our diseases is from Isa 53.4. Jesus' miracles are not simply the sensational workings of an extraordinary man but rather the fulfilment of the Scriptures; cf. 11.2–6.

Even though 8.17 is a possible rendering of Isa 53.4, it cannot be rightly said that the NT verse captures the true sense of the OT text. In Isaiah the servant suffers vicariously, carrying infirmities in himself; in the Gospel he heals the sick by *taking away* their diseases. In the OT the distress seems to be mental or spiritual; in Matthew physical illnesses are the subject. So a text about vicarious suffering has become a text about healing. Can Matthew be delivered from the charge of eisegesis? Perhaps he understood the healing ministry to be a type of Jesus' redemptive suffering; or maybe the association between sin and the distasteful reality of disease was so intimate (cf. Jn 9.2) that the healing of sickness could be conceived of as a taking away of sins. There is also the possibility that there was precedent in Jewish circles for a literal interpretation of Isa 53.4. Certainly the tradition in *b. Sanh.* 98a–b, although rather different in sense from Mt 8.17, seems to take the OT prophecy literally: 'Surely he has borne our griefs and carried our sins, yet we did esteem him stricken with leprosy, and smitten of God and afflicted.'

By associating the servant motif with the ministry of miracles, Matthew shows us that Jesus' healings are not self-serving. The miracles flow from Jesus' meekness and mercy, from his compassion. His portion is with lepers and demoniacs, and he identifies himself with humanity in its suffering.

The Cost of Discipleship (8.18–22)

Mt 8.1–17 has demonstrated the great authority of Jesus, to which the proper response to this authority is 'following', which accordingly becomes the theme.

Mt 8.18–22 happily precedes the stilling of the storm, which is a parable, a symbolic illustration of what it means to 'follow' Jesus. So a story about discipleship is prefaced by teaching on discipleship.

The parallelism between 8.19–20 and 8.21–2 is antithetical, not synthetic. (i) While it is a scribe who addresses Jesus in 8.19, a disciple comes forward in 8.21. (ii) While Jesus is addressed as a teacher in 8.19, in 8.21 he is called 'Lord'. (iii) While the scribe in 8.19 asks to follow Jesus, in 8.21 Jesus asks the disciple to follow him. These contrasts are striking. The would-be follower in 8.19–20 bears a title ('scribe') which often belongs to Jesus' opponents; he calls Jesus 'teacher' – an appellation which does not in itself connote faith and which is used by unbelieving scribes in 12.38; and he asks if he may come with Jesus, which accords with how Jewish students picked teachers, not with how Jesus selects his disciples; cf. 4.18–22; 9.9. In contrast to all this, 8.21–2 has to do with a disciple who calls Jesus 'Lord' and is beckoned to discipleship by Jesus himself: 'Follow me'. It appears that 8.18–22 first offers a negative example and follows with a positive presentation of genuine discipleship.

18. Jesus must move on. Are we to imagine that the great crowds around Peter's house have become troublesome and that Jesus is seeking repose? Or is Jesus' movement a challenge to the crowds to follow him?

Seeing great crowds around him, Jesus gave orders to go over to the other side. Jesus makes the decision to take a boat. He is in command of the situation. No one advises him or has to bring circumstances to his attention.

19. Teacher. Although Jesus is, for Matthew, the teacher par excellence, 'teacher' remains only a minor christological title. The disciples, in fact, never employ it. By contrast, outsiders, in particular the Jewish leaders, often do. It seems to be the equivalent of 'rabbi' and is usually addressed to Jesus out of respect. It seems a good guess that Matthew, despite his strong emphasis on Jesus' teaching, did not turn 'teacher' into a major christological title in part because it, like 'rabbi', was too common to set Jesus apart.

20. Jesus answers with a hard saying which presupposes that he is an itinerant and that those who follow him will have to live on the road, uncertain whether the night will bring a friendly haven or not. Matthew will have understood 8.20 in terms of the contrast between the Son of man on earth and the Son of man in his kingdom. Before coming in glory with his angels to judge the quick and the dead, the Son of man must first suffer humiliation and be rejected.

Foxes have holes, and birds of the air have nests; but the Son of Man has nowhere to lay his head. Cf. *m. Qidd.* 4.14: 'R. Simeon b. Eleazar says, Have you ever seen a wild animal or bird practising a craft, yet they are sustained without care, and were they not created for no other purpose than to serve me? But I was created to serve my maker. How much more then ought I to be sustained without care? But I have done evil, and forfeited my sustenance.'

Matthew's line is likely an intimation of Psalm 8, which is seemingly the only place in Jewish literature where 'son of man' and 'the birds of the air' are found together. This Psalm proclaims the honour and glory of mortals (literally 'the son of man'), who have dominion over the beasts of the field and 'the birds of the air'. Jesus, however, declares that the son of man is worse off than the birds and beasts, for he, unlike they, is without a home. So far from his head being crowned with glory and honour, Jesus finds no place to rest. Such a cynical, ironic revision of Psalm 8 has numerous parallels in Jewish literature (see already Ps 144.3 and Job 7.17–18).

In Matthew, 'the Son of man' appears thirty times, thirteen with reference to the future coming of the Son of man, ten with reference to his death and resurrection, seven with reference to his earthly activity. The title seems to be used primarily of Jesus not in his relationship to God (cf. 'Son of God') or to believers alone (cf. 'Lord') or to unbelievers alone (cf. 'rabbi') but to the world at large. This is why in the First Gospel the Son of man is the eschatological judge (13.41; 19.28; 24.30, 39; 25.31); why he will come publicly and be seen by all (10.23; 24.27, 30; 25.31; 26.64); why Jesus answers enemies and outsiders by referring to himself as the Son of man (11.19; 12.32, 40; 26.24, 64); why it is as the Son of man that Jesus suffers at the hands of others (the passion predictions); and why the ransom for many is paid by Jesus as the Son of man (20.28).

Decisive for Matthew's understanding of the Son of man is the apocalyptic vision of Dan 7. The dependence of 24.30 and 26.64 upon Daniel's version of the eschatological judgement would have been manifest to our knowledgeable evangelist, and he would not have missed the allusion to Dan 7.13 created by the linking of the Son of man with 'come' in 10.23; 16.28; 24.44; and 25.31. There are several additional verses which may well allude to Dan 7: 9.6; 19.28; 28.3; 28.18. Even if the First Evangelist knew Aramaic and so was aware of the idiomatic usage of '(the) son of man' to mean 'one' or 'a human being', he must also have believed that Jesus often used the words to allude to Dan 7 (and therefore that his words were sometimes susceptible of being interpreted on two different levels).

21. A second man appears. He too (having just heard the interchange in 8.19–20?) wants to follow Jesus. He feels bound, however, to fulfil a familial obligation – burial of his father. The request, if taken at face value, is quite reasonable and in accord with the filial piety enjoined by the decalogue. Moreover, burial of the dead was in Judaism considered an act of loving-kindness and imitation of the deity (some taught that God buried Moses).

Another of his disciples said to him. It is perhaps odd that a 'disciple' is being called to follow Jesus. One has the impression from 4.18–22 and 9.9 that discipleship is defined precisely as following Jesus, so would a disciple not already be following Jesus? Perhaps by 'disciple' is meant 'one who became a disciple'. Or maybe 8.21–2 has to do with continuing in a discipleship already entered into: the decision for Jesus must be made again and again. Or maybe 'disciple' is here used in a very loose sense, so that Jesus is calling an individual who already believes in him to full-time work.

First let me go and bury my father. Cf. 1 Kgs 19.20 ('Let me kiss my father and my mother, and then I will follow you' – so Elisha to Elijah). If the father is already dead, the disciple is not asking for an indefinite period of time but perhaps for only a few hours.

22. 'The sayings of the wise are like goads' (Eccles 12.11), but this remark seemingly discourages a deed of loving-kindness and leaves one truly nonplussed.

Follow me. For Matthew and his Christian readers, faith in Jesus and following Jesus were probably conterminous ideas: to have faith in Jesus was to follow him. But with regard to the historical Jesus, the two must be distinguished. Jesus proclaimed the kingdom to all Israel. He called only a few, however, to follow him. Discipleship in that sense was a special 'office', the result of a personal, concrete encounter. For the purpose of furthering his mission, Jesus chose a select group to be with him and to engage in missionary work. These alone 'followed' him.

and let the dead bury their own dead. In the story of Elijah calling Elisha, which should here be recalled, the latter asks the former for permission to say farewell to his parents (1 Kgs 19.19–21). The LXX and Josephus take the text to imply that such permission was granted. This makes for a striking contrast with our passage. Jesus demands that discipleship take absolute precedence over everything else. His command brooks no delay, even if the result is the slighting of one's parents; cf. 4.18–22.

Who are the dead who should bury the dead? If they are the physically dead, then, since the dead can do nothing, the meaning must be paradoxical and ironic: let the business of burial take care of itself. It is better, however, to think of the spiritually dead. The figurative use of 'dead' is well-attested in the NT and texts from its world. So the buriers of the dead are those who have rejected Jesus and his proclamation. They love father and mother more than Jesus (10.37) and have chosen death instead of the life of the kingdom. 'Let the living dead who are in the world bury those dead in the body' (John Climacus).

Jesus' disquieting demand has long scandalized commentators, who have freely exercised their imaginations to revise their sense. Maybe, some have mused, the Aramaic has been mistranslated. Or perhaps the Greek has suffered corruption. Maybe the man's father is sick and not yet dead, so that the inquirer will not be free to follow Jesus for days or even weeks; or perhaps the father is hale and hearty, and his son is saying that he has to stay home to take care of his parents in their old age. Or maybe the father has just now died and Jesus is disallowing the obligatory six days of bereavement. Again, perhaps Jesus knows that the man has brothers who will take care of the dead man. Or maybe the potential disciple is involved in exhumation and a secondary burial.

It would be imprudent to dismiss such suggestions as impossible. It would be even more imprudent to embrace any of them as likely. They all stand under the suspicion of being rationalizations designed to extract the offence.

The traditional commentators, patristic, Catholic, and Protestant, have typically and rightly refused to read 8.21–2 as a general or normative remark about burial or as an attack on the commandment to honour father and mother. They have rather understood Jesus' imperative to reflect only a concrete moment, to be a one-time only requirement, a demand made to one individual in a unique situation. In other words, exegetical tradition has understood Jesus' demand to be not universal but particular. It is part of a call story and no more enjoins a general neglect of burial or burial customs than summoning the sons of Zebedee away from their father's boat was a swipe at the fishing industry. Jesus, with the consciousness of a prophet, called a certain individual away from a sacred obligation, because at that moment something else was more important, something to be attended to immediately.

* * * * *

(i) Jesus heals a leper, a Gentile, a woman with fever. He does not heal a priest, a Pharisee, or a Sadducee. Why not? It cannot be because there is no love for the enemy: 5.38–48 excludes that. The answer is instead that Jesus consciously sides with those without status and power in traditional Jewish society. He aids not those at the top but those on the bottom. Implicit, yet still unmistakable, is a dissatisfaction with the world as it is. The Christian Lord is not at home in a place where God's will is not done as it is in heaven. Things have gone awry and need to be righted. By showering his compassion on the unfortunate and downtrodden, Jesus rejects the status quo. His eschatological orientation is accordingly understandable. The evils of the present move one to look to God's future.

(ii) The quotation of Isa 53.4 in 8.17 serves notice that Jesus' ministry fulfils the oracles of Deutero-Isaiah. This was already hinted at in 3.17 and in 5.3–12, and it will become even clearer in 11.2–6 and 12.18–21. By drawing so much attention to Jesus' role as Isaiah's servant, Matthew lends balance to his christological portrait. One could come away from the First Gospel with an image of Jesus as the fearful, majestic, transcendent Son of man who will return to judge the world (cf. 16.27; 24.30 etc.). But the allusions to and quotations from Isaiah show Jesus to be a more sympathetic, understanding figure. He knows sorrow and is acquainted with grief. He is the servant who preaches to the poor and does not break a bruised reed.

(iii) The compassion present in 8.17 ('he bore our diseases') is strikingly juxtaposed with 8.18–22, where Jesus is a harsh master. The scribe is not welcomed by the Son of man, and the disciple is told to let the dead bury their own dead. In this way Matthew informs us that Jesus' compassion is not sentimental. The merciful servant issues excruciating orders. The kindly saviour is the Lord who asks much. Jesus freely dispenses grace, but he is not to be presumed upon. Love gives and demands in equal measure.

A SECOND TRIAD OF MIRACLE STORIES (8.23–9.17)

^{23}And when he got into the boat, his disciples followed him. ^{24}And behold, a great windstorm arose on the sea, so that the boat was being swamped by the waves. But he was asleep. ^{25}And they went and woke him up, saying, 'Lord, save us! We are perishing!' ^{26}And he said to them, 'Why are you afraid, O you of little faith?' Then arising he rebuked the winds and the sea, and there was a great calm. ^{27}And the men marvelled, saying, 'What sort of man is this, that even the winds and the sea obey him?'

^{28}When he came to the other side, to the region of the Gadarenes, two demoniacs coming out of the tombs met him, so fierce that no one could pass that way. ^{29}And behold, they cried out, 'What have you to do with us, O Son of God? Have you come here to torment us before the time?' ^{30}There was a large herd of swine feeding at some distance from them. ^{31}And the demons begged him, 'If you cast us out, send us into the herd of swine.' ^{32}And he said to them, 'Go!' So they came out and entered the swine; and behold, the whole herd rushed down the steep bank into the sea and perished in the waters. ^{33}The herdsmen ran off, and going away into the town, they told everything that had happened to the demoniacs. ^{34}And behold, all the town came out to meet Jesus; and seeing him, they begged him to leave their neighbourhood.

9 ^{1}And getting into a boat, he crossed over and came to his own town. ^{2}And behold, they brought to him a paralysed man, lying on a bed. And when Jesus saw their faith, he said to the paralysed man, 'Take heart, son. Your sins are forgiven.' ^{3}And behold, some of the scribes said to themselves, 'This man is blaspheming.' ^{4}But Jesus, knowing their thoughts, said, 'Why do you think evil in your hearts? ^{5}For which is

easier, to say, "Your sins are forgiven," or to say, "Stand up and walk"?' [6]But that you might know that the Son of Man has authority on earth to forgive sins – he then said to the paralytic – 'Rise up, take your bed and go to your home.' [7]And he rose up and went to his home. [8]When the crowds saw this, they were afraid, and they glorified God, who had given such authority to people.

[9]As Jesus was walking along, he saw a man named Matthew sitting at the tax booth. And he said to him, 'Follow me.' And he got up and followed him. [10]And as he reclined at table in the house, many toll-collectors and sinners came and were sitting with him and his disciples. [11]When the Pharisees saw this, they said to his disciples, 'Why does your teacher eat with toll-collectors and sinners?' [12]But when he heard this, he said, 'Those who are well have no need of a physician, but those who are sick. [13]Go and learn what this means, "I desire mercy, not sacrifice". For I have come to call not the righteous but sinners.'

[14]Then the disciples of John came to him, saying, 'Why do we and the Pharisees fast often, but your disciples do not fast?'[15]And Jesus said to them, 'Can the wedding guests mourn as long as the bridegroom is with them? The days will come when the bridegroom is taken away from them, and then they will fast. [16]No one sews a piece of unshrunk cloth on an old cloak, for the patch pulls away from the cloak, and a worse tear is made. [17]Neither is new wine put into old wineskins; otherwise, the skins burst, and the wine is spilled, and the skins are destroyed. But new wine is put into fresh wineskins, and so both are preserved.'

Parallels: Mk 2.1–22; 4.35–41; 5.1–20; Lk 8.22–39; 5.17–39; Jn 3.29–30

If 8.1–22, Matthew's first miracle triad, contains three healing stories, 8.23–9.17, Matthew's second miracle triad, is different; it offers three diverse types of miracles: a sea rescue (8.23–7), an exorcism (8.28–34), and a healing (9.1–8). Following these three miracle stories are the call of Levi and its sequel (9.9–13) and the paragraph about fasting (9.14–17). This sequence, three miracle stories + added material, also occurs in 8.1ff. and 9.18ff. See p. 117.

Jesus Stills the Storm (8.23–7)

This miracle story is a parable about discipleship. (i) The verb, 'follow', links 8.23–7 with 8.18–22: in both places disciples follow or are called to follow their master. Surely the figurative use of the verb in the former paragraph colours the usage in the second. (ii) Already in the OT the subduing of the raging flood by Yahweh illustrates the experience of Israel (Ps 29.3; 65.7 etc.); and the sea and its storms can symbolize chaos or the world and its difficulties (Ps 65.5; 69.1–2; Isa 43.2 etc.). (iii) 'Little faith', which occurs in v. 26, is associated with discipleship; see 6.30; 14.31; 16.8. (iv) The disciples address Jesus as 'Lord' (8.25). This encourages readers to identify with those in the boat. (v) The identification of the boat with the little ship of the church is found in patristic exegesis.

Mt 8.23–7 draws upon the story of Jonah. Both stories involve:

1. Departure by boat
2. A violent storm at sea
3. A sleeping main character
4. Badly frightened sailors
5. A miraculous stilling related to the main character
6. A marvelling response by the sailors.

Our our story shows that 'a greater than Jonah is here' (12.41): Jesus is more than a prophet (cf. 8.27) because in rebuking the roaring waves he exercises the power of Yahweh; cf. Ps 65.7; 89.8–9; Isa 51.9–20. It is striking that, unlike Jonah, Jesus does not pray to God but directly addresses the storm.

23. his disciples followed him. Bengel wrote: 'Jesus had an itinerant school: and in that school his disciples were much more solidly instructed than if they had dwelt under the roof of a single college, without any anxiety or trial.'

24. windstorm is literally 'earthquake'.

swamped by the waves. We are to imagine the boat sunk in a great trough.

But he was asleep. Cf. Jon 1.5. The ability to sleep untroubled is, in the OT, a sign of faith in the protective power of God (Lev 26.6; Job 11.18–19; Ps 3.5; etc.). There were, furthermore, moments of disaster or peril when it seemed as though God were asleep, and his people sought to 'wake him up' (Ps 35.23; 44.23–4; 59.4; Isa 51.9).

25. Are we to recall that at least four of the disciples were fishermen and that they would not have been greatly troubled unless the storm was out of the ordinary?

Lord, save us! We are perishing! Cf. Jon 1.14. These words are, in Jonah, addressed to God. In Matthew, Jesus receives the cry for help.

26. Jesus now acts to save. After speaking to the disciples he commands the winds and sea, which dutifully obey him. The emphasis is not on the stilling of the storm but rather on the faith of the disciples in a difficult situation.

Why are you afraid, O you of little faith? Cf. 14.31. The disciples come to Jesus and asked for help; they appeal to him as to a guardian angel. Why then are they of 'little faith'? We are probably to see in the exclamation, 'We are perishing', evidence of the sort of anxiety rebuked in 6.24–34.

Then arising he rebuked the winds and the sea. Having calmed the souls of the disciples, Jesus now rises and calms the winds and sea, speaking to them as though they were conscious beings.

Although the degree to which Matthew thought of the winds and sea as being subject to supernatural or demonic powers is unclear, he may not have conceived of them as we do, that is, as lifeless elements. The primitive 'science' preserved in *1 En.* 72–82 reveals plainly enough that the sun, the moon, the stars, the winds, the seasons and other natural phenomena were commonly anthropomorphized by Jews and thought of as ruled by heavenly or supernatural creatures.

And there was a great calm. Cf. Jon 1.15. As God once overcame the powers of chaos and limited the sea (cf. Job 38.8–11; Ps 33.7; Prov 8.22–31; Jer 5.22; 31.35), so Jesus overcomes the swirling tempest in the Sea of Galilee. Note that the 'great calm' – which undoes the 'great windstorm' – is established instantaneously. There is no period during which things get progressively calmer. As in the healing stories so here too: Jesus' power works its full effect immediately.

In the OT the coming of the eschaton is depicted in terms of Yahweh's victory over the cosmic sea. For example, victory over the nations in the last days is compared with victory over the sea (Isa 17.12–14); and the future final conflict between Yahweh and 'the adversary' is expressed in similar terms (Isa 50.2–3). It is probably over against this tradition that we are to understand the description of the sea, the terror of the disciples, and the action of Jesus in 8.23–7. The cosmic forces of evil that threaten the order of creation are brought under the control of one who has authority over them, and who, in the latter days, exercises the sovereign power of God. In his sovereign word the elements have found their master.

27. And the men marvelled, saying. Cf. 9.33; 21.20; Jn 7.15; Acts 2.7. The people marvel because the stilling of the storm has revealed a previously unknown power of Jesus. Until now, he has only healed the sick and cast out demons.

What sort of man is this? The answer will come in 14.22–32, the sea-walking epiphany: 'Truly you are the Son of God.'

Jesus Heals Two Demoniacs (8.28–34)

28. Gadarenes. Gadara belonged to the Decapolis and was located about six miles southeast of the Sea of Galilee. The population was mostly Gentiles, but Jews also lived there.

so fierce. Chrysostom: 'the sea was not in such a storm as they.'

29. O Son of God. The demons, like the devil (4.3, 6), have supernatural knowledge: they know Jesus' true identity without being told. Contrast 9.27, where the disciples still wonder who Jesus is.

Have you come here to torment us before the time? 'The time' refers to the great assize, when evil spirits, along with wicked human beings, will receive recompense from the Son of man; cf. 25.41. So here is an element of 'realized eschatology': the eschatological judge has already appeared, and evil is already being punished; cf. 12.28.

30. There was a large herd of swine feeding at some distance from them. The demoniacs are usually thought of as Gentiles. Although this is not stated, their proximity to pigs argues for it.

31. If you cast us out. The demons do not tell Jesus what to do; they instead display diffidence.

send us into the herd of swine. In accordance with the belief that evil spirits can leave one body and enter another, the demons now think about a new home; cf. 12.43–5; Mk 9.25.

32. Jesus speaks for the first time. He utters one little word: 'Go!' The result is dramatic. The herd thunders over a cliff and perishes in the water. The sovereign power of Jesus could not be more effectively presented.

and perished in the waters. Evidently some spirits preferred dry localities; cf. 12.43. This may explain why Jesus sends the demons into water: he is tormenting them. On the other hand, there are other texts in which demons or spirits are associated with water; so one could conceivably argue that Jesus is sending the demons back to whence they came, back to the watery chaos; cf. 8.23–7. He is restoring order on the land.

34. They begged him to leave their neighborhood. The crowd does not utter an acclamation, nor is it curious; it is rather disturbed. Is this because the swine have stampeded and perished?

Jesus Heals a Man Sick with Palsy (9.1–8)

1. And came to his own town. 'His own town' is Capernaum, not Nazareth; see 4.13. Chrysostom accurately represents Matthew's conviction: 'That which gave him birth was Bethlehem; that which brought him up, Nazareth; that which had him continually inhabiting it, Capernaum.'

2. And when Jesus saw their faith, he said to the paralysed man. In Mark the faith Jesus sees has been demonstrated by the digging through the roof: the sick men's friends have overcome difficulty. In Matthew all we read about is the bringing of the paralytic to Jesus:

details are not given. This is a bit odd. Everywhere else in Matthew when a person's faith is commented upon, it is in view of what he or she has said or because of his or her persistence (8.10; 9.22, 29; 15.28). Does Matthew not presuppose knowledge of the fuller account in Mark?

As in 8.5–13, the story of the centurion, it is not the sick person who displays faith. The centurion's faith gains healing for his servant, and the faith of the paralytic's friends saves the paralytic. Yet perhaps too much should not be made of this. For it is not implied that the lame man was being carried to Jesus against his will. Presumably he was a consenting party.

Your sins are forgiven. The passive might be considered a divine passive: God has forgiven the man's sins. In this case, Jesus would only be declaring God's forgiveness. Verse 6, however, disallows this interpretation, for it clearly states that the Son of man has authority to forgive sins.

Would the idea of someone forgiving sins have been extraordinary in first-century Judaism? Certainly the scribes in Mk 2.7 affirm that God alone can forgive sins. But the action of Jesus in 9.2 is not without precedent. 4QprNab. contains this: 'The words of the prayer which Nabonidus prayed, the king of [the] la[nd of Bab]ylon, the [great] king, [when he was smitten] with the evil disease by the decree of the [Most High] Go[d] in Teima: ["With the evil disease] was I smitten (for) seven years, and unlike [man] was I made; [and I prayed to the Most High God,] and an exorcist remitted my sins for Him; he (was) a Jew fr[om (among) the deportees. He said to me,] 'Make (it) known and write (it) down, to give glory and gr[eat hono]ur to the name of Go[d Most High"'.'

3. This man is blaspheming. Matthew does not explain why the outraged scribes believe Jesus has blasphemed, that is, spoken evil. But it cannot be because they have misunderstood Jesus, missing the divine passive and so erroneously supposing that Jesus himself forgives sin. Verse 6 states that the Son of man does indeed have authority on earth to forgive sins. So Jesus does more than announce God's forgiveness. It seems best to take our clue from Mark's text: 'Who is able to forgive sins but God alone?' In Mark and probably Matthew, Jesus has taken to himself what some, despite 4QprNab., reckon to be a divine prerogative. He has acted not as a channel of forgiveness but as its source; cf. Jn 10.33.

4. knowing their thoughts implies paranormal or telepathic knowledge. Jesus can read minds.

5. or to say, 'Stand up and walk'? It is easier to pronounce sins forgiven than to command someone to walk, this because only the latter can be objectively verified. But Jesus can in fact heal the paralytic. So he can do the harder thing, and this should cause his critics to wonder whether he cannot also forgive sins. The point is the more forceful given the close connection between sin and sickness in ancient Judaism.

6. But that you might know that the Son of Man has authority on earth to forgive sins. This is probably editorial clarification, not a word of Jesus. 'On the earth' can be taken in several different ways. It can stress the fact that the Son of man, the judge of the last day, has already appeared (cf. Dan 7.13–14). But it might also indicate the period of the earthly ministry: even before the resurrection Jesus forgives sins. Or there could be a contrast between heaven and earth: God forgives in heaven, Jesus on the earth. Yet another possibility finds a claim to exclusivity. Jesus is *the only one* on the earth with the power and right to forgive sins. On this interpretation he has replaced the temple in Jerusalem and its priests. 'A greater than the temple is here.'

Jesus Calls Matthew (9.9–13)

Mt 9.9, which is an extraordinarily brief story, exhibits the same structure as 4.18–22. Jesus is (i) walking along; (ii) he sees an individual, whose name is given; (iii) this individual is going about his daily tasks; (iv) Jesus calls the individual to discipleship; and (v) he immediately follows. The dependence of this arrangement upon 1 Kgs 19.19–21 (Elijah's call of Elisha) is obvious.

9. As Jesus was walking along, he saw a man named Matthew sitting at the tax booth. 'Matthew' occurs five times in the NT, everywhere but here in a list of the twelve (Mt 10.3; Mk 3.18; Lk 6.15; Acts 1.13). There is nothing here or elsewhere in our Gospel to suggest that Matthew authored it.

And he said to him, 'Follow me'. Matthew does not choose Jesus. Jesus chooses Matthew.

And he got up and followed him. No motive is given for Matthew's obedience. Readers feel that Jesus' word compels.

10. in the house. Whose house is it? There are three possibilities: Jesus' house (so apparently Mk 2.15), Matthew's house (so Lk 5.29), or Peter's house. Although commentators have traditionally thought of Matthew's house, the first and third options seem most likely.

many toll-collectors and sinners came and were sitting with him and his disciples. The 'sinners' (cf. 9.11, 13; 11.19; 26.45) are Jews who, in the eyes of others, have abandoned the law and denied God's covenant with Israel.

12. Those who are well have no need of a physician, but those who are sick.

The words reproduce a well-known secular proverb which, in its Matthean context, is a parable with transparent meaning: the sick are the toll-collectors and sinners, the strong those who oppose Jesus, and the physician is Jesus.

13. Go and learn what this means. 'Go and learn' is a rabbinic expression which is particularly appropriate when its audience is considered. In its present context it conveys irony. The Pharisees never go and learn. Always misunderstanding and raising objections, they receive no education.

'Go and learn' introduces a precept the Pharisees know only too well, so their failing scarcely lies in scriptural ignorance. The problem, rather, is a lack of imagination. They cannot see how Hos 6.6 is applicable to the situation that has made them indignant. They cannot see how the words, 'I desire mercy, and not sacrifice', justify Jesus' outreach to sinners. And so is it throughout our narrative. Jesus never informs the Jewish leaders of ideas or principles they do not already know. On the contrary, he typically responds to criticism by recalling the OT or by appealing to common wisdom or common sense. Persuaded that all is not what it seems to be, Jesus invites his opponents to use their imaginations, to ponder a creative reinterpretation of their tradition. He is, in other words, trying to push their thoughts beyond conventional interpretations, trying to encourage their minds to construe the old in an inventive fashion. Thus what we appear to have implicit in the First Gospel is an anticipation of the profound notion so memorably taught by Blake, and later by the English writer Charles Williams: sin is a consequence of not exercising the imagination.

I desire mercy, not sacrifice. The words are found in Hos 6.6. That the Pharisees should be answered by a citation from the OT is particularly appropriate, for they prided themselves on their knowledge of and faithfulness to God's revelation in the Torah.

The meaning of the text is: cultic observance without inner faith and heartfelt covenant loyalty is vain. The Pharisees are castigated because their objections show that despite their concern with religion their hearts are far from the God they think they honour; cf. 23.25–6.

For I have come to call not the righteous but sinners. What precisely the sinners are called to is left unsaid. Is it to repentance? Is it to the kingdom of heaven? Is it to discipleship? Readers also do not know the status of the 'righteous'. There would seem to be three different possibilities. (i) Jesus does not call the righteous because he knows it would do no good: they are too stubborn to heed his proclamation; cf.

13.14–15. (ii) All the emphasis lies on the 'sinners' and one should not draw any inferences at all about the status of the righteous. (iii) Jesus calls sinners only, it being presupposed that everyone is a sinner; cf. 7.11; Rom 3.9–18. The 'righteous' would then simply be those who failed to see that they were no better off than everyone else; cf. Lk 18.9–14.

The Question about Fasting (9.14–17)

After feasting in a manner offensive to some, Jesus defends his behaviour as regards fasting and characterizes the present as a time of celebration.

14. By referring only to 'the disciples of John', Matthew makes 9.14–17 the third story in a row in which a different religious group has shown itself to be at cross purposes with Jesus: the scribes in 9.1–8, the Pharisees in 9.9–13, the disciples of John the Baptist in 9.14–17.

Why do we and the Pharisees fast often. We are to think of the voluntary, self-imposed fasts that many pious Jews observed every week. Matthew must have believed that Jesus kept the fast for the day of atonement: it was commanded by Scripture (Lev 16.1–34; Num 29.7–11); and the temptation story tells about a lengthy fast of Jesus. So the failure to fast like the disciples of John and the Pharisees was not, in Matthew's eyes, a failure to fast altogether. What Jesus and his disciples probably did not do, and what Matthew and his community probably did not do, was fast regularly on Mondays and Thursdays. The custom of non-obligatory fasting on these two days had already established itself among the first-century Pharisees.

but your disciples do not fast? Cf. 11.19, where John's asceticism is contrasted with Jesus' freedom in eating and drinking.

15. Can the wedding guests mourn as long as the bridegroom is with them? Cf. Isa 62.4–5. The answer to Jesus' rhetorical question is obvious: wedding guests do not fast during the bridal celebrations. In like manner, Jesus' disciples cannot fast because they enjoy a time of celebration as long as the Messiah is with them.

The days will come when the bridegroom is taken away from them, and then they will fast. Cf. Joel 2.16. The reference is to the post-Easter period.

16. for the patch pulls away from the cloak means: 'because the patch of unshrunk cloth draws the fill (that is, the overlapping section of the unshrunk cloth) from the cloak'.

and a worse tear is made. The deficiency of the old is made manifest when it puts on the new.

17. Neither is new wine put into old wineskins. Wineskins were typically made of goat hides.

otherwise, the skins burst. Fermentation will swell the wine and burst the old wineskin.

But new wine is put into fresh wineskins. The wine is newly made, the wineskins unused.

and so both are preserved. In its broader context, which concerns fasting, this clause makes for a positive relation between an old practice (fasting) and the newness brought by Jesus. The wineskins are symbols of something from the past, and of the need to preserve them. After all, Jesus has explicitly endorsed fasting in the post-Easter period, so the old has hardly been cancelled. The concern expressed by v.17 would seem to be the same as the expressed in 5.17–20: Jesus does not destroy Judaism but fulfils it (cf. 13.52).

* * * * *

(i) The Sermon on the Mount has already demonstrated the authority of Jesus' teaching; cf. 7.28–9. Mt 8–9 next demonstrates the authority of his actions. In 8.23–7 Jesus can command the storm to cease. In 8.28–34 he can cast out demons with the simple word, 'Go'. In 9.1–8, he can both heal a paralytic and forgive his sins. And in 9.9 Jesus can, with two words, compel a stranger to follow him. In sum, Jesus' authority is such that his word is deed; cf. 8.9. His command is 'compulsion' and is immediately obeyed by nature (8.23–7), by demons (8.28–34), and by people (9.9). The power of Jesus' divine authority is seemingly unbounded, as is its sphere; cf. 28.18 and the comments on 7.29.

(ii) A second major theme of 8.13–9.17 is mercy. In 8.28–34 Jesus reaches out to two men – demoniacs dwelling in a graveyard – who were clearly forsaken by society. In 9.1–8 he compassionately heals a paralytic by saying to him, 'Take heart, my son; your sins are forgiven.' In 9.9–10 Jesus calls a social outcast – Matthew the toll-collector – and then reclines at table with 'sinners'. And in 9.13–14 the merciful physician explicitly proclaims that he came for the sick, and in order to call sinners.

(iii) The three miracles stories in 8.23–9.8 are closely related in that each lays emphasis upon the reaction of the onlookers. In 8.23–7 the result of Jesus' miracle is wonder and questions: Who is this? The answer is left open. In the next episode, 8.28–34, the response is negative: the people beg Jesus to leave their region; they cannot abide his presence. Lastly, in 9.1–8, the response is positive: the crowds glorify God. The effect of such disparate reactions to the same man and his work is to suggest that the meaning of a miracle lies in the eye of the beholder. Put otherwise, one must have eyes to see and ears to hear. Miracles will not compel unbelief to relinquish its doubt.

A THIRD TRIAD OF MIRACLE STORIES (9.18–34)

[18]While he was saying these things to them, behold, a leader (of the synagogue) came in and knelt before him, saying, 'My daughter has just died; but come and lay your hand on her, and she will live.' [19]And getting up, Jesus followed him, as did also his disciples.

[20]And behold, a woman who had suffered from haemorrhages for twelve years came up behind him and touched the fringe of his garment, [21]for she said to herself, 'If I only touch his garment, I will be made well.' [22]Turning and seeing her, Jesus said, 'Take heart, daughter; your faith has made you well.' And instantly the woman was made well.

[23]When Jesus came to the leader's house and saw the flute players and the crowd making a commotion, [24]he said, 'Go away; for the girl is not dead but sleeping.' And they laughed at him. [25]But when the crowd had been put outside, he went in and took her by the hand, and the girl got up. [26]And the report of this went throughout that district.

[27]And as Jesus went on from there, two blind men followed him, crying and saying, 'Have mercy on us, Son of David!' [28]When he entered the house, the blind men came to him; and Jesus said to them, 'Do you believe that I am able to do this?' They said to him, 'Yes, Lord.' [29]Then he touched their eyes, saying, 'According to your faith be it done to you.' [30]And their eyes were opened. And Jesus sternly charged them, 'See that no one knows of this.' [31]But going away they spread the news about him throughout that district.

[32]As they were going away, a mute demoniac was brought to him. [33]And when the demon had been cast out, the one who had been mute spoke; and the crowds were amazed, saying, 'Never has anything like this been seen in Israel.' [34]But the Pharisees said, 'He casts out demons by the prince of demons.'

Parallels: Mt 12.22–4; 20.29–34; Mk 3.22; 5.21–43; 10.46–52; Lk 8.40–56; 11.14–15; 18.35–43

Mt 9.18–34 consists of three progressively shorter miracle stories (9.18–26, 27–31, 32–4) in which Jesus heals five people: the woman with a haemorrhage and the ruler's daughter (9.18–26), two blind men (9.27–31), and a demoniac (9.32–4). There is a numerical advance over the two preceding sections. Three people are healed in 8.1–15, three in 8.23–9.8, five in 9.18–34.

Jesus Heals a Ruler's Daughter and a Woman with a Haemorrhage (9.18–26)

18. Jesus is apparently still at table in 'the house'; cf. 9.10.

behold, a leader (of the synagogue) came in and knelt before him, saying. As with the magi (2.11), so too with this notable authority: people prostrate themselves before Jesus.

My daughter has just died. The man believes not that Jesus can heal his sick daughter but that he can raise her from the dead.

but come and lay your hand on her. Unlike Mark and Luke, Matthew prefers to write of Jesus' 'hand' (singular; cf. 8.3; 12.49; 14.31). The plural is reserved for 19.13–15, where the subject is not healing but the blessing of children. Perhaps our author thought of Jesus' right hand as his more powerful and therefore as the hand he used in healing. It is also possible that Matthew was influenced by OT usage. In the OT, the mighty and creative 'hand of God' is almost always singular. So the First Gospel may assimilate to an OT image, with the result that the hand of Jesus is like the hand of God.

19. Jesus, immediately following the ruler, says nothing. His response is action.

20. The story is now unexpectedly interrupted.

who had suffered from haemorrhages for twelve years. A uterine haemorrhage is probably meant, although the text remains discreetly silent about the details.

came up behind him and touched the fringe of his garment. The notion that healing power can be transmitted through touch is common; see on 8.3 and 9.28. It does not seem to matter whether the healer is laying on hands or whether, as here, the patient is touching the healer. Moreover, the spread of divine power from a healer to clothing or cloth is well attested; cf. Acts 19.12. This last idea seems to presuppose that there is some sort of energy which can be stored in physical objects and subsequently drained.

21. Confidence in the helpful kindness of Jesus – and not special merit or achievement – is what counts

If I only touch his garment, I will be made well. 'Only' (cf. 14.36) serves to underline Jesus' power: '*only*' a touch will suffice. Cf. 8.8, where the centurion says to Jesus: 'Only speak the word.'

22. Turning and seeing her, Jesus said. Just as the Father knows his children's requests before they ask him (6.8), so too, apparently, does Jesus know what people need before they ask.

23. and saw the flute players. Cf. Josephus, *Bell.* 3.437 ('for thirty days the lamentations never ceased in the city, and many of the mourners hired flute-players to accompany their funeral dirges');

m. Ketub. 4.4 ('R. Judah says: Even the poorest in Israel should hire not less than two flutes and one wailing woman'); *m. Šabb.* 23.4 ('If a Gentile brought the flutes on the Sabbath an Israelite may not play dirges on them unless they had been brought from nearby'); *m. B. Mes.* 6.1 ('pipers for a bride or for a corpse').

the crowd making a commotion should be envisaged as consisting of both professional mourners and friends offering food and consolation; cf. Jer 16.7; Ezek 24.17, 22; Hos 9.4. The custom of hiring professional mourners for money had long been established; cf. 2 Chr 35.25; Eccles 12.5; Jer 9.17–22; Amos 5.16. Such mourners evidently were available at a moment's notice. They lamented and composed poems that served as funeral dirges.

24. for the girl is not dead but sleeping. The words, 'she is not dead but sleeping', have occasioned much discussion. Some have inferred that, as a matter of history, the girl was not dead but in a deep trance. Such speculation can never be dismissed out of hand. The tendency of the tradition to magnify the power of Jesus is undeniable. Nonetheless, 'she is not dead but sleeping' is in itself scarcely strong reason for diagnosing a coma. How did Jesus know the child's real state before seeing her? Furthermore, in Jn 11.11–14 Jesus can both affirm that 'Lazarus is dead' and that he 'sleeps'. This offers a perfect parallel for our passage, in which the girl is dead but, in view of what is about to happen, can be said to be merely 'sleeping'. In any event, one can hardly miss Matthew's intention. According to 11.5 Jesus raised the dead, and 9.18–26 is the only possible illustration of this in the First Gospel.

25. But when the crowd had been put outside. Despite its laughter, the crowd is subject to Jesus' command. For parallels to excluding the public from a miracle see 1 Kgs 17.19 (a resurrection); 2 Kgs 4.4, 33 (a resurrection); Mk 7.33; 8.23; Acts 9.40 (a resurrection). The idea underlying many of these passages is not too far from Mt 7.6: pearls are not to be thrown before swine; certain doctrines and practices need to be kept private.

and the girl got up. In rising up the girl rises from the dead.

26. Matthew neglects to answer the questions of curious readers. What did the girl say? How did her family respond? Did Jesus say anything at all?

And the report of this went throughout that district. Cf. 9.31; 14.35. 'That district' must be the region around Capernaum.

Jesus Heals Two Blind Men (9.27–31)

The colourless story of Jesus healing two blind men has no true parallel in Mark or Luke and is almost certainly a redactional creation. It most resembles the healing of blind Bartimaeus, Mk 10.46–52, which presumably served as its inspiration. Two circumstances led to the story's creation. First, Matthew needed a third triad of miracle stories with which to conclude Mt 8–9. Second, in view of the prophecy quoted in 11.5 ('the blind receive their sight and the lame walk'), he wanted a story about Jesus healing the blind.

27. And as Jesus went on from there. The precise referent is ambiguous. Are we to think of the ruler's house? or of Capernaum? or of the territory around Capernaum (cf. 9.26)?

two blind men followed him, crying and saying. Given the close connexion between sin and sickness in Jewish tradition, it is no surprise to learn that blindness was often regarded as a punishment for wrong-doing (Gen 19.11; Exod 4.11; Deut 28.28–9; 2 Kgs 6.18; etc.). Moreover, Lev 21.20 prohibits a man with defective sight from joining the priesthood; and in 11Qtemple 45.12–14 we read, concerning Jerusalem: 'No blind people may enter it all their days lest they defile the city in whose midst I dwell.' Clearly blindness for an ancient Jew could involve not simply poverty and hardship but also religious alienation. Thus for those who composed the Dead Sea Scrolls, physical disabilities had serious spiritual consequences. Some humanitarian provisions for the blind were, however, made by the Torah. Lev 19.14 prohibits putting a stumbling block before the blind, and Deut 27.18 curses those who mislead a blind man 'on the road'. Jesus' ministry to the blind is to be interpreted in part as an extension of such humanitarian concern. At the same time, Matthew, as probably Jesus before him, will have seen in cures of the blind the fulfilment of the eschatological expectation of Isa 35.5: 'the blind shall receive their sight'; cf. Isa 29.18; 42.7, 16.

Have mercy on us, Son of David! Cf. 15.22; 17.15; 20.30–1; and *T. Sol.* 20.1 ('King Solomon, son of David, have mercy on me'). Although Matthew thought of 'Son of David' as a messianic title, there is another side to the term. Jesus several times heals as David's 'son' (9.27; 12.23; 15.22; 20.30–1). This intrigues because, with one exception, 'son of David' is always, in the OT, used of Solomon, who was later renowned as a mighty healer, exorcist, and magician. Especially significant in this regard is the *Testament of Solomon* (second century AD?). Its use of 'son of David' in connexion with Solomon the healer does not appear to be under Christian influence. Matthew, it seems reasonable to suppose, both knew the Jewish legends about Solomon's powers and probably intended to present Jesus in their light.

28. Do you believe that I am able to do this? The lesson is that of 21.22: 'whatever you ask in prayer you will receive – if you have faith.'

They said to him, 'Yes, Lord.' The blind men profess faith and even call Jesus 'Lord' (see on 8.6). It is, therefore, rather odd that they turn around and disobey his command.

29. Then he touched their eyes, saying. Cf. 20.34.

31. The blind men who have hailed Jesus as David's son and who have had their request granted now openly disobey him. Instead of keeping quiet (9.30), they spread the news of Jesus' act. Their disobedience, like the frequent failure of the twelve, shows that first-hand observation or experience of the supernatural scarcely guarantees faithful discipleship. Miracles eliminate neither little faith nor unbelief.

Jesus Heals a Demoniac (9.32–4)

This exceedingly concise and comparatively unremarkable pronounce-ment story, in which Jesus' opponents make the pronouncement, is a redactional doublet of 12.22–3. It serves several functions. (i) It completes Matthew's third triad in chapters 8–9. (ii) It prepares for 11.5, which quotes Isa 11.5 as a summary of Jesus' work. (iii) The crowds' declaration, 'Never has there appeared anything like this in Israel,' appropriately brings chapters 8–9 to a climax. While Matthew must know that people other than Jesus have worked miracles, he is anxious for us to understand that the success of Jesus' ministry of miracles was in certain respects unprecedented. (iv) Mt 9.34 records the negative reaction of the Pharisees. This helps prepare for the missionary discourse, where the theme of opposition is prominent.

33. And when the demon had been cast out, the one who had been mute spoke. Instead of writing that the man was healed, Matthew writes that the demon was cast out. The phraseology, along with the notice that the man was a 'demoniac', sets the stage for 9.34, where the Pharisees accuse Jesus of being in league with the prince of demons.

Never has anything like this been seen in Israel. Coming as they do at the end of chapters 8–9, the words probably refer not to the miracle just worked but to the whole series of miracles Matthew has recounted. Bengel wrote: 'the nation in which so many things had been seen.'

34. But the Pharisees said, 'He casts out demons by the prince of demons.' The words anticipate 12.24 and 27 and supply an antecedent for 10.25: 'If they called the master of the house Beelzebul, how much more those of his household.' The Pharisees' statement is to be closely associated with the utterance of the crowds. The crowds speak, then the Pharisees speak. The latter are responding not so much to Jesus himself but to the assertion that 'never has there appeared anything like this in Israel'. That is, the Pharisees, the leaders, are addressing the crowds and trying to convince them that their assertion is wrong; cf. 12.23–4. As throughout the First Gospel, the leaders, transparent symbols of the rabbis and synagogue leaders of Matthew's day, are the major obstacle between the masses and faith in Jesus.

* * * * *

(i) Like the first and second triads, the third triad of miracle stories in Mt 8–9 underlines the theme of faith; see 8.10, 26; 9.22, 28. But 9.28 introduces an idea not previously explicit. For Matthew, faith is faith in Jesus. Jesus asks the two blind men: 'Do you believe that I am able to do this?' Jewish faith in God presupposes God's omnipotence and anticipates God's saving acts. Matthew's Christian faith is a bit different. It sees Jesus as the concrete manifestation of the divine omnipotence and therefore expects God's saving acts to come through him. In other words, faith is not general faith in God but involves looking to Jesus as the embodiment and channel of God's power and grace; cf. 11.27; 28.18. Jesus himself thus becomes an object of faith; cf. 18.6.

(ii) The Pharisees do not deny Jesus' mighty works. The biting assertion which closes 8.1–9.34 – 'He casts out demons by the prince of demons' – assumes the successful expulsion of evil influences. So the burning issue in 9.34 is not what Jesus does but what his deeds mean. One gets the same impression elsewhere. Matthew is nowhere concerned to uphold the historical veracity of his narrative by calling upon eye-witnesses or by otherwise gaining the reader's confidence (contrast Lk 1.1–4). What is controversial is not the essentials of Jesus' story but whether one should side with the Christian *interpretation* of that story.

THE MISSIONARY TASK AND ITS MESSENGERS (9.35–10.4)

[35]**And Jesus went about all the cities and villages, teaching in their synagogues, and preaching the good news of the kingdom, and healing every disease and every sickness.** [36]**Upon seeing the crowds, he had compassion for them, because they were harassed and helpless, like sheep without a shepherd.** [37]**Then he said to his disciples, 'The harvest is plentiful, but the labourers are few.** [38]**Pray then the Lord of the harvest to send out labourers into his harvest.'**

10 [1]**And summoning his twelve disciples, Jesus gave them authority over unclean spirits, to cast them out, and to cure every disease and every sickness.**

[2]**The names of the twelve apostles are as follows: first, Simon, who is**

called Peter, and Andrew his brother; and James the son of Zebedee and John his brother; ³Philip and Bartholomew; Thomas and Matthew the toll collector; James the son of Alphaeus and Thaddaeus; ⁴Simon the Cananaean and Judas Iscariot, who also betrayed him.

Parallels: Mk 3.15–19; Lk 6.13–16; 9.1; Acts 1–13

Mt 9.35–10.4 is a door that closes off one room and opens another; it belongs equally to what comes before and to what comes after. If it introduces the missionary discourse, it also closes chapters 5–9, with their focus on the words and deeds of Jesus.

This introduction to the second major discourse resembles 4.23–5.2, the introduction to the first major discourse. Both 4.24–5.2 and 9.35–10.4 consist of two major parts, the first having to do with Jesus and the Jewish multitudes (4.23–5; 9.35–8), the second with Jesus and his disciples (5.1–2; 10.1–4). Especially noteworthy is the fact that 4.23 and 9.35 are nearly identical and form an important *inclusio*.

The other passage 9.35–10.4 resembles is 8.16–22, which follows the miracle stories in 8.1–15. Both paragraphs conclude a miracle triad, contain summary statements about Jesus' healing ministry, and allude to or cite Scripture (8.17; 9.36).

The Missionary Task (9.35–8)

This passage offers the reader three images of Jesus. The first is of him wandering about cities and villages, carrying out his ministry of teaching, preaching, and healing (v. 35). The second is of him seeking the crowds and feeling compassion for them (v. 36). The third is of him speaking to his disciples, explaining to them the situation and what they must do (vv. 37–8). The three images become increasingly contracted. We go from Jesus wandering about cities and villages, to Jesus seeing the crowds, to Jesus speaking to his disciples. In this way the narrative naturally gives rise to 10.1–42. The tasks that the twelve are to perform (vv. 37–8 + 10.1–42) are rooted in Jesus' compassion for the multitude (v. 36) and result from the need for the ministry of teaching, preaching, and healing to be carried out by more than one individual (v. 35).

35. The missionary work of the disciples is introduced by describing the missionary work of Jesus. This is because the two tasks are of a piece. The disciples of Jesus do what he does.

And Jesus went about all the cities and villages, teaching in their synagogues, and preaching the good news of the kingdom, and healing every disease and every sickness. This, with minor variations, reproduces 4.23.

36. Having travelled through cities and villages (v. 35), Jesus knows the condition of the multitudes: they are lost. His response to this sad fact is neither anger nor resignation. Rather is it compassion and action. He sees the people as though they were sheep without a shepherd, as victims, as harassed and cast down; and, in accordance with his messianic mission, he seeks to help.

like sheep without a shepherd. The noun 'shepherd' appears in 9.36; 25.32; and 26.31. In 25.32, as the eschatological judge, Jesus acts like a shepherd who separates the sheep from the goats. In 26.31, he is the shepherd of Zech 13.7; being struck, his sheep (= the disciples) scatter. In 9.36, Israel is without a true shepherd, and implicitly this must be Jesus; cf. 2.6: Jesus is the messianic ruler who will 'shepherd' Israel.

The notice that Israel appeared to Jesus as shepherdless sheep reflects Matthew's estimate of the Jewish leadership. The scribes and the Pharisees and the others in positions of power and responsibility have, for Matthew, not performed properly, and they are one of the major causes of the people's downfall. Cf. Chrysostom: Jesus words are a 'charge against the rulers of the Jews, that being shepherds they acted the part of wolves. For so far from amending the multitude, they even marred their progress.'

37. The harvest is plentiful, but the labourers are few. Everywhere else in the synoptic tradition, as in the prophets and Jewish apocalyptic literature, the harvest is typically a metaphor for the divine judgement, and the harvesters, those who gather, are God and the angels (Isa 18.4; Jer 51.53; Hos 6.11 etc.). Here, however, the harvest is a metaphor for mission, and the disciples of Jesus, with their preaching of the kingdom, are the harvesters. So the eschatological harvest has been moved from the future to the present.

Because the harvest is, in the OT and other Jewish sources, so frequently associated with eschatological themes, and because the connexion is maintained in the NT, including Matthew, 9.34–5 puts what follows in an eschatological context. The mission of the twelve and of the post-Easter church belongs to the latter days. It is not simply a prelude to the end but itself part of the complex of events that make up the end. This means that the evangelist and his community perceived their own time as eschatological time.

38. Having observed the tragic situation – the harvest is great, the labourers few – Jesus does not weep and grieve but asks for prayer. Faith responds to the situation of crisis by turning towards God; cf. 24.20; 26.41.

Pray then the Lord of the harvest to send out labourers into his harvest. Because the disciples of 9.37 are most naturally identified with the twelve (see 10.1–4), the 'workers' (cf. 10.10) are probably, in

Matthew's mind, to be identified with the missionaries of the post-Easter period. If so, their existence is an answer to prayer. Which is to say: the post-Easter mission is grounded not only in the activities of Jesus and the twelve but also in the prayer request of Jesus.

The Twelve Apostles (10.1–4)

This pericope consists of two parts. The first is a general summary of Jesus' charge to his 'twelve disciples' (v. 1). It anticipates v. 8 and stands as a heading for the discourse that follows. The second part is a list, given in six parts, of the names of the twelve (vv. 2–4). This list introduces the original audience for vv. 5–42.

The list of the students of a teacher was conventional in both the Jewish and Graeco-Roman worlds. Compare, for example, *m. 'Abot* 2.8 ('Five disciples had Rabban Johanan b. Zakkai, and these are they: R. Eliezer b. Hyrcanus, and R. Joshua b. Hananiah, and R. Jose the Priest, and R. Simeon b. Nathaniel, and R. Eleazar b. Arak') and Diogenes Laertius 8.46 (a list of the pupils of Philolaus and Eurytus). Unlike a genealogy, in which the names outline a pre-history, a list of students indicates a post-history. In our gospel the genealogy in 1.2–17 shows Jesus' pre-history to lie in Abraham's descendants, while the list of disciples in chapter 10 shows his post-history to be in the church with Peter at its head.

1. Jesus summons twelve individuals and gives them authority for tasks which he himself has already performed. The *imitatio Christi* is implicit.

summoning. The initiative lies with Jesus. He makes the decisions and issues the call.

his twelve disciples. Cf. Mk 6.7. Of the four canonical evangelists, only Matthew uses the phrase, 'the twelve disciples'. He takes their existence and status for granted.

Mt 10.1–4 combines into one paragraph material that, in Mark, belongs to two very different scenes (Mk 3.13–19; 6.7). Although the evangelist knows that, according to Mark, Jesus called the twelve some time before he sent them out, it would not serve his literary and theological ends to follow his predecessor in this regard. From 4.23 on the evangelist wants Jesus alone to be in the spotlight. Only after reciting Jesus' words and deeds (chapters 5–9) do the disciples fully come into the picture. This is because Jesus and the disciples are two different subjects, and Matthew, with his proclivity for thematic as opposed to historical and chronological thinking, wants to handle one theme at a time. So Jesus, the model, comes first, the disciples second.

Jesus gave them authority over unclean spirits. Cf. 12.43. Jesus is the sole source of authority for his followers. What they have comes from him. It is consistent with this that no reason is given for his choice. Prior accomplishments merit no mention. What counts is Jesus' will.

to cast them out makes explicit what remains only implicit in Mark: the purpose of having authority over unclean spirits is to cast them out. Perhaps the point needed to be made unambiguous because authority over unclean spirits could theoretically have been used to make those spirits do one's bidding – something Matthew would have found abhorrent.

and to cure every disease and every sickness. Matthew now repeats a phrase used of Jesus in both 4.23 and 9.35, and thereby drives home once again the correlation between Jesus' deeds and those of his followers: the disciples do what their master does.

2. The names of the twelve apostles are as follows. The word 'apostle' appears only here in the First Gospel. Our author seemingly identifies 'the twelve' with 'the apostles'. No stress, however, is laid on the equation.

first, Simon, who is called Peter. On 'Simon, who is called Peter' see on 16.13–20. 'First' refers not to his having been called first or to his being the first to see the risen Lord or to his being the first on the list. Rather does it indicate his privileged status. He is the first among equals, the chief of the apostles. Just as Judas, the last on the list, is the most dishonoured, so is Peter, the first, the most honoured.

and Andrew his brother. See on 4.18.

and James the son of Zebedee and John his brother. Matthew, like Luke, omits the enigmatic 'whom he surnamed Boanerges, that is, sons of thunder'.

3. Philip and Bartholomew. Philip is, in the synoptics, nothing more than a name. In John he is a major character; see 1.43–51; 6.5; 12.20–2; 14.8.

Bartholomew is, like Philip, only a name in the synoptics. Unlike Philip, he is never mentioned by John. Some have identified him with the Nathanael of the Fourth Gospel, but the reasons for this equation are not compelling. According to a legend in Eusebius, Pantaenus, upon arriving in India, found that Matthew's Gospel (in Hebrew letters) had preceded him there, having been left by Bartholomew.

Thomas, who is traditionally credited with taking Christianity to India, is named in the synoptics only in the lists of the twelve. In John he appears on several occasions, in 11.16; 14.5; 20.24–9; and 21.2. In three of these places he is called 'twin'. We do not learn, however, whose twin he was. If we discount the strange, ancient tradition that he was Jesus' twin, we necessarily remain in the dark.

Matthew the toll collector. Matthew is labelled 'the toll collector' because of the story in chapter 9. The vocation of no other apostle is here given. Our evangelist probably did not know what the other apostles did, with the exceptions of Peter, Andrew, James, and John.

James the son of Alphaeus and Thaddaeus. About James the son of Alphaeus we know next to nothing, although he could be identified with James the son of Mary (27.56; Mk 15.40; 16.1; Lk 24.10) or with Levi's brother (according to Mk 2.14 Levi was also a son of Alphaeus). He is not James 'the just', the brother of the Lord (1 Cor 15.7; Gal 1.19). As for Thaddaeus, he too is a faceless figure.

4. Simon the Cananaean is the same as 'Simon the Zealot' (Lk 6.15; Acts 1.13). 'Cananaean' derives not from 'Canaanite' or 'Cana' but from the Aramaic word for 'zealot' or 'enthusiast'. Although it is widely held that Simon at one time belonged to the party of the Zealots, it is very doubtful whether 'zealot' came to refer distinctively to revolutionaries before the Jewish war in the sixties (cf. Gal 1.14); and 'zealot' may simply be adjectival in Lk 6.15 and Acts 1.13: 'the zealous one' (cf. 4 Macc. 18.12).

Judas Iscariot, who also betrayed him. The enigmatic Judas Iscariot, who naturally comes last in the apostolic catalogue and who is the only apostle to have his future role noted, appears five times in the First Gospel: in 10.4; 26.14–16 (where he strikes the deal to deliver up Jesus); 26.20–5 (where he is singled out by Jesus as his betrayer); 26.47–56 (where he leads the crowd to arrest Jesus); and 27.3–10 (his suicide). Except for 27.3–10, Matthew's material comes from Mark, and most of the major motifs associated with Judas in Mark also appear in Matthew: Judas delivers Jesus up (10.4; 26.25; 27.3) and is 'one of the twelve' (10.4; 26.14, 47), and what he does is somehow ordained by or in accordance with the Scriptures (26.53–6; 27.9–10). Matthew has, however, made at least four contributions of his own. He has emphasized Judas' repentance (27.3), underlined his greed (26.14–16), told us of his bleak end (27.3–10), and added to the parallels between Judas and Ahithophel, the trusted friend who betrayed David and then went out and hanged himself.

* * * * *

By harking back to 4.23 and forming an *inclusio*, the passage makes Jesus' words (5–7) and deeds (8–9) the fundamental context for understanding Mt 10. The twelve are to preach and to heal (10.7–8). In this they are clearly following in the footsteps of Jesus. More particularly, since 5.1–7.27 gives content to the command to preach the gospel of the kingdom (10.7), and since 8.1–9.34 gives content to the command to 'heal the sick, raise the dead, cleanse lepers, cast out demons' (10.8), 5.1–9.34 is for the missionary example and precedent.

Matthew's Jesus is in some sense the first Christian missionary and the standard to be followed. The bearers of the gospel are, in their own situations, to proclaim what Jesus proclaimed and to do what Jesus did. It is no surprise that chapter 10 is full of parallels between Jesus and his followers (cf. 10.6, 7, 8, 17, 18, 24–5).

INSTRUCTIONS AND PROSPECTS FOR MISSIONARIES
(10.5–25)

[5]These twelve Jesus sent out, charging them: 'Go nowhere among the Gentiles, and enter no town of the Samaritans, [6]but go rather to the lost sheep of the house of Israel. [7]As you go, preach, saying, "The kingdom of heaven has come near." [8]Heal the sick, raise the dead, cleanse the lepers, cast out demons. You received without payment; give without payment. [9]Do not take gold or silver or copper in your belts [10]or bag for your journey or two tunics or sandals or a staff; for the labourer deserves his food. [11]Whatever town or village you enter, find out who in it is worthy, and stay there until you leave. [12]As you enter the house, greet it. [13]If the house is worthy, let your peace come upon it; but if it is not worthy, let your peace return to you. [14]If anyone will not receive you or listen to your words, shake off the dust from your feet as you leave that house or town. [15]Amen I say to you, it will be more tolerable for the land of Sodom and Gomorrah on the day of judgement than for that town.

[16]'Behold, I send you out like sheep into the midst of wolves. So be wise as serpents and innocent as doves. [17]Beware of people, for they will hand you over to councils and flog you in their synagogues; [18]and you will be dragged before governors and kings because of me, as a testimony to them and the Gentiles. [19]When they hand you over, do not worry about how you are to speak or what you are to say; for what you are to say will be given to you at that time. [20]For it is not you who speak, but the Spirit of your Father speaking through you. [21]Brother will hand over brother to death, and a father his child, and children will rise up against parents and have them put to death; [22]and you will be hated by all because of my name. But the one who endures to the end will be saved. [23]When they persecute you in one town, flee to the next. For amen I say to you, you will not have gone through all the towns of Israel before the Son of Man comes.

[24]'A disciple is not above his teacher, nor a slave above his master. [25]It is enough for the disciple to be like his teacher, and the slave to be like his master. If they have called the master of the house Beelzebul, how much more will they malign those of his household!'

Parallels: Mk 6.8–11; 13.9–13; Lk 6.40; 9.2–5; 10.1–12; 12.11–12; 21.12–19; Jn 13.16; 14.26; 15.20

Mt 10.5–25 consists of three progressively shorter subsections: vv. 5–15, 16–23, 24–5. The first, which is dominated by the theme of movement from place to place, issues instructions to missionaries and tells them about their reception and rejection by others. The second, a list of hardships headed by v. 16, prophesies tribulation. It is built around three key imperatives: 'beware', v. 17; 'do not worry', v. 19; 'flee', v. 23. The third subsection forewarns missionaries that they will be treated as Jesus was treated. It makes explicit the theme of the imitation of Christ, a theme implicit in the two previous sections. Altogether, 10.5–25 paints a bleak picture: the future holds hard work and fierce persecution. In this way the whole unit prepares for vv. 26–31, where consolation is the theme.

The Missionary Task (10.5–15)

5. The prohibition not to go to the Gentiles or to the Samaritans is given special prominence by virtue of its initial position in the discourse. And it anticipates 15.24, where Jesus makes it plain that his mission is to Israel alone.

These twelve Jesus sent out, charging them. Matthew probably uses 'the twelve' instead of 'the disciples' or 'the apostles' because Jesus' words confine the mission to Israel: the number of apostles corresponds to the number of tribes; cf. 19.28.

Go nowhere among the Gentiles created, for obvious reasons, problems for the church Fathers. Many of them allegorized the words and applied them to pagan doctrine or behaviour.

and enter no town of the Samaritans. This line is the only one in Matthew to mention the Samaritans or Samaria. The impression left by the First Gospel is that Jesus never entered Samaritan territory (contrast Luke and John).

The Samaritans were the inhabitants of Samaria, the territory between Judea and Galilee. Traditionally their roots have been traced back to the Israelites who were not exiled when the northern kingdom fell in 722 BC, or to the aliens who were settled in Israel by the Assyrian conquerors. Recent scholarship, however, has questioned the traditional view and made it possible to think of the split between Jews and Samaritans as taking place relatively late – in the period from the third century BC to the first century BC. One fact remains undisputed: before the time of Jesus and Matthew, hostility between Jews and Samaritans was commonplace. The causes of enmity were several and included regional prejudices, the erection of a temple on Mount Gerizim, its destruction by a Hasmonaean, John Hyrcanus, in 128 BC, and Samaritan acceptance of the Pentateuch alone as the authoritative word of God.

Why does 10.5 mention the Samaritans? The status of the Samaritans was uncertain. On the one hand, their forefathers were Jewish. On the other hand, they were regarded as racially mixed. For this reason, a command to go to Jews but not Gentiles might be thought unclear. What about the Samaritans? Are they Jews or Gentiles? Verse 5 dispels the doubt. The Samaritans are not Jews; treat them like Gentiles.

But there may be more than this in the verse before us. In Acts the Christian mission proceeds in three stages. The followers of Jesus first preach in Jerusalem and Judea; they then move on to Samaria; finally they reach out to the Gentiles (cf. Acts 1.8). While the scheme is undoubtedly Lukan, it has every chance of being historically correct, which means that others besides Luke probably thought of the gospel as going first to the Jew, then to the Samaritan, then to the Gentile. If so, Mt 10.5–6 might have been formulated under the impact of the historical sequence.

6. The negative injunction is now followed by a positive imperative: Go to the lost sheep of the house of Israel. The reason for disregarding the Samaritans and Gentiles stems not from prejudice (as 28.16–20 will make clear) but from the immediate needs of God's people, Israel.

but go rather to the lost sheep of the house of Israel. Cf. 15.24. The sheep are probably lost largely because their leaders have gone astray. 'House of Israel' may be either a partitive genitive or an explicative genitive. If the former, then the disciples' mission is limited to a portion of Israel (presumably the sinners and outcasts). If the latter, then the disciples are being sent to all Israel, and the people as a whole are characterized as lost sheep. The case for an explicative genitive seems stronger. Not only does 'the lost sheep of the house of Israel' stand over against 'the Gentiles' (all of them) and 'the Samaritans' (all of them), but in Isa 53.6; Jer 50.6; and Ezek 34 all the people of Israel are lost sheep.

The tension between 10.5–6 and 28.16–20, which sends the disciples into all the world, is dissolved by recognition that the post-Easter mission to the Gentiles is a consequence for Matthew of the relative failure of the pre-Easter mission to Israel. 'To the Jew first and also to the Greek' is the idea, with Easter marking the point at which the mission goes beyond the borders of Israel. This theological idea reflects the historical fact that the Gentile mission did not begin until after the resurrection. Further, the focus of Jesus upon his own people is a sign of God's covenantal faithfulness. Before offering salvation to Gentiles, the Christ offered salvation to Israel. The sending of the Messiah to Israel, in fulfilment of the OT, is, then, a demonstration of God's love for the chosen people.

7. Having been instructed on the location of their actions, the disciples now receive the message they are to deliver: the kingdom of heaven has drawn near. The words are those Jesus himself has used (4.17; cf. 9.35). In carrying on the missionary task, the disciple must be like the master; cf. 10.24–5.

As you go, preach, saying. The preachers, like Jesus, are itinerants.

The kingdom of heaven has come near. See on 4.17. The proclamation of 10.7 is not only the proclamation of the twelve but also the proclamation of Matthew's church. This follows from the obvious transparency of chapter 10: while it is addressed to the historical twelve, it simultaneously addresses later missionaries. There is only one gospel. The proclamation of the pre-Easter epoch and the proclamation of the post-Easter epoch differ, apart from the all-important fact that it is only in the latter that the crucifixion and resurrection can be proclaimed as already accomplished, in the audience addressed. It is only after the resurrection that Gentiles are sought out. The content of the preaching is in a real sense the same. So the Christian missionary repeats the words of the Lord and the message of the twelve apostles.

8. Heal the sick. The good news of the kingdom is spread by believers following the example of the Messiah.

raise the dead. Cf. 9.18–26 and 11.5. There is no good reason for taking the language metaphorically.

cleanse the lepers. Cf. 8.1–4 and 11.5. Nowhere in the NT does anyone but Jesus heal a leper.

cast out demons. Cf. 8.28–34 and 9.32–4

You received without payment; give without payment. These words presuppose that believers should act towards others just as God has acted towards them. Because the power to heal is a gift from God, it in turn must be made a gift for others. Cf. 2 Kgs 5.15–16.

9–10. These two verses contain a list of prohibitions (vv. 9–10a) followed by an explanation (10b). The disciples can and should leave behind gold and silver and copper. They are not even to take along a travel bag or an extra tunic or sandals or a staff – the normal and necessary accoutrements of the traveller; cf. Exod 12.11; Josh 9.3–6. Preaching a kingdom 'not of this world', they have unloosed their ties to the present age. They are to be 'like slaves that minister to the master not for the sake of receiving a bounty' (*m. 'Abot* 1.3).

By going about without possessions the disciples not only put themselves beyond suspicion but also become examples of trust in God's providential care; cf. 6.24–34. They are, further, signs that God is working not through the rich or powerful but through the poor and powerless; cf. 5.3–12.

Do not take gold or silver or copper in your belts. It was common custom to keep coins in one's belt or girdle.

or bag for your journey. The prohibition of a traveller's bag is the one point on which 10.9–10 and its synoptic parallels agree. Perhaps it is significant that the Hellenistic wandering philosophers carried such bags. Early Christian preachers may have felt a need to distinguish themselves from Cynics.

or two tunics or sandals or a staff. To carry an extra tunic would be a luxury; cf. Lk 3.11. To be without sandals would be a sign of poverty; cf. Deut 25.10; Lk 15.22. The 'staff' was not only a walking aid but also used to ward off animals and human attackers. Perhaps, then, the lack of a staff is a sign of pacifism.

for the labourer deserves his food. Cf. 1 Cor 9.14, 17–18; 1 Tim 5.18. Missionaries may receive food and accept free lodging, but they should not ask for anything more. Cf. *Did.* 11.6: 'when he departs let the apostle receive nothing except bread, until he finds shelter; but if he asks for money, he is a false prophet.' (Montanus, at the end of the second century, was evidently the first to put missionaries under salary.)

The disciples, who are here identified with the 'workers' of 9.37–8, are to live off what is given to them by those who favourably receive them and their message. One is reminded of 6.25–34. If one takes care of God's business, one will be taken care of by God. There is no need to be anxious about food or drink or clothing.

11. The theme becomes the reception and rejection of the missionaries and their response to such. The disciples are not to stay just anywhere. They are to be careful in choosing lodging.

and stay there until you leave. To stay in one place would cut the time spent looking for lodging and cancel the suspicion that the disciples want to take as much as possible from as many as possible. Further, to be content where one is prevents the making of invidious comparisons between households.

12. As you enter the house, greet it. The command to 'greet' a house is the idiomatic equivalent of the command to say, 'Peace to this house'.

13. Let your peace come upon it. The disciples do not make a wish but instead offer a gift, one that can be accepted or rejected. One must wonder whether the offer of peace reflects more than social convention. Not only does our passage ride roughshod over other social conventions, but the concept of *shalom* had strong eschatological associations in ancient Judaism. The messianic or eschatological age was often represented as a time of unprecedented peace: 'there will be deep peace and understanding' (*Sib. Or.* 2.29); 'all peace will come upon the land of the good' (*Sib. Or.* 5.780). Already in the OT the coming day of the Lord is anticipated as a day of universal peace (Mic 5.5; Nah 1.15). Particularly noteworthy is Isa 52.7, a passage which 11QMelch links to an eschatological figure and which the targum associates with the revelation of the kingdom of God: 'How beautiful upon the mountains are the feet of him who brings good tidings' (cf. Acts 10.36; Rom 10.15; Eph 6.15; all three of these texts significantly enough are about preaching the gospel). For Matthew and his tradition the apostolic greeting of peace was probably a sign of the inbreaking of the kingdom, a symbol of God's eschatological work of establishing reconciliation and *shalom*.

let your peace return to you. Peace is here spoken of as though it had an objective existence and as though it were subject to the disciples' commands; cf. Isa 45.23; 55.10–11. The disciples do not lose their peace if they give it to an unworthy house. When the message of the kingdom is rejected, it is not the proclaimers that suffer loss but those who do not believe.

14. shake off the dust from your feet as you leave that house or town. According to some, the disciples are to shake off from their cloaks the dust their feet have stirred up. According to others, however, the disciples are to wipe their feet or shake off the dust that cleaves to their feet. In favour of the first alternative, both Neh 5.13 and Acts 18.6 involve the shaking of garments as a sign of renunciation. In favour of the second alternative, the Greek of the synoptics most naturally brings to mind the image of dust on the feet, and this must be the decisive consideration. It may nevertheless be observed that the shaking of clothing and the cleaning of feet essentially mean the same thing. Both are public demonstrations of the breaking off of communion and the forfeiting of responsibility; cf. the handwashing of 27.24. So the main point is clear. The disciples will no longer have anything to do with the place that rejects the messengers of God's kingdom. They will without guilt leave it to its fate.

15. It will be more tolerable for the land of Sodom and Gomorrah on the day of judgement than for that town. Sodom and Gomorrah are, in the biblical tradition, remembered as cities whose wickedness was so great that God determined to destroy them and make them a 'burned-out waste' (Gen 13.13; 18.20; 19; Deut 29.23). Their overthrow became proverbial and stood as a warning of God's wrath towards sinners; cf. Isa 1.9; Jer 23.14; Amos 4.11; 2 Pet 2.6. In the present text, Jesus' prophecy assumes that greater privileges require greater responsibility. It is an unprecedented honour to hear the disciples, and incomparable failure to reject them. To whom much is given, from them much will be required.

The Missionaries' Afflictions (10.16–23)

There are a number of items in 10.16–23 which show us that the text here goes beyond the historical situation of the twelve to include the situation of missionaries in Matthew's own day. The evangelist has accordingly passed from the past to the present without explicitly noting this. This has struck many as strange. The phenomenon, however, occurs elsewhere in early Christian literature. Moreover, the unheralded transition from past to present results naturally from Matthew's typification of the twelve: they stand for the Christian readers – especially missionaries – of Matthew's time. All that Jesus says to the twelve he says to the church; and the mission of the church is a continuation of the mission carried out in Jesus' lifetime.

16. This verse, which incorporates two proverbial expressions, stands as the heading of 10.17ff.; Jesus prophesies the fate of those who are like sheep in the midst of wolves.

Behold, I send you out like sheep into the midst of wolves. In 7.15, the false prophets have sheep's clothing but are inwardly ravenous wolves. In 10.16, by contrast, a few sheep are scattered among wolves.

So be wise as serpents and innocent as doves. Cf. Gen 3.1, where the serpent is more crafty or prudent than all beasts. What exactly is meant by 'innocent'? The observation that the dove is 'innocent' because it is not a bird of prey does not take us very far. The Greek word translated 'innocent' literally means 'unmixed', and in early Christianity it comes close to meaning 'child-like simplicity'; cf. Rom 16.19; Phil 2.15. So the disciples, with a single-minded devotion to duty – a devotion made manifest by a lack of equipment – have no guile. Like children, their intent is obvious to all. Such 'simplicity' is not inconsistent with the call for practical prudence, the object of which is simple survival; cf. 10.23.

The rabbis applied the proverbial adage about being wise as serpents and innocent as doves to Israel's situation amidst the Gentiles. This matters because the image of sheep in the midst of wolves was similarly applied. One strongly suspects, then, that the two parts of 10.16 implicitly reinterpret traditional images. The sheep are no longer the Jews but the disciples of Jesus, the wolves no longer the Gentiles but Jews hostile to the Christian mission; and those who are wise and innocent are not Jews surrounded by Gentiles but rather Jesus' followers in a situation of persecution. As elsewhere, imagery and privileges traditionally associated with Israel are now associated with the church; cf. 5.13–16; 21.43.

17. Following the general warning and admonition in 10.16, the evangelist next offers paraenesis and a detailed description of missionary tribulation. Despite prudence (10.16b), the disciple cannot avoid persecution. Against unjust suffering there is no inbred immunity. It can even be said that suffering as much as anything will characterize the missionary; cf. 5.10–12. As with the master, so with his disciple.

The material in 10.17–22 is taken primarily from Mk 13.9–13. This fact is a key for the interpreter. Mk 13 is above all a description of the woes preceding the second advent of Jesus, and Matthew's treatment of that chapter in Mt 24 reveals that he understood and accepted its eschatological orientation. Further, nothing in chapter 10 tones down the eschatological nature of the Markan material. On the contrary, 10.22 explicitly mentions 'the end' and 10.23 refers to the *parousia*. It follows that Mt 10 views the pre- and post-Easter missions as belonging to the eschatological affliction, the period of trial and tribulation which heralds the coming of God's new world.

Beware of people. The reference is to all people, both Jews and Gentiles.

for they will hand you over to councils. 'Councils' are probably local (Jewish) councils, not the lesser sanhedrins known from rabbinic sources. The verb (cf. 4.12) links the disciples' fate with Jesus' fate (cf. 10.4): both are 'handed over'.

and flog you in their synagogues. The verb is used of Jesus in 20.19. Here it refers specifically to the punishment of flogging as decreed in Deut 25.1–3.

18. The mention of sanhedrins and synagogues (v. 17) leads to the mention of governors and kings. This reflects the story of Jesus: he was first delivered to a Jewish council and then taken to the governor.

And you will be dragged before governors and kings because of me. 'Governors' means here imperial governors or Roman procurators. Matthew uses 'governor' often of Pontius Pilate (27.1, 11 etc.)

as a testimony to them and the Gentiles. The disciples, through what they say, do, and suffer, become witnesses to the truth. In other words, they spread the gospel about Jesus even after they are handed over; cf. the position of Paul in Philippians. The text assumes that to speak to governors and kings is to speak to the people they represent, that is, to 'the Gentiles' in general. A 'testimony' before the former is simultaneously a 'testimony' before the latter. (This is why v. 18 does not necessarily envisage activity outside Palestine. The Gentiles had representatives in the land of Israel.)

19. Do not worry about how you are to speak or what you are to say. 'Do not worry' recalls 6.25–34 and the reasons there given for not fretting overmuch. Throughout chapter 10 it is presupposed that Christian missionaries suffer passively. When delivered up and arrested they do not resist. Their only action is speaking – and then not in their own defence but in order to proclaim the gospel. Mt 10 thus illustrates the humility enjoined by the beatitudes and the meekness demanded by 5.38–48.

For what you are to say will be given to you at that time. This is not a command but reassurance. Perhaps Matthew wanted his readers to recall the encouraging words of the Lord to Moses: 'I will be with your mouth and teach you what you shall speak' (Exod 4.12).

20. When standing before courts and synagogues, governors and kings, the missionaries are not alone. The 'Spirit' of their Father is with them, as it was with the prophets.

but the Spirit of your Father speaking through you. Perhaps one should recall the baptismal story, where the Spirit comes down and a divine voice speaks. In any event, elsewhere in Matthew Jesus is the possessor of, or vehicle for, God's Spirit: 3.16; 12.18, 28. So once again we have a parallel between Jesus and his apostles: both are vessels of the Spirit.

21. The subject now becomes familial strife (cf. 10.34–6), and 'here again the consolation is at the doors' (Chrysostom). If vv. 21–2a and 23a–b speak of tribulation, vv. 22b and 23c–d speak of salvation.

Brother will hand over brother to death, and a father his child, and children will rise up against parents and have them put to death. Cf. Mic 7.6, which 10.35–6 quotes. The theme belongs to eschatological expectation.

The reference to being delivered over to death is striking. The language is very strong indeed. One is initially inclined to dismiss it as hyperbole. One should remember, however, that late first-century Christians did have stories about those who gave their lives for the gospel – Stephen, Paul, and Peter, for instance, not to mention John the Baptist and Jesus himself. Even if death for the Christian cause was an unlikely prospect for Matthew's readers, they had sufficient examples to make the possibility seem real to them.

22. And you will be hated by all because of my name. Cf. 24.9. The disciples of Jesus will encounter opposition from every quarter. There is no safe haven, in or out of Palestine. Regarding 'because of my name': what the world hates is not the disciples but their behaviour as followers of Jesus. It is precisely in so far as believers speak and act as did their Lord that they encounter opposition.

But the one who endures to the end will be saved. Despite all appearances, the tested and afflicted disciples are really the ones who will be saved and delivered from death to life. All is not what it seems to be.

23. On the lips of Jesus, a saying such as this would have been encouragement to disciples or missionaries whose future included suffering in the eschatological tribulation: take heart, for salvation is near to hand. But what of Matthew? The attempts to interpret 10.23 as a fulfilled prophecy have been numerous. According to some, Matthew saw in the destruction of Jerusalem the realization of the prophecy in 10.23. According to others, the word found its fulfilment for Matthew in the resurrection of Jesus. Chrysostom thought of the pre-Easter reunion of Jesus with his disciples after they returned from their missionary assignment. Calvin seemingly thought of Pentecost. Against all these interpretations, there is every reason to urge that Matthew identified the coming of the Son of man with the coming of the kingdom of God in its fullness. According to the First Gospel, when the Son of man comes, the angels will be sent forth, all people will be requited according to their deeds, and Jesus will sit on his throne; cf. 13.41; 16.27; 24.27–44; 25.31. This is the series of events to which 10.23 most likely refers.

The major objection to this interpretation is that it seemingly makes Matthew's Jesus a false prophet. Obviously the Son of man did not come in glory before the apostles completed their mission to Israel. But the supposed contradiction rests upon a questionable assumption, namely, that Matthew believed the mission to Israel to be completed. Our evangelist nowhere informs us that the apostles finished their work in Israel. Indeed, while the missionaries are commanded to go out (10.5–6), they are never said to return (contrast Mk 6.30; Lk 10.17). This striking circumstance is a clue to the reader. The mission to Israel, which began in the pre-Easter period, has never concluded. It continues – which is why the command to go to 'all nations' (28.19) includes Israel. Hence, the application of 10.23 to the *parousia* could not, from Matthew's perspective, result in an unfulfilled prophecy.

When they persecute you in one town, flee to the next. Cf. 23.34. There is here no eagerness for martyrdom. In contrast to the attitude of Ignatius and some Christian martyrs, the message of the kingdom is evidently to be preached even if it means that the missionaries are to flee as though they were cowards.

For amen I say to you, you will not have gone through all the towns of Israel before the Son of Man comes. One should flee because the coming of the Son of man is near. Cf. 24.22: God will shorten the days of eschatological tribulation for the sake of the elect. Whether 'the towns of Israel' includes the diaspora is not clear.

Disciple and Teacher, Servant and Master (10.24–5)

Taken with what comes before it, 10.24–5 declares the necessity of suffering: people persecuted the master, surely they will persecute his servants.

24. A disciple is not above his teacher. The sentiment may well have been proverbial.

nor a slave above his master. Cf. Jn 13.16. There is for our author no negative connotation to the idea of being a servant or slave. Jesus himself was a servant; cf. 20.28. Christian service is perfect freedom. Cf. Philo: 'To be the slave of God is the highest boast of man, a treasure more precious not only than freedom, but than wealth and power and all that mortals most cherish.'

25. Although never the teacher's equal, the disciple can aspire to be like the teacher, and the servant can aspire to be like the Lord. The theme is the imitation of Christ: Christians must follow Christ's example. It should be stressed, however, that in Matthew the idea is neither simplistic nor literal. Our author would hardly have commended the Cerinthians and Ebionites for using 10.25 to urge that, because Jesus was circumcised, Christians should be also. Matthew's text moves much more in the direction of the words attributed to Isaac the Syrian: 'If anyone should ask how to acquire humility, he would answer: "It is enough for the disciple to be as his master, and the servant as his lord." See how much humility was shown by Him who has given us this commandment and who gives us this gift; imitate Him and you will acquire it.'

If they have called the master of the house Beelzebul, how much more will they malign those of his household! Cf. 1 Pet 4.1. It is precisely because the disciples are members of the Christian household that they are persecuted.

Beelzebul is probably an ancient name for the Canaanite god Baal, the Lord of the heavens. In Ugaritic texts he is known as 'Exalted one, Lord of the earth'. In the NT, he is the prince of demons (cf. 12.24), the commander in charge of demonic hordes. In the *Testament of Solomon* he is said to have once been 'the highest-ranking angel in heaven' (6.1–2). This suggests identification with Satan, and its seems likely that by NT times 'Beelzebul' was one of Satan's several names, along with 'Asmodeus', 'Belial', and 'Mastemah'. (Dante identified Satan and Beelzebul: Milton did not.)

* * * * *

(i) Matthew's words to missionaries are permeated by eschatological motifs which show that Christian suffering belongs to the 'messianic woes' and will only be ended when – and this will be sooner rather than later – the Son of man comes on the clouds of heaven (10.16–23). All of this follows from a plain reading of the text and a knowledge of the eschatological expectations of Judaism and Christianity. For Matthew, the missionary endeavour takes place in the latter days, and the sufferings of Christian missionaries are to be interpreted as a manifestation of the birth pangs which herald the advent of God's new world.

(ii) The *imitatio Christi* runs like a bright thread throughout 10.5–25. The disciples, like Jesus, go only to the lost sheep of the house of Israel (10.5; 15.24). They preach the same message Jesus preached (10.7; cf. 4.17). They heal the sick, raise the dead, cleanse lepers, and cast out demons (10.8) – all of which Jesus did (8.2–4, 14–17, 28–34; 9.18–26). They wander from town to town, just like Jesus (10.11; cf. 4.23–5); and, like their master, they stay in the homes of others (10.11; cf. 8.14–16; 9.10?). The apostles also suffer like Jesus. They flee (see on 10.23), are delivered up before councils, are flogged, and are dragged before governors (10.17–19; cf. 26.57–27.31). They in addition are betrayed by those closest to them, which recalls the betrayal of Jesus by one of the twelve (10.21; cf. 26.47–56).

That Matthew was conscious of these parallels is clear from two facts. The first is 10.25, which concludes our section: it is enough for the disciple to be like the master. This makes the imitation of Christ explicit. Equally telling is the arrangement of chapters 5–10. Before the apostles are told what to say and do (10), the narrative recounts what Jesus said (5–7) and did (8–9). Thus 5–9 is the hermeneutical key to 10. The acts of the apostles are given meaning by the acts of Jesus. In him the Sermon on the Mount has become flesh. The Christian Lord is, for Matthew, the incarnation of proper Christian behaviour and therefore its model. His words and deeds supply an example that demands and fortifies at the same time.

THERE IS NO NEED TO FEAR (10.26–31)

[26]'So have no fear of them; for nothing is covered up that will not be revealed, and nothing hidden that will not be made known. [27]What I say to you in the dark, utter in the light; and what you hear whispered, proclaim from the housetops. [28]Do not fear those who kill the body but cannot kill the soul. Fear rather him who can destroy both soul and body in hell. [29]Are not two sparrows sold for a penny? Yet not one of them will

fall to the ground without your Father. [30]**And even the hairs of your head are all numbered.** [31]**So do not be afraid. You are of more value than many sparrows.'**

Parallels: Mk 4.22; Lk 8.17; 12.2–9

The primary function of 10.26–31 is manifest. The passage is surrounded on all sides by difficult commands and ominous prophecies. These are put in perspective by encouragement; cf. the function of 6.25–34 and 7.7–11. Despite rejection, persecution, and even the prospect of death, the true follower of Jesus need not fear. God is the sovereign Lord, and what befalls God's own must somehow be within the divine will. The course of discipleship may seem to be a mighty maze, but it is not without sense, even if that sense escapes human understanding. Beyond this, earthly life is not what ultimately matters, for it is temporal and to be swallowed up by the things of eternity. Gaining the whole world is nothing if it is followed by losing the world to come.

26. So have no fear of them. This line sets the theme: notwithstanding all appearances, there is no need to have fear or suffer despair. The imperative is repeated three times, which recalls the very similar threefold use of 'Do not worry' in 6.25–34.

for nothing is covered up that will not be revealed, and nothing hidden that will not be made known. Cf. Mk 4.22; Lk 8.17; 1 Cor 4.5 ('Therefore do not pronounce judgement before the time, before the Lord comes, who will bring to light the things now hidden in darkness and will disclose the purposes of the heart'). Jesus now backs off from the frightening scenes he has just painted and directs the mind's eye towards the grand eschatological future. He thereby puts everything in perspective and gives the true interpretation of the disciples' predicament. It is not just that 'time brings all to light'. Rather, on the last day God will see to it that the truth will be victorious. The eschatological judgement will be public and all lies exposed, so those on the side of the truth need have no fear.

27. Although that which is hidden will be revealed (v. 26), this is something the disciples should not simply wait for or expect. They themselves are called to bring it about proleptically, to make known the truth and those who belong to it. They do this by preaching.

What I say to you in the dark, utter in the light. Christian missionaries, no matter what situation they find themselves in, are not to keep quiet but must plainly declare all they have learned from and about Jesus. The gospel is not to be hid under a bushel. The truth must be fully served even now, even if its full revelation belongs only to the future. (The contrast between light and darkness is simply the contrast between the pre- and post-Easter periods.)

and what you hear whispered, proclaim from the housetops. Roofs were typically flat and used for various activities.

28. The subject now switches from eschatological revelation to the meaning of death. But the underlying thought remains the same: all is not what it appears to be. God's eschatological future will reveal the true meaning of earthly events.

Do not fear those who kill the body. A situation of possible martyrdom is presupposed. Cf. 4 Macc. 13.14 ('Let us not fear him who thinks he kills'); Sextus, *Sent.* 363b ('As a lion has power over the body of a sage, so too does a tyrant, but only over the body'); *T. Job* 20.3 (the devil has authority over Job's body, not his soul).

but cannot kill the soul. 'Soul' is here the disembodied soul which can survive bodily death and later be reunited with a resurrected body. The conception, whether due to the influence of Hellenism or whether a faithful continuation of OT thought, is 'dualistic'. Ambrose rightly conveys the sense: 'We do not fear him who can carry off our clothing, we do not fear him who can steal our property but cannot steal us.'

Fear rather him who can destroy both soul and body in hell. The disciples should fear God, not people, for only the former has any real power. Further, the fear of God will eliminate the fear of all else. As Augustine put it: 'Let us fear prudently that we may not fear vainly.'

Mention of the death of both body and soul in Gehenna may allude to the universal resurrection, when all, both good and evil, will stand before the throne of God; cf. Rev 20.11–15. See further 5.29–30, where the whole body goes into Gehenna. Most often in Matthew the punishment of the wicked is eternal. How then can Jesus here speak of their destruction? There are two possibilities. (i) The punishment of the wicked is said to be eternal because its results are eternal, not because the wicked consciously persist forever. (ii) There is no consistency because the purpose of the texts about hell is not to offer details about future states but rather to warn of dreadful consequences.

29. Mt 10.26–7 encourages by invoking eschatological revelation, 10.28 by calling to mind the deathless soul. Mt 10.29–31 next offers, by means of an *a fortiori* argument, a third means of consolation: God is sovereign, so whatever happens must, despite appearances, somehow be within God's will. 'Nothing happens without God' (Origen). This disallows the false supposition that God's will is done only in the future, as 10.26–8 might be taken to imply. The heavenly Father is not just the guarantor of the fantastic dream which is the eschatological future, but is also the sovereign Lord of the trying and mundane present.

Are not two sparrows sold for a penny? 'Penny' translates 'assarion', a small copper Roman coin worth about one-sixteenth of a denarius (a day's wage; cf. 20.1–16). Its lack of value was proverbial. Sparrows were part of the diet of the poor and were the cheapest of all the birds. For their insignificance see Ps 84.3.

Yet not one of them will fall to the ground without your Father. Cf. *Gen. Rab.* on 33.18: 'Not even a bird is caught without the will of heaven; how much less the soul of a son of man.' 'Without your Father' means 'without your Father's will'. 'On the earth' could be influenced by Amos 3.5: 'Does a bird fall in a snare on the earth when there is no trap for it?'

30. And even the hairs of your head are all numbered. The question, How many hairs does one's head have?, was probably proverbial and at home in Jewish wisdom; cf. *Apoc. Sed.* 8.6: 'Since I created everything, how many people have been born, and how many have died and how many shall die and how many hairs do they have?' Like so many Jewish wisdom texts which contrast God's omniscience with human ignorance through the naming of things only God can count, 10.30 implies that only God can count hairs ('are numbered' is the divine passive); cf. Ps 40.12; 69.4 and recall the biblical statements about 'the sands of the sea'. The effect is intellectual consolation. One may not understand the events that befall humanity and how they can be permitted by the divine will; but if one does not even know the number of concrete hairs on one's own mundane head, how can one presume to judge the Creator, who is beyond comprehension? 4 Ezra 4.10–11 puts it this way: 'You cannot understand the things with which you have grown up; how then can your mind comprehend the way of the Most High?' Similarly, 10.30 reminds readers that while believers may not understand the trying events that befall them and how such can be permitted by the divine will, comfort may be found in this: that God knows what human beings do not.

31. This verse does not exclude the prospect of martyrdom but rather implies that, if it comes, it will be in accord with God's will. Although God may not nip evil in the bud, ultimately good will out.

You are of more value than many sparrows. God who, in the words of St Basil the Great, 'lives in the highest and cares for the humblest', cares even for the sparrow. How much more deeply then must God feel for those made in the divine image? They must be of incomparable value.

* * * * *

(i) Mt 10.26–31 poses the problem of evil in a most acute fashion. A theodicy is first attempted by means of eschatology. What matters is not the pain of the present but one's fate in the world to come: 'Fear him who can destroy both soul and body in Gehenna'. But lest readers falsely infer that God's will is to be done only in the future, vv. 29–31, through the illustration of the sparrow and an argument *a fortiori*, assert that God is sovereign even now, so whatever happens must, despite all appearances, somehow be within the divine will. This, however, poses the unanswerable problem. How can God be sovereign Lord of this world with all its ills and wrongs? The question is responsible for the placement of v. 30. Perhaps proverbial, with the meaning that God's knowledge admits no rival, it has been inserted in order to qualify the eschatological solution to the problem of evil: that solution – which Matthew fully accepts – does not solve all the difficulties. One must, in the end, follow the path taken by Job and confess human inability to fathom the depths. God is a mystery and knows what creatures do not. In that should lie solace. 'But indeed all the hairs of your head are numbered.'

(ii) Mt 10.26–31 concerns itself neither with human integrity nor with the truth as such. The passage is instead an appeal to the handmaiden of faith's certainty, which is the imagination, the faculty that looks beyond the present to the future and beyond the temporal to the eternal. Faith judges the here and now by pondering what is to come (so vv. 26–8). It sets itself upon the divine outcome and from there surveys the ache and doubt and turmoil that history hands the faithful. And from that anticipated conclusion it gains boldness for the moment and confidence even in the face of death. Hope engenders freedom, above all freedom from fear. Furthermore, faith, seeing not 'with but through the eyes' (Blake), has the ability to see beneath the surface or face of the world (so vv. 29 and 31). One may never be able to 'find bottom in the uncomprehensive deeps' (cf. v. 30), but it is sometimes given to human beings to glimpse the heavenly in the earthly, which permits faith to make its unlikely extrapolation: God cares even for the sparrow. There is, then, no need to fear. The hand of God, although invisible, is always there.

CONFESSION, CONFLICT, COMPENSATION (10.32–42)

[32]'Everyone, then, who acknowledges me before others, I also will acknowledge him before my Father in heaven; [33]but whoever denies me before others, I also will deny him before my Father in heaven.

[34]'Do not think that I have come to bring peace on earth. I have not come to bring peace but a sword. [35]For I have come to set a man against his father, and a daughter against her mother, and a daughter-in-law against her mother-in-law; [36]and a person's enemies will be members of

his own household. [37]The one who loves father or mother more than me is not worthy of me, and the one who loves son or daughter more than me is not worthy of me. [38]And whoever does not take up his cross and follow me is not worthy of me. [39]The one who finds his life will lose it, and the one who loses his life for my sake will find it.

[40]'The one who receives you receives me, and the one who receives me receives the one who sent me. [41]The one who receives a prophet in the name of a prophet will receive a prophet's reward; and the one who receives a righteous person in the name of a righteous person will receive the reward of the righteous; [42]and whoever gives to one of these little ones even a cup of cold water because he is a disciple, amen I say to you: none of these will lose their reward.'

Parallels: Mk 8.34; 9.41; Lk 9.23; 10.16; 12.8–9, 51–3; 14.25–7; 17.33

The third portion of the second major discourse, which falls into three paragraphs (10.32–3, 34–9, 40–2), is distinguished by a total dearth of imperatives, even though imperatives are everywhere implicit. Every sentence describes either a particular circumstance or the consequence of a particular activity.

Confession and Denial before Others (10.32–3)

Matthew now returns to the task of exhortation. The demand is for courage. One must confess Jesus no matter the upshot. The motivation is eschatological consequences. One wants to pass, not flunk, the last assize.

32. This sayings alludes to Dan 7:13–14 and its context, for it (i) concerns the last judgement; (ii) speaks of the Son of Man (Daniel speaks of 'one like a Son of Man'); (iii) depicts this figure as being 'before' the divine court; and (iv) speaks to a situation of persecution.

Everyone, then, who acknowledges me before others. In chapter 10 the disciples are literally on trial: they appear in councils and synagogues and before governors and kings (cf. 10.17–20). So confession takes place in a court.

I also will acknowledge him before my Father in heaven. Readers will imagine Jesus sitting on a throne at the last judgement; cf. 19.28; 25.31–46.

33. Promise (v. 32) now gives way warning (v. 33).

But whoever denies me before others, I also will deny him before my Father in heaven. Peter's denial of Jesus before others later on disallows literalism here: repentance and forgiveness change the rules.

Verses 32–3 have very different meanings depending upon the

potential audience one assigns to them. If we envision Jesus' declaration as a general religious proposition, as something he could have uttered before a large Galilean audience, then it would entail that whoever accepts Jesus is saved, and that whoever does not accept him is not saved. Such a sweeping declaration of general import would be, one might fairly claim, a step toward Cyprian's unecumenical conviction that outside the church there is no salvation. One can, however, take the context of vv. 32–3 seriously and see them as instead part of the missionary discourse, as addressed to Jesus' co-workers. The verses then becomes a warning to disciples to stick to their task, an exhortation to loyalty – not something close to 'I am the way, the truth, and the life; no one comes to the Father but by me' (John 14:6).

Tribulation and Familial Division (10.34–9)

Mt 10.34–9 returns to two themes already introduced: eschatological tribulation and division within families. The effect is twofold. First, the eschatological context of suffering is emphasized, its inevitably within the end-time scenario established. Second, the priority of Jesus and his way over against all earthly ties, including the strongest, family ties, is inculcated.

Mt 10.34–6 is declarative, 10.37–9 paraenetic; and the one is the basis for the other. Vv. 34–6 set forth the character of Jesus' coming, which brings not peace but a sword; his arrival witnesses the fulfilment of the eschatological prophecy in Mic 7.6: enemies can be those of his own household. Vv. 37–9 then draw out the implications of vv. 34–6: one must not love father or mother more than Jesus and his cause. One must instead prepare to face domestic strife, to take up the cross, to lose one's life in this world.

34. Do not think that I have come to bring peace on earth. The time of eschatological peace, when the lion will lie down with the lamb (Isa 11.6), when swords will be beaten into ploughshares (Isa 2.4), when God will make a covenant of peace with Israel (Ezek 34.25), is not yet.

I have not come to bring peace but a sword. The sword signifies both personal strife and public persecution, and extends to the thought of martyrdom.

Mt 10.34 is about the proper interpretation of the present, and the main point is that the time of Jesus and his church is not, despite the presence of the kingdom, the messianic era of peace. It is instead the eschatological tribulation. Jesus has not come 'to turn the hearts of fathers to their children and the hearts of children to their fathers' (Mal 4.6). Rather, his coming coincides with the kingdom of heaven suffering violence. Utopia still belongs to the future. One is reminded of Paul's rebuke of the Corinthians: now is not the time to be filled or rich; the present is not the time for strength or honour. Rather is it the time for suffering, for hunger, for homelessness, for being reviled (1 Cor 4.8–13).

35. For I have come to set a man against his father, and a daughter against her mother, and a daughter-in-law against her mother-in-law. The lines takes up Mic 7.6, which was drawn upon to describe the discord of the latter days. *m. Sota* 9.15 reads as follows: with the footprints of the Messiah, 'children will shame the elders, and the elders will rise up before the children, for the son dishonours the father, the daughter rises up against her mother, the daughter-in-law against her mother-in-law: a man's enemies are those of his own house.' Similar statements are found elsewhere. The conviction that the great tribulation would turn those of the same household against one another was widespread. It follows that 10.35, like 10.34, comprehends the ministry of Jesus and the time of the church in terms of the eschatological woes. Jesus' appearance coincides with – or, rather, causes – a crisis that divides even the members of one household, separating the faithful from the unfaithful; cf. 1 Cor 11.18–19. So the eschatological trial, the time of the fulfilment of Mic 7.6, has broken in with the appearance of Jesus; and before the messianic age of peace establishes itself, all must pass through affliction and suffer pain; cf. Acts 14.22. As chaos and darkness came before the first creation, so division and strife must come before the second creation: the last things are as the first. Thus, for the present, conflict, not concord, reigns.

36. This line continues the quotation of Mic 7.6.

37. The subject now shifts slightly, from Jesus' effect upon families to what the disciple should do.

The one who loves father or mother more than me is not worthy of me, and the one who loves son or daughter more than me is not worthy of me. These words inevitably recall the command to honour father and mother in Exod 20.12 = Deut 5.16. Chrysostom, with reference to the Lukan parallel, which commands one to hate parents (Lk 14.26), asked, 'What then? Are not these things contrary to the Old Testament?' He answered: 'It is a sacred duty to render them [parents] all other honours; but when they demand more than is due, one ought not to obey ... [Jesus is] not commanding simply to hate them, since this were quite contrary to the law, but rather "When one desires to be loved more than I am, hate him in this respect".' This is correct interpretation. Although Jesus upholds the imperative to honour parents (15.4–6; 19.19), there is a hierarchy of demands. Just as the first part of the Decalogue, which concerns the honour due to God, precedes the second, which has to do with social relations, so too is it in the synoptics: discipleship to Jesus trumps parental obligation; cf. 4.18–22; 8.18–22.

38. The self-denial involved in sacrificing familial bonds when necessary is an instance of taking up one's cross and losing one's life in this world.

And whoever does not take up his cross and follow me is not worthy of me. Cf. 16.24. 'Cross' is in the first instance a vivid metaphor which stands for utter self abnegation. The disciples must voluntarily deny themselves (10.39); they must selflessly engage in Christian service – even if it ruins their families. Beyond this, the afflictions attendant upon self-denial will, in some cases, include suffering and death (cf. 10.17–25), with the result that the cross as metaphor may give way, as it did for Jesus, to the cross as literal object.

39. The one who finds his life will lose it, and the one who loses his life for my sake will find it. This is not a naïve declaration of present possibilities but an expression of eschatological hope. To lose one's life in this world is to win it in the world to come; to lose one's life in the world to come means that one has tried to win it in this world.

On Welcoming Missionaries (10.40–2)

The missionary discourse winds down with promissory words in which the disciples are not active but passive: they are received and served; contrast vv. 37–9. One is reminded of the opening section, 10.5–15, which also treats the reception of the gospel and its emissaries. Mt 10.40–2, however, broaches a theme absent from 10.5–15: namely, that of compensation. Those who welcome the eschatological messengers of Jesus in effect welcome Jesus himself and gain for themselves reward. With this thought, which makes the decision for or against the missionaries equivalent to the decision for or against Jesus, chapter 10 comes to its close.

40. It is hazardous to divine in 10.40–2 anything much about Matthean church order. Some have seen a descending gradation of offices: 'you' refers to the apostles, 'prophets' to itinerants, 'righteous people' to community leaders, 'little ones' to lay members. But the parallelism in 10.41 is probably synonymous parallelism: the prophet and righteous person are one and the same.

The one who receives you receives me. Cf. Jn 13.20. The words have two effects. To begin with, they magnify the apostolic mission. It is not just that the cause of Jesus and his demands live on in the Christian missionaries. Rather, behind the ever-changing faces of the preachers of the gospel is the Son of God himself, and behind him God the

Father. The authority of the exalted Jesus and his presence have been given to the disciples (cf. 28.16–20), with the result that they have become, to use a Pauline metaphor, members of his body. Master and servant are, in some sense, one. Second, if the missionaries are truly persuaded that those who receive them – reception involves both hospitality and faith in their message – truly receive Jesus, then it would hardly be thinkable to give up the missionary task, no matter how great its pains. The work, by its very nature, requires perseverance.

And the one who receives me receives the one who sent me. Cf. Jn 13.20 and *Mek.* on Exod 18.12: 'everyone who welcomes his fellow man is as though he had welcomed the Shekinah.'

41. The one who receives a prophet in the name of a prophet will receive a prophet's reward. The prophets are itinerant Christian teachers.

42. And whoever gives to one of these little ones even a cup of cold water because he is a disciple. 'Little ones' was probably a term Jesus applied to his disciples. He may have picked it up from apocalyptic circles (cf. Zech 13.7; *1 En.* 62.11; *2 Bar.* 48.19), but its precise background is unclear. The appellation could be a natural development of characterizing faithful Israelites as God's sons or children. Or it may have something to do with King David, who, despite being small (1 Sam 16.11) and the 'least' of his brethren (*LAB* 59.2), became the exalted king. In any case the appropriateness of 'little ones' on Jesus' lips cannot be missed. He stressed God's fatherhood, said positive things about children, promised that the lowly would be exalted, treated his disciples as those with much to learn, and knew that his followers were, by worldly standards, of little account.

Amen I say to you: none of these will lose their reward. The hospitable but hardly extraordinarily generous act of giving a cup of cold water to a hot and thirsty missionary simply because he is a missionary for Jesus brings reward. The thought, which focuses on one's motive, not the size of one's deed, fittingly closes chapter 10 by showing that even those who do not set out for the mission field can still participate in the Christian mission. By supporting the messengers of the gospel, they share in the great task that is the topic of chapter 10. In this way Matthew demonstrates his desire to make every part of his gospel relevant to every reader. Some might be tempted to pass over 10.1–42 on the grounds that it is addressed to missionaries only. But 10.42 is an invitation for all the faithful to involve themselves in whatever way they can with the apostolic mission. If the invitation is accepted, Mt 10 cannot but become meaningful even to those who stay at home.

* * * * *

(i) Mt 10.32–42 addresses topics already addressed by 10.5–25. For instance, the themes of familial division, eschatological trial, endurance in suffering, and the reception of missionaries are treated in both sections. It is for this reason that the concluding observations made in the commentary on 10.5–25 also apply, *mutatis mutandis*, to 10.32–42. Matthew's repetition, however, is hardly redundancy. Repetition is the key to learning, and if 10.32–42 reiterates previous paragraphs, it is because the evangelist is trying to underline without a pencil. Certain points need to be driven home, certain themes highlighted, certain lessons not forgotten. Now it is not coincidence that the majority of these points or themes or lessons common to 10.5–25 and 32–42 have to do with suffering and persecution. Matthew knows that the most troublesome side of his faith is the painful difficulties it brings – the persecution by authorities, the ridicule by friends, the disapproval by families. This is why 10.26–31 functions as it does to proffer comfort and encouragement. The same pastoral motivation also explains why 10.32–42 exhorts believers to make the good confession and warns them about the hatred that may come from those nearest to them. Suffering foreseen (cf. 10.34–6) is more easily endured, and pain is lessened when beyond it lies reward; cf. 10.32, 39.

(ii) There is a second notable way in which 10.32–42 makes a contribution beyond 10.5–25. The latter is explicitly addressed to itinerants, and it is largely specialized instruction: the missionary should do this, the missionary should do that. But, to state the obvious, not all Christians were missionaries, and concrete advice on where to go and not to go, on what to take and not to take, would not have been of self-evident relevance for many of Matthew's readers. So 10.5–25 would seem to have a smaller potential audience than, say, the Sermon on the Mount. Mt 10.32–42 is different. Although still ostensibly directed to the missionary, the whole section could be heeded equally by each and every believer. All must confess Jesus, take up the cross, and put faith above family. Thus 10.32–42 is, much more than 10.5–25, appropriate for everyone, without consideration of status or office. That Matthew was in fact concerned to make his discourse pertinent to all is shown by the very last verse: 'And whoever gives to one of these little ones even a cup of cold water only because he bears the name of Christ, truly I say to you, he will not lose his reward.' The 'little ones' are Christian missionaries, so 10.42 is not a word for them but for others – those who, although not itinerants, may, if they will, share in and further the Christian mission by supporting the heralds of the gospel. What the verse reveals, therefore, is Matthew's attention to the non-missionary. Such attention has helped form the entire section, beginning with 10.32. Although firstly addressed to the missionary, others are, in 10.32–42, hardly out of the picture.

THIS GENERATION: INVITATION AND RESPONSE (11.1–30)

11 [1]And it happened when Jesus had finished instructing his twelve disciples, that he went on from there to teach and to preach in their cities. [2]When John heard in prison about the deeds of the Christ, sending word by his disciples [3]he said to him, 'Are you the one who is to come, or should we expect another?' [4]And answering Jesus said to them, 'Go and tell John what you hear and see: [5]the blind receive their sight and the lame walk, the lepers are cleansed and the deaf hear, and the dead are raised and the poor have good news preached to them. [6]And blessed is the one who takes no offence at me.'

[7]As they were going away, Jesus began to speak to the crowds about John: 'What did you go out into the wilderness to see? A reed shaken by the wind? [8]But what then did you go out to see? A man dressed in soft robes? Behold, those who wear soft robes are in the houses of kings. [9]But what did you go out to see? A prophet? Yes, I tell you, and more than a prophet. [10]This is the one about whom it is written, "Behold, I am sending my messenger ahead of you, who will prepare your way before you." [11]Amen I say to you, among those born of women no one has arisen who is greater than John the Baptist; yet the least in the kingdom of heaven is greater than he. [12]From the days of John the Baptist until now the kingdom of heaven has suffered violence, and the violent take it by force. [13]For all the prophets and the law prophesied until John. [14]And if you are willing to accept it, he is Elijah, who is to come. [15]The one who has ears, let him hear!

[16]'But to what will I compare this generation? It is like children sitting in the marketplaces and calling to one another, [17]"We played the flute for you, and you did not dance; we wailed, and you did not mourn." [18]For John came neither eating nor drinking, and they say, "He has a demon." [19]The Son of Man came eating and drinking, and they say, "Behold, a glutton and a drunkard, a friend of toll-collectors and sinners!" Yet wisdom is vindicated by her deeds.'

[20]Then he began to upbraid the cities in which most of his deeds of power had been done, because they did not repent: [21]'Woe to you, Chorazin! Woe to you, Bethsaida! For if the deeds of power done in you had been done in Tyre and Sidon, they would have repented long ago in sackcloth and ashes. [22]But I say to you, on the day of judgement it will be more tolerable for Tyre and Sidon than for you. [23]And you, Capernaum, will you be exalted to heaven? No, you will be brought down to Hades.

For if the deeds of power done in you had been done in Sodom, it would have remained until this day. ²⁴But I say to you that it will be more tolerable on the day of judgement for the land of Sodom than for you.'

²⁵ At that time Jesus said, 'I thank you, Father, Lord of heaven and earth, because you have hidden these things from the wise and the intelligent and have revealed them to infants. ²⁶Yes, Father, for such was your gracious will. ²⁷All things have been handed over to me by my Father; and no one knows the Son except the Father, and no one knows the Father except the Son, and anyone to whom the Son chooses to reveal him. ²⁸Come to me, all you who are weary and are heavy laden, and I will give you rest. ²⁹Take my yoke upon you, and learn from me; for I am meek and lowly in heart, and you will find rest for your souls. ³⁰For my yoke is easy, and my burden is light.'

Parallels: Mk 1.2; Lk 7.18–35; 10.12–15, 21–2; Jn 3.35; 10.15; 13.3; 17.2, 25, 29

Mt 11.2–20 considers the relationship of Jesus and John. Mt 11.21–4 illustrates the apparent failure of Jesus' mission. Mt 11.25–30 introduces his real success.

The Baptist's Question (11.1–6)

Following a transitional sentence (11.1), Matthew relates a pronouncement story which looks back on the whole of Jesus' public ministry to date.

1. This verse simultaneously concludes the preceding discourse and resubmerges the reader in the narrative flow.

And it happened when Jesus had finished instructing his twelve disciples. Cf. 7.28; 13.53; 19.1; 26.1. 'The twelve disciples' creates an *inclusio* with 10.1.

he went on from there to teach and to preach in their cities. It is odd, immediately following Jesus' charge to the twelve, to read that he 'went on from there to teach and to preach in their cities'. The disciples' pre-Easter mission is never recounted, and they do not make another appearance until chapter 12. The omission is striking and has called forth several explanations. For some, the focus on Christology simply overshadows all else. For others, the disciples have in fact been sent out and are still away: this is why they are not mentioned in chapter 11. Another possibility is this: while the missionaries are commanded to go out (10.5–6), they are never said to return because such a notice might lead to seeing in 10.23 an unfulfilled prophecy and further be wrongly taken to imply an end to the Jewish mission.

2–3. John the Baptist, though in prison, hears about 'the deeds of the Christ'. His curiosity is piqued, and he sends messengers to Jesus. His question must reflect waning faith, for John has already perceived Jesus' identity (3.13–17).

When John heard in prison about the deeds of the Christ. 'The deeds of the Christ' (cf. 11.19) are defined in 11.4 as what has been heard and seen and described in 11.5 as healing and preaching; so the phrase refers back not only to the miracle chapters, 8–9, but also to the Sermon on the Mount, 5–7; and it interprets both Jesus' authoritative words and his mighty deeds as messianic. So the phrase is comprehensive and summarizes the content of 4.23ff. Even chapter 10 is included insofar as the disciples' words and deeds are in effect a re-enactment or continuation of their master's words and deeds. In sum, 11.2 makes a closure (4.23–11.2) and prepares for the following chapters, whose theme is the response of people to 'the deeds of the Christ'.

Are you the one who is to come, or should we expect another? Jesus' deeds do not match those of the somewhat judgemental figure portrayed by John in Mt 3.10–12.

It is surprising enough that the John who, in 3.14, confesses his need to be baptized by Jesus, now asks about the Coming One. But matters are even more problematic if the emphatic testimony given by the Baptist to Jesus in Jn 1 be taken into account. One can understand why Christian exegetes have traditionally not been able to accept 11.2 at face value. Tertullian was the exception. According to him, John's doubts were genuine. Most of the Fathers convinced themselves that John was inquiring for the sake of his disciples. Others have held that John asked in order to lure Jesus into making a public declaration, or that John did not doubt Jesus' identity but only his way of manifesting himself.

5. Borrowing the language of several passages in Isaiah (cf. 26.19; 29.18; 35.5–6; 42.7, 18; 61.1), Jesus answers John by calling attention to the marvellous events that have been happening: the blind see, the lame walk, and so on. The list consists of six items which are, in typical Matthean fashion, arranged in three pairs: a and b, c and d, and e and f. (Luke has the six items but not the triad.) The reader's thought inevitably turns back to what has gone before. Jesus heals blind men in 9.27–31. He cures a lame man in 9.1–8. A leper is cleansed in 8.1–4. A deaf man regains his hearing in 9.32–4. Mt 9.18–26 recounts a resurrection. And 4.17, 23; 5.3; 9.35; and 10.7 record preaching to the poor. Our gospel is arranged so that the various threads of chapters 4–10 are woven together in 11.2–6. The passage thus interprets 4–10 as a whole: Jesus is the Coming One of John's preaching, the Messiah of prophecy who, through his proclamation to the poor and his miraculous and compassionate deeds, brings to fulfilment the messianic oracles uttered so long ago by Isaiah the prophet. All of 4–10 is prophecy come to pass.

The influence of the Isaianic texts upon 11.5 is not confined to the vocabulary: it extends to the very form or structure of the sentence. Isa 29.18–19; 35.5–10; and 61.1–2 are lists. So is Mt 11.5.

4Q521 2 + 4 ii 12 (4QMessianic Apocalypse) contains a fascinating parallel: '[for the heav]ens and the earth will listen to his Messiah, [and all] that is in them will not turn away from the holy precepts ... For the Lord will observe the devout, and call the just by name, and upon the poor he will place his spirit, and the faithful he will renew with his strength. For he will honour the devout upon the throne of eternal royalty, releasing prisoners, giving sight to the blind, lifting up those who are bowed down. Ever shall I cling to those who hope. In his mercy he will jud[ge,] and from no one will the fruit [of] good [deeds] be delayed, and the Lord will perform marvellous acts such as have not existed, just as he sa[id], for he will heal the badly wounded and will make the dead live, he will proclaim good news to the meek, give lavishly [to the needy], lead the exiled and enrich the hungry [...] and all [...].' Although this list in 4Q521 is far from identical to the recitation of Jesus' deeds in Matthew, it does appear that phrases from Isa 61:1–2 were sometimes used to paint a picture of eschatological fulfilment.

the blind receive their sight and the lame walk. Cf. Isa 61.1; also 29.18; 35.5; and 42.7, 18. 'The lame walk' alludes to Isa 35.6: 'the lame man will leap like a hart.'

the lepers are cleansed and the deaf hear. Cf. Isa 35.5: 'The ears of the deaf unstopped.' There is no mention of lepers in Isaiah. Perhaps one is to infer that Jesus' works go even beyond what the OT anticipates. Or maybe an Elisha typology lies in the background; cf. 2 Kgs 5.

and the dead are raised and the poor have good news preached to them. 'The dead are raised' probably alludes to Isa 26.19 ('thy dead shall live, their bodies shall rise'). 'And the poor have good news preached to them' draws upon LXX Isa 61.1. The proclamation to the poor comes at the end because it gives meaning to – that is, interprets – the miracles done by Jesus. Moreover, the miracle that heals only the body does not accomplish as much as the word that heals mind and heart and brings eschatological salvation.

John has, according to v .2, already heard of 'the deeds of the Christ'. What then is the function of v. 5? Being a summary of what is already known to both John and the reader, is it not superfluous? The answer is no, for the verse contains more than a list of miracles: it also supplies a hermeneutical suggestion. Jesus' language directs one to Isaiah and is therefore an invitation to put Jesus' ministry and Isaiah's oracles side by side.

6. And blessed is the one who takes no offence at me. Exactly why John might be offended is not stated, although one thinks first of the discord between Jesus and popular messianic expectation.

'Blessed is the one who takes no offence at me' makes explicit the christological presupposition of 11.5: the works of eschatological salvation are being done through the speaker; neither those works nor the good news he preaches can be separated from him. Recognition of Jesus makes one blessed.

Jesus' Testimony to the Baptist (11.7–15)

This passage opens with Jesus asking three questions. The first question (v. 7c) is answered by another (v. 7d). The other two questions (vv 8a, 9a) are answered initially by a question (vv. 8b, 9b), then by a clarifying declaration (vv. 8c, 9c). Because the second clarifying declaration (v. 9c) identifies John as 'more than a prophet', the way is cleared for a precise statement of John's identity. Four points are made. John is the figure foretold by Mal 3.1 (v. 10); he is the greatest of those born among women (v. 11); he is the turning point in salvation-history (vv. 12–13); and he is Elijah (v. 14).

7. As they were going away. When John's followers exit the stage the scene changes, as does the subject of the discourse. The crowd appears (v. 7b) and the question is no longer, Who is Jesus? but rather, Who is John?

What did you go out into the wilderness to see? One wonders whether the crowds in the wilderness are intended to evoke messianic expectation; cf. 24.26.

A reed shaken by the wind? The meaning probably is that the people did not go to the Jordan banks to gaze upon an everyday sight; cf. Job 40.21; Isa 19.6; 35.7. One should not, however, altogether exclude another possibility. To one steeped in the Hebrew OT, the image of reeds blown by the wind might have recalled Exod 14–15, where God sends forth a strong wind to drive back the Sea of Reeds. The meaning of Jesus' query would then be: Did you go into the wilderness to see a man repeat the wonders of the exodus? Certainly people at a later time did just that, as we know from Josephus.

A man dressed in soft robes? John, of course, wore camel's hair and a leather girdle. The point is that when people went to see him they were not expecting to feast their eyes upon worldly splendour. (Some would see an implicit depreciation of Herod's courtiers.)

9. A prophet? Cf. 21.26; Lk 1.76: John is a 'prophet of the Most High'. In the first century, the word 'prophet' was plastic. It could refer to one able to tell the future or to one who, like the biblical prophets, interpreted the contemporary social-political situation, usually with an emphasis upon God's judgement. 'Prophet' could also call to mind certain eschatological figures: either Elijah or the prophet-like Moses. And from Josephus we learn about men such as Theudas, the Egyptian, and others – self-proclaimed prophets – who led large movements and sought to perform acts of deliverance similar to those performed by Moses and Joshua. John was no doubt thought of by many as a prophet in several or all of these senses.

Yes, I tell you, and more than a prophet. John is not only a prophet but himself the object of prophecy, for he is the messenger foretold by Malachi, Elijah (11.10, 14).

10. Behold, I am sending my messenger ahead of you. LXX Exod 23.20 agrees exactly with Matthew. LXX Mal 3.1 is similar: 'Behold, I will send out my messenger.' In the OT, Exod 23.20 refers not to Moses but to God's angel, who led Israel safely to the promised land. So when the text is applied in the NT to eschatological preparation, one inevitably sees a typology: entrance into the kingdom is like the entrance into Canaan.

who will prepare your way before you. Cf. Mk 1.2. Dependence upon LXX Mal 3.1 seems unlikely. The Hebrew is a more likely source for our line.

11. Amen I say to you, among those born of women no one has arisen who is greater than John the Baptist; yet the least in the kingdom of heaven is greater than he. Mt 11.7–11a heaps praise upon John the Baptist, making him indeed the greatest among those born of women – and then v. 11b turns round and makes him less than the least. In this way his greatness, which is no longer the subject, becomes a foil for the surpassing greatness of the kingdom.

The meaning of v. 11b is disputed. The problem concerns 'the least in the kingdom of heaven'. The options include: (i) Jesus, with reference to his humility, to his being younger than John, or to his being John's disciple, is speaking of himself: he is the least. Chrysostom, while observing that some identified 'the least' with angels or the apostles, adopts this interpretation and writes of Jesus' 'condescension'. (ii) 'The least in the kingdom' means 'anyone now in the kingdom of heaven'. This understanding, which excludes John from the present kingdom, is the most popular with modern commentators. In some of the Fathers it is combined with NT texts according to which Christians are born not of the flesh but of God, which makes a contrast with John, who was only 'born of woman'.

(iii) 'The least in the kingdom of heaven' really means 'anyone in the kingdom of heaven (when it comes)'. On this view, which has the most to commend it, Jesus is contrasting the least in the future kingdom with the greatest of all before the kingdom. In other words: 'the least in the kingdom will be greater than the greatest is now'. This interpretation does not exclude John from the kingdom.

12. From the days of John the Baptist until now the kingdom of heaven has suffered violence, and the violent take it by force. This is one of the NT's great conundrums. The differences between the two canonical versions reveal that, even at the beginning, Matthew and Luke probably found contrary meaning in Jesus' words. Clearly any interpretation will have to be offered with appropriate modesty. But one good possibility is that the line evokes the expectation of the eschatological tribulation: the suffering of John and of the saints after him is interpreted in terms of the messianic woes, the eschatological tribulation of the latter days. In other words, the great redemption must be preceded by a conflict between the forces of good and the forces of evil, and this conflict has already been joined, from the days of John the Baptist until now.

13. For all the prophets and the law prophesied until John. Many have detected in 11.13 a denigration of the law. Indeed, it has been common for Christian interpreters to assume that Jesus was implicitly abolishing the authority of Moses when he said that 'the law and the prophets were until John'. According to Tertullian, the burdens of the law ceased with John; and in another place the same author informs us that some early Christians used our verse as reason for disregarding OT legislation. Now the presence of the kingdom does, in Matthew, displace the Mosaic law from centre stage: the Torah is no longer the criterion for salvation. But this in itself involves neither abolition of Moses nor any sort of antinomianism. Mt 11.12–13 is about the kingdom, not the law and the prophets. So 'the law and the prophets prophesied until John' is simply another way of saying that the kingdom of God has entered the present. One dispensation has given way to another. What that means for the Mosaic Torah is an open question not answered by 11.12–13. For that one must read the rest of the Gospel.

14. This draws out the implication of the citation in 11.10 and discloses what Matthew thinks is most important about John: he is Elijah *redivivus*.

And if you are willing to accept it does not convey doubt or hesitation or unimportance. Nor are the words an appeal for faith or a call to take especial care. The conditional indicates either that what Jesus is about to say is new or that not all accept its truth.

he is Elijah, who is to come. Cf. 17.12–13. The words would almost certainly have sent Matthew's readers back to Malachi's paragraph about Elijah (Mal 3.23). This is fitting. If 11.12–13 says that the old dispensation of the law and the prophets concluded with John, 11.14 conjures up the final passage in the prophetic corpus.

Some early Christians used 11.14 as one of their proof texts for reincarnation. Matthew, one is confident, would not have accepted their interpretation. For one thing, Elijah, according to Jewish tradition, had not died but ascended. For another, reincarnation was foreign to early Jewish tradition. How then did Matthew understand the equation, John = Elijah? Given that stories about the Baptist's infancy seem to have circulated in the early church (cf. Lk 1–2), the First Evangelist is not likely to have thought of a man descending from heaven. Perhaps, then, he thought of the Baptist as holding Elijah's *office*, so that John came 'in the spirit and power of Elijah'; cf. Lk 1.17.

15. The one who has ears, let him hear! This imperative, which is found often in the Jesus tradition, apparently floated from one context to another. It typically functions as a hermeneutical warning and/or to mark the conclusion of a paragraph or other literary unit. Here the words serve notice that one subsection (11.7–15) has ended and that another (11.16–19) is about to begin. The phrase harks back to those prophetic texts which refer to people who have ears but hear not (Isa 6.9; Jer 5.21; Ezek 12.2). The point is that it takes more than an ear in order to hear with understanding. What is required is inner attention, concentration, discernment. Words, unless heeded, go in one ear and out the other.

'To What Shall I Liken This Generation?' (11.16–19)

With this paragraph Matthew closes the discussion on John the Baptist. There is logic in the arrangement. The identity of Jesus (11.2–6) makes his estimation of John (11.7–15) authoritative. So the reader has been confronted first by the truth about Jesus and then by the truth about John. What then follows is a record of how their contemporaries responded to them.

16. But to what will I compare this generation? 'This generation' is a technical term referring neither to the Jewish people nor to humanity in general but to Jesus' or Matthew's contemporaries, their 'generation'. The expression has its roots in the OT, where the generation in the wilderness is called 'faithless', 'evil', 'sinful', 'perverse', and 'crooked'; cf. Deut 1.35; 32.5, 20. In the rabbis that particular generation came to be seen, along with the generation of the flood, as especially corrupt. This is the spirit in which 'this generation' is used in the gospels. The term refers firstly not to chronological duration but to character, and it is pejorative. Further, Lk 17.22–37 and Mt 24.34–44 compare Jesus' time with the days of Noah, and the vocabulary used in Mk 8.38; 9.19; 12.39; and Mt 17.17 = Lk 9.41 is clearly taken from OT descriptions of the generation in the wilderness; cf. Deut 1.35; 32.5, 20. So a typological perspective informs the synoptic usage. Jesus' contemporaries are like the generation of the flood in so far as God's judgement fell – unexpectedly – upon the one and will fall – unexpectedly – upon the other. And Jesus' contemporaries are like the generation of the wilderness in that just as God's mighty acts of salvation did not prevent grumbling and rebellion in the wilderness, so is it with Jesus' deeds and his generation. What distinguishes the NT usage is its christological context: it is the rejection of Jesus that makes 'this generation' so sinful.

It is like children sitting in the marketplaces and calling to one another. Children play games in which girls on flutes invite boys to dance the wedding dance and in which wailing boys call upon girls to sing a funeral dirge. But the boys do not respond to the flutes, nor the girls to the wailing. Both groups refuse to play the game. This brings the response: 'We played the flute for you, and you did not dance; we wailed and you did not mourn.' In what way does this parallel the situation of John and Jesus? Most commentators, identifying the children who call with John and Jesus, have put forward some such interpretation as this: John, the ascetic and herald of judgement, called for mourning and repentance. Jesus announced joy and the presence of the kingdom and invited others to enter it with him. Both invitations fell upon deaf ears. Instead of repenting or rejoicing, people chose to ignore God's messengers. So it did not matter how or in what guise God made appeal.

There are serious problems with this understanding of our parable. (i) Mt 11.16 likens 'this generation' to the children who play and wail, not their audience. (ii) 'We played the flute for you and you did not dance' (usually taken to refer to Jesus) comes before 'We wailed and you did not mourn' (usually taken to refer to John). Yet John made his appeal before Jesus appeared. (iii) The parallelism between 11.17 and 18–19 naturally inclines one to associate John with the first line, 'We played the flute for you and you did not dance', Jesus with the second line, 'We wailed and you did not mourn'. (iv) The children who complain in v. 17 are like those who speak their complaint in vv. 18 and 19 ('He has a demon', 'Behold, a glutton ...'). For these reasons, then, one may identify the piping and wailing children with 'this generation'. The contemporaries of John and Jesus are like disagreeable children who complain that others will not act according to their desires and expectations. When the Baptist came neither eating nor drinking but sternly demanded repentance in sackcloth and ashes, people instead wanted to play at making merry: 'We played the flute for you and you did not dance.' When Jesus came, preaching good news and entering into joyous fellowship with others, people demanded that he fast (cf. 9.14–17) and exclude 'sinners' from his company: 'We wailed and you did not mourn'.

18. For John came neither eating nor drinking. 'Neither eating nor drinking' is not to be taken literally. It is simply the antithesis of 'eating and drinking', a phrase which connotes carefree excess; cf. Isa 22.13; Mt 24.38, 49; 1 Cor 15.32.

and they say, 'He has a demon'. Nowhere else do we learn that John was thought by some to be possessed. Yet the charge is historically likely. Jesus himself was similarly smeared (cf. 12.22–32), and the Baptist's ragged appearance and unconventional behaviour would have been consistent with a diagnosis of possession.

19. The Son of Man came eating and drinking, and they say, 'Behold, a glutton and a drunkard'. The language recalls Deut 21.18–22, a passage containing legislation regarding a rebellious son who disobeys parents.

a friend of toll-collectors and sinners! Cf. 9.11. It may be that 'glutton and drunkard' stands in synthetic parallelism with 'friend of toll-collectors and sinners'. If the first phrase has in view Jesus' well-known habit of holding festive table-fellowship, the second could refer to the disreputable company typically imagined to participate.

Yet wisdom is vindicated by her deeds. If, as it appears, the deeds of Sophia are the deeds of the Messiah (11.2), then the text identifies Jesus with Wisdom. So it is Jesus who is vindicated by his works. What does that mean? Despite the poor response of people, the works of God in Jesus have made plain to all his identity (cf. 11.2–6) and the need to respond to him favourably. If people will disbelieve (cf. the following pericope, 11.20–4), that is not Wisdom's fault, that is not Jesus' doing: the blame lies with those who have ears but do not hear. Were Wisdom to be brought to trial with the crime of not stirring Israel to faith, she would be acquitted. Her works, that is, Jesus' works, exonerate her by bearing testimony to her labour for others.

Woes on the Cities of Galilee (11.20–4)

The woes belong to a large complex whose theme is the decision for or against Jesus. Thus 11.20–4 carries forward the disappointment registered at the end of 11.16–19, a unit whose subject is the rejection of John and Jesus by 'this generation'; and it makes for a contrast with the following pericope, which concerns those who accept Jesus (11.25-30).

20. Then he began to upbraid the cities in which most of his deeds of power had been done, because they did not repent. 'Deeds of power' recalls the 'deeds' of 11.2 and 19 and refers to sensational, supernatural events which have religious meaning and merit a religious response. The 'cities' are obviously Jewish cities (cf. 10.5-6) and the subject is *Jewish* rejection of Jesus. Since Jesus himself called for repentance (4.17), those who fail to repent are guilty of disobedience to him.

21. What follows is, in Bengel's words, 'a prelude to the last judgement'.

Woe to you, Chorazin! Woe to you, Bethsaida! Whereas 'woe to me' or 'woe to us' expresses fear or anguish, woes not in the first person convey a threat or warning.

Chorazin, which is to be identified with the ruins called Khirbet Kerâzeh, two miles from Capernaum, is mentioned only here in the NT. Bethsaida (= 'house of the fisher'), a city located close to the northern tip of the Sea of Galilee and identified today with the ruins of et-Tell, is named nowhere else in Matthew. Our evangelist has done nothing to make the reader ready for mention of the two cities. He has not, for example, told us of any miracles done in those two places; nor has he told us that some of Jesus' disciples hailed from Bethsaida; cf. Jn 1.44; 12.21.

For if the deeds of power done in you had been done in Tyre and Sidon, they would have repented long ago in sackcloth and ashes. Tyre and Sidon were both important coastal cities on the Mediterranean. In Isa 23 the former is denounced in a prophetic oracle, and in Ezek 28 both are rebuked and the certainty of divine judgement upon them is proclaimed. Thereafter it evidently became common for the two cities, which were thought of as arrogant centres of wealth, to be spoken of together – like Sodom and Gomorrah – and sometimes in warnings of judgement; cf. Jer 25.22; 27.3; 47.4; Joel 3.4; Zech 9.1-4.

'Sackcloth' is a dark (cf. Rev 6.12) haircloth used as a garment of mourning and penitence; cf. 2 Kgs 19.2; Jon 3.5. 'Ashes' were also an element in mourning rituals; cf. 2 Sam 13.19; Job 42.6; Jer 25.34. The combination 'sackcloth and ashes' became a fixed phrase betokening sincerity; cf. Esra 4.3; Isa 58.5; Dan 9.3.

The declaration in 11.21 gains force because, while Chorazin and Bethsaida were Jewish cities, Tyre and Sidon were not. So Jesus, with the hyperbole of a prophet, is exclaiming that Jews failed to respond to phenomena which would have persuaded even pagans – and, what is more, even notoriously wicked pagans.

22. But I say to you, on the day of judgement it will be more tolerable for Tyre and Sidon than for you. Having delivered the indictment (v. 21), Jesus now utters the verdict. Cf. 10.15, where Jesus avows that it will be easier for Sodom and Gomorrah on the day of judgement than for the city that rejects the apostles.

23. And you, Capernaum, will you be exalted to heaven? The line alludes to Isa 14.13, although verbal agreement with the Greek is lacking: 'You (the king of Babylon) said in your heart: I will ascend to heaven.' Capernaum (cf. 4.13; 8.14) is, according to Matthew, Jesus' 'own city' (9.1). This makes its lack of repentance all the more terrible, and also proves the truth of the proverb: 'A prophet is not without honour except in his own country' (13.57). Yet note that Jesus' harsh words do not prevent him from returning to Capernaum; see 17.24.

The commentators have discussed at some length the meaning of 'will you be exalted to heaven?' Most have thought of Jesus' presence: he exalted Capernaum by residing there. Others have referred the expression to the city's geographical situation, to its prosperity, or to its pride. Of the various proposals, the last has the most to commend it, for pride is the subject in Isa 14.13. Even this, however, may read too much into the text. The phrase under discussion might be wholly rhetorical; that is, Capernaum's exaltation may not be concrete but rather hypothetical, serving simply to introduce her abasement.

No, you will be brought down to Hades. This is from Isa 14.15. 'Hades' is used by Matthew only two times, in 11.23 and 16.18. The word frequently translates *sheol* in the LXX and its first meaning is 'netherworld', the place where the dead reside. But by the first century 'Hades' seems to have merged, at least in some minds, with 'Gehenna', the place of damnation and punishment for the wicked. In 11.23, however, 'Hades' is not, any more than the 'heaven' of the same verse, to be taken literally. It functions rather as part of a figure of speech. So far from scaling the heights, Capernaum is poised for a catastrophic fall and the deepest abasement.

For if the deeds of power done in you had been done in Sodom, it would have remained until this day. On Sodom see 10.15. Perhaps 'would have remained until this day' alludes to Sodom's complete obliteration.

In the first century Sodom was no longer a city. Tyre and Sidon, on the other hand, although they had in the past been sacked and burned to the ground, were still inhabited; cf. Acts 12.20; 21.3. One wonders, then, whether 11.20–4 does not intentionally bring together the living wicked and the wicked dead.

24. But I say to you that it will be more tolerable on the day of judgement for the land of Sodom than for you. We can be fairly certain that Jesus first preached his gospel in the hope that he would be heard and heeded. He can hardly have launched a mission and sent forth messengers fully persuaded that all the effort would be wasted and that 'this generation' would by and large disbelieve him. What follows? When Jesus' preaching and mighty deeds did not generate a corporate repentance, disappointment must have been acute. The presumption is confirmed by 11.21–4. The text is a testimony to dashed expectations. Chorazin and Bethsaida and Capernaum are condemned because something was expected of them, something which they failed to produce. Mt 11.21–3 is a witness not only to unbelief but to a belief undone. The pathos the passage conveys has its source in the distance between promise and fulfilment, and the sound it records is that of the waves of hope crashing against the hard rocks of uncooperative reality.

The Great Thanksgiving (11.25–30)

The thematic connexion between 11.25–30 ·and 11.2–24 is clear enough. Mt 11.2–19 culminates in a parable about the rejection of John and Jesus, and 11.20–4 declares judgement against Galilean cities for their failure to repent. Mt 11.25–30 continues the theme of response. Its three stanzas, however, go beyond the refrain of failure. Rejection is not the whole story. If 'this generation' does not follow John and Jesus, and if Chorazin and Bethsaida and Capernaum do not acknowledge Jesus' miracles, there are still the 'infants' who perceive what is happening.

In 11.19 Jesus is Wisdom. The same equation is apparently implicit in the present passage. There are, in any case, some very intriguing parallels between the Jesus of 11.25–30 and Sophia in Wisdom literature. Only the Father knows the Son, just as only God knows Wisdom (Job 28.12–27; Ecclus 1.6–9; Bar 3.32). Only the Son knows the Father, just as only Wisdom knows God (Wisd 8.4; 9.1–18). Jesus makes known hidden revelation, just as Wisdom reveals divine secrets (Wisd 9.1–18; 10.10). And if Jesus invites others to take up his yoke and find rest, Wisdom issues precisely the same call: Ecclus 51.23–30; cf. Prov 1.20–3; 8.1–36; Ecclus 24.19–22.

The primary background of 11.25–30 is, however, in traditions about Moses. The declaration about Father and Son knowing each other is grounded in Exod 33.12–13, where God knows Moses and Moses prays that he might know God. The promise of rest in 11.28 is modelled upon Exod 33.14. Further, in deeming himself to be 'meek' (v. 29), Jesus is taking up a chief characteristic of Moses (see Num 12.3); and in referring to his 'yoke' (v. 29) he is using a term often applied to the law which was given through Moses. Thus what we have in Mt 11.25–30 is a presentation of Jesus in Mosaic colours; and it is the similarities as well as the differences between the Messiah and the lawgiver which clarify the text's meaning.

25. Following 11.20–4 one might expect a complaint. Jesus instead offers a prayer of thanksgiving. Like the prayer in Jn 11.41–2, it is uttered aloud for the sake of those standing nearby.

I thank you, Father, Lord of heaven and earth. 'I thank you' covers the entirety of 11.25–30. It would hardly be prudent to restrict the compass to the hiding of revelation from the wise and understanding. Jesus offers thanks for the giving and hiding of revelation, for the knowledge given to the Son, and for the possibility of rest.

because you have hidden these things from the wise and the intelligent and have revealed them to infants. God has, in effect, 'made wise the simple' (Ps 19.7). Cf. Wisd 10.21 ('because wisdom opened the mouth of the dumb, and made the tongues of babes speak clearly') and Ecclus 3.19 (v. 1: 'Many are lofty and renowned, but to the meek he reveals his secrets').

'The wise and intelligent' also appear together in Isa 29.14 and 1 Cor 1.19. One is to think of the worldly wise, people of secular sophistication who, though seemingly sagacious, are yet far from wisdom. Already in the OT there is a tendency to use 'wise' and 'understanding' in pejorative contexts: it is recognized that those who profess to be devoted to Wisdom often neglect her, and that they are sometimes the most insensitive of all (Job 5.13; Isa 5.21). As for the present verse, Matthew may well have thought of the scribes and Pharisees in particular (so Chrysostom) – and of the 'infants', conversely, as those unlearned in Torah. This would fit well with v. 27: Jesus has his own tradition which is not that of the scribes and Pharisees.

Verse 25 may well be based upon Isa 29.14, a verse Paul quotes in 1 Cor 1.19: 'the wisdom of their wise will perish, and the discernment of their discerning will be hid.' But the thought is common enough in Jewish texts. Revelation does not come to all. It comes only to those who have prepared themselves to receive it – to the pure in heart and the poor in spirit; cf. Job 28.28; Ps 25.14. This is because religious knowledge is a function of being and has a moral dimension. Such knowledge can not be grasped by either dispassionate or neutral observers. In Paul's words, spiritual things are only discerned by the spiritual (1 Cor 2.14–15); or, in the Johannine idiom, only those who love God can know God; cf. 1 Jn 4.8. While knowledge, like wealth, may 'puff up' (1 Cor 8.1), finding God requires the annihilation of pride. And in any case, 'if you understand it, it is not God' (Augustine).

Strength of mind then does not guarantee spiritual knowledge; cf. 1 Cor 1.20–1. As with so much else, so too is it here true that the first shall be last, the last first. (Our text, one must add, scarcely extols stupidity. There is in it no criticism of intellectuals as such, only of the proud and arrogant. Piety is not ignorance, faith is not obscurantism. Recall especially that the parables challenge understanding.)

26. Yes, Father, for such was your gracious will. Cf. 1 Cor 1.21: 'For since, in the wisdom of God, the world did not know God through wisdom, it pleased God through the folly of what we preach to save those who believe.'

27. This makes explicit the christological dimensions of 11.25–6: the revelation to 'infants' has come through Jesus.

All things have been handed over to me by my Father. Cf. 28.18; Jn 3.35 ('the Father loves the Son and has given all things into his hand'). 'All things' refers firstly to the 'these things' of 11.25; but it goes beyond that to include the whole revelation of God in Jesus. Embodied in Jesus are the eschatological truths which heretofore have only been longed for in prophecy. This means, to speak concretely, that the First Gospel, which purports to be a record of Jesus' words and deeds, itself by implication lays claim to being revelatory. That is, in so far as Jesus makes known the truth, Matthew's gospel is, on its own terms, a vehicle of eschatological revelation.

and no one knows the Son except the Father, and no one knows the Father except the Son. The Father acknowledges, takes account of, and concerns himself with the Son; the Son acknowledges, takes account of, and concerns himself with the Father. Thus they know each other.

It is a bit peculiar to read that 'no one knows the Son except the Father'. Perhaps it is assumed – as in 16.13–20 and Gal 1.15–16 – that the identity or nature of the Son can only be known through divine revelation. Or perhaps the words in question are rhetorical over-statement, occasioned by the need to balance 'no one knows the Father' (a literary desideratum) and by the failure of so many people to recognize Jesus (a historical circumstance). It may also be that no one knows the Son except the Father because only the Father completely knows the 'all things' delivered to the Son.

and anyone to whom the Son chooses to reveal him. The mutual knowledge of Father and Son is for the benefit of others. The Son, by grace, makes known to others what the Father has made known to him. We are not far from Jn 1.18 ('No one has ever seen God; God the only Son, who is in the bosom of the Father, he has made him known') and Jn 14.9 ('He that has seen me has seen the Father'). To quote

Origen, Jesus 'reveals the Father by himself being understood; for whoever has understood him understands as a consequence the Father also'.

In Exod 33.12–13 God 'knows' Moses by name, and Moses in turn prays that he may 'know' God. The full text is: 'Moses said to the Lord, "See, you say to me, 'Bring up this people'; but you have not let me know whom you will send with me. Yet you have said, 'I know you by name, and you have also found favour in my sight.' Now therefore, I pray thee, if I have found favour in your sight, show me now your ways, that I may know you and find favour in your sight"'.' As in Mt 11.25–30, we here have the notion of reciprocal knowledge. Further, ancient Jews would have supposed the mutual knowledge to be exclusive; cf. Deut 34.10.

28. Come to me, all you who are weary and are heavy laden, and I will give you rest. As Augustine somewhere has it, 'Christ is the true Sabbath.' The closest OT parallel is Exod 33.14, where God says to Moses: 'and I will give you rest.' This is being alluded to by our text, as the dependence of v. 27 upon Exod 33.12–13 shows. Note that whereas in the OT text it is God, not Moses, who gives rest, in the NT Jesus gives it. Once more, then, Jesus is greater than Moses.

Who precisely are the weary and the heavy laden? There would seem to be three options: those suffering under the burdens imposed by the Pharisaic establishment (cf. 23.4); those suffering from the costly demands of discipleship (cf. 10.16–39); or those suffering under the weight of sin (general patristic opinion). Most modern commentators favour the first option: even though they may rest and not carry physical burdens on the Sabbath, those under the Pharisaic yoke labour and bear a heavy load. Yet one wonders whether it is really necessary to be so exclusively specific. Mt 11.28 may simply assume that the yoke of Christ alone brings true rest, and that therefore all who have not come to Jesus must be deprived of rest.

'Rest' has OT wisdom affinities, but an eschatological interpretation lies near to hand. The messianic age was to be a time of rest, and it was sometimes conceived of as a great Sabbath; cf. Heb 4.9. Also, in Jewish eschatology the end is as the beginning, the first creation is as the last – and after the first creation God rested (Gen 2.2). So given the NT's 'realized eschatology' or 'eschatology in the process of realization', one might anticipate that eschatological 'rest' would become a present reality. It is in Heb 4.1–13, to which Mt 11.28 is kindred: the Son offers eschatological rest to those who join his cause.

29. Take my yoke upon you. This imperative is synonymous with the summons 'Come to me' (v. 28), for the same promise (rest) is attached to each. 'Yoke' came to be a metaphor for obedience, subordination, servitude; and Jewish teachers commonly spoke of the yoke of the Torah and the yoke of the commandments. But no Jewish teacher ever told another: Take up my yoke. This, however, is precisely what Jesus does. He is, therefore, playing not only the part of Wisdom but also the part of Torah; or, rather, he is Wisdom, he is Torah, the full revelation of God and of God's will.

and learn from me; for I am meek and lowly in heart. Cf. Num 12.3 (the meekness of Moses); 2 Cor 10.1 ('the meekness and gentleness of Christ'). 'Learn from me' – which is yet one more indication that in 11.25–30 Jesus is the functional equivalent of Torah: the Sages learned Torah, the disciples learn Jesus – has as its immediate antecedent the revelation spoken of in 11.25–7. But because that revelation encompasses Jesus' sayings and acts, one thinks of all that he has said and done.

and you will find rest for your souls. This is a quotation from Jer 6.16.

30. For my yoke is easy, and my burden is light. The words are paradoxical. No yoke is comfortable, no burden light. But just as the pious Jew found the commandments not burdensome but liberating, so too should the disciples be able to say: 'his commandments are not grievous' (1 Jn 5.3). How one should conceptualize this is not clear, although 11.30 may hang in the air without explanation because it simply records the voice of experience. While the imperatives of Jesus must appear harsh to the uninitiated, the truth is grasped only in the living.

* * * * *

(i) Matthew's understanding of John the Baptist can be fittingly summarized by three basic assertions: John is Jesus' forerunner; John is subordinate to Jesus; John's words and career run parallel to Jesus' words and career. These three ideas colour the material in 3.1–17, and they are no less prominent in 11.2–19. To begin with, 11.2–19 is in great measure a statement about John's role as forerunner. John looks for the Coming One (11.3). He prepares the way for Jesus (11.10). And he fulfils the office of Elijah, which is the prelude to the Messiah's coming (11.14). Hence the Baptist is no independent figure. He is instead wholly christianized: everything he does points ahead to Jesus. Second, 11.2–19 makes John's subordination perfectly clear. The least in the kingdom is greater than he (11.11). Moreover, by making inquiry of Jesus and wondering whether he might not be the Coming One, the Baptist acknowledges Jesus' authority and his superior status. Finally, not only does 11.12–13 place John and Jesus in the same era of salvation-history, but 11.2–19 puts the lifework of John and Jesus side by side and calls attention to the similarities or parallels amidst the differences. Both fulfil prophecy (11.5–6, 10). Both are out of step with 'this generation' (11.16–17). Both are rejected (11.16–19). Both are insulted (11.18–19).

(ii) Taking a bird's eye view of the First Gospel, 11.1–19 marks a turning point in the plot. Mt 1.1–4.22, conceived as a whole, is a preface or prologue to the public ministry. The genealogy, the infancy stories, the material on the Baptist, the temptation, the return to Galilee, and the call of the first disciples – all these serve to establish Jesus' identity as Son of God and Messiah. Following 4.22, the next three chapters give us Jesus' authoritative and revelatory words (5.1–7.29). After that, 8.1–9.34 recounts Jesus' marvellous and salvific acts. And then, subsequent to the missionary discourse, in which the apostles are commanded to do what Jesus has done and to preach what Jesus has preached (9.35–10.42), there is 11.1–19. The passage opens with a reference to 'the deeds of the Christ'. The comprehensive phrase, which summarizes the basic content of the public ministry up to chapter 11, belongs, in effect, to a question: What does one make of 'the deeds of Christ'? Is Jesus the one who is to come, or should we expect another? The all-important question brings Mt 1–10 to a close and introduces the rest of the gospel. The issue now becomes *response to Jesus*. The subject is explored in various ways in chapters 11–12 (the woes on Galilee, the great invitation, the controversy dialogues), and also in chapter 13, where the mysteries of faith and unbelief are pondered by means of parables.

(iii) Mt 11.25–30 is a capsule summary of the message of the entire gospel. In this passage, Jesus reveals that he is the revealer. That is, he reveals that, as the meek and humble Son of the Father, he fulfils the calling of Israel, embodying in his own person Torah and Wisdom and thus making known the perfect will of God.

TWO SABBATH CONTROVERSIES AND THE SERVANT OF DEUTERO-ISAIAH (12.1–21)

12 [1]At that time Jesus went through the grainfields on the Sabbath. His disciples were hungry, and they began to pluck heads of grain and to eat. [2]When the Pharisees saw it, they said to him, 'Behold, your disciples are doing what is not lawful to do on the Sabbath.' [3]He said to them, 'Have you not read what David did, when he and his companions were hungry, [4]how he entered the house of God and ate the bread of the Presence, which it was not lawful for him or his companions to eat, but only for the priests? [5]Or have you not read in the law that on the Sabbath the priests in the temple break the Sabbath and yet are guiltless? [6]I say to you,

something greater than the temple is here. [7]If you had known what this means, "I desire mercy and not sacrifice," you would not have condemned the guiltless. [8]For the Son of man is lord of the Sabbath.'

[9]And leaving that place he entered their synagogue. [10]And behold, there was a man with a withered hand, and they asked him, saying, 'Is it lawful to heal on the Sabbath?' so that they might accuse him. [11]He said to them, 'Who among you, if he owns one sheep and it falls into a pit on the Sabbath, will not lay hold of it and lift it out? [12]Of how much more value is a person than a sheep! So it is lawful to do good on the Sabbath.' [13]Then he said to the man, 'Stretch out your hand.' And he stretched it out, and it was restored, whole like the other.

[14]But the Pharisees, going away, took counsel against him, that they might destroy him. [15]Jesus, becoming aware of this, withdrew. And many crowds followed him, and he healed all of them,[16]and he ordered them not to make him known. [17]This was to fulfil what had been spoken through the prophet Isaiah: [18]'Behold my servant, whom I have chosen, my beloved, with whom my soul is well pleased. I will put my Spirit upon him, and he will proclaim justice to the Gentiles. [19]He will not wrangle or cry aloud, nor will anyone hear his voice in the streets. [20]He will not break a bruised reed or quench a smouldering wick until he successfully brings forth judgement. [21]And in his name the Gentiles will hope.'

Parallels: Mk 2.23–3.12; Lk 6.1–11, 17–19

The Son of Man Is Lord of the Sabbath (12.1–8)

1. At that time is not intended to supply chronological information but to serve as a thematic bridge: it helps associate 11.25–30, which is introduced by 'at that time' and which proclaims Jesus as the giver of rest, with 12.1–8, where Jesus is Lord of the Sabbath.

His disciples were hungry anticipates v. 3 and thereby increases the parallelism between the situation of David and the situation of Jesus.

2. The Pharisees object to the disciples' action. Are not Jesus' followers neglecting a fundamental demand of the decalogue, one of the obligations of the covenant? Are they not breaking a command-ment God kept (Gen 2.2)? Are they not doing away with one of the signs that separates Jew from Gentile?

Behold, your disciples are doing what is not lawful to do on the Sabbath. The law permitted the poor to glean from the corners of the fields (Lev 19.9–10; Deut 23.24–5). Exod 34.21, however, commands: 'Six days you shall work, but on the seventh day you shall rest; in ploughing time and in harvest you shall rest.' The action of Jesus' disciples was, in accordance with the strictness of the times, interpreted by some as a violation of this statute. According to *m. Sabb.* 7.2, thirty-nine classes of work – including reaping – were prohibited. Yet how many of these were in fact in force in the first century, and who would have enforced them, and upon whom, are questions to which we do not have the answers. Jewish tradition in any case had long recognized that exceptional circumstances sometimes allowed the non-observance of the Torah. So the question is not, Can there be exceptions to the Sabbath halakah? It is rather, What constitutes a legitimate exception? It is over this – a question which different Jews answered differently – that there is controversy.

3–4. In a manner reminiscent of rabbinic debate, Jesus answers the objection with a question and appeals to Scripture. Specifically, he appeals to David's breach of the law in 1 Sam 21. There are two obvious points of correlation. In both instances a righteous individual breaks a commandment, and both times he does so out of hunger. Also implicit is a third point of comparison: Jesus, the Messiah and descendant of David, is like his ancestor the king. It is even possible to find a fourth parallel. For there is some rabbinic evidence (albeit late) which places David's act on a Sabbath, when the old showbread was being replaced by the new.

Some rabbis, by affirming that he was in peril and near starvation, sought to justify David's act. Perhaps Jewish scholars in Jesus' day had already concerned themselves with the problem. If so, Jesus might have been appealing to a text whose implications were known to be controversial.

how he entered the house of God. This agrees with Mk 2.26, except that Mark has these words at the end: 'when Abiathar was high priest'. Lk 6.4 also omits the remark about Abiathar. Probably both the First and Third Evangelists recognized Mark's error. The high priest in question was Abiathar's son, the lesser known Ahimelech (see 1 Sam 21.1).

and ate the bread of the Presence. 'The bread of the Presence' refers to the 'showbread', the twelve loaves of bread which were arranged in two rows upon the table before the Holy of Holies. The loaves were baked on Friday, taken into the temple on the morning of the Sabbath, and offered as a thank offering.

which it was not lawful for him or his companions to eat. See Lev 24.9: 'And it shall be for Aaron and his sons, and they shall eat it in a holy place, since it is for him a most holy portion out of the offering ...'

but only for the priests? The example of David illustrates the possibility of breaking the law for the sake of some greater good, just as the following example of the priests in the temple (12.5–6) illustrates the possibility of observing one commandment at the expense of another. But there is also a christological point. Both 12.5–6 and 8 make christological assertions, and 12.3–4, over against 1 Sam 21.1–6, emphasizes David's active role and puts the priests in the background. So Jesus' authority is illustrated by David's authority. If David could act as he did, surely Jesus, in a manner of uncertain infringement, can act similarly.

5. If the priests serving on the Sabbath in the Temple are guiltless, how much more innocent are Jesus' disciples, who are serving something greater than the temple?

Or have you not read in the law. When addressing the crowds, Jesus says, 'You have *heard*'. When the leaders are being spoken to he says, 'Have you not *read*?'

that on the Sabbath the priests in the temple break the Sabbath and yet are guiltless? In order to fulfil Num 28.9–10, the priests had to offer sacrifices on the Sabbath and thereby violate the prohibition of Sabbath work. How does their action justify the disciples? First, the priests prove that Scripture allows at least one exception to the general Sabbath rule. Second, since the violation of the Sabbath is done for the sake of the temple, this shows that the temple service takes precedence over Sabbath observance; if then there is something which is greater than the temple (as 12.6 asserts), it follows that it too may take precedence over observing the Sabbath.

6. I say to you, something greater than the temple is here. 'I say to you' underlines the theme of christological authority. 'Something greater' is not the kingdom, Jesus' interpretation of the law, or the community of disciples, but rather Jesus himself.

7. Matthew now inserts Hos 6.6, a verse already cited in 9.13.

If you had known what this means. The meaning is, 'Do you not know what this means?' (cf. Jn 13.12). Although the Pharisees read, they do not understand.

I desire mercy and not sacrifice. The citation does not establish a moral law/ritual law antithesis; nor is Jesus asserting that the Pharisees should have mercy on the disciples. One also hesitates to find here a reference to the 'love commandment'. The point seems rather to be that if mercy is greater than the temple cult (sacrifice), and if the temple cult can trump the Sabbath when necessary, then mercy should likewise trump the Sabbath when necessary.

8. This concluding line might be thought to have the effect of rendering much of the foregoing irrelevant. If Jesus the Son of man is Lord of the Sabbath, if he stands not under but above the Sabbath, then his dictate is law, and what is the need of argument? But 12.8 does help to complete the thought of 12.6. 'Something greater than the temple is here' is explained by 'the Son of man is Lord of the Sabbath.'

A Sabbath Healing (12.9–14)

9. Jesus leaves the outdoors for the indoors, entering a synagogue. It is still the Sabbath.

10. a man with a withered hand remains vague. Luke adds that the hand in question was the right hand. This accentuates the handicap, the right hand being more important.

Is it lawful to heal on the Sabbath? The Essenes and the author of *Jubilees* would have answered no. According to the *Mishnah*, circumstances dictate the ruling: life in immediate danger should be saved. This does not, however, cover our story, for the man could presumably have been healed at a later time. Closer to Jesus is *Eccles Rab.* 9.7, where Abba Tahnah raises the showing of mercy to a leper above correct Sabbath observance.

so that they might accuse him. The Pharisees, who here as so often play a false part, question Jesus in order to entrap him. They are not honestly seeking another's halakhic judgement but rather an occasion to be used against Jesus in court ('accuse' is a technical legal term meaning 'bring charges'). In view of 12.14, one thinks of the statute in Exod 31.14: 'Every one who profanes it [the Sabbath] shall be put to death.' One should note, however, that in the accounts of the trial of Jesus his perceived violations of the Sabbath are not brought up at all.

11. Jesus answers his critics with a counter-question that appeals to human sentiment. The argument is once more *a fortiori*. One is reminded of the addition in 12.5–7 (also an argument *a fortiori*). But the point is not Jesus' halakhic logic or his status as a first-rate debater. The legal debates in this chapter and elsewhere remain relatively unsophisticated. This is because Jesus always goes straight to the heart of the matter. His brevity and clarity focus on 'the weightier matters of the law' (23.23). This excludes long, drawn-out debate. It also explains why he appeals more frequently to human instincts than to legal niceties.

if he owns one sheep. Whether 'one' simply means 'a' (sheep), or whether it is intended to reinforce the argument ('[only] one sheep') is unclear.

will you not lay hold of it and lift it out? Cf. Prov 12.10 ('A righteous man has regard for the life of his beast'). Perhaps Deut 22.4 is in the background: 'You shall not see your brother's ass or his ox fallen down by the way, and withold your help from them; you shall help him to lift them up again.' Opinion surely differed as to whether one should help an animal out of a pit on the Sabbath. CD 11.13–14 seems to exclude such action. The rabbis discussed the issue and tended to agree that one could not pull an animal out of a pit or use instruments but that one could throw in food for the day or even toss in something which the animal could use to climb out. Perhaps most first-century Galileans would have used normal means to extricate an animal from a pit on the Sabbath, whatever the Pharisees or others may have taught.

12. The conclusion Jesus now draws illustrates 12.7: 'mercy' takes precedence over 'sacrifice'.

So it is lawful to do good on the Sabbath. Cf. Diognetus, *Ep.* 4.3: 'as if He forbade us to do any good thing on the Sabbath day, is not this profane?' If one may do good to a sheep on the Sabbath, and if human beings are of more value than sheep, then it is permitted on the Sabbath to do good to a human being. Thus Jesus has acted on principle. He has not overthrown the law.

13. Having justified his action beforehand, and having convicted his hearers of hypocrisy (for would they not help a beast?), Jesus now heals the disabled man. But note that Jesus does not stretch forth his hand, touch the man, or help him up (contrast 8.3, 15; 9.25 etc.). He simply speaks. Thus his act of healing is far less provocative than his words in vv. 11–12.

and it was restored, whole like the other. Cf. the healings in 1 Kgs 13.1–10 (where Jeroboam's 'withered' hand is healed by the prayer of a prophet so that it becomes as it was before) and *T. Sim.* 2.11–14 (where Simeon prays to the Lord for the restoration of his 'withered' right hand).

14. Jesus has not, in Matthew's view, done anything to violate the Sabbath. That the Pharisees think otherwise is not clearly stated but is implied: they are sufficiently distraught to begin contemplating Jesus' death. Thus, by doing good to another, Jesus has put his own life in jeopardy.

Jesus the Servant (12.15–21)

This paragraph is structurally reminiscent of 8.16–17. In both places we have a summary of Jesus' healing activity followed by a formula quotation from Isaiah. In both cases the OT text has to do with the suffering servant.

15–16 constitutes yet one more summary of Jesus' ministry.

becoming aware of this may highlight Jesus' supernatural knowledge.

18–21. The following formula quotation, from Isa 42.1–4, 9, is

probably Matthew's independent translation of the Hebrew, with
some influence from the LXX and the targum. The evangelist
evidently latched on to the passage because it serves so remarkably
to illustrate the nature of Jesus' ministry in Israel. Jesus is the
unobtrusive servant of the Lord. God's Spirit rests upon him. He does
not wrangle or quarrel or continue useless strife. He seeks to avoid
self-advertisement and to quiet the enthusiasm that his healings
inevitably create. He has compassion upon all, especially upon the
'bruised reed' or 'smouldering wick'. And he brings salvation to the
Gentiles.

**Behold my servant, whom I have chosen, my beloved, with whom my
soul is well pleased.** Cf. the divine voice in 3.17 and 17.5. Here 'servant'
is not associated with Jesus' passion but has a much broader reference.
Indeed, 'servant' is here a comprehensive title. It covers Jesus' entire
ministry, all that he says and does; cf. 8.17. He is the humble, suffering
servant not only at the end but from the beginning.

I will put my Spirit upon him recalls the baptism and links up nicely
with the next paragraph, where the theme is Jesus and the Spirit.

and he will proclaim justice to the Gentiles. Is Matthew thinking of
Jesus as the judge of all nations and peoples (cf. 25.31–46)?

He will not wrangle or cry aloud means, in its present context, that
Jesus, instead of quarrelling unprofitably with his opponents, goes on
about his business, and instead of seeking publicity asks people not to
make him known; cf. 8.4; 9.30.

nor will anyone hear his voice in the streets. This makes sense in the
light of 12.16: 'He asked them not to make him known.' Should one
also imagine a contrast with 6.5, where the 'hypocrites' make
themselves seen and heard in the streets?

He will not break a bruised reed or quench a smouldering wick. Do
the 'bruised reed' and the 'smouldering wick' stand for any group of
people in particular? The commentaries suggest several possibilities:
the apostles, Gentiles, Christians, the poor in Israel. More probably
one should think in general of the undistinguished – Jew and Gentile,
Christian and non-Christian – at society's margin. They are
paradigmatically represented by the toll-collectors and sinners,
harassed outcasts who were the objects of Jesus' tenderness and
compassion. Jesus accepted the 'bruised reed' and the 'smouldering
wick' as they were and bade them to lay aside the miseries of the past
and to recognize the possibilities opened by the future. Implicit is the
idea that there is always hope for human beings, however wretched or
unremarkable they may seem.

Until he successfully brings forth judgement probably anticipates the
universal judgement (25.31–46). But the Greek word translated

'judgement' can also mean 'justice', in which case Jesus is being presented as the one who establishes God's will and righteousness in the world.

And in his name the Gentiles will hope. One thinks especially of the Gentile magi at the beginning and of the commission to go into all the world at the end.

* * * * *

(i) The Sabbath is mentioned in Matthew only four times: in 12.1–8 (plucking grain on the Sabbath); 12.9–14 (healing on a Sabbath); 24.20 (fleeing on a Sabbath); and 28.1 (the women at the sepulchre). While the last is of no theological significance, the other texts show us, first, that Matthew presupposed continued observance of the Sabbath by Christians, and second, that he was concerned with what was 'lawful' on the Sabbath (12.1–14). Unfortunately, our gospel does not spell out the differences between the Sabbath observance of Jews and Christians in Matthew's area. We also do not know whether the evangelist was familiar with (Gentile) Christians who honoured Sunday instead of Saturday. It does, however, seem reasonable to suppose, in view of Matthew's additions in 12.1–14, that there was conflict between Matthew's community and others over the nature of true Sabbath observance. Furthermore, there would seem to be two tendencies detectable in the Matthean redaction. On the one hand, the concern with what is lawful (12.2, 4, 10) and the insertion of the halakhic argument in 12.5–6 evidence a desire to remain faithful to the Sabbath and its OT legislation. Matthew has taken care to prevent Jesus' position from being interpreted as radical or antinomian. On the other hand, there is a distancing of Jesus and his church from a perceived legalism. When Jesus quashes the objections of the Pharisees, he is attacking an over-developed casuistry. He is asserting that the 'commandments of people' can prevent faithful observance of the 'commandments of God' (cf. 15.3). God wills the Sabbath to be honoured, but not at the expense of 'doing good' (12.10).

(ii) The quotation of Isa 42 is the longest in the gospel, and it is linked in several intriguing ways with its present context. These facts reveal the great importance for Matthew of Jesus' role as servant, an importance with its correlation in Matthew's understanding of God's primary demand: love of neighbour; cf. 7.12; 19.19; 22.39. Such love is defined as unselfish service of others; cf. 5.43–8. To love is to serve and to serve is to love. Thus Matthew's emphasis upon the love commandment goes hand in hand with his desire to interpret Jesus with the christological category of servant. As the perfect embodiment of God's moral demand, Jesus the servant lives the commandment to love.

AN OBJECTION STORY, A TESTING STORY, A CORRECTION STORY (12.22–50)

²²Then a blind and mute demoniac was brought to him, and he cured him, so that the one who had been mute could speak and see. ²³And all the crowds were amazed and said, 'Can this be the Son of David?' ²⁴But the Pharisees, upon hearing this, said, 'It is only by Beelzebul, the ruler of the demons, that this man casts out demons.' ²⁵Knowing their thoughts, he said to them, 'Every kingdom divided against itself is laid waste, and no city or house divided against itself will stand. ²⁶And if Satan casts out Satan, he is divided against himself; how then will his kingdom stand? ²⁷And if I cast out demons by Beelzebul, by whom do your sons cast them out? They, then, will be your judges. ²⁸But if I by the Spirit of God cast out demons, then the kingdom of God has come upon you. ²⁹Or how can one enter a strong man's house and plunder his goods, unless he first binds the strong man? Then indeed he can plunder his house. ³⁰The one who is not with me is against me, and the one who does not gather with me scatters. ³¹Therefore I say to you, every sin and blasphemy will be forgiven people, but blasphemy against the Spirit will not be forgiven. ³²And whoever speaks a word against the Son of man will be forgiven, but whoever speaks against the Holy Spirit will not be forgiven, either in this age or in the age to come. ³³Either make the tree good, and its fruit good; or make the tree bad, and its fruit bad. For the tree is known by its fruit. ³⁴You brood of vipers! How can you speak good, when you are evil? For out of the abundance of the heart the mouth speaks. ³⁵The good person out of his good treasure brings forth good, and the evil person out of an evil treasure brings forth evil. ³⁶I say to you, on the day of judgement people will render account for every careless word they utter. ³⁷For by your words you will be justified, and by your words you will be condemned.'

³⁸Then some of the scribes and Pharisees answered and said to him, 'Teacher, we wish to see a sign from you.' ³⁹But he answered them, 'An evil and adulterous generation seeks for a sign, but no sign will be given to it except the sign of the prophet Jonah. ⁴⁰For just as Jonah was three days and three nights in the belly of the whale, so for three days and three nights will the Son of man be in the heart of the earth. ⁴¹The people of Nineveh will rise up at the judgement with this generation and condemn it, because they repented at the proclamation of Jonah, and behold, something greater than Jonah is here. ⁴²The queen of the South will rise up at the judgement with this generation and condemn it, because she came from the ends of the earth to listen to the wisdom of Solomon, and behold, something greater than Solomon is here. ⁴³When the unclean spirit has gone out of a person, it wanders through waterless regions

looking for a resting place, but it finds none. [44]Then it says, "I will return to my house from which I came." And when he comes he finds it empty, swept, and put in order. [45]Then he goes and brings with him seven other spirits more evil than himself, and they enter and live there. And the last state of that person is worse than the first. So will it be also with this evil generation.'

[46] While he was still speaking to the crowds, behold, his mother and his brothers stood outside, seeking to speak to him. [47]Someone said to him, 'Behold, your mother and your brothers are standing outside, asking to speak to you.' [48]But he replied to the one who told him this, 'Who is my mother, and who are my brothers?' [49]And pointing to his disciples, he said, 'Here are my mother and my brothers! [50]For whoever does the will of my Father in heaven is my brother and sister and mother.'

Parallels: Mt 9.32–4; 16.1–4; Mk 3.22–35; 8.11–12; Lk 6.43–5; 11.14–32; 12.10; Jn 6.20; 7.20; 10.20

Jesus and Beelzebul (12.22–37)

This drawn-out objection story consists of an exorcism followed by three responses: the crowd's response to Jesus, the Pharisees' response to the crowd, and Jesus' response to the Pharisees. Whereas the responses of the crowd (a question) and that of the Pharisees (an accusation) are narrated quite briefly, Jesus' response is extended. It consists of (i) three rebuttals followed by a warning (vv. 25–30); (ii) a passage on the unforgivable sin (vv. 31–2); and (iii) a little paragraph on fruits and words (vv. 33–7).

23. And all the crowds were amazed and said, 'Can this be the Son of David?' If the Pharisees will shortly assert that Jesus casts out demons by the prince of demons, the crowds instead wonder whether Jesus might not be the Davidic Messiah. The real enemies of Jesus are the Pharisees, who are sure of themselves, not the uncertain populace.

24. The Pharisees respond not so much to Jesus' exorcism as to the crowds. The narrative accordingly implies that what the Pharisees are interested in above all is keeping others from belief.

It is only by Beelzebul, the ruler of the demons, that this man casts out demons. The Pharisees refer to Jesus not in the second person but in the third person, as 'this man', which connotes contempt. They are not arguing with the healer but with the onlookers.

On Beelzebul see on 10.25. The attempt to discredit Jesus by claiming that he did his miracles through the agency of an evil spirit was probably made on more than one occasion; cf. Jn 7.20; 8.48, 52; 10.20. It presupposes Jesus' undoubted success at exorcism. His opponents evidently did not deny his seemingly miraculous deeds but rather took the course of attributing them to a dark power; cf. Deut 13.1–5.

25. Every kingdom divided against itself is laid waste. Jesus' words – which sound proverbial – take for granted that Satan, like God, has a kingdom, a well-ordered and organized host of powers and influences that heed the beck and call of their dark Lord. Over against the kingdom of God is the kingdom of Satan.

and no city or house divided against itself will stand. For all practical purposes this is synonymous with the previous clause. From the largest collective to the smallest, internal division wreaks havoc.

26. And if Satan casts out Satan, he is divided against himself; how then will his kingdom stand? The Pharisees have charged Jesus with casting out demons by the prince of demons. That is, they have assigned Jesus' power to evil forces, not God. Jesus responds by constructing a *reductio ad absurdum* which affirms Satan's rational behaviour. Would it make sense for the devil to give a human being power if that power was in turn used to ransack the kingdom of demons? Once one grants that Jesus has in fact delivered souls from spiritual bondage and given them their health, it is foolhardy to see him in league with Satan. Satan would not knowingly and willingly destroy his own dominion.

27. And if I cast out demons by Beelzebul, by whom do your sons cast them out? They, then, will be your judges. 'Your sons' is not to be taken literally. The phrase rather refers to members of the Pharisaic sect or to Pharisaic sympathizers. 'Your judges' alludes to the eschatological assize.

Jesus' reasoning is crystal clear. The Pharisees assign two similar activities – Jesus' exorcisms and the exorcisms of others – to two radically different sources. Jesus brands this as irrational. Similar effects have similar causes; and good does not come from evil (cf. 12.33–7).

Ironically, when the tables were later turned and the church Fathers were required to account for the success of non-Christian exorcists and miracle workers, they responded precisely as the Pharisees in our story and referred to demons. Furthermore, the difficulty of attributing genuine miracles to unbelievers, that is, to the 'sons' of the Pharisees, led to the untenable exegetical opinion that 'your sons' should be identified with the apostles. 'We have miracles, you have magic' seems to have been the rule in the ancient world.

28. It is illogical, many presume, to refer to the successful exorcisms of others (12.27) and then to claim that Jesus' exorcisms are special signs of the presence of the kingdom. But the inference made in 12.28

is not from exorcisms in general to the presence of the kingdom. How could Jesus ever have contended that the kingdom of God had come simply because a few demons had been cast out? If exorcisms were not exactly everyday affairs, they were hardly unknown until Jesus. No, the force of his assertion must lie elsewhere, and that can only be in his very presence. What matters is that *Jesus* casts out demons. In other words, the saying is a veiled testimony to his eschatological role. As so often, Jesus implicitly asserts the mystery and magnitude of his own person but gives himself no title. He does not say that the kingdom has come because the Messiah or the Son of man is present and ransacking Satan's kingdom. He says simply, 'I cast out demons.' The listener should be moved to ask, 'Who then is this?'

But if I by the Spirit of God cast out demons, then the kingdom of God has come upon you. Jesus accepts the miracles of others but holds his own to be of different import because of his identity. What is decisive is not the exorcisms but the exorcist. The coming of Jesus inaugurates the fulfilment of eschatology.

29. Jesus' third argument takes the form of a parable. The point is that so far from belonging to Satan's kingdom and using Satan's power, Jesus has attacked that kingdom and overcome its power.

Or how can one enter a strong man's house and plunder his goods. Cf. Isa 49.24 ('Can the prey be taken from the mighty, or the captives of a tyrant be rescued?') and *Ps. Sol.* 5.4 ('For a man will not take booty from a strong man'). 'The house of the strong man' is Satan's kingdom. 'His goods' or 'possessions' are the people he has under his sway: those possessed by demons.

unless he first binds the strong man? Just as demons may bind people (cf. Lk 13.16), so may people bind demons. Whether Jesus himself or Matthew after him thought in terms of a specific time when the devil was overcome and bound is uncertain, but such an idea could well lie behind the synoptic temptation stories; cf. also Lk 10.18.

30. the one who does not gather with me scatters. Contrast Mk 9.40. The imagery seems to be that of gathering and scattering sheep, though some commentators have thought of harvesting. The words refer neither to the devil nor to Jewish exorcists. Jesus is speaking theoretically and in general of those who align themselves against God's kingdom. The gist of the hyperbole is that there is no middle ground. One must align oneself either with God or with Satan.

31–2. The argument of 12.22–30 has ended. Jesus, however, continues to speak. He drops his defensive posture and takes up the offensive. His words are warnings to those who have not accepted the import of what has just been said.

every sin and blasphemy will be forgiven people, but blasphemy

against the Spirit will not be forgiven. 'Sins' are offences against fellow human beings, 'blasphemies' offences against God. That 'all sins and blasphemies will be forgiven' is to be taken literally and considered a revolutionary utterance is exceedingly doubtful. The statement, which looks forward to the last judgement, is simply a way of declaring God's readiness to forgive.

The notion that some sins are more grievous than others was a common Jewish conviction. Also well-attested is the notion of an unforgivable sin; cf. 1 Sam 3.14. But the rabbis, who wondered much about Exod 20.7 ('The Lord will not hold him guiltless who takes his name in vain'), disagreed as to whether blasphemy was such a sin.

And whoever speaks a word against the Son of man will be forgiven, but whoever speaks against the Holy Spirit will not be forgiven, either in this age or in the age to come. As it stands, these words have no obvious meaning. The distinction between speaking against the Son of man and speaking against the Spirit does not hold up because Jesus is the bearer of the Spirit (3.16; 12.18, 28), so to speak against one would be to speak against the other. Perhaps we have here an example of a saying whose Greek form (with 'Son of man' used as a title for Jesus) misrepresents the Aramaic original (with 'son of man' meaning just 'a human being').

The history of the interpretation of 12.31–2 is one of tragic misapprehension. The *Didache* is fairly faithful to the tradition as it is found in the synoptics: 'And every prophet speaking by the Spirit you will not tempt or condemn; for all sins shall be forgiven, but this sin shall not be forgiven'. Here blasphemy against the Spirit is opposition to the Spirit's inspiration. Similar is Ambrose, who makes the sin against the Holy Spirit identical with denying the Spirit's dignity and power and attributing to Beelzebub the casting out of demons. Other, less credible identifications of the unpardonable sin include rejection of the gospel (Irenaeus), slander of God's servants (the *Gospel of Bartholomew* 5.4), and denial of Jesus' divine nature (Athanasius). But the dominant idea in church history is that the sin against the Holy Spirit is the 'sin unto death' of 1 Jn 5.16, that is, post-conversion relapse. Novatian, for example, argued that those who recanted the faith under torture had sinned against the Holy Spirit and were lost for ever. As Jerome observed, this does not take the synoptic context very seriously, for there it is unbelievers (at least in Matthew and Mark) who are running the risk of damnation. But Jerome's exegesis did not, unfortunately, steer the course of Christian discussion on the matter. Augustine, in his attempt to uphold God's desire to forgive all everything, devoted a whole sermon to the subject (*Sermon* 71) and affirmed that the text has to do with impenitence lasting until death; it is resistance of the Spirit throughout one's life. His interpretation, which made blasphemy against the Spirit not a specific act but a state of enmity, and one possible for Christians, became quite influential. Much later, John Bunyan's *Grace abounding to the Chief of Sinners* shows us how Jesus' word could come to haunt and torment sensitive and pious souls who agonized over the possibility that they had committed the unpardonable sin. Sadly, there have even been individuals who have taken their own lives, evidently persuaded that they, due to some wrong thought to be the sin against the Holy Ghost, were beyond the pale of mercy (e.g. the English Puritan John Child).

Jesus' statement that a certain sin will not be forgiven in the world to come was later taken by some to imply the possibility of other sins that could be forgiven after death (an idea also found in rabbinic literature). Our text was thus one of the proofs of purgatory. Theologians up through the nineteenth century continued to discuss the issue, usually in connexion with 1 Pet 3.18–22.

33. The possible supposition that blasphemy cannot really have eternally evil consequences, because it consists only of words, is now seemingly countered by a statement on the connexion between words and the inner life. To speak evil is to be evil. Those therefore who have spoken evil of Jesus have revealed their true character.

Mt 12.33 heads a small subsection, reminiscent of 7.16–20, which is tripartite. Three subjects are treated: trees and fruit (v. 33), words and the heart (vv. 34–5), and words and the judgement (vv. 36–7).

For the tree is known by its fruit. Cf. 7.20. There is a close parallel in Ecclus 27.6: 'The fruit discloses the cultivation of a tree; so the expression of a thought discloses the cultivation of a man's mind.'

34. You brood of vipers! This harsh address, which prefaces a new thought, appears again in 3.7 and 23.33.

How can you speak good, when you are evil? Cf. 7.16 and *Tabula of Cebes* 40.2 ('no good thing comes from evils').

For out of the abundance of the heart the mouth speaks. Cf. 15.18.

on the day of judgement people will render account for every careless word they utter. This is possible because God knows all; cf. 6.4.

37. For by your words you will be justified, and by your words you will be condemned. Because words come from the heart, the judgement of an individual will be according to his or her words. Cf. 11.19; 15.11; Lk 19.22.

An Evil and Adulterous Generation (12.38–45)

Mt 12.38–45 is a testing story. After Jesus is asked by the scribes and Pharisees for a sign, he responds with a speech which takes up three points, the first being the sign to 'this generation' (the sign of Jonah; 39–40), the second being the sayings about past generations (vv. 41–2), and the third being the fate of 'this generation' (vv. 43–5).

38. Jesus' speech in 12.22–37 has not made converts. The scribes and Pharisees do not want words but a stupendous miracle, validation of Jesus' lofty claims. Of course the irony here, from Matthew's perspective, is that Jesus has already worked more than enough miracles to persuade an open mind; cf. 11.2–4.

we wish to see a sign from you. Cf. 16.1. Because they lack faith, the scribes and Pharisees want to see convincing evidence. Just as Moses and Aaron did signs which moved Israel to belief (Exod 4.30–1), so should Jesus now prove that God is on his side by performing some spectacular marvel. But readers know that even as the signs of Moses did not persuade Pharaoh, so nothing will persuade Jesus' opponents.

39. An evil and adulterous generation seeks for a sign. Cf. 16.4. 'Evil and adulterous generation' recalls the descriptions of the generation in the wilderness in Deut 1.35 and 32.5. 'Adulterous' appears only three times in the synoptics, each time as a qualifier of 'generation' (12.39; 16.4; Mk 8.38). It is used in its OT sense: 'unfaithlessness (to Yahweh)'; cf. Isa 52.3; Jer 3.10; Ezek 23; Hos 1–3; 5.3–4.

but no sign will be given to it except the sign of the prophet Jonah. The genitive may be appositive (Jonah himself is the sign) or it may qualify the sign as that experienced by Jonah (who was remembered as a prophet from Galilee; cf. 2 Kgs 14.25 with Josh 19.13).

40. The sign of Jonah is now explained: just as Jonah was in the belly of the sea monster three days and three nights, so shall the Son of man be in the belly of the earth three days and three nights. Matthew's text seems to make explicit what is implicit in the speeches in Acts, namely, that the resurrection is God's one great sign to Israel; cf. Acts 2.24, 32, 36; 3.15 etc.

For just as Jonah was three days and three nights in the belly of the whale, so for three days and three nights will the Son of man be in the heart of the earth. There is no explicit reference to the deliverance of Jonah or to Jesus' resurrection. But the figure of three days and nights posits an end to the time in the earth and so suggests the resurrection.

Jesus did not, according to Matthew's own narrative, stay in the tomb three days and three nights. But the 'three days and three nights' comes straight from Jonah, and we can allow Matthew some poetic licence. Further, ancient Jews often counted parts of days as wholes. So our verse can hardly be turned into the key to setting the day of Jesus' death.

41–2. The people of Nineveh will rise up at the judgement with this generation and condemn it, because they repented at the proclamation of

Jonah, and behold, something greater than Jonah is here. Cf. Jon 3.2. Clearly readers are supposed to know Jonah's story. 'Rise up' refers to the resurrection. The scene painted is the universal judgement.

Who or what is the 'greater' that is 'here'? In the light of 12.6, where Jesus is greater than the temple, one supposes that Matthew thought of Jesus himself (cf. Jn 4.12; 8.53). The connexion between 12.40 and 41 makes this plain, for since Jonah and Jesus have been compared in v. 40, one wants to make the same comparison in v. 41.

The contrast Jesus draws between Nineveh's repentance and the faithlessness of Israel was probably a traditional Jewish theme. In *Mek.* on Exod 12.1, Jonah leaves the land of Israel with this excuse: 'For since the Gentiles are more inclined to repent, I might be causing Israel to be condemned.' Put otherwise, if the Israelites were to hear Jonah, they would show badly, for they, unlike the pagans, would not repent in sackcloth and ashes.

The queen of the South will rise up at the judgement with this generation and condemn it, because she came from the ends of the earth to listen to the wisdom of Solomon, and behold, something greater than Solomon is here. The 'queen of the South' is the queen of Sheba, whose story is told in 1 Kgs 10.1–13; 2 Chr 9.1–12. The OT knows her only as 'the queen of Sheba', but 'the queen of the south' does occur in other sources. Note that, according to 1 Kgs 10.1, the queen of Sheba came to Solomon 'to test him with hard questions'. So like the Pharisees she tested a king. But unlike them, she could see the truth.

43–5. The wider context is Jesus' relationship to 'this generation', and what has happened is that unbelief has won out. Jesus has not converted Israel. What follows? From those to whom much has been given much will be required. Israel has had the opportunity to see and hear one greater than Jonah and one greater than Solomon. All to no avail. Therefore her judgement will be the harsher; cf. Heb 10.28–9. The last state will be worse than the first.

When the unclean spirit has gone out of a person, it wanders through waterless regions looking for a resting place, but it finds none. The demon finds no rest in isolation because it is its nature to torment others. Evil always seeks to enlarge itself.

And the last state of that person is worse than the first. The words sound proverbial; cf. 27.64; Jn 5.14.

So will it be also with this evil generation. There is no reason to think that 12.45b should call any particular occurrence to mind, although interpreters have, from time to time, identified the last things that are worse than the first with the fall of Jerusalem and its aftermath or with the state of Judaism since the resurrection. It seems preferable to think less concretely of the sorry state of 'this generation' in general, that is, the sorry state of those who have rejected the proclamation of Jesus and of the church.

Jesus' True Family (12.46–50)

46. While he was still speaking to the crowds. Jesus is no longer addressing the Jewish leaders (as he was in 12.22–45), but the crowds. Thus we pass from controversy narratives to what amounts to an invitation; cf. 11.25–30. Note the parallel with 12.1–21, where again two controversy stories are followed by a pericope about the crowds.

49. Jesus stretches forth his hand toward his disciples and declares that they are his mother and brothers. The words do not dissolve family bonds but rather relativize them. They do this by revealing that there are even stronger bonds.

Here are my mother and my brothers. The elevation of one's spiritual family over one's physical family is found elsewhere in ancient Judaism. Already in Deut 33.9 Levi is commended for saying 'of his father and mother, "I regard them not".' The Essenes in particular seem to have thought of their community as a replacement for the traditional family. For Jesus, the break with family was probably spurred on by both personal experience and eschatological expectation; see on 10.34–7. The kingdom demanded all of Jesus and those who followed him. This is why Jesus was 'a eunuch for the kingdom of heaven' (19.12).

50. For whoever does the will of my Father in heaven. This is the only line in 12.46–50 in which 'father' is used. Some would take this to reflect an historical fact: by the time of his public ministry, Jesus' father, Joseph, was dead. While this inference is probably correct, the omission also makes a theological point. There is, as 23.9 states so plainly, only one father in the ecclesia, namely, God.

* * * * *

(i) Jesus' ministry of exorcism is subject to two radically different interpretations. How, then, does one get to the truth? The text implies that there are good reasons for embracing one view of Jesus rather than another (12.25–39). Yet Matthew also knows that rational persuasion has its limitations, as becomes clear in 12.33–7 and 38–45. Thus, even though the sign of Jonah, which is the resurrection of Jesus, will be made known to 'this generation', it will not believe. Faith in Matthew has a moral dimension, and it cannot abide with ill will and disagreeable natures; for good fruit cannot be found on a bad tree (12.33). In line with this, the confession of Jesus as the Messiah is in the last analysis not a question of right understanding but of a good heart. Despite Socrates, sin is more than ignorance. Even scriptural knowledge will not save if the heart is corrupt.

(ii) Mt 12.22–45 proclaims the presence of salvation and underlines the unprecedented opportunity of the present time. The kingdom of God has come. The domain of Satan has been plundered. One greater than Jonah and Solomon has appeared. And a spectacular and unrivalled sign has been given to all – Jesus' resurrection. Hence God has, in the Son (cf. 11.25–30), spoken louder than ever before. It follows that *now* is the day of salvation in a sense untrue of any past moment. And it is not surprising that failure to hear and respond in the present means that 'the last things become worse than the first'. The greater the opportunity missed, the greater the loss suffered.

(iii) In 4.21–2 James and John leave their father when Jesus calls them to discipleship. In 8.22 Jesus tells a follower that he should not attend to his father's burial but should rather 'leave the dead to bury their own dead'. And 10.34–7 foretells that those who further the gospel will find themselves opposed by their own family members. The picture drawn by these texts is disturbing. Faith in Jesus would seem to entail, at best, a loosening of family ties, at worst renunciation of one's parents and siblings. Admittedly, this hard truth is understandable given Matthew's view of things. If faith matters above all else, then whatever hinders faith must be forsaken. Still, the circumstance is not a happy one, and just understanding its necessity might not bring much consolation. What will bring consolation, however, is the fact that the leaving behind of one's natural family will coincide with adoption into another family, and this is in large part the message of 12.46–50. Although religious commitments may well weaken family ties, the disciple will not thereby be left alone, without a family. Rather, the Christian will join the household of faith, the church, in which there is a father (God) and in which there are many brothers and sisters (cf. 23.8).

THE PARABLE OF THE SOWER AND ITS INTERPRETATION
(13.1–23)

13 **¹In that same day Jesus, upon leaving the house, sat beside the sea. ²And great crowds gathered to him, so that he got into a boat and sat there; and the whole crowd stood on the shore. ³And he spoke many things to them in parables, saying: 'Listen! A sower went out to sow. ⁴And as he sowed, some seeds fell along the path, and the birds came and devoured them. ⁵Other seeds fell on rocky ground, where they did not have much soil, and immediately they sprang up, since they had no depth of soil. ⁶But when the sun rose, they were scorched; and since they had no**

root, they withered away. [7]Other seeds fell upon thorns, and the thorns grew up and choked them. [8]Other seeds fell upon good soil and brought forth grain, some a hundredfold, some sixty, some thirty. [9]He who has ears, let him hear!'

[10]And coming the disciples said to him, 'Why do you speak to them in parables?' [11]Answering he said, 'To you it has been given to know the secrets of the kingdom of heaven, but to them it has not been given. [12]For to the one who has will more be given, and he will have in abundance; but from the one who has not, even what he has will be taken away. [13]Because of this I speak to them in parables, so that seeing they do not perceive, and hearing they do not hear, nor do they understand. [[[14]With them indeed is fulfilled the prophecy of Isaiah that says: "You will indeed hear, but never understand, and you will indeed look, but never perceive. [15]For this people's heart has grown dull, and their ears are heavy of hearing, and they have shut their eyes, lest they should see with their eyes and listen with their ears and understand with their heart and turn for me to heal them."]] [16]But blessed are your eyes, for they see, and your ears, for they hear. [17]Amen I say to you, many prophets and righteous people longed to see what you see, but did not see it, and to hear what you hear, but did not hear it.

[18]'Hear then the parable of the sower. [19]When anyone hears the word of the kingdom and does not understand it, the evil one comes and snatches away what is sown in his heart. This is what was sown along the path. [20]As for what was sown on rocky ground, this is the one who hears the word and immediately receives it with joy; [21]yet he has no root in himself but endures only for a while, and when tribulation or persecution arises on account of the word, immediately he falls away. [22]As for what was sown among thorns, this is the one who hears the word, but the cares of the world and the love of wealth choke the word, and it becomes unfruitful. [23]But as for what was sown on good soil, this is the one who hears the word and understands it. He indeed bears fruit and yields, in one case a hundredfold, in another sixty, and in another thirty.'

Parallels: Mk 4.1–20; Lk 8.4–15

The Parable of the Sower (13.1–9)

Jesus' famous parable of the sower, which is perhaps more fittingly designated the parable of the four soils, heads a chapter whose leading theme is the kingdom of heaven and its reception in the world. The subject comes up for treatment at this juncture because of the rejection so far experienced by Jesus and his disciples. The pressing question is, Why has Israel not embraced her Messiah? Why has the good news of the kingdom engendered so much opposition? One answer to these questions is given in 4.3–9 – the most important parable in chapter 13 – and its interpretation: the kingdom of God does not force itself upon people; it is invitation, not compulsion; a human response is required. If Jesus' ministry has not brought about what one might have anticipated, the fault lies neither with him nor with God but with human sin and hardened hearts. In this way, then, the parable of the sower comes to function as an apologetic, even a sort of theodicy, explaining the evil that has befallen Israel.

1–2. In that same day Jesus, upon leaving the house, sat beside the sea. On 'the house', which may be Peter's, and which Jesus enters in 13.36, see on 9.10; cf. 12.46. On 'he sat', which signals that Jesus is about to teach, see on 5.1.

and the whole crowd stood on the shore. The standing of the crowds (cf. Exod 20.18) is probably intended to create a visual contrast: Jesus alone sits.

3. And he spoke many things to them in parables, saying. 'Parable', whose usual sense in Greek literature is 'comparison', has several meanings in the NT, including maxim or proverb, comparison or similitude, and story or tale embodying some truth. Along with several others, each of these meanings is also attested for the Hebrew *mashal*, and the OT uses of this word are crucial for understanding the NT's use of parable. When Jesus spoke 'in parables', he was relating himself to a literary tradition firmly rooted in the OT, one which lived on in apocalyptic literature and the rabbis.

Unfortunately, throughout much of church history Jesus' parables have been understood as deliberately mysterious and involved allegories in which every character and action must be deciphered like a cryptogram. If today things are different, if today the excesses of the old hermeneutical method are almost universally acknowledged, much of the credit must go to Adolf Jülicher and his massive, two-volume work, *Die Gleichnisreden Jesu* (originally published in 1888 and 1899). The book marked a dramatic turn in the discussion of Jesus' parables. Jülicher argued that there is a world of difference between an allegory on the one hand and a parable on the other. Whereas the latter is a narrative based on everyday life whose elements combine to make an instructive picture with simple or self-evident meaning, the former is a story whose features all stand for something extrinsic to the narrative. And Jesus, Jülicher contended, spoke in parables, not in allegories.

Despite the giant step forward it represents, *Die Gleichnisreden Jesu* was considerably marred by its adherence to the liberal theology of the day. Jülicher tended to interpret the parables as pedagogical illustrations of general moral and religious truths. For example, he took the parable of the labourers in the vineyard (Mt 20.1–16) to teach that all are equal in God's eyes and so equally treated by him. This approach gave both Christology and eschatology inadequate consideration. Jülicher also failed to take sufficiently into account the rabbinic corpus of parables, which often illuminates Jesus' words.

Jülicher's first failing – his viewing the parables as little more than illustrations of religious and moral truisms – was probably most effectively countered and called into question by C. H. Dodd's influential book, *The Parables of the Kingdom* (first edition, 1935). In this Dodd tried to relate the parables not to religion in general but to Jesus' ministry in particular. For Dodd, Jesus taught a realized eschatology which is consistently reflected in his parables. To illustrate: the parable of the sower implies that the ministry of Jesus is the time of the eschatological harvest, while the parable of the bridegroom (Mk 2.18–19 par.) teaches that the messianic time has commenced; and the parable of the pearl (Mt 13.45–6) means that the great treasure of the kingdom of God can be possessed even now. The parables proclaim the presence of the kingdom and set forth the unprecedented opportunity afforded Jesus' hearers.

After Dodd the next major contribution to the study of the parables came from Joachim Jeremias: *The Parables of Jesus* (first published in German in 1947). Taking up where Dodd left off, Jeremias replaced 'realized eschatology' with 'eschatology in the process of realization', a phrase which perhaps the majority of NT scholars have found apt. Jeremias also made a contribution by underlining the fact that several of Jesus' parables seem to be variants of stories preserved in rabbinic texts and that one may sometimes discern the meaning of a synoptic parable by discovering the new twist Jesus evidently gave to an old tale. Even more importantly, however, was Jeremias' consistent attempt to interpret the parables in their setting in the life of Jesus. This was an emphasis begun by Dodd, but Jeremias carried it forward. Indeed, the entire first half of *The Parables of Jesus* is given over to uncovering ten 'laws of transformation' which effected the shape of the parables in their transmission from Jesus to gospel. Jeremias' one goal was to get back to the historical Jesus.

Although much important work has been done since Jülicher, Dodd, and Jeremias, their contributions remain the most influential, so some critical comment upon them is necessary. First, the emphasis of Dodd and Jeremias and many after them upon the setting of the parables in the life of Jesus has tended to direct attention away from the texts as they stand, as well as away from the interpretations of the evangelists. While certainly understandable as part of the quest of the historical Jesus, the interpretation of the parables in their present literary contexts remains a legitimate concern, and it is the chief concern of this commentary.

Second, the meaning of the parables must not be too rigidly restricted to one point of comparison. Both Dodd and Jeremias, following in the footsteps of Jülicher, tended to confine the meaning of any given parable to a single application. Metaphorical language, however, has an affective component which goes beyond the straightforward imparting of information. In addition, one cannot eliminate from the parables every trace of allegory. Allegory is not always obscure; it is well-attested in ancient Palestinian literature, and several synoptic parables can only with great difficulty be altogether purified of allegorical features. This last is true in part because Jewish tradition, which is full of stock metaphors (such as 'father' and 'fruit'), makes it almost inevitable that certain words be understood as tropic.

The third point is that Dodd was probably incorrect to assert that in Jesus' parables 'all is true to nature and to life'. There are quite a few texts which seem to give the lie to this generalization. Indeed, their number is such that one is tempted to turn the tables and make the atypical features a key to interpreting a number of the parables. When a man who has worked one hour is paid the same as a man who has worked all day (20.1–16), and when a mustard seed becomes not a large plant but a *tree* (Mt 13.31–2), is not the point precisely that God's ways are not our ways and the workings of the kingdom do not always follow the laws of this world? Jülicher's justified attack upon allegorical extremism led him to stress the true-to-life character and realism of the events narrated in Jesus' parables. But he went too far. Anomalous elements must not be ignored or eliminated. They are instead to be understood as rhetorically appropriate, a method for stating surprising convictions about God's mysterious ways. Everyday situations were not always enough to illustrate the radical nature of the kingdom, and Jesus on occasion imaginatively resorted to painting unlikely or impossible scenarios.

Lastly, one wonders whether it is not a mistake to insist that all of the synoptic parables be approached with one method or with one fixed set of expectations as to what a parable must be. Indeed, some of the parables are allegorical, others functions as exemplary stories, and still others employ true-to-life metaphors.

Listen! A sower went out to sow. When the sower goes out in order to sow, has he already ploughed the field, or will that come later? The issue has been much discussed, with uncertain result. One cannot reach a decision on the basis of presumed common practice, for ancient texts reflect both orders. It may, moreover, have been common to plough both before and after one sowed.

4. And as he sowed, some seeds fell along the path. Paths sometimes marked the boundaries of ownership. But paths also evidently ran through the middle of fields.

and the birds came and devoured them. Cf. Gen 40.17 and *Jub.* 11.11 ('And the prince Mastema sent ravens and other birds to eat up the seed that had been sown in the land . . .').

6. and since they had no root, they withered away. Cf. Jn 15.6 9: 'If a man does not abide in me, he is cast forth as a branch and withers.'

7. The reader is next informed that some seed will fall among thorns and be choked. This would appear to mark an advance over the fate of the first two groups of seed. If the seed on or beside the road never germinates, and if the seed on rocky soil springs up only for the briefest period, the seed among thorns grows some time before it is overcome. The lifetime of the various seeds becomes greater as one moves toward the parable's climax.

8. some a hundredfold, some sixty, some thirty. Is the estimation of the yield fantastic? According to some, a good harvest may yield up to tenfold, so the abnormal numbers – thirty, sixty, one hundred – witness to a true miracle. But according to Varro, *R.R.* 1.44.2, seed in Syria could yield a hundredfold; and other texts point in the same direction. In trying to evaluate the issue one would like to know how the yield in the gospels is computed. Is it according to the number of seeds or grains on each stalk, or the proportion of stalks to grain planted, or the number of seeds produced for each seed planted, or something else again? Despite our desire to know, the text is mute. Perhaps, then, it is legitimate to look outside the NT for a solution. There are Jewish and Christian passages which refer to the exceedingly great harvests expected in the messianic age. Papias is quoted as having foretold that 'a grain of wheat shall bring forth ten thousand ears, and every ear shall have ten thousand grains . . .'. The fanciful descriptions in *b. Ketub.* 111b–12a are equally ludicrous (e.g. it will take a ship to carry one grape!). Compared to these texts, the numbers in the gospels do not seem obviously out of the ordinary. So maybe the yield in our parable is not spectacularly overdone.

9. He who has ears, let him hear! Cf. 11.15 and 13.43.

The Reason for Speaking in Parables (13.10–17)

Although the disciples have, as shall soon be made clear, religious understanding, the parable of the sower moves them to ask a question. They want to know why Jesus speaks in parables. Why not instead teach in a straightforward manner? Their query gives Jesus the opportunity to discourse upon the differences between these who have been given the secrets of the kingdom of heaven and those who have not.

11. To you it has been given to know the secrets of the kingdom of heaven. Cf. the agraphon in Clement of Alexandria ('For the prophet says: Who shall understand a parable of the Lord save he that is wise and knowledgeable and loveth his Lord? For it is given to few to contain all things; for it is not as grudging that the Lord commanded in a certain gospel: My mystery for me and for the sons of my house') and *Ps.-Clem. Hom.* 19.20 ('And Peter said: "We remember that our Lord and teacher, commanding us, said, 'Keep the mysteries for me and the sons of my house'." Wherefore also he explained to His disciples privately the mysteries of the kingdom of Heaven').

The 'mystery' is the *presence* of the kingdom in Jesus and his ministry. This mysterious presence is a circumstance which is recognized only by the minority: by those who, because they follow Jesus, understand his words.

In their preoccupation with wondering how God can justly give knowledge to only a select group, some commentators have failed to see that the emphasis of the text lies not on privation but on God's gift. Mt 13.16–17 and the remainder of the chapter make this manifest. The normal state of humanity is ignorance of God's eschatological secrets. Human beings as human beings do not know the truth about the kingdom of heaven. If therefore some have come to know that truth, it can only be because of God's gracious dealings with them. Mt 11.25 and 16.17 make the same point: eschatological knowledge is the gift of God. Mt 13.10ff. is a testimony to God's kindness. Cf. Chrysostom: Jesus does 'not bring in necessity or any allotment made carelessly and at random, but implies them to be the authors of all their own evils, and wishing to represent that the thing is a gift, and a grace bestowed from above'.

12. This verse illustrates further the differences between the disciples and those who do not understand the mysteries of the kingdom; it accentuates the distinction between those who perceive and those who do not. 'To him who has will more be given' refers to the disciples, who have understanding and will be given more understanding. 'To the one who has not, even what he has will be taken away' refers to those not privy to the secrets of the kingdom: they do not and will not understand. Thus it is explained why the parables hide and reveal at the same time. Their effect – illumination or darkness – depends upon the status of the hearer. Knowledge leads to knowledge, ignorance to ignorance. Like begets like.

13. that seeing they do not perceive. Matthew's 'that' makes the parables a *response* to unbelief: they are uttered *because* people see and do not see, because they hear and do not hear. This puts the emphasis unambiguously on human responsibility. More particularly, it makes the parables a consequence of the unbelief that has withstood Jesus' gracious teaching and salvific ministry. For Matthew, Jesus did not speak in parables to outsiders until hostility raised its ugly head.

and hearing they do not hear, nor do they understand. If by and large the disciples in Mark cannot 'understand' much before Jesus rises from the dead, in Matthew they can, at least with Jesus' aid; cf. 13.51; 15.15–20; 16.9–12; 17.10–13. In this way Matthew blurs the line between the pre- and post-Easter periods. The result is that Christian readers may identify more readily with the disciples. Also, the stress on understanding well serves Matthew's view of the apostles as the authoritative bearers of Jesus' teaching.

[[**14–15.** These verses are probably a post-Matthean interpolation whose source is perhaps Acts 28.26–7.]]

16–17. In contrast with others (13.11), the disciples truly see and hear. In thus accurately perceiving they are, Jesus boldly proclaims, beholding what the prophets and the righteous of old only longed to see, namely, the eschatological revelation of God – which for Matthew includes Jesus' parables.

Worth comparing are the beatitudes in *Ps. Sol.* 17.50 ('Blessed are those who will be in those days, in that they will see the good fortune of Israel which God will bring to pass in the gathering of the tribes') and 18.7 ('Blessed will they be who will be in those days, in that they *will* see the goodness of the Lord which he will perform for the generation that is to come'). In these two texts those who *will* see the messianic age are blessed. Jesus, however, declares that salvation has come *now*. What was once only in the future, a matter of hope, is now in the present, a matter of experience.

Amen I say to you, many prophets and righteous people longed to see what you see, but did not see it. Cf. Jn 8.56 ('Your father Abraham rejoiced that he was to see my day; he saw it and was glad'); Heb 11.13 ('These all died in faith, not having received what was promised, but having seen it and greeted it from afar'); and 1 Pet 1.10 ('The prophets who prophesied of the grace that was to be yours searched and inquired about this salvation'). 'Righteous people' is here an inclusive term which covers all the just who looked forward to the coming of the Messiah.

and to hear what you hear, but did not hear it. While references to 'seeing' the Messiah or the world to come are common in Jewish literature, the reference to 'hearing' in connexion with eschatology recalls not Jewish parallels but rather 11.4–5: 'Announce to John what you see *and hear* ... the deaf *hear* ... and the poor have good news preached to them.' The emphasis upon *hearing* eschatological events seems to have been characteristic of Jesus, the preacher and teacher. Cf. his use of 'He who has ears to hear, let him hear'.

Two texts from the *Mekilta* may shed some light on 13.16–17. *Mek.* on Exod 15.2 reads as follows: 'R. Eliezer says: Whence can you say that a maidservant saw at the sea what Isaiah and Ezekiel and all the prophets never saw? It says about them: "And by the ministry of the prophets have I used similitudes"' (Hos 12.10). *Mek.* on Exod 19.11 has this: 'Another interpretation: *In the sight of all the people.* This teaches that at that moment the people saw what Isaiah and Ezekiel never saw. For it is said: "And by the ministry of the prophets have I used similitudes"' (Hos 12.10). In these passages the witnesses of the exodus and the people at Sinai are said to have seen what the prophets did not see. Not only that, but those who did not see are associated with 'similitudes'. If Matthew knew this tradition or something similar, it may have encouraged him to bring together the saying about prophets and wise men with Jesus' words on parables. This would have been all the more natural given the beginning–end equation: if the prophets did not witness God's great miracles at the beginning of salvation-history, neither did they apprehend the consummation; rather, their visions of God were unclear; they saw only 'parables'.

The Interpretation of the Parable of the Sower (13.18–23)

Matthew's allegorical interpretation of the parable of the four soils agrees in all essentials with Mk 4.13–20, from which it was taken (cf. also Lk 8.11–15).

19. The seed is 'the word of the kingdom', and its fate is now considered. Interestingly enough, nowhere in what follows is the sower clearly identified. The broader Matthean context, however, as well as 13.37 ('he who sows ... is the Son of man'), encourage one to think of Jesus. The issue is Israel's response to Jesus and his proclamation. **When anyone hears the word of the kingdom and does not understand it, the evil one comes and snatches away what is sown in his heart.** 'The word of the kingdom' seems to mean, 'the preaching of the kingdom'. Birds are frequently associated with the devil or demonic beings in Jewish tradition. In *Jub.* 11.11, Mastema sends ravens and birds to devour seed sown in the land. In *Apoc. Abr.* 13, Azazel manifests himself to Abraham in the form of an unclean bird. In *b. Sanh.* 107a, Satan is seen by King David in the likeness of a bird. These texts (cf. also Rev 18.2) make the allegorical equation of birds with Satan less artificial than it otherwise might seem. Recall also Satan's status as the 'prince of the power of the air' (Eph 2.2).

20. this is the one who hears the word and immediately receives it with joy seems to equate the hearer of the word with the seed, this in contrast to v. 19, where the seed is the word and the soil represents an individual. The interpretation of the parable of the sower is not consistent in all its details.

* * * * *

When Mt 13.1–23 is preached today it is usually for the purpose of exhorting believers. While such an application is far from hermeneutically unlawful, it does inevitably miss the main point for Matthew. His version of the parable of the sower is not aimed at exhortation. Its purpose is rather to offer an explanation. The passage has to be understood within its wider context, this being chapters 11–12. These two chapters relate in some detail the failure of Jesus' ministry to effect repentance in corporate Israel. A difficult question is thus engendered, a question not unlike that addressed in Rom 9–11: how does one explain the failure of so many of Jesus' hearers to come to faith? Matthew was, like Paul before him, faced with the dilemma of a Messiah rejected by his people – in opposition to all Jewish eschatological expectation. What was his response? Just as Paul believed that God would, in the end, redeem his people, so too did the First Evangelist probably hope for Israel's eschatological redemption. But this conviction by itself hardly explained the unexpected response to Jesus himself or the unbelief of so many Jews in Matthew's day: and it is precisely to these failures of faith that Mt 13.1–23 is intended to speak. Although the word of the kingdom is preached to all, all do not respond in the same way. Some believe, some do not. The reason? Opportunity does not guarantee response, proclamation does not abolish sin. This is the main message of 13.1–23, which in effect offers something similar to the free will defence for the problem of evil. For Matthew, Israel's failure, the root of her trouble, does not lie with God. It lies rather with people who are free to harden their hearts. Therefore, unless or until God overrides wills, the gospel will meet a mixed reception.

THREE MORE PARABLES (13.24–43)

[24]**He put before them another parable: 'The kingdom of heaven may be compared to the situation of a man who sowed good seed in his field.** [25]**Now while people were sleeping, an enemy came and sowed weeds among the wheat and then went away.** [26]**So when the plants came up and**

bore grain, then the weeds appeared also. [27]And the slaves of the householder came and said to him, "Lord, did you not sow good seed in your field? From whence, then, did these weeds come?" [28]He said to them, "An enemy has done this." The slaves said to him, "Then do you want us to go and gather them?" [29]But he said, "No, lest in gathering the weeds you uproot the wheat along with them. [30]Let both of them grow together until the harvest, and at harvest time I will tell the harvesters, Gather the weeds first and bind them in bundles to be burned, but gather the wheat into my barn".'

[31]Another parable he put before them: 'The kingdom of heaven is like a mustard seed that a man took and sowed in his field. [32]It is the smallest of all the seeds, but when it has grown it is the greatest of shrubs and becomes a tree, so that the birds of the air come and make nests in its branches.'

[33]Another parable he spoke to them: 'The kingdom of heaven is like yeast that a woman took and mixed in with three measures of flour until all of it was leavened.'

[34]All these things Jesus told the crowds in parables, and without a parable he told them nothing. [35]Thus was fulfilled what had been spoken through the prophet: 'I will open my mouth to speak in parables; I will proclaim what has been hidden from the foundation of the world.'

[36]Then leaving the crowds he went into the house. And his disciples came to him, saying, 'Explain to us the parable of the weeds of the field.' [37]Answering he said, 'He who sows the good seed is the Son of man. [38]The field is the world, and the good seed are the sons of the kingdom. The weeds are the sons of the evil one, [39]and the enemy who sowed them is the devil. The harvest is the end of the age, and the harvesters are angels. [40]Just as the weeds are gathered and burned up with fire, so will it be at the end of the age. [41]The Son of man will send his angels, and they will gather out of his kingdom all causes of sin and all evildoers, [42]and they will throw them into the furnace of fire, where there will be weeping and gnashing of teeth. [43]Then the righteous will shine like the sun in the kingdom of their Father. He who has ears, let him hear!'

Parallels: Mk 13.31–4; Lk 13.18–21

The Parable of the Weeds (13.24–30)

In several respects the parable of the tares carries forward themes already treated in 13.1–23. It is not just that certain motifs – sowing, seeds, soil, kingdom, obstacles to growth, the devil or the evil one – are repeated. Rather, and beyond this, both parables make it plain that while the victory of God's kingdom is sure, *the way from here to there is hampered by unbelief and its effects.* In other words, both address the same problem of evil, which is the failure of the gospel to win the hearts of all, and both answer in a similar fashion. More precisely, and taking into account the broader context, the first two parables in Matthew 13 help explain unbelief in Jesus and the dilemma of a rejected Messiah. Just as seed may fall upon different types of soil, and just as weeds may be sown among wheat, so too is it with Jesus' ministry: the good comes with the evil. The one major difference between the sower and the tares is that while the former focuses on human responsibility, the latter points to the evil one: the devil must share the responsibility for the apparent failure of God's word.

Most modern commentators assume that 13.24–30 and its interpretation address a situation in Matthew's community. Either that community was concerned with opposition to the gospel in its own day or it was worried about the character of some of its members and what to do about them. Neither idea, however, is expounded in the interpretation in 13.36–43 – which in fact quite plainly identifies the field with the world, not the church; and instead of conjuring up some hypothetical historical setting, the literary context should be the key to interpretation. When this natural requirement is observed, 13.24–30 can be seen to relate to the plot of the gospel as a whole. It is part of the answer to the difficult situation – disbelief in Jesus – depicted in chapters 11–12.

25. an enemy came and sowed weeds among the wheat and then went away. Mt 13.39 will identify the enemy with the devil. One is reminded of 13.19, which takes the birds of the air to symbolize the evil one. In both instances God's work of sowing is countered by Satanic opposition. Note that in 13.25 the devil does what the Son of man does: he sows. Thus the devil is made out to be an imitator, a maker of counterfeits. The result is that just as there are wolves in the midst of sheep (7.15), so too are there weeds in the midst of wheat.

27. And the slaves of the householder came and said to him. The householder – Jesus has already been pictured as a 'householder' in 10.24–5 – is the same person as the sower. The slaves, however, are not identified, and they are not mentioned in the interpretation.

Lord, did you not sow good seed in your field? This summarizes the action of 13.24b, from whence the vocabulary derives. 'Lord' is implicitly christological because in 13.37 the householder (who, we must assume, sowed the seed) will be identified as the Son of man.

29. The servants are instructed not to pull up the weeds, lest the wheat also be pulled up. The assumption seems to be that the number of weeds is so great that their roots have entwined with the roots of the wheat, with the result that one could not pull up the one without pulling up the other. (Or, less likely, the weeds have been discovered too late in the season, so their roots have had opportunity to mingle with the wheat.)

The Parable of the Mustard Seed (13.31–2)

This is a parable of contrast. It illustrates, by reference to the growth of a mustard seed, a vital truth about God's kingdom: a humble beginning and secret presence are not inconsistent with a great and glorious destiny. The focus is neither on the smallness or insignificance of a present circumstance, nor on the greatness of God's future (on both points instruction was unnecessary). Rather, the emphasis falls upon their juxtaposition, on two seemingly incongruent facts, the one being the experience of Jesus and his followers in the present (cf. the mustard seed), the other being their expectations of the future; cf. the tree in which the birds of heaven nest. Our parable is an invitation to contemplate these two things in the light of the mustard seed's story. The point is that despite all appearances, between the minute beginning and the grand culmination there is an organic unity. Indeed, the one (the tree/the eschatological climax) is an effect of the other (the seed/God's activity in Jesus and his disciples). The end is in the beginning.

32. It is the smallest of all the seeds, but when it has grown it is the greatest of shrubs and becomes a tree. According to Pliny, the mustard seed 'germinates at once'. Certainly a seed that grows into a ten-foot herb in one season, as some mustard plants do, has a very rapid growth rate.

the birds of the air come and make nests in its branches. Cf. Ezek 17.23; 31.5–6; Dan 4.10–12, 20–1. The image of a large tree with birds nesting in it or under it was a traditional symbol for a great kingdom. In addition to the passages already cited see Judg 9.7–15. Jewish tradition could also think of the messianic community as a planting, one which would spread throughout the earth; see *Ps. Sol.* 14.2–3; 1QH 6.14–16; 8.4–8.

While mustard plants in Palestine grow up to ten feet, and while birds eat their seeds and sometimes use their leaves for shelter, the plants do not provide nesting places for birds. Once again the unrealistic nature of our parable is manifest. Mt 13.31–2 is not a simple collection of observations about mustard seeds and plants.

Did Matthew think of the birds of heaven as standing for Gentiles? One guesses that he did, in view of 21.43: 'the kingdom of God will be taken away from you and given to a nation producing the fruits of it.'

The Parable of the Leaven (13.33)

This parable is much like that preceding it. The introductions (vv. 31a–b, 33a–b) are very similar; both parables recount the story of someone hiding something which then becomes great; and both have to do with an organic process. These similarities signal an identity of theme. Both parables teach that the coming of the kingdom begins not with a grand, public spectacle but with a hidden presence. In this way the character and nature of Jesus' ministry, including its failure in Israel, can be understood. Eschatology commences not with a bang but with little more than a whimper.

33. The kingdom of heaven is like yeast. In ancient sources leaven (we are to think of old, fermented dough) is used figuratively of either a corrupting influence or – much less frequently – of a beneficial influence.

that a woman took and mixed in with three measures of flour until all of it was leavened. The woman in our parable is not herself a symbol, although some have equated her with the Holy Spirit, wisdom, Mary, or the church. She is no more symbolic than 'the man' of v. 31.

Why is the measure specified? Why *three* measures? The quantity is excessive. It would provide a meal for over a hundred people. So 'three measures' suggests a feast, which Jesus often used to symbolize the kingdom.

Cf. 1 Cor 5.6: 'Do you not know that a little leaven leavens the whole lump?' This could reflect knowledge of Jesus' parable. But most commentators regard the words (which also appear in Gal 5.9) as proverbial. Perhaps, then, Jesus' parable was based upon the proverb preserved in Paul. If so, it would be one more instance of Jesus using a negative image in a positive fashion.

The negative associations of leaven are so prominent in Scripture and other ancient sources that some earlier exegetes understood the parable of the leaven to predict the corruption of the church in the world. While this exegesis can hardly be sustained, some modern scholars have tried to retain the negative connotations of leaven by proposing that Jesus intended it to reflect the disreputable character of many of the members of the kingdom.

The Use of Parables (13.34–5)

Drawing upon Mk 4.33–4 and Ps 78.2, Matthew now composes a formula quotation which makes a general statement about Jesus' use of parables. Two ends are thereby served. First, Jesus' parabolic manner of speaking is grounded in OT prophecy. Just as Jesus' birth, childhood, ministry, and death are all foretold in the Scriptures, so too does the OT look forward to the Messiah uttering in parables mysteries hidden from the foundation of the world. Second, vv. 34–5 serve, in a manner reminiscent of vv. 10–17, as a transition which notifies the reader of a switch in audience. Jesus at this juncture speaks not to the crowds and the disciples but to the disciples alone. He is turning away from those who do not understand towards those who do.

35. I will open my mouth to speak in parables; I will proclaim what has been hidden from the foundation of the world. Matthew was attracted to Ps 78.2 because of the phrase, 'in parables'. That he paid much attention to the verse's broader context is not manifest, and it could be claimed that in this verse Matthew has misused the OT, especially as Ps 78.1–4 is clearly about an open revelation, not mysteries revealed to a select few. On the other hand, it can be urged that since Ps 78.1–4 is about the history of Israel, and since for Matthew that history is recapitulated in Jesus' life, the novel application of Ps 78.2 is not arbitrary; cf. the discussion of the use of Hos 11.1 in Mt 2.15.

For Matthew the meaning of Ps 78.2 is not, despite 13.12–13, that Jesus speaks in parables in order to hide things from the crowds. Rather, his parables are revelatory (cf. 13.52), even when some cannot grasp them.

The Interpretation of the Parable of the Weeds (13.36–43)

Returning to a private location, Jesus now answers his disciples' request for an interpretation of the parable of the weeds. He complies by giving them a list of allegorical equations (vv. 37–9), by reciting a short account of the last judgement (vv. 40–3a), and by uttering a general admonition (v. 43b).

36. Then leaving the crowds he went into the house. Esoteric teaching demands a private setting.

Explain to us the parable of the weeds of the field. The title, 'the parable of the weeds', shows us that Matthew is thinking primarily not of the salvation of the righteous but of the wicked and their fate. The subject is not reward but punishment.

37–9. Matthew's Jesus meets the disciples' request by first compiling a list of seven allegorical equations.

He who sows the good seed is the Son of man. 'The Son of man' is chosen because it is in this role that Jesus will act as the judge on the final day.

The field is the world. Much exegetical blood has been spilled over these words. The reason is that the parable of the weeds has often been viewed as treating of church discipline, and more specifically as being instruction to refrain from trying to create a church purified of sinners. Augustine championed this view in fighting the Donatists, and the text has been similarly used down the centuries. It seems unlikely, however, that our text should have much bearing on properly ecclesiastical issues, for (i) Matthew equates the field with the world, not the church; (ii) the Matthean context has nothing to do with church discipline (contrast chapter 18); and (iii) chapter 18 does not shy away from offering firm instructions on excommunication.

and the good seed are the sons of the kingdom. In 8.12 'the sons of the kingdom' is an ironic appellation for Jews who will be cast out into the darkness. Here the phrase describes the faithful. The antithetical applications are striking. It has been suggested that the use of the one title to tag two different groups should warn church members that they, like unbelieving Jews, can lose their privileged status. The point would certainly be consistent with Matthew's view of things.

The weeds are the sons of the evil one. 'The sons of the evil one' underlines the power of the devil in the world and the responsibility he bears for human failing, two themes Matthew wishes to bring out at this point in his story, for he is still largely concerned with coming to grips with Israel's response to Jesus.

and the harvesters are angels. It is characteristic of Matthew to associate the Son of man with angels (13.41; 16.27; 25.31).

40. Mt 13.24–30 told a story. Mt 13.37–9 then supplied a lexicon of sorts explaining the meanings of seven figures in that story. Mt 13.40–3 now takes those meanings and with them constructs a second narrative. In other words, the story in 13.24–30 uses the figures on one side of the equations in 13.37–9, while 13.40–3 uses the figures from the other side:

13.24–30	13.37–9	13.40–3
sower	sower = Son of man	Son of man
field	field = world	world
good seed	good seed = sons of the kingdom	sons of the kingdom
weeds	weeds = sons of the evil one	sons of the evil one
enemy	enemy = the devil	the devil
harvest	harvest = judgement	judgement
harvesters	harvesters = angels	angels

The result is two stories with one meaning. (As a matter of fact the story in vv. 40–3 only takes up the separation of the wheat and tares, recounted in v. 30; it passes over the verses leading up to this.)

41–2. and they will gather out of his kingdom all causes of sin and all evildoers. 'His kingdom' is most naturally equated with the church; but 13.38 equates the field with the world. So either the kingdom encompasses the world in so far as it is proclaimed everywhere, or the harvesting immediately follows the coming of the future kingdom, when the world and the kingdom will be identical.

and they will throw them into the furnace of fire. This phrase, used again in 13.50, is from Dan 3.6.

where there will be weeping and gnashing of teeth. On this Matthean refrain see on 8.12.

43. Then the righteous will shine like the sun in the kingdom of their Father. Cf. the transfiguration in 17.2, which Matthew may have had in mind here: the transfiguration of Jesus shows forth the eschatological glory which all the saints will share.

* * * * *

(i) The parable of the weeds and its interpretation suggest that human failure is part of a wider problem, namely, the cosmic struggle between God and Satan. Those who oppose the Messiah are 'sons of the devil', that is, they are his planting. Thus their (from Matthew's perspective) irrational lack of faith is part and parcel of an even greater mystery, that of transcendent or non-human evil. Second, the parable of the tares addresses the question of theodicy by putting evil in eschatological perspective, by reminding one that the bad endures only for a season. The tares will eventually be plucked up, the wheat gathered. It is, then, history's end which will give the answers to the difficult theological questions history, including the history of Jesus, raises.

(ii) The parables of the mustard seed and leaven, cut from the same cloth, stand in continuity with the parable of the weeds in that they too place God's triumph only in the future. For the present the kingdom is a mysterious, hidden entity, whose chief feature seems to be weakness. But according to our similitudes what matters is not the beginning but the end. The kingdom of God may not begin with success, but success is its divinely ordained destiny. If leaven leavens the whole lump, and if a little mustard seed becomes a tree, similarly will the kingdom, however obscure now, become, in the end, the measure of all things.

THREE MORE PARABLES AND THE CONCLUSION OF THE DISCOURSE (13.44–52)

[44]'The kingdom of heaven is like treasure hidden in a field, which someone found and hid; then in his joy he goes and sells all that he has and buys that field.

[45]'Again, the kingdom of heaven is like a merchant seeking fine pearls. [46]On finding one pearl of great value, he went and sold all that he had and bought it.

[47]'Again, the kingdom of heaven is like a net that was thrown into the sea and caught fish of every kind. [48]When it was full, they drew it ashore, sat down, and put the good into baskets but threw out the bad. [49]So will it be at the end of the age. The angels will come out and separate the evil from the righteous [50]and throw them into the furnace of fire, where there will be weeping and gnashing of teeth.

[51]'Have you understood all these things?' They answered, 'Yes.' [52]And he said to them, 'Therefore every scribe who has been instructed in the kingdom of heaven is like the master of a household who brings out of his treasure what is new and what is old.'

Parallels: none

In contrast with the surrounding verses, which speak of dread judgement, the two parables which open our section – vv. 44 and 45–6 – have to do with finding the kingdom and giving all one has to obtain it. Thus the focus of vv. 44–6 is on the present, not on the future, and readers are led to envision the actions of believers, not the deeds and fate of unbelievers.

The Hidden Treasure (13.44)

The parable, by reference to a once-in-a-lifetime discovery, to an event one only dreams about, expresses the incomparable worth of the kingdom and the necessity to do all one can do to gain it. One gladly risks everything to take advantage of the unexpected opportunity presented by the presence of God's salvific kingdom with all its blessings; cf. the call stories in chapters 4, 8, and 9. (While some exegetes stress the value of the kingdom, others put the emphasis upon the appropriate reaction. But these are equally important.)

treasure hidden in a field. In a day before safe-deposit boxes, it seems to have been common enough for people to bury valuables in the ground, especially in times of political instability and crisis.

which someone found and hid. Our parable presupposes that the kingdom is not yet revealed to everyone. This fits well with the rest of the chapter. The revelation of God in Jesus is not perfectly vivid to all; it can only be perceived by those with ears to hear and eyes to see.

Commentators have long discussed whether the finder of the treasure acts immorally or unlawfully when he covers it up and seeks to make it his own. Some have defended his actions as above reproach. Others have thought him immoral. It is not easy to assess the issue. What is the status of the finder? What is he doing in the field? How is the treasure discovered? How did it come to be where it is? What kind of treasure is it? Who owns the field? How did the owner come to own the field? Without knowing such details one is hesitant to evaluate the legal or moral situation and even uncertain as to the value of discussing such. Certainly Jesus' failure to remark on them makes one wonder how important they can be. Further, whether or not 13.44 was originally associated with 13.45–6 (the parable of the pearl), it seems altogether likely that both texts were composed in order to make the same point. There is, however, nothing at all scandalous or illegal about the merchant's purchase of the magnificent pearl. When he goes and sells all that he has, he may be acting strangely, but he is not being immoral. Can it really be so different with the finder of the treasure?

then in his joy he goes and sells all that he has and buys that field. Since it takes all that he has for the man discovering the treasure to procure the field, it is often concluded that he is poor. If this is a correct inference, there would be a contrast with the next parable, in which the main figure, the pearl merchant, is presumably well-to-do. Cf. the contrast in 13.31–3: one parable has to do with a man, the other with a woman.

The Pearl of Great Price (13.45–6)

When the kingdom is encountered, a decision is required; that decision may require sacrificing all one has; but all one has no longer means anything compared to the kingdom.

45. a merchant seeking fine pearls. 'Pearls' were more valued by the ancients than they are by us, and several commentators have suggested that pearls once held the place that diamonds do now. 'Seeking' implies that the kingdom does not manifest itself to all, but only to those who search it out: 'Seek and you will find.' In context, the lesson may be that Israel has not welcomed the Messiah because she has not sincerely sought the kingdom. (This interpretation does not, of course, exclude a paraenetic application for Matthew's Christian readers.)

The pearl is surely to be identified with the kingdom. Those exegetes who have equated the costly pearl with Jesus are therefore incorrect. Nonetheless, their mistake is a small one. Matthew's gospel makes it plain enough that to find the kingdom is to find Jesus and that to find Jesus is to find the kingdom.

The Drag-Net and Its Interpretation (13.47–50)

The third and final parable of 13.44–52, a parable which in so many ways recalls the weeds, returns readers' thoughts to the last judgement, a topic already treated at length in vv. 36–43. The main point is quite simple: the wicked will, in the end, be separated from the righteous and suffer due punishment. The fate of the righteous is not contemplated at all; rather is attention directed towards what becomes of the unrighteous. So vv. 47–50 make known the tragic end of those who reject Messiah Jesus. (That our parable has anything to do with the mixed state of Matthew's church is not apparent.)

47. a net that was thrown into the sea. The drag-net was either pulled between two boats or drawn to land by ropes after being dropped offshore; cf. Lk 5.4–7.

and caught fish of every kind. 'Of every kind' underlines the universality of the judgement and perhaps also hints at the Gentile mission.

48. sat down, and put the good into baskets but threw out the bad. Would Matthew and his readers have thought of 'good' and 'bad' fish as clean and unclean fish (cf. Lev 11.9–12)? And is the reference to sitting supposed to allude to the fact that at the last judgement the judge or judges will be seated (cf. 19.28; 25.31)?

49. An interpretation of vv. 47–8 – really of only v. 48b – is now offered.

So will it be at the end of the age. The interpretation which follows is rather artificial, and even if Jesus' parable originally had to do with the eschatological judgement (a disputed issue), his meaning could hardly have matched Matthew's. For one thing, whereas in vv. 47–8 it is fishermen who cast, gather, and sort, in vv. 49–50 the angels sort, which implies also that they cast and gather, for their role is allegorically that of the fishermen. But in what sense angels can be said to cast and gather is mystifying. Furthermore, while 'and throw them into the furnace' makes sense in connexion with weeds (13.42), fish were not fired but rather tossed back or used as fertilizer.

The angels will come out and separate the evil from the righteous. This restates 13.41.

50 relates the final fate of the wicked. In contrast with vv. 36–43, the fate of the righteous is left unremarked. This shows where Matthew's interest lies. He is concerned with the problem of evil and its ultimate solution, as well as with delivering a warning.

Conclusion: The Discipled Scribe (13.51–2)

51. The major point is that the disciples have indeed understood Jesus' discourse and therefore qualify as skilled scribes.

Have you understood all these things? The verb recalls vv. 13, 19, 23 and in the light of these indicates that the disciples are among those who hear the word and bear much fruit. 'These things' harks back to v. 34 ('all these things Jesus told the crowds in parables') and anticipates v. 56 ('from where then did this man get all these things?') The words are accordingly comprehensive and refer to all of chapter 13.

52. Jesus responds to the disciples' affirmation by declaring them to be scribes discipled for the kingdom of heaven, individuals who will bring forth from their storehouses things new and old. Matthew probably thought of the words as including himself, his Lord, the twelve, and all Christian scribes or teachers. One also supposes that he thought of all these together as forming some sort of counterpart to the Jewish rabbinate.

every scribe who has been instructed in the kingdom of heaven is like the master of a household. It is altogether probable that Matthew belonged to a 'school' of Christian scribes, who perhaps carried on their activities in a Christian synagogue. They were no doubt prominent leaders of Matthew's church.

Given that his gospel is so much concerned with the last things, it may well be that Matthew thought of himself and his fellow Christian scribes as holding an office whose members had been entrusted with eschatological secrets. The authors of several apocalypses, including *1 Enoch*, 4 Ezra, *2 Baruch*, *2 Enoch*, and *3 Enoch*, were held to have been scribes. Ecclus 39.1–3 is also pertinent: 'He who devotes himself to the study of the law of the Most High will seek out the wisdom of all the ancients, and will be concerned with prophecies; he will preserve the discourse of notable men and penetrate the subtleties of parables; he will seek out the hidden meanings of proverbs and be at home with the obscurities of parables.'

It has on occasion been suggested that just as Mk 14.51–2 (the flight of the naked young man) might be an autobiographical insertion, so too may Mt 13.51–2 be the author's signature: he was a scribe, so 13.51–2 is a self-portrait.

who brings out of his treasure what is new and what is old. The picture painted is evidently of a householder bringing forth – for guests? – food, articles of clothing, and other necessities from his storehouse.

But what is meant by 'new' and 'old'? The suggestions can be represented thus:

The old	The new
the old revelation (Torah, OT)	the new revelation in Jesus
Jewish tradition/teaching	Christian tradition/teaching
Jesus' teaching	the teaching of Christians
Jesus' parables	Matthew's interpretations
the OT	Christian interpretation of the OT
eschatological revelation (hidden)	eschatological revelation (revealed)
observations about the world	Jesus' parabolic teaching
Jewish Christian tradition	Gentile Christian tradition
understanding before hearing the parables	understanding after hearing them

Although these options are ranked in the order of their probability (the most probable first, the least probable last), it must be confessed that the contrast remains cryptic. All one can say with certainty is that the ability to teach things new and old rests upon the ability to understand Jesus' teaching.

* * * * *

Commentators of an earlier time were often encouraged to divine in the seven parables of Mt 13 a prophetic outline of church history. The approach remained popular until the twentieth century. One has no difficulty understanding the reason. The opening parable (the sower) has to do with the beginning of the gospel in the preaching of Jesus and the apostles, the last (the net) with the great assize, and in between are parables which describe the kingdom with metaphors of growth (the weeds, the mustard seed, the leaven). So the sequence is: beginning – growth – culmination.

If scholars nowadays do not take chapter 13 to be an allegorical representation of ecclesiastical history, this is in part because the interpretation is inevitably anachronistic: it must read into the text events which could not possibly have been on the minds of a first-century author and his readers. The old interpretation is nonetheless to be commended for its recognition of two facts, the first being that the discourse – like the other major discourses – exhibits a thematic unity, the second being that it – again like the other major discourses – winds up on an eschatological note. It is particularly important to recognize that, with regard to the first point, no parable in Mt 13 is out of place. The subject of the chapter as a whole is the kingdom and its fate in the world. The sower describes the initial proclamation of the gospel and its mixed reception. The weeds continues in the same vein, emphasizing the mysterious role of transcendent evil. The mustard seed and the leaven then follow, making plain the certainty of the kingdom's ultimate victory despite all appearances. It is subsequent to this that we have the twin parables of the hidden treasure and the pearl and, lastly, that of the net. The first two appropriately succeed 13.1–43 by offering paraenesis: buy, sell, seek. Granted the kingdom's value and its sure eschatological triumph, one must strive to be unlike the people denounced in Mt 11 and 12 and the unfruitful seeds described in 13.1–23. One must, recognizing the truth about the kingdom, do all to gain the one thing needful. The necessity for such action is, in turn, underlined by 13.47–50: judgement will come upon those who reject the kingdom; cf. the function of 7.24–7; 18.23–35; 25.1–46. There is, accordingly, a shift of emphasis between 13.1–43 and 13.44–50. Whereas the passages in the former are more descriptive, those in the latter are more paraenetic.

THE REJECTION AT NAZARETH (13.53–8)

[53]**When Jesus had finished these parables, he went away from there.** [54]**And coming to his own country he taught them in their synagogue, so that they were amazed and said, 'Where did this man get this wisdom and these mighty works?** [55]**Is not this the carpenter's son? Is not his mother called Mary? And are not his brothers James and Joseph and Simon and Judas?** [56]**And are not all his sisters with us? Where then did this man get all these things?'** [57]**And they took offence at him. But Jesus said to them, 'A prophet is not without honour except in his own country and in his own house.'** [58]**And he did not do many mighty works there, because of their unbelief.**

Parallels: Mk 6.1–6; Lk 4.16–30; Jn 4.44; 6.43; 7.15; 10.39

Following the preceding parables, 13.53–8 illustrates that the failure to understand leads not to indifference but to hostility. Those who do not grasp the secrets of the kingdom of heaven necessarily find Jesus offensive.

53. When Jesus had finished these parables. See on 7.28. The statement seemingly implies that the material in chapter 13 was spoken at one time; but Matthew, who put together the discourse from disparate sources, certainly knew otherwise, so his language should not be pressed.

he went away from there. Whenever Jesus finishes a major discourse, he immediately moves on to a new location; see 8.1; 11.1; 13.53; 19.1;

26.6. Discourse and narrative do not share the same geographical space.

54. And coming to his own country. In view of 2.22–3, the reader is to think of Nazareth, not Capernaum; cf. Lk 4.16.

he taught them in their synagogue is the last notice of Jesus teaching in the synagogue. This should not be misunderstood to mean a formal break with that institution. By placing the story of rejection where he has, that is, after chapters 11–13, the evangelist has made it plain that Jesus continued his ministry to the Jewish synagogue despite all opposition. Notwithstanding the fact that the need for a new religious institution has become obvious and will soon be realized (cf. 16.13–20), Jesus does not abandon his people. He still speaks to them and stills heals their infirm; cf. 14.34–6; 15.1–20, 29–31; 26.55; etc. Perhaps Matthew saw his Lord's persistence in this matter as precedent for missionaries in his own day: the existence of the church and the hostility of Israel did not provide an excuse for abandoning the Jews.

so that they were amazed and said. See further on 7.28–29, although here as opposed to there the amazement or perplexity appears to be negative.

Where did this man get this wisdom and these mighty works? Cf. Jn 7.15: 'How is it that this man has learning when he has never studied?' In 21.23–7, the question, 'The baptism of John, whence was it?', has for its answer either 'from heaven' or 'from men'. In 13.54 another alternative is implicit, that set forth in 12.22–30: God or Beelzebul; cf. 9.34; 10.24–5. The question before the synagogue is whether the inspiration for Jesus' words and deeds comes from God or Satan. While the sympathetic reader of Matthew knows the answer, the subject is an open one for the speakers.

55. The crowd continues to ask questions which attempt to explain away the extraordinary by associating it with the familiar. How can Jesus' reputation be harmonized with his humble origins? (It is implied that Jesus' family was not extraordinary.)

Is not this the carpenter's son? Cf. Jn 6.42: 'Is not this Jesus, whose father and mother we know?' According to Matthew, Jesus was the son of a carpenter. According to Mark, Jesus himself was a carpenter. How are the two texts to be explained? There are several possibilities. (i) Jesus and his father were both carpenters: the son was his father's apprentice. Both Matthew and Mark are correct. (ii) Menial labour was thought degrading and it was therefore unedifying to imagine Jesus as a carpenter; so his father was turned into such. This does not explain why Matthew did not simply drop the reference altogether and write, 'Is not his mother called Mary ...?' (iii) Mark's text has 'son' with Mary, not Joseph: 'Is this not the son of Mary?' Some have accounted for Mark's odd phrase by supposing that Joseph was long since dead. Others have discovered in the phrase an allusion to the virgin birth. A few have thought that 'the son of Mary' might have functioned as a slur: the circumstances of Jesus' birth were known to have been unusual, for there was doubt as to the father, so people contemptuously referred to Jesus as the son of his mother, implying illegitimacy; cf.1.18–19. In such a case, Matthew might have found 'the son of Mary' potentially disturbing and therefore have rejected it. (iv) The evangelist, in accordance with his interest in Jesus' legal descent from David, wanted to mention Jesus' father, not just his mother, and the easiest way to do this was to turn Mark's 'the carpenter' into 'the son of the carpenter'.

Is not his mother called Mary? And are not his brothers James and Joseph and Simon and Judas? Cf. 12.46, 48–9; Jn 2.12; and Acts 1.14 (all of which mention Jesus' mother and his brothers). Besides James, who became a leader of the Jerusalem church, the brothers of Jesus are mentioned by name in the NT only in 13.55 par. and Jude 1.1. For James see Acts 12.17; 15.13; 21.18; 1 Cor 15.7; Gal 1.19; 2.9, 12; Jas 1.1; Jude 1 (all referring to one and the same person). Paul refers to 'the brothers of the Lord' in 1 Cor 9.5 and implies that those besides James were itinerants. Jn 7.5 relates that before Easter even Jesus' brothers did not believe him.

There has been much discussion concerning the 'brothers' (and 'sisters') of Jesus. Later Christian belief in Mary as ever-virgin rendered problematic the thought that he had blood brothers and sisters. So it came to be widely imagined that James and the rest were either cousins, that is, Mary or Joseph's nephews and nieces, or half-brothers, that is, the children of Joseph by an earlier marriage. It is true that 'brother' need not mean 'blood brother' but can have broader meaning: 'kinsman' or 'relative'; cf. Gen 29.12; 24.48. The Greek word, however, normally means '(blood) brother', and one can explain the conviction that the 'brothers' and 'sisters' of Jesus were not the children of Mary by seeing it as a consequence of belief in Mary's perpetual virginity. In line with this, the manner of expression in 1.25 (Joseph did not know Mary 'until she had borne a son') and Lk 2.7 (Jesus was Mary's 'first-born son') would probably have been avoided had the evangelists already thought Mary ever-virgin. Further, Tertullian could hold that Jesus' brothers and sisters were Mary's offspring without expressing any awareness that he was in this departing from tradition.

It must, nonetheless, be confessed that the issue is not so simply resolved. If, as is not unnatural, one equates 'Mary the mother of James the younger and of Joseph/Joses' (Mk 15.40 = Mt 27.56) with

'Mary the wife of Clopas' (Jn 19.25), it would seem to follow that the brothers named in Mk 6.3 and Mt 13.55 were not the sons of Jesus' mother but another Mary. The same inference is to hand if one doubts, for the reason that 'Mary the mother of James and of Joses' (Mk 15.40) is an unexpected circumlocution for Jesus' mother, that the Mary of Mk 15.40 can be the Mary of Mk 6.3. It is accordingly at least *possible* that Jesus' 'brothers' and 'sisters' were not the children of Mary by Joseph; but nothing more definite can be hazarded.

56. And are not all his sisters with us? Only in Mt 13.56 and Mk 6.3 do we hear of the 'sisters' of Jesus. We know nothing about them at all, for after departing the synoptic stage they disappear into the backstreets of history, where only ecclesiastical fable can henceforth trace them. The silence of the NT may imply that they never became Christians.

57. And they took offence at him signifies a denial of faith which has eschatological importance. The citizens of Nazareth, by being 'offended' at Jesus, have passed eschatological judgement upon themselves.

A prophet is not without honour except in his own country and in his own house. Cf. Lk 4.24; Jn 4.44; Dio Chrysostom 47.6 ('all the philosophers held life to be difficult in the homeland'); and Apollonius of Tyana, *Ep.* 44 ('until now my own country alone ignores me'). What we have in the gospels is probably a Jewish version of the common sentiment that great people are rejected by their own.

58. because of their unbelief. Unlike the disciples, who have 'little faith' (see on 6.30), the congregation in Nazareth has no faith at all.

* * * * *

Coming as it does after the episodes of rejection in chapters 11 and 12 and after the little 'theodicy' of seven parables in chapter 13, 13.53–8, which supplies a concrete example of people hearing but not hearing and seeing but not seeing (cf. 13.13), shows us that unbelief does not correspond to any geographical pattern: Jesus is rejected in the north as well as the south, in his home town as well as in the capital. There is no safe haven, no sacred space uncontaminated by hostility; there is no one group of people that will, as a unit, embrace Jesus. Opposition is ubiquitous. The lesson neatly complements 12.46–50, the passage which immediately precedes 13.1–52. For if in 13.53–8 one learns that geographical and social ties are not what really matter, in 12.46–50 it is similarly taught that family ties may be relaxed by commitment to Jesus. Hence the great parable discourse is framed by two texts which relativize the significance of standard social connexions.

Mt 13.53–8 links up not only with what precedes but also with what follows. In 13.57 Jesus implicitly proclaims himself a prophet, and in 14.5 the people (correctly) hold John to be a prophet. The upshot is clear. John's fate, which is recounted in 14.1–12, is that of a prophet, and it must therefore lie ahead for Jesus. To be a prophet means to suffer rejection, and to suffer rejection means, ultimately, to suffer death.

THE DEATH OF JOHN THE BAPTIST (14.1–12)

14 [1]**At that time Herod the tetrarch heard reports about Jesus;**[2]**and he said to his servants, 'This is John the Baptist. He has been raised from the dead, and this is why these powers are at work in him.'** [3]**For Herod had taken John into custody, bound him, and put him in prison on account of Herodias, his brother Philip's wife,** [4]**because John said to him, 'It is not lawful for you to have her.'** [5]**And while he wanted to put him to death, he feared the crowd, because they regarded him as a prophet.** [6]**But when Herod's birthday came, the daughter of Herodias danced before the company, and she pleased Herod,** [7]**with the outcome that he promised on oath to grant her whatever she might ask.** [8]**Now she, being instructed by her mother, said, 'Give me the head of John the Baptist here on a platter.'** [9]**And the king was grieved, yet out of regard for his oaths and for the guests, he commanded it to be given.** [10]**And sending orders he had John beheaded in the prison.** [11]**The head was brought on a platter and given to the girl, who brought it to her mother.** [12]**His disciples came and took the body and buried it; then they went and told Jesus.**

Parallels: Mk 6.14–29; Lk 3.19–20; 9.7–9

Having, in the parable discourse (13.1–52), examined the root of causes of unbelief, the evangelist is now about the task of showing how the failure to gain faith will manifest itself. For this 14.1–12 is paradigmatic. Unbelief begets not only misunderstanding (vv. 1–2) but also violent opposition to Jesus and those on his side (vv. 3–12; cf. also 13.53–8).

1. Herod is Herod Antipas, the Son of Herod the Great

tetrarch originally designated one who ruled a quarter of a region, but by the first century was commonly used of any petty ruler of a dependent state. Herod was the tetrarch of Galilee and Peraea from 4 BC to AD 39.

2. He has been raised from the dead, and this is why these powers are at work in him. The report that some took Jesus to be John the Baptist risen from the dead (cf. 16.14) has generated much speculation. Some have thought it evidence for a Jewish belief in a dying and rising eschatological prophet. Others have asked whether reincarnation may not have gained a foothold in first-century Judaism. The evidence for this idea in ancient Jewish circles is, however, rather scant, as is the evidence for a dying and rising prophet; and in any case it would have been possible to think of Jesus as John resurrected only if one did not know that the two were alive at the same time or that one had baptized the other. Should one then suppose that the real meaning of our verse is more figurative – Jesus possessed the same supernatural inspiration that had been at work in John? On this interpretation, which makes Jesus, so to speak, John's alter ego, one could appeal to 2 Kgs 2.9–15, where Elisha is given a 'double share' of Elijah's 'spirit', as well as to Lk 1.17, where John the Baptist is said to come 'in the spirit and power of Elijah'. Nevertheless, in view of 16.14, one is inclined to take the text more literally: some superstitiously believed that John had come back to life and was now known as Jesus.

3. taken John into custody adds to the parallelism between the Baptist and Jesus, because 'take into custody' occurs several times in the passion narrative with reference to the latter (21.46; 26.4, 48, 50, 55, 57).

bound him, and put him in prison. Josephus, *Ant.* 18.119, contains another account of John's imprisonment and execution. Josephus plainly states that the Baptist was 'brought in chains to Machaerus', to the fortress-palace rebuilt by Herod the Great and located east of the Dead Sea, thirteen miles southeast of Herodium. Ruins are still visible today. Although it is often claimed that the synoptic accounts assume that John was executed at the court in Tiberias, not at Machaerus, this is not perfectly clear.

on account of Herodias, his brother Philip's wife. Herodias was indeed Herod's relative, but she was, according to Josephus, the wife of Herod, son of Mariamme II, not Philip, the tetrarch who married Salome. Many modern commentators have accordingly attributed an understandable error to Matthew. Of the various attempts to establish harmony with Josephus on the point, the most plausible is that Herod, son of Mariamme II, was named Herod Philip.

4. The reason for John's arrest is given: he rebuked Herod's illicit union. The Baptist thus illustrates 10.26–31: he spoke the truth aloud, fearing God instead of those who can kill only the body.

It is not lawful for you to have her. John presumably denounced Herod not because he had divorced his first wife (the daughter of Aretas) or because he was guilty of polygamy but because he had married his (living) brother's wife; cf. Lev 8.16; 20.21. According to the gospels, this was the cause of his arrest. Josephus tells a different story. In his account, the Baptist was arrested because he incited the people to the point of sedition. Some commentators have maintained that between the synoptics and John there is in this regard a contradiction. Yet neither source can be credited with passing on anything more than an outline of selected events, which makes it possible to see the two as being complementary on the matter. Indeed, given the political situation, a denunciation of Herod's marriage may well have been politically explosive.

5. And while he wanted to put him to death, he feared the crowd, because they regarded him as a prophet. Cf. 21.26, which Matthew has here anticipated: 'But if we say, "From people", we are afraid of the crowd; for all hold John to be a prophet.' The crowd's opinion that John is a prophet is quite correct from Matthew's viewpoint. In fact, 'for they held him to be a prophet' is the key to the story, at least as it appears in the First Gospel. Matthew has just finished recounting an episode in which Jesus speaks only one sentence: 'A prophet is without honour ...'. Thus 13.53–8 and 14.1–12 depict the inevitable, tragic lot of the true prophet; cf. 23.29–39.

6. she pleased Herod. Cf. Est 2.9.

9–10. The Baptist is beheaded without a trial.

And the king was grieved, yet out of regard for his oaths and for the guests, he commanded it to be given. And sending orders he had John beheaded in the prison. John dies a shameful death, the death of a criminal. In this he is like Jesus.

The reference to Herod grieving makes sense only in Mark, where Herod hears John gladly; contrast Mt 14.5, where Herod wants to kill John. But the reference to grief may have been retained for a very good reason. Throughout 14.1–12 the fate of John foreshadows that of Jesus. So it is not beside the point to recall that in Matthew Pilate is Jesus' *reluctant* executioner, and he finally orders the crucifixion only after pressure is brought to bear upon him; see 27.1–26. So just as Pilate is disinclined to do away with Jesus, so is Herod Antipas disinclined to do away with John.

12. then they went and told Jesus. This creates a close link between 14.1–12 and 14.13–21; the execution of John in the former supplies the motive for Jesus' withdrawal in the latter. The problem, however, is that 14.1–12 is told as a flashback. Here then Matthew has been clumsy in putting his sources together.

* * * * *

Although it stands out from the rest of the gospel by being a story about someone other than Jesus, the episode of John's imprisonment and martyrdom is not just an interesting aside, an odd, slack moment in Matthew's narrative. This is because the Baptist is no independent character. He is instead a passenger on the vessel of Jesus' career, and his words and life are in the service of another. Such was the case in chapters 3 and 11, and so is it here. Mt 14.1–12 is, in fact, a christological parable. On its surface the passage is about John; but its organic connexion with Jesus' story is unmistakable. First of all, by illustrating the fate of a true prophet (martyrdom), John's sad end foretells what is in store for Jesus. Hence the juxtaposition with 13.53–8, where Jesus the prophet is rejected by his own, is hardly accidental. Second, 14.1–12 not only sheds light upon what has gone before (13.53–8), it also portends in some detail exactly what is to happen in the passion narrative. The following parallels between John's passion and that of Jesus are to be observed:

John	Jesus
Herod the tetrarch is responsible for John's death	Pilate the governor is responsible for Jesus' death
John is seized (14.3)	Jesus is seized (21.46 etc.)
John is bound (14.3)	Jesus is bound (27.2)

Herod
   fears the crowds
   because they hold John
   to be a prophet (14.5)
	The chief priests and Pharisees
	   fear the crowds
	   because they hold Jesus
	   to be a prophet (21.46)

Herod is asked by another
   to execute John
   and is grieved so to do (14.6–11)
	Pilate is asked by others
	   to execute Jesus
	   and is reluctant so to do
	   (27.11–26)

John is buried by his disciples (14.12)	Jesus is buried by a disciple (27.57–61)

THE FEEDING OF THE FIVE THOUSAND (14.13–21)

[13]**Jesus, hearing this, withdrew from there in a boat to a place in the wilderness by himself. But when the crowds heard it, they followed him on foot from the towns. [14]And as he went ashore, he saw a great crowd; and he had compassion upon them and healed their sick. [15]When it became evening, the disciples came to him and said, 'This is a deserted place, and the hour is now late; send the crowds away so that they may go into the villages and buy food for themselves.' [16]Jesus said to them, 'They need not go away. You give them something to eat.' [17]They replied, 'We have nothing here but five loaves and two fish.' [18]And he said, 'Bring them here to me.' [19]Then he ordered the crowds to sit down on the grass. Taking the five loaves and the two fish, he looked up to heaven and he uttered a blessing and broke the loaves, and he gave them to the disciples, and the disciples gave them to the crowds. [20]And all ate and were**

satisfied; and they took up what was left over of the broken pieces, twelve baskets full. [21]**And those who ate were about five thousand men, besides women and children.**

Parallels: Mk 6.32–44; Lk 9.10–17; Jn 6.1–15

As it stands in Matthew, the story of the feeding of the five thousand is above all about the compassionate Jesus and his supernatural ability to meet the lack of those in physical need. One may compare 1 Kgs 17.8–16 (Elijah and the jar of meal); 2 Kgs 4.1–7 (Elijah and the vessels of oil); 4.42–4 (Elijah feeds one hundred men); Lk 5.1–11 (the miraculous draught of fish); Jn 2.1–11 (the wedding at Cana); 21.4–8 (the miraculous draught of fish); and *b. Ta'an.* 24b–5a (a bread miracle). Typically these miracles are not initiated by requests but by the spontaneous act of the miracle-worker. Further, the miracle itself is usually left undescribed, its facticity inferred from subsequent circumstances.

If 14.13–21 is a gift miracle which is firstly about the compassionate Christ making physical provisions, there are also important secondary themes:

(i)   The feeding of the five thousand is an allegory of the Eucharist, as can be seen from the following parallels:

14.13–21	26.20–9
when it became evening	when it became evening
to sit down	sat
taking	taking
bread	bread
uttered a blessing	blessing
broke	broke
gave ... to the disciples	gave ... to the disciples
ate	eat

(ii) Jesus' compassionate provision of bread and fish prefigures the coming eschatological feast. The Eucharist itself, with which our story has striking parallels, was thought to be a foretaste of the meal in the kingdom of God; and both bread (or manna) and fish (or Leviathan) are associated with the messianic feast in many Jewish texts; cf. *2 Bar.* 29.3–8; 4 Ezra 6.52. Note that, in Jn 6.1–59, the feeding of the five thousand is understood by the people as a *messianic* miracle of the prophet-like Moses.

(iii) Most commentators have observed the parallels between the gospel miracle and the story in 2 Kgs 4.42–4: 'A man came from Baalshalishah, bringing the man of God bread of the first fruits, twenty loaves of barley and fresh ears of grain in his sack. And Elisha said, "Give to the men, that they may eat." But his servant said, "How am I to set this before a hundred men?" So he repeated, "Give them to the men, that they may eat, for thus says the Lord, 'They shall eat and have some left'." So he set it before them and they ate and had some left, according to the word of the Lord.' There is no denying the similarities.

Elisha takes (barley) bread and ears of grain	Jesus takes bread and fish
Elisha commands, 'Give to the men, that they may eat'	Jesus commands: 'Give to them something to eat'
Objection of servant	Objection of disciples
The people eat and food is left over	The people eat and food is left over

Given that in the broader context of the First Gospel (13.53–14.12) Jesus is interpreted in the category of prophet, informed readers may understand 14.13–21 to depict Jesus as the eschatological prophet.

13. Jesus, hearing this. Because the motive for withdrawal has become John's execution, the reader no longer thinks of Jesus and his disciples as seeking rest in a spiritual corner: they rather are going into hiding.

withdrew from there in a boat to a place in the wilderness by himself. 'By himself' is quite appropriate here. For with the death of John the curtain has begun to fall upon Jesus too, so he must turn his immediate attention towards his disciples, towards those who will carry on after he is gone.

15. In the evening Jesus' disciples, little knowing what is soon to happen, ask the master to dismiss the crowd. Their request is rooted in common sense and perhaps even compassion; it is not a sign of lack of faith. It in any case makes the need of the entire crowd – and not just the sick – known to the reader: they have no food.

16. You give them something to eat. The sentence is obviously modelled upon the command of Elisha in 2 Kgs 4.42–3: 'Give to the people that they may eat.' The reader who catches the allusion will be prepared for what follows.

17. We have nothing here but five loaves and two fish. Cf. 1 Kgs 17.12 ('I have nothing baked, only a handful of meal in a jar, and a little oil in a jug'); 2 Kgs 4.2 ('Your maidservant has nothing in the house, except a jar of oil'); 4.42 ('twenty loaves of barley and fresh ears of grain'), 43 ('How can I set this before a hundred people?'). Whereas in Mark the disciples initially fail to understand what Jesus has in mind – which is why they ask about buying bread – in Matthew they do understand, which is why they count the loaves and fish. Their deficiency is no longer in comprehension but in faith.

The numbers 'five' and 'two' have often been given symbolic import. The most common interpretation has it that the five loaves stand for the five books of Moses, the two fish for the psalms and the prophets or the apostles and the gospel (= the NT). Matthew's text, however, does nothing to foster such an approach.

19. After directing the crowd to sit down, Jesus, acting like the host at a regular Jewish meal, takes the bread and fish, looks up to heaven, offers a blessing, and distributes the food to his disciples, who in turn distribute it to the crowd.

Taking the five loaves and the two fish, he looked up to heaven and he uttered a blessing. For looking to heaven while praying – something relatively rare in Jewish texts – see Ps 123.1; Mk 7.34; Lk 18.13; Jn 11.41; 17.1. It is an outward sign of an inward dependence. Matthew is not likely to have thought of the food itself as being blessed, although he may have understood the blessing to be the means of multiplication. Did he assume that Jesus uttered the traditional Jewish blessing: 'Blessed are You, O Lord our God, King of the world, who brings forth bread from the earth'?

and broke the loaves, and he gave them to the disciples. Cf. 26.26.

and the disciples gave them to the crowds. Has Matthew made the disciples intermediaries in order to highlight the correspondence between the course of events and Jesus' command in 14.16 ('You give them something to eat')? Or did the author want us to think of the disciples as representatives of church leaders, through whose hands the Eucharist is given?

20. As in many gift miracles, there is a remark on the overabundance of leftovers; cf. 1 Kgs 17.16; 2 Kgs 4.6–7, 44; 8.8–9; Lk 5.6–7; Jn 21.6, 11.

And all ate and were satisfied. Cf. Jn 6.11–12. 'Satisfied' is used in the fourth beatitude in connexion with the hungry who will be satisfied in the eschatological kingdom. If one may link that verse to this, the satisfaction of the multitude may be thought of as foreshadowing the satisfaction of the messianic banquet.

and they took up what was left over of the broken pieces. Cf. Jn 6.12. The subject is probably the twelve, not the crowds.

twelve baskets full. Matthew has dropped Mark's mention of fish, perhaps because fish are not present in 26.26–9, the account of the Last Supper. Our story does not, as might be expected, conclude by observing that the crowds marvelled; contrast Jn 6.14–15. Maybe readers are to suppose that the people were ignorant of what had taken place. Maybe the epiphany was made known only to the disciples.

Those who find symbolic significance in the numbers of 14.13–21 generally understand the twelve baskets to stand for the twelve apostles or the twelve tribes of Israel.

21. besides women and children. Cf. LXX Num 17.14; Judg 20.15, 17; Mt 15.38. In Exod 12.37 one reads that the number of souls in the wilderness was six hundred thousand men on foot, 'besides women and children'. Moreover, when Moses, in Num 11.21, wonders how he is to feed the people that have come forth from Egypt, his words are these: 'the people among whom I am number six hundred thousand (men) on foot; and thou hast said, "I will give them meat..."'. As in Matthew, the number of individuals to be fed is not given, but only the number of men; cf. Exod 12.37. Maybe the concluding words of 14.13–21 allude to the way the people in the wilderness were counted.

* * * * *

(i) The feeding of the five thousand echoes the institution of the Eucharist. Concerning this fact, two observations are in order. First, there are other instances of Matthew using the literary device of foreshadowing. In chapters 1–2, for example, the story of the peril of the new-born Messiah clearly foreshadows the passion narrative, and the same is true of the account of the Baptist's martyrdom in 14.1–12. Thus the parallelism between 14.13–21 and 26.20–9 is hardly exceptional. Rather, Matthew consistently looks towards the end, and the conclusion colours all that comes before. Second, it is significant that both feeding stories (14.13–21; 15.32–9) appear in the section 13.53–17.27, the fourth major narrative section of the gospel. This is the section in which the stewardship of the kingdom is transferred from Israel to the church (see 16.13–20, the story of Peter's confession and its sequel). It is then most appropriate that 14.13–21 and 15.32–9, which are transparent symbols of a Christian service, should be told only after the need for a new religious community has become manifest, and precisely in the section in which that need is met.

(ii) The allegorical reading of 14.13–21 in terms of the Eucharist does not discount the equal emphasis upon Jesus as the one who can meet mundane, physical needs. Our pericope displays Jesus' concern for such 'non-religious' needs and demonstrates his ability to act in accord with that concern.

THE LORD OF THE SEA WALKS ON THE WAVES (14.22–33)
AND HEALS THE SICK AT GENNESARET (14.34–6)

[22]And immediately he compelled the disciples to get into the boat and to go before him to the other side, while he dismissed the crowds. [23]And after he had dismissed the crowds, he went up the mountain by himself to pray. When evening came, he was there alone, [24]but by this time the boat, beaten by the waves, was many stadia from the land, for the wind was against them.[25]And early in the fourth watch of the night he came walking toward them on the sea. [26]But when the disciples saw him walking on the sea, they were terrified, saying, 'It is a ghost!' And they cried out in fear. [27]But immediately Jesus spoke to them and said, 'Take heart, it is I; do not be afraid.' [28]Peter answered him, 'Lord, if it is you, command me to come to you on the water.' [29]He said, 'Come.' So Peter got out of the boat, started walking on the water, and came toward Jesus. [30]But when he noticed the strong wind, he became frightened, and beginning to sink, he cried out, 'Lord, save me!'[31]Jesus immediately reached out his hand and caught him, saying to him, 'O man of little faith, why did you doubt?' [32]And when they got into the boat, the wind ceased. [33]And those in the boat worshipped him, saying, 'Truly you are the Son of God.'

[34]And when they had crossed over, they came to land at Gennesaret. [35]And when the people of that place recognized him, they sent word throughout the region and brought all who were sick to him, [36]and they begged him that they might touch even the fringe of his cloak; and as many as touched it were healed.

Parallels: Mk 6.45–56; Jn 6.16–25

The history-of-religion parallels are both close and numerous. In 2 Kgs 2.14 and 6.6 Elisha defies the law of gravity in performing water miracles, and there are several places in the OT where reference is made to God walking on the waves or sea (see below). In *P. Berol.* 1.120 we read of a demon with the power to tread upon rivers and seas. Lucian, *Philops.* 13, refers to a magician who was imagined by people to march on the sea. *PGM* 1.121 contains instructions on how to pass over water without assistance. The Buddhist text, *Jâtaka* 190, tells the tale of a disciple who walked upon the water when he meditated upon the Buddha and who sank when he did not. The *Apophthegmata Patrum* preserves the story of a certain hermit Bessarion crossing the river Chrysoroas on foot. In the seventeenth century, according to Sabbatean sources perhaps influenced by the Gospels, Sabbatai Sevi, when to all appearances drowning, rose from the sea; and on another occasion he calmed a sea storm.

22. And immediately he compelled the disciples to get into the boat and to go before him to the other side. Is the reader to presume that the disciples, anticipating the storm, are afraid to cross without Jesus and therefore need to be pressed? Or does Jesus' intention to perform and permit what follows suffice to explain the action? Whatever the answer, there is an edifying lesson to hand: there is no need to fear if one is in danger out of obedience to Christ's command.

23. And after he had dismissed the crowds. We are given no clue as to why it was necessary to dismiss the crowd.

he went up the mountain by himself to pray. Cf. 6.5–6; Lk 9.28; Jn 6.15. Jesus' retreat to the mountain is not an indispensable part of its context: the story of him walking on the sea would develop as well without a specific remark on his whereabouts before he takes to the water. So one might have expected Matthew, given his penchant for abbreviating miracle stories, to have omitted the mountain. That he has not done so perhaps indicates its significance for him. Mt 14.23 recalls both 5.1–2 and 17.1–8, and in these last a Moses typology is in evidence. Further, that Jesus is on the mountain by himself recalls the situation of Moses on Sinai (cf. Exod 24.2); and the OT records that the lawgiver prayed on Sinai (Exod 32.30–4). So it is quite possible that 14.23 is part of Matthew's Moses typology.

24. for the wind was against them. In Jewish tradition it is God alone who can rescue from the sea. Note especially Exod 14.10–15.21; Ps 107.23–32; Jon 1.1–16; and Wisd 14.2–4.

25. in the fourth watch of the night he came walking toward them on the sea. Cf. Jn 6.19. The period between 6 p.m. and 6 a.m. was divided by the Romans into four equal periods or watches; cf. Mk 13.35; Lk 12.38. So the fourth watch was the last (and the darkest), the time between 3 a.m. and 6 a.m. This implies that the disciples struggled without Jesus for some time.

The crux to understanding the Christology of 14.22–33 is the fact that walking on the sea has its background in the OT, where Yahweh the omnipotent creator treads upon the waters. See Job 9.8 (MT: 'who trampled the waves (or: back) of the sea (monster)'; LXX: 'and walking on the sea as if on ground'); MT Hab 3.15 ('You did trample the sea with your horses, the surging of many waters'); Ps 77.19 ('Your way was through the sea, your path through the great waters; yet your footprints were unseen'). By *walking* on the sea Jesus overcomes the powers of chaos and subdues them, like Yahweh in Job 9.8. And by *crossing* the sea so that his disciples may in turn cross safely, Jesus is again acting like Yahweh, who according to Ps 77.19 prepared the way for the Israelites to pass through the Sea of Reeds. In sum, Jesus' walking on the water demonstrates his divine powers and his ability to save those in peril. The theophanic action of Yahweh is the epiphanic action of Jesus.

26. It is a ghost! Perhaps the disciples are perturbed because they think they see the ghost of a dead Jesus, or maybe – the Greek is literally 'phantom' – they think they see an angel or a demon. In any case the use of 'ghost' underlines the note of fear in the face of the extraordinary, the numinous.

And they cried out in fear. Cf. Ps 77.17: 'when the waters saw thee, they were afraid.'

27. it is I recalls the mysterious, divine 'I am' of the OT (Exod 3.14; Isa 41.4; 43.10; 47.8, 10). By walking on and subduing the sea Jesus has manifested the numinous power of Yahweh. In the idiom of 11.27, the Son has made known the Father.

b. B. Bat. 73a passes on the tradition that clubs engraved with 'I am that I am, Yah, the Lord of Hosts, Amen, Amen, Selah' will subdue waves that would otherwise sink a ship. While certainly not directly comparable to the synoptic story, this rabbinic tradition does reflect the conviction that the inscrutable 'I am' contains within itself the power to make a stormy sea subside.

28. This verse and the next three, which constitute a story within a story, have no parallel in any of the other gospels.

Lord. Here the title seemingly reflects an awareness that Jesus shares in the sovereign lordship of Yahweh.

29. Jesus not only has the authority to walk on the sea but also the ability to share his power and authority with others; cf. 11.27; 28.18.

He said, 'Come'. Even though Peter will falter, Jesus has acknowledged the propriety of the disciple's desire to act as his Lord acts.

30. Peter, suddenly perceiving the strength of the wind, takes the measure of his perilous situation and begins to waver: his faith has been wrecked by the force of the storm. This in turn prevents him from participating in Jesus' divine power and so he, like a rock, starts to sink, crying out to the Lord for help. Cf. Ps 69.1–3: 'Save me, O God! For the waters have come up to my neck. I sink in deep mire, where there is no foothold; I have come into deep water, and the flood sweeps over me. I am weary with my crying. . .'

Lord, save me! Cf. 8.25.

31. reached out his hand and caught him. In Ps 18.15–16, the taming of the sea by Yahweh is followed by this: 'He reached from on high, he took me, he drew me out of many waters.' Similarly, in Ps 144.5–8, a request for a public divine demonstration ('Bow your heavens, O Lord, and come down! Touch the mountains that they smoke!') introduces a plea for deliverance from the waters of distress: 'Stretch forth your hand from on high, rescue me and deliver me from the many waters ...'. So the pattern, theophany + deliverance from water, would have been familiar to readers of the psalms.

little faith helps make the incident of 14.28–31 typical. Peter is an example of the believer who suffers from lack of faith in Jesus: after taking the first few steps of a difficult endeavour he falters when opposition begins to buffet. But – and this is what counts for the evangelist – Jesus is there to save *despite* inadequate faith.

why did you doubt? Bengel commented: Peter 'is not blamed for leaving the vessel, but for not abiding in firm faith. He was right in exposing himself to trial; but he ought to have persevered.'

32. And when they got into the boat, the wind ceased. Just as walking on the sea is, in the OT, an attribute of Yahweh alone (see above), so too is the stilling of the storm a power the Scripture assigns only to God. See Job 26.11–12 ('The pillars of heaven tremble, and are astounded at his rebuke. By his power he stilled the sea; by his understanding he smote Rahab'); Ps 65.7 ('who stills the roaring of the seas, the roaring of their waves, the tumult of the peoples'); 89.9–10 ('You do rule the raging of the sea; when its waves rise, you still them. You did crush Rahab like a carcass, you did scatter thy enemies with your mighty arm'); 107.29 ('he made the storm be still and the waves of the sea were hushed'); Jon 1.15; Ecclus 43.23 ('By his counsel he stilled the great deep ...'). Once again, Matthew's story has christological implications. Jesus is the conduit of divine power and authority.

33. The story ends with 'those in the boat' – that is, all the disciples save Peter – worshipping Jesus, the Son of God. Cf. the endings of the sea rescue narratives in Exod 14.31; Ps 107.31–2; Jon 1.16.

And those in the boat worshipped him, saying, 'Truly you are the Son of God.' The title, 'Son of God', here refers to Jesus not in his capacity as a simple wonder-worker but in his status as revealer of the Father. What matters is not that Jesus has done the seemingly impossible but that he has performed actions which the OT associates with Yahweh alone.

Readers have learned already of Jesus' status as Son of God; cf. 2.15; 3.17; 4.3, 6; 8.29. It is, however, only in 14.33 that the disciples themselves make the confession of the church. Thus the unfolding of the gospel witnesses a growth in their knowledge, a growth which will reach its pre-Easter maturity in 16.16. In short, the disciples are beginning to catch up with readers.

34. Subsequent to the walking on the sea we are informed, in an independent pericope, that Jesus healed many in the area or city of Gennesaret. The passage is characterized by brevity and lack of detail. No names are named, no individual characters are introduced; we are simply told that Jesus healed the masses. This reinforces the impression, conveyed throughout Matthew, that Jesus did not neglect the common individual but rather identified with ordinary, and especially helpless, people.

And when they had crossed over, they came to land at Gennesaret. 'Gennesaret' (in the NT only in 14.34 = Mk 6.53 and Lk 5.1) is probably the name for the fruitful and well-forested valley on the northwest shore of the Sea of Galilee, south of Capernaum and north of Tiberias (modern El-Ghuweir). There is a glowing description of the place in Josephus, *Bell.* 3.516–21. 'Gennesaret', however, might also be taken to have been a town which gave its name to the surrounding region as well as to the adjacent Sea of Galilee (which is called the Sea of Gennesaret in Lk 5.1). What our evangelist thought is unclear.

36. Given Matthew's dislike of magical practices, it is surprising to find here no remark on faith or Jesus' teaching or preaching. But perhaps in this connexion it is worth noting that while the crowds are allowed to touch Jesus' garments, we never read of him encouraging them in this. It may even be against his will; yet his compassion is such that he permits it.

* * * * *

(i) Throughout Matthew Jesus exercises powers and displays attributes traditionally connected with God alone. In the present pericope, Jesus both walks on the sea and subdues its rage, and these are acts which the OT assigns to Yahweh exclusively. In addition, Jesus is bold enough to refer to himself with the loaded and numinous 'I am'. In view of all this, it does not quite suffice to say that, for our author, God has acted through Jesus the Messiah. It seems more accurate to assert that, in Matthew's gospel, God shares divine attributes with his Son. The step towards the later ecumenical creeds, which affirm Christ's deity, appears undeniable.

(ii) So often the First Evangelist, while addressing christological issues with his right hand, is at the same time delivering teaching on discipleship with his left. And so is it here. If 14.22–33 is first of all about Jesus, his authority and identity, it is also a parable about Christian faith in the face of difficulties. The stormy sea – so often a symbol of chaos and evil in the biblical tradition – represents the troubles in which believers will inevitably find themselves when they obey Jesus' commands. The boat, perhaps, represents the church. Jesus' walking on the water and coming to his disciples conveys the thought that he will not forget or abandon his own but will come to deliver them from evil. And Peter's actions, through which he displays his little faith, teach that what counts is Jesus' saving presence, not the

Christian's strength of will or courage; and furthermore that faith is in fact participation in Jesus' divine power.

(iii) The part of Peter in 14.22–33 merits three remarks. First, there is here no portrait of a faultless hero: the apostle doubts and he sinks. Greatness and frailty go hand in hand. Second, it may well be, as commentators have often held, that 14.22–33 should be viewed partly as a rehearsal for Peter's role in the passion narrative. Just as other stories in chapter 14 point forward to the gospel's conclusion, so too may Peter's bold entrance into the water, his subsequent sinking, and his eventual rescue by Jesus foreshadow the apostle's overconfident confession (26.30–6), his denial of the Lord (26.69–75), and his final restoration; cf. 28.16–17. Third, because the narrative section, 13.53–17.27, is dominated by the founding of the church (16.13–20), and because Peter is the rock on which that church is built (16.18), it is most fitting that, from this point on, Peter should begin to be singled out in various ways from the rest of the apostolic band; cf. 15.15; 16.22–3; 17.4, 24–5.

THE PHARISAIC TRADITION; CLEAN AND UNCLEAN (15.1–20)

15 **¹Then Pharisees and scribes came to Jesus from Jerusalem, saying, ²'Why do your disciples transgress the tradition of the elders? For they do not wash their hands when they eat.' ³Answering he said to them, 'And why do you transgress the commandment of God for the sake of your tradition? ⁴For God said, "Honour your father and your mother," and, "Whoever speaks evil of father or mother, let him die." ⁵But you say that if any one tells his father or mother, "What you might have gained from me is given to God," then that person need not honour his father. ⁶So, for the sake of your tradition, you make void the word of God. ⁷You hypocrites! Well did Isaiah prophesy rightly about you when he said: ⁸"This people honours me with their lips, but their heart is far from me; ⁹in vain do they worship me, teaching as teachings the precepts of people." '**

¹⁰And calling the crowd he said to them, 'Hear and understand. ¹¹It is not what goes into the mouth that defiles the person, but it is what comes out of the mouth that defiles the person.' ¹²Then coming the disciples said to him, 'Do you know that the Pharisees took offence when they heard this word?' ¹³Answering he said, 'Every plant that my heavenly Father has not planted will be uprooted. ¹⁴Let them alone; they are blind guides of the blind. And if a blind person leads another blind person, both will fall into a pit.' ¹⁵Peter answering said to him, 'Explain to us this parable.' ¹⁶He said, 'Are you also still without understanding? ¹⁷Do you

not see that whatever goes into the mouth enters into the stomach and goes out into the sewer? [18]But what comes out of the mouth proceeds from the heart, and this defiles the person. [19]For out of the heart come evil intentions, murder, adultery, fornication, theft, false witness, blasphemy. [20]These are what defile the person, but to eat with unwashed hands does not the person.'

Parallels: Mk 7.1–23; Lk 6.39

Mt 15.1–20 serves three major functions. It is first an attack on Pharisaic tradition: that tradition does not have the same authority as Scripture, so it must be judged by Scripture and where necessary rejected (vv. 1–9). There is secondly the attack on the Pharisees themselves: their lives exhibit hypocrisy and they cannot be followed (vv. 12–14; cf. 16.5–12). The third major thrust of 15.1–20 is the teaching on purity: what matters above all is the defilement effected by the human heart (vv. 10f., 15–20). There is no obvious thematic link between 15.1–20 and the surrounding material.

Matthew does not teach the abolition of OT purity laws. Not only would such an interpretation run afoul of 5.17–20, but the decisive statement in Mk 7.19 ('thus he declared all foods clean') is not in Matthew. Further, the insertion of vv. 12–14 (a discussion of the Pharisees) as well as the editorial conclusion (v. 20: 'but to eat with unwashed hands does not defile the person') reveal that the evangelist's concern is not with the OT but with the Pharisees and their tradition.

1. Then Pharisees and scribes came to Jesus from Jerusalem. On the Pharisees – only here in Matthew are they named before the scribes – see p. 40, and on the scribes p. 24. The appearance here of Jerusalem (which has not been named for ten chapters) reinforces its hostile character – it is home to Jesus' opponents – and points ahead to the passion narrative.

2. Why do your disciples transgress the tradition of the elders? 'Tradition' refers to the Pharisees' extrabiblical traditions, many of which later came to be codified in the Mishnah. These traditions had a controversial status before AD 70. The Sadducees repudiated them. So did those responsible for composing the Dead Sea Scrolls. Cf. Josephus, *Ant.* 17.41, which probably preserves a criticism of Nicolas of Damascus: the Pharisees pretend to observe the laws of which God approves. Behind this accusation may well lie the polemic that the laws which they *do* observe are of their own making – in which case Mt 15.1–20 would in part contain a conventional criticism. However that may be, Jesus and the gospel writers were not alone in rejecting the

Pharisaic *paradosis* as a later innovation. That the Pharisees themselves were sensitive to the criticisms directed against them is apparent from the fact that they used such expressions as 'tradition of the elders' and 'tradition of the fathers'. These grounded the tradition in the authoritative past, which is just what we might expect from a Hellenistic school.

For they do not wash their hands when they eat. The custom of washing the hands with water before meals was not primarily hygienic but rather a means of removing ceremonial defilement and ritual impurity. Already in Exod 30.17–21 the Aaronic priesthood is instructed to wash hands and feet before going into the tent of meeting; and in Lev 15.11 uncleanness is not transmitted by one with a discharge if he has rinsed his hands with water. Before the end of the second temple period, a non-priestly interest in purity had evolved so that the custom of washing hands before prayer and meals and reading Torah was widely practised (not just by Pharisees), even if Mark's statement, 'For the Pharisees, and all the Jews, do not eat unless they wash their hands' (7.3), is usually regarded as hyperbole. Cf. Jn 2.26: 'there were there six stone jars of water standing there, according to the purification of the Jews, each holding twenty or thirty gallons.' We do not, however, know to what extent the developed legislation in the Mishnah, which covers such topics as what sort of water can be used for purification, what vessels are appropriate, and so on, was observed in first-century Palestine or exactly who would have observed it.

3. And why do you transgress the commandment of God for the sake of your tradition? Cf. 2 Chron 24.20; *T. Levi* 14.4 ('you want to destroy the light of the law which was granted to you for the enlightenment of everyone, teaching commandments which are opposed to God's just commandments'); *T. Asher* 7.5 ('heeding not God's law but human commandments').

4. For God said. These words show that Jesus is not attacking the Torah. The commandment of Moses is the commandment of God.

Honour your father and your mother. Cf. Exod 20.12; Deut 5.16. From what follows, the imperative to honour parents clearly includes financial assistance; cf. Prov 28.24; 1 Tim 5.4.

Whoever speaks evil of father or mother, let him die. The citation of Exod 21.17 serves the purpose of stressing the seriousness of breaking the fifth commandment. To dishonour one's parents is a crime meriting severe punishment.

5. But you say. This stands in antithesis to 'For God said' (v. 4).

given to God. This is a substitution for Mark's longer 'korban, an offering'. 'Korban' originally meant 'sacrifice' or 'offering'. In time it came to refer to a ban which involved the withdrawing of something from profane or common use, the treating of it as though it were dedicated to the temple. From the Mishnah we learn that a korban vow formula could function as a legal fiction which entailed no actual sacrifice, and also that the word itself was sometimes used as a secular word of protestation. Scholars debate to what extent these facts as well as the Mishnah's various rulings on korban vows are useful for studying the first century. Particularly discussed, because of its bearing on the gospels, is the question: when did the rabbis come to make allowances for ill-considered vows and permit alleviation? *m. Ned.* 9.1 implies that by reason of the honour due father and mother, one can repent of a korban vow, and other mitigating circumstances are considered elsewhere. But it seems safe to assume, in the light of Mark's account, that at least some first-century teachers held a korban vow to be binding regardless of the circumstances of its utterance, or at least binding in the situation presupposed by Matthew and Mark.

what you might have gained from me. The Mishnah plainly reveals how common it was, at least at the time of its composition, to pronounce a korban vow for the purpose of not sharing property with others; and it contains texts in which the vow deprives one's relatives.

6. for the sake of your tradition, you make void the word of God. The korban vow is supposed to constitute service to God. Such service, however, can never be isolated from service to fellow human beings. If the korban vow does nothing save deprive the needy, then it is not in accord with service to God, which demands as its invariable corollary love of neighbour.

8–9. This people honours me with their lips. This and the following words are from Isa 29.13.

10. Jesus now ceases to address his opponents and turns to the crowd. This coincides with a change in his argument. In vv. 3–9 he has responded to the charge about his disciples not keeping Pharisaic tradition. The issue there is authority. Beginning with v. 10 the broader issue of defilement becomes the subject.

he said to them. Jesus proceeds to give the crowd teaching. But, as in chapter 13, he interprets or explains his teaching only to insiders.

Hear and understand. Jesus' invitation to the crowd to hear and understand should caution those who refer to Matthew's attitude towards 'the Jews'. In the present passage Jesus rebukes only the Pharisees. He treats the crowd differently. It is not reprimanded but instead given teaching. Clearly the Pharisees and the Jewish masses are for Matthew two different groups; they should not be lumped together as one entity.

11. This antithetical proverb or wisdom saying is the crucial declaration in 15.1–20.

It is not what goes into the mouth that defiles the person, but it is what comes out of the mouth that defiles the person. Cf. Menander, frag. 540 ('all that brings defilement comes from within'); Philo, *Spec. leg.* 3.209 ('for the unjust and impious man is in the truest sense unclean'); *Pseud.-Phoc.* 228 ('purification of the soul, not of the body, makes atonement': there are textual variants). 2 Chron 30.18–20 has this: 'For a multitude of the people, many of them from Ephraim, Manasseh, Issachar, and Zebulun, had not cleansed themselves, yet they ate the passover otherwise than as prescribed. For Hezekiah had prayed for them saying, "The good Lord pardon every one who sets his heart to seek God, the Lord the God of his fathers, even though not according to the sanctuary's rules of cleanness." And the Lord heard Hezekiah, and healed the people.' Here the efficacy of the heart which seeks God is such that it overrules cultic defilement. Without rejecting the cult, the lesson that purity of heart matters above all else is clearly taught. Also pertinent is *Num. Rab.* 19.18, where Johanan b. Zakkai is reported to have said: 'It is not the dead that defiles nor the water that purifies. The Holy One, blessed be He, merely says: "I have laid down a statute, I have issued a decree. You are not allowed to transgress my decree"; as it is written, "This is the statute of the law".' Johanan is saying, as did Maimonides later, that purity and impurity depend upon the intention of the heart. They do not inhere in objects. So while the cultic commands remain valid, they are translated into ethics: one becomes unclean only through a deliberate choice to disobey God's declared will (= Scripture). Here we are near the gospels. Defilement is caused not by what is external but by disposition, intent.

That which goes into the mouth is, as the following will elucidate, food and drink, that which comes out the evil things produced by an evil heart.

The line was originally composed as a moral pronouncement or exhortation, not halakah; it was exhortation aimed at people perceived as preoccupied with the literal observance of Torah and tradition to the neglect of the weightier matters of the law (cf. 23.23), and Matthew's understanding is not fundamentally different. If so, the saying assumes the continuing validity of the cult, and its gist is that the disposition of the heart determines all else; cf. 6.22–3. There is a certain parallel with the OT prophets. It was once fashionable to read the prophets as enemies of the Jerusalem cult. Now it is understood that declarations such as Hos 6.6 – 'I desire mercy, not sacrifice' – were never intended to set aside the Mosaic commandments. Despite their extreme formulation, they must be interpreted as rhetorical injunctions to upright behaviour.

It is often thought that the first half of our saying refers to cultic defilement, the second to ethical defilement. It is preferable, however, to adopt a different interpretation, one which assigns to 'defile' the same meaning in both lines. According to this interpretation, food cannot really defile because true defilement is a function of morality. What matters before God is the heart; cf. 5.21–8. This does not make one indifferent to actions or all external circumstances. Rather, the meaning of such must be determined by its relationship to what is internal. Nothing which goes into a person can of itself defile, for true defilement is effected by intention. Such teaching, while it relativizes the ritual law, does not of necessity set it aside.

In 5.27–8 we read: 'You have heard that it was said, "You will not commit adultery." But I say to you that everyone who looks at a woman in order to lust after her has already committed adultery with her in his heart.' Mt 15.11 could be formulated similarly. 'You have heard that it was said: "It is what goes into a man that defiles a person." But I say to you: what comes out of a person defiles a person.' Just as the condemnation of lust does not mean indifference to the physical act of adultery, so too does the branding of the heart as the source of defilement not mean the dismissal of the laws of Leviticus.

12. Unlike the disciples, who must ask Jesus for his meaning, the Pharisees evidently think they comprehend. At least their reaction reflects a conclusion about what has been said.

Do you know that the Pharisees took offence when they heard this word? It is not 'the Jews' who are offended. Matthew's Jesus is not attacking Judaism as a whole but only Pharisaic tradition.

13. The general effect of vv. 13–14 is to make plain that the Pharisees are not just wrong about handwashing and korban. There is much else in their tradition that must be rejected.

Every plant that my heavenly Father has not planted will be uprooted. Cf. 3.10; Lk 17.6. Isa 60.21 reads: 'Your people shall all be righteous; they shall possess the land for ever, the shoot of my planting, the work of my hands ...' (cf. 61.3). This is one of many texts in which the people of God are spoken of as God's planting. But what we have in Mt 15.13 is the polemical proposition that not all in Israel are God's planting. The Pharisees, offended by the Messiah, show themselves not to be God's own. Hence they will be uprooted (cf. 13.29) at the final judgement.

14. they are blind guides of the blind. And if a blind person leads another blind person, both will fall into a pit. Cf. Lk 6.39. For falling into a pit as a symbol of misfortune or calamity see Ps 7.15; Prov 26.27; Isa 24.18; Jer 48.44; *T. Reub.* 2.9 (the spirit of intercourse 'leads the young person like a blind man into a pit ...').

15. Peter answering said to him, 'Explain to us this parable.' In Mark we read that 'his disciples' (in the house) asked Jesus about 'the parable'. In Matthew, Peter is the sole speaker. 'Parable' is fitting here because Jesus' declaration is extraordinary speech which is difficult to understand.

In Acts 10–11, 15 and Gal 2, Peter is involved in debates over the meaning of ritual impurity and its bearing upon the Gentile question. One must wonder whether Matthew's tradition associated the apostle with this topic and whether this encouraged his being mentioned precisely here. Was Peter remembered as having issued teaching on the matter of clean and unclean?

17. Jesus asks a second question, this about things entering the mouth. He is here expounding the first part of the saying in v. 11 (on what does not defile). In the next verse (v. 18) he will turn to the second part (on what does defile).

18. Having explained what does not defile a person, Jesus now declares what does, affirming that 'the treasuries of evil things are in ourselves' (Philo).

But what comes out of the mouth proceeds from the heart, and this defiles the person. Cf. Rom 10.8 for the close connexion between heart and mouth.

19. The evils sown by the heart in the subterranean regions of human nature are now catalogued. They are seven in number (in Mark, thirteen).

evil intentions. Cf. Ezek 38.10; Jas 2.4. Although the list opens with 'evil intentions' (the only double-membered entry), it goes on to cite six concrete actions. Perhaps implicit is the truth that behind every public evil there lurk the sinful, wicked thoughts which are its roots; cf. Gen 6.5. Indeed, maybe 'evil intentions' is Matthew's Greek equivalent for the *yeṣer hara'*, the evil impulse, which the rabbis generally located in the heart.

murder, adultery, fornication, theft, false witness, blasphemy. Matthew's list has (for mnemonic or catechetical reasons?) been influenced by the second table of the decalogue (as have the lists in 1 Cor 5.9–10; 1 Tim 1.9–10; and *Barn.* 19). After 'evil intentions', the catalogue refers to murder, adultery, unchastity, theft, bearing false witness, and blasphemy. This resembles the sixth through ninth commandments, which concern murder, adultery, theft, and bearing false witness – commandments which immediately follow the injunction to honour father and mother; cf. Mt 15.4. The differences are two: Matthew has two words for sexual sins (cf. Mk 10.19; 1 Cor 6.9; Heb 13.4) and two words for sinful speech; cf. the pairs in Rom 13.13. He has, in other words, slightly expanded the inventory while staying close to both the content and order of Exod 20.13–17. Perhaps he wanted a total of seven entries, seven being the number of completeness.

20. Matthew's closing words have the effect of making the whole discussion turn around the question of the Pharisaic tradition rather than the written law; the washing of hands before meals was not enjoined in the latter, only the former.

* * * * *

(i) Matthew believed that the law and the prophets were still valid (5.17–20). He also believed that the Gentiles had come to a full share in God's salvation (28.16–20). In holding together these two beliefs he exhibited the qualities which Edmund Burke considered characteristic of the sound statesman: the disposition to preserve and the ability to reform; cf. 13.52. There was preservation because, despite acceptance of the Gentile influx, the Jewish Torah was not abandoned; cf. 15.4–9. There was reformation because, in the light of the Messiah's teaching, Jewish tradition had to be critically evaluated and in some measure rejected.

We unfortunately do not know very much about the everyday, concrete realities of Matthew's community. For example, how did law-observant Jews relate to uncircumcized Gentiles? We can only guess. Perhaps, however, we can make a good guess. Notwithstanding the fact that many – not all – pious, non-Christian Jews refused to eat with Gentiles, we detect in our Gospel no evidence of segregated groups. This makes the existence of separate fellowships (cf. Gal 2) improbable. On the other hand, that there was a total disregard of traditional law, so that Jewish Christians had no scruples at all concerning what they ate, is most unlikely. Unlikelier still is a scenario in which Gentile Christians observed all the laws of Judaism (Matthew nowhere mentions circumcision). We are left, then, with the likelihood that Gentile believers kept a minimum number of OT commandments, sufficient to allow fellowship with Jews. Such *may* have been the situation in Antioch before the crucial debate between Peter and Paul. More importantly, one is put in mind of the so-called 'Apostolic Decree' (Acts 15.20, 29; 21.45; cf. Rev 2.15, 20). This decree, which, according to the best manuscripts, prohibited four things – eating meat sacrificed to idols, eating blood, eating strangled animals, and intercourse with near kin – recalls the Holiness Code of Lev 17–18, which lays down rules not only for Israelites but also for the 'strangers that sojourn among them' (Lev 17.8). The decree was clearly designed to allow Gentiles and law-abiding Jews to share a common religious life. Whether or not Matthew's community knew and observed the

'Apostolic Decree' one cannot be sure. Yet Matthew was probably composed in Antioch, and Acts has the decree being taken there (Acts 15.23, 30). Even if the decree was not followed by Matthew's church, a similar rule of compromise probably was.

(ii) 'What comes out of the mouth proceeds from the heart, and that defiles the person.' This line reminds one of so much in the Sermon on the Mount, which refers several times to the 'heart' and demands that it be pure and focused in intent. This stress on the heart, on the interior life of religion, on intention and attitude, is indeed found throughout Matthew and is a chief characteristic of the whole. At the heart of Matthew is the demand for integrity, for harmony between thought and act, for heeding the inner meaning of the commandments.

THE CANAANITE WOMAN (15.21–8)

[21]**Leaving that place Jesus withdrew to the district of Tyre and Sidon.** [22]**And behold, a Canaanite woman from that region came out and cried, 'Have mercy on me, O Lord, Son of David. My daughter is wickedly tormented by a demon.'** [23]**But he did not answer her a word. And his disciples came and urged him, saying, 'Send her away, for she keeps shouting after us.'** [24]**Answering he said, 'I was sent only to the lost sheep of the house of Israel.'** [25]**But she came and knelt before him, saying, 'Lord, help me.'** [26]**Answering he said, 'It is not fair to take the children's bread and to throw it to the dogs.'** [27]**She said, 'Yes, Lord, yet even the dogs eat the crumbs that fall from their masters' table.'** [28]**Then answering Jesus said to her, 'O woman, great is your faith! Let it be done for you as you desire.' And her daughter was healed instantly.**

Parallels: Mk 7.24–30

Chrysostom compared the sequence – debate with scribes and Pharisees over food laws (15.1–20) followed by the story of Jesus and the Canaanite woman (15.21–8) – with the sequence in Acts 10: following Peter's vision about clean and unclean things, the apostle visits the Gentile Cornelius and welcomes him into the faith. Is the comparison apt? It assumes that both 15.1–20 and 21–8, in different ways, treat the same theme, namely, the place of Israel and Gentiles in salvation-history. Although many exegetes, ancient and modern, would concur, one has reservations. If 15.1–20 does not clearly abolish OT laws, then it is difficult to see how it bears on the Gentile problem. Indeed, one could perhaps even argue that the trailing of 15.1–20 by vv. 21–8 guarantees that the former will not be interpreted in any antinomian fashion, for in the latter the primacy of the Jews and of God's covenant with them are unequivocally upheld. There is in any event nothing in 15.1–20 or 21–8, considered by themselves, to indicate that God has rejected Israel.

Mt 15.21–8 shows that, despite the priority of Israel, Jesus was, on an exceptional occasion, willing to share messianic blessings with a non-Jew because of her faith. But the tension, which is almost a general principle, between Matthew's particularism and his universalism remains unresolved and unclarified. Should Christian missionaries follow Jesus' example and confine themselves to Israel? Or should they preach to Gentiles in the hope that they will come to faith? And what is required of Gentiles once they have come to faith? Must they keep the law or are they free of all Jewish legislation? These questions are not addressed by 15.21–8, a text which recounts a quite exceptional situation and which leaves the status of the Gentiles hanging in the air. It is only with 28.16–20 that any clarity is achieved. Not until his conclusion does Matthew's commitment to the law-free Gentile mission become explicit, and not until the end do the differences between pre- and post-Easter praxis become plain.

21. Jesus, following his debate with the scribes and Pharisees (15.1–20), heads for the region of Tyre and Sidon. Whether he actually arrives there is unclear.

22. a Canaanite woman. Chrysostom: 'the evangelist speaks against the woman, that he may show forth her marvellous act, and celebrate her praise the more. For when you hear of a Canaanitish woman, you should call to mind those wicked nations, who overset from their foundations the very laws of nature. And being reminded of these, consider also the power of Christ's advent.'

from that region came out translates Greek that could also be rendered by 'came out from that region', which would mean that a Gentile is on Jewish territory seeking out Jesus. One can hardly decide whether Jesus has or has not departed from Jewish territory.

Have mercy on me, O Lord, Son of David. It is surprising that a non-Jew addresses Jesus as 'Son of David'. Is one to infer that already the woman is acknowledging that Jesus is the Jewish saviour, his mission to Israel? However that may be, all three times the woman addresses Jesus she calls him 'Lord'. This helps keep her boldness in check. She may debate with Jesus, but that does not diminish her recognition of his superiority.

23. Jesus reacts to the cries of the woman for her child with stony silence, as though he has not heard anything. Why? He is not mulling over her words, nor is it beneath him to talk with a woman. Rather, he is either turning her down or trying her faith. The disciples, then, in view of Jesus' tacit refusal, take it upon themselves to ask their master to dismiss the woman. Perhaps they want to avoid contact with a Gentile, or maybe the woman has become a bother.

Send her away, for she keeps shouting after us. Cf. 14.15; 19.13. Some have taken 'send away' to mean not 'dismiss' but 'set free'. On this interpretation, the disciples want Jesus to favour the woman's request. Some support for this can be found in the seeming absence of a connexion between vv. 23 and 24 if the former be understood to invite a simple dismissal. Why respond to the disciples with 'I was sent only to the lost sheep of the house of Israel' if they have just asked Jesus to get rid of the woman? One nonetheless wonders whether it is natural to read so much in the imperative.

24. Although he does not dismiss the woman as requested, Jesus declares unequivocally the absolute priority of Israel for his mission: 'I was sent only to the lost sheep of the house of Israel.' The words seemingly exclude the Gentile petitioner from the benefits of Jesus' healing ministry. At best she has been challenged to show that her request is grounded in an authentic faith and is more than a self-seeking hope in magic.

the lost sheep of the house of Israel. This phase, which anticipates and so interprets the 'children' of v. 26, can be interpreted in at least four different ways. (i) A few exegetes have thought of spiritual Israel, Israel according to the spirit. But nothing in Matthew justifies anything save an ethnic understanding of 'Israel'. (ii) One might think of the ten lost tribes. This, however, renders 10.5–6 senseless, for there the lost sheep of Israel are located in Jewish territory: they are not scattered abroad. (iii) Some have taken the phrase to refer only to the lost within Israel, the assumption being that many or most were not lost. (iv) The most popular and surely most credible interpretation has it that 'the lost sheep of the house of Israel' was intended by Matthew to characterize the Jewish nation as a whole. It was by and large lost (with the emphasis probably not on sinfulness but lack of leadership).

25. Instead of letting Jesus' first pronouncement still her desire, the woman ignores what has been said and, kneeling, again asks for help. To what she owes her enormous faith so quickly acquired we are not told; but her tenacity, like that of the widow of Lk 18.1–8, has, understandably, often been taken by expositors to be an instructive example of perseverance in faith; and more than one commentator has recalled the tale of Jacob wrestling with the angel. (One assumes that the woman has heard the conversation of 15.23–4; but some exegetes have pictured Jesus and the twelve being out of her hearing, so that v. 25 is a response not to the words of v. 24 but to the silence of v. 23a.)

26. 'The more urgent she makes her entreaty, so much the more does he also urge his denial' (Chrysostom). Jesus responds to the

Canaanite woman by uttering a little parable which, totally devoid of conciliatory overtones, almost inevitably strikes the modern Christian as too off-putting, even cruel, as designed to wound a human heart.

It is not fair to take the children's bread and to throw it to the dogs. Cf. Jesus' initial, negative response to the nobleman's request in Jn 4.46–54; also the commentary on Mt 8.7. The parable implicitly assumes that Jesus is a Jew, the woman a Gentile, and probably further that the word 'dog' was sometimes used as an appellation for Gentiles. Mt 15.26 also presupposes the equation, 'the children' = Israelites; and it may even be that the bread should be considered a symbol of salvation; cf. the feeding stories. That the table (in v. 27) too is symbolic, intended to allude to the Lord's table (cf. 1 Cor 10.21), is, however, too much.

The Greek word translated by 'dog' is actually the diminutive of the word used in 7.6. The distinction is that the diminutive, connoting familiarity, probably refers to a pet or house-dog as opposed to a stray or wild dog.

27. Despite Jesus' discouraging words, the woman, so far from displaying resentment or becoming sullen, remains insistent and offers a riposte: the dogs eat the crumbs that fall from their masters' table. Her words take up Jesus' parable and extend it. The woman dutifully recognizes both the priority of Israel and Jesus' obligation in that regard. She accepts her secondary status among the house-dogs. At the same time, she raises the possibility of being fed even now, along with the children.

Yes, Lord. For the third time the woman addresses Jesus as Lord. This places her spirited exchange within the confines of faith: she confesses Jesus' superiority even as she argues her case with him.

yet even the dogs eat the crumbs that fall from their masters' table. The food the dogs eat consists of the small scraps that have fallen (by accident) to the floor – although some interpreters have thought of the bread with which the hands were wiped after a meal.

28. Jesus, although he has not really changed his mind about anything – his mission is still only to the lost sheep of Israel, and the priority of Israel in salvation-history remains uncontested – finally gives in to the woman. The reason is not her wit, which has entangled Jesus in his own words, but rather her great faith – the real miracle of our story – along with her recognition of the divinely ordained division between Jew and Gentile.

great is your faith! Let it be done for you as you desire. Cf. 8.13; 9.29.

And her daughter was healed instantly. The exorcism – which at this point is really incidental – is described as a healing, and there is no trace of any exorcistic ritual.

* * * * *

(i) That Matthew has *two* sayings limiting Jesus' mission to Israel (10.5–6; 15.24) emphasizes the biblical doctrine of Israel's election. God, according to our gospel, has kept faith with Israel. The Messiah was, in accordance with the Scriptures, sent first of all to the chosen people. Even in the face of opposition and disbelief, and even after prolonged conflict, Jesus continued to direct his mission to the leaderless sheep of Israel. What does all this say about our author? Despite his knowledge of the post-Easter Gentile mission and his experience of Jewish opposition in his own time, Matthew remained faithful both to the intent of the historical Jesus and to the particularism of the OT. He unequivocally granted, indeed strenuously upheld, the central place of Israel in God's dealings with humanity.

(ii) Just as Paul, in Romans, had to argue vigorously, in combating Gentile arrogance, for the continuing importance of Israel in God's plan, so too may it have been for our evangelist. Although 28.16–20 extends the missionary horizon to all peoples, it does not shut out Israel: 'all the nations' includes the Jews. If so, the missions to Jew and Gentile are to be carried on at the same time. Some confirmation for this can perhaps be gleaned from this, that although in chapter 10 missionaries are commanded to go forth into Israel, they are never said to return; that is, their mission is never made out to be over – which would be more than consistent with the existence of a continuing mission to Israel in Matthew's place and time. It is also noteworthy that 15.24 comes as late as it does. Even after he has met opposition from so many Jewish quarters, Jesus remains preoccupied with his people. His persistence in this regard cannot but be exemplary. It is true that in 21.43 we read of the kingdom passing from its custodians; but it is delivered into the hands of the church, made up of Gentiles *and Jews*. Thus the Jewish element is hardly a thing of the past. Beyond this, the First Gospel – and in this it is in harmony with Paul – seems on occasion to foresee a special role for Israel in the eschatological drama. One should not, therefore, come away from Matthew with the notion that Israel's election no longer counts for anything. Notwithstanding the rejection of the Messiah, the Jews, in some mysterious way, remain divinely advantaged. In the church there is, to use a Pauline phrase, neither Jew nor Greek, and yet there is a continued place for the Jewish people as such.

THE FEEDING OF THE FOUR THOUSAND (15.29–39)

29 And leaving there, Jesus went beside the Sea of Galilee; and going up on the mountain he sat there. 30 And great crowds came to him, bringing

with them the lame, the maimed, the blind, the mute, and many others; and they put them at his feet, and he cured them, [31]so that the crowd was amazed when they saw the mute speaking, the maimed whole, the lame walking, and the blind seeing. And they glorified the God of Israel. [32]Then calling the disciples Jesus said to them, 'I have compassion for the crowd, for they have been with me now for three days and have nothing to eat; and I do not want to send them away hungry, lest they faint on the way.' [33]And the disciples said to him, 'Where in the wilderness will we get enough bread to feed so great a crowd?' [34]And Jesus said to them, 'How many loaves do you have?' They said, 'Seven, and a few small fish.' [35]And commanding the crowd to sit down on the ground, [36]he took the seven loaves and the fish, and after giving thanks he broke them and gave them to the disciples, and the disciples gave them to the crowds. [37]And all of them ate and were satisfied. And they took up the broken pieces left over, seven baskets full. [38]Those who had eaten were four thousand men, besides women and children. [39]And sending away the crowds, he got into the boat and went to the region of Magadan.

Parallels: Mk 7.31–7; 8.1–10

The meaning for Matthew of 15.29–39 is in great measure the same as the meaning of 14.13–21. The story first of all speaks about the compassionate Christ making physical provision for his own. At the same time, it also points forward to both the Eucharist and the eschatological banquet. The story may also be intended to present Jesus as the eschatological prophet; the one major difference between the account of the feeding of the five thousand and that of the four thousand is that the latter alone is intended to express the conviction that the coming of Jesus began to fulfil the eschatological promises associated in Jewish tradition with Mount Zion; see below.

29. And leaving there, Jesus went beside the Sea of Galilee. Despite 4.15 ('Galilee of the Gentiles'), the phrase, 'the Sea of Galilee', does not in itself bring Gentiles to mind.

and going up on the mountain he sat there. Cf. 5.1–2; 14.23; 23.2; Jn 6.3. Should we suppose that the following story takes place where the Sermon on the Mount was delivered?

The mountain of our pericope is a place of gathering, healing, and feeding. In addition, the miracle itself anticipates the messianic banquet while vv. 30–1 recall both the prophecy of Isa 35.5–6 and the pregnant clauses of Mt 11.5; thus the broader context has to do with eschatological fulfilment. All this suggests a Mount Zion typology. For in Jewish expectation Zion is the eschatological gathering site of scattered Israel, a place of healing, and the place of the messianic feast. Furthermore, it is worth remarking that if there is in fact an allusion to Isa 35.5–6 in Mt 14.30–1, that OT passage is part of a prophecy about the pilgrimage of Israel to Mount Zion.

How is it that 'the mountain' can here be interpreted in terms of a Zion typology while elsewhere there is a Sinai background (see on 5.1–2; 14.23; and 17.1)? Already in the OT, Sinai and Zion motifs are merged: see, for instance, Ps. 68. Decisive above all else in this connexion is the expectation in Isa 2.2–3: 'law will go forth out of Zion'. Here Mount Zion functions as the eschatological Sinai, the mountain of law-giving. The upshot is that by associating the mountain with Sinai and Zion at the same time, that is, by making Jesus the new Moses in whose coming the promises made concerning Zion have begun to find fulfilment, the First Evangelist was not entering virgin territory. Rather was he simply following a path laid out already by Jewish tradition.

30. and they put them at his feet. One wonders, given the statements about feet in 5.35; 22.44; and 28.9, whether the position at Jesus' feet does not imply his lordship.

when they saw the mute speaking, the maimed whole, the lame walking, and the blind seeing. Cf. 11.5; also Isa 35.5–6; Mk 7.37 ('And they were astonished beyond measure, saying, "He has done all things well; he even makes the deaf hear and the dumb speak" '); *Mek.* on Exod 20.18 (where it is recorded that at Sinai there were no blind, dumb, deaf, or lame individuals).

And they glorified the God of Israel. So also 9.8, without 'Israel' (which is, obviously, the Jewish people, not the patriarch). 'The God of Israel' (only here in Matthew) is a conventional title which occurs often in the OT and books inspired by it; see Exod 5.1; 1 Kgs 1.48; 1 Chr 16.36; Ps 41.13; Isa 29.23 etc. In these and other texts the appellation, 'the God of Israel', is on the lips of Jews; and, with few exceptions, it is used in acclamations (it was clearly liturgical). The use of the title is not evidence for a Gentile crowd.

32. for they have been with me now for three days and have nothing to eat. 'Three days' is just an approximate period of time. Whether or not the words are designed to bring to mind the biblical tradition that God helps or saves people after three days, they make it manifest that if any brought provisions, they have by now been spent.

and I do not want to send them away hungry, lest they faint on the way. Matthew has 'on the way' in 5.25; 15.32; 21.8, and 32. He does not seem to lend it any symbolic significance.

33. Where in the wilderness will we get enough bread to feed so great a crowd? 'Wilderness' designates an uninhabited region and often stands in contrast to 'city'. Here the thought is: there are no nearby villages in which to buy food.

34. Seven, and a few small fish. The disciples are disparaging their sparse provisions.

35. And commanding the crowd to sit down on the ground. As in 14.19, Jesus, obviously in charge, once again orders the crowd to recline on the ground.

36. he took the seven loaves and the fish, and after giving thanks he broke them and gave them to the disciples, and the disciples gave them to the crowds. Cf. 14.19. The notice that Jesus gave the food to his disciples who in turn handed it on to the crowd could well have been intended as an allusion to the Eucharist. In early practice the elements were given to the deacons for distribution.

37. And all of them ate and were satisfied. So also 14.20a.

And they took up the broken pieces left over, seven baskets full. See on 14.10. Nothing important arises from the fact that 15.37 uses a different word for 'basket' than does 14.10.

38. Those who had eaten were four thousand men, besides women and children. See on 14.21.

39. and went to the region of Magadan. This differs substantially from Mk 8.10 ('he came into the district of Dalmanutha'). Why the geographical alteration? Both names are otherwise unattested. The location of Dalmanutha remains unknown, although it must have been near Lake Gennesaret. If Magadan is not to be identified with Magdala (the modern Tarichaeae; cf. 27.56: Mary Magdalene), a town which the Talmud puts near Tiberias on the west side of the Sea of Galilee, then its identity is also unknown. It is possible that Matthew and Mark accurately present us with two different names for some small, insignificant hamlet, in which case Matthew's knowledge of Galilee might be reckoned considerable. One should also not discount the possibility that Mark's text is corrupt and that Matthew, recognizing this, substituted an educated guess.

* * * * *

In view of the many similarities in both Matthew and Mark between the feeding of the five thousand and the feeding of the four thousand, one must ask, why the repetition? Why tell a story about Jesus which, in all essentials, has already been told, and quite recently at that? As repetition makes for emphasis, the major themes of 14.22–33 are underlined in 15.29–39 by way of reiteration; that is, their recurrence calls attention to their importance. But 15.29–39 does more than just repeat 14.22–33 and its motifs. The pericope has an independent contribution to make. Verses 29–31 make the feeding of the four thousand the vehicle of an idea not found in the feeding of the five thousand, namely, that in Jesus the Messiah the eschatological promises surrounding Zion have begun to be fulfilled. The gathering of the Jewish crowds, the healing of the sick, the allusion to Isa 35.5–6, the feeding of many, and the mountain setting are all at home in Jewish texts about Mount Zion. Perhaps it is even fair to infer from 15.29–39 that Jesus has, for Matthew, *replaced* Zion as the centre of God's dealings with God's people. However that may be, it is in 15.29–39, not 14.22–33, that Matthew's interest in the prophecies made to Zion and his conviction that they have found their fulfilment in Jesus come to the surface.

REQUEST FOR A SIGN FROM HEAVEN (16.1–4)

16 ¹And the Pharisees and Sadducees came, and testing him they asked him to show them a sign from heaven. ²Answering he said to them, 'When it is evening, you say, "It will be fair weather, for the sky is red." ³And in the morning, "It will be stormy today, for the sky is red and threatening." You know how to interpret the appearance of the sky, but you cannot interpret the signs of the times. ⁴An evil and adulterous generation seeks for a sign, but no sign will be given to it except the sign of Jonah.' And leaving them he departed.

Parallels: Mt 12.38–9; Mk 8.11–13; Lk 12.54–6

Despite everything Jesus has said and done, the sceptical leaders remain unmoved and seek to entrap him by making a request he will not fulfil. We have here a vivid picture of sad individuals who, professing to want evidence, in fact refuse to see the proofs right in front of their noses.

There may be a thematic connexion with 15.32–9, the feeding of the four thousand. The miraculous feeding harks back to the similar miracle performed by Elijah in Kings, while 16.1–4 mentions Jonah. This is interesting because the two prophetic figures were linked in Jewish tradition. According to 1 Kgs 17, Elijah healed the son of a widow, and this son was later identified with Jonah. Further, the healing of the widow's son by Elijah was in fact a resurrection, and for Matthew the sign of Jonah is the resurrection of Jesus. Perhaps, then, a typology lies behind the sequence in 15.32–16.4, the thought being that while 'this generation' vainly asks for a sign, it has been sent one no less remarkable than Elijah and will in the end be favoured with a sign reminiscent of what Jonah experienced.

1. The Pharisees and Sadducees – an unlikely alliance united in common cause against a perceived enemy (cf. 3.7) – tempt Jesus, asking for a sign from heaven. (In 12.38 it is the scribes and Pharisees who do this.) Obviously they do not really want Jesus to give them a compelling sign. They seek rather to make him stumble and lose face with the people. They are hypocritically asking for something they believe he cannot deliver. To sympathetic readers, who have just finished with the feeding of the four thousand, the request for a marvellous sign is ludicrous, a symptom of acute spiritual blindness.

And the Pharisees and Sadducees came. On the Pharisees and Sadducees see p. 40.

testing him they asked him to show them a sign from heaven. The assumption is that what Jesus has heretofore said and done is insufficient to compel belief. His sceptical opponents want rather some kind of sign in or from the heavens (such as a heavenly voice) as opposed to all the earthly signs Jesus has until now reportedly worked. Probably one should think of an unambiguous, eschatological sign, one so dramatic or cosmic in scope as to preclude the need for interpretation; cf. 24.27–30, where sun and moon are darkened and stars fall.

2–3. When it is evening, you say, 'It will be fair weather, for the sky is red.' And in the morning, 'It will be stormy today, for the sky is red and threatening.' If the saying about the meaning of a red sky at dawn and dusk was proverbial, perhaps it was especially associated with sailors, for whom the question of what the day would bring held special meaning.

but you cannot interpret the signs of the times. Jesus is referring to 'the (last) times (set by God)', which demand personal decision.

4. Jesus concludes his response by cryptically denying the request and then departing. The sign of Jonah – to be given in the future – is enough. God will not be put on display nor compel belief.

but no sign will be given to it except the sign of Jonah. The resurrection of Jesus is, according to Matthew, the sign that shall be given to 'this generation'; cf. 12.38–9. Is there supposed to be irony in the circumstance that the Sadducees dogmatically denied the resurrection of the dead?

How one is to harmonize the statement that *only* the sign of Jonah will be given with Matthew's conviction that Jesus' miracles were signs (cf. 11.1–24; 16.3–4) is far from clear. Did the evangelist draw a distinction between signs in general and a sign from heaven, that is, between signs such as Jesus' exorcisms and the type of irresistible sign some wanted?

And leaving them he departed. Jesus leaves the Sadducees and

Pharisees (who perhaps are to be thought of as uninterested in continuing the subject). He does not stay on in a vain attempt to persuade them of the truth but leaves the incorrigible to their own devices. In the event, even the resurrection will not persuade them; cf. 28.11–15.

* * * * *

The chief lesson in 16.1–4 is this: despite the proverb, seeing is not believing. If the Sadducees and Pharisees have not been persuaded by Jesus' miracles heretofore, neither will they be won over by a spectacular sign from heaven; cf. Lk 16.31. The truth is that one does not see until one believes. For the faith that holds the soul also rules one's perception. It is thus vain to expect hardened hearts and firmly fixed minds to be melted by demonstrations of power. In our gospel, accordingly, miracles, while pointers to God's presence in Jesus (cf. 11.2–4), are always therapeutic or salvific, that is, worked for the benefit of others. They are never straightforward, overpowering marvels aimed at convincing sceptics; cf. 13.56: 'he did not do any mighty works there because of their unbelief.'

THE LEAVEN OF THE PHARISEES AND SADDUCEES
(16.5–12)

[5]**And when the disciples came to the other side, they had forgotten to bring any bread.** [6]**Jesus said to them, 'Take heed and beware of the leaven of the Pharisees and Sadducees.'** [7]**They discussed it with one another, saying, 'We brought no bread.'** [8]**And Jesus, knowing this, said, 'You of little faith, why are you talking about having no bread?** [9]**Do you not yet perceive? Do you not remember the five loaves for the five thousand, and how many baskets you gathered?** [10]**Or the seven loaves for the four thousand, and how many baskets you gathered?** [11]**How can it be that you fail to perceive that I did not speak about bread? Beware of the leaven of the Pharisees and Sadducees!'** [12]**Then they understood that he had not told them to beware of the leaven of bread, but of the teaching of the Pharisees and Sadducees.**

Parallels: Mk 8.14–21; Lk 12.1

6. Take heed and beware of the leaven of the Pharisees and Sadducees. Leaven, as will be explained shortly (v. 12), is a metaphor for teaching. Probably in the background is the common use of leaven to symbolize a corrupting influence, an evil tendency which, although insignificant to start with, quickly multiplies to corrupt the whole; see on 13.33.

8. And Jesus, knowing this, said. Whether Matthew is here thinking of Jesus overhearing a conversation or instead reading minds is unclear.

You of little faith is appropriate because the disciples have done more than just misunderstand Jesus' saying. They have also – oddly enough, given all that they have witnessed – come to wonder about their provisions.

11. Jesus' concluding question – 'How is it that you fail to perceive that I did not speak about bread?' – makes everything clear: leaven is not to be understood literally. So Jesus can restate his warning without any possibility of being misunderstood: 'Beware of the leaven of the Pharisees and Sadducees.'

12. Then they understood that he had not told them to beware of the leaven of bread, but of the teaching of the Pharisees and Sadducees. 'The teaching' refers to all that the Jewish leaders say which hinders trust in Jesus and support for his cause.

* * * * *

Matthew could have used 16.5–12 to emphasize either Jesus' miraculous ability to meet physical needs, or his pedagogical skills, or both. These two themes, however, remain subsidiary. What stands out in the passage is the admonition about the Pharisees and Sadducees. The warning is repeated twice, frames the discourse as an *inclusio*, and is interpreted in the conclusion (leaven = teaching). It is clearly the main point. The explanation for this is presumably Matthew's historical setting. There was, evidently, still a need for him to warn readers about the Jewish leaders, that is, rabbis and synagogue authorities. It is altogether likely that Matthew knew Christians who still attended Jewish synagogue and that he himself engaged Jewish intellectuals in theological discussion. So there was a practical need to issue a clear admonition about the Jewish leaders.

JESUS, THE MESSIAH AND THE SON OF GOD, FOUNDS HIS CHURCH (16.13–20)

[13]**When Jesus came into the district of Caesarea Philippi, he asked his disciples, 'Who do men say that the Son of man is?'** [14]**They said, 'Some say John the Baptist, others Elijah, others Jeremiah or one of the prophets.'** [15]**He said to them, 'But who do you say that I am?'** [16]**Simon Peter answered, 'You are the Christ, the Son of the living God.'** [17]**Jesus answering said to him, 'Blessed are you, Simon son of Jonah! For flesh**

and blood has not revealed this to you, but my Father in heaven. [18]And I say to you, you are Peter, and on this rock I will build my church, and the gates of Hades will not prevail against it. [19]I will give to you the keys of the kingdom of heaven, and whatever you bind on earth will be bound in heaven, and whatever you loose on earth will be loosed in heaven.' [20]Then he sternly charged the disciples not to tell anyone that he was the Christ.

Parallels: Mk 8.27–30; Lk 9.18–21; Jn 6.67–71

This episode's primary function is, within the broader context of Matthew's whole narrative, to record the establishment of a new community, one which will acknowledge Jesus' identity and carry forward his work. The event has been occasioned by the rejection of Jesus by corporate Israel, a rejection chronicled in the previous chapters.

The major themes have their collective root in Davidic messianism, above all in Nathan's famous oracle to David, preserved in 2 Sam 7.4–16 and 1 Chr 17.3–15. Jesus is confessed as both Christ and Son of God; he builds a new church or temple; and he gives to Peter the keys to the kingdom of Heaven. These are all Davidic motifs. In 2 Sam 7 and 1 Chron 17 it is promised that one of David's descendants will rule over Israel as king (and therefore as anointed one), that he will be God's son ('I will be his father, and he will be my son'), that he will build a temple ('he shall build a temple for my name'), and that 'his kingdom' will be forever. This oracle was, before Jesus' time, understood to refer not just to Solomon but to Israel's eschatological king. Mt 16.13–20 presupposes its fulfilment in Jesus. Moreover, the giving of the keys of the Kingdom of heaven to Peter has its closest OT parallel in Isa 22.22: 'And I (God) will place on his (Eliakim's) shoulder the key of the house of David; he shall open, and none shall shut; and he shall shut, and none shall open.' Although this verse does not appear to have received a messianic interpretation in Judaism, 'the house of David' did have messianic associations, and the text is about the activity of a man second only to the king. That it lies behind Mt 16.19 is altogether likely. In sum, 16.13–20 records the eschatological realization of the promises made to David.

13. When Jesus came into the district of Caesarea Philippi. Caesarea Philippi was a Gentile town located on a terrace on the southern foot of Mount Hermon, over twenty miles north of the Sea of Galilee. The city was associated with the god Pan, who there had a cave shrine. Augustus gave it to Herod the Great in 20 BC. Herod's son, Philip, upon becoming tetrarch of the area, had the city enlarged and renamed, in honour of Augustus and himself. (The double name served to distinguish the place from Caesarea (Maritima) on the coast.) As is indicated by the expression in Mark and Matthew – 'the villages of Caesarea Philippi' – the city ruled over its surrounding territory.

14. In response to Jesus' query, the disciples observe that he has been identified with John the Baptist, with Elijah, with Jeremiah, and with 'one of the prophets'. The common denominator is the prophetic office.

others Elijah. Although some identified John the Baptist with Elijah (11.14; 17.12–13), Jesus' miracles and his preaching of repentance no doubt reminded many of Elijah and encouraged speculation that the Nazarene's ministry should be associated with expectations about the Tishbite.

others Jeremiah. There would seem to be three explanations for mentioning Jeremiah. (i) The text could be referring to a Jewish eschatological expectation, one which some connected with Jesus. Our sources, however, know nothing of an expected return of this prophet. (ii) Is Jeremiah simply an example or specification of 'one of the prophets', chosen because his book stood at the head of the latter prophets? (iii) More probable is the proposal that some noticed parallels between Jesus and Jeremiah. Both Jesus and Jeremiah were prophets of judgement and spoke against the temple. Both were thought of as having Mosaic traits. Both were figures of suffering, and both were martyrs. There are also several places in the First Gospel where Jesus borrows from the sayings of Jeremiah.

or one of the prophets. 'Or one of the prophets' makes plain what the three previous identifications have in common. John the Baptist was a prophet; cf. 11.9. Elijah was a prophet. And Jeremiah was a prophet. Thus the one fact upon which opinion concurs is that Jesus is a prophetic figure.

16. Simon Peter answered. Because Jesus has asked the disciples what they think, Peter, in his response, has been made out as their spokesman and representative. Certainly this is the situation in Mark, as well as in Luke. In Matthew, however, all the attention immediately becomes focused on Peter (vv. 17–19). Peter alone is said to be blessed, and he alone is named as the rock upon which the church is to be built. If he were just a spokesman we would instead have statements about the disciples as a group.

You are the Christ. On the background and meaning of 'Christ' see on 1.1. The definite article and the entire context leave no doubt that we have here not a name but a title: 'the Messiah'. Although this is the first time in Matthew that the disciples have called Jesus 'the Messiah', readers have known the truth from the beginning (1.1, 16–18; 2.4; 11.1–2).

the Son of the living God. It has been debated whether 'Son of God', whose truth as applied to Jesus will shortly be confirmed again by the voice at the transfiguration (17.4), is here intended to be a messianic title (in favour of this one could appeal to Hebrew parallelism) or whether it refers instead to the secret, personal relationship Jesus alone has with the Father (cf. 11.27; so the vast majority of commentators). But these are not mutually exclusive alternatives. Surely Matthew could have seen in 'Son of God' both messianic associations and a reflection of the unique relationship reflected by 11.27.

Because all the disciples have already confessed Jesus to be the Son of God (14.33; cf. 11.27), one wonders why the present confession is treated as a break-through attributable only to divine revelation. Has Peter done anything more than just reiterate an insight already expressed? One way around the difficulty is to place all the emphasis upon the confession of Jesus as Messiah: Peter is not being praised for his confession of Jesus as the Son of God, but for being the first to perceive Jesus' messianic identity (which would entail that the earlier confession was incomplete). But whether one should drive such a clear wedge between the two titles is far from obvious, and certainly most exegetes have not thought of Peter being praised only for part of his confession. A second way around the difficulty is to surmise that the earlier confession of Jesus as the Son of God was not borne of the fullest conviction. Yet of this the text says nothing. Perhaps, then, it is best to explain the inconcinnity in terms of sources. Maybe the fact that there are two confessions of Jesus as Son of God, the second of which is presented as though it were a new or fresh insight, is due to Matthew's imperfect assimilation of his sources, which presented him with two different Son of God confessions.

17. Peter's confession begets a beatitude: Jesus declares Simon blessed. The language recalls 11.27. But whereas there we read of the Son revealing the Father, here the Father reveals the Son.

Blessed are you, Simon son of Jonah! 'Bar Jona' transliterates the Aramaic for 'Son of Jonah'. But in Jn 1.42 Simon is said to have been 'the son of John'. It seems likely that Simon, perhaps because there was another Simon in the apostolic band, was called 'son of John' or 'son of Jonah' and that Matthew's tradition inadvertently turned 'John' into 'Jonah' (the name of a biblical prophet) or, alternatively, John's tradition inadvertently turned 'Jonah' into the much more popular 'John'.

For flesh and blood has not revealed this to you, but my Father in heaven. Cf. Gal 1.15–16; Ignatius, *Phil.* 7.2 ('I did not know from human flesh'). 'Flesh and blood' came to be a technical term in rabbinic texts, meaning 'human agency' in contrast to divine agency.

18. Jesus continues, giving Simon a new name (Peter, the rock) and speaking for the first time of 'my church', which will be built upon the rock against which the gates of Hades will not prevail. The verse is among the most controversial in all of Scripture. The literature it has generated is immense, and not a little of it rather polemical.

Verse 18 has a background in Genesis. Of the OT figures to receive a second name, the most memorable are Abram and Jacob. The former was given the new name Abraham to signify that he would be the father of a multitude (Gen 17.1–8). The latter was renamed Israel, by which the people that would spring from him would be known (Gen 32.22–32). Particularly intriguing are the parallels between Gen 17 and Mt 16. In both cases we are witnessing the birth of the people of God (the Jews in the one case, the church in the other). In both that birth is associated with one particular individual (Abraham, then Peter), and in both that individual has a name which symbolizes his crucial function (Abraham is taken to mean 'father of a multitude', Peter to mean the 'rock' on which the church is founded). The Peter of Mt 16 is like Abraham.

Buttressing this inference is Isa 51.1–2: 'Hearken to me, you who pursue deliverance, you who seek the Lord; look to the rock from which you were hewn, and to the quarry from which you were digged. Look to Abraham your father and to Sarah who bore you; for when he was but one I called him and I blessed him and made him many.' Here Abraham, like Peter, is a rock. So just as the OT figure whose name was changed in order to signify the coming into being of the people of God was likened to a rock, so too in Matthew is the birth of the church accompanied by Simon gaining a new name, Peter.

In 3.9, John the Baptist takes up Isa 51.1–2 in order to issue a warning: 'Do not presume to say to yourselves, "We have Abraham as our father"; for I tell you, God is able from these stones to raise up children to Abraham' (3.9). In this saying the Baptist holds forth the possibility that God can bring forth a new people, not from the old rock or quarry (Abraham and Sarah) but from elsewhere. What we seem to have in Mt 16.17–19 is the realization of John's dire prophecy. Here the new people of God is brought into being, not hewed from the rock Abraham but instead founded on the rock Peter.

you are Peter. This matches 'you are the Christ'. And just as Peter spoke revelation, so now does Jesus. But does this mean that Peter only now gets his new name? This is the judgement of perhaps most commentators, and no one else but the narrator uses 'Peter' until 16.17. Furthermore, the first notice of Simon is followed by this: 'who is called Peter' (4.18). The note does not indicate when or why he received this name. Certainly he does not receive it in 4.18. It is most natural to think that 4.18 looks forward to 16.17, that 16.17 explains a fact 4.18 mentions but leaves unexplained. This is confirmed by the parallels between Mt 16.17–19 and Gen 17.1–8 (see above). These gain their full force only when one thinks of 16.17–19 as recounting the giving of a new name.

And on this rock I will build my church. This line has been the object of much heated debate and much wasted ingenuity. 'This rock' has been identified variously with Peter's faith or confession, with his preaching office, with the truth revealed to him, with the twelve apostles, with Jesus, with Jesus' teaching, and even with God himself. All this is special pleading. The most natural interpretation of the Greek is that of Roman Catholic tradition: the rock is Peter.

It is possible that there is a mythological background to the imagery of the rock. 'My church', interpreted in the light of 2 Sam 7, evokes the idea of a temple, and the conception of the people of God as a temple was well known in both Judaism and early Christianity. This is important because in Jewish tradition the rock at the base of the temple on Zion is at the centre of the world. It links heaven and the underworld, being the gate to the former as well as the portal to Hades, the realm of the dead. Note that in 16.18c mention is made of the 'gates of Hades'. Perhaps, then, the informed reader should imagine the church at the centre of the cosmos, sitting above the powers of evil.

'I will build' is used again in both 26.61 and 27.40, where people claim that Jesus threatened to tear down the temple and then rebuild it or raise it up. What is the relationship between the three verses? The key is the evangelist's treatment of Mk 14.58, from which he has omitted 'not made with hands'. This last is usually, and rightly, taken to refer to the Christian community. Why its omission by Matthew? One can scarcely maintain that he rejected the conception of the church as a temple (it is implicit in 16.18). Rather, Mk 14.58, interpreted of the church, might be thought to put its founding in the post-Easter period ('after three days'), which would create tension with Mt 16.18, which places the church's birth before the resurrection. The difficulty is solved by modifying Mk 14.58 so that one thinks more readily of Jesus alone being raised up; cf. Jn 2.19–22. (Perhaps Matthew felt justified in his editing by the circumstance that Mk 14.58 is attributed to false witnesses and could therefore reasonably be held to be a misrepresentation of something Jesus said.)

and the gates of Hades will not prevail against it. Cf. Isa 28.15–19 (where the cornerstone laid in Zion will withstand the assault of water while those who have made a covenant with Sheol and death will be swept away) and 1QH 6.19–31 (here the speaker has journeyed to the

gates of death but finds refuge in a city founded on a rock). The notion
that the underworld or the realm of the dead was locked by gates was
common in the Ancient Near East and appears already in the *Epic of
Gilgamesh*.

The spectrum of opinion on these words, which in the early church
were so often used against heretics, and which later came to serve as an
apology for tradition, is unusually broad. But readers should likely
think of the end-time scenario, when the powers of the underworld will
be unleashed from below, from the abyss, and rage against the saints;
cf. Rev 6.8; 11.7; 17.8. The promise is that even the full fury of the
underworld's demonic forces will not overcome the church. One may
compare Rev 9.1–11, where the demonic hosts, under their king
Abaddon, come up from the bottomless pit to torment humanity.
They prevail against all save those with the seal of God. Also worth
comparing is 1QH 6.22–9. In this the author faces the gates of death
but is delivered by entering a fortified city founded on a rock. The
context is the great eschatological conflict.

19. I will give to you the keys of the kingdom of heaven. Cf. Isa 22.22;
Rev 1.18 and 3.7 (Jesus has the keys of Death and Hades as well as the
key of David); *3 Bar.* 11.2 (the angel Michael is the 'holder of the keys
of the kingdom of Heaven'); *3 En.* 18.18 ('Anapi'el YHWH the prince
keeps the keys of the palaces of the heaven of Arabot); 48 C 3
(Metatron has the keys to the treasure chamber of heaven). Heaven
was conceived of as having gates or doors. It is not obvious, however,
that we have that image in Mt 16.19. For in the synoptics 'the
kingdom of heaven' is not equated with the heavenly world. Maybe
then the image is of the gates to the future city of God.

**and whatever you bind on earth will be bound in heaven, and
whatever you loose on earth will be loosed in heaven.** Cf. 18.18 and Jn
20.23. Peter is the authoritative teacher without peer. He has the
power to declare what is permitted and what is not permitted. Cf.
23.13: 'But woe to you, scribes and Pharisees, hypocrites! For you
shut people out of the kingdom. For you do not go in nor allow those
who want to go in to do so'. Here, as the context proves, the scribes
shut the door to the kingdom by issuing false doctrine. The image is
closely related to 16.19, and the inference lies near to hand that just
as the kingdom itself is taken from the Jewish leaders and given to the
church (21.43), so are the keys of the kingdom taken from the scribes
and Pharisees and given to Peter. Supportive of this is the broader
context of Peter's confession. In the immediately preceding 16.5–12
Jesus warns: 'Beware of the leaven of the scribes and Pharisees.'
Matthew takes this to be about the *teaching* of the scribes and
Pharisees. It would make good sense for the evangelist, in the very

next paragraph, to tell a story in which Jesus replaces the Jewish academy with his own 'chief rabbi'.

* * * * *

(i) Mt 16.13–20 begins by moving the reader to draw a comparison between Jesus and great heroes from the past: Elijah, Jeremiah, and John the Baptist. It at once becomes apparent that the contrasts are greater than the similarities. Even if Jesus is undeniably a prophet, he is greater than all other prophets. Indeed, even more than John the Baptist is he more than a prophet. Jesus is 'the Christ, the Son of the living God'. As such he is not one in a series. He rather stands alone. He is the realization of the messianic hopes of Judaism, the fulfiler of the Davidic promises, the culmination of salvation-history. He also builds the church, which is the eschatological temple, and he speaks of the inability of the powers of Hades to overcome those who follow him. He has the keys to the kingdom and the power to give them to another. Are we not dealing in 16.13–20 with a person who cannot adequately be described in purely human categories (cf. the 'I am' of 14.22–33)? Here we have Davidic messianism, but with a difference. As Jewish messianism had anticipated, the Messiah in Matthew is certainly a human figure. But he is also God's Son. Unfortunately, we do not know how the First Evangelist conceptualized this, how exactly he thought of the person of Jesus. Did he conceive of him as transcending the traditional messianic categories in such a way that use of the term 'essential deity' is justified? Or would 'functional deity' be better? The application of the word 'God' to Jesus is extremely rare in the NT, and it is not found in the First Gospel. Is it, however, there implied? Should one hazard that 'deity' was a significant implication of Matthew's Christology, as it was of John's?

(ii) Mt 16.13–20 is the crucial pericope in Matthew's fourth narrative section. The first narrative section, 1.1–4.23, introduced us to Jesus. The second, 8.1–9.38, recounted Jesus' mighty acts and witness to Israel. The third section, 11.1–12.50, recorded the negative response of corporate Israel to the Messiah's activities. What we then have in the next narrative section, 13.53–17.27, is the consequence of the rejection of the Messiah: the people of God are founded anew. In other words, the birth of the ecclesia – of Jew and Gentile – is traced directly to the failure of Israel to live up to its eschatological calling. The underlying logic of the narrative is explicitly formulated in 21.43, which speaks of the kingdom being taken from its Jewish custodians and given to the church.

(iii) The parallels between 16.13–20 and Gen 17.1–8 indicate that Peter functions as a new Abraham. He is the first of his kind, and he stands at the head of a new people. Peter is, like Abraham, a rock (cf. Isa 51.1–2), and the change in his name denotes his function. What follows? Peter is not just a representative disciple, as so many Protestant exegetes have been anxious to maintain. Nor is he obviously the first holder of an office others will someday hold, as Roman Catholic tradition has so steadfastly maintained. Rather, he is a man with a unique role in salvation-history. The eschatological revelation vouchsafed to him opens a new era. His person marks a change in the times. His significance is the significance of Abraham, which is to say: his faith is the means by which God brings a new people into being.

THE PASSION AND RESURRECTION PREDICTED (16.21–3)

[21]From that time, Jesus began to show his disciples that he must go to Jerusalem and suffer many things from the elders and chief priests and scribes, and be killed, and on the third day be raised. [22]And Peter took him aside and began to rebuke him, saying, 'Far be it from you, Lord! This will never happen to you.' [23]But turning he said to Peter, 'Get behind me, Satan! You are a stumbling block to me; for you are not perceiving divine things but human things.'

Parallels: Mk 8.31–3; Lk 9.22

Once it has become evident that Israel as a corporate body is not going to heed Jesus, two tasks remain for God's rejected servant. First, he must establish a new community, the church, and give her instruction. Second, he must give his life as a ransom for many. Having begun the first task, in the previous passage, Jesus next turns his eyes towards the second.

21. that he must go to Jerusalem and suffer many things from the elders and chief priests and scribes, and be killed. 'Must' (cf. 17.10; 24.6; 26.54), which in Matthew is the functional equivalent of 'it is written', expresses the conviction that Jesus' passion is the realization in time of a destiny stored up for and dictated to the Messiah by the Scriptures, which convey God's will. In connexion with a prophecy of suffering and resurrection, the use of 'must' could call to mind several OT texts, including Ps 22; 34.19–22; 89.38–45; 118.10–25; Isa 52–3; Dan 7; Hos 6.2; and Zech 13.7–9.

On the chief priests and scribes see p. 24. The 'elders', together with the chief priests and scribes, made up the membership of the Sanhedrin in Jerusalem. The order of the present verse – elders, chief priests, scribes – is unusual because unattested elsewhere. Two observations.

First, the Pharisees are not mentioned here. This is because they play no role in the passion narrative. Second, Matthew does not speak of the Jews rejecting Jesus. Only the leaders are named.

and on the third day be raised. Cf. Hos 6.2. With one exception (27.63), Matthew consistently prefers the more precise 'on the third day' over the less precise 'after three days' (which does not, if taken literally, harmonize with his passion narrative).

22. Imagining that Jesus 'was the Christ as the generality of men supposed' (Irenaeus), Peter, playing the fool and not understanding the secret purposes of God, imprudently counters his Lord. Perhaps readers may imagine, emboldened by the promise that the gates of Hades will not prevail against the church, the apostle does not yet recognize that the way to life is through death. This gives Matthew's Jesus the opportunity to stress, in the strongest way possible, the necessity of messianic suffering. 'Unless a grain of wheat falls into the earth and dies, it remains alone; but if it dies, it bears much fruit.' Peter's fancies and Jesus' subsequent rebuke (v. 23) also forcefully demonstrate the difficulty of apprehending the difficult ways of God.

And Peter took him aside and began to rebuke him, saying. Cf. *Gen. Rab.* on 22.7, where Samael 'rebukes' Abraham and tries to turn him away from sacrificing his son Isaac.

23. Get behind me is probably just a rebuke meaning 'get away from me'. But it is possible that Jesus is telling Peter to get back in line, to quit taking the lead, to become a follower so that he might once more learn what discipleship is all about.

You are a stumbling block to me. 'Stumbling block' here means 'temptation to sin'. Peter, up against what Paul called 'the stumbling block of the cross' (cf. Gal 5.11; also 1 Cor 1.23), himself has become a stumbling block, an obstacle tempting Jesus to leave the path that goes through Gethsemane and Golgotha.

for you are not perceiving divine things but human things. Cf. Rom 8.5; Phil. 3.19; and Col 3.2. Chrysostom: 'Let them hear, as many as are ashamed of the suffering of the cross of Christ. For if the chief apostle, even before he had learnt all distinctly, was called Satan for feeling this, what excuse can they have, who after so abundant proof deny his economy? I say, when he who had been so blessed, who made such a confession, has such words addressed to him; consider what they will suffer, who after all this deny the mystery of the cross.'

* * * * *

(i) As everything in our gospel takes its meaning from its relation to the events recounted in chapters 26–8, it is not surprising that 16.21–3, the first formal passion prediction, only makes explicit a fact previously foreshadowed and implied in a dozen different ways, namely, that Jesus must go to Jerusalem, be rejected by the Jewish establishment, die, and then rise from the dead. Already the reader knows of the opposition of Jerusalem and the Jewish leaders (2.1–6; 9.32–4; 12.1–8, 14), of Jesus' willingness to take up the role of the suffering servant of Isaiah (12.15–21), of his determination to die and redeem his people (1.21; 9.15), and of his coming triumph over death (12.40). Mt 16.21–3 is, accordingly, a knot in the narrative where various threads are drawn together.

(ii) The divine 'must' of 16.21 should not be taken to mean that Jesus' fate is inevitable, something which will befall him whether he likes it or not. The rebuke of Peter shows plainly enough that the Messiah goes to his death as a free individual; his destiny is one he chooses for himself.

(iii) The jarring juxtaposition of 16.13–20, where Jesus congratulates Peter with a makarism, and 16.21–3, where Jesus rebuffs Peter as Satan, is full of edifying lessons which exegetes throughout the centuries have rightly unfolded. To begin with, Peter's pre-eminence makes his misunderstanding in effect universal: if even the favoured Simon, rock of the church and recipient of divine revelation, did not grasp the truth, then, we may assume, that truth was hidden from all. God's intentions for Jesus were so dark and mysterious that they simply could not, before the event, be comprehended. This in large part explains why Jesus is such a lonely figure in Matthew and why he is trailed throughout the gospel by misapprehension and even opposition. God's ways are inscrutable. At the same time, the darkness of the pre-Easter period is only revealed to be such by the light diffused by Easter, so the readers of the gospel must know themselves to live in a special time, one no doubt demanding unprecedented responsibilities. Another lesson is to be found in this, that Peter's fall from the heights shows him to be anything but an idealized figure. Like David and so many other biblical heroes, the apostle serves as a warning that privilege and even divine election will not keep one from evil mischief. Finally, Peter must also, again like David and so many others, be intended to stand as a symbol of God's ever-ready willingness to bestow forgiveness on the imperfect. For as soon as Peter has been quickly dismissed for words better left unsaid, Jesus selects him, along with two others, to be witnesses of the transfiguration. Thus Peter, so far from being punished for his misguided thoughts, is immediately granted a glimpse of the glorified Christ. Readers may see in this a triumph of grace.

THE COST OF DISCIPLESHIP (16.24–8)

[24]Then Jesus said to his disciples, 'If any one wants to follow after me, let him deny himself and take up his cross and follow me. [25]For whoever wants to save his life will lose it, and whoever loses his life for my sake will find it. [26]For what will it profit a person if he gains the whole world but forfeits his life? Or what will a person give in return for his life? [27]For the Son of man is about to come with his angels in the glory of his Father, and then he will repay everyone for what he has done. [28]Amen I say to you, there are some standing here who will not taste death before they see the Son of man coming in his kingdom.'

Parallels: Mt 10.38–9; Mk 8.34–9.1; Lk 9.23–7; Jn 12.5

True discipleship is not an easy achievement because it is a 'following' (v. 24) of the master's example. If Jesus endured both suffering and crucifixion (16.21–3), likewise must his disciples give up their lives and carry a cross (vv. 24–5). Furthermore, following Jesus in such a manner is accomplished primarily through a surrender or denial of self – which, in the context of the gospel as a whole, means above all obedience to another's will. Hardly anything more difficult could be asked. The effort, however, shall prove more than worthwhile, for what matters is not gain in this world (v. 26) but reward in the world to come (v. 27), which is not far off (v. 28).

24. Then Jesus said to his disciples. It would not be appropriate for Jesus to demand of the crowds, who have not decided for or against him, what he demands of his closest followers.

let him deny himself and take up his cross and follow me. Cf. 10.38. The first two verbs – 'deny' and 'take up' – are in the past tense, the third – 'follow' – in the present. This suggests that the decision to renounce the self and to take up one's cross stands at the beginning of the disciple's journey and is then followed by a continued determination to stick to the chosen path. One first picks up the cross and then one carries it, following the path to death first walked by Jesus.

25. As the 'for' indicates, v. 25 elucidates v. 24: one must take up one's cross because it is only through the loss of life – that is, displacement of the ego from the centre of its universe and the accompanying willingness to give up personal ambition and even to suffer and, if need be, die for God's cause – that eschatological life is gained. Maybe the best commentary is Gal 2.20: 'I have been crucified with Christ. It is no longer I who live ...'.

For whoever wants to save his life will lose it, and whoever loses his life for my sake will find it. Cf. 10.39; Jn 12.25. 'For my sake' means in effect that the disciple is Jesus' possession. The lord of the self has become another.

26. The ultimate value of a person's life as compared with all else is now proclaimed by two questions whose negative answers are too obvious to be made explicit. What good is even the greatest possession if there is no possessor to enjoy it? The point is not the surpassing value of human beings as such but rather life as the prerequisite for enjoying anything. There is no value in gaining the present world if the cost is loss of life in the world to come; cf. 6.19–24.

For what will it profit a person if he gains the whole world but forfeits his life? Cf. Eccles 1.3 ('What does a person gain by all the toil at which he toils under the sun?') and *2 Bar.* 51.15 ('For what then have men lost their life, and for what have those who were on the earth exchanged their soul?') 'His life' is the true self, that part which can survive death. Combined with 'forfeits', it calls to mind the final judgement; cf. 16.27.

Whether or not 16.26a par. was based upon a proverbial sentiment, its truth, if one believes God to be lord of the future, is patent. Those who gain this world at the cost of the next are dangers to their own souls, fools without peer. This life offers no certainties, no permanent security, no lasting inheritance: 'No mortal can in solid reality be lord of anything' (Philo). Nothing belongs to human beings in the end; rather, human beings belong to death. To seek worldly possessions and power at the expense of everlasting treasure (6.19–21) is an unconscionable blunder, with sin as its only possible explanation; cf. Lk 12.16–21.

Or what will a person give in return for his life? Even if one has gained the whole world, it cannot be returned in exchange for participation in eternal life. Worth comparing is Ps 49.7–9: 'Truly no one can ransom himself, or give to God the price of his life, for the ransom of his life is costly and can never suffice, that he should live forever ...'. Perhaps our text was first formulated with this line in view. If so, vv. 26a and b could well have originated together, and their basis would be the OT, not secular wisdom.

27. Mt 16.13–20 largely concerns Jesus' identity: he is the Messiah and the Son of God. Mt 16.21–3 then tells of his upcoming passion and resurrection. Finally, 16.27–8 is about Jesus' future as the eschatological judge, the Son of man of Dan 7. The sequence is: identity, history, future.

For the Son of man is about to come with his angels in the glory of his Father. Cf. 24.30–1; 25.31; 26.64. 'In the glory of his Father' (cf. 6.29 – Solomon's glory; 25.31 – the Son of man's glory) makes its impact first from the immediately preceding lines, which are about suffering and death, and the earthly fate of the speaker. The future will stand in stark contrast to the present. If now the Son of man and his followers are rejected, forced to suffer, and even executed, things to come will see the world turned upside down. The Son of man, once rejected and despised, will participate in God's eschatological story. Then, second, 'in the glory of his Father' gains meaning from what follows, where the appearance of Jesus bathed in light is an anticipation of his eschatological glory.

and then he will repay everyone for what he has done. Very similar words also appear in Rom 2.6; 2 Tim 4.14; Rev 2.23; 22.12 (both sayings of the risen Lord). In view of all these and other texts (Prov 24.12; Ecclus 35.22 etc.), we have to do with a stereotyped phrase or expression rather than a scriptural citation or allusion.

That there is any final contradiction between 16.27 and Paul's doctrine of justification by faith is not obvious. For one thing, Paul himself, in Romans, could write that God 'will render to everyone according to his works' (Rom 2.6; cf. 1 Cor 3.10–15; 2 Cor 5.10). For another, Matthew no less than Paul believed that salvation was God's gift. If there is no antithesis between faith and works, then there need be no contradiction between justification by faith and judgement according to works.

28. The section winds up with an asseveration whose interpretation has long divided exegetes.

there are some standing here who will not taste death before they see the Son of man coming in his kingdom. Cf. Jn 8.51–2. Of believers it is said that they, at the end, will enter into the kingdom. But of Jesus it is said that he will come 'in his kingdom'. Instead of entering the kingdom, as others do, he brings it with him.

What does Mt 16.28 mean? (i) The reference could be to the following story, the transfiguration, where Jesus is transfigured into light. (ii) Calvin took 16.28 to be a prophecy not of the transfiguration but of the resurrection. (iii) A few have identified the coming of the Son of man in 16.28 with the post-Easter outpouring of the Holy Spirit. (iv) Gregory the Great argued for fulfilment in the early triumph of Christianity. (v) Some connect 16.28 with the destruction of Jerusalem in AD 70: this last was the Son of man's judgement of Israel. (vi) Mt 16.28 refers to the Second Coming, which Matthew still hoped was near.

One's choice would clearly seem to be between (i) and (vi). As to which one of these is correct, one is hard pressed to say. But perhaps the two are complementary. The resurrection is, for Matthew, an eschatological event. Both the resurrection and the *parousia* are, moreover, associated with Danielic Son of man imagery; cf. e.g. 24.30;

28.18. Consequently, the resurrection is a foretaste of the second advent, a preview of what is to come. More than this, it is the first act in the eschatological instalment of Jesus. This makes it possible to suppose that, from Matthew's perspective, 16.28 looks forward at the same time to both the resurrection and the *parousia*. In other words, it foretells both, because they are the two halves of one event: the eschatological glorification and vindication of the Son of man.

* * * * *

Our text drives home the point that the disciples must not passively observe their Lord and what he does. They are not to be seated spectators watching from the grandstand the actions foretold in 16.21–3. Rather must they themselves enter the arena after their Lord. For Matthew, Jesus is not a substitute but a leader. He does not do something for those who do nothing. Instead he commands, 'Follow me' (4.18–22; 9.9). This authoritative call leaves no room for considerations of convenience or even self-preservation. Discipleship is a doing of what is right, no matter how irksome the privations, no matter how great the dangers (cf. the missionary discourse). Faith means obedience, and obedience is the grave of the will. 'Not as I will, but as you will.'

THE TRANSFIGURATION (17.1–8)

17 ¹And after six days, Jesus took with him Peter and James and his brother John and led them up a high mountain, by themselves. ²And he was transfigured before them, and his face shone like the sun, and his clothes became white as light. ³And behold, there appeared to them Moses and Elijah, talking with him. ⁴And Peter answered and said to Jesus, 'Lord, it is good that we are here. If you wish, I will make three dwellings here, one for you, one for Moses, and one for Elijah.' ⁵While he was yet speaking, behold, a bright cloud overshadowed them, and a voice from the cloud said, 'This is my beloved, with whom I am well pleased; listen to him!' ⁶When the disciples heard this, they fell on their faces and became exceedingly afraid. ⁷But Jesus came and touched them, saying, 'Rise and do not be afraid.' ⁸And raising their eyes they saw no one but Jesus alone.

Parallels: Mk 9.2–10; Lk 9.28–36; 2 Pet 1.17–18

The text may have a chiastic arrangement. One can correlate the narrative introduction with the narrative conclusion, the transfiguration of Jesus with the words of Jesus, the response of Peter with the response of the disciples:

    a.   Narrative introduction (1)
       b.   Jesus is transfigured (2–3)
          c.   Peter's response (4)
             d.   The divine voice (5)
          c.   The disciples' response (6)
       b.   Jesus speaks (7)
    a.   Narrative conclusion (8)

If this analysis is correct, the voice from heaven is the structural centre.

The story recalls Exodus 24 and 34, which tell of Moses' transfiguration on Mount Sinai. That Jesus is transfigured into light 'after six days' corresponds to what happens to Moses in Exodus 34.29–35 (cf. Exodus 24.16, where God calls to Moses out of the cloud on the seventh day). Further, there is a special group of three named witnesses as in Exodus 24.1, and if a divine voice speaks from a bright cloud when Jesus is transfigured, the same thing happens in Exodus 24.15–18 and 34.5. All this takes place, moreover, on a mountain, just as it does in Exodus 24 and 34. Not only does Moses show up but so does Elijah, and they are the only figures in the Old Testament to speak with God on Mount Sinai (called Horeb in Kings), so their presence together makes one think of that mountain and the epiphanies there. As so often in early Christian literature, then, Jesus is like Moses, and his history is something like a new exodus.

The heavenly voice, which, like the voice at the baptism, seems to mix Psalm 2.7 ('I will tell of the decree of the Lord: He said to me, "You are my son; today I have begotten you"') and Isaiah 42.1 ('Here is my servant, whom I uphold, my chosen, in whom my soul is well pleased'), is probably designed to reinforce the idea that Jesus is like Moses. For Deuteronomy 18.15 and 18, which Acts 3.22–23 sees as fulfilled in Jesus, foretell the coming of one like Moses, to whom the people should 'listen'.

While the transfiguration as it stands in Matthew is first of all a picture of Jesus as a new and greater Moses, this fact scarcely eliminates the presence of other important themes. For instance, 17.1–8 recalls the baptism and confirms Peter's confession; it foreshadows the resurrection and anticipates the *parousia*. Nonetheless, the Mosaic motifs are the key to Matthew's story, and attempts to give other themes pride of place do not persuade.

1. And after six days. 'After six days' is not only ambiguous – is the reference to 16.13? or to 16.21? or to 16.24? – but is also quite anomalous for the synoptic tradition: chronological precision before the passion narrative is rare. An allusion to Exod 24.16 (see above) is probable.

Jesus took with him Peter and James and his brother John. In Exod 24.1, Moses separates himself from the people and takes with him seventy elders and a special group of three people whose names are given: Aaron, Nadab, and Abihu.

a high mountain corresponds to Sinai, which both Philo and Josephus make the highest mountain in its region. None of the synoptic evangelists seems to have been interested in locating with any precision the mount of transfiguration, and none names it. Christian tradition from an early time pointed to Mount Tabor.

2. And he was transfigured before them. Even though the primary background for the synoptic picture of Jesus transfigured is in the change Moses experienced on Sinai, it may not be irrelevant to keep in mind the expectation that the bodies of the righteous will, in the end, undergo a transformation, for the transfigured Jesus is probably intended to show forth what believers will become; cf. 13.43.

and his face shone like the sun. Although the OT does not compare Moses' face to the sun, Philo says that dazzling brightness flashed from Moses like 'rays of the sun', and *Sifre Num.* 140 declares that 'The face of Moses was as the face of the sun.' Cf. also *LAB* 12.1: Moses' 'face surpassed the splendour of the sun and the moon.'

and his clothes became white as light. The supernatural brightness of the clothes of divine or heavenly beings or of the resurrected just is a common motif in the biblical tradition; see Dan 7.9 (of the Son of man); *1 En.* 14.20 (the gown of God); 63.15–16 (the garments of the righteous); Mk 16.5 (an angel's robe); Rev 3.4–5; 7.9 (white garments of the saints); etc. Like God, who 'covers himself with light as with a garment' (Ps 104.2), those who belong to God are also destined to shine like the sun.

3. And behold, there appeared to them Moses and Elijah, talking with him. Moses and Elijah are the only two OT figures who encountered God on Sinai/Horeb.

4. it is good that we are here. It is unclear whether Peter is pleased because of what he is experiencing or because he has an opportunity to serve Jesus and Moses and Elijah.

I will make three dwellings here. Peter no longer speaks for the others but of himself alone: he will build the tents or booths.

one for you, one for Moses, and one for Elijah. The comment is obscure. Some think that there might be a connection with the feast of booths, which Jewish tradition sometimes associated with eschatological expectation. Is Peter then expressing his conviction that the transfiguration is a harbinger of the end of the world? Cyril of Jerusalem wrote: 'Peter, thinking perchance that the time of the kingdom of God was even now come, proposes dwellings on the

mountain, and says that it is fitting there should be three tabernacles
... But he knew not, it says, what he was saying, for it was not the time
of the consummation of the world, nor for the saints to take
possession of the hope promised to them.' Others have simply
surmised that Peter wishes to prolong the blessed moment, or that
his request comes from a desire to observe the feast that is at hand, or
that he assumes that the saints in heaven have dwellings and so will
need them when on earth. Whatever Peter has in mind, and whatever
his mistake might be – that he wants to linger when he cannot? that he
wants to build the booths instead of letting God take things in hand?
that 'one for you and one for Moses and one for Elijah' implies the
parity of the three named? – the cloud and its voice interrupt him. His
is not to teach but to listen.

5. The proceedings are now interrupted by a cloud and then by a
heavenly voice which, repeating the divine declaration of the baptism,
but here addressed to the disciples instead of Jesus, proclaims Jesus to
be God's Son and the suffering servant.

a bright cloud overshadowed them. Cf. Exod 30.45; Ezek 1.4 ('a great
cloud with brightness round about it'); Rev 14.14 ('a white cloud');
Liv. Proph. Jer. 14 ('a cloud as of fire'); 18 ('a cloud like fire, just like
the ancient one'); *T. Abr.* A 9.8 ('a cloud of light').

a voice from the cloud said. Cf. 2 Pet 1.18: 'and this voice we heard
from heaven'. The places in which God speaks from a cloud are few and
far between; cf. Exod 24.16. This strengthens the Exodus connexion.

This is my beloved, with whom I am well pleased. Cf. 3.17; also Ps
2.7; Isa 42.1; 44.2; 2 Pet 1.17. The agreement with the voice at the
baptism is perfect. So 3.17 and 17.5 say precisely the same thing, which
makes for emphasis. Furthermore, it is fitting that Jesus should be
presented as servant of Yahweh in a pericope so influenced by Mosaic
motifs, for Moses was known as the servant *par excellence*; cf. Exod
14.31; Num 12.7–8.

listen to him refers to Deut 18.15 and 18 and shows Jesus to be the
prophet like Moses. For other texts where Jesus is presented as the
object of Moses' prophecy of a future prophet see Acts 3.22 and 7.37.

The command to hear or obey Jesus probably pertains not solely to
the future ('listen to him from now on'), but also looks back to the
episode at Caesarea Philippi and Jesus' words about suffering.

**6. When the disciples heard this, they fell on their faces and became
exceedingly afraid.** Cf. Exod 34.30: those who saw Moses' face were
afraid to come near. The motif of falling on one's face in fear is a
standard part of heavenly ascent or revelation stories. But here there is
more, for there is a contrast between Jesus' face, which is shining, and
the faces of the disciples, which are hidden.

Mark places the awe felt by the disciples early in the narrative, immediately after the transfiguration and the vision of Moses and Elijah: not the fact that Jesus commands but his transfiguration itself is emphasized. Luke makes the descent of the cloud the occasion for fear (Lk 9.34). With Matthew it is otherwise. He reserves the experience of awe on the part of the disciples until immediately after the words, 'Listen to him'. It is the divine word which is awesome.

7. But Jesus came and touched them. Only here and in 28.18 does Jesus approach anyone. In both cases he approaches his disciples and he is in an exalted state.

8. they saw no one but Jesus alone. Evidently Moses and Elijah have been taken away to heaven by the cloud; cf. Josephus, *Ant.* 4.326: while Moses 'was yet communing with them, a cloud of a sudden descended upon him and he disappeared in a ravine.'

The history of the interpretation of the transfiguration is rather interesting. In 2 Peter the story is employed as an apologetic. It vindicates belief in Jesus as God's beloved Son and as the recipient of divine honour and glory. It also serves to uphold what 2 Pet 1.19 calls 'the prophetic word', which word, given the content of 2 Peter, probably refers to the promises of the second advent or, more precisely, to the transfiguration as an anticipation of and therefore prophecy of that advent. That is, Christ's glory at his first coming assures believers that his promise of a glorious second coming is most sure; cf. 3.1–18. In the second-century *Apocalypse of Peter* (chapter 17) the transfiguration is recounted in response to the disciples' request that they behold the fate of the righteous after death. Furthermore, when Peter asks where the righteous ones dwell and inquires about their world, the scene expands to include the paradise of God, with its lights and flowers and trees and fragrances and fruits. So here the transfiguration is a preview of what heaven will be like and an illustration of the glory that awaits the Christian. Perhaps the most common interpretation in Christian history is that found in *Acts of Peter* 20 and *Acts Thom.* 143: the transfiguration is a revelation of Christ's heavenly or divine nature, of Jesus as he always was and is. On this view, Jesus was not really changed; rather, the disciples were enabled to perceive what was always the case; cf. the story in 2 Kgs 6.15–17. This interpretation has often been put forward with Phil 2.6–7 in mind.

Most traditional approaches to the transfiguration can be assigned to one of two categories: either the emphasis is upon Christ's divinity or it is upon his humanity. In the latter case the transfiguration represents what all believers will experience at the resurrection. But in the Hesychiasts of Byzantium the two traditions are fused. Gregory

Palamas identified the light of Tabor with the ineffable, uncreated light of Christ which bathes the whole cosmos and which can yet be seen in the chambers of the heart by those who say the Jesus Prayer and accomplish poverty of spirit: that is, by those in the process of being deified through participation in the divine life. So the light of the transfiguration belongs to Christ as God but at the same time transforms human beings into their divine destiny.

* * * * *

(i) In 17.1–8 the great light of 4.16 becomes visibly radiant to those called, in 5.14, to be the light of the world. For Matthew the first purpose of the manifestation is to recall Exod 24 and 34 and certain events in the life of Moses. The point of this is not simply Christological, although that is important: Jesus is the prophet like Moses (cf. Deut 18.15, 18) who, as the unique Son of God, surpasses Moses. Also significant is the closely related eschatological theme: 'as it was in the beginning, so shall it be in the end'; 'as the first redeemer, so the last redeemer.' When Jesus, in circumstances strongly reminiscent of Exod 24 and 34, goes up on a mountain and is transfigured into light, the reader is to infer that history has come full circle, that the eschatological expectations of Judaism have begun to find their fulfilment. The eschatological prophet, the one like Moses and Elijah, has appeared, and the light of the resurrection and *parousia* has already shone forth. Israel's primal history is being recapitulated by her Messiah, God's Son, the eschatological embodiment of true Israel.

(ii) The transfiguration, with its wealth of theological associations, relates itself in diverse ways to the immediately preceding narrative. To begin with, the story illustrates 16.24–8 by first showing the glory of the *parousia* foretold in vv. 27 and 28 (cf. 2 Pet 1.16–18), and second by making concrete the resurrection hope of those who follow the hard commands of Jesus issued in vv. 24–6. As for 16.21–3 (the prophecy of Jesus' passion and vindication), 17.1–8 illumines this by anticipating Jesus' exaltation as well as by interpreting the suffering which must come first as that of the servant written of by the prophet Isaiah. Moving backward yet one more pericope, there is also a close connexion with 16.13–20, for both at Caesarea Philippi and on the mount of transfiguration Jesus is proclaimed to be the Son of God. There is, to be sure, a major difference in that in the earlier story the Son of God confession comes from Peter, whereas in the latter God himself speaks. But this only makes 17.1–8 set the divine seal of approval over Peter's pronouncement. Further, the two pericopae are alike insofar as both qualify sonship with suffering service; just as

16.13–20 is followed by 16.21–3, which holds forth the necessity for suffering, so 17.1–8 interprets Jesus' sonship in terms of Isaiah's servant ('in whom I am well pleased'; cf. Isa 42.1).

(iii) The transfiguration has a sort of dark twin in the accounts of the crucifixion. In the one case, there are three named male disciples (Peter, James, and John), in the other three female disciples are named (Matthew: two Marys and the mother of the sons of Zebedee; Mark: two Marys and Salome). In the one case Jesus is elevated on a mountain, in the other he is elevated on a cross. In the one case there is a private epiphany, in the other there is a public spectacle. In the one case Jesus is transfigured into light, in the other case a supernatural darkness descends. In the one case Jesus's garments are illumined, in the other they are stripped off. In the one case Jesus is glorified, in the other he is shamed. In the one case Elijah appears, in the other case Elijah does not appear. In the one case two saints appear beside Jesus (Moses and Elijah), in the other two criminals hang beside him. In the one case God confesses Jesus, in the other God abandons Jesus. In the one case a divine voice declares Jesus to be God's Son, in the other a pagan soldier makes this confession. In the one case there is reverent prostration before Jesus, in the other the onlookers mock Jesus with prostration.

The curious confluence of similar motifs and contrasting images creates pictorial antithetical parallelism, something like a diptych in which the two plates have similar outlines but different colors. If one scene were sketched on a transparency and placed over the other, many of its lines would disappear.

Together the two scenes interestingly illustrate the extremities of human experience. One is spit and mockery, nails and nakedness, blood and loneliness, torture and death. The other makes visible the presence of God and depicts the divinization of human nature. So Jesus embodies the gamut of human possibilities; he is the coincidence of opposites. Perhaps this is one of the reasons the canonical Jesus has always been so attractive and inspiring. He shows forth in his own person both the depths of pain and anguish which human beings have known, as well as that which all long for – transfiguration into some state beyond such pain and anguish. Jesus is the paradigm of both despair and hope; he is humanity debased and humanity glorified.

ELIJAH AND JOHN (17.9–13)

⁹And as they were coming down the mountain, Jesus commanded them, 'Tell no one about the vision until after the Son of man has been raised from the dead.' ¹⁰And the disciples asked him, saying, 'Then why do the

scribes say that Elijah must come first?' [11]Answering he said, 'Elijah does come, and he will restore all things. [12]But I say to you that Elijah has already come, and they did not know him, but rather they did to him whatever they pleased. So also the Son of man is about to suffer at their hands.' [13]Then the disciples understood that he was speaking to them of John the Baptist.

Parallel: Mk 9.11–13

This story first of all deprives Jewish critiques of 'realized eschatology' of one forceful objection: namely, since Elijah has not yet come, the eschatological scenario cannot be unfolding. Beyond that, the passage emphasizes yet once more the parallels between Jesus and his forerunner, John, thus adding to that Matthean theme. Lastly, the command to keep silence until the Son of man is raised from the dead (v. 9) underlines the differences between the pre- and post-Easter epochs and the impossibility of preaching the whole truth about Jesus until he has completed his mission.

9. And as they were coming down the mountain. The line, like 8.1, recalls LXX Exod 34.29 and so adds to the Sinai parallels.

Tell no one about the vision until after the Son of man has been raised from the dead. The three apostles are unique and authoritative bearers of the kerygma. In the light of the resurrection and after the cross they will be able to tell the whole truth about Jesus.

10. Then why do the scribes say that Elijah must come first? This alludes to LXX Mal 3.22–3: 'I will send to you Elijah the Tishbite before the great and glorious day of the Lord comes; he will restore the heart of a father to his son . . .'.

11. Jesus begins his response to the disciples' question by agreeing with the scribal expectation: Elijah is to come and restore all things.

Elijah does come, and he will restore all things. In its present context, the future tense, 'will restore', is not likely to mean that Elijah is still to come or will come again. 'Will restore' simply agrees with what the OT and the scribes say. Many Christian interpreters, however, have taken Matthew's text to mean that Elijah has come and will come. Historically this has been one way of avoiding the contradiction between the synoptic identification of John with the Tishbite and the Baptist's denial that he was Elijah (Jn 1.21): John the Baptist fulfilled the rôle of Elijah in preparation for the first advent, the historical Elijah will return to prepare for the second advent; cf. Rev 11.1–13.

The precise nature of Elijah's task of restoration is left unstated and we cannot tell what Matthew had in mind, for there were differing notions. Mal 4.5–6 has Elijah reconciling families. The LXX (3.22–3) adds that the prophet will also reconcile 'the heart of a man with his neighbour'. In Lk 1.17, Elijah is thought of as one who will turn 'the disobedient to the wisdom of the just, to make ready for the Lord a people prepared'; cf. 4 Ezra 6.26. The idea that Elijah would preach repentance was presumably common (cf. Rev 11.1–13; *Pirqe R. El.* 43), and it probably encouraged the identification of John with Elijah. In Ecclus 48.10 the prophet is expected 'to restore the tribes of Jacob', which may mean ingathering the diaspora (cf. Tg. Ps.-J. on Deut. 30.4) or purifying a remnant. According to rabbinic texts he will explain points in the Torah which baffled or divided the rabbis. There are also places where Elijah is expected to restore the bottle of manna, the bottle of sprinkling water, and the bottle of anointing oil (e.g. *Mek.* on Exod 16.33). Finally, already by Matthew's time Elijah – who in the OT raises the dead – may have been expected to inaugurate the resurrection or reawaken the dead (note that in Mark the disciples' question about Elijah follows directly a discussion about the resurrection of the dead).

12. Jesus next makes a claim for 'realized eschatology': Elijah has in fact already come. But Jesus goes on to observe that Elijah's mission, to restore the people of God, was met with opposition, and that this same opposition will lead to the death of the Son of man.

Elijah has already come. The reader of the gospel immediately equates Elijah with John the Baptist, for the equation has already been made; see on 11.14.

and they did not know him. This explains why Elijah was rejected: his identity, like that of Jesus, remained hidden to most.

but rather they did to him whatever they pleased. As with the previous clause the identity of the subjects ('they did') is not specified. Are 'they' the Jewish people as a whole, or their leaders, or Herod and Herodias (cf. 14.1–12)? In view of the next line, where the Son of man also is made to suffer by 'them', one may do best to think of those in charge, that is, those with political and religious authority.

13. An editorial remark on the disciples' understanding draws the paragraph to its close.

Then the disciples understood that he was speaking to them of John the Baptist. This is the second time Matthew makes the equation of John with Elijah explicit (the first being 11.14). No other NT writer does so even once.

* * * * *

Mt 17.9–13 seeks to answer a Jewish objection against Christian claims, adds to the numerous parallels already drawn between John and Jesus, and marks out Peter and James and John as authorities for the Jesus tradition. The passage also, through the identification of John with Elijah, may be intended to form an *inclusio* with 11.14 ('he is Elijah who is to come'), indicating that the central section of the gospel is coming to its close. Lastly, one should consider the ways in which vv. 9–13 not only balance vv. 1–8 but are also like 16.13–23. If the transfiguration presents Jesus as the glorified Son of God, the sequel announces the suffering of the Son of man. This mirrors 16.13–23, where the confession of Jesus as Son of God and the promise of his church's triumph are followed by a passion prediction concerning the Son of man (16.21–3). The pattern – the Son of God triumphant/the Son of man suffering – may be illustrated in this fashion:

	16.13–20	16.21–3	17.1–8	17.9–13
Son of God	Jesus is confessed as Son of God and his church is promised victory		A voice from heaven proclaims the glorified Jesus to be the Son of God	
Son of man		The Son of man must be killed		The Son of man must suffer

JESUS HEALS AN EPILEPTIC (17.14–20)

[14]**And when they came to the crowd, a man came toward him, kneeling before him** [15]**and saying, 'Lord, have mercy on my son, for he is an epileptic and he suffers terribly. For he often falls into the fire and often into the water.** [16]**And I brought him to your disciples, but they could not heal him.'** [17] **And Jesus answered and said, 'O faithless and perverse generation, how much longer am I to be with you? How much longer must I bear with you? Bring him here to me.'** [18]**And Jesus rebuked him, and the demon came out of him, and the boy was cured from that hour.** [19]**Then the disciples came to Jesus privately and said, 'Why could we not cast it out?'** [20]**He said to them, 'Because of your little faith. For amen I say to you, if you have faith as a grain of mustard, you will say to this mountain, "Move from here to there," and it will move; and nothing will be impossible for you.'**

Parallels: Mk 9.14–29; Lk 9.37–43

This account of the successful exorcism of a demon of epilepsy is in Matthew on its way to becoming a pronouncement story. The tale is told primarily for the sake of Jesus' provocative declaration in v. 20. The focus – in complete contrast to Luke's presentation – is not on Jesus as healer or any other Christological theme, but on discipleship and faith. In Matthew the lesson is not what Jesus can do but what his followers can do.

15. The man asks Jesus to have mercy on his son, whose epileptic condition is described; cf. the pleas in 8.5–13; 9.18–26; and 15.21–8.

an epileptic and he suffers terribly is not a purely physical affliction. The problem is caused by a malign spirit.

For he often falls into the fire and often into the water. That the child falls into the fire and water indicates that his behaviour is perversely self-destructive.

16. but they could not heal him. One recalls the incident in 2 Kgs 4, where Gehazi, Elisha's disciple, is unable to resurrect a dead child. Only Elisha himself can perform the miracle. Whether one should here speak of an allusion to that OT story is uncertain.

The disciples' inability is all the more a failure given that, in 10.1, Jesus gave them the authority to cast out unclean spirits. The implication is that their lack of success stems not from strict incapacity but from not exercising an authority they in fact possess.

17. O faithless and perverse generation. Who exactly is Jesus speaking of when he refers to an unbelieving and perverse 'generation' (not 'race'; cf. Deut 32.5, 20)? The father is hardly to the fore. According to Chrysostom, Jesus' words pertain to the crowd. Others, however, contend that only the disciples are thus rebuked. It seems best to conflate the two interpretations. Jesus is casting a mournful eye over his disciples who have, by their 'little faith', retrogressed to the spiritual level of the multitude.

how much longer am I to be with you? Cf. Jn 14.9: 'Have I been with you so long, and yet you do not know me?'

How much longer must I bear with you? The words, which recall the divine and prophetic complaints in Num 14.27 and Isa 6.11, express exasperation and function as a reprimand. It is almost as though Jesus has been wasting his time, and his task – soon to come to its end – is thankless.

18. And Jesus rebuked him, and the demon came out of him, and the boy was cured from that hour. Jesus' healing word is always, in the First Gospel, instantly efficacious.

20. Because of your little faith. For 'little faith' see p. 102.

if you have faith as a grain of mustard, you will say to this mountain, 'Move from here to there,' and it will move; and nothing will be

impossible for you. Cf. 7.7–11; 21.21. On 'grain of mustard', a symbol of the smallest quantity, see p. 218. One wonders whether the organic image implies that faith can grow; cf. 13.31–2, a passage which has often been connected with 17.20 and so interpreted. However that may be, Matthew's novel placement of the saying about faith moving mountains is, at first glance, problematic. The logion, taken by itself, seems to be calling for any faith at all, however small (see below), whereas in Mt 17 the disciples are rebuked not for being without faith but for having little faith. Perhaps we should postulate behind Matthew two competing notions of faith, the one being saving faith (whose antithesis is unbelief), the other the special faith required to perform great miracles. If so, the disciples have the former but not the latter.

'To move mountains' was, for obvious reasons, a proverbial expression for the impossible or improbable. A literal interpretation is clearly ludicrous, although in Christian tradition the miracle of actually moving physical mountains has been attributed to certain saints (e.g. Gregory Thaumaturgus). The saying takes its force from a paradoxical juxtaposition: the insurmountable is accomplished by the infinitesimal. To uproot a mountain– a striking image and absurd task – is utterly impossible. But it can be done by something as small as a grain of mustard, if that something is genuine faith in God. For with God the impossible is possible, and faith may become the opportunity for God's power to manifest itself.

* * * * *

The primary lesson in 17.14–20 is that faith enables, lack of faith cripples. This is because faith is the pre-condition for God's acting in the world. Cf. 13.58: 'And he did not do many mighty works there, because of their unbelief.' Such faith is not, it must be added, a power in and of itself: it is not positive thinking or any other active force, nor does it give its possessor power to wield. Faith, as trust and hope, instead calls upon God or Jesus to act on its behalf: 'Lord save, we perish!'

JESUS AGAIN PROPHESIES HIS DEATH AND RESURRECTION (17.22–3)

²²As they were gathering in Galilee, Jesus said to them, 'The Son of man is going to be delivered into human hands, ²³and they will kill him, and he will be raised on the third day.' And they were greatly distressed.

Parallels: Mk 9.30–2; Lk 9.43–5

For a third time, and without adding more details, Jesus plainly prophesies his end. There does not seem to be any firm link with the pericopae immediately on either side.

22. As they were gathering in Galilee. Mt 19.1 is being anticipated: Jesus is in Galilee for the very last time.

The Son of man is going to be delivered into human hands. Cf. 26.45 and Aristobulus in Eusebius, *Praep. ev.* 8.10.8: 'it is possible for people speaking metaphorically to consider that the entire strength of human beings and their active powers are in their hands.' In the present context, the passive probably refers not principally to Judas but points rather to God, as Origen already contended: 'as in the case of Job, the Father first delivered up the Son to the opposing powers, and ... then they delivered Him up into the hands of men, among which men Judas also was ...'

23. and they will kill him. The verb is used elsewhere both of the deaths of prophets (23.34, 37) and the deaths of Christian disciples (10.28; 24.9). Thus Jesus stands at the end of one line of martyrs and at the beginning of another.

One must contrast 17.23 with 16.21–3. After the passion prediction at Caesarea Philippi, the reaction on Peter's part is absolute refusal to accept Jesus' prospective end: 'Far be it from you, Lord!' By 17.23 this is no longer the response. Now the disciples, having listened to Jesus (cf. 17.5), understand and are reconciled to the inevitable. They grieve precisely because they know all too well what the future holds.

* * * * *

(i) The First Evangelist might have passed over Mk 9.30–2 as a doublet, a text not needed in view of 16.21–3 (= Mk 8.31–3). That he has not done so but has instead chosen to follow Mark and let Jesus speak once again of his coming passion and resurrection is consistent with the fact that the gospel's conclusion is Matthew's Rosetta stone, by which all else is deciphered. Repetition of the passion predictions does more than emphasize Jesus' prophetic powers and make plain the voluntary nature of his suffering. It also connotes necessity and destiny (cf. the 'must' of 16.21) and, in terms of plot, pushes the reader forward in anticipation: the key to everything must lie in the end. Matthew is a passion narrative with an extended introduction.

(ii) If in 28.18 Jesus will declare, 'All authority in heaven and on earth has been delivered to me (by God)' (cf. LXX Dan 7.14, where the one like a son of man is given eternal authority), here, in 17.22–3, the Son of man speaks of being delivered into the hands (that is, authority) of sinful people. The poles of experience represented by the two texts are worlds apart, a fact which holds much pathos for Matthew's readers. God gives the Son of man into the hands of others, and God gives the Son of man universal authority. It is the burden of the gospel to demonstrate that these two opposing acts, so far from being contradictory, are, in God's hidden but sovereign will, the two complementary halves of the same divine purpose.

THE TEMPLE TAX (17.24–7)

[24]When they came to Capernaum, the collectors of the half-shekel tax went up to Peter and said, 'Does your teacher not pay the tax?' [25]He said, 'Yes.' And when he came to the house, Jesus spoke to him first, saying, 'What do you think, Simon? From whom do the kings of the earth take toll or tribute? From their sons or from others?' [26]And when he said, 'From others,' Jesus said to him, 'Then the sons are free. [27]But lest we offend them, go to the sea and cast a hook, and take the first fish that comes up, and when you open its mouth you will find a stater; take that and give it to them for me and for you.'

Parallels: none

This miracle story is located at the end of chapter 17 primarily for two reasons. First, Matthew has just recounted a story which, in its Markan setting, is followed by notice that Jesus and his disciples went to Capernaum (see Mk 9.30–3), and the story about Peter and the coin in the fish's mouth was presumably set in that city before Matthew's telling of it (the temple tax was collected in or near a person's place of residence, and Peter and perhaps Jesus were officially residents of Capernaum). Second, it is in the narrative section stretching from 13.53 to 17.27 that Peter comes into prominence, this because the section records the founding of the church on the chief apostle. Matthew has placed his other special passages about Peter in this section.

24. When they came to Capernaum. The text requires a location where fish can be readily obtained; Capernaum was on the Sea of Galilee.

Does your teacher not pay the tax? The temple tax was intended to support the sacrificial system in Jerusalem. According to the Mishnah, the tax was to be paid annually, in the month of Adar (February–March) by all adult Jewish males over twenty years of age. But the Dead Sea Scrolls and a few rabbinic texts supply evidence that there was some dispute as to precisely who was to pay – for instance, are priests liable? – and how often (the Essenes made a one-time contribution). Although apparently of post-Exilic origin, the temple tax was regarded by the Pharisees at least as firmly grounded in Scripture (Exod 30.11–16; cf. Neh 10.33–4). After AD 70 the tax, now known as the *fiscus iudaicus*, was diverted by the Romans to support the temple of Jupiter Capitolinus.

25. And when he came to the house, Jesus spoke to him first, saying. On 'the house' and its identity – is it Peter's house? Jesus' house? or someone else's? – see p. 135.

What do you think, Simon? Is Simon being addressed because it is his house?

From whom do the kings of the earth take toll or tribute? 'The kings of the earth' is an old expression with pejorative connotations. It is antithetical to 'the king of heaven' (= God). The phrase is found often in the Psalms as well as in Revelation and apocalyptic literature in general. It is inclusive: that is, it encompasses all earthly rulers (not just the Romans).

From their sons or from others? The opposition between 'sons' and 'others' has been understood to designate different groupings – a king's nation versus all other nations, a king's household versus all outsiders, or a king's immediate family versus everyone else. The first option is unlikely because kings did in fact exact taxes from their own people. The second fails because the evidence that a king's household could be described as his 'sons' does not seem to exist. This leaves the third view: the sons are the king's family, the others those outside his family.

Who are the sons in the implicit interpretation of the parable? That is, who are God's sons? Most commentators assume that they must be equated with Jesus' followers or all Christians. But others have argued that we should think of the Israelites. This seems the best interpretation both for the historical Jesus and for the evangelist Matthew.

26. Then the sons are free. The major thrust of Jesus' parable is this. The sons of earthly kings do not pay toll or tribute, and Jesus and his disciples are, as members of Israel, sons of God. So they should be exempt from any taxes levied in God's name – 'the sons are free'. What is thereby rejected is not the temple cult but instead the idea that taxation is the appropriate means of maintaining that divine institution.

27. Jesus' command well fits the previous teaching. The tax will be paid but not out of money to hand. So Jesus fulfils his obligation without clearly endorsing the legitimacy of a tax. One might even go further and affirm that the miracle of the fish shows that God will provide for the upkeep of the temple; that is, God will supply people with what they need if they wish to support the temple.

Lest we offend them. Cf. 1 Cor 8.9–13. 'Them' refers not to the kings of the earth but to the tax collectors and to the authorities they represent. What Jesus and his followers should avoid, if at all possible, is offending the devout people who, in collecting the temple tax, believe themselves to be serving God. Voluntary payment should be made in order to prevent others from inferring that Peter or Jesus has rejected the temple cult.

and when you open its mouth you will find a stater. 'Stater' designates a Greek silver coin worth four drachmas or two didrachmas – not a large sum.

take that and give it to them for me and for you. Bengel wrote: 'A manifold miracle . . . 1, Something shall be caught; 2, and that quickly; 3, there shall be money in a fish; 4, and that in the first fish; 5, the sum shall be just what is needed; 6, it shall be in the fish's mouth.' The story ends, however, without informing the reader that Peter went and did as Jesus commanded. No miracle is recorded. This striking fact, which has been taken to show that Matthew was interested only in the passage's halakhic content, has also led to the suggestion that Jesus' words were not intended to be taken literally: they were merely a fanciful remark on the lack of ready money. But readers most naturally assume that Peter, as a faithful disciple, did as the Lord commanded him. A figurative interpretation is really not much more satisfactory than the idea that 'and there you will find a stater' really meant to get a stater from the sale of a fish or the supposition that Jesus was using a metaphor: as a fisher of people go out and get a rich convert!

* * * * *

(i) Whether Paul knew the tradition behind 17.24–7 cannot be known. His actions do, however, illustrate our text's rejection of theocratic taxation. Paul asked for contributions for the poor in Jerusalem, but he was adamant about the voluntary nature of the work. It seems likely that, in an analogous fashion, the evangelist Matthew thought Jesus' words about the temple tax to be applicable to the church and so disclaimed legalism with respect to the gathering of ecclesiastical funds. God does not tax God's children; rather does he supply benefits to them. For Matthew this must have meant that church giving should be a matter of charity dependent upon the free will of the people.

(ii) 'Lest we offend them.' The temple tax is to be paid, not because it is something God requires but because refusal may cause offence. The lesson is clear. Personal freedom is delimited because it must be responsibly exercised, which means it must take into account the effect upon others. As Paul so plainly recognized, freedom does not mean licence. The freedom of sonship is not any sort of antinomianism; it is not the abnegation of tasks or responsibilities. The believer belongs not just to God but also to the church and to the world. Hence one's actions must always be weighed with regard to their broader consequences. 'None of us lives to himself' (Rom 14.7); 'if food causes my brother to stumble, I will never eat meat, lest I cause my brother to fall' (1 Cor 8.13); 'We endure anything rather than put an obstacle in the way of the gospel of Christ' (1 Cor 9.12). Freedom is a task.

ON CHILDREN AND LITTLE ONES (18.1–14)

18 [1]**At that time, the disciples came to Jesus and asked, 'Who is the greatest in the kingdom of heaven?'** [2] **And calling a child, he put him among them,** [3]**and he said, 'Amen I say to you, unless you turn and become like children, you will never enter the kingdom of heaven.** [4] **Whoever humbles himself like this child, he is the greatest in the kingdom of heaven.** [5] **Whoever welcomes one such child in my name welcomes me.**

[6] **'But whoever puts a stumbling block before one of these little ones who believes in me, it would be better for him were a great millstone fastened around his neck and he were drowned in the depth of the sea.** [7] **Woe to the world because of stumbling blocks! For it is necessary that stumbling blocks come, but woe to the person by whom the stumbling block comes!** [8] **And if your hand or your foot causes you to stumble, cut it off and throw it away. It is better for you to enter life maimed or lame than to have two hands or two feet and to be thrown into the eternal fire.** [9] **And if your eye causes you to stumble, tear it out and throw it away. It is better for you to enter life with one eye than to have two eyes and to be thrown into the Gehenna of fire.**

[10] **'See to it that you do not despise one of these little ones. For I say to you, in heaven their angels always behold the face of my Father in heaven.** [12] **What do you think? If a man has a hundred sheep, and one of them has gone astray, does he not leave the ninety-nine on the hills and go in search of the one that went astray?** [13] **And if he finds it, amen I say to you, he rejoices over it more than over the ninety-nine that never went astray.** [14] **So it is not the will of your Father in heaven that one of these little ones should be lost.'**

Parallels: Mt 5.29–30; Mk 9.33–7, 42–50; Lk 9.46–8; 14.34–5; 15.3–7; Jn 3.3, 5; 13.20; 17.1–2

Mt 18.1–14 consists of three subsections, vv. 1–5 (on greatness), vv. 6–9 (on offences), and vv. 10–14 (on the lost sheep). The first, which contains three key declarations (vv. 3, 4, 5), features the catchword 'child/ren'. The second subsection, which has three main parts (vv. 6, 7, 8–9), is united by the proverbial 'better' form, which is used three times (vv. 6, 8, 9). The third subsection does not feature any catchword, but 'one of these little ones' and 'Father in heaven' both occur twice, in vv. 10 and 14, at the beginning and end.

Mt 18.1–14 is a block of moral teaching which has special bearing on relations among church members. Verses 1–5 demand humility. Verses 6–9 demand the elimination of all stumbling blocks, whether placed before others or before oneself. And vv. 10–14 demand exceptional kindness towards all believers, including – or especially – the 'least'.

'Child' and 'little one' are the key terms holding the section together. How they relate to each other is disputed. While it is manifest that Jesus opens the chapter by referring to literal children, by vv. 10–14 he is clearly using 'little ones' as a designation for believers. The problem is finding the point of transition. Where does the subject switch from children to believers? It seems best to identify the shift in subject with the shift in vocabulary. 'Child' is the key word in vv. 1–5, 'little one' in vv. 6–14. Evidently, then, the first paragraph, 18.1–5, concerns literal children while the next two paragraphs, 18.6–9 and 10–14, have to do with believers. The use of 'believe' in v. 6 reinforces this conclusion. Only after v. 5 do we find explicit indication that believers are in the picture.

Exegetes are divided over whether chapter 18 is addressed to all Christians equally or first of all to ecclesiastical leaders. Three considerations imply that the discourse is aimed at every Christian disciple. First, the content of the directions does not demand a special audience. Humility, kindness, and a willingness to forgive others are required of every believer. Second, unlike chapter 10, where Jesus, addressing a special group, namely, missionaries, speaks to 'the twelve apostles', his audience here is simply 'the disciples'. Third, there is a tendency on Matthew's part to avoid as much as possible specialized instruction relevant for only a minority.

On Children (18.1–5)

This memorable pronouncement story offers moral counsel. One should turn and become like little children, for only by this means will one enter the kingdom (v. 3). One should humble oneself as a child, for in the kingdom the humble will be great (v. 4). And one should welcome children 'in my name', for to receive such is to receive Jesus himself (v. 5). The sequence is: entrance into the kingdom, greatness in the kingdom, service in this world.

1. Whether the disciples' question about greatness comes up because of the prominence of Peter in 17.24–7 is not clear. Matthew's text does not even reveal whether the disciples have themselves in mind or are simply speaking in general.

Who is the greatest in the kingdom of heaven? Some see a reference to the future, that is, to who *will be* the greatest in the coming kingdom. Others suppose that the disciples are fretting about the present. Yet it may be unwise to set the two interpretations against one another and choose between them. Do not the disciples assume that any hierarchy in the future kingdom will be reflected in some way in the structure of the church, and that greatness in the kingdom means greatness even now?

2. Jesus responds with an enacted parable. He calls a child and sets him in the disciples' midst. The verbal is here aided by the visual.

3. Amen I say to you, unless you turn and become like children, you will never enter the kingdom of heaven. Cf. 5.20; Mk 10.15 (= Lk 18.17); Jn 3.3, 5. To become a child has nothing to do with innocence or simplicity or sinlessness. Rather, as v. 4 proves, Jesus is calling for humility, for what Chrysostom called the 'mother, root, nurse, foundation, and centre of all other virtues'. The point, of course, is not that children are self-consciously humble but that they are, as part of society at large, without much status or position. The followers of Jesus, reflecting upon this illustration, are to rid themselves of all pride – 'the root, the source, the mother of sin' (Chrysostom) – and forget about worldly standing.

4. Whoever humbles himself like this child, he is the greatest in the kingdom of heaven would probably have struck many first-century Jewish ears as surprising. Even if Christian exegetes have tended, for theological reasons, to overestimate the denigration of children in ancient Judaism, one does not find Jewish texts in which children are examples or models to be imitated. Further, for those who took knowledge of and obedience to the law to be the essence of piety, the unlearned child would scarcely have been a natural illustration of religious greatness. Were then the synoptic declarations about children intended to provoke puzzlement and/or reflection?

5. The pericope concludes with a promise about receiving children. The narrative logic is a bit awkward. The child is no longer a model to be imitated (as in vv. 3–4) but the object of one's action. Perhaps the continuity between vv. 4 and 5 lies in this, that the reception of a child (v. 5) is really an illustration of the humility enjoined by v. 4.

Whoever welcomes one such child in my name welcomes me. To receive a child in Christ's name is to perceive Christ in that child and act accordingly. We have here the same principle as in 25.31–46: the

Son of man unites himself to others, especially the weak and insignificant, so that to show kindness to them is to show kindness to him.

We should not overlook the fact that if, in 18.5, Jesus commands the reception of children, it is not very long before he enacts his own words, for in 19.13–15 he does this very thing himself. Once more, therefore, Jesus unites word and deed in his own person and thereby becomes the model to be imitated.

On Offences (18.6–9)

This paragraph consists of sayings which use the verb 'cause to stumble' or the noun 'stumbling block'. The tone is not one of promise as in vv. 3–5, but of warning. Verse 6 demands that one does not offend 'one of these little ones' and offers for motivation the spectre of severe divine punishment. The reference is no longer to literal children (as in vv. 1–5) but to certain members of the Christian community. Next verse 7 speaks of stumbling blocks in general and contains two woes. The subject is wider than the little ones. Finally, vv. 8–9 turn attention from others towards oneself: one must guard against one's own members and the spiritual damage they can wreak.

6. Switching from 'child' to 'little one', and with that from literal children to the 'little ones' who believe, Jesus now warns, in the strongest possible language, against causing others to stumble.

But whoever puts a stumbling block before one of these little ones who believe in me.

'Puts a stumbling block before' means to pervert and mislead, intellectually and morally. Here, in view of the consequent punishment, it must signify causing others to lose their faith and fall away from God.

'One of these little ones' appears four times in Matthew (10.42; 18.6, 10, 14). The expression has been taken to refer to missionaries (as in 10.42), catechumens, recent converts, young Christians, or lowly Christians – those lightly esteemed by others. A firm decision one way or the other is impossible.

a great millstone fastened around his neck and he were drowned in the depth of the sea. 'Great millstone' designates a large, heavy millstone worked by donkey power as opposed to a handmill millstone. The picture of such a giant millstone being thrown into the sea, signifying a dark, eternal grave out of all reach, may have been common, for it occurs also in Rev 18.21; cf. Jer 51.63–4. Moreover, the figure of a millstone around the neck was for Jews, like that of an albatross around the neck for us, proverbial: it referred to suffering or difficulty.

The merging of the two images – millstone around the neck, millstone in the sea – is, however, something evidently not found elsewhere.

On the lips of Jesus, 18.6 could have been about literal children, the disciples or 'the poor' of the beatitudes. In Matthew the general meaning is not in doubt: 'these little ones' are believers ('who believes in me'), and to harm them is to harm oneself, for one cannot cause others to stumble without causing oneself to stumble. Salvation is part of a social process, and there can be no thoughtlessness towards others: 'Our life and our death is with our neighbour; if we gain our brother, we have gained God, but if we scandalize our brother, we have sinned against Christ' (Anthony the Great).

Whether our evangelist had a particular group of believers – catechumens, recent converts etc. – in mind cannot be determined (see above). One can, however, confidently state that the Pauline application of the 'stumbling block' sayings in Rom 14.13 and 1 Cor 8.13 – the apostle applies them to weak believers – is not foreign to the spirit of Mt 18.

For it is necessary that stumbling blocks come. Why is it necessary that there be 'stumbling blocks'? The verse does not inform us. But 24.10–11 foretells stumbling blocks for the latter days, and these stand under the eschatological necessity: before the good triumphs, evil must flourish; cf. 24.6. Thus 'stumbling blocks' are inescapable.

woe to the person by whom the stumbling block comes. Judas is a perfect illustration of the tragic man through whom offence comes. If 'stumbling blocks' in general are inevitable and necessary (v. 7b), this does not entail that any particular individual is bound to commit them. One may, our passage assumes, exercise the will in such a way as not to lead others into sin. There is no escape from responsibility.

8–9. These two verses, with their parallels in 5.29–30, are variant expressions of the same theme; they shift the subject and have been thought a bit disruptive (v. 10 would follow v. 7 nicely). The declaration in v. 6 has to do with offending others, that in v. 7 with offences in general. But the imperatives in vv. 8–9 demand that one rid the self of whatever in it leads to sin: response to temptation from one's members must be swift, sure and severe. Perhaps the connexion with vv. 6–7 is to be found in this, that occasions of sin in oneself lead to the stumbling of others; thus in order to avoid offending one's brother, one must first take care of oneself. In this connexion, one wonders whether vv. 8–9 are not similar in function to 7.3–5, the parable of the log and splinter, where in order to correct a brother one must first be free of his faults. Similarly here, before one undertakes to reprove a fellow believer (vv. 15ff.), one must be free of personal 'stumbling blocks'.

cut it off and throw it away. Cf. 5.30. Although amputation was practised by ancient physicians, a literal interpretation is wholly improbable. Mutilation of the physical body is no more the burden of this sentence than it is the point of the logion on eunuchs in 19.10–12.

than to have two hands or two feet and to be thrown into the eternal fire. Cf. 5.29; also Sextus, *Sent.* 13 ('Cast away every part of the body which leads you to intemperance; for it is better to live temperately without it than to perish whole').

The text concerns the relation between present action and the future kingdom, signified by 'life'. The war with sin in the here and now determines one's final destiny. Every obstacle in the way of 'life' is to be eliminated, no matter what the personal cost. Nothing matters but the treasure of the kingdom; cf. 13.44. No sacrifice can be too great. The self must suffer what Symeon the New Theologian labeled 'a life-giving mortification'.

The Lost Sheep (18.10–14)

In Lk 15.3–7, where this parable is paired with that of the lost coin, the audience is the scribes and Pharisees, and Jesus is attempting to justify himself in the face of their criticism. Why does he associate with disreputable folk? There the lost sheep represents a lost sinner, and the joy of finding is God's joy at his conversion. In Matthew, by contrast, the parable of the lost sheep is addressed to disciples and oriented towards ecclesiastical concerns. All members of the church are specially cared for by God, including 'the little ones'. Hence one should not despise 'the little ones'.

The parable forwards the theme of the *imitatio Dei*. The shepherd recovering his lost sheep illustrates God's concern for the little ones, and such concern is the paradigm and illustration for a similar human concern; cf. 18.14: divine love for the lost invites human love for the lost.

10. 'One of these little ones' recalls the opening sentence of the previous paragraph (v. 6), as does 'see to it that you do not despise'. At the same time, the switch from 'puts a stumbling block' to 'despise' informs readers that they have come to a new subsection. Verse 10 therefore gathers up what has gone before while it also prepares for what follows.

in heaven their angels always behold the face of my Father in heaven. Cf. 5.8, which promises the pure in heart that they will see God. The motive for not despising little ones is that their angels always behold the face of the Father in heaven. It is assumed that the value of the little ones on earth is revealed by their having incorporeal representatives in heaven.

The belief that God, out of love for mankind, has appointed for every person an angel is well-attested in Jewish sources; cf. Ps 34.7. It may ultimately derive from the Iranian idea of guardian spirits; or perhaps it is an individuation of the idea that each nation has its heavenly counterpart. One assumes that the angels of Mt 18.10 are at least intercessors, mediators between God and the little ones. Whether they are also to be thought of as creatures who come and go between heaven and earth ('ascending and descending') and perform the functions Raphael performs for Tobias (in the book of Tobit) is disputed, although that is the dominant tradition in Christian exegesis.

Because the little ones of 18.10 are not literal children but believers, one may not infer that the angels see God because those in their care are innocents and that therefore such angels will gradually lose privileged access when those innocents grow up and grow into sin. This idea would in any event not fit first-century Judaism because it did not see children as sinless. The presence of angels in heaven representing the little ones – who may even have strayed – is an expression of God's compassion for those in the ecclesia.

The notion, often supported by appeal to Mt 18.10, that each individual Christian has a guardian angel has been a significant element in popular Christian piety, although it is true that the cult of the saints has worked to lessen the attention paid to angels. The church Fathers discussed whether Mt 18.10 implies that every individual has an angel (Chrysostom said yes); whether adults or just children are guarded; whether wickedness can drive one's guardian angel away (Origen and Jerome thought so); whether evil individuals have over them evil angels or spirits; whether one's guardian angel was received at birth or baptism; and whether one could be looked after by more than one angel. The subject first received systematic treatment at the hands of the twelfth-century theologian Honorius Augustodunensis, who supposed each soul to be given an angel at the moment of conception. Aquinas taught that guardian angels come from only the lowest angelic ranks. Calvin, in his cautious discussion of the theme (*Inst*. 1.14.6–7), did not claim to know whether each believer has an angel; but, citing Mt 18.13 and Lk 16.22 (Lazarus is carried to Abraham's bosom by angels), he held for certain 'that each of us is cared for not by one angel merely, but that all with one consent watch for our safety'. He took note in his analysis of the 'vulgar imagination', which assigns a bad angel as well as a good angel to every person. Schleiermacher regarded the Biblical references to guardian angels as incidental and affirmed that their existence is a matter of indifference for conduct and dogmatics. Later Rudolf Bultmann, with his demythologization programme, took the next step and denied altogether the existence of disembodied spirits. But his contemporary, Karl Barth, devoted much energy to the subject of angels and regarded them as real beings created to serve God and his redemptive purposes. He nevertheless held the idea of individual guardian angels to be 'suspicious' and did not find it evidenced by Mt 18.10.

12. The parable proper begins with this verse, which poses two questions. The first question serves to engage one's attention ('What do you think?'). The second question is rhetorical and presumes a positive response ('If a man has a hundred sheep ...').

If a man has a hundred sheep, and one of them has gone astray. Cf. Ps 119.176 ('I have gone astray like a lost sheep'); 1 Pet 2.25. Throughout Christian history the man with the sheep has been identified with Jesus himself, and our parable has often been conflated with Jn 10. One guesses that the First Evangelist likewise identified the shepherd with Jesus and took the logic of the parable to be this: God approves of the actions of the shepherd Jesus who set out for the lost little ones, and those who believe in Jesus must do what he did. Such an interpretation is natural in the light of 9.36; 15.24; and 26.31 (in these Jesus is likened to a shepherd) as well as early Christian tradition in general (e.g. Lk 12.32; Jn 10.1–21).

does he not leave the ninety-nine on the hills and go in search of the one that went astray? Cf. 1 Sam 17.28 ('with whom have you left those few sheep in the wilderness?') and *Mek.* on Exod 19.21 ('If only one of them [the Israelites] should fall it would be to Me as though all of them fell ... Every one of them that might be taken away is to Me as valuable as the whole work of creation.') Commentators have not been at one over the question Jesus raises. Would a shepherd normally have taken the risk of leaving his flock to rescue a solitary beast? If not, then the point would be the great value of the one stray: it is so valuable that the security of the others must be gambled. Attempts have been made to avoid this conclusion by postulating either mistranslation from Aramaic or circumstances not mentioned (maybe the ninety-nine have just been counted and are therefore safe in the sheepfold). In any case, Jesus' parable presupposes assent from the hearer, which disallows finding untypical or strange behaviour. The point is not the taking of some unusual risk but the great joy at recovering the one stray. The failure to relate what happened to the ninety-nine is just a consequence of sticking to the point.

14. So it is not the will of your Father in heaven that one of these little ones should be lost. The will of God concerning the little ones – that they should not perish – becomes an imperative for the believer. The disciple must be like God (cf. 5.48): that is, must act as the divine shepherd (Ps 23) acts and so share in his activity of saving the lost.

* * * * *

(i) Mt 18.1–14 demands certain qualities requisite for the performance of God's will within the ecclesia. The passage is particularly concerned with those attributes and actions which will check the impulse to judge others and which will make correction, necessary as it will be (18.15–20), a true act of charity (cf. vv. 21ff.), so that there is a hedge around 18.15–20, a buffer of grace, which reflects deep pastoral concern.

(ii) Genuine humility (cf. vv. 3–4), special kindness towards children (v. 5), refraining from offending others, especially the weak or marginal (vv. 6–7), serious self-control (vv. 8–9), and heartfelt, loving concern for all fellow believers, including 'these little ones' (vv. 10–14) – all of these virtues are called forth in view of their communal relevance. In other words, Jesus' various imperatives have in view not the solitary individual but the one in relation to the many. Nothing could make clearer that the Matthean Jesus demands no flight from the world. Believers live for the common good. Indeed, there is no alternative to this, for salvation itself requires humility (vv. 3–4), and humility is, most concretely, service towards others (v. 5). Matthew would have agreed that 'we are members one of another' (Eph 4.25), and eagerly embraced the maxim that those who go to hell do so on their own, while those who go to heaven cannot but do so in the company of a multitude.

(iii) The various injunctions delivered in 18.1–14 all centre upon either one or two related virtues: love of others and self-effacement. The two go hand in hand, not only because self-effacement without love is vain (1 Cor 13.3) but because Matthew associates both with the theme of imitation. Concerning love, Jesus commands the imitation of God (5.45–8), and this entails that one love others, for God is chiefly characterized by unbounded love and mercy (cf. 5.43–8). In the present context God's love is clearly expressed in vv. 10–14, and no less clear is it that Jesus' disciples must follow suit as best they are able (Evagrius: 'Nothing so makes a person resemble God as doing good to others.'). As for self-effacement, this follows not so much from the imitation of God as from the imitation of Christ (a theme implicit in v. 5 and, more obviously, in vv. 12–13, if one thinks of the shepherd as Jesus). Jesus is meek and lowly in heart (11.29); he does not wrangle or cry aloud (12.19); and he gives his life as a ransom for many (20.28). These facts become imperatives for believers, who are to take up the cross like Jesus (10.38; 16.24). The least becoming the greatest has no better illustration than Jesus himself; cf. 20.26–8.

RECONCILIATION AND FORGIVENESS (18.15–35)

[15]'If your brother sins against you, go and tell him, when the two of you are alone, his fault. If he heeds you, you have regained your brother. [16]But if he does not heed, take one or two others along with you, so that every word may be confirmed by the evidence of two or three witnesses. [17]If he refuses to listen to them, tell it to the church; and if he refuses to listen even to the church, let him be to you as a Gentile and a toll-collector. [18]Amen I say to you, whatever you bind on earth will be bound in heaven, and whatever you loose on earth will be loosed in heaven. [19]Again, amen I say to you, if two of you agree on earth about anything they ask, it will be done for them by my Father in heaven. [20]For where two or three are gathered in my name, there am I among them.'

[21]Then Peter came and said to him, 'Lord, how often will my brother sin against me and I yet forgive him? As many as seven times?' [22]Jesus said to him, 'Not seven times, but, I tell you, seventy times seven times.

[23]'For this reason the kingdom of heaven may be compared to the situation of a king who wished to settle accounts with his slaves. [24]When he began the reckoning, one who owed him ten thousand talents was brought to him; [25]and, as he could not pay, his lord ordered him to be sold, with his wife and children and all his possessions, and payment to be made. [26] So the slave fell on his knees before him, saying, "Have patience with me, and I will pay you everything." [27]And out of pity for him, the lord of that slave released him and forgave him the debt. [28]But that same slave, as he went out, came upon one of his fellow slaves who owed him a hundred denarii; and seizing him by the throat he said, 'Pay what you owe.' [29]Then his fellow slave fell down and pleaded with him, "Have patience with me, and I will pay you." [30]But he refused and he went and threw him into prison until he should pay the debt. [31]When his fellow slaves saw what had happened, they were greatly distressed, and they went and reported to their lord all that had taken place. [32]Then his lord summoned him and said to him, "You wicked slave! I forgave you all that debt because you pleaded with me, [33]and should you not have had mercy on your fellow slave, as I had mercy on you?" [34]And in anger his lord handed him over to the torturers until he should pay his entire debt. [35]So my heavenly Father will also do to every one of you, if you do not forgive your brother or sister from your heart.'

Parallels: Mt 16.19; Lk 17.3–4; Jn 20.23

Mt 18.15–35 falls into three sections of unequal length. The first paragraph runs from v. 15 to v. 20 and outlines the method for admonishing one who has sinned. This is followed by vv. 21–2, which call for a spirit of unbounded forgiveness. The whole unit ends with the parable of the unforgiving servant, vv. 23–35.

Reproving Another (18.15–20)

This paragraph sets down the community rules for dealing with trouble between Christians. If one has sinned against another, the offended party should first seek reconciliation in private. If this initial attempt fails, the offended should next seek the aid of another believer, maybe two (cf. Deut 19.15), and try again. If that likewise does not produce results, the matter must be brought before the whole community. If, after that, and despite all the well-intentioned effort, the sinner remains recalcitrant, that one should be treated as 'a toll-collector and Gentile'. Description of this whole procedure, recounted in vv. 15–17, is followed by three verses which ground the authority of the church in theological propositions.

15. How does a Christian respond to a personal offence committed by a fellow believer? One is to seek reconciliation by bringing the wrongdoer to penitence. In other words, the offended is to imitate the shepherd of vv. 10–14 and go after the one stray sheep.

If your brother sins against you. The sin – which must be both serious and intentional to be subject to the following regulations – is specifically that committed against another. Further, the offence is not of a public nature, otherwise the initial concern for privacy would be out of place.

go and tell him when the two of your are alone, his fault. Cf. Lev 19.17, where rebuking another is closely related to love of neighbour.

If he heeds you, you have regained your brother. Note that 'brother' underlines the familial character of the Christian community (cf. 12.46–50) and strengthens the link to Lev 19.17, where 'your brother' occurs. Concerning 'regained', Bengel aptly wrote: 'The healed body of a sick man does not become the property of the physician; a house does not become the property of him who extinguishes the fire in it . . . But the man whom I have *gained* becomes in some sense my own.'

16. take one or two others along with you. There is a parallel of sorts in the Talmud: 'Samuel said: Whoever sins against his brother, he must say to him, I have sinned against you. If he hears, it is well; if not, let him bring others, and let him appease him before them' (*y. Yoma* 45c). In this, however, it is the offending person who takes the initiative, not the offended. Matthew's text is closer to the Dead Sea Scrolls, where reproof of an erring brother is made in front of witnesses before the leaders of the community are presented with the problem.

so that every word may be confirmed by the evidence of two or three witnesses. This alludes to Deut 19.15. 'Two or three' probably means 'two or more', but not more than a few. In time this text came to be thought of as enshrining a general principle with wide relevance. Thus, for example, Deut 19.15 played a role in the eschatological expectation of 'two witnesses' (Rev 11), and in *T. Abr.* 13, rec. A, the OT verse is cited as support for the idea that there will be three judges or groups of judges in the afterlife – Abel, the angels, God. In addition, some ancient and modern commentators have, perhaps rightly, claimed that the two or three witnesses of 2 Cor 13.1 are in fact not individuals but rather Paul's three visits to the community. Whether that be so or not, Mt 18.16 is not the only ancient text to enlarge the original horizon of Deut 19.15; and both 2 Cor 13.1 and 1 Tim 5.19 prove that Matthew was not the first to draw on Deut 19.15 with reference to church discipline.

17. If he refuses to listen to them, tell it to the church. The local community is here meant, not the church universal. Its role is not to condemn but to assist and add authority to the one who has spoken critically of another.

and if he refuses to listen even to the church, let him be to you as a Gentile and a toll-collector. To treat someone as a Gentile and toll-collector would involve the breaking off of fellowship and hence mean exclusion from the community – no doubt in hope that such a severe measure (it would have dire social and probably economic consequences) would convict sinners of their sin and win them back; cf. 2 Thess 3.14; Titus 1.13. The passage is therefore about excommunication. Once someone has refused to heed the whole church, there can be no appeal to a higher authority: the matter has been settled.

The command to reprove a brother has a long history in Jewish literature. The key text is Lev 19.15–18, which includes: 'You shall not hate your brother in your heart, but you shall reprove your neighbour, lest you bear sin because of him.' The second imperative in v. 17 – 'you shall reprove your neighbour' – has parallels in the wisdom tradition (cf. Prov 3.12; 25.9–10; 27.5–6; Ecclus 20.20), as does the command not to hate one's brother in the heart (cf. Prov 10.18; 26.24–5). The two themes are brought together in Ecclus 19.13–20.2, where reproving another is an antidote for anger; cf. Lev 19.17: 'lest you bear sin because of him.' These themes are also taken up in *T. Gad* 6.3–5: 'Love one another from the heart ... and if anyone sins against you, speak to him in peace. Expel the venom of hatred, and do not harbour deceit in your heart. If anyone confesses and repents, forgive him. If anyone denies his guilt, do not be contentious with him, otherwise he may start cursing, and you would be sinning doubly. In a dispute do not let an outsider hear your secrets ...' The parallels to Mt 18.15–17 are remarkable, and include mention of the possibility that the offender may not repent.

T. Gad 6 has nothing to do with a formal or judicial process. In the Dead Sea Scrolls it is otherwise. The rebuke commanded by Lev 19.17 becomes, presumably because of Lev 19.15, part of a formal procedure. If one has a complaint against another, one first takes up the matter with him; that is, one reproves him according to Lev 19.17. If this does not have its intended effect, then the matter must be brought before the community. This brings us very close to Matthew's text. Whether or not one should postulate sectarian influence upon Matthew's tradition is unclear. One cannot, however, doubt that Mt 18.15–17 has a long pre-history in Judaism.

18. whatever you bind on earth will be bound in heaven, and whatever you loose on earth will be loosed in heaven. Cf. 16.19, where Peter has the authority to 'bind' and 'loose' by issuing authoritative halakah. Here the halakhic decisions of the community have the authority of heaven itself. In context the reference is to the church's verdict on the behaviour of an individual Christian. (Verse 18 closely follows v. 17. It does not apply to the actions described in vv. 15 and 16.)

19. if two of you agree on earth about anything they ask, it will be done for them by my Father in heaven. The notion that the prayer of several outweighs the prayer of one was probably a commonplace. 'On earth' qualifies 'you', not 'agree', just as 'in heaven' qualifies 'my Father'; cf. vv. 10, 14. On the connexion between omnipotent prayer and the forgiveness of one's brother (the topic of the next paragraph) see p. 96. That connexion holds here. The power of the community depends upon the spiritual harmony of its members, a harmony which must include the practice of forgiveness (vv. 21–35). One is reminded of *Gos. Thom.* 48. 'If two make peace with each other in this one house, they will say to the mountain, "Move away," and it will move away.'

20. The paragraph ends with a promise that the risen Christ will be present where two or three are gathered 'in his name'. Following upon v. 19, the meaning is that the community's prayer becomes Jesus' prayer, and his prayer cannot but be answered.

For where two or three are gathered in my name. 'Two or three' presumably means, as in v. 16, 'two or more'. Most commentators assume that 'gathered in my name' refers to the act of coming together as Christians: 'For where two or three are gathered with reference to me'. But it is worth considering whether 'in my name' is not here used as in 7.22: 'in the power of my name'; cf. 1 Cor 5.40.

there I am among them. Just as the presence of the risen Christ is not confined to any particular space or time, so is it independent of numerical considerations. Verse 20 especially recalls a saying in *m. 'Abot* 3.2: 'But if two sit together and words of the Law (are spoken) between them, the Divine Presence rests between them ...' Similar is the saying in *m. 'Abot* 3.3: 'If three have eaten at one table and have spoken over it words of the Law, it is as if they had eaten from the table of God.' It is possible that these rabbinic sayings were called forth by the gospel saying as a kind of counterblast, but more probably they express a rabbinic commonplace – which would make Mt 18.20 a Christified bit of rabbinism. Cf. *Mek.* on Exod 20.24 and *m. 'Abot* 3.6: 'R. Halafta b. Dosa of Kefar Hanania said: If ten men sit together and occupy themselves in the Law, the Divine Presence rests among them, for it is written, God stands in the congregation of God. And whence (do we learn this) even of five? Because it is written, And has founded his group upon the earth. And whence even of three? Because it is written, He judges among the judges. And whence even of two? Because it is written, Then they that feared the Lord spoke one with another; and the Lord hearkened and heard. And whence even of one? Because it is written, In every place where I record my name I will come unto thee and I will bless thee.' Again, although one might conjecture that this last was prompted by the saying preserved in Matthew, it seems more likely that the rabbinic texts cited are independent of Christianity, and that Mt 18.20 is a Christian reformulation of a rabbinic sentiment. Jesus, the 'effulgence' of God's glory (Heb 1.3), has simply been substituted for the *shekinah*, and gathering together 'in my name' for study of the Torah. As in the Mishnah, so in Matthew: the zone of the sacred is not dictated by geography but is mobile. The difference is that holy space is 'Christified' in the gospel and is entered into by gathering in Christ's name.

In church history Mt 18.20 has been employed in sundry ways. It has not only, for instance, been cited as support for the authority of church councils, but also quoted as a justification of Free Churches (Christ is present for any two or three gathered in his name: no institution is required). But the saying has also been a stumbling block for certain Christians. The mention of 'two or three' troubled early Christian solitaries and was used against them. Is not Christ also present with one?

On Reconciliation (18.21–2)

Following the instructions on excommunication is a pronouncement story which serves as commentary. Its function is to be a hedge against rigidity and absolutism, to balance the hard teaching of the previous paragraph. The concern is to avoid any calculus of 'less and more' and to make explicit the attitude that is necessary if one is to undertake the hard task of correcting another. Forgiveness, like love, must be limitless. Without such forgiveness the community cannot correct the wayward, cannot pray as a united force, and cannot have Christ in its midst.

It is sometimes affirmed that vv. 21–2 stand in tension with what has gone before. How can one display unlimited forgiveness and yet undertake proceedings which may end in a brother's expulsion? But in Jewish tradition reproof and love belong together and are not perceived as antithetical, in part because the classic text on reproof, Lev 19.17, is followed immediately by the command to love one's neighbour as oneself (Lev 19.18). Beyond that, membership in the Christian community clearly disallows, for Matthew, certain types of behaviour. The community would cease to be if it did not insist on such. Thus the spirit of forgiveness cannot mean blindness and indifference to sin within the church (cf. Paul).

21. The effect of the juxtaposition with vv. 21–2 is to inculcate an attitude of forgiveness in the midst of the necessary but unpleasant proceedings just described. Rabbinic texts show that the sages were well-acquainted with the need to forgive an offender more than once. There are, however, passages which recommend limiting forgiveness, for example to three times. The understandable assumption here is that justice demands that mercy be bounded. *If* the notion that one might forgive another three times was part of common wisdom (we can only guess this), then Peter's proposal might have seemed excessively generous, in which case Jesus' proposal would be doubly so.

22. Jesus answers Peter's question by calling for what is in effect unlimited forgiveness.

but seventy times seven times. Gen 4.24 ('If Cain is avenged sevenfold, truly Lamech seventy-seven fold') is recalled because it refers to a blood-feud carried on without limit. Jesus demands the antithesis of this.

The Greek translated 'seventy times seven' can also mean seventy-seven. Both numbers amount to the same thing. One is not being commanded to count but to forgive without counting. The quality of Christian forgiveness requires that it should not be conceived in quantitative terms.

The Parable of the Unforgiving Servant (18.23–35)

Between the introduction (v. 23a) and the conclusion (v. 35), the parable consists of three scenes (vv. 23b–7, 28–30, 31–4), each having the same form: situation (vv. 23b–5, 28, 31); words (vv. 26, 29, 32–3); and response/action (vv. 27, 30, 34).

Some have said that 18.23–35 is not an apt illustration of vv. 21–2, for the king in our parable forgives only once, not seventy plus (or times) seven. This criticism misses the mark. It was surely as obvious to Matthew – who after all was responsible for the present setting of the parable – as it is to us that 18.23–35 does not illustrate precisely the same lesson. Rather, although both have to do with forgiving, they have different emphases. Mt 18.21–2 is a memorable call for repeated forgiveness. Mt 18.23–35 is a vivid reminder that the failure to forgive is failure to act as the heavenly father acts; cf. 5.48. Between the two themes there is scarcely any real tension.

23. The introduction sets the stage for the opening scene: a king wished to settle accounts with his servants. The reader, for whom 'king' and 'servant' are stock images for God and God's people, immediately thinks in terms of theological truths. While this does not entail a one-to-one correspondence between the actions of the king and the actions of God, it does turn the parable into a lesson about divine and human relationships.

24. one who owed him ten thousand talents was brought to him. The line helps point the reader to religious realities, for the equation of sin with debt was well known. The talent was a unit of coinage with relatively high value, equal in the first century to about 6,000 drachmas. The sum of 10,000 talents is fantastic. Josephus says that the total Judean tax for one year totaled only 600 talents. The parable uses an inflated figure in order to magnify God's munificence.

25. his lord ordered him to be sold, with his wife and children and all his possessions, and payment to be made. The practice of enslaving individuals on account of unpaid debts was common in the Graeco-Roman world and Judaism; cf. Exod 22.2; 1 Sam 22.2; Isa 50.1; Amos 2.6.

28. What follows mirrors vv. 24–7, except that the response of the unmerciful servant is not the response of the master. The striking similarities show up the differences.

who owed him a hundred denarii. The denarius, a Roman silver coin, had approximately the same value as the Greek drachma. According to 20.1–16, it was the standard day's wage for a labourer. A hundred denarii is a trifle compared to what the unmerciful servant owed his lord.

29. Have patience with me, and I will pay you. This request, unlike that in v. 26, is reasonable. The debt is sufficiently small that it could be paid back in time.

30. The plea for patience is ignored. The debtor is thrown in prison. The action is as surprising as the master's forgiveness of the unforgiving servant, not because it is unlawful or unjust but because it trumpets hypocrisy. The wicked servant asked for and benefited from mercy yet refuses to bestow it. He has broken the 'golden rule' of 7.12 and treated another as he would not wish to be treated.

and he went and threw him into prison until he should pay the debt. The requisite legal proceedings have been passed over as irrelevant to the story line.

31. All that has taken place is now related to the master by fellow servants, who recognize the terrible hypocrisy of a man who receives kindness but does not give it.

32–3. because you pleaded with me. The master forgave the unmerciful servant his debt out of pure generosity. The one forgiven should have acted in kind. The one act of mercy should have begotten another.

and should you not have had mercy on your fellow slave, as I had mercy on you? Beneath this remark is the idea that God's goodness should be imitated; cf. 5.48. The forgiven slave, however, has acted otherwise, with the result that he undoes the fifth beatitude: the unmerciful will not receive mercy. One recalls Browning: the sole death is 'lack of love from love made manifest'.

34. We do not now read that the wicked servant asked for mercy (contrast vv. 26 and 29). He knows he stands condemned. There is no protest when the angry master hands the evil servant over to torturers and the last punishment becomes worse than the first.

until he should pay his entire debt. Here we have the principle that like is punished by like. The unmerciful servant put another in prison for a debt unpaid (v. 30). This is now his own punishment. He too is put in prison, and for the same cause. As the parable now stands, with the debt amounting to 10,000 talents, the punishment must be perpetual, for a debt so immense could never be repaid. So the situation is a transparent symbol of eschatological judgement.

35. The parable ends with a warning which makes the moral of the parable impossible to miss. Cf. 6.15: 'if you do not forgive people their trespasses, neither will your Father forgive you your trespasses'; also Jas 2.13: 'judgement is without mercy to him that shows no mercy.'

from your heart expresses sincerity and excludes all calculation.

* * * * *

'Let him be to you as a Gentile and toll-collector.' These words, decidedly harsh and unpleasant, are nonetheless embedded in a section filled with kindness. The sinner is to be offered at least three opportunities to repent (vv. 15–17). And the one offended is to have forgiven the offender, no matter what – for Jesus demands forgiveness without measure (vv. 21–2). The motivation for such unbounded generosity is imitation of the Father in heaven; cf. 5.48. As God has forgiven undeserving Christians, so must they likewise forgive others (vv. 23–35). 'Freely you have received, freely give' (10.8). The appropriate attitude towards a wayward believer is like that of a shepherd seeking a stray sheep. The shepherd does not want to punish the stray but instead bring it back to the fold (cf. vv. 12–14). All this reveals two things. First, for Matthew, excommunication, when it comes, will be self-imposed exile. The community, if it is to be true to itself, if it is forbearing, anxious about the welfare of all its members, and animated by a spirit of forgiveness, will give sinners more than a fair chance. If, despite everything, excommunication follows, that can only be because the one excommunicated has finally refused to live within the law of the church. Second, it is clear that chapter 18, including 18.15–35, has been shaped by Matthew's pastoral concern. The main teaching is in vv. 15–20, on excommunication. Verses 21–2 and the long parable in vv. 23–35 are subsidiary: they function as a kind of commentary. In a way reminiscent of 6.25–34; 7.7–11; and 10.26–31, the harsh demands in vv. 15–20 are tempered by the radical teaching on forgiveness in vv. 21–35. Those who involve themselves in deciding whether someone is to be expelled must live and breathe a spirit of forgiveness. The process of expulsion is too serious a matter to be left in the hands of any but the meek and merciful, who know that they themselves are the unworthy recipients of God's constant mercy and forgiveness.

MONOGAMY, DIVORCE, CELIBACY (19.1–12)

19 ¹And when Jesus had finished these words, he departed from Galilee and entered the region of Judea beyond the Jordan. ²And large crowds followed him, and he healed them there.

³And Pharisees came to him, testing him and asking, 'Is it lawful to divorce one's wife for any cause?' ⁴He answered, 'Have you not read that he who made them at the beginning "made them male and female" ⁵and said, "On account of this a man will leave his father and mother and be joined to his wife, and the two will become one flesh?" ⁶So they are no longer two but one flesh. What therefore God has joined together, let no one separate.' ⁷They said to him, 'Why then did Moses command one to

give a certificate of divorce and to send her away?' ⁸ He said to them, 'Because of your hardness of heart Moses allowed you to divorce your wives, but from the beginning it was not so. ⁹And I say to you, whoever divorces his wife, except for unchastity, and marries another, commits adultery.'

¹⁰ His disciples said to him, 'If such is the case of a man with his wife, it is better not to marry.' ¹¹But he said to them, 'Not everyone can accept this word, but only those to whom it is given. ¹² For there are eunuchs who have been so from birth, and there are eunuchs who have been made eunuchs by others, and there are eunuchs who have made themselves eunuchs for the sake of the kingdom of heaven. He who is able to receive this, let him receive it.'

Parallels: Mt 5.31–2; Mk 10.1–12; Lk 16.18; 1 Cor 7.7–13

The theme of divorce has already been considered, in the Sermon on the Mount (5.31–2); but the declaration there made, without explanation, is now elucidated. The subject of celibacy has not previously appeared, although in 1.24–5 Joseph refrains from 'knowing' Mary for a time, and in 10.34–5 the prospect of alienation from family is raised.

1. Jesus leaves Galilee, which will not see him again until after the resurrection (28.7, 16). The earthly ministry there, which commenced with 4.12, has now concluded, and the trek to the holy city has begun.

And when Jesus had finished these words. Cf. 7.28; 11.1; 13.53; 26.1.

he departed from Galilee and entered the region of Judea beyond the Jordan. Cf. 13.53; Jn 10.40–2. Neither 'Judaea' nor 'the region beyond the Jordan' has been mentioned since chapters 3 and 4, which recount the commencement of the ministry. So the story begins to come full circle. The places around which the action centred at the beginning (2.3; 3.1; 4.25) will be the focus of activity at the end.

2. A major discourse has just ended (18.1–35). This does not mean, however, that the focus ceases to be Jesus' speech. While vv. 1–2 do tell us what Jesus did, with v. 3 and continuing through 20.28, the narrative element is severely circumscribed. Attention remains upon oral instruction.

3. The temptation is to contradict the Torah; cf. v. 7.

Pharisees came to him, testing him and asking. The query presupposes Jewish law, so the only question concerns the husband divorcing his wife. Jesus is being asked to give his interpretation of Deut 24.1.

Is it lawful to divorce one's wife for any cause? 'For any cause' reflects the Jewish scholastic debates. Both the schools of Hillel and

Shammai regarded divorce as lawful. They disagreed however over what constituted just cause, for their interpretations of Deut 24.1 differed. Matthew's 'for any cause' appears to have as its background something akin to the Hillelite position, according to which many things constituted grounds for divorce. The question is whether Jesus holds a less liberal position.

4. Jesus directs his opponents to Gen 1.27 and so responds to the question about divorce by raising the issue of monogamy.

Have you not read that he who made them at the beginning 'made them male and female'? The final five words in Greek agree with LXX Gen 1.27 = 5.2. 'At the beginning', which recalls Gen 1.1, entails that the circumstances recalled obtained before sin disturbed things; cf. v. 8. Regarding 'have you not read', which is particularly fitting in a debate with learned opponents: the Pharisees have of course read Genesis 1. The rhetorical question invites contemplation of the creation and reconsideration of the implications of Gen 1.27: Did God not establish monogamy?

Gal 3.28, which may be part of a baptismal formula, alludes to Gen 1.27. The theme of the passage is reunification, and the myth of the androgyne could lie in the background. The point in any event is that man and woman are no longer two but (in Christ) one: just as, in Mt 19, Gen 1.27 is cited, in connexion with Gen 2.24, to underline the unity of man and wife. Both Paul and the gospel text cite Gen 1.27 when the subject is unification.

5. Jesus continues by quoting another Scripture, Gen 2.24. Again the created order is a guide for the moral order.

On account of this a man will leave his father and mother and be joined to his wife, and the two will become one flesh. The quotation presupposes a knowledge of the OT context: 'on account of this' refers to Eve coming from Adam's rib (not to Mt 19.4).

Mal 2.16 ('I [Yahweh] hate divorce' or, alternatively, 'One who divorces because of hate ...') takes us some way towards Jesus' rejection of divorce. It is true that some consider the prophetic passage in which the words are embedded to be about spiritual unfaithfulness rather than literal divorce. But historically such has not been the understanding of most interpreters, and a first-century Jew would probably have understood Mal 2.16 to be about divorce. Beyond that, the section which Mal 2.16 concludes (namely 2.10–16), begins with a reference to God's creation of humanity (v. 10: 'Did not one God create us?'), and continues a few verses later with an apparent allusion to Gen 2.24: 'Did he not make one?' It has therefore been argued that the rejection of divorce is based upon a reading of the creation story. Perhaps, then, Jesus interprets Deut 24.1 in the light of Malachi: that is, Deut 24.1 is subordinated to the intention of God in creation because the intention of God in creation is the reason given for God hating divorce in Mal 2.

6. they are no longer two but one flesh. As in Genesis, the meaning of 'one flesh' is not perfectly clear; but perhaps the best guess is that in both places the phrase implies that man and wife become as closely and truly related as those with the same parents.

8. Jesus answers the Pharisees not by quoting Scripture but by explaining Deut 24.1: that is, by elucidating why God allowed Moses to permit divorce.

Because of your hardness of heart Moses allowed you to divorce your wives. The main point is not that the teaching of Genesis is from God, that in Deuteronomy from Moses. Rather, the instructions in Deut 24.1 were given for hardness of heart (= moral and spiritual petrification); that is, they were a 'concession' to the post-fallen state. Jesus here distinguishes between legislation that corresponds directly to God's perfect will in an ideal world, and legislation issued in response to humanity's fallen, sinful state. Jesus demands conformity to the will of God as it was expressed before the fall. Probably in the background is the beginning = end equation. The coming of the kingdom is the beginning of the restoration of paradise, the union of creation and redemption, the final realization of what God intended from the beginning.

There is an important parallel to Mt 19 in Deut 17.14–20, the law of the king. The passage accepts kingship and promulgates divine precepts for it, yet still regards it as an imperfect institution chosen by Israel, not God; cf. Judg 8.22–23; 1 Sam 8.4–22. Here too, then, the Torah is conceived as containing divine 'concessions' or 'compromises'.

but from the beginning it was not so. The idea that priority in time may indicate a priority in God's will is found only here in the gospels. There are no true rabbinic parallels. Gal 3.15–20 does, however, offer something similar. There Paul argues that the promise to Abraham is somehow more fundamental than the law, which came later. Whether this type of argument shows Paul's knowledge of the Jesus tradition or has some other explanation or is coincidence we do not know. But there is also an OT parallel of sorts. The editor of the Deuteronomic history subordinates the unconditional covenant with David to the prior conditional covenant made with Moses.

9. The main point of the passage is given in an apodictic statement which resembles 5.32.

whoever divorces his wife, except for unchastity, and marries another, commits adultery. 'Except for unchastity' justifies the envisaged action of the 'just' Joseph in 1.18–25. In our gospel divorce is not adultery only when the marriage bond has already been broken by unfaithfulness.

The problem of whether 19.9 allows remarriage for the innocent party (so traditionally most Protestants) cannot, as Augustine conceded, finally be answered. Grammatical reflections cannot decide. Patristic opinion, burdened by a less than enthusiastic view of marriage, disallowed remarriage and so understood our text accordingly. The link with vv. 10–12, which have to do with sexual abstinence, has recently been thought to uphold this interpretation: the eunuchs for the kingdom of heaven are those who have separated from their spouses because of *porneia* and do not remarry. But the saying about eunuchs is not a command but a qualified recommendation: not all are given the gift (see on v. 12). So if 19.10–2 is closely associated with v. 9, it might appear that some are free to remarry. There is also the issue of whether something like the later distinction between separation (divorce *a mensa et thoro*) and divorce (*a vinculo*) would have made much sense in Matthew's Jewish environment. The Jewish divorce bill contained the clause, 'You are free to marry again.' To obtain a divorce was to obtain permission to remarry. In line with this, 5.32 simply assumes that divorce leads to remarriage (to divorce a wife is to make her commit adultery, because she will take another spouse).

10. The Pharisees disappear (their response is irrelevant). In place of their hostility is an exclamation of the disciples.

His disciples said to him, 'If such is the case of a man with his wife, it is better not to marry.' The disciples' observation is unexpected and does them no credit. Just as they will wrongly rebuke people for bringing a child to Jesus in the next paragraph, and just as they will wonder 'Who then can be saved?' in the paragraph after that, so here too: they misunderstand. The correct inference from Jesus' exaltation of monogamy is hardly the general recommendation of celibacy. But the disciples, holding a view of marriage and divorce akin to that in Ecclus 25.16–26, and reasoning that a lifetime of commitment to one woman is more burdensome than no involvement at all, reach a conclusion also reached by certain Essenes and Greek and Roman philosophers: it is better not to marry.

11. But he said to them, 'Not everyone can accept this word, but only those to whom it is given.' The crux of the line is 'this word'. Does it refer to vv. 3–9, or to v. 9 (Jesus teaching on divorce), or to v. 10 (the disciples' inference from Jesus' teaching), or does it anticipate or introduce v. 12 (the saying about eunuchs)? Or can no sense be made of the passage because disparate traditions have been merged? A reference to vv. 3–9 or 9 is unlikely. It would make v. 12 address those who have separated from their wives and enjoin them to remain single: but v. 9 does not clearly exclude the prospect of remarriage if there has been divorce for adultery. Further, the gift of celibacy is something exceptional, something that cannot be accepted by everyone; but surely Jesus' teaching on divorce is for all. And one could not in any case speak of a *command* not to remarry: vv. 11–12 contain only a recommendation.

Does 'this word' then point forward to v. 12? This is possible. But a connexion with v. 10 is to be preferred. The disciples' remark in v. 10 functions as a transitional sentence. They have drawn an inference about celibacy from Jesus' teaching on marriage. Jesus does not go back to the subject of marriage but takes up the question of celibacy ('this word'). His main thrust may be seen in the contrast between the disciples' unqualified generalization and his own denial of universal applicability – a denial consistent with our book's relatively positive view of marriage. Note how the qualifications are piled up: 'not all', 'those to whom it is given', 'he who is able'. Bengel wrote: 'Jesus opposes these words [vv. 11–12] to the universal proposition of his disciples.' Matthew does use the saying on eunuchs to confirm celibacy as a calling, but his emphasis – in contradiction to the disciples – is upon its special character. Note well that, if he had so desired, he could easily have remarked that Jesus himself, the moral model *par excellence*, was celibate. That he did not is significant. One is reminded not only of 1 Corinthians 7, where Paul qualifies an ascetic generalization of the Corinthians ('It is good for a man not to touch a woman') but also of 1 Corinthians 12: there are varieties of gifts, and just as not all are apostles or prophets or teachers, so all are not eunuchs.

12. 'To that ... general argument against contracting matrimony which the disciples gave, namely, the inconvenience which seemed to them to result from its indissolubility, Jesus opposes the legitimate, particular, and only good reason ...' (Bengel).

The saying about eunuchs exhibits a pattern typical of the wisdom tradition: the first two lines relate concrete facts about the everyday world and serve to introduce or illustrate the third line, which proclaims a truth – much less concrete – from the moral or religious sphere; cf. Prov 17.3; 20.15; 27.3. In the present instance our maxim mentions three types of eunuchs. The first two are taken for granted: they are known entities (see below). They thus serve to illustrate the third type, which is novel.

there are eunuchs who have been so from birth, and there are eunuchs who have been made eunuchs by others. According to the rabbis there

were two sorts of eunuchs, those of human device and those of
nature's making. The first type was spoken of as being 'eunuch of
man'. The second type was spoken of as being 'eunuch of the sun', that
is, from the first seeing of the sun, a eunuch by birth. The 'eunuch of
man' was a male who had either been literally castrated or who had,
sometime after birth, lost the power to reproduce, whether through
disease, injury, or other debilitating factor. The 'eunuch of the sun'
was one who had been born with defective male organs or one who
had otherwise been rendered impotent by the circumstances of his
birth.

**there are eunuchs who have made themselves eunuchs for the sake of
the kingdom of heaven.** In addition to the two sorts of eunuchs just
introduced there is a third type, one accounted for only by religion.
Members of this class are not literal castrates nor impotent by nature.
They are indeed unmarried, not because they cannot take a wife but
rather because they *will* not – because the duty placed upon them by
the kingdom of heaven is such that it is best discharged outside the
confines of marriage. For these people, the good and valuable thing
that marriage undoubtedly is (cf. vv. 3–9) must be sacrificed in view of
the demand made upon them by something greater.

It is worth comparing Paul's attitude, as voiced in 1 Corinthians 7
and 9. The apostle knew that he, like the other apostles and the
brothers of the Lord and Cephas, had the right to be accompanied by
a wife (9.5). Yet he had not, he boasted, made use of that right, for in
his case it would only have been an obstacle in the way of the gospel
(9.12). Paul evidently believed that, at least in his own case, it was
expedient not to marry. While he might have taken a wife, and while
he certainly had the right to have one, his own particular calling would
only have suffered under the anxieties and responsibilities of married
life.

He who is able to receive this, let him receive it. The notion that
celibacy or continence is a special gift or grace was common in the
early church.

* * * * *

(i) The Marcionites, the Encratites, and the Eustathians rejected
marriage; and they were all, for this reason and others, labelled
heretics by the Christian majority. Most Christian bodies have
regarded marriage either as a covenant made between two people
and God, or as a sacrament. And yet beginning with the *Shepherd of
Hermas*, the apocryphal acts, and the Montanists (including the later
Tertullian), and continuing through Augustine, Pope Siricius, and the
Council of Trent, it has been common in Christendom to view celibacy

as a higher state than marriage. Jerome – who took Mt 19.10–12 to indicate that 'Christ loves virgins more than others' – could assert that virginity is better because it was Adam's condition before the fall; and Methodius of Olympus affirmed that Christian virgins will 'carry off the highest honours'. But thoughts such as these do not appear in Matthew. In the First Gospel, which perhaps is too Jewish to permit redemption to eclipse creation, marriage is part of the natural order, and the natural order is, despite the coming eschatological change, from God. Furthermore, if the preceding interpretation of 19.10–12 is sound, we find here the spirit of Jovinian, who argued that monasticism is not to be rated superior to life in the world. God created man and woman to be one flesh, and God joins people in marriage. God also calls some to celibacy: not because women are evil or male communal life advantageous or cultic purity desirable, but simply because service to the kingdom sometimes demands such. Thus the same God stands equally behind married and unmarried. So the assertion that it is, in general, expedient or profitable not to marry, is not endorsed but corrected. Just as there is no command to marry, so there is no command to be celibate. Not all are able to live outside marriage – and precisely because God has not called them to such. It is not too much to say that Mt 19.1–12 is, like Gregory of Nazianzus' famous words on the benefits of both celibacy and marriage, an attempt to balance the scales: both those yoked in marriage and those called to be eunuchs for the kingdom are equal members of Jesus' church. 'Each has his own special gift from God, one of one kind and one of another' (1 Cor 7.7).

(ii) If chapter 18 concerns itself with properly ecclesiastical issues, chapter 19 addresses everyday existence. Mt 19.1–12 opens a series of paragraphs which treat, in order, marriage and divorce (vv. 1–9), celibacy (vv. 10–12), children (vv. 13–15), and money (19.16–20.16). So between the end of his work in Galilee and the last struggle in Jerusalem, Jesus gives counsel on key social concerns. There is in all this a certain parallelism with 6.1–7.12. There, in the Sermon on the Mount, Jesus first discusses properly cultic issues (6.1–18: almsgiving, prayer, fasting) and subsequently speaks on social issues (6.19–7.12 what to do about wealth, how to treat one's neighbour). Does the common sequence reflect a catechetical order?

JESUS AND THE CHILDREN (19.13–15)

[13]Then were brought to him little children so that he might lay his hands on them and pray. But the disciples rebuked them. [14] Jesus, however, said, 'Let the little children come to me, and do not prevent them; for to

such as these belongs the kingdom of heaven.' [15] **And laying his hands on them, he went away.**

Parallels: Mk 10.13–15; Lk 18.15–17

Following the discussion of marriage and celibacy, children are now the subject. They should be received because 'to such as these belongs the kingdom of heaven'. Interpreted in the light of 18.3, this teaches humility, by which is meant lack of concern for worldly status: to be childlike is to be without power or position. So there are two lessons: respect children, embody humility.

13. Children are put forward so that Jesus might lay hands on and pray for them. The disciples, acting as though unaware of 18.1–5 and of the kindness shown by Jesus to little ones in 9.18–26; 15.21–8; and 17.14–21, disapprove. The reason for their attitude is not given, but that matters little: their error affords Jesus the opportunity to clarify.

Then were brought to him little children. The verb means either 'were brought' (appropriate for larger children) or 'were carried' (appropriate for smaller children). Who is doing the bringing is unsaid (should we think of the crowds of 19.2?).

so that he might lay his hands on them and pray. One suspects that liturgical language has affected the text. 'To lay hands on them and pray' has a traditional ring.

14. Jesus rebukes the disciples, delivering an authoritative pronouncement consisting of imperative + prohibition + explanation.

for to such as these belongs the kingdom of heaven. The kingdom belongs to 'such as these', that is, to those in the situation of children. Although 'belongs' could indicate the kingdom's presence, it may also carry future sense. But is the distinction without a difference? Those who enjoy the kingdom now will also enjoy it in the future, and *vice versa*.

15. Jesus now incarnates his own speech.

laying his hands on them. Some think our narrative was designed to vindicate infant baptism. Tertullian already knew such an interpretation, which has been very common in church history, and Jn 3.5 links the saying in Mk 10.15 = Mt 18.3 with baptism. Yet how soon infants came to be baptized is uncertain, and in any case customs must have differed from place to place. Note should nonetheless be taken of Matthew's language. In the second century and probably earlier baptism was preceded and/or accompanied by a laying on of hands *and prayer*. So one wonders whether Matthew's original audience would have been put in mind of baptism.

Mt 19.13–15 par. has been used in church history to justify giving communion to children and to counter belief in the damnation of unbaptized infants. It has also been employed when speaking of the slaughtered infants in Matthew 2 as 'martyrs' and to authenticate the religious experiences of children. But there is no evidence for thinking that any of these things were issues for the synoptic evangelists.

* * * * *

(i) The declaration that the kingdom belongs to such as children takes on meaning from the positive way children are presented elsewhere in Matthew. In 14.13–21 and 15.29–39 Jesus miraculously feeds a crowd, among which are children. In 15.21–8 he heals a child. In 18.3 he tells his followers to be like children. And in 21.15 children, recognizing that Jesus is the Son of David, shout 'Hosanna'. So throughout the Gospel readers feel sympathy for children. They are objects of Jesus' mercy. They are to be imitated. And they can receive miraculous insight. Within the macrocontext, then, Mt 20.13–15 comes as no surprise at all.

(ii) If in 19.10 the disciples assert that it is better not to marry, in 19.13 they belittle children. Both judgements are consistent with a negative view of family life – and in both cases Jesus offers correction. In 19.11–12 he makes it plain that celibacy is not for everyone, and in 19.13–15 he affirms that children are to be welcomed. So 19.13–15, in its present context, reinforces 19.11–12 and so confirms the high view of marriage put forward in 19.1–9.

WEALTH AND THE KINGDOM (19.16–30)

[16]**And behold, someone came up to him and said, 'Teacher, what good deed must I do to have eternal life?'** [17]**And he said to him, 'Why do you ask me about what is good? One is good. If you desire to enter into life, keep the commandments.'** [18]**He said, 'Which ones?' And Jesus said, 'You shall not murder. You shall not commit adultery. You shall not steal. You shall not bear false witness.** [19]**Honour your father and mother. Also, you shall love your neighbour as yourself.'** [20]**The young man said to him, 'I have observed all these; what do I still lack?'** [21]**Jesus said to him, 'If you wish to be perfect, go, sell your possessions, and give the money to the poor, and you will have treasure in heaven. Then come, follow me.'** [22]**When the young man heard this word, he went away grieving, for he had many possessions.**

[23]**Then Jesus said to his disciples, 'Amen I say to you, it will be hard for a rich person to enter the kingdom of heaven.** [24]**Again I say to you, it is easier for a camel to go through the eye of a needle than for someone**

who is rich to enter the kingdom of God.' ^{25}When the disciples heard this, they were greatly astounded and said, 'Who then can be saved?' ^{26}But Jesus looked at them and said, 'For mortals this is impossible, but for God all things are possible.'

^{27}Then Peter said in reply, 'Behold, we have left everything and followed you. What then will we have?' ^{28}Jesus said to them, 'Amen I say to you, at the regeneration of all things, when the Son of man is seated on the throne of his glory, you who have followed me will also sit on twelve thrones, judging the twelve tribes of Israel. ^{29}And everyone who has left houses or brothers or sisters or father or mother or children or fields, for my name's sake, will receive a hundredfold, and will inherit eternal life. ^{30}But many who are first will be last, and the last first.'

Parallels: Mk 10.17–30; Lk 18.18–30

Continuing the subject of domestic affairs, our scholastic dialogue has for its theme wealth and the kingdom. The topic has already been extensively treated in the Sermon on the Mount. Indeed, the declaration about the impossibility of serving both God and mammon (6.24) is here concretely demonstrated. The subjects of treasure in heaven (6.19–21), generosity (6.22–3), eschatological reversal (5.3–12), and perfection (5.48) also resurface here. Mt 19.16–30 is a narrative illustration of important portions of the Sermon on the Mount.

The Rich Man and Jesus (19.16–22)

This is a call story with an unhappy ending, for the one called cannot relinquish his present earthly goods for future heavenly treasures. The tragic dimension is, however, lessened by the alternative ending, in which the disciples are promised reward for having forsaken all.

16. Jesus is addressed as 'teacher' and asked, with apparent sincerity, 'what good thing must I do in order to have eternal life?' The speaker (who is not yet said to be rich) hopes that Jesus knows the will of God, and his question presupposes dissatisfaction with or uncertainty concerning what other teachers have said.

Teacher, what good deed must I do to have eternal life? The inquirer seems naïve, as though he thinks maybe one great deed will earn God's favour.

17. Jesus responds by (a) raising a question; (b) making a theological assertion; and (c) uttering an imperative.

Why do you ask me about what is good? One need not ask about 'the good' because the good is clear and can be known: God has revealed the commandments.

One is good. Cf. Deut 6.4. The 'one' is God, and the sense is this: the commandments (= 'the good' of the previous clause) are good because they are from the one who is good, God. Humanity's sinfulness is implicitly acknowledged (cf. 7.11), as is the derivative nature of every so-called good thing in this world: God is the source of all goodness; cf. Ps 16.2.

If you desire to enter into life. Jesus replaces the man's 'have' with his own 'enter', which implies that the inquirer must make a pilgrimage instead of a purchase.

keep the commandments. Because God alone is good, the only question is what God says and wills.

18–19. Jesus, upholding the Torah (cf. 5.17–20), tells the man to keep the second table of the decalogue (the table on social relations: Exod 20.12–16; Deut 5.16–20) and, in accord with Leviticus, to love his neighbour as himself. In all this there are four prohibitions and two positive imperatives. The omission of the first table is perhaps surprising; but the issue at hand will prove to be social, and certainly Calvin was correct to observe that right action (as depicted by the second table) is proof of right religion (as outlined by the first table).

He said, 'Which ones?' The great number of the commandments, which implies that some might seem to be more important than others, makes the question possible.

you shall love your neighbour as yourself. This is from Lev 19.18; cf. 5.43; 22.39. For discussion of the meaning of 'neighbour' (in Matthew the term is inclusive: no one is excluded) and of the love commandment see pp. 84–85, 381–82.

Lev 19.18 is cited by the NT more than any other verse from the Pentateuch: Mt 5.43; 19.19; Mk 12.31 par.; 12.33; Rom 12.9; 13.9; Gal 5.14; Jas 2.8. This fact is nicely accounted for if Jesus himself summed up the law's demands by citing Lev 19.18. But why was Lev 19.18 independently brought into association with commands from the decalogue by Matthew (19.18–19), by Paul (Rom 13.9; cf. Gal 5.14), and by James (2.8, 11)? Perhaps Judaism had already done the same, or perhaps it was natural to connect what were thought of as two summaries of the Torah, or perhaps we have here traces of a common catechism.

The question, 'Which (commandments)?', might imply the unimportance of parts of the Torah: that is, that only some are required for salvation. Jesus' response dispels that notion. He quotes the decalogue and Lev 19.18. The former was thought of as a summary of or heading for the whole law, whereas the latter (or the chapter to which it belonged) was sometimes said to contain the Torah *in nuce*. Thus v. 19 directs attention not to isolated texts but to parts that stood for the whole.

20. The man, although he boldly claims to have kept the commandments, confesses his own lack. He is indeed looking for something.

I have observed all these. Obviously the speaker believes he has faithfully observed the law. But Jesus' citation of Lev 19.18 undoes his presumption: the keeping of the second half of the decalogue is one thing, the loving of one's neighbour *as oneself* something else again.

what do I still lack? Luther wrote: 'What you lack is everything. For you would be devout, and yet you refuse to give up your goods for my sake, and to suffer with me. Therefore Mammon is your God, and you prefer it to me.'

21. Jesus demands not alms but everything. This is not an imperative of the decalogue or the OT but something new, a novel charge engendered by the nature of discipleship and the greater righteousness announced by 5.20.

If you wish to be perfect. Verse 21 raises two fundamental issues: the nature of perfection, and the question of whether two kinds of believers are envisaged. Concerning this last there has always been a tendency to sort Christians into two grades, one better or more advanced than the other. One thinks of the so-called 'religious' in Roman Catholicism, and also of 'the perfect' among the Manichees and Bogomils. Jerome contrasted the 'half-hearted' with 'the perfect' and defined the latter as the impoverished with 'nothing beside Christ'. Similar sentiments are more than easy to document. But did Matthew understand 19.21 to mean that Christians who sold all could be perfect while others would be stuck with 'a second degree of virtue' (Jerome)? It is better to follow Calvin: 'Our Lord is not proclaiming a general statement that is applicable to everyone, but only to the person with whom He is speaking.' Mt 5.48 and 19.21 (the only two verses in Matthew to use 'perfect') are naturally related, and there is nothing in the former to hint that only a few are to be 'perfect'. All are called to imitate the divine love. Mt 19.16ff. is, moreover, a call story, like those in 4.18–20; 8.18–22; and 9.9: the rich man is being invited to follow Jesus in a specific situation. This circumstance determines what is asked of him. One can no more generalize v. 21 than turn 8.22 ('leave the dead to bury their own dead') into a general order to neglect the deceased.

But what then is meant by 'perfect'? It can hardly be a reference to sinlessness, although such an idea would not have been foreign to ancient Jews. In 5.48 the connotation of completeness is foremost. But whereas in the Sermon on the Mount it is the completeness of love, here it is the completeness of obedience. The rich man would be perfect if he exhibited wholehearted obedience to Jesus. This, then, is the point to be generalized: all are called to be perfect, by which is meant that all are called to obey the divine word that comes to them.

go, sell your possessions, and give the money to the poor. The man's wealth is to be given to the poor (= hired labourers, widows, orphans, beggars), not contributed to a common religious fund; and nothing is said about poverty as a sign of sanctity or self-sufficiency. One is put in mind of the praise of charity in *b. B. Bat.* 9a ('Charity is equivalent to all the other religious precepts combined') and 10a ('Charity saves from death').

Mt 19.21, so often in church history associated with 16.24 – to renounce possessions is to take up the cross – has had a life-changing impact upon several important Christian figures. Origen, Anthony of Egypt, Cyprian, Francis of Assisi, and countless others have, in seeking 'perfection', given away their private possessions. That there were already some in the earliest Christian communities who did likewise is a safe inference; cf. Acts 2.43–7. But neither then nor later has the counsel to sell everything been taken by any but a handful to be a blanket command applicable to all. Sometimes, however, as with the Pelagians, the Eustathians, and the Manichees, it has been taught that at least all rich people should give up their wealth.

treasure in heaven stands in contrast to 'possessions': one belongs to this world, the other to the world to come.

Then come, follow me. Following Jesus would be the man's salvation.

22. The man's desire is insufficient for action: he is an example of velleity. Unable to relinquish familiar security for the uncertainties of discipleship, he sadly and silently leaves the story.

he went away grieving. That the man grieves proves his conscience is alive: he does not do the good he wants; cf. Rom 7.19.

he had many possessions. Why the man is unable to free himself from the swirl of wealth is not stated; but the text, which pictorially proves 6.24, assumes that wealth is a snare. As throughout the First Gospel, failure is not failure to believe but failure to obey.

Wealth and Salvation (19.23–6)

23. Jesus turns from the rich man to his disciples, giving commentary on what has just happened.

it will be hard for a rich person to enter the kingdom of heaven. God's kingdom is hard to reach if one is rich, for one is almost inevitably inclined to trust in the security of wealth rather than in God alone.

24. A second, more vivid declaration, one with its proof in what has just occurred, complements the first.

it is easier for a camel to go through the eye of a needle than for someone who is rich to enter the kingdom of God. Cf. *b. Ber.* 55b (one never dreams of 'an elephant going through the eye of a needle') and *b. B. Me* 38b (in Pumbditha 'they make an elephant pass through a needle's eye'). Many have tried to reduce the absurdity of the image in 19.24 par. (i) A few mss. and versions have the similar-sounding 'rope' or 'ship's cable'. (ii) The same result has been obtained in modern times via conjectures about the original Aramaic. (iii) Ancient walled cities had small gates built within or beside the larger gates, so that when the latter were closed individuals could still go in and out; and some have affirmed that such a gate could have been referred to as the 'needle's eye'. Presumably a camel could pass through such a gate, but just barely, and only after its load had been removed.

There is, however, no need to depart from the plain meaning of the text, which goes on to speak about what is *impossible*. As Jerome, put it, 'one impossibility is compared with another.' The absurd juxtaposition is actually characteristic of Jesus; cf. Mt 23.24, which refers to *swallowing* a camel – another ludicrous contrast of large and small.

The eye of the needle has often been associated with the narrow way of Mt 7.13–14. Clement of Alexandria wrote of 'the camel which passes through a strait and narrow way sooner than the rich man'. There is, however, nothing to indicate that Matthew himself linked the two verses.

25. Who then can be saved? The question uncritically presupposes, against the whole weight of the Jesus tradition, that wealth is a sign of divine favour; so if not even the rich man, blessed as he is by God, can enter the kingdom, who can? Matthew presents the disciples as obtuse: it is as though they have not heard the Sermon on the Mount.

26. For mortals this is impossible, but for God all things are possible. Cf. Gen 18.14 ('Is anything too hard for the Lord?'); Lk 1.37; Mk 9.23. The idea that nothing is impossible 'with' God lies behind the commendation of omnipotent prayer in 17.20 and 21.21–2. Here the notion is antithetical to that of human impotence: regarding salvation, only God has strength – just as, with regard to goodness, God and human beings belong to different categories (cf. v. 17). The text evokes Paul.

Mt 19.26 speaks only of the possible, not the probable. Divine omnipotence does not guarantee anybody's salvation. The verse is misunderstood if received as comfort for the rich. It does not cancel vv. 23–4.

Eschatological Reward (19.27–30)

Peter asks how things stand with itinerants like himself who have, in contrast with the rich man, forsaken all. His self-interest is evident. Jesus responds first by offering congratulations. But the praise will soon enough be balanced with the caution of 20.1ff.: if the twelve are examples of the last becoming first, they need to beware, lest they likewise become examples of the first becoming last.

28. at the regeneration of all things, when the Son of man is seated on the throne of his glory, you who have followed me will also sit on twelve thrones, judging the twelve tribes of Israel. The sitting of the Son of man also appears in 25.31 and 26.64. Perhaps the appearance of the plural, throne*s*, in Dan 7.9 was thought to imply that there was one throne for God, another for the Son of man.

The link between throne and glory was an old one. But the throne of the Son of man is not a well-attested motif; see *1 En.* 62.5 ('when they see that Son of man sitting on the throne of his glory'); 69.29 ('that Son of man has appeared and seated himself upon the throne of his glory'). It is in fact referred to in first-century Christian literature only by Matthew, and one must wonder whether this betrays a knowledge of *1 Enoch*, especially given the prominence of the glory of God's throne in *1 En.* 36–71 and its connexion with the Son of man sitting on his throne in 62.5 and 69.29.

What is meant by 'judging'? Many have understood the verb to refer not to lordship but to a one-time judgement: Israel will be judged – some would say condemned – by the twelve at the consummation. In support of this conclusion, many ancient Jewish and Christian texts foresee a group of saints judging the world in the sense indicated. Further, 19.28 recalls 25.31, which introduces a depiction of the last judgement. But it is better to hold that sitting on thrones designates the exercise of authority over a period of time. As the twelve phylarchs once directed the twelve tribes under Moses, and as Israel was once ruled by judges, so shall it be at the end: cf. Lk 22.28–30.

How did Matthew understand the new age? Did he, like Papias and Justin Martyr, look forward to a literal messianic kingdom on this earth? Or did he anticipate, after the eschatological birth pangs, a new or renewed earth? Or did he anticipate both, one to come after the other? Although there is no real evidence that Matthew had a double expectation or that he expected an earthly messianic kingdom, the data do not admit of certainty. Yet that very fact shows that Matthew was not much interested in the details of future cosmological states. For him the future was above all two things: the Messiah and Israel.

The 'regeneration' for him meant the world in which the Messiah reigns, a world with a redeemed Israel.

29. Jesus now makes a promise that broadens out to include not only Peter and his fellows, but all who have left families.

everyone who has left houses or brothers or sisters or father or mother or children or fields for my name's sake, will receive a hundredfold, and will inherit eternal life. 'Will receive' puts all the reward in the future. The present is the vale of soul-making, the future the time of reward.

There is tension between 19.29 on the one hand and 19.1–15 + 19 ('honour your father and mother') on the other: in the former those who have forsaken wife and children for Christ are commended, whereas in vv. 1–15 + 19 marriage is a divine institution, parents are to be honoured, and children are to be valued. But 19.10–12 supplies one possible key to harmonization, for it implies that different callings entail different behaviour. Just as, within the universal demand for perfect obedience, some are called to celibacy and others to marriage, so too within that same universal demand are some called to poverty, others to almsgiving.

30. Although in origin perhaps a secular proverb about fickle fortune, in Matthew the chiastic generalization came to portend the divine future.

many who are first will be last, and the last first. Cf. 20.16 (with reverse order); *b. B. Bat.* 10b ('a world upside down, the upper below and the lower above'). Reversal aphorisms and lists appear in the OT (e.g. 1 Sam 2.4–5) and are common in ancient near eastern wisdom literature. They were naturally taken over by Jewish apocalyptic, Jesus, and the early church to paint pictures of eschatological reversal; cf. Lk 6.20–6; the book of Revelation is eschatological reversal writ large.

Who are the first and the last? Suggestions include the Pharisees and sinners, Jews and Gentiles, those converted late in life and those converted early, the rich and the poor, the rich and the 'perfect', the twelve and other disciples. It is possible that the logion nicely finishes vv. 16ff., where the rich man has failed but Peter and the others succeeded: many who are first (including the rich man, an example of disobedience) will be last (= excluded at the judgement), while the last (including the impoverished disciples, models of obedience) will be first (= enter the kingdom and receive reward). But it seems better to interpret 19.30–20.16 as a caution against thinking oneself among the first. We thus have congratulations followed by warning – something analogous to what appears in 16.13–28.

* * * * *

Clement of Alexandria's *Who Is the Rich Man Who Will Be Saved?* is the most famous commentary on Mt 19.16–30 par. It is also pretty good commentary, even though the philosophical idiom is foreign to Matthew. For Clement, 'salvation does not depend on external things, whether they be many or few, small or great, illustrious or obscure, esteemed or disesteemed; but on the virtue of the soul, faith, hope, love, brotherliness, knowledge, meekness, humility, and truth ...'. Clement does not deny that riches are seductive and dangerous, that they are an obstacle on the way to God: quite the contrary. But he observes that many other things are also obstacles, and 'it is no great thing or desirable to be destitute of wealth, if without special object'. Wealth is therefore not to be eliminated on principle but rather used according to the needs of the hour: 'make friends for yourselves by means of unrighteous mammon' (Lk 16.9). The problem, of course, is that those who seek to use wealth for good ends so often become not its master but its slave; cf. Mt 13.22. As Bernard of Clairvaux wrote of the rich man in Mt 19: he 'did not own his possessions: they owned him; if he had owned them, he could have been free of them'. What is therefore demanded of the faithful is neither ascetic renunciation nor acceptance of a communistic ideal but, as Clement saw, *freedom for obedience*, that is, the freedom to do what God 'wishes, what he orders, what he indicates'. The rich man did not have such freedom. The so-called 'perfect', however, do; for while they do not hate wealth, they are, in effect, truly indifferent towards it; and such indifference, generated by a consuming love for God and spiritual things (cf. Mt 6.33), enables them to do what the rich man could not: namely, respond in wholehearted obedience to the demands of Christ. That such a reading is correct is strongly suggested by Mt 27.57–61, where Joseph of Arimathea is both a rich man and a disciple. The two things cannot be mutually exclusive.

THE GENEROUS EMPLOYER (20.1–16)

20 **[1]For the kingdom of heaven is like the situation of a householder who went out early in the morning to hire labourers for his vineyard. [2]After agreeing with the labourers for a denarius a day, he sent them into his vineyard. [3]And going out about the third hour, he saw others standing idle in the marketplace. [4]And he said to them, 'You too go into the vineyard, and whatever is right I will give to you.' So they went. [5]Going out again about the sixth hour and ninth hour, he did the same. [6]And about the eleventh hour he went out and found others standing around. And he said to them, 'Why do you stand here idle all day?' [7]They said to him, 'Because no one has hired us.' He said to them, 'You too go into the vineyard.'**

[8]And when evening came, the owner of the vineyard said to his manager, 'Call the labourers and give them their pay, beginning with the last and then up to the first.' [9]And when those hired about the eleventh hour came, each of them received a denarius. [10]And when the first came, they thought that they would receive more, but each of them also received a denarius. [11]And upon receiving it, they grumbled against the landowner, [12]saying, 'These last worked only one hour, and you have made them equal to us who have borne the burden of the day and the scorching heat.' [13]But he replied to one of them, 'Friend, I am doing you no wrong. Did you not agree with me for a denarius? [14]Take what belongs to you and go. I choose to give to this last just as I give to you. [15]Am I not allowed to do what I choose with what belongs to me? Or is your eye evil because I am good?' [16]So the last will be first, and the first last.

Parallels: Mk 10.31; Lk 13.30

In its present context, 20.1–15 has been construed as (i) a parable of the last judgement which functions as a warning against boasting or presuming oneself to be among the first; (ii) a supplement to 19.16–30, illustrating how the last (cf. the disciples and those who come at the eleventh hour) become first and how the first (cf. the rich man and those hired at the first hour) become last; (iii) a denial of special reward for charismatics; (iv) a contrast between Jews and Gentiles or between Jewish Christians and Gentile Christians – the Gentiles in both cases being the latecomers; (v) an allegory of human life and times of conversion (childhood, adolescence, etc.); (vi) an allegory about world history or salvation-history; (vii) an allegory about spiritual progress; and (viii) a pictorial representation of 21.31: the toll-collectors and prostitutes (= the last) go into the kingdom of God before the Pharisees (= the first).

An interpretive decision – which is between (i) and (ii): the other proposals are foreign to the immediate context – must begin with this observation: Matthew framed 20.1–15 with 19.20 and 20.16. These seem to teach eschatological reversal. Yet is our parable about such reversal? Whereas the last are indeed treated as the first, the first do not become last. The point seems to be not reversal but equality, or rather that the last are given so much. Perhaps then 20.1–15 only illustrates 19.30b and 20.16a (the last will be first), but not 19.30a and 20.16b (the first will be last); or perhaps 19.30 and 20.16 are just roundabout ways of saying that all are equal. In either case, because the 'workers' (cf. 9.38) hired at sunrise gain a reward, it is difficult to identify them with those outside the kingdom; so interpretation (ii) is doubtful. Further, it is best, as the 'for' of v. 1 requires, to see continuity with 19.30, which is a warning to the faithful. Thus 20.1–15 first teaches that the promise of reward should not become ground upon which to stand. Interpretation (i) is correct.

Often cited for comparison is a parable attributed to R. Ze'ra in *y. Ber.* 2.8: 'Sweet is the sleep of the labourer whether he has eaten much or little. Like a king who had hired many labourers, one of whom so distinguished himself by industry and skill that the king took him by the hand and walked up and down with him. In the evening the labourers came, and the skilful one among them, to receive their pay. The king gave them all the same pay. Wherefore those who had worked the whole day murmured, and said: "We have worked the whole day, and this man only two hours, and yet he also has received his whole pay." The king answered: "This man has done more in two hours than you in the whole day."' Despite the attribution to a rabbi who flourished much later than Jesus, and despite the fact that in the rabbinic parable pay is still according to merit, it is possible that both Jesus and R. Ze'ra drew upon a traditional parable and that both modified it in different directions.

There is also a striking if neglected OT parallel. In the face of protest, David, in 1 Sam 30.21–5, decides to reward equally soldiers who fought and those who, because of exhaustion, did not. The narrative ends: 'For as his share is who goes down into the battle, so shall his share be who stays by the baggage. They shall share alike. And from that day forward he [David] made it a statute and an ordinance for Israel to this day.' The verbal links between this and Mt 20.1–15 are, however, insignificant, so we have no proof that the one directly influenced the other.

1. For the kingdom of heaven is like the situation of a householder makes the parable an explication of 19.30 and so about eschatological judgement and rewards.

who went out early in the morning to hire labourers for his vineyard. 'His vineyard' (cf. vv. 4, 7; 21.28, 41), in which the day-labourers work, recalls esp. Isaiah 5 and Jeremiah 12 and so encourages one to think of God and Israel.

2. The first four groups (vv. 2–5) really constitute one group over against those hired last.

agreeing with the labourers for a denarius a day. For 'denarius' see p. 309. Rabbinic sources show that the denarius was a common wage for one day's manual labour: it is neither generous nor miserly.

3. about the third hour would be around 9 a.m.

the marketplace (literally 'agora', as in 11.16; 23.7) of a Palestinian village was something like a modern near eastern bazaar. Presumably this was also the scene of the transaction in v. 1.

4. whatever is right I will give to you. The reader is further drawn into the story by wondering what a fair wage will be.

5. Going out again about the sixth hour and ninth hour, he did the same. The sixth and ninth hours would be roughly 12 p.m. and 3 p.m. For this sort of narrative compression, which reflects relative unimportance, see Mt 22.26; 26.44.

6. about the eleventh hour. The eleventh hour, which would be about 5 p.m.– not long before sundown – interrupts the sequence of hours. The unexpected hour draws attention to itself and hints at more unexpected things to come.

7. no one has hired us. Whether the claim was true – unemployment was a problem then as now – or false is irrelevant: the only point is the men's availability.

You too go into the vineyard. Nothing is to be made of the circumstance that no agreement on wages is mentioned: this is not the proof of a special trust the workers have. Rather, mention of their recompense at this juncture would extend the narrative unnecessarily and diminish the dramatic tension.

8. when evening came. Given 24.43, one might be put in mind of the last judgement.

owner is literally 'lord' and so encourages the reader to identify the figure with God (or just possibly Jesus).

beginning with the last and then up to the first. The use of 'first' and 'last' recalls 19.30 and points ahead to v. 16. The last are paid first so that the first can see all that has occurred. According to OT law, 'the wages of a hired servant shall not remain with you all night until the morning' (Lev 19.13; cf. Deut 24.14–15).

9. If in vv. 1–7 the lord of the vineyard goes out to hire workers, in vv. 8–15 the workers come to him.

each of them received a denarius. The payment is that agreed upon with the first workers in v. 2. The lord of the vineyard is unexpectedly generous.

10. they thought that they would receive more, but each of them also received a denarius. The response of the workers is wholly natural: the more work, the more pay is the first rule of all economics.

11–12. they grumbled against the landowner, saying, 'These last worked only one hour, and you have made them equal to us who have borne the burden of the day and the scorching heat.' Cf. the complaint in Lk 15.28–30. One naturally sympathizes with the workers: it is not just to pay the same wage for different efforts. Bengel, however, got it right: 'The feeling of the discontented labourers concerning the whole day resembles that of Peter, when he indiscreetly alluded to the difference between himself and that rich man'; cf. 19.27.

13. The parable concludes with the householder's words, which amount to two arguments, one based on legal rights, the other on goodness; and the final question invites the reader into the story: am I like the murmuring workers?

Friend, I am doing you no wrong. 'Friend' either underlines the civility of the speaker – in contrast to the protestor who uses no address – and/or simply indicates that the householder does not know the man's name.

14. The accuser now becomes the accused.

Take what belongs to you and go. The third 'go' of the narrative is not an invitation (as in vv. 4 and 7) but a dismissal: the worker is told to go out of the vineyard (contrast v. 2) because he cannot accept the large-hearted actions of the employer.

I choose to give to this last just as I give to you. The householder's motivation for his action is given in the next verse: 'I am good'. This recalls 19.17 ('One there is who is good') and solidifies the equation that householder = God.

15. **Am I not allowed to do what I choose with what belongs to me?** Whether the Greek means 'with (what is mine)' (so most) or 'on (my estate)', the legal principle is valid and becomes all the more so when applied to God, whose decisions cannot be questioned: the divine will should determine all else (6.10; 26.42).

Or is your eye evil because I am good? On the 'evil eye' (= lack of generosity) see p. 99. The meaning is: 'Do you begrudge my generosity?' How can one complain about kindness?

16. Matthew's Jesus now adds editorial commentary.

So the last will be first, and the first last. Cf. 19.30. The last become first through no merit of their own; the first become last by opposing grace.

* * * * *

(i) Many older commentators took the successive groups of labourers to represent stages in salvation-history. This interpretation misses the point entirely. Nearer the truth is that interpretation which discerns in 20.1–16 the lesson that those converted late in life will not suffer disadvantage. The main teaching is indeed about how God rewards human beings according to an unexpected goodness (although that teaching functions as much as warning as encouragement; cf. 19.30). Hence the less deserving may receive as much as the more deserving. Like the Spirit, the divine grace blows where it wills and that destroys all human reckoning and therefore all religious presumption. It is a truth that must be absorbed after the heady promises of 19.28–9: hope should never become self-satisfaction.

(ii) Reading 19.16–30 one might suppose that salvation is according to works: one must obey the Torah and Jesus Christ. But 20.1–15 disallows this simplistic interpretation. For it clearly teaches, albeit in a picture, that there is no necessary proportion between human work and divine reward; or, as Isaac the Syrian provocatively put it, 'How can you call God just when you come across the Scriptural passage on the wage given to the workers?' The parable makes for continuity between the Jesus tradition and Paul.

ANOTHER PASSION PREDICTION (20.17–19)

[17]**And as Jesus was going up to Jerusalem, he took the twelve disciples aside by themselves, and he said to them on the way,** [18] **'Behold, we are going up to Jerusalem, and the Son of man will be delivered to the chief priests and scribes, and they will condemn him to death,** [19] **and they will hand him over to the Gentiles to be mocked and scourged and crucified; and on the third day he will be raised.'**

Parallels: Mk 10.32–4; Lk 18.31–4

This short pericope consists of a brief narrative introduction (Jesus and his disciples are on the way to Jerusalem (v. 17)) followed by a detailed prediction of what will soon happen to the Son of man (vv. 18–19). The prediction itself, prefaced by a remark on present circumstances ('we are going up to Jerusalem'), summarizes the major events subsequent to Gethsemane. Their order is that of the passion narrative, except in the latter the scourging comes before the mocking:

the handing over to authorities	(26.47–56)
the authorities' verdict	(26.57–68)
the handing over to Pilate for	(27.1–14)
mocking	(27.29, 31, 41)
scourging	(27.26)
crucifixion	(27.33–50)
the resurrection	(28.1–20)

Mt 20.17–9 moves the story forward by taking Jesus closer to Jerusalem and by forecasting for a third time, and so emphasizing, upcoming events. As compared with the earlier passion predictions (16.21; 17.22–3; cf. also 17.12), the mention of condemnation to death, deliverance to Gentiles, mocking, scourging, and crucifixion are new. As Jesus nears his end, its shape becomes plainer and plainer. Also plainer and plainer is Jesus' foreknowledge, which is not vague but exact.

17. Jesus now speaks privately, as befits his solemnity. The verse implies that he and the disciples are travelling with others; one thinks of Galileans going to the capital for Passover.

And as Jesus was going up to Jerusalem, he took the twelve disciples aside by themselves, and said to them on the way. It was common to speak of 'going up' to Jerusalem: one ascended both physically (the city was elevated) and spiritually.

18–19. These two verses emphasize humiliation; there is no glory in martyrdom.

we are going up. That Jesus is on his way now makes the following words more urgent: the prediction pertains not to some distant future but to the coming days.

to Jerusalem. So far Jerusalem has, among other things, collaborated with Herod the Great (2.1–12), been the site of a Satanic temptation (4.5), and sent forth Pharisees to test Jesus (15.1). The repetition of v. 17 ('Jesus was going up to Jerusalem'/'we are going up to Jerusalem') adds emphasis, but Jesus' own words also mark an advance over the narrative: he uses the first person plural. Thus he is not journeying alone. Rather are the disciples going with him. It is their calling to endure what he endures (16.24; 20.23 etc.).

the Son of man will be delivered to the chief priests and scribes. The chief priests and the scribes – whose responsibility Matthew accentuates here and subsequently – are first introduced in 2.1–12, where they collaborate with the wicked Herod. In the passion narrative they collaborate with another, Pilate, and the end is like the beginning.

they will hand him over to the Gentiles. Mt 27.1–2, where the chief priests and presbyters 'hand over' Jesus to Pilate. Clearly the 'Gentiles' are represented by their governor.

to be mocked and scourged and crucified. Cf. 27.26, 29, 31, 41.

on the third day he will be raised. So also 17.23; cf. 16.21.

* * * * *

Mt 20.17–19 is surrounded by two sizeable paragraphs having to do with eschatological rewards. But it is not a foreign body disrupting the continuity of chapter 20. The passage not only illustrates 19.30–20.16 but also prepares for 20.20–8. How so? Regarding the connexion with 19.30–20.16, Jesus, as his passion prediction proves, is the chief illustration of the eschatological principle that the last will be first. As for the link with 20.20–8, three points may be made. (i) Mt 20.22–3 refers to 'the cup' that Jesus is about to drink (vv. 22–3) without elaborating on what that cup is. Such elaboration, however, is unnecessary because Jesus, in 20.17–19, has made all plain. The cup is the content of the third passion prediction. (ii) Verse 28 illumines exactly *why* Jesus is willing to drink 'the cup' despite his knowledge that it means mockery, scourging, and crucifixion: his life, given to death, will be 'a ransom for many'. (iii) The tragic solemnity of 20.17–19 is a perfect foil for 20.20; for following Jesus' announcement of pain and suffering we do not next read that his disciples showed concern for him, but only that some people were preoccupied with their own self-centred hopes: who is to be at the right and the left? The loneliness of the passion narrative begins here.

FALSE AMBITION AND TRUE SERVICE (20.20–8)

[20]**Then the mother of the sons of Zebedee came to him with her sons, and kneeling before him, she asked for something from him.** [21]**And he said to her, 'What do you want?' She said to him, 'Command that these two sons of mine may sit, one at your right and one at your left, in your kingdom.'** [22]**But Jesus answering said, 'You do not know what you are asking. Are you able to drink the cup that I am about to drink?' They said to him, 'We are able.'** [23]**He said to them, 'You will drink my cup, but to sit at my right and at my left is not mine to grant, but it is for those for whom it has been prepared by my Father.'**

[24]**And when the ten heard it, they were indignant at the two brothers.** [25]**But Jesus, calling them, said, 'You know that the rulers of the Gentiles lord it over them, and their great ones exercise authority over them.** [26]**It will not be so among you. But whoever wishes to be great among you must be your servant,** [27]**and whoever wishes to be first among you must be your slave –** [28]**just as the Son of man came not to be served but to serve, and to give his life as a ransom for many.'**

Parallels: Mk 10.35–45; Lk 22.24–7; Jn 13.4–5, 12–17

Mt 19.30–20.16 appends warnings to Jesus' promise of eschatological rewards, and 20.20–8 continues in the same vein. Jesus discourages all vanity derived from the hope of participating in God's victory; and he shifts attention to the hard tasks of life in the here and now, for which the Son of man's life-giving service is paradigmatic.

20. Then closely connects the following with the preceding pericope: the passion prediction is trailed by an expression of personal aspiration. One remembers that following the first passion prediction, Peter expresses his opposition (16.22) and that, after the second, the disciples argue over who is greatest (18.1). So following all three predictions there is an inability to take in the idea that Jesus must suffer, that the crown of thorns must come before the crown of victory.

the mother of the sons of Zebedee came to him with her sons, and kneeling before him, she asked for something from him. In contrast with Mk 20.35, the mother of the sons of Zebedee makes the request, not the sons themselves. It is customary to affirm that the evangelist made the mother the inquirer in order to put the sons in a better light: not only do they not make the request but they are, it is perhaps implied, sufficiently young that their mother still looks after them; and she, in turn, as the history of exegesis shows, can be excused because of her parental affection and love for her sons. One wonders, however, whether Matthew's desire to spare the twelve was so great; otherwise why did he so certainly include so much unflattering material? Chrysostom, moreover, took the mother's words to discredit her sons: 'the request was theirs, and being ashamed they put forward their mother.' Perhaps there is influence from 1 Kgs 1.15–21, where Bathsheba appears before king David. The king inquires, 'What do you desire?' She in turn asks for the throne for Solomon. The Greek uses 'kneeling' of the mother (v. 16; cf. v. 31) and 'sit' of the sons (vv. 17, 20; cf. v. 30).

21. Is the reader to imagine that the following request – an illustration of individual ambition in religious disguise – was made in view of Peter's shortcomings (16.22–3; 19.27–20.16), that these last made possible the thought of others becoming pre-eminent? In any case Jesus has already bestowed special privilege upon the two sons of Zebedee (17.1ff.) – and will again (26.36–46).

What do you want? A question on Jesus' lips is rare in Matthew. But here, especially in view of what immediately follows, the counter-question to one bowed before him makes Jesus sound like a king. The request, which is not about the last judgement or the messianic feast but about eschatological rule and places of honour – proximity implies favour – rightly recognizes Jesus' destiny and correctly assumes great authority on his part; and it harmonizes with Jesus' invitation to pray for great things (17.19–20). Still, the request is misdirected (cf. v. 23) and takes no account of what has just been predicted.

Command that these two sons of mine may sit, one at your right and one at your left, in your kingdom. Cf. 19.28; also 2 Sam 16.6 ('all the people and all the mighty were on the right and on the left of the king [David]'); *T. Abr.* 12.8 (the recording angels – angelic attorneys – are on the right and on the left of the eschatological judge); Josephus, *Ant.* 6.235 (Jonathan on David's right, Abner on his left).

Although crowds will soon hail Jesus as the Davidic Messiah, Jerusalem will not see Jesus mount a throne but a cross, and those at his right and left will not be glorified apostles but crucified criminals (27.38). That Matthew intends an allusion to this last scene seems probable: he has modified Mk 10.37 and 15.27 par. so that in both places the wording is exactly the same.

22. You do not know what you are asking. Jesus turns from the mother to the sons, assuming that they concur with her request.

Are you able to drink the cup that I am about to drink? The 'cup' should not be equated with 'temptations' or (with reference to 26.27) given a sacramental interpretation; nor can there be any real connexion with the drink given to Jesus on the cross (27.34, 48). It is also improbable that 'cup' refers simply to death. The targumim do know the expression, 'to taste the cup of death'; but our text speaks of 'drinking'. Additionally questionable is the straightforward equation of 'cup' with martyrdom. It is preferable to turn to the OT, where 'cup' is often used figuratively in texts about suffering, especially suffering God's wrath or judgement. Such usage can also be found in intertestamental literature and Revelation. That this is the proper background for understanding Mt 20.22 par. is confirmed by the parallel in Mk 10.38–9, which speaks of 'baptism' and by this refers not to death but to being overwhelmed by trouble. The cup that Jesus will drink (cf. 26.39), and that his disciples should be prepared to drink (cf. Mk 9.49), is the cup of eschatological sorrow, which will be first poured out upon the people of God. Jesus himself faces God's judgement.

We are able. The boast foreshadows 26.31–5, where the disciples will vainly affirm their determination not to forsake Jesus. There is also an ironic connexion with 26.36–46, the story of Gethsemane: there the sons of Zebedee can do nothing but sleep while Jesus struggles with drinking his cup.

23. You will drink my cup. This creates an interesting verbal link with 'prepared by my Father': despite his intimate relationship with God, Jesus' fate is the cup of wrath.

to sit at my right and at my left is not mine to grant. Here we find one of the few limitations ascribed to Jesus in Matthew; some sort of subordinationism is implied. How this comports with 28.18 is not explained.

but it is for those for whom it has been prepared by my Father. Does 'prepared' (cf. 25.34, 41; 1 Cor 2.9) refer to a past decision (a divine decree, a sort of predestination), or does this read too much into the text?

24. when the ten heard it, they were indignant at the two brothers. One naturally supposes that 'the (other) ten' (cf. v. 17 and the precise 'eleven' of 28.16) are indignant not because they think as Jesus does but because they think like the sons of Zebedee: they are jealous, wanting the best places for themselves. It is as though Jesus' speech in chapter 18, given in response to a quarrel over greatness in the kingdom, has had no effect.

25. This verse marks a transition from focus on the future to focus on the present.

the rulers of the Gentiles lord it over them, and their great ones exercise authority over them. The 'rulers' of the Gentiles and 'the great ones' (cf. v. 26; Rev 19.5) – the first-century Mediterranean reader would inevitably think of the Romans – are counter examples; they do precisely what the Son of man does not (v. 28).

26. It will not be so among you. Historically, certain Anabaptists have cited this verse and the next as reason for Christians not to seek positions of governmental authority.

But whoever wishes to be great among you must be your servant. Cf. 23.11; Cicero, *De officiis* 1.90 ('those who teach that the higher we rise, the more humbly we should walk are clearly giving correct advice'); *m.* '*Abot* 1.13 ('a name made great is a name destroyed'). 'Great' recalls v. 25 and especially 5.19: 'will be called great in the kingdom of heaven'. 'Servant' makes a model of individuals without status or rights.

28. As the climax to vv. 20–8, and as the last word he speaks before going up to Jerusalem, Jesus refers to the Son of man in whom word and deed are one, the true king whose one aim is to benefit his subjects. He himself, destined to have authority in heaven and on earth, is the outstanding example of the first who makes himself last. And his precedent is imperative.

the Son of man came not to be served but to serve, and to give his life as a ransom for many. This probably alludes to Isa 53.10–13. 'Ransom', meaning deliverance by payment, is used in non-biblical Greek primarily of the manumission of slaves and release of prisoners of war. In the LXX, where the meaning is invariably 'ransom-price', it translates several Hebrew roots and appears in various contexts: of the half-shekel poll tax (Exod 30.12); of payment to save one's life after one has killed another (Exod 21.28–32); of buying back mortgaged property (Lev 25.26); of buying an enslaved relation (Lev 25.51–2); and of the redemption of the first-born (Num 18.15). 'Many' may refer to the church. Because, however, the variant of our saying in 1 Tim 2.6 has 'all'; because 'many' elsewhere in the NT sometimes seem to mean 'all' (e.g. Rom 5.15, 19); and because one can identify the 'many' as all except the Son of man, one should probably give 'many' comprehensive meaning.

Mt 20.28 is only one of a network of Matthean texts that cite or allude to Isa 52.13–53.12, the fourth servant song: 8.17 (quoting Isa 53.4); 26.27–8 (alluding to Isa 53.12); 27.12 (alluding to Isa 53.7), and 57 (alluding to Isa 53.9). Taken together these texts strongly suggest that Matthew (i) saw the entire chapter as a picture or forecast of the Messiah and (ii) did not miss, and did not expect his readers to miss, the OT allusion in 20.28.

Mt 20.28 makes Jesus an atonement offering, a substitution, a ransom for sins. But almost every question we might ask remains unanswered. What is the condition of 'the many'? Why do they need to be ransomed? To whom is the ransom paid – to God (so John of Damascus and Calvin), to the devil (so Origen and Gregory of Nyssa), or to no one at all (so Gregory Nazianzus and Abelard)? Is forgiveness effected now or at the last judgement or both? How is it appropriated? Does the theme of imitation extend beyond 20.28a to 20.28b (cf. Col 1.24; 1 Pet 4.13)? Even when 1.24 and 26.26–9 are taken into account, it is impossible to construct a Matthean theory of the atonement. We have in the Gospel only an unexplained affirmation. But perhaps that is inevitable. For the ancients atonement and its attendant themes were firstly matters of experience, not rational reflection.

* * * * *

(i) Mt 20.20–8 communicates next to nothing on the subject of rewards. Who will sit at Jesus' right or left? And on what basis will the Father make his choice (v. 23)? What will it mean to be 'great' or 'first'? The questions go unanswered. The reason is that the text is really about Christology. We read here that Jesus will reign in 'his kingdom', that he will drink a cup of wrath, that he has come not to be served but to serve, and that he will give his life as a ransom for others. Although our scene opens with the spotlight on the wife of Zebedee and her two sons, they soon leave the stage; and regarding the rest of the disciples, the most important thing we learn about them is that they should be *like Jesus*; cf. vv. 26–8. So our text is thoroughly christocentric: all revolves around the Son of man. What matters is his life, his example, his death, his destiny. Only in the light of these things does the passage generate meaning.

(ii) Mt 20.28 is a particularly apt conclusion. When the mother of the sons of Zebedee, at the beginning of the pericope, envisages James and John sitting on the right and left of Jesus in the kingdom, the reader is reminded of 19.28, where the twelve are promised thrones beside the Son of man. It is therefore fitting that the paragraph culminates in a declaration about the Son of man. But here, as opposed to 19.28, the subject is not the Son of man's glory but his service unto death. As in vv. 20–3, visions of grandeur give way to forecasts of suffering and death, for the king cannot rule from his throne until he has, through self-sacrifice, rescued his people.

THE HEALING OF TWO BLIND MEN (20.29–34)

[29]**And as they were leaving Jericho, a great crowd followed him.** [30]**And behold, two blind men were sitting by the way. Hearing that Jesus was passing by, they shouted, 'Lord, have mercy on us, Son of David!'** [31]**The crowd rebuked them, telling them to be quiet. But they cried out the more, 'Lord, have mercy on us, Son of David!'** [32]**And Jesus stopped and called them, saying, 'What do you want me to do for you?'** [33]**They said to him, 'Lord, let our eyes be opened.'** [34]**Being moved with compassion, Jesus touched their eyes, and immediately they received their sight and followed him.**

Parallels: Mt 9.27–31; Mk 10.46–52; Lk 18.35–43

As compared with the longer Mk 10.46–52, Matthew has turned one blind man into two, added 'Lord' on three occasions (vv. 30, 31, 33), made explicit the element of compassion (v. 34), and increased parallelism (cf. v 29 with v. 34, v. 30 with v. 31).

29. From this point on the topography of the narrative becomes much more detailed.

And as they were leaving Jericho, a great crowd followed him. Jesus leaves Jericho before we hear that he entered it. The modern Jericho (er-Riha) is not located at precisely the same spot as either ancient Jericho (Tell es-Sultan) or NT Jericho (about sixteen miles NW of Jerusalem). The latter, which was renovated by Herod the Great, who had a palace there, was over a mile south of ancient Jericho.

30. two blind men were sitting by the way. The two blind men, who sit, are not participants in the festal pilgrimage: they are social outsiders. Whereas Mark's parallel has one blind man, Bartimaeus, Matthew has two unnamed blind men. Why the change? Should we postulate independent tradition? or imagine a contrast with James and John in 20.20–8? or suppose that a double healing is all the more marvellous and so particularly appropriate as the climax of Jesus' ministry of miracles? Or is there assimilation to 9.27 (although then one must ask why there are two men in that pericope)?

'By the way' (cf. 21.8) refers to the pilgrims' route to Jerusalem. Perhaps one should remember that Passover probably was (like our Christmas) a special time for charitable giving, so the blind men appear to be in the right place at the right time. They look, however, not to the crowd but to Jesus for help; and their request is not for money.

Hearing that Jesus was passing by. The line implies that Jesus is the talk of the crowd.

Lord, have mercy on us, Son of David! Cf. 9.27; 15.22; Mk 10.47 ('Son of David, Jesus, have mercy upon me'); *T. Sol.* 20.1 ('King Solomon, son of David, have mercy upon me'). On 'Son of David', which links up nicely with the following pericope, see p. 142. Christian readers who make the same confession will sympathetically identify with the blind men.

31. The crowd rebuked them. The motive for the rebuke – which Jesus, as in 19.13, cancels – is not given, but one supposes that the crowd, hardened to roadside beggars, thinks the men a nuisance; cf. 20.13. In any case this is the first time the anonymous crowd is really at odds with Jesus. This hints at things to come.

But they cried out the more, 'Lord, have mercy on us, Son of David!' The lesson of persistence is obviously close to hand.

32. Jesus stopped and called them. There is no longer any attempt to keep the so-called messianic secret: the blind men are not instructed to be quiet; contrast 8.4; 9.30. Is this because the public ministry is just about finished?

What do you want me to do for you? Jesus' question – he knows the answer already – expresses his own readiness to serve (cf. v. 28) and simultaneously challenges the men to reiterate their faith in concrete form.

34. followed him. The ability to follow is proof of the healing.

* * * * *

(i) Mt 20.29–34, in which Jesus is thrice acclaimed Son of David, prepares for the entry into Jerusalem, where Jesus is again so acclaimed. In this preparation there is subtle irony. For if in 20.30–1 the crowd rebukes the two blind men who call out to the Son of David, in 21.9 the crowd itself acclaims Jesus to be David's Son. In other words, the crowd does precisely what it seeks to prevent others from doing. Its fickleness is plain; and when the reader comes to 21.9, the crowd's sincerity and understanding – although not the truth of its confession – will be suspect.

(ii) Mt 20.29–34 and its synoptic parallels have frequently been allegorized, to wit: the two blind men represent the spiritually blind; when such hear about Jesus and cry out for salvation, obstacles arise; but to those with persistence in faith, Jesus gives sight, that is, brings salvation; after which they must follow Jesus, that is, enter into discipleship. Whether the text was composed to promote such an interpretation one cannot know. It is not, however, impossible: both blindness and sight often carry the requisite symbolic meanings in Jewish and early Christian literature, including Matthew. Nonetheless, manifest signs of an allegorical or symbolic interpretation are absent.

(iii) One wonders whether there might not be a lesson intended in the juxtaposition of 20.20–8 and 20.29–34. In the former, two privileged insiders (James and John) make a request through a third party (their mother). The request is prefaced by no title of respect or majesty, it concerns the eschatological future, and it involves personal exaltation (to sit and the right and left of the Messiah). In the latter, two outsiders (the blind men) make a request that a third party (the crowd) tries to stifle. That request is prefaced by titles of respect and majesty, concerns the present, and is for something necessary that is taken for granted by most (simple sight). Is it perhaps implied that petitions are more likely to be heard when addressed directly, with respect, and for things truly needful?

THE PROPHET-KING ENTERS JERUSALEM (21.1–11)

21 [1]**And when they drew near to Jerusalem and had arrived at Bethphage, at the Mount of Olives, Jesus sent two disciples,** [2]**saying to them, 'Go into the village opposite you, and immediately you will find a donkey tied, and a colt with her. Untie them and bring them to me.** [3]**And if anyone says anything to you, say: "Their Lord needs them." And he will send them immediately.'** [4]**This happened in order to fulfil the word through the prophet, saying,** [5]**'Tell the daughter of Zion, Behold, your king is coming to you, meek, and mounted on a donkey, and on a colt, the foal of a donkey.'** [6]**The disciples went and did as Jesus had directed them.** [7]**They brought the donkey and the colt, and put their garments on them, and he sat on them.** [8]**Most of the crowd spread their garments on the road, and others cut branches from the trees and spread them on the road.** [9]**And the crowds that went before him and that followed were shouting, 'Hosanna to the Son of David! Blessed is he who comes in the name of the Lord! Hosanna in the highest!'** [10]**And when he entered Jerusalem, the whole city was stirred up, asking, 'Who is this?'** [11]**The crowds were saying, 'This is the prophet Jesus from Nazareth in Galilee.'**

Parallels: Mk 11.1–10; Lk 19.28–40; Jn 12.12–19

Our pericope pulls forward several threads from the previous chapters: the theme of prophetic fulfilment (vv. 4–5; cf. 1.22–3 etc.); Jesus' trek to Jerusalem (vv. 1, 10; cf. 16.21; 20.17); his 'meekness' (v. 4; cf. 11.29); and his status as 'king' (v. 5; cf. 2.1–12), 'Son of David' (v. 9; cf. 1.1–18), 'the coming one' (v. 9; cf. 3.11; 11.3), and 'prophet' (v. 11; cf. 13.57). But 21.1–11 also contains two firsts: (i) Jesus' public claim (albeit indirect, through actions, not words) to his own messianic kingship and (ii) recognition by a group ('the crowds') of that kingship; contrast 16.13–4. Together these two firsts (Jesus' claim and the crowds' response) function to challenge Jerusalem, to force her to render a decision: who is this person (cf. v. 10)? All that follows depends upon the city's answer to that question.

Mt 21.1–11 par. is one of many texts that recount the triumphal arrival (*parousia*) of a ruler or military hero. Such texts, which mostly depict military triumphs, tend to exhibit a cluster of motifs, including the approach of the king, public acclamation/celebration (sometimes with song), entrance of city, and cultic activity (including the cleansing of cultic pollution) – all items found in our passage and its sequel. Moreover, 1 Macc 13.49–53, like Mt 21.8, refers to branches. Thus the synoptic story belongs to a type. Three points, however, should be observed. First, Jesus' entry is not one of military triumph. Indeed, our story gains much of its force from the fact that the central figure, the kingly Son of David, is 'meek' and has not in any conventional sense conquered anybody or anything, nor is he about to do so. Second, the synoptics lay great stress on the king's animal(s), and this has parallels only in 1 Kgs 1.32–40 and Zech 9.9. In the other sources cited the mode of transportation is not so much as mentioned. Third, Jesus does not sacrifice in the temple but there protests against abuse of the cult. So this last does not validate him; he rather invalidates it, or rather those who run it.

1–2. If David went from Jerusalem to the Mount of Olives amid cries of lamentation (2 Sam 15.30), Jesus, the Son of David, goes from the Mount of Olives to Jerusalem amid shouts of jubilation.

Bethphage was a small village of Olivet; its location is uncertain, although proposals have not been wanting. In the Talmud, 'Outside the wall of Bethphage' means 'outside Jerusalem'; it was therefore ritually part of the holy city. That the place is mentioned in the Gospels may be explained by its probable etymology, 'house of (unripe) figs'; for the entry into Jerusalem and the cleansing of the temple issue in the story of the barren fig tree.

the Mount of Olives or Olivet is the two and a half mile (= four kilometre) ridge with three major summits just east of Jerusalem, across the Kidron Valley, or the middle summit of that ridge (et-Tur). As the name implies, in antiquity the area was covered with olive trees. OT references include 2 Sam 15.30; 1 Kgs 11.7; 2 Kgs 23.13; Ezek 11.23; Zech 14.4. Grave remains from the sixth century BC to the fourteenth century AD have been uncovered. It is probable that the site was home to a cult honouring the god of death, Nergal, but this fact does not much illuminate the NT texts. On the Mount of Olives and eschatological expectation see on 24.3; 27.51–3. The place was associated both with judgement and the resurrection. How closely it was linked with messianic expectation in the first century is impossible to say.

Jesus sent two disciples, saying to them. The following instructions, which reflect a king's authority, indicate that riding the donkey will be a deliberate, symbolic act.

Go into the village opposite you. 'The village' is probably Bethphage, not Bethany.

you will find a donkey tied, and a colt with her. Cf. 1 Sam 10.1–9 (Samuel's prophecy of coming events, including the finding of lost donkeys). The otherwise superfluous 'tied' probably alludes to Gen 49.11 ('binding his foal to the vine and his donkey's colt to the choice vine'). This line was given a messianic interpretation in Judaism and the church Fathers.

Rabbinic literature makes the donkey a messianic animal. Zech 9.9 was the key text in this development. It in turn arose out of the use of the ass in the Ancient Near Eastern royal ceremony. 1 Kgs 1.33 (cf. 38) supplies an OT example: Solomon rode David's donkey to Gihon to be anointed king; cf. 2 Sam 18.9; 19.26. For the mules of nobility see Judg 5.10; 10.4; 12.13–14; 2 Sam 13.29. Riding on a mule for ceremonial entry into a city is already an act of kingship in a text from the royal archives of Mari; and there is a Sumerian text in which those 'who are raised with the sons of the kings' are referred to as those who ride donkeys.

3. The imperatives of Jesus – who is completely in charge of events – continue to pile up; and his seemingly supernatural knowledge of circumstances continues to be exhibited.

And if anyone says anything to you, say: 'Their Lord needs them.' Some have equated 'their Lord' with God, others with the beasts' owner, who was (on this interpretation) with Jesus. It is preferable to see the title as a self-designation. The messianic beasts belong to Jesus because he is the Lord Messiah who recovers the lordship of Adam over the animals; cf. Gen 1.26–31. For Matthew of course the truth is that Jesus is not only lord of the beasts but also of Jerusalem itself.

Isa 1.3 (LXX: 'The ox knows his owner, and the ass his master's crib; but Israel does not know me') might lie behind our text. Later Christians drew upon the verse to put an ass in the Bethlehem stable at the birth of Jesus.

4. **This happened in order to fulfil the word through the prophet, saying.** Is no prophet named because the quotation is mixed, or because 'Zechariah' would add nothing of theological significance?

5. **Tell the daughter of Zion, Behold, your king is coming to you, meek, and mounted on a donkey, and on a colt, the foal of a donkey.** The first few words of this conflated quotation are from Isa 62.11 and agree with the LXX. Was the beginning of Zech 9.9 ('Rejoice greatly, daughter of Zion') deemed inappropriate in view of Jerusalem's hostility and/or the destruction of Jerusalem in AD 70? Or do we have here a lapse of memory or the unconscious assimilation of like texts ('daughter of Zion' is common to both)? Origen satisfied himself by speaking of 'abbreviation'. According to others, however, 'Say to the daughter of Zion' makes plain that the entrance and acclamation demand a response from Jerusalem. The next several words are from LXX Zech 9.9, although there has been abbreviation: 'righteous and saving is he' does not appear; cf. Jn 12.15. This puts all the emphasis upon Jesus' meekness and the animals and, in view of upcoming events, mutes any notion of triumphalism. The final six words follow MT Zech 9.9 rather than the LXX.

'Daughter of Zion' here means 'the people of Jerusalem', who should hear the word spoken to them and welcome their king. Their response, however, is not to rejoice (as the uncited introduction to Zech 9.9 has it), but rather to question (v. 10).

On 'meek' see p. 67. Here the word adds to the Moses typology and characterizes Jesus as a king who does not conquer. Thus the entry proves Jesus to be innocent of military ambition. He accordingly rides not a war horse (cf. *Ps. Sol.* 17.33) but an ass. While his chosen animal, because of its royal associations, hardly shows him to be poor, it does prove him to be a man of peace. One is reminded of the eastern iconographic tradition in which Jesus rides his donkey side-saddle: that is the posture of a woman, not a warrior.

The Semitic parallelism of MT Zech 9.9 requires that the 'donkey' and the 'colt, the foal of a donkey', be the same animal (the LXX is ambiguous). In Matthew, however, the one animal has become two. Several explanations have been forwarded. (i) The evangelist simply misread the OT (Hebrew or Greek). (ii) He knew, because he was there or learned from one who was, that in fact there were two asses; or at least he had non-Markan tradition to that effect. (iii) The newness of the colt (Mk 11.2) implied the presence of its mother. (iv) Mt 21.5 is part of a wider phenomenon, that of Matthew's tendency to multiply by two. (v) Matthew was thinking of an oriental throne supported by two animals. (vi) Matthew read Zech 9.9 in the light of 2 Sam 16.1–4, where there are two asses for David's household to ride upon.

Rabbinic texts contain numerous tendentious renderings of Scripture which ignore the rules of poetry in favour of excessively literal interpretation. When one adds that some rabbis found two animals in Zech 9.9; that David was presented with two asses (2 Sam 16.1–2); that 'colt, the foal of a donkey' reinforces the impression of

Jesus' meekness; and that LXX Hab 3.2 declares that 'he will be made
known in the middle of two animals', deliberate, theological alteration
– not ignorance of how Hebrew poetry works – seems likely. One
should not forget, furthermore, that rabbinic Judaism used Exod 4.19
to illustrate the principle that the last redeemer (Messiah) will be as the
first (Moses): 'And Moses took his wife and his sons, and set them
upon a donkey. Similarly will it be with the latter Redeemer, as it is
stated, lowly and riding upon a donkey.' Although this particular
tradition is not attested early in the rabbinic corpus, the general
principle it enshrines is: namely, that the Messiah will be like Moses.
Further, the typological use of Exod 4.19–20 in Matthew's infancy
narrative is seemingly proof that the OT text already belonged to
messianic speculation by the first century. This matters because (i)
throughout the First Gospel Jesus is assimilated to Moses; (ii) Moses
was firmly associated with riding an ass; (iii) Matthew's interest in
Exod 4.19–20 is established by its influence upon chapter 2, where the
parallelism between Jesus and Moses is manifest; and (iv) LXX Exod
4.19–20 uses the plural: Moses travelled with ass*es*. One suspects that
Matthew, just like the later rabbis, read Zech 9.9 in the light of Exod
4.19–20, so that it was natural, given the plural in LXX Exod 4.19–20,
to find two animals in the ambiguous LXX Zech 9.9.

6. The disciples went and did as Jesus had directed them. Cf. LXX
Exod 12.28; Mt 1.24; 26.19.

**7. They brought the donkey and the colt, and put their garments on
them, and he sat on them.** Is the image of the disciples draping the
animals with saddle clothes, upon one of which Jesus sits? Or is
Matthew's language inexact? Or is the picture indeed of Jesus
somehow riding on two asses? Whatever the answer, Jesus, unlike
the normal pilgrim, does not approach the city on foot. Instead he
rides. This reflects his extraordinary status: the king sits.

8. Most of the crowd spread their garmemts on the road. In Matthew
Jesus' entry is a popular triumph (contrast Mark and Luke, where the
messianic aspect is more restrained): the parabolic act of riding the
donkey in accordance with Zechariah's prophecy is rightly interpreted
by the crowd as an implicit claim to be the messianic Son of David.
For strewn clothing before a king see 2 Kgs 9.13; Aeschylus, *Ag.* 855–
957 (Clytemnestra talks Agamemnon into walking on purple); *Acts
Pilate* 1.2 (he 'spread his kerchief on the ground and made him [Jesus]
walk on it like a king'); Tg. Sheni Est 8.15 (Mordecai walks on strewn
purple as he is proclaimed king). As clothes represent their wearers,
their position beneath another's feet means submission.

others cut branches from the trees and spread them on the road. In
Mark the reader thinks of straw or leaves placed upon the ground, the

significance of which is not obvious. In Matthew we read of branches, something fitting for a religious procession. That Matthew thought of palm branches in particular (so John) is not said.

9. Hosanna to the Son of David! Cf. MT 2 Sam 14.4; 2 Kgs 6.26; Ps 118.25. Jesus enters Jerusalem not as the Son of God or the Son of man but as the Son of David; cf. 20.30; 21.5. This may reflect the evangelist's conception of Jerusalem as 'the city of David'. Although 'Hosanna' is composed of two words meaning 'save now' or 'save, (we) pray' (cf. MT 1 Sam 14.4), there is evidence that, in Matthew's day, it could also mean 'praise'.

Blessed is he who comes in the name of the Lord! The line is from Ps 118.26. 'In the name of the Lord' may go either with 'blessed' or with 'the coming one'. In the former case people would be blessing 'the coming one' in the name of the Lord. In the other Jesus would be coming 'in the name of the Lord'. Whichever alternative is adopted, the eschatological application of the same line in 23.39 makes the entry foreshadow the *parousia*.

If, in 21.1–11, the chanting of Ps 118 by crowds approaching Jerusalem is followed by their confession of Jesus as a prophet and his protest in the temple, the citation of the same verse in 23.37–9 is bound up with the charge that Jerusalem kills the prophets and the declaration that 'your house' is forsaken. Thus 21.1–11 and 23.37–9 have more in common than the same Scripture. In both the capital (i) fails to acclaim Jesus with the words of Ps 118; (ii) is blind to the appearance of God's prophet; and (iii) has a defiled temple. The difference between the two passages lies in this: that in the first there are some who rightly acclaim Jesus and recognize who he is. The contrast serves to underline Jerusalem's culpability.

Psalm 118 was, according to rabbinic sources, recited during Passover, Tabernacles, and Hanukkah. Originally it may have been a royal processional psalm of thanksgiving, perhaps part of the annual enthronement ritual. If so, and if the psalm's ancient function was known to Matthew and his first readers, that would only have underlined for them the royal dimension. But we cannot be sure, just as we cannot be sure that a messianic interpretation was current in first-century Judaism.

10–11. We are not told what Jesus made of the crowd's reception, but rather about how 'the city' reacted.

the whole city was stirred up, asking, 'Who is this?' The question, 'Who is this?', means not, 'What is this man's name?' but 'What should we make of this person?' The crowd's confession is neither inadequate nor anticlimactic. Rather does it (i) prepare for the prophetic act in the next pericope; (ii) expand the christological perception of the crowd: Jesus is not just the Son of David (v. 9); (iii) supply a foil for the ignorance of those in Jerusalem; and (iv) add to the parallels between Jesus and Moses (Moses was both a prophet and king in Jewish tradition, and 'the prophet' presumably adverts to the eschatological prophet like Moses promised by Deut 18.15, 18; cf. Jn 6.14).

* * * * *

(i) Our narrative serves so well to introduce the subsequent chapters because, as the following parallels make plain, it is largely composed of themes, expressions, and key words that punctuate those chapters:

21.1–11		*21.12–28.10*
21.1, 10	Jerusalem	23.37 (*bis*)
21.1	Mount of Olives	24.3; 26.30
21.2–3	sending ahead of disciples for preparation	26.17–18
21.4	scriptural fulfilment	26.56; 27.3–10
21.5	citation of or allusion to Zech 9–14	21.12–13; 26.15–16, 26–9,30–5; 27.3–10, 51–3
21.5	Jesus as king	27.11, 29, 37, 42
21.6	'the disciples did as Jesus commanded them'	26.19
21.8, 9, 11	'crowd(s)'	21.26, 46, etc.
21.9	'Hosanna to the Son of David'	21.15
21.9	Jesus as David's Son	22.42–4
21.9	'Blessed is he that comes in the name of the Lord'	23.39
21.10	'the city'	21.17, 18; 23.37; 26.18; (27.53); 28.11
21.10	Who is Jesus?	26.63; 27.11
21.11	Jesus as 'prophet'	21.46; 26.68
21.11	'of Nazareth'	26.71
21.11	Galilee	26.32; 27.55; 28.7, 10, 16

Mt 21.1–11 is not just the entry into Jerusalem: it is also the entry into

the remainder of the narrative. By anticipating upcoming events and introducing or reiterating certain themes, the passage strengthens the unity of Matthew 21–8 and prods the reader to interpret the text in the light of itself.

(ii) Kingship does not mean glory. Jesus, in his Mosaic meekness, does not insist on his rights as Jerusalem's king; and Jerusalem, for her part, can do no more than wonder, 'Who is this?' Thus the passage, which records no real triumph, holds much irony and pathos. 'The daughter of Zion', for whose sake Jesus comes, does not comprehend the tumult before her gates or understand that her king has come and that prophecy has been fulfilled. Even the momentary acclamation that Jesus does receive is from those going up to the capital, not from those within it. In short, 21.1–11 is already haunted by the spectre of upcoming events; or, put alternatively, 21.1–11 prepares for and anticipates the dark days ahead: Jerusalem is not the happy goal of Jesus' journey but the way to death and disgrace. As Jesus leaves the sympathetic pilgrims to encounter the hostility of the holy city, he is exchanging his royal mount for a criminal's cross. His exit will not be as his entrance.

(iii) Our story cites two eschatological scriptures, Ps 118.25–6 and Zech 9.9. The former is again cited with reference to the *parousia* in 23.39, and thus it is possible that 21.1–11 is, like 17.1–8 and 28.16–20, a sort of proleptic *parousia*, a foreshadowing of Jesus' eschatological entry into kingly glory. One is emboldened in this idea not only by the mention of 'the Mount of Olives', a location charged with eschatological associations, but also by Jesus' status here as the eschatological Mosaic prophet, and by the fact that the very word, *parousia*, used four times in chapter 24 with reference to the Son of man's return, was, in the Hellenistic world, a technical term for a king's arrival or visit. Moreover, a ruler's *parousia* was typically accompanied by flattering speech (cf. 21.9, 11), a donkey for the baggage (cf. 21.1–7), street improvements (cf. 21.7?), and petitions (cf. 20.29–34).

THE PROPHET-KING IN THE TEMPLE (21.12–17)

[12] And Jesus entered the temple and drove out all who were selling and buying in the temple, and he overturned the tables of the money-changers and the seats of those who sold doves. [13] And he said to them, 'It is written, "My house will be called a house of prayer"; but you make it a den of robbers.' [14] And the blind and the lame came to him in the temple, and he healed them. [15] But when the chief priests and the scribes saw the wonderful things that he did and the children crying out in the temple,

'Hosanna to the Son of David,' they were indignant [16]and said to him, 'Do you hear what these are saying?' And Jesus said to them, 'Yes. Have you never read, "Out of the mouths of infants and nursing babies you have brought perfect praise"?' [17]And leaving them he went out of the city to Bethany, and he lodged there.

Parallels: Mk 11.11, 15–17; Lk 19.39–40, 45–6; Jn 2.13–17

Having entered the capital as king, Jesus, now playing the prophet, next enters the temple, the centre of the world and the symbol of Jewish national identity, and there, through violent deed and scriptural word, declares divine disfavour. The disfavour is not directed against the temple as such but against those who have corrupted the institution, who have prevented the temple from being what God intended it to be, a house of prayer.

12. This verse seemingly implies that, whatever else Matthew took 'meek' to mean (cf. 11.29; 21.5), he did not believe it inconsistent with forceful behaviour.

the temple refers to the whole temple complex. One should think of the outer court, into which Gentiles were permitted. This court was the large enclosure which surrounded the court of women and the court of priests.

all who were selling and buying. The former are the sellers of sacrificial animals and oil and meal, the latter probably not their worshipping customers but the temple treasurers and staff, who bought supplies and engaged in other economic activities. It has been doubted whether trade in sacrificial animals was carried out in the temple court itself. Rabbinic sources locate the shops on the Mount of Olives. But Zech 14.21 already refers to traders in the temple, and *m. Šek*. 1.3 has money-changers in the temple.

he overturned the tables of the money-changers and the seats of those who sold doves. Because temple dues were paid in Tyrian half-shekels and shekels, not Greek or Roman coinage (which had pagan mottos; cf. 22.15–22), money-changers were a necessity. According to *m. Šek*. 1.3, the tables for money-changers were placed in the temple on 25 Adar, that is, three weeks before Passover. So the synoptic chronology makes Jesus' action coincide with a time when financial operations were conspicuous. For the selling of doves see Lev 5.7, 11; 12.6, 8; 14.22; 15.14, 29; Lk 2.24. They were the offering of the poor, and there is a tradition in *m. Ker*. 1.7 in which R. Simeon b. Gamaliel protested against their high cost.

It is possible that Matthew saw in Jesus' deed a fulfilment of Mal 3.1ff. ('Suddenly the Lord whom you seek will come to his temple ...

he will purify the Levites'; cf. Mt 11.10). But because this text is neither clearly cited nor alluded to, it would be wiser to speak more generally of the (partial or initial?) fulfilment of the eschatological hope, found in several places, that the temple and/or its staff will be purified. Yet even that may read too much into the text. The word 'cleansing' connotes restoration; but Matthew's text does not imply this. Jesus simply protests; he does not 'cleanse' or 'restore' anything. Moreover, precisely what he is protesting against – exorbitant prices? the conducting of commercial transactions in the wrong place? something else? – is not evident. The text, to our frustration, tells us nothing more than that something was wrong.

13. My house will be called a house of prayer is from Isa 56.7. For people going up to the temple for the explicit purpose of praying see Lk 18.10; cf. 2 Macc 10.26; Ecclus 51.14; Lk 2.37. One recalls that the incense of the temple symbolized prayer (cf. Ps. 141.2; Rev 5.8), and that Jews outside Jerusalem prayed when the morning and afternoon burnt offerings – which were accompanied by prayers (Acts 3.1) – were made, a fact underlining the intimate link between sacrifice and prayer.

but you make it a den of robbers is not an exact quotation but rather draws upon the language of Jer 7.11, which belongs to a prophecy of the temple's destruction. Here is where the weight of the story lies, in the sorry state of the temple. 'Robber' means more than 'swindler': the word connotes force. Perhaps it is not irrelevant to observe that in 27.47 the representatives of the high priests carry clubs and swords. Some have even thought 'robber' refers to zealots or anti-Roman revolutionaries, in which case Jesus would be attacking such. But the violence more probably pertains to economic extortion; and in any case 'den of robbers' is here, as in Jeremiah, not to be taken literally: it is just a way of saying that the temple harbours people who, from Jesus' point of view, are criminals.

14. And the blind and the lame came to him in the temple, and he healed them. This is the last time Jesus heals anybody in Matthew. David, in 2 Samuel 5, is told by the Jebusites: 'You cannot enter here: even the blind and the lame will drive you away' (v. 6). Verse 8 then reads: 'On that day David said: "Whoever would attack the Jebusites, let him get up the water shaft to attack the lame and the blind, those whom David hates." Therefore it is said, "The blind and the lame shall not enter the house" '; cf. Lev 21.18. Perhaps Matthew's text implicitly contrasts the first David with the Son of David, Jesus.

'The blind and the lame' recalls the catalogue of healings in 11.5 and the list in 15.30–1; cf. also 9.27–8; 12.22; 20.30. Just as 1QSa 2.8–9 excludes the blind and the lame from the messianic banquet, so *m. Hag.* 1.1 excludes them from the temple, or at least from certain parts of it; and MMT (= 4Q394–8) 14.57–62 does the same for the blind and deaf. Did Matthew believe Jesus contradicted this type of discrimination? Or should we simply think of the needy who were a regular sight at the temple (cf. Jn 9.1; Acts 3.1)?

15–16. As in 2.2–3 and 12.23–4, the confession of Jesus as Son of David provokes vigorous opposition. This probably reflects the hostility of the Judaism of Matthew's experience to the proclamation of Jesus as the Messiah.

when the chief priests and the scribes saw the wonderful things that he did and the children crying out in the temple, 'Hosanna to the Son of David', they were indignant and said to him, 'Do you hear what these are saying?' The rhetorical question makes the leaders miserably ungenerous: they even complain about the blind and lame being healed. The chief priests and scribes, although named in the passion predictions (16.21; 20.18), have not been active since their conspiracy with Herod the Great. Their appearance here portends another attempt on Jesus' life.

Ps. 118.25–6, quoted in v. 9, is here again recalled. Interestingly enough, Ps 118.26 has this: 'We bless you from *the house of the Lord.*' Did Matthew or his tradition locate the children's praise in the temple in order to achieve a proleptic fulfilment of this prophecy (which remains future in 23.39)?

Both the identity of those crying 'hosanna' and the place of their crying serve to confirm God's approval of Jesus. For not only were the words of little children sometimes regarded as oracular but temples, the traditional links between heaven and earth, were widely thought of as places of special revelation. Note that in Mt 21.16 God is the author of the praise ('you have brought'). We have here inspired utterance: the acclamation is a miracle.

Jesus said to them, 'Yes. Have you never read?' As in 19.13–15, Jesus defends children against their detractors.

Out of the mouths of infants and nursing babies you have brought perfect praise. So LXX Ps 8.3. The 'infants' (cf. 11.25) and 'babies' are the counterparts of the chief priests and scribes, and represent the response of faith.

The *Mekilta* on Exod 15.1 links Ps. 8 with the song of Exod 15. The exegetical conflation is not peculiar to the *Mekilta;* the two texts were often brought together, and from this developed the well-attested belief that, at the Red Sea, children praised God. The pre-Matthean genesis of this tradition is vouched for by Wisd 10.21, according to which, when Israel crossed the Red Sea, Wisdom 'opened the mouth of the dumb, and made the tongues of babes speak clearly'. Matthew, it follows, inserted into his story of Jesus a motif – the supernatural singing of children as recorded in Psalm 8 – that recognizably belonged to another story, the story of Moses. Given, then, Matthew's fondness for drawing parallels between Moses and Jesus and between the exodus and the Christ event, this fact should colour one's interpretation of 21.12–17.

17. leaving them he went out of the city to Bethany, and he lodged there. The first verb possibly carries symbolic meaning: Jesus, having had the last word, is once and for all turning his back on the priests and scribes. 'Bethany' (meaning uncertain) was a village on the eastern side of the Mount of Olives, approximately two miles (= three kilometres) east of Jerusalem (cf. Jn 11.18). It may be equated with the OT Ananiah (see Neh 11.32) and the modern El-Azarieh (cf. 'Lazarus'). Both the synoptics and John agree that Jesus stayed in Bethany during Passover week (Mk 11.11–12; 14.3; John 12.1, at the home of Mary and Martha). Festal pilgrims often stayed, because of overcrowding, outside Jerusalem proper.

* * * * *

(i) Matthew, writing after AD 70, had no need to attack the Jerusalem temple, nor did he. Rather did he assume its propriety, that is, its foundation in Torah, and its one-time sanctity: God intended the temple to be a house of prayer (21.13), a place for the offering of sacrifices (5.23–4), and a holy site sanctifying the objects within it (23.16–22). If the temple had ceased to be these things, and then ceased to be altogether, the explanation was that God's judgement had come upon Jerusalem: the corruption of the priests and others (21.13; 23.35) and the rejection of Jesus (21.42–3; 22.7) brought destruction (24.2). In all this Matthew falls in line with late first-century Jewish thought: 4 Ezra, *2 Baruch*, and the *Apocalypse of Abraham*, for instance, likewise attribute Jerusalem's tragic demise and the levelling of its sanctuary to Jewish failing. Furthermore, if in Matthew the former functions of the temple have been supplanted by both Jesus and his community, Johanan ben Zakkai evidently used Hos 6.6 ('I desire mercy, not sacrifice') to offer a rabbinic replacement for the temple cult. What is unique to Matthew, then, is neither its interpretation of the destruction of Jerusalem as a divine judgement provoked by sin, nor its proffering of substitutes for the defunct cult, but its christological and ecclesiological slant on those things: Jesus himself and his church absorb the functions that were peculiar to the temple.

(ii) Mt 21.1–17, like the beatitudes and so much else in our gospel, trumpets eschatological reversal. The pericope tells of the meek king who heals those without status (the blind and the lame), the meek king who is praised by those without power (children). Opposed to him are Jerusalem, the great and glorious centre of the nation, and the chief priests and scribes, men of authority, prestige, and influence. So things are upside down. Those who appear to be in charge truly are not, and judgement will soon overtake them, whereas those who appear to be powerless are welcomed by the Messiah, and they will inherit the earth.

THE CURSED FIG TREE (21.18–22)

[18]In the morning, when he was returning to the city, he was hungry. [19]And seeing a fig tree by the side of the road, he went to it and found nothing at all on it but leaves. And he said to it, 'May no fruit ever come from you again!' And the fig tree withered at once. [20]When the disciples saw it, they marvelled, saying, 'How did the fig tree wither at once?' [21]Jesus answered and said to them, 'Amen I say to you, if you have faith and do not doubt, you will not only do what has been done to the fig tree, but even if you say to this mountain, "Be taken up and cast into the sea," it will be done. [22]And whatever you ask for in prayer you will receive, if you have faith.'

Parallels: Mk 11.12–14; 20–6; Jn 14.13–14; 15.7; 16.23

The action against the fig tree is a visual illustration, an enacted parable that inaugurates judgement against that for which it stands, Jerusalem and/or the temple. Nonetheless, only vv. 18–19 focus on judgement. Verses 20–1 have to do with heroic deeds of faith.

18. In the morning, when he returned to the city, he was hungry. In view of what follows, 'he was hungry' (cf. 4.2) turns the tree's barrenness into a failure to serve Jesus.

19. That Jesus now acts 'gratuitously' shows that his deed is symbolically charged.

And seeing a fig tree by the side of the road. We are to envisage a wild fig tree: Jesus does not curse another's property; contrast 8.28–34.

found nothing at all on it but leaves. 'But leaves' means that the tree's appearance is deceptive: the leaves should be a sign of fruit.

And the fig tree withered at once does not correspond exactly to the imprecation, which was about fruit. Yet how else but by withering could the tree visibly and immediately show the effect of Jesus' words?

For the withered fig or fig leaf as a symbol of judgement see Isa 34.4; Jer 8.13 (of Judah: 'no figs on the fig trees, foliage withered'); 24.1–10 (of those Jews not taken into captivity); Hos 2.12 (the wasting of vines and fig trees is part of Israel's punishment; cf. Joel 1.7). In

Matthew the story of the fig tree represents neither God's wrath against the unfaithful in general nor displeasure with Israel as a whole, but rather judgement against Jerusalem and/or those in charge of the temple. Matthew, however, supplies no interpretation; and the commentary (vv. 21–2) highlights something else altogether.

20. How did the fig tree wither at once? In Mark, Peter tells Jesus to look at the cursed tree. In Matthew the disciples direct no imperative to Jesus but, like good pupils, ask a question.

21. even if you say to this mountain, 'Be taken up and cast into the sea', it will be done. In the present context, the mountain could be identified with the Mount of Olives or with the 'mountain of the house of the Lord' (= the temple mount); and some have identified 'the sea' with the Dead Sea. Such speculations, however, appear to be absent from patristic literature, and perhaps that should sound caution.

22. And whatever you ask for in prayer you will receive, if you have faith. Cf. 18.19. Jesus' sayings about faith must be instances of Semitic hyperbole, the sort of thing one finds all the time in the rabbis, in the same class with a camel going through the eye of a needle. They are a poetic and memorable way of exhorting people to pray more and with more confidence. The gospel in any case deconstructs a literal interpretation by offering, in its story of Gethsemane, an example in which Jesus himself has his prayer unanswered; cf. 2 Cor 12.8–9.

* * * * *

Mt 21.18–22 falls between two paragraphs having to do with the temple. In the first Jesus makes a protest, in the second the priests protest against Jesus. So the immediate context encourages us to interpret the cursing of the fig tree as a prophetic act of judgement: the divine wrath has begun to manifest itself against the Jerusalem temple, and the way is being prepared for another people who will produce genuine 'fruit'; cf. 21.43. But there is more to our pericope than this. For one thing, we should find in the extravagant promise for prayer an illustration of Matthew's tendency to balance judgement with kindness. For another, 21.13 refers to the temple as 'a house of prayer', and it is not coincidence that the next pericope has to do with petition. The old temple had, for Matthew, passed away, its place taken by the ecclesia. So the sequence in 21.12–22 (judgement of the old place of prayer, promise of prayer's efficacy within the church) reflects (i) the course of salvation-history and (ii) the replacement of fixed holy space by a portable community; cf. 18.20. With the old house of prayer gone, it was appropriate to give instruction on prayer in the new temple, the Christian community.

THE CHIEF PRIESTS AND ELDERS QUESTION JESUS' AUTHORITY (21.23–7)

²³**And when he entered the temple, the chief priests and the elders of the people came to him as he was teaching, and they said, 'By what authority are you doing these things, and who gave you this authority?'** ²⁴**Jesus answered and said to them, 'I also will ask you one question. If you tell me the answer, then I also will tell you by what authority I do these things.** ²⁵**The baptism of John – whence was it? From heaven or from people?' And they argued with one another, 'If we say, "From heaven," he will say to us, "Why then did you not believe him?"** ²⁶**But if we say, "From people," we are afraid of the crowd; for all hold John to be a prophet.'** ²⁷**So they answered Jesus, 'We do not know.' And he said to them, 'Neither will I tell you by what authority I do these things.'**

Parallels: Mk 11.27–33; Lk 20.1–8

The purpose of the narrative is not to highlight a pronouncement of Jesus but rather to (i) add to the dramatic tension between Jesus and his opponents and (ii) characterize the latter. Moreover, trailing upon the protest in the temple and the cursing of the fig tree, the passage illustrates why Jerusalem and its temple are doomed: the chief priests and elders have turned a deaf ear to God's eschatological envoys.

23. We are apparently back in the outer court, or in one of the surrounding porticos.

the chief priests and the elders of the people came to him as he was teaching. On the 'chief priests' see p. 24, and on 'the elders of the people' p. 272.

By what authority are you doing these things, and who gave you this authority? 'These things', while including the protest in the temple, must also embrace the other actions of Jesus in Mt 21 (including the entry into Jerusalem), as well as his teaching; so the question – which Jesus has already answered by his provocative deeds – is about Jesus' presumption both to act as messianic king and to teach as he does in the subsequent pericopae. It follows that were Jesus to answer, 'I do these things by human authority,' he would contradict his own bold behaviour, but that were he to answer, 'I do these things by divine authority,' he would be laying explicit public claim to messianic status, perhaps thereby blaspheming (cf. 26.64–5), or perhaps thereby violating the idea that God alone will reveal the Messiah, but in any case certainly risking Roman investigation of sedition. Obviously a clever trap has been laid.

24. The opponents' two questions provoke Jesus to compose two counter questions. As usual, he does not publicly make plain statements about his own person.

25. Jesus circumvents his dilemma by moving attention from himself to his opponents. The question is no longer what he thinks but what the chief priests and the elders think.

The baptism of John is an instance of synecdoche: the reference is to John's prophetic ministry.

From heaven means 'from God'; it is analogous to the rabbinic 'from Sinai'.

from people in effect means 'not from God'. Implicit is a comparison between John's prophetic authority (cf. v. 26) and Jesus' prophetic authority; cf. vv. 11, 46. On the level of Matthew's text, John the Baptist has testified to Jesus (3.14); so acceptance of John requires acceptance of Jesus.

Our pericope implies the same source for John's authority as for Jesus' authority. It also records that John was held to be a prophet (v. 26), that the Jewish leaders did not recognize his prophetic authority, and that they feared to speak the truth about John for fear of the crowds. In all this John is like Jesus; for Jesus is similarly regarded as a prophet (vv. 11, 43), he too finds his authority unrecognized by the Jewish leaders, and in his case also these last fear to speak the truth for fear of the crowds (v. 43).

And they argued with one another. The following verses give us the thoughts of the chief priests and elders. But one can hardly object that the narrator is reading minds: the thoughts of Jesus' opponents are manifest from their deeds.

If we say, 'From heaven', he will say to us, 'Why then did you not believe him?' The text presupposes that the chief priests and elders did not submit to John's baptism. When Jesus' opponents consider answering, 'From heaven,' perhaps they suspect the truth but cannot honestly face the implications. Their motivation for keeping silent in any event is fear of entrapment. As Calvin remarked: 'They do not inquire what is true, nor do they put the question to their own conscience.' Cf. Bengel: 'That is an evil mind which, in a holy subject, does not look at the truth but assumes what serves its purpose.'

26. Just as the opening question seemingly left Jesus with only two unsatisfactory responses, so too now are the Jewish leaders left with two unpalatable possibilities. Dilemma matches dilemma.

if we say, 'From people', we are afraid of the crowd; for all hold John to be a prophet. Cf. 14.5 (Herod's fear to put John to death); 21.46 (the fear of the Jewish leaders to arrest Jesus). For John as 'prophet' – something the crowd has just called Jesus – see 11.7–15. The crowd's estimation is not only correct: it is also in line with Jesus' estimation (11.9).

27. We do not know. To avoid losing an argument (v. 25) or raising the ire of the crowd (v. 26), the chief priests and elders feign ignorance. But in this there is no victory. To confess no estimate of John not only reveals blindness to the obvious but also amounts to denial of his prophetic authority. The leaders accordingly indict themselves.

Neither will I tell you by what authority I do these things. Jesus' authority is not placed in doubt by his refusal to answer; rather is it indirectly confirmed: he need not submit to questioning at the hands of the chief priests and elders. His refusal is in fact veiled affirmation.

* * * * *

Mt 21.23–7 is not so much about Jesus (the main point is certainly not that he was a skilled debater or clever philosopher) or John the Baptist as it is about the chief priests and elders. Its first purpose is to characterize certain principals in the subsequent drama. Here we learn that the leaders, upset by Jesus' deeds, inquired of him 'without reason or respect, a thing that was plain to all' (Calvin); and further that, out of cowardly expediency, they respond to his questions by lying against the truth, thereby demonstrating that their own authority is purely human. As if that were not enough, they show themselves to be spiritually less perceptive than those over whom they presume to preside as privileged members of the sanhedrin: the multitudes – here sharply distinguished from their leaders – at least recognize John's prophetic status. On the literary level the effect of all this is to set the passion of Jesus within a moral context: Jesus' death is not the upshot of an unfortunate misunderstanding on the part of uninformed authorities; instead is it brought about by the plotting of self-serving individuals of ill will. The passion narrative, in other words, depicts a struggle between good and evil.

THE TWO SONS (21.28–32)

[28]'What do you think? A man had two sons. And going to the first he said, "Child, go today and work in the vineyard." [29] He answered, "I will not." But later he changed his mind and went. [30] The father went to the other and said the same thing. And he answered, "I (will go), lord." But he did not go. [31] Which of the two did the will of his father?' They said, 'The first.' Jesus said to them, 'Amen I say to you, the toll-collectors and the prostitutes are going into the kingdom of God ahead of you. [32] For John came to you in the way of righteousness, and you did not believe him; but the toll-collectors and the prostitutes believed him. And even when you saw it, you did not afterward repent and believe him.'

Parallel: Lk 7.29–30

The passage falls into two parts, vv. 28–30 (a parable) and vv. 31–2 (commentary/application). Both parts open with questions (vv. 28a, 31a). The first question, which is purely rhetorical, is followed by a very short parable which relates two encounters and their issues. The differences and similarities between the two encounters and their issues are formally reflected by the dissimilarities within the parallelism:

The first encounter and issue	*The second encounter and issue*
The father went to one son	The father went to the other son
The father said: Go work in the vineyard	The father spoke as before
The son answered: 'I will not'	The son answered: 'I (will go), lord'
But later he changed his mind and went	But he did not go

Mt 21.28–30 is a polemical parable which is allegorically interpreted in vv. 31–2: the father represents God; the first son represents toll-collectors and prostitutes, those who were lax in the law but came to obey God through John's ministry; the second son represents the chief priests and the elders, those who, despite their religious profession, disobeyed God by not believing in John. The main function in the broader context is to characterize the Jewish leaders who oppose Jesus.

28. What do you think? 'You' = the chief priests and elders of the people (v. 23), so the following story continues the previous dialogue.

A man had two sons. The usual Greek word for 'son' (*huios*) is probably avoided because, in other parables, it is allegorically associated with Jesus, who plays no allegorical role in this parable.

Child, go today and work in the vineyard. 'Child' is a form of familiar address, a term of affection which makes the subsequent refusal more dramatic.

30. The second son behaves differently from the first:

	word	*deed*
first son	a curt refusal	yet he works
second son	a respectful yes	yet he does not work

The brothers contradict not only themselves but each other.

'I (will go), lord.' But he did not go. The use of 'lord' adds pathos, for it makes the contradiction between word and deed more acute. Further, taken with vv. 31 and 32 one is inevitably reminded of 7.21: 'Not every one who says to me, "Lord, Lord," will enter the kingdom of heaven; but only the one who does the will of my Father who is in heaven.' Three items are shared: 'lord', entrance into the kingdom, and doing the will of the father. Mt 21.28–32 is thus an illustration of 7.21. Note that the absence of 'repented' in v. 30 (contrast v. 29) hints that the second son never had any intention of doing what he indicated verbally: he did not agree to work and then change his mind. He simply spoke empty words.

31.They said, 'The first.' The answer, which is inevitable, becomes a trap by which the speakers pass judgement on themselves. Contrast v. 26, where they were prudent enough to refrain from returning an answer.

In 21.23–22.46 Jesus asks his opponents several questions, to which the answers given are: 'we do not know' (21.27); 'the first' (21.31); 'he will put those wretches to a miserable death, and let out the vineyard to other tenants who will give him the fruits in their season' (21.41); 'Caesar's' (22.21); 'the Son of David' (22.42); and, finally, silence (22.45). These answers are invariably dictated by the question and show no creativity or wit. They are, with one exception, brief and colourless. Two display ignorance (21.27; 22.45) and two are blatantly self-incriminating (21.27, 41). We are left with the impression that while Jesus' opponents were adept at laying traps, they were also good at falling into them. Contrast the answers that Jesus skilfully crafts: they are uniformly creative and clever, memorable and colourful; and they avoid entanglement either by turning a question back on others (21.23–7) or by moving the discussion to another level (22.15–22; 22.23–33). Clearly Jesus' spiritual authority gives him a rhetorical sovereignty.

the toll-collectors and the prostitutes is a phrase that occurs in the NT only here and in v. 32 (but cf. 9.10–11). It is likely that Jesus himself was accused of being in the company of harlots: in the Graeco-Roman world the slur, often baseless, was commonly made against men who banqueted with women. Perhaps that memory or the memory that John baptized prostitutes informed Matthew's choice. In any case their mention is effective: the chief priests and the elders – like Matthew's readers – would have had nothing but utter disdain for prostitutes. These last were, like toll-collectors, outside the law and, additionally, were associated with the Roman soldier camps. To put them ahead of the Jewish leaders dramatically proves that those leaders 'could not be further from the position they boasted of' (Calvin): they were beneath both the unjust and the unchaste.

32. This verse demonstrates that, like the first son in the parable, the chief priests and elders know what is needful. Ignorance therefore cannot excuse them.

the way of righteousness (cf. 22.16, 'the way of God') is a traditional

Jewish expression. In the present context it means 'the right way' or 'the righteous way of life', that is, the moral demands of divine revelation that lead to God and eternal life.

In 3.15 Jesus declares that his baptism by John is a fulfilling of all righteousness. There, as here, 'righteousness' = the will of God. In both places, then, John is (like Jesus) an example of righteous behaviour, a moral model.

you did not believe him. The assertion takes up the language of 21.25 and so confirms the allegorical identification of the second son with the chief priests and elders. It also unmasks the agnosticism of v. 27: the chief priests and elders certainly did come to a decision about John.

the toll-collectors and the prostitutes believed him. That John was accepted by 'toll-collectors and prostitutes' further assimilates him to Jesus, who was embraced by 'toll-collectors and sinners'.

even when you saw it, you did not afterward repent and believe him draws the threads of the narrative together by echoing vv. 25 and 29 as well as the other parts of v. 32; it thus makes an effective conclusion. 'Even when you saw it' refers to the previous clause and implies that the leaders decided against John twice: once when John began his ministry (cf. 3.7ff.), and once after that ministry had moved sinners to repentance.

* * * * *

Chrysostom urged that the two children of our parable 'declare what came to pass with respect to both the Gentiles and the Jews. For the former, not having become hearers of the law, showed forth their obedience in their works; and the latter having said, "All that the Lord shall speak, we will do, and will hearken" (Exod 19.8), in their works were disobedient.' This interpretation of our parable in terms of salvation-history has dominated Christian exegetical history. The list of its proponents is long. And it is not implausible: 21.43 can be taken as confirmatory, and as both toll-collectors and prostitutes were generally reckoned as being beyond the bounds of Torah they were appropriate symbols for Gentiles.

Some recent exegetes, however, have rightly begun to question the consensus of the past. Nothing so far in 19.1ff., the fifth narrative section, has directly addressed Jewish/Gentile relations. Indeed, the section has encouraged the reader rather to think in terms of believing and unbelieving Israel. Our parable, moreover, is explicitly about different responses to John the Baptist, not Jesus or the Christian kerygma. The most natural interpretation, then, is that which finds in our pericope (i) depiction of a divided Israel; (ii) illustration of the first (the chief priests and elders) becoming last and the last (toll-collectors and prostitutes) becoming first; and (iii) characterization of Jesus' opponents as hypocrites. The advent of the Messiah's forerunner, like the advent of the Messiah himself, compels Israel to make a decision that splits it asunder: there are believers and unbelievers. The former tend to come from disenfranchised groups, whereas the latter include individuals of power and prestige who sinned knowingly.

THE PARABLE OF THE WICKED TENANTS (21.33–46)

[33]**'Hear another parable. There was a householder who planted a vineyard, and he put a fence around it, and he dug a wine press in it, and he built a watchtower, and he leased it to tenants and went away to another country. [34]When the season of fruits drew near, he sent his slaves to the tenants to get his fruit. [35]But the tenants, seizing his slaves, beat one, killed another, and stoned another. [36]Again he sent other slaves, more than the first; and they did the same to them. [37]After that, he sent his son to them, saying, "They will respect my son." [38]But when the tenants saw the son, they said to themselves, "This is the heir; come, let us kill him and gain his inheritance." [39]So they took him and threw him out of the vineyard, and they killed him. [40]So when the owner of the vineyard comes, what will he do to those tenants?' [41]They said to him, 'He will put those wretches to a miserable death, and lease the vineyard to other tenants who will give him the fruits in their season.' [42]Jesus said to them, 'Have you never read in the scriptures: "The stone that the builders rejected has become the cornerstone; this was the Lord's doing, and it is marvellous in our eyes"? [43]Therefore I say to you, the kingdom of God will be taken away from you and given to a people that produces the fruits of it.' [[[44]The one who falls on this stone will be broken to pieces; and it will crush anyone on whom it falls.]] [45]When the chief priests and the Pharisees heard his parables, they perceived that he was speaking about them. [46]And wanting to arrest him, they yet feared the crowds, because they regarded him as a prophet.**

Parallels: Mk 12.1–12; Lk 20.9–19

Mt 21.33–40 is an allegory about faithlessness and judgement. Its character as an allegory does not mean that it is not true-to-life – it largely seems to be – or that every element has a symbolic meaning, only that equations for the main elements can be given:

> vineyard stands for Israel/Jerusalem/kingdom
> householder stands for God

tenant farmers stand for leaders of Jerusalem/Israel
fruit stands for what is owed to God
rejection of servants stands for rejection of prophets
sending + rejection of son stand for sending + rejection of Jesus
tenants punished stands for Jerusalem destroyed
new tenants stand for the church

Our parable and its interpretation combine the traditional motif of the rejection and even murder of the prophets with the traditional metaphor of Israel as God's vineyard. What is new is the joining of the two themes in the service of Christology: the rejection of Jesus is the climax in the story of rebellion against Israel's God.

33. The scene is set by borrowing from LXX Isa 5.2, although the order of events recounted is not the same:

Matthew	*LXX Isa 5.2*
planting vineyard	raising fence
	digging trench
raising fence	planting vineyard
digging winepress	building tower
building tower	digging winepress

The transparent use of Isa 5.2 means that we have an allegory: as in Isaiah 'the vineyard of the Lord of hosts is the house of Israel' (Isa 5.7), and the owner must be God.

he put a fence around it, and he dug a wine press in it, and he built a watchtower. Fences were built around vineyards to keep out animals and human intruders. Towers were elevated lookouts and perhaps also supplied shelter for tenants (cf. 2 Chr 26.10; Isa 1.8); and indeed a wine press has been uncovered just north of ancient Nazareth with beautiful walled terraces and three circular stone towers. So the details of v. 33 should probably not be regarded as evidence of special care for the vineyard and so as a symbol of God's love for Israel (although most interpreters have imagined otherwise). They simply make plain that the owner made a substantial investment and should have expected a good return. Cf. Isa 5.3: 'What more was there to do for my vineyard?'

he leased it to tenants and went away to another country. Absentee landlords – often Gentile foreigners – were common in first-century Palestine. Here we may think of a vineyard in Galilee owned by a man living outside of Galilee. His absence requires that others be responsible.

In Matthew's allegorical interpretation, the wicked tenants are the leaders in Jerusalem, including the priests. It is therefore of interest to observe that the targum on Isa 5.2 refers both to the sanctuary and the altar and that, according to *b. Suk.* 49a, ' "And planted it with the choicest vine" refers to the temple' (cf. *t. Suk.* 3.15). Moreover, 4Q500 depends upon Isa 5.1–7 and appears to locate the Lord's vineyard on the temple mount. Thus an application of Isa 5.2 to the temple was already known in the first century.

34. When the season of fruits drew near, he sent his slaves to the tenants to get his fruit. Cf. 22.2; also Ignatius, *Eph.* 6.1 ('Everyone whom the master of the house sends to do his business ought one to receive as him who sent him'). 'The season of fruits' = harvest, presumably the harvest five years after the planting (Lev 19.23–5).

35. The tenants do not respect the owner. They desire only their own gain – which will bring their own loss.

seizing his slaves, beat one, killed another, and stoned another. 'Killed' appears in Matthew often – of the deaths of prophets (23.34, 37), John (14.5), disciples and Christians (10.28; 24.9), and Jesus (16.21; 17.23; 26.4); thus the word points to a sad continuity in salvation-history. 'Stoned' appears again of the stoning of prophets in 23.27. It is appropriate here because it (i) refers to a mode of execution which involved the participation of a group and so speaks of communal responsibility; (ii) makes for an ironic wordplay with v. 43 ('stone'); and (iii) gives the order of the verbs (beat, kill, stone) 'a climax, in which the third step is an atrocious species of the second' (Bengel): stoning was a brutal and shameful death, one legislated as punishment for blasphemy, idolatry, divination, child sacrifice, adultery, and sabbath violation.

36. The act of sending is repeated. But more slaves means redoubled effort.

Again he sent other slaves, more than the first. Cf. 22.4. 'More than the first' makes the second sending more significant than the first, just as the third will be more significant than the second. Hence the phrase adds to the dramatic development (it is not an allegorical element indicating some particular historical episode or period). The reader is unsure whether another year has passed and so another harvest, or whether action is taken immediately upon news of the first servants.

37. After that, he sent his son to them. Presumably the man's son would have legal authority whereas the slaves would not.

38. they said to themselves recalls 21.25 and encourages the identification of the wicked tenants with the Jewish leaders: both groups consist of conspirators.

This is the heir; come. Jesus 'the son' is also called 'the heir' in Heb 1.2, and there too he comes 'last', after the sending of 'the prophets' to 'our fathers'.

let us kill him and gain his inheritance. It has been suggested that, as

Jesus spoke the parable, the activity of the tenants presupposes that the owner is dead; so if the son is killed, no other claim to the vineyard will be made. But in Matthew at least vv. 40–1 disallow this. Perhaps the assumption is that attempts to gather revenue have been so costly that no more will be made, or that the son has already been deeded the property. Or do we have here an instance of irrational behaviour?

40. So when the owner of the vineyard comes, what will he do to those tenants? Most commentators have thought of the destruction of Jerusalem in AD 70; cf. 22.7.

41. The owner's patience will be exhausted by the murder of his son, and he will act according to the *lex talionis*: murder calls forth murder.

They said to him, 'He will put those wretches to a miserable death, and lease the vineyard to other tenants who will give him the fruits in their season.' Cf. *Apoc. Pet.* E 2 ('If it does not then bear fruit, we will immediately remove its roots from the garden and plant another one in its place'). Matthew's line emphasizes the culpability of the Jewish leaders: they speak their own condemnation; cf. 21.31. It further stresses their wickedness, introduces new keepers of the vineyard – not Gentiles but the church, or perhaps church leaders – who will give the owner what is his (cf. v. 43), and inserts an allusion to Ps 1.3.

42. The scriptural proof text from the Psalms – which amounts to another prediction of Jesus' passion and resurrection – declares that the rejected one (the son = Jesus = the stone) is subsequently vindicated by God. The theme shifts from revenge to triumph.

Have you never read in the scriptures. The indictment obviously concerns not knowledge of Scripture but understanding and taking it to heart.

The stone that the builders rejected has become the cornerstone; this was the Lord's doing, and it is marvellous in our eyes. So Ps 118.22. The proverbial-sounding line, which is secondary in this context, belonged to early Christian apologetical tradition and emphasized Jesus' rejection by unbelievers and his vindication by God. In the OT it appears to be about Israel, rejected by the nations; or, less probably, about the Israel's king. Here the subject is Jesus himself, rejected by the Jewish leaders, vindicated by God.

The image is probably not of a foundational cornerstone but rather an elevated copestone or the last stone at the top of a corner, for (i) Ps 118.22 is, in *T. Sol.* 22–3, quoted of the stone that completes Solomon's temple; (ii) the Syriac translation of Ps 118.22 and Symmachus concur that the stone is the head of the building; and (iii) patristic witnesses, including Hippolytus, Tertullian, and Aphraates, identify our stone with the crown of a building.

Implicit here, as in 16.13–20, is the notion of the church as a new temple. The idea is particularly appropriate at this juncture because Jesus has just indicated, in vv. 12–22, that judgement hangs over the temple in Jerusalem; and our parable has just foretold the destruction of Jerusalem, including its temple. Thus the end of the old temple coincides with a new temple.

43. Therefore I say to you, the kingdom of God will be taken away from you and given to a people that produces the fruits of it. Cf. 1 Sam 15.28 ('The Lord has torn the kingdom of Israel from you this day and has given it to a neighbour of yours'); 7.27 ('The kingdom ... will be given to the people of the saints of the Most High'); Mt 13.12; 25.28–9; 1 Pet 2.9 ('a holy nation' = the church). This verse stands in tension with the parable, in which the issue is not production of fruit but who should profit from that fruit. While a few exegetes have taken the transference of the kingdom to take place at the last judgement, it is more common to think of the 'people' (= the church and/or its leaders) gaining the kingdom upon the death and resurrection of Jesus, because vv. 41 and 42 have reminded the reader of those two events. As in v. 42, the main verbs are divine passives: God is the implicit subject.

[[**44.** This verse, which is missing in several early, important witnesses, appears to be secondary, a scribal addition from Lk 20.18.]]

45. The distinction between the hypocritical leaders and the crowds they seek to persuade is apparent in this verse. Note too the irony: having just themselves uttered what will happen to those who killed the householder's son, they now invite the same fate by scheming to kill the Son of God.

When the chief priests and the Pharisees heard his parables, they perceived that he was speaking about them. That the leaders grasp part of the meaning of the parable means that Jesus has answered their question about authority (v. 23): he claims to have been sent by God just as were the prophets of old.

46. wanting to arrest him, they yet feared the crowds. Cf. 21.26.

they regarded him as a prophet. The remark appropriately concludes the pericope by recalling the story-line, in which the son is, allegorically, the last of God's prophetic envoys.

* * * * *

(i) Mt 21.28–32, 33–46 and 22.1–14 share similar themes, related constructions, and much common vocabulary. The parallels do more than forge an artistic unity: they also create a thematic coherence by encouraging readers to expect similar meaning, which expectation is fully met. All three parables are about failure: the failure to work in a vineyard (vv. 28ff.), the failure to hand over the produce of a vineyard

(vv. 33ff.), and the failure to attend a king's celebration (22.1ff.). On the allegorical level, moreover, all three failures are, as the parallels hint, the very same failure: namely, the failure of the Jewish leaders to heed God's messengers.

(ii) Mt 21.33–46 should not be summarized as an allegory about God's rejection of the Jews and the Gentiles' acceptance of Jesus. First, the parable itself identifies the tenants not with the Jews in general but with the Jewish leaders in particular, with those who had the power of capital punishment. Second, the parable's context is the conflict between Jesus and the leadership of Israel, not Jesus and Judaism. Third, it is not the vineyard = Israel that suffers judgement, but the tenants in charge of the vineyard. Fourth, whereas Isaiah 5 has to do with all Israel and Judaea, some Jewish tradition associates the OT text especially with the temple; and it should be remembered that 21.18–22 connects the temple with the theme of producing fruit. So it is misguided to interpret the parable as though it concerns ethnic relations. 'The kingdom of God will be taken away from you' refers to the Jewish leaders, the new 'people' to the church, consisting of Jews and Gentiles. Furthermore, nothing at all is implied about the eschatological fate of Israel. While many exegetes have found in our passage the final dismissal of the Jews, that is eisegesis.

INVITATIONS TO A ROYAL WEDDING FEAST (22.1–14)

22 [1]**And again Jesus spoke to them in parables, saying:** [2]**'The kingdom of heaven is like the situation of a king who gave a wedding feast for his son.** [3]**And he sent his slaves to call those who had been invited to the wedding feast, but they would not come.** [4]**Again he sent other slaves, saying, "Say to those who have been invited: Look, I have prepared my dinner, my oxen and my fat calves have been slaughtered, and everything is ready; come to the wedding banquet."** [5]**But they made light of it and went away, one to his farm, another to his business,** [6]**while the rest seized his slaves, mistreated them, and killed them.** [7]**The king was angry. He sent his troops, destroyed those murderers, and burned their city.** [8]**Then he said to his slaves, "The wedding is ready, but those invited were not worthy.** [9]**So go into the main streets, and invite everyone you find to the wedding feast."** [10]**Those slaves went out into the streets and gathered all whom they found, both good and evil; so the wedding hall was filled with guests.** [11]**But when the king came in to see the guests, he noticed a man there who was not wearing a wedding robe,** [12]**and he said to him, "Friend, how did you get in here without a wedding robe?" And he was speechless.** [13]**Then the king said to the attendants, "Bind him hand and foot, and throw him into the**

outer darkness, where there will be weeping and gnashing of teeth."
¹⁴For many are called, but few are chosen.'

Parallels: Lk 14.15–24

Mt 22.1–10 is an allegory much influenced by 21.33ff. The king is God. His son is Jesus; cf. 21.37–8. The royal wedding feast is the eschatological banquet. The dual sending of the servants is, as in the preceding parable, the sending of God's messengers. The murder of the servants represents the murder of the prophets and Jesus; cf. 21.35–9. And the third sending of servants is the mission of the church, in which good and evil stand side by side until the end. All this has been evident throughout the history of exegesis. Here the traditional allegorical interpretation has been correct.

It is possible that our parable was partly inspired by a traditional parable. *Y. Sanh* 6.23c has this: 'Two pious men lived together in Ashkelon, devoting themselves to the study of the Law. One of them died and no honour was paid to him at his funeral. Bar Mayon, a tax collector, died and the whole town honoured his funeral. The remaining pious man was deeply disturbed and cried out that the wicked in Israel did not get their deserts. But his dead companion appeared to him in a dream and told him not to despise the ways of God in Israel. He himself had committed one evil deed and hence had suffered dishonour at his funeral, whereas Bar Mayon had committed one good deed and for that had been honoured at his. What evil deed had the pious man committed? On one occasion he had put on his phylacteries in the wrong order. What good deed had the tax collector done? Once he had given a breakfast for the leading men of the town and they had not come. So he gave orders that the poor were to be invited to eat it, lest it should go to waste. After some days the pious man saw his dead companion walking in the garden of paradise beside fountains of water; and he saw Bar Mayon the tax collector lying on the bank of a river; he was striving to reach the water and he could not.' Given that this is a variant of the tale in Lk 16.19–31, perhaps Jesus mined one folk tale for two parables

1. Jesus is still speaking to the chief priests and scribes; cf. 21.45.

in parables either refers to the three parables in 21.28–22.14 or simply means 'parabolically'.

2. a king who gave a wedding feast for his son. 'Wedding feast' and 'son' link our parable to 25.1–13 (the parable of the ten virgins) and 21.33–45 (the parable of the wicked tenants) respectively. The reader naturally identifies the son with Jesus, this because (i) the son of the previous parable is Jesus; (ii) in 9.15 and 25.1 Jesus is the bridegroom;

(iii) God is often king in Matthew (cf. 5.35 and 'kingdom of God') and Jesus is his son (3.17 etc.); and (iv) other early Christian texts speak of the eschatological wedding feast of Jesus Messiah (e.g. Rev 19.7, 9). In the background is the Jewish expectation of a messianic feast.

3. he sent his slaves. Matthew's text assimilates to 21.34. Here, as there, the servants stand for God's messengers.

to call those who had been invited to the wedding feast refers not to an invitation but to a notice that an occasion for which invitations have already been issued is about to begin; this means that, when the refusal of the high honour comes, people are going back on a previous promise – which fact reminds us of the disobedient son in 21.30 (he first says yes and then does otherwise), and of the tenants in 21.35–6, who make an agreement but do not abide by it. Presumably the celebration would go on for a couple of days or more.

4. The king, out of kindness, repeats his summons. This time a description of the feast adds incentive to attend.

5. one to his farm, another to his business. In Luke three individuals concoct excuses. One must go and see a field newly purchased, another must examine a newly purchased yoke of oxen, and another has just been married. The first two add: 'I pray you, have me excused.' In Matthew all this is severely abbreviated, every note of politeness is absent, and even the lame excuses – which could have no allegorical meaning – are gone. Guilt has been heightened.

Matthew does not implicate all those invited to the feast equally. Some are not hostile but indifferent. This reflects recognition that Israel is not at one in its response to God's messengers. Some repent. Some are apathetic. Others became violent.

6. What follows seems an absurdly exaggerated response, but it accords with Matthew's passion narrative: the crucifixion of the Son of God is both monstrous and inexplicable.

the rest seized his slaves, mistreated them, and killed them. Cf. 21.35. For the mistreatment of a king's messengers see 2 Sam 10.4.

7. The king now treats those who have mistreated his servants as though they are rulers of a city, not ordinary citizens. This furthers the allegory.

The king was angry. He sent his troops, destroyed those murderers, and burned their city. Cf. Isa 5.24–5 (where God's wrath against Israel is expressed as fire) and *Exod Rab.* on 12.19 ('God was like a king who made festivities in honour of his son and slew his enemies'). The line reflects the destruction of Jerusalem in AD 70.

In Jud 1.7ff. king Nebuchadnezzar sends messengers to ask people to join him. The people refuse. The king then becomes angry and determines to kill those who sent his servants back empty-handed.

There is, especially given the lack of significant verbal parallels between Judith's story and Mt 22.1–14, no reason to postulate a literary connexion. Rather do we have here a literary motif; cf. 2 Sam 10–11. Particularly common are three items: the sending of soldiers, the killing of inhabitants, and the burning of their city.

8. The wedding is ready, but those invited were not worthy. Bengel: 'the past [tense] ... leaves the unworthy behind more significantly.'

9. The command to go and invite 'whomever you find' stands for the universal mission of the church.

10. both evil and good. The order, 'evil' before 'good', perhaps makes the former emphatic. Conceptually close is 13.47–8 (although there not the church but the world is in view). For Matthew, as for Augustine against the Donatists, the church is a mixture not to be sorted out by anyone save God at the end.

11. This line allegorically describes the last judgement, which extends to those within the church. The one man obviously stands for a whole class.

when the king came in to see the guests, he noticed a man there who was not wearing a wedding robe. Because of Rev 19.8 ('for the fine linen is the righteous deeds of the saints'), the wedding garment has often been equated with good works or the doing of righteousness: to enter God's palace one must have pious and righteous works. But one may also equate the wedding garment with the resurrection body or its garment of glory, which were typically imagined to be luminous and angelic. This second interpretation harmonizes with 13.43, according to which the saints will shine like the sun. In either case the guest is not properly prepared for the messianic feast.

A third interpretation is also possible. The garment might be identified with the baptismal garment. Certainly later Christian tradition spoke of baptismal 'robes'; and disrobing before and dressing after baptism are already presupposed in Paul's epistles. Yet this interpretation, which requires that the guest without a wedding garment is not a member of the community but rather an unbaptized outsider, eliminates the hortative dimension of the text and improbably gives us instead a lesson on the necessity for baptism.

12. how did you get in here without a wedding robe? The verse assumes that the man could and should have worn the proper garment, and that his doing otherwise was an insult to the king and therefore the guests.

he was speechless. Cf. the silence of the Sadducees in 22.34. Silence here implies no excuses.

13. This verse is not part of the allegory but an added piece of eschatological teaching: the 'outer darkness' is hell, not an earthly prison.

Bind him hand and foot. 'What else does the binding of hand and foot mean than the utter privation of power?' (Bernard of Clairvaux).

throw him into the outer darkness. Mt 22.11–13 may presuppose a Jewish tradition about the evil Azazel. According to *1 En* 10.4–5, God instructed the angel Raphael to bind Azazel 'hand and foot and throw him into the darkness'. And according to *Apoc. Abr.* 13.14, the fallen Azazel lost his heavenly garment, which will be given to Abraham. All this is strikingly close to our text, in which, in the context of the eschatological banquet, God instructs his angels (cf. above) to cast into the darkness the man without a wedding garment. Given the possibility that Matthew knew *1 Enoch* and that the book was otherwise well known in early Christian circles, literary influence is likely. But how does acceptance of the thesis influence interpretation of the text? Certainly we cannot equate the ill-prepared man with Azazel. Rather should we think of his fate as akin to that of Azazel. Just as the righteous will wear garments of glory and so be like the heavenly angels, so will the wicked be unclothed and suffer like the fallen angels.

14. The reader may think of Judas, who was 'called' (10.1–4) but not 'chosen'.

many are called, but few are chosen. Cf. 4 Ezra 8.1 ('The Most High made this world for the sake of many, but the world to come for the sake of the few'), 3 ('Many have been created, but few will be saved;' cf. 7.47–8; 8.55); *2 Bar.* 44.15 ('For the coming world will be given to these, but the habitation of the many others will be in the fire'); Plato, *Phaed.* 69c ('Many bear the emblem [of the cult], but the devotees are few'); and *b. Mena* 29b ('the righteous men therein [in the world to come] are few'). Our line does not appropriately conclude the parable if the words are taken literally and the reference is to the king's final invitations; for we read of only one guest being cast out. So it seems better either to give the words a Semitic meaning ('All are called but not all are chosen') and/or to apply the verse to the entirety of the parable: many were indeed called, for a summons went out three times; but only some (those asked at the end) responded. In either case the use of 'chosen' coheres nicely with the rest of the parable, in which the king = God has been the chief actor and in total control from the beginning. Still, it is quite clear from the parable that individuals make their own choices: the parable itself does not teach an Augustinian doctrine of election, and we do not have here either the pessimism of 4 Ezra or a numerical estimate of how many will fail the last judgement. Rather we have exhortation. It is not enough just to be called. In the words of Eph 4.1, one must walk 'worthy of the calling'.

* * * * *

Mt 22.1–14 carries forward the two main points of the previous two parables: first, the polemic against the Jewish leaders is, through the introduction of vv. 6–7, continued, and second, the theme of the kingdom passing from the people of Israel to a non-ethnic entity with a universal mission is reiterated; cf. 21.31, 41. But 22.1–14 also includes something new. Vv. 11–14 turn attention from outsiders to insiders, from opponents to the church. In this we again see Matthew's pastoral concern. The evangelist was all too aware that criticism of others as well as the doctrine of election (cf. v. 14) are both fraught with moral peril; for the former tends to nourish complacency – censure of our enemies always makes us feel better about ourselves – while the latter can beget feelings of superiority. Matthew, however, understood that while censure has its necessary place in moral instruction, and while election is of the essence of Judaism, the two things can foster illusions. Thus it is that Christian readers of 22.11–14, who necessarily identify with those at the king's banquet, cannot read the text and feel self-satisfaction over the wrath that overtakes others. They must, as the homilies on this text throughout the centuries prove, instead ask whether they are like the man improperly clothed, whether they are among 'the many' despite profession to be among 'the few'. God's judgement comes upon all, including those within the *ecclesia*. The author of 1 Peter well understood this when he wrote that judgement begins with the household of God.

GIVING TO CAESAR (22.15–22)

[15]**Then the Pharisees, upon departing, took counsel that they might entrap him in his speech.** [16]**And they sent to him their disciples, along with the Herodians, saying, 'Teacher, we know that you are true, and that you teach the way of God in accordance with truth, and care not for anyone; for you do not regard people with partiality.** [17]**Tell us, then, what you think. Is it lawful to pay taxes to Caesar, or not?'** [18]**But Jesus, knowing their malice, said, 'Why do you put me to the test, you hypocrites?** [19]**Show me the coin for the tax.' And they brought him a denarius.** [20]**Then he said to them, 'Whose image is this, and whose inscription?'** [21]**They answered, 'Caesar's.' Then he said to them, 'Give then to Caesar the things that are Caesar's, and to God the things that are God's.'** [22]**When they heard this, they were amazed; and they left him and went away.**

Parallels: Mk 12.13–17; Lk 20.20–6

This pericope open a series of discussions that runs through the remainder of chapter 22. The first discussion pits Jesus against Pharisees and Herodians (vv. 15–22); the second against the Sadducees (vv. 23–33); the third against a Pharisaic lawyer (vv. 34–40); and the fourth against the Pharisees (vv. 41–6). Taken together, the four passages continue the negative characterization of Jesus' opponents, the Jerusalem leaders, a characterization that has been to the fore since 21.23. But there is also a special connexion with the parable of the vineyard. This last concerns the giving to God of 'fruits in their season'. That too is the subject of our paragraph.

15–16. 'Entrap' is used because to answer 'Yes' to the subsequent question – as we would expect of one rumoured to be a friend of toll-collectors (11.19) – would alienate nationalists opposed to taxation, whereas 'No' – the expected answer of one who made himself out to be the 'king of the Jews' – would open Jesus to the charge of sedition. Jesus faces a dilemma.

And they sent to him their disciples. The Pharisees' 'disciples' are mentioned only here in the First Gospel.

the Herodians. The identity of the 'Herodians' is, despite their being conveniently described in most of the commentaries, unknown. It is possible they were Essenes, for Josephus tells us that the Essenes won the favour of Herod the Great. However that may be, there is insufficient evidence to prove that the Pharisees would have answered the question posed to Jesus in one way (it is not permitted), the Herodians in another (it is permitted), so that each party represents one horn of the dilemma.

Teacher, we know that you are true. 'You are true' = 'you speak the truth'. This comment and those that follow are not only hypocritical (v. 18) but ironic: Jesus' opponents speak the truth unwittingly. The words serve, moreover, to distinguish Jesus from his adversaries: unlike him they are not 'true' but rather 'hypocrites' (v. 18). Their flattery additionally flaunts their irrationality; for it should be as obvious to them as to the reader that Jesus cannot be moved by adulation.

you teach the way of God in accordance with truth. Cf. Jn 14.6 ('I am the way and the truth'). 'The way of God' means 'the way (= behaviour) demanded by God', that is, the demands of the Jewish halakah. The phrase makes Jesus like John the Baptist, who came 'in the way of righteousness' (21.32).

and care not for anyone; for you do not regard people with partiality. Because the speakers are hoping Jesus might speak like a usurper of the government, they, 'in saying, "You care not for anyone," and "You regard not the face of anyone," were hinting at Herod and

Caesar' (Chrysostom). In other words, v. 16 is designed to embolden Jesus to speak his mind, without regard for the consequences.

17. Tell us, then, what you think. The line emphasizes not what the law says (see v. 17b) but what Jesus himself thinks, which is what the opponents want to hear.

taxes to Caesar refers to the Roman *census*, a tax upon agricultural yield (*tributum soli*) and personal property (*tributum capitis*). The *tributum capitis* was collected through census, or registration (Lk 2.1–5; Acts 5.37), and probably amounted to one denarius a year. Although Jewish authorities (including the sanhedrin) helped farm the tax, many Jews resented it and objected on religious grounds. Indeed, although Roman taxation had been a reality since 63 BC, the census of AD 6 or 7, when Judaea came under direct Roman control, encouraged the revolt of Judas of Galilee; and resentment of Roman taxation also surely contributed to the unrest that culminated in the later revolt against Rome. Thus the question of our verse, a question that, in one form or another, always arises outside a theocracy, was a real one for first-century Jews. It was hardly formulated for this occasion.

18. Jesus recognizes the daggers in his opponents' smiles.

hypocrites prepares for chapter 23 and refers first to insincerity: kind words disguise ill intent.

19. The story would be coherent without vv. 19–21a. But the use of a visual aid, of non-verbal communication, adds drama, while the coin being in the possession of Jesus' opponents highlights the insincerity of their query: at least they have no qualms about using pagan money, and even bring a coin with the emperor's image and blasphemous inscription into the holy precincts of the temple.

Show me the coin for the tax. Evidently Jesus and his followers have no money on them, or at least not the right type of coin.

they brought him a denarius. The denarius was the coin in which taxation was calculated and paid. Many Jews would have used the coin without much thought, despite its having a 'graven image'. Certainly that is the presupposition of our verse: Jesus' hearers will have a silver coin to hand. Copper coins without Caesar's image were, however, produced for daily use and, according to Hippolytus, the Essenes refused to use the denarius, 'saying that they ought not either to carry, or behold, or fashion an image'.

20. Jesus clearly speaks while holding up the coin, showing no hesitation in handling or looking at Caesar's coin.

Whose image is this, and whose inscription? The denarius of our story is almost certainly one minted in Lugdunum in Gaul. It had on the obverse a head of Tiberius laureate with the words, *TI CAESAR DIVI AVG F AVGVSTVS* (that is, *Ti[berius] Caesar Divi Aug[usti]*

F[ilius] Augustus), and on the reverse the words *PONTIF MAXIM* with a seated lady (*pax* personified, perhaps as the emperor's mother, Livia). A hoard of coins discovered on Mount Carmel in 1960 contained at least thirty such denars.

21. Instead of trapping Jesus, the Pharisees and Herodians have been trapped by him.

They answered, 'Caesar's.' The answer is a foregone banality which contrasts with the memorable words that follow. The opponents, although they speak, have nothing to say.

Give then to Caesar the things that are Caesar's, and to God the things that are God's. The verb literally means 'give back' and was used of paying debts (cf. Lk 7.42); so the thought may well be that in giving the coin to Caesar one is simply returning to him what is his. In any case one recalls 21.41 (where the same verb is used) and according to which the Jewish leaders have not rendered to God what is God's due. Thus Jesus' imperative serves firstly to indict his opponents.

Jesus' words distance him from those who opposed supporting Rome. At the same time, the inclusion of giving to God what is his relativizes the political obligation. There is here no firm principle of loyal submission to the state. Implied rather is a reservation regarding the state, and a lack of reservation regarding God. While obedience to God can, as in the current instance, coexist with doing what the state requires, obligation to the former obviously overshadows obligation to the latter. So there is no simple yes or no, no straightforward rule, but the imperative to weigh the demands of two (very unequal) authorities, one of which endures, one of which passes away. When those demands are not at odds (as here), obligations to both can be met; cf. Rom 13.1–7; 1 Pet 2.17. In cases of conflict, however, it is manifest which authority requires allegiance. Our text has rightly been cited to curb the powers of the state. God, who after all determines what is Caesar's and what is not, is sovereign over the state, albeit in a non-theocratic fashion. In the end, no one can serve two masters (6.24), and all that truly matters is obedience to God.

Beginning with Tertullian, many have identified 'the things that are God's' with human beings. If coins with Caesar's image and inscription belong to Caesar, then human beings created in God's image (Gen 1.26) belong to God.

Many have found our passage in harmony with the Lutheran doctrine of the two kingdoms: life has two spheres, the sacred and the secular, each with its own demands. It should be kept in mind, however, that the two spheres can hardly be kept apart, and that although Jewish tradition tended to view governments as divinely placed, and while Christian tradition followed, it is not clear that this thought belongs to our pericope. Indeed, some commentators have argued that 'render to God' so outweighs 'render to Caesar' as to make the latter ironic or unimportant, a matter (as Kierkegaard had it) of indifference. While they go too far, our passage remains cryptic, and theological assertions about God's relationship to the state will wisely ground themselves in other scriptures (e.g. Romans 13). There is here no precise theory of governmental authority.

22. Jesus' opponents, unable to offer rebuttal, simply marvel and so implicitly concede defeat.

* * * * *

(i) Whether one considers Jesus' answer to his opponents to be clever or profound or both, the performance is impressive and unforgettable. Jesus not only avoids a well-conceived trap but additionally communicates his own teaching. Further, that teaching is expressed in the briefest compass. Here again is the speaker of the Sermon on the Mount, the man able to put worlds into aphorisms. Readers not only feel admiration but also know that here is a teacher without peer; and that feeling and knowledge in turn reinforce our Gospel's portrait of Jesus as the great instructor, whose teachings are to be observed until the end of the age.

(ii) Matthew's post-70 Christian readers must have read 22.15–22 in the light of the Jewish war. Unlike those who rebelled against Rome, Jesus did not advise revolution against the state: and that despite the fact that, as the passion predictions reveal, he expected the state to execute him.

(iii) Mt 22.15–22, continuing upon 21.23–22.14, is more polemic against the Jewish leaders. Here they take counsel against Jesus, seek to manipulate him through flattery, behave as 'hypocrites', and fail to confess their defeat when outdone: they simply move on. The negative characterization could hardly be bleaker. In this way the pericope anticipates chapter 23, or, more precisely, offers partial justification for the attack there unleashed.

THE SADDUCEES AND THE RESURRECTION (22.23–33)

[23]**That same day Sadducees came to him, claiming that there is no resurrection; and they asked him a question, saying,** [24]**'Teacher, Moses said, "If a man dies, having no children, his brother should marry the widow, and raise up children for his brother."** [25]**Now there were seven brothers among us. The first married, and he died; and being childless he left his wife to his brother.** [26]**Likewise also the second and the third, down to the seventh.** [27]**After them all, the woman herself died.** [28]**In the**

resurrection, then, whose wife of the seven will she be? For all of them had her.' ²⁹Jesus answered and said to them, 'You are wrong, because you know neither the scriptures nor the power of God. ³⁰For in the resurrection they neither marry nor are given in marriage, but are like angels in heaven. ³¹And as for the resurrection of the dead, have you not read what was said to you by God, ³²"I am the God of Abraham, the God of Isaac, and the God of Jacob"'? He is God not of the dead, but of the living.' ³³And when the crowd heard it, they were astounded at his teaching.

Parallels: Mk 12.18–27; Lk 20.27–40

If the Pharisees raise a political issue, the Sadducees pose a theological riddle. Although the two parties disagree regarding resurrection, they are one in opposing Jesus.

23–4. The Sadducees, despite addressing Jesus as 'teacher', do not seek instruction. Rather are they insincere and malicious.

Sadducees came to him. On the Sadducees and their denial of the resurrection see p. 4. They were probably not genuine annihilationists but, in harmony with many OT texts, rather believed in a shadowy existence in Sheol.

claiming that there is no resurrection. The denial of resurrection is not just speculation regarding the distant future. It instead directly opposes the teaching of Jesus (16.21; 17.9 etc.) as well as the foundational Christian proclamation.

If a man dies, having no children, his brother should marry the widow, and raise up children for his brother. This line combines the teaching of the Levirate law in Deut 25.5 with the concrete example in Gen 38.8 and refers to the only sort of 'resurrection' the Sadducees recognized.

25. In accordance with rabbinic custom, example follows precept. We are given a concrete example of the law applied – but an example in which its end is not achieved: no children are begotten. How much currency the argument had we do not know. Knowledge of the Sadducees and their propaganda is scanty. But one guesses that they probably did enjoy creating contradictions between the Torah and the hope of resurrection.

28. The preamble is concluded. The question, which assumes that polyandry is unacceptable and implies that the resurrection is foreign to the teachings of Moses and the Pentateuch, follows.

29. Jesus treats his opponents' cunning objection as the product of culpable ignorance and bad theology; cf. 1 Cor 15.34.

You are wrong, because you know neither the scriptures nor the power of God. Perhaps one should associate 'the Scripture' with vv. 31–2, and 'the power of God' with v. 30, so that the two themes of our line are treated in reverse order. The Sadducees in any case deny the resurrection because they imagine the eschatological future which others profess to be mundane and terrestrial. But their materialistic view of reanimation is not the refined view of Jesus, according to whom Israel's God is the omnipotent who will transform the saints.

30. Jesus first responds to the argument against the resurrection, after which he will prove the resurrection from Scripture.

For in the resurrection they neither marry nor are given in marriage, but are like angels in heaven. Cf. *b. Ber.* 17a (Rab: 'In the world to come there is no … propagation'). 'Neither marry nor are given in marriage' means '(Men) neither marry nor are (women) given in marriage'. 'In heaven' modifies 'angels', not 'God'; and 'for' grounds the assertion in Jesus' knowledge of the future. 'In the resurrection' means not 'at the resurrection' but 'in the resurrected condition (of the just)'. The argument moves from the general to the particular. If in general people will be like angels, then the marital bond in particular will be transcended, for angels (who are immortal) live without marriage.

Although Jesus may have been the first to dispute the Sadducees with the argument of 22.30, the general content was conventional. There are many old texts in which human beings do what angels do or are, in one way or another, likened to angels (in this life); and the thought that eschatological destiny will be angelic is well-attested.

The thought that angels do not engage in sexual intercourse does not depend upon their being sexless or androgynous, for they were typically thought of as male. *Jub.* 15.27 even informs us that the angels were born circumcized. According to the old interpretation of the myth in Gen 6.2, the wicked angels engaged in sexual intercourse with human females. The other angels (that is, those referred to in our verse) were those who 'restrained themselves' (*2 Bar.* 56.14), remaining chaste. As sex was largely thought of as serving the purpose of procreation, not pleasure, and as angels were thought of as deathless, intercourse for them was unnecessary and would only have been self-indulgence. So too will it then be for the righteous who, upon gaining eternal life, will no longer need to reproduce.

The impact of Mt 22.30 par. upon early Christianity was considerable. Largely under its influence the Christian life was popularly conceived to be an imitation of the angels. In particular, the exhortation to asceticism was often supported by appeal to the model of the angels; and virginity especially was espoused as in accordance with the angelic standard. Mt 22.30 has, however, not played much of a role in modern Christian thought or practice. Whereas belief in both incorporeal spirits and the value of chastity once made our verse a prized possession, under the influence of the Reformers' rejection of the superiority of virginity, Protestantism's neglect of the angels, post-Enlightenment scepticism regarding unseen spiritual beings and even the life to come, and the modern inability to sympathize much with asceticism, 22.30 and its presuppositions have become problematic for many. The verse has gone from being significant to marginal.

31. In passing from the *manner* of the resurrection to its *fact*, Jesus does not cite Dan 12.1–3 (or other possible biblical proof texts for the resurrection), but a Pentateuchal text. He accordingly meets the Sadducees, who recognize the authority of the Pentateuch, on their own ground.

32. The argument seemingly implies not resurrection but continued existence and therefore an interim state. The two things were, however, not mutually exclusive; indeed, many no doubt took the one to imply the other. Cf. the argument in *b. Sanh.* 90b: R. Eliezer ben R. Jose urged: '"(Because he has despised the word of the Lord, and has broken his commandment,) that soul shall be utterly cut off; his iniquity shall be upon him." Now as he shall be utterly cut off in this world, when shall his iniquity be upon him? Surely in the next world.' This is presented as refuting the sectarians who 'maintained that resurrection is not deducible from Torah'. But to our minds only continued existence is established.

I am the God of Abraham, the God of Isaac, and the God of Jacob. The quotation is from the famous Exod 3.6.

He is God not of the dead, but of the living. The argument, whose conclusion sounds proverbial, seems to come down to this: God does not say, 'I *was* the God of Abraham etc.' but 'I *am* the God of Abraham etc.', even though Abraham and the others are dead at the time of the pronouncement. They therefore cannot have ceased to be.

33. The conclusion (i) emphasizes Jesus' authority as teacher, a leading motif of Mt 21–2, and (ii) distinguishes again the crowds from their leaders.

* * * * *

(i) Mt 22.23–33 expands the front of Jesus' opposition in Jerusalem by the introduction of the Sadducees, and reiterates once more that the God of the Christians is the God of Abraham, Isaac, and Jacob: that is, of the Jews.

(ii) That the saints will be like angels implies that the eschatological future will be less an earthly paradise than something transcendent, a time and place in which the boundaries between heaven and earth will become indistinct.

THE GREATEST AND FIRST COMMANDMENT (22.34–40)

[34]When the Pharisees heard that he had silenced the Sadducees, they gathered together, [35]and one of them, a lawyer, questioned him in order to test him: [36]'Teacher, which commandment in the law is the greatest?' [37]He said to him, 'You shall love the Lord your God with all your heart, and with all your soul, and with all your mind. [38]This is the greatest and first commandment. [39]And a second is like it: You shall love your neighbour as yourself. [40]On these two commandments hang all the law and the prophets.'

Parallels: Mark 12.28–31; Luke 10.25–8

A representative of the Pharisees, one of their 'lawyers', continues the series of hostile challenges begun in 21.23. Again the issue regards the Torah, and again Jesus speaks the truth without becoming ensnared. His summary of the law and the prophets, which recapitulates the unifying theme of his own words and deeds, simply unites, against all possible complaint, two traditional Jewish summaries: the commandment to love God (part of the Shema, Judaism's closet thing to a creed) and the commandment to love neighbour (which Rabbi Akiba reportedly called 'the greatest principle in the law': *Sifre* on Lev 19.18).

34. The Pharisees, despite their agreement with Jesus' teaching on the resurrection, are in truth on the side of the Sadducees, and so they now take up where the latter left off.

When the Pharisees heard that he had silenced the Sadducees, they gathered together. This makes the 'lawyer' of v. 35 an emissary of the Pharisees. Some have found here an allusion to Ps 2.2: 'the rulers take counsel together against the Lord and against his anointed.'

35. one of them, a lawyer, questioned him in order to test him. 'Lawyer', that is, 'teacher of the law', is the equivalent of 'scribe'. We may think of a learned Pharisee, an expert in the law. His question regarding an exegetical issue is thoroughly rabbinic, and it is not precisely clear in what sense there is a temptation. Are we to suppose that the lawyer expected Jesus to answer by annulling part of the law (cf. 5.17–20) or by denigrating certain statutes? Perhaps the verb simply indicates bad faith. In any case there can be no political repercussions.

36. Teacher, which commandment in the law is the greatest? Cf. Jas 2.8; *Sifre* on Lev 19.18 (R. Akiba: Lev 19.18 is 'a major principle in the Torah').

37. Jesus' remark is not polemical; contrast 22.29.

You shall love the Lord your God with all your heart, and with all

your soul, and with all your mind. This is a quotation from Deut 6.5, a text recited in the morning and evening by pious Jews. Love of God, like love of neighbour, is not firstly an attitude or affection but – as the example of Jesus shows – a way of life, the sweat of labour for others, 'the free service of our wills' (Calvin). This is why, unlike an emotion, it can be commanded, and why, as Tertullian wrote, it is visible.

The three faculties, 'heart', 'soul', and 'mind', first of all represent the entire person; so the demand is for total allegiance: one should love God with every globule of one's being.

39. Jesus, although asked for the greatest commandment, answers with two which are inextricable. Cf. 1 Jn 4.20–1 and Philo's contention that the two halves of the decalogue, halves which concern love of God and love of neighbour, are incomplete in themselves (*Decal.* 109–10).

And a second is like it. 'Second' is 'purely numerical', that is, second in the order given but not second in importance; and 'like it' here means 'equally great or important'. So the following commandment is no less important than the first: both together qualify as 'the greatest' imperative; cf. 7.12. Their equality reflects their unity.

You shall love your neighbour as yourself. This is from Lev 19.18. The positive and unqualified endorsement of Lev 19.18 (cf. 19.19) supports the view that 5.43–8 does not, despite much modern exegesis, abrogate an OT imperative. Surely Matthew's Jesus does not criticize a scriptural text (5.43–8) and then subsequently (22.39–40) call it the greatest commandment.

Matthew does not clarify 'as yourself'. Augustine found here approval of self-love, and even put love of self alongside love of God and neighbour. But there is no support for such a reading elsewhere in Matthew, which has so much to say about denying and losing and crucifying the self (10.38–9; 16.24–6). The point is simply that, as in 7.12, one treats others as one wishes to be treated.

Although the text leaves unclear how the two commandments to love relate to one another, theologians through the centuries have made up this lack. Evagrius Ponticus argued that love of neighbour is love of God because it is love of the image of God. Theodoret of Cyrrhus urged that, as contemplation is to action, so love of God is to love of neighbour: the one is the foundation of and inspiration for the other. We imitate what we love; so to love God is to imitate the One whose love is catholic (5.43–8). Ailred of Rievaux, on the contrary, contended that 'love of neighbour precedes love of God': the latter grows out of the former. Luther argued that while our neighbour is needy, God needs nothing, so true service of God must always be for the sake of the neighbour: 'Even the preaching of His glory and our praising and thanking Him take place on earth in order that our neighbours may be converted and brought to God thereby.' Harnack thought that the Gospel places love of neighbour beside love of God because 'the love of one's neighbour is the only practical proof on earth of that love of God which is strong in humanity.'

Often cited as a parallel to our verse is *b. Šabb.* 31a, where Hillel, in response to the request to teach the Torah while standing on one foot, answered with this: 'What you hate for yourself, do not do to your neighbour. This is the whole law. The rest is commentary.' This is even closer to Matthew than the commentaries indicate; for in Jewish and Christian tradition the golden rule (or its negative form) was thought synonymous with Lev 19.18. See *Tg. Yer 1* on 19.18 and cf. the verdict in *Sifre* on Lev 19.18: Lev 19.18 'is the encompassing principle of the Torah.'

40. The conclusion reveals that the Torah's foundation and end is, in our idiom, 'moral monotheism' or 'theistic humanism'. Religion and ethics are one. There is no self-contained piety.

Matthew probably interpreted the double commandment to love as a summary of the decalogue: (i) Philo thought of the decalogue as a summary of the law that could itself be summarized in terms of love of God and love of neighbour; (ii) Lev 19.18 was used by early Christians, including Matthew, to summarize the latter half of the ten commandments (see on 19.19); and (iii) the interpretation, attested as early as the second century, is common throughout Christian history.

On these two commandments hang all the law and the prophets. Cf. Rom 13.8–10; Gal 5.14. 'Hang' means 'depend upon'. Matthew's line harks back to 7.12b, and what is true there regarding the golden rule as 'the law and the prophets' holds here too: the double commandment to love is not a principle from which all of the law's commands can be deduced, nor does it replace the Torah, nor is it the hermeneutical key to interpreting the law or for determining the validity or importance of different commandments. Rather is it simply the most basic or important demand of the law, a demand which in no way replaces Torah but instead states its true end. Love the Lord your God and love your neighbour: all the rest is commentary. Matthew's text, in other words, postulates that the Torah is in harmony with itself: its twin commandments to love God and neighbour are at one with its other commandments; and the suspension of the law and prophets on the commandments to love simply means that all imperatives are to be performed for the sake of God and neighbour. Cf. *b. Ber.* 63a, where Prov 3.6 ('In all your ways acknowledge him') is cited as a 'short text ... upon which all the essential principles of the Torah hang'.

* * * * *

(i) Lev 19.18 is quoted three times in our Gospel, more than any other OT text: 5.43; 19.19; 22.39. The first citation expands the meaning of neighbour to make it universal: even the enemy is to be loved. The second citation reveals Lev 19.18's status as a fundamental summary of the moral demands of the decalogue. The third brings the love of neighbour into intimate connexion with the commandment to love God and thus, in typically Matthean fashion, fuses religion and ethics.

(ii) Mt 22.34–40 recalls the Sermon on the Mount. In the former Jesus is asked for his teaching on Torah, speaks of what is demanded in relationship to God, and clarifies what is required in relationship to neighbour. In the latter Jesus first teaches about the Torah (5.17–48), then about properly religious topics (6.1–18), and then about the ethical or vertical dimension of discipleship (6.19–7.12). The similarities are even closer because 22.34–40 concerns 'the law and the prophets', and the same phrase constitutes an *inclusio* that marks off 5.17–7.12 as the central core of the Sermon on the Mount. So 22.34–40 and the Sermon on the Mount address the same three topics: the law, what is owed God, and how to behave towards one's neighbour. Moreover, the teaching is in each case similar: Jesus' words fulfil the law and the prophets (5.17–48; 7.12; 22.40); religious duties are to be performed not for human approval but grow out of the intimate relationship with the heavenly Father, out of love for and devoted service to God (6.1–18; 22.37); and the neighbour is to be loved and treated as one loves and treats oneself (7.12; 22.39).

DAVID'S SON AS DAVID'S LORD (22.41–6)

[41]**When the Pharisees were gathered together, Jesus asked them,** [42]**'What do you think of the Messiah? Whose son is he?' They said to him, 'The son of David.'** [43]**He said to them, 'How then is it that David by the Spirit calls him Lord, saying,** [44]**"The Lord said to my Lord, 'Sit at my right hand, until I put your enemies under your feet' "?** [45]**If then David calls him Lord, how can he be his son?'** [46]**And no one was able to answer him, nor did anyone dare from that hour to ask him any more questions.**

Parallels: Mark 12.35–7; Luke 20.41–4

Jesus abandons his defensive posture for the offensive. His questions, unlike those of his opponents, go to the heart of things, for they concern Christology. The answer of the Pharisees, 'David's', is only half the truth. The other half, unpronounced by Jesus but clear from the rest of the narrative, is: God's.

41–2. As in 16.13 and 21.28, Jesus initiates the discussion.

When the Pharisees were gathered together may, like 22.34, be designed to recall Ps 2.2.

What do you think of the Messiah? Whose son is he? The first question is completed by the second, so that the meaning is: 'Whose son is the Messiah?' Although the question is designed to draw forth a conventional answer, 'Son of David', it simultaneously hints at another title, 'Son of God'.

They said to him, 'The son of David.' Cf. Jn 7.24. Once more Jesus' opponents do nothing more than state the obvious: they have no profundity to contribute. On 'Son of David' see p. 2. Here the title harks back especially to 21.9 and 15. Hence we have no academic discussion; rather, Jesus is posing a riddle about himself.

43. How then is it that David by the Spirit calls him Lord. Cf. LXX 2 Sam 23.2 ('The Spirit of the Lord speaks in me' [David]); Acts 1.16; 28.25; 2 Pet 1.21. 'By the Spirit' (= by inspiration of the Spirit) makes Psalm 110 prophetic and implies the text is inspired Scripture. For David as prophet see 11QPs^a 27.10–11 ('And the total [of psalms and songs] was 4,050. All these he spoke through prophecy which was given him from before the Most High'); Acts 2.30; Josephus, *Ant.* 6.8.2 ('the Deity abandoned Saul and passed over to David, who, when the divine Spirit had removed to him, began to prophesy').

44. David himself made the Christian confession.

The Lord said to my Lord, 'Sit at my right hand, until I put your enemies under your feet'. This quotes Ps 110.1, with some influence from LXX Psalm 8, a Psalm which is cited in 21.16 in connexion with the Son of David and which evidently has messianic meaning in the targum.

Psalm 110 was, according to current scholarly opinion, a pre-exilic, royal psalm. It pledges a Jerusalem monarch that he will reign with Yahweh's power and authority, overwhelm enemies, and fulfil priestly functions. The LXX interprets the promises to include a divine begetting, and some pre-Christian Jews probably gave it messianic sense. *T. Job* 33 uses it to describe Job's heavenly enthronement, and evidence indicates it was applied to the Hasmoneans. The rabbis referred Psalm 110 to Abraham, David, the Messiah, and, according to Justin Martyr, Hezekiah.

Early Christian sources often cite and allude to Psalm 110. The verse is employed most often for the image of Jesus at God's right hand. But that image is variously employed to depict the subjection of powers to Jesus (e.g. 1 Cor 15.25); to describe Jesus' glory or vindication (e.g. Mt 26.64); to raise questions about the messianic Son of David (e.g. Mt 22.41–6); and to characterize Jesus' priesthood (e.g. Heb 8.1).

45. Perhaps we are to surmise that the Pharisees' messianic expectation (v. 42) is, like the Sadducees' idea of resurrection, feeble and unimaginative.

If then David calls him Lord, how can he be his son? The argument makes two assumptions: (i) in accordance with Jewish tradition, David composed Psalm 110 (cf. the superscription) and (ii) Psalm 110 is messianic. It follows that David wrote about '(the) Lord' (= God) speaking to 'my Lord', and that this last must be the messianic Son of David; cf. v. 42. We have here an apparent contradiction. For how can one standing at the right hand of God and addressed as 'Lord' be David's 'son'? A son may address his father as 'Lord' (cf. 21.29), but a father does not so speak to his son. The silence of the Pharisees shows that they have no solution to the riddle, even though it is superficial for the Christian reader, who knows that all is resolved in Jesus, to wit: although the Messiah is of the lineage of David, he will also be exalted to God's right hand and there reign as 'Lord'. The 'Son of David' – neither the title nor its content is rejected or denigrated – is therefore not an earthly king or David's simple successor, but a descendant of the former king whose destiny surpasses his forebear. Beyond this, Jesus is already, before Easter, God's Son, in which capacity he is even now greater than David or any son of David; cf. 12.42: 'greater than Solomon', David's son.

That the Son of David is in fact 'Lord' is an idea prepared for by earlier passages. In 9.27–8; 15.22; and 20.31–3, those who cry out to Jesus the Son of David also hail him as 'Lord'.

46. This is the end of all debate with learned opponents, whose scholastic impotence contrasts with Jesus' teaching authority. The next chapter is addressed to the crowds and the disciples.

* * * * *

(i) Mt 22.41–6, which records the Messiah's teaching about the Messiah, effectively closes the section that commenced with 20.29 by taking up phrases and themes that have gone before. Observe the following connexions:

> 'gather' + Pharisees (v. 41): cf. 22.34
> the Pharisees (v. 41): cf. 21.45; 22.15, 34
> 'ask' (vv. 41, 46): 22.23, 35
> 'What do you think?' (v. 41): cf. 21.28; 22.17
> 'son' (v. 42): cf. 21.37–8; 22.2
> 'son of David' (vv. 43–4): cf. 20.30–1; 21.9, 15
> 'lord' (v. 46): cf. 20.30–1; 21.3
> inability to answer Jesus (v. 46): cf. 21.25–7

Also artistically admirable is the circumstance that those who have been asking all the questions are finally forced into silence by a question asked of them.

(ii) Our pericope is a concatenation of Christological themes. The subject is 'the Son of David'. But the question, 'Whose son is he?,' reminds the reader that Jesus is also the Son of God. Moreover, both 'Messiah' and 'Lord' appear here; and it may further be worth remarking that, in 26.64, Ps 110.1 is cited to depict Jesus' vindication as the Son of man of Daniel 7. All this is most appropriate: the fundamental theme of 20.29–22.46 is response to Jesus, that is, evaluation of who he is – so what ending could be more fitting than one which sets forth Jesus' manifold identity?

WARNINGS ABOUT THE SCRIBES AND PHARISEES (23.1–12)

23 [1]Then Jesus said to the crowds and to his disciples, [2]'The scribes and the Pharisees sit on Moses' seat. [3] So practise and observe whatever they teach you. But do not do as they do, for they do not practise what they teach. [4]They bind heavy burdens, hard to bear, and lay them on the shoulders of others, yet they themselves will not move them with their finger. [5]They do all of their deeds to be seen by others; for they make their phylacteries broad and their fringes long. [6]They love to have the place of honour at banquets and the best seats in the synagogues, [7]and to be greeted with respect in the market places, and to be called rabbi by others. [8]But you are not to be called rabbi, for you have one teacher, and you are all brothers. [9]And call no one your father on earth, for you have one Father: the one in heaven. [10]Nor are you to be called instructors, for you have one instructor, the Messiah. [11]The greatest among you will be your servant. [12]Whoever exalts himself will be humbled, and whoever humbles himself will be exalted.'

Parallels: Mk 12.37–40; Lk 11.46; 14.11; 20.45–7

1–2. As in the Sermon on the Mount, Jesus addresses the crowds and the disciples.

Then Jesus said to the crowds and to his disciples. Only the crowds – who have previously overheard Jesus' criticism of Jewish leaders – and the disciples are exhorted. The vices of the scribes and Pharisees are so hardened that imperatives would be wasted upon them: the incorrigible do not repent.

The scribes and the Pharisees. Not all Pharisees were authoritative instructors of Torah, so originally our saying is not likely to have named them. One might infer that Matthew was simply ignorant of the distinction between scribes and Pharisees, especially as throughout his Gospel the Jewish leaders are lumped together. More plausible is the guess that the unified front against Jesus reflects a unified Jewish front in Matthew's experience; and further that Matthew's tendency to focus on the Pharisees indicates that his Jewish adversaries were known as heirs of the Pharisees. Perhaps indeed all the scribes known to him were Pharisaic.

Moses' seat is ambiguous. It may either refer to a literal chair for synagogue authorities or be a metaphor for teaching authority; cf. the professor's 'chair'. In any case only here are the Jewish leaders presented in a positive light

3. At the beginning the theme of hypocrisy is sounded. But the chapter ends with the accusation of murder. Hence things go from bad to worse.

practise and observe whatever they teach you. Cf. 28.20. Mt 23.3 – the only time Matthew seemingly construes the Jewish leaders in a positive light – stands in tension with 16.11–12 and other passages which counter Pharisaic teaching. What is the explanation? Some have suggested we have here a pre-Matthean tradition out of harmony with the rest of the Gospel, others that the command belongs only to the pre-Easter period, still others that it is ironic. It is also possible to regard the 'all' as hyperbole; the sentence indicts the scribes and the Pharisees by parading their inconsistencies. 'Practise what they preach' is then less practical imperative than proof of a bad character which cannot be excused by ignorance. The focus is not upon Christian obedience but upon the opponents' knowledge, which condemns them. Yet another possibility is that 'whatever they teach you' refers to their reading of Scripture, 'they do' to Pharisaic doctrine and practice.

But do not do as they do, for they do not practise what they teach. Cf. 21.28–32. This line and others in chapter 23 reveal that much of the conflict between Matthew's community and its Jewish opponents was perceived to centre not on words but deeds. Here the scribes and Pharisees are not criticized for having the wrong tradition, but for not living according to the tradition they confess.

To label one's opponents hypocrites or charlatans was standard fare for ancient polemics, Jewish and Graeco-Roman. It goes without saying that the charge was always credible, for hypocrisy belongs to the human condition and so can always be found in the enemy camp.

4. They bind heavy burdens, hard to bear, and lay them on the shoulders of others. Cf 11.29; Acts 15.10, 28. No coherent image emerges, although the mention of 'shoulders' should perhaps connote 'yoke'.

If Jesus' commandments are 'light' (11.30; cf. 1 Jn 5.3), those of his opponents are, by implication, 'heavy'. The reader inevitably thinks of the halakhic rules Jesus counters in chapters 12 and 15. Even so, as Calvin realized, it is not a question of hard rules versus easy rules, or even more versus less. The Sermon on the Mount, especially 5.20, blasts that notion. The opponents' yoke is, from Matthew's point of view, so heavy probably because (i) as v. 23 avows, it takes insufficiently into account justice, mercy, and faith and (ii) its proponents, as the next line states, lift no finger to help; contrast the ever-present aid of the gracious risen Jesus: 28.20.

they themselves will not move them with their finger. Obviously few things are easier than moving a finger; so not to do even that is to do nothing. Commentators disagree whether the Pharisees do not even lift a finger to help those they have burdened or whether they themselves do not do what they ask of others. The latter option harmonizes with v. 3b ('they do not do'). But the former is to be preferred; for 'them' refers back to the 'heavy burdens', and these are on the shoulders of others.

5. The failure to lift a finger to help others springs from wrong motivation: the scribes and Pharisees do not wish to serve but to be applauded for pious show.

They do all of their deeds to be seen by others. Cf. 6.1; also Josephus, *Ant.* 17.41 (presumably quoting Nicolaus of Damascus: the Pharisees take too much pride in themselves). The generalization sums up vv. 5b–7. The 'all' is rhetorical.

they make their phylacteries broad and their fringes long. Cf. *Ps. Sol.* 4.2 (ostentation is a characteristic of the author's opponents); Josephus, *Bell.* 2.140 (where we learn that the Essenes were not to outdo each other in garments or finery). It was common to accuse opponents of seeking glory or of being 'men-pleasers'. Phylacteries are not amulets but *tefillîn*, the two black leather boxes containing parchment Scriptures that, since at least the second century BC, were commonly worn on the upper left arm and forehead following the literal understanding of Exod 13.9, 16; Deut 6.8; 11.18. Their ostentatious and superstitious use is attested. To enlarge *tepillîn* might mean either widening the strap or increasing the box size; but perhaps we should give the verb chronological sense: the time spent wearing them was increased beyond the usual period. Fringes made of blue and/or white threads were worn on the four corners of the rectangular outer garment, in accord with Num 15.38–9 and Deut 22.12. The presumption is that the scribes and Pharisees who make their tassels long – the Torah prescribed no length or number, and the schools of Shammai and Hillel debated the issue – do so to draw attention to their piety. The attack clearly is against not a scriptural ordinance but its observance for self-glorification. Recall 9.20 and 14.36: Jesus himself wears tassels on his garment.

In Num 15.38–9, the tassels are sewn into garments so that they may be looked upon, thus reminding one of the commandments of the Lord, and that one should 'do' them. Verse 40 continues: 'So you shall remember and do all my commandments'. But the scribes and Pharisees, according to Mt 23.2–3, do not do the commandments. Thus on them the fringes do not serve their lawful purpose.

6–7. They love to have the place of honour at banquets and the best seats in the synagogues, and to be greeted with respect in the market places, and to be called rabbi by others. Cf. Lk 14.7–11; also Josephus, *Ant.* 17.229 (Caius was made to 'sit first of all'); 1QS 2.14–20 (before the Messiah 'shall sit the heads of the thousands of Israel, each according to his standing in their camps ... and all the clan heads of the community, together with the wise of the holy community, shall sit before them, each according to his degree of honour'); Suetonius, *Aug.* 44 (the Senate ordered that the front row of seats in theatres be reserved for senators); I. Kyme = CIJ 2.738 (a 'seat of honour' was bestowed by a synagogue upon a female benefactor); *t. Ber.* 5.5 ('when there are two couches the more important guest reclines first and the other above him'). The desire for 'the first place' at dinners (cf. Jn 13.23–5; Jas 2.2–3) – that is, the place nearest the host – and for the 'first seats' in the synagogues is self-explanatory, as is the wish to be 'greeted' by those of lower rank – that is, hailed as important.

8. Unlike the scribes and Pharisees (v. 7), authorities in the church are to shun titles. Such titles are inconsistent with the demand for humility and mutuality and the need to restrict certain appellations to God and Christ. Believers are equals, and none should be exalted by unnecessary adulation. It is implied that the scribes and Pharisees, whose leadership *functions* at least are mirrored in Matthew's community, enjoy wrongful flattery and think in hierarchical terms.

you are not to be called rabbi. Contrast 23.7; Jn 3.10; Acts 13.1. Unequivocal evidence for 'rabbi' as a technical term to designate the authoritative leaders of emerging rabbinic Judaism comes from the late second century AD. Many have, to be sure, found such usage in Matthew 23 and John. But it is possible that all four canonical Gospels consistently use 'rabbi' without its later technical meaning, as nothing more than a term of respect. Still, it is clear from the context of Mt 23.8 not only that 'rabbi' was associated with Matthew's Jewish opponents but that it was especially linked with teachers (cf. Jn 1.38); and it is altogether likely that the word evolved into a title near the end of the first century. Our verse, then, is responsive: it is a Christian reaction to a late first-century development in Judaism.

you have one teacher. Cf. Jn 13.13; Ignatius, *Magn.* 9.1 ('Jesus Christ, our only teacher'); *Eph.* 15.1 ('there is then one teacher'). As v. 10 shows, the 'one teacher' is the Messiah. Perhaps Isa 54.13 is in the background: 'All your sons will be taught by the Lord.' The logic in any event seems to be that authority is grounded in the risen Jesus; therefore, all earthly authority is derivative, rooted outside itself, which fact should impart humility to the bearers of such derivative authority.

you are all brothers. Possibly, like Mt 13.46–50, Matthew here records a democratizing impulse.

9. call no one your father on earth. Does the prohibition (i) oppose calling Jewish synagogue leaders 'father' or (ii) counter calling Christian leaders such or (iii) dispute using honorifics for dead worthies? 'Father' is used of instructors in the OT wisdom tradition, and Paul could regard himself as the 'father' of his converts (1 Cor 4.15). The titular use of 'father', however, is first associated with rabbis of Matthew's period, which corresponds nicely with Matthew's setting in life. Nonetheless, examples of 'father' as a direct address to a rabbi are rare in rabbinic literature, which typically reserves the honorific for early scholars (e.g. 'Abba Saul'). So if one were to judge solely by that corpus, interpretation (iii) might be best: Matthew took himself to be combatting a new habit of memorializing late teachers with 'father'. But this scarcely fits the context of 23.9, whose theme is humility – what does humility have to do with what one calls the dead? – and whose other prohibitions relate to then-current titles. It seems preferable to infer that certain religious authorities were indeed sometimes called 'father' by their lessers and that either interpretation (i) or (ii) could be correct.

10. This is probably a restatement of v. 8 for emphasis or clarification – although some would find here an expansion to include specifically Hellenistic titles of honour.

Nor are you to be called instructors. The Greek noun means 'leader' or 'guide', and most often academic leader or guide: that is, 'teacher', 'tutor', 'professor'. It frequently implies honour or dignity. Many suspect v. 10 to be a clarifying variant of v. 8. But some have guessed that Matthew's tradition opposed the use of two different titles – perhaps rabbi and *morêh*.

you have one instructor, the Messiah. Cf. v. 8. Only here in the canonical Gospels does Jesus refer to himself as the Messiah. Although one might urge a less literal interpretation, the injunctions against 'rabbi', 'father', and 'instructor', taken together, constitute a general prohibition against all ecclesiastical titles. There is no more room for 'bishop' or 'the most reverend' than 'rabbi'. If so, one could scarcely find a biblical text so little heeded. Indeed, the practical difficulty of getting along without titles is such that one wonders whether our verse was ever more than someone's unrealized hope – although occasionally some individuals have eschewed honorifics (e.g. Francis of Assisi). Certainly pre-Reformation exegetical history offers only isolated protests based upon our text, the most famous being Jerome, *In Ep. ad Gal.* 2, the authenticity of which was, on the ground of its offensive content, disputed.

11. This verse and the next issue a general call for humility, the paradigm example of which is Jesus (20.26–8). It is presupposed that humility 'is something which is capable of being learned and practised by all' (John Cassian).

The greatest among you will be your servant. 'Domination is forbidden; service is imposed' (Bernard of Clairvaux). Cf. 20.26–7; Mk 9.35; Lk 9.48; 1 Cor 9.19.

12. The section ends on an eschatological note which reminds us of the sad maxim that 'many people want to be pious but few are prepared to be humble' (La Rochefoucauld).

All who exalt themselves will be humbled, and all who humble themselves will be exalted. 'Not only does he forbid setting heart upon the first place but he requires following after the last' (Chrysostom). Cf. 18.4; also Job 22.29; Prov 29.23; Isa 10.33; Ezek 21.26; *Ahiqar* 60 (Linenberger: 'If [yo]u wis[h] to be [exalted], my son, [humble yourself before Šamaš], who humbles the [exalted] and [exalts the humble]'); Diogenes Laertius 1.69 (Zeus humbles the exalted and exalts the humbled); Lk 1.52; 2 Cor 11.7; Jas 4.6; 1 Pet 5.5; *b. 'Erub.* 13b ('The Holy One exalts him who humbles himself and humbles him who exalts himself'). Our line reproduces a common wordplay and a common sentiment and must be reckoned proverbial. But the eschatological orientation is characteristic of Jesus and the early church: we have here not worldly wisdom but God's judgement. The passives are divine and refer to God's eschatological verdict. The verse thus accomplishes two things: it (i) establishes that the prohibition against titles is motivated by the need for humility and (ii) underlines the seriousness of the matter.

* * * * *

(i) Mt 23.1–12 condemns hypocrisy (v. 3), religious show (vv. 4–6), and self-exaltation (v. 7). It commends obedience to the truth (v. 3), mutuality (v. 8), and humility (vv. 11–12). In all this there is nothing new, only repetition for emphasis. The same vices and virtues have been assailed and praised before, especially in chapters 5–7 and 18. It is not the ethical teaching that distinguishes 23.1–12 but (a) the concentration of vices in the scribes and Pharisees and (b) the eschewing of titles. Both are explained by Matthew's historical setting: his community thought of itself as competing with the heirs of Pharisaism, who thus became polemical objects. At the same time, the opposition to titles was surely also given earnest by a growing ecclesiastical authority, which can otherwise be documented. One inevitably thinks of Ignatius of Antioch and his strong words about his own office. Opposition to honorifics would have well served to counter presumptuous hierarchical dignity.

(ii) Two groups, one represented by 'them', the other by 'you', are at the centre of 23.1–12. What is the chief distinction between the two? Those directly addressed ('you') are told that they have one teacher, one father, and one master. Hence Christology and theology shape their behaviour. It is otherwise with those whose conduct is condemned. Those who sit on Moses' seat and lengthen their fringes and love to be called 'Rabbi, rabbi' are not, in our passage, related either to God or Christ. Rather are they related to other people, and their behaviour is dictated not by authentic religious considerations but by perceived public opinion. Our passage thus depicts the same antithesis as Eph 6.6: there are on the one hand those who seek to please people and who live according to appearances and then there are, on the other hand, 'the servants of Christ who do the will of God from the heart.'

(iii) The Jewish character of 23.1–12 is remarkable. Here we read of 'Moses' seat', 'phylacteries', 'tassels', the 'chief seats' in 'synagogues', and people being called 'rabbi, rabbi'. Not one of these things is explained. Knowledge of them is rather assumed. This is more than consistent with the author and his community being mostly Jewish. Would a Gentile have left intact an imperative to obey those on Moses' seat? Could a man writing for a Gentile church have refrained from elucidating v. 5? Perhaps indeed a significant portion of Jewish-Christians in Matthew's community still attended Jewish synagogue.

SEVEN WOES (23.13–33)

[13]'But woe to you, scribes and Pharisees, hypocrites! For you shut people out of the kingdom. For you do not go in nor allow those who want to go in to do so.

[15]'Woe to you, scribes and Pharisees, hypocrites! For you traverse sea and land to make a single convert, and whenever one becomes a proselyte, you make that one twice as much a son of Gehenna as yourselves.

[16]'Woe to you, blind guides, who say, "Whoever swears by the temple

it is nothing, but whoever swears by the gold of the temple is obligated by the oath." [17]You blind morons! For which is greater, the gold or the temple that sanctifies the gold? [18]And you say, "Whoever swears by the altar is obligated by nothing, but whoever swears by the gift that is on the altar is obligated by the oath." [19]How blind you are! For which is greater, the gift or the altar that sanctifies the gift? [20]The one then who swears by the altar swears by it and by all upon it. [21]And the one who swears by the sanctuary swears by it and by the one who dwells in it. [22]And the one who swears by heaven swears by the throne of God and by him who sits upon it.

[23]'Woe to you, scribes and Pharisees, hypocrites! For you tithe mint, dill, and cumin, and have neglected the weightier matters of the law – justice and mercy and faith. It is these you ought to have practised without neglecting the others. [24]You blind guides! Straining out a gnat and swallowing a camel!

[25]'Woe to you, scribes and Pharisees, hypocrites! For you clean the outside of the cup and of the plate, but inside they are full of extortion and self-indulgence. [26]You blind Pharisee! First clean the inside of the cup, so that the outside also may be clean.

[27]'Woe to you, scribes and Pharisees, hypocrites! For you are like whitewashed tombs, which on the outside appear beautiful, but inside they are full of the bones of the dead and of all uncleanness. [28]So you also outwardly appear righteous to others, but inside you are full of hypocrisy and lawlessness.

[29]'Woe to you, scribes and Pharisees, hypocrites! For you build the tombs of the prophets and decorate the graves of the righteous, [30]and you say, "If we had lived in the days of our ancestors, we would not have taken part with them in shedding the blood of the prophets." [31]Thus you testify against yourselves that you are descendants of those who murdered the prophets. [32]Fill up, then, the measure of your ancestors. [33]You snakes, you brood of vipers! How can you escape from the judgement of Gehenna?'

Parallels: Lk 11.52, 47, 42, 39–41, 44, 47–8

Mt 23.13–35, in which the judge of the last day humbles the exalted in illustration of v. 12, has as its primary purpose the drawing of a firm line between two social groups, one of which is severely criticized. The scribes and the Pharisees, here for Matthew representatives of the leaders of emergent rabbinic Judaism, are stridently opposed and depicted as hopelessly corrupt, wherefore their eschatological doom is sure. The debasement of antagonists serves to (i) indirectly vindicate those who oppose them and (ii) exhibit, through counter-examples, what the church is not. Only in a secondary sense does one have here criticism to be internalized by the disciples. Exegetical and sermonic history has, to be sure, justly used the verses to illustrate Christian failings. But in Matthew's situation the synagogue was still across the street, and there was yet competition for adherents. In that circumstance woes addressed to scribes and Pharisees would not have been understood by faithful readers as directed firstly towards them.

Almost every commentator observes the contrast between the blessings near the beginning of Jesus' ministry (5.3–12) and the woes in chapter 23. Whether the evangelist intended such a contrast is uncertain. It is true that much of chapter 23 recalls the Sermon on the Mount. There is, on the other hand, no evidence of redactional assimilation of one passage to the other.

The First Woe (23.13)

This woe appropriately prefaces the series as a sort of summary of the whole: the scribes and Pharisees, despite their religious efforts, neither enter the kingdom nor allow others to do so. They are not leaders but misleaders.

13. hypocrites is justified by vv. 3–7.

you shut people out of the kingdom. Cf. the gate to life of 7.14 as well as 16.18, where Jesus gives Peter the keys to the kingdom. As appears from the next clause, the scribes and Pharisees shut out not only themselves but, what is more grievous, also others. This then indicts them as not simply wrong but contagiously wrong.

How they shut out others is not here clarified, although most commentators think of the heavy burdens of v. 4, the human traditions which divert attention from the vital issues of belief and conduct requisite for salvation (on this interpretation those shut out are Jews). But one might also think of the persecution of Christian missionaries: to hinder the proclamation of the good news is to shut the doors of the kingdom (on this interpretation Gentiles too might be excluded). This makes for greater continuity with the next woe, which concerns proselytes.

you do not go in nor allow those who want to go in to do so. Cf. CD 6.12 ('they bar the door'); b. Šabb. 31b ('one who possesses learning without the fear of heaven is like a treasurer who is entrusted with the inner keys but not with the outer; how is he to enter?'). 'Nor allow those who want to go in to do so' must mean: 'nor do you permit those who would otherwise enter to enter.' Our verse assumes the authority stated by vv. 2–3: the scribes and the Pharisees are in charge of others' religious lives, for they are the custodians of the Torah, wherein is made known God's will.

The present tenses probably imply the presence of the kingdom. But that hardly requires equating the kingdom with the church: elsewhere the two are distinguished. The present tense, moreover, implies the future tense, just as the future tense would imply the present: those who will enter the kingdom are those who already belong to it, and *vice versa.*

The Second Woe (23.15)

Jesus now indicts the scribes and Pharisees, not because they are missionaries, but because their missionary activity, which makes others like themselves, has tragic effects. The problem is not conversion to Judaism but conversion to Judaism without the Messiah.

15. you traverse sea and land to make a single convert. To compass 'sea and (dry) land' – a biblical idiom connoting completeness – to make one convert is frightfully ironic when juxtaposed with the previous verse: the converts of the scribes and Pharisees do not enter the kingdom but are shut out. The rest of our verse spells out this irony.

The current consensus seems to be that available evidence does not establish Judaism as much of a proselytizing religion before or after AD 70. Certainly our verse, which is hyperbolic invective, can scarcely be turned into good evidence for such. So it has been suggested that some famous conversion may lie in the background. But 'a single convert' simply implies extraordinary determination: even for just one convert great effort will be expended. Whether composed before or after AD 70, 23.15 probably had in view attempts to turn into full converts the so-called 'God-fearers'. One recalls the Judaizing of the Galatians.

whenever one becomes a proselyte, you make that one twice as much a son of Gehenna as yourselves. 'Son of Gehenna' – probably a traditional Semitism meaning 'destined for' or 'worthy of' Gehenna (cf. v. 14) – appears only here in Matthew. Although the rhetoric is virulent and hyperbolic and so of tenuous connexion with historical experience, the reader thinks of the enthusiastic zeal of the convert. Cf. Justin Martyr, *Dial.* 122: 'the proselytes not only do not believe but twofold more than yourselves blaspheme his name ... for in all points they strive to be like you.'

The Third Woe (23.16–22)

This woe falls into three parts, the first two of which (vv. 16–17, 18–19) stand in near perfect parallelism, the third of which (vv. 20–2) is triadic:

1   Woe to you, blind guides, who say,
       'Whoever swears by the temple it is nothing
           but whoever swears by the gold of the temple is
          obligated,'

2   You blind morons!
              For which is greater,
                  the gold or the temple that sanctifies
                  the gold?

3   And you say,
       'Whoever swears by the altar it is nothing
           but whoever swears by the gift on it is obligated.'

4   How blind you are!
              For which is greater,
                  the gift or the altar that sanctifies
                  the gift?

5   The one swearing by the altar
       swears by it and all upon it.

6   And the one swearing by the temple
       swears by it and by the one who dwells in it.

7   And the one swearing by heaven
       swears by the throne of God and by him who sits upon it.

The argument resembles yet differs from 5.33–7. In the Sermon on the Mount, oaths are attacked. Here their use is assumed. In both passages, however, there is the common assertion that to swear by one thing is to swear by another. Indeed, both assert that to swear by heaven is to swear by God's throne.

16. We now turn from generalizations (vv. 13–15) to specific halakah. Verses 16–19 argue against the distinction between binding and non-binding oaths. Vv. 20–2 assert that all oaths are binding because all oaths relate themselves to God.

blind guides. Cf. 15.14 (of the Pharisees). These 'blind leaders', who imagine themselves to be rather 'leaders of the blind' (Rom 2.19 – a traditional expression?), lead the 'sons of Gehenna' (v. 15) who do not enter the kingdom (v. 13). There is no satisfying explanation why the introduction to this woe is different from the others.

Whoever swears by the temple it is nothing, but whoever swears by the

gold of the temple is obligated by the oath. Those here criticized regard oaths by the temple as non-binding, oaths by its gold as binding. There is no evidence, beyond our text, of this teaching, although there are comparable distinctions; and we know that a superstitious fear of valid oaths begot substitute oath forms (which many rabbis opposed). Perhaps our passage is caricaturing rhetoric. More plausible, however, is the suggestion that Matthew's opponents regarded as valid only oaths employing the divine name, divine attributes, or the word, 'korban'. If so, the temple gold and the altar gift were binding as part of an oath because they were connected with the term *korban*, while the Temple and the altar, though holy objects, were illegitimate substitutions in an oath formula.

We do not know precisely what 'gold of the temple' means. It could refer to the temple treasury, to the gold utensils and tables, to the golden plates of the entire façade, or to all of these things at once.

17. You blind fools! The contradiction with 5.22 (where use of 'fool' is forbidden) dissipates only if one assumes that (i) Jesus is, because of his special status, exempted from the prohibition or (ii) 5.22 pertains only to 'brothers'. Neither explanation is satisfying. We seem to have here a real contradiction, which then becomes a reason for viewing 5.22 as being hyperbolic, or as less than all-encompassing, or a command that can be trumped by something more important.

For which is greater, the gold or the temple that has made the gold sacred? Neither this verse nor the following enlightens us about Matthew's attitude toward the temple cult. The whole point is instead rejection of the distinction between binding and non-binding oaths, which distinction implies that not all assertions are equally bound to the truth. That was perceived as contrary to Jesus' teaching; cf. 5.33–7.

19. For which is greater, the gift or the altar that makes the gift sacred? Cf. Exod 29.37 ('whatever touches the altar will become holy') and *m. Zeb.* 9.1 ('the altar makes holy whatsoever is prescribed as its due').

20–1. Verses 20–2 imply that distinctions between various types of oaths are irrelevant; what matters is telling the truth, which should require no oath (5.33–7). If one is not believed without an appeal to God, what good is such appeal?

So whoever swears by the altar, swears by it and by everything on it; and whoever swears by the sanctuary, swears by it and by the one who dwells in it. For God's presence in the temple see Ps 135.21. That God's name is not mentioned in an oath means nothing. Substitutions are evasions, for all the time it is God who is thought of, though it is only something connected with God that is mentioned.

22. whoever swears by heaven, swears by the throne of God and by the

one seated upon it. Cf. 5.34; also Isa 66.1 ('heaven is my throne') and *Mek*. on Exod 17.16 ('The Holy One swore by the throne of his glory'). There has until now been no mention of swearing by heaven. The line seems like an afterthought.

The Fourth Woe (23.23–4)

In this woe the scribes and Pharisees are culpable not because their halakah is wrong (contrast vv. 16–22) but because they leave the most important parts of their own halakah undone. The problem is not tithing or straining gnats, but swallowing camels and a lack of justice, mercy, and faith. The lesser things, however useful or needful, should never eclipse the greater.

23. you tithe mint, dill, and cumin. Only food properly tithed was lawful for the Pharisee to eat. For the tithing of dill and cumin see *m. Ma'as*. 4.5 and *m. Dem*. 2.1. Rabbinic sources do not, however, seem to know of the tithing of mint. More general legislation – none of which mentions herbs – appears in Lev 27.30–3; Num 18.21–32; Deut 14.22–9 (this was later taken to include dill and cumin); 26.12–15; cf. 2 Chr 31.5–12; Neh 10.37–8; 12.44; 13.5, 12; Mal 3.6–12. Occasionally it is suggested that our text presupposes the knowledge that the tithing of herbs was part of oral, not biblical, tradition.

the weightier matters of the law – justice and mercy and faith. Cf. Mic 6.8 ('What does the Lord require of you but to do justice and to love kindness and to walk humbly with your God?'). 'The weightier [= more important, not more difficult] matters of the law' recalls 7.12 and 22.34–40, in which the law and the prophets are summed up in a word. Related summaries appear in rabbinic tradition, and it is only Christian prejudice which finds in 23.23 a break with Judaism. There are certainly rabbinic texts which declare, according to the logic that God gave them all, the equality of the commandments; but there are also texts which distinguish between more important and less important, or between fundamental and peripheral. One recalls Hillel's declaration in *b. Šabb*. 31a ('What is hateful to you, do not do to your neighbour; that is the whole Torah; all the rest is commentary'). Also relevant are *t. Pe'a* 4.19 ('Charity and deeds of loving-kindness outweigh all other commandments in the Torah') and *b. Mak*. 23b–24a (in which various authorities reduce the 613 commandments: David to eleven, Isaiah to six, Micah to three, Isaiah to two, Amos and Habakkuk to one).

It is these you ought to have practised without neglecting the others. The extra-canonical halakah on tithing is neither dismissed nor belittled but affirmed; and v. 24 does not negate this. Tithing is not undone by the weightier matters of the law but subordinated to them. Thus the line distinguishes perceived weaknesses of Pharisaism from criticism of the Jewish tradition itself.

24. Hyperbole exhibits absurdity. The scribes and Pharisees play on the seashore of religion while the great ocean of fundamental truth lies all undiscovered before them.

blind guides. The repetition of the phrase (cf. v. 16) forms an *inclusio* that marks off the third and fourth woes as a subunit. The words are also appropriate here because the ability to strain gnats (see the next line) requires good eyes; so perhaps it is implied that the scribes and Pharisees cannot even do that very well.

Straining out a gnat and swallowing a camel! The reference is to straining wine, as in Amos 6.6. According to Lev 11.41, 'every creeping thing that creeps upon the earth is an abomination; it shall not be eaten.' This verse was understood to require the straining of wine so as to keep out small insects. When it is added that the camel, like the gnat, was reckoned unclean (Lev 11.4), the point of v. 24 becomes plain: while the scribes and Pharisees strain their wine and so do not swallow the tiniest bugs that defile, they overlook the larger things that defile, that is, they swallow the camel (a proverbially large beast: 19.24). The picture is admittedly absurd, but that (i) lodges it in the memory and (ii) makes the scribes and Pharisees look ridiculous.

All too often the straining of gnats is regarded as picayunish and, in the end, insignificant, which fact in turn might entail that tithing is also insignificant. But one wonders whether the KJV's typographical error, 'straining at', has not subconsciously encouraged this mis-interpretation, which contradicts the end of v. 23. The straining of gnats was thought to be commanded by Moses, and our verse does nothing to upset that assumption. The thought is instead that the scribes and Pharisees do the lesser things of the law to the neglect of the greater things. The sin is not observance of the small but disregard of the large.

The Fifth Woe (23.25–6)

This woe adds to the charge that the scribes and Pharisees do the less important thing to the neglect of the more important; specifically, they cleanse the outside of the cup and plate but neglect the inside; that is, they appear on the outside to be righteous (cf. vv. 2–7, 23a) but inside are full of extortion and intemperance.

Verses 25–6 are about neither the literal purity of vessels nor the legal teaching of the Pharisees, nor is v. 25 to be understood literally, v. 26 figuratively. The two verses rather speak of the scribes and

Pharisees metaphorically, as though they were dirty cups and dishes. The text concerns not utensils but people who are clean on the outside (= righteous to all appearances) but impure on the inside; cf. the meaning of vv. 27–8.

The saying carries forward a theme found in the Sermon on the Mount. There anger (an internal disposition) is said to be the root of murder (an external act), and lust (another internal disposition) is made out to be the cause of adultery (another external act); thus the focus for moral reformation must be the heart. As 6.22–3 has it, the light or darkness within determines how one behaves in the world. One also recalls 15.11, which states that it is not what goes into the mouth (an external thing) that defiles but what comes out (words from the heart) that pollutes; cf. 15.18–20; also 7.17–18; 12.33, 35. Mt 23.25–6 is just one more expression of this way of looking at things. In other words, the scribes and Pharisees are impure in heart.

25. The scribes and Pharisees are like cups and plates that are clean only on the outside, which means not really clean at all.

For you clean the outside of the cup and of the plate, but inside they are full of extortion and self-indulgence. Cf. 15.18. The accusation charges the scribes and Pharisees with economic and sexual sins; cf. Amos 2.6–8. Both were standard fare for ancient polemic, and one is reminded of the similar charges levelled by pagans against Christians of the second and third centuries, or by the author of the *Testament of Moses* (a Pharisee?) against his opponents (Sadducees?); see *T. Mos.* 7.5–10: 'they consume the goods of the poor' and say: 'we shall have feasts, even luxurious winings and dinings.'

26. The metaphor of v. 25a is continued and a chiasmus formed: outside–inside–inside–outside.

First clean the inside of the cup, so that the outside also may be clean. Cf. v. 32 (the only other imperative in the seven woes); 10.25; *2 Clem.* 12.2 (Jesus said: the kingdom will come when 'the outside [will be] as the inside'); *Gos. Thom.* 22 ('when you make the inner as the outer ... you will enter the kingdom').

The Sixth Woe (23.27–8)

'The metaphor changes, but the subject remains the same' (Calvin), as is made plain by the catchword connexions with 25–6: 'inside', 'outside', 'clean', and 'full of'.

27. The scribes and Pharisees are likened to tombs, which they regard as unclean.

you are like whitewashed tombs which on the outside appear beautiful. Cf. Ezek 13.10–16; 22.28; Armenian *Ahiqar* 2.2 ('For she is like unto a sepulchre which is fair on the upper side and below is full of the rottenness and bones of the dead'). Although most commentators think of the 'whitewashing' of grave markers, there is no evidence that whitewash was thought of as beautiful. On the contrary, *b. B. Kam.* 69a likens 'lime', that is, whitewash, to the colour of bones. Further, graves so marked do not hide but rather announce their contents. So the reference may instead be to plastered monuments or tombstones. Porous limestone structures were often plastered with lime to smooth surfaces and add a sheen. One may thus picture beautiful monuments and their finished splendour. Perhaps indeed we should think of a magnificent façade, like that of the so-called 'Tomb of James' or the so-called 'Tomb of Zechariah'.

inside they are full of the bones of the dead and of all uncleanness. Cf. Ps 5.9 ('their throat is an open sepulchre'); Ignatius, *Phil.* 6.1 (Judaizers are 'tombstones and sepulchres of the dead').

28. The scribes and Pharisees, although preoccupied with matters of purity, are themselves sources of impurity.

lawlessness is ironic here because the scribes and Pharisees proudly purport to uphold the law.

The Seventh Woe (23.29–33)

After the opening refrain, vv. 29–30 contain three observations: 'you build', 'you decorate', and 'you say'. There follows an inference (v. 31), an ironic imperative (v. 32), and a rhetorical question (v. 33).

29. The following woe is spoken by one who was buried without pomp and circumstance, by one who instructed a would-be disciple to let the dead bury their own dead (8.22). And it is spoken to people who think they will rest easier when Jesus becomes like the prophets of old – dead.

scribes and Pharisees. This, with the exception of 27.62, is the last mention of the Pharisees in Matthew, and the very last time Jesus speaks to them. They quit the stage in disgrace, with judgement looming over their heads.

you build the tombs of the prophets and decorate the graves of the righteous. There was an upsurge in tomb building during the Hellenistic period, and our sources tell us about several well-known tombs and elaborate monuments: 1 Macc 13.27–30 (memorials built over tombs by Simon Maccabee for his family); Josephus, *Ant.* 7.390–2; 13.249 (David; cf. Acts 2.29); 18.108 (Philip the Tetrarch's tomb); 20.95 (Queen Helena of Adiabene's pyramid); *Bell.* 4.531–2 (the tombs 'of fine marble and exquisite workmanship' alleged to belong to Abraham and his kin); 5.506 (Ananus the High Priest).

30. If we had lived in the days of our ancestors, we would not have taken part with them in shedding the blood of the prophets. For another contrary-to-fact denial of guilt see 26.35; and for 'blood' = 'shedding of blood' see 27.24. The scribes and Pharisees refer to those who murdered the prophets as 'our fathers'. They deny, however, that they themselves, had they been alive then, would have been complicit in their fathers' deeds. The contrast between their profession and their deeds (which are detailed forthwith) well suits Matthew's emphasis upon hypocrisy, the gulf between word and deed. It is 'the way of hypocrites to honour God's holy ministers and true-living teachers after they have died, but in their lives to abhor them' (Calvin).

31. This verse simply draws out a claim made in v. 30: the scribes and the Pharisees acknowledge their descent from those who murdered the prophets. It is assumed that offspring resemble their parents (cf. Jn 8.44) – an inference which v. 34 will confirm.

those who murdered the prophets. 'Murder' recalls the decalogue (cf. 5.21; 19.18) and anticipates v. 35. The scribes and the Pharisees witness against themselves that they are 'sons' of those who murdered the prophets. There is probably here a play on the broad meaning of 'sons': it can refer either to literal descendants or to those who share a set of characteristic features (cf. Qumran's 'sons of light' and Paul's 'sons of Abraham'). For the murder of God's messengers see 5.10–12; Acts 7.51–2; 1 Thess 2.15–16.

It was common in Jewish polemic to associate one's enemies with past generations acknowledged by all to be evil; see, for example, 11.20–4; 24.37–9; Josephus, *Bell.* 5.566; *T. Levi* 14.6. In this way present controversy (who is on God's side?) was clarified through association with an unambiguous past.

32. Now that the true character of the scribes and Pharisees has been asserted, they are sardonically exhorted to act accordingly, to murder the Messiah and his heralds.

Fill up, then, the measure of your ancestors. Cf. 1 Thess 2:15–16; *Gos. Pet.* 5.17 ('and they fulfilled all things and completed the measure of their sins on their head'). 'Measure' = 'measure of sins'. For prophetic texts containing ironic imperatives to do wrong see Isa 8.9–10; Jer 7.21; Amos 4.4–5.

The verse presupposes that God can store up only so much wrath; there then comes a point when it must be let loose. Cf. Gen 15.16; Dan 8.23; 9.24 Aq.; *Jub.* 14.16; 2 Macc 6.14; 1 Thess 2.15–16. It is commonly asserted that our line inverts the Jewish belief that eschatological judgement will fall when the sins of Gentiles reach a certain level, exhausting God's long suffering: here instead (as only, it is alleged, in Christian sources) the end comes because of Israel's guilt.

But in addition to the non-eschatological *LAB* 29.13 ('and when the sins of my people [Israel] have reached full measure'), it may be noted that Qumran's so-called Second Ezekiel (4Q385–9, frags 4–6) has this: 'I [God] have hidden my face from [them (that is, the children of Israel) until] they fill up their sins. This will be the sign for them, when they fill up sin . . .' See also 11QTemple 59.3–13 and recall *b. Sanh.* 98a, according to which the Son of David will come to a generation who is either totally worthy *or totally guilty*. Clearly Jesus and/or the early Christians were not the first to make Israel responsible for the eschatological fulfilment of sin.

33. The sinful actions of the addressees are such that eschatological judgement must fall upon them: there can be no escape.

You snakes, you brood of vipers! How can you escape the judgement of Gehenna? This is a redactional insertion based upon the Baptist's words to the Pharisees and Sadducees in 3.7 (whence 'offspring of poisonous snakes', 'escape', and the interrogative form); cf. further 12.34 (also of the Pharisees). Again, then, Jesus speaks as did John, and his message is that of his forerunner: the Pharisees cannot escape eschatological wrath; cf. Rev 6.15–17. It follows that the character of the Pharisees has not changed, that the ministries of John and Jesus have been without effect, that poisonous they remain. 'The judgement of Gehenna' (a rabbinic phrase) means 'the judgement whose verdict will be Gehenna, the place of wrath'. 'Gehenna' (instead of 'the coming wrath', as in 3.7) forges a link with v. 15: the scribes and Pharisees will share the miserable fate of their proselytes: the sons of those who murdered the prophets will become the sons of Gehenna.

* * * * *

(i) Mt 23 is full of conventional accusations. In Matthew's world one's opponents were, as a rule, blind, foolish, impious, hypocritical, and much else besides. That is, the language of vilification was as stereotyped as the language of praise. We accordingly no more have here a fair account of Pharisaic Judaism than we have such an account of Christianity in the pagan polemic of the second, third, and fourth centuries. Further, the ferocity of rhetoric in Jewish texts, and especially the volatile language of the Dead Sea Scrolls, shows Matthew's polemic need not signal a break with Judaism. So far from that being the case, Mt 23 is less a Christian critique of Judaism than it is a Jewish-Christian critique of Jewish opponents – and therefore no more 'anti-Semitic' than the Dead Sea Scrolls.

(ii) The seven woes, which commence with halakhic disagreements and culminate in the murder of God's messengers, mirror the plot of the whole Gospel, in which religious disputes lead to Jesus' death.

Furthermore, although chapter 23 strikes the reader as distinctive, this is not because its content is new: the woes constitute a climax, not a novum. All of the major accusations and assertions have already been made, as the following reveals:

	Matthew 23	*Matthew 1–22*
Woes upon contemporaries	vv. 13, 15, etc.	11.21; 18.7 (*bis*)
Condemnation of Pharisaic hypocrisy	vv. 13, 15, 25–8 etc.	15.7; 22.18
Failure of scribes and Pharisees to enter the kingdom	v. 13	5.20
The Pharisees as blind guides	vv. 16, 24	15.14
Refutation of Pharisaic halakah	vv. 16–22	15.1–11; 16.5–12
To swear by one thing is to swear by another	vv. 16–22	5.33–7
The Pharisees neglect the more important and heed the less important	vv. 23–4	12.1–8; 15.1–20
The Pharisees are deficient in mercy	v. 23	9.10–13; 12.1–8
Condemnation of discrepancy between outward appearance and impure inward state	vv. 27–8	6.1–18
The Pharisees are a 'brood of vipers' destined for hell	v. 33	3.7
The scribes are murderers	v. 31–3	16.21; 20.18

Even the polemical harshness of 23.13–33 is (as recollection of 22.1ff. proves) not unique; new only is its concentrated repetition.

(iii) The woes as a whole do not proclaim the judgement of Israel. Only in v. 34 or v. 36 does the polemic clearly pass beyond the leaders to embrace their followers. Israel is not the subject of 23.13ff.

(iv) The Jewish character of 23.13ff. is, like that of 21.1–12, remarkable. As compared with Luke's woes, only those in Matthew refer to Jewish proselytes, oaths by the temple and its altar, 'the weightier matters of the law', the practice of whitewashing tombs or sepulchres, and flogging in synagogues; and Matthew alone has the Semitic expression, 'son of Gehenna'. Whether all these differences are due to Matthean reaction, or whether some of them should be explained as Lukan omission of things foreign to Gentiles, one fact is plain: Matthew 23 appears to have been written by a Jewish author for a Jewish-Christian audience.

(v) The woes, although part of a discourse addressed to disciples and crowds, are spoken directly to the scribes and Pharisees. Moreover, the emphatic second person plural appears only in Matthew, not in Luke. These facts, along with the concrete nature of the halakhic disputes and the intensity of the emotions expressed, plainly reveal that the heated polemic of 23.13ff. was for Matthew no relic of an earlier time. Nor were the woes simply a literary device, Christian parenesis disguised as polemic against opponents. Rather, the woes were forged by a heartfelt bitterness, by the hostile feelings of a Jewish-Christian group estranged from its mother community.

(vi) Mt 23.13ff. was not composed largely as a warning to Christians, lest they follow in the path of those here condemned. Certainly hypocrisy, a vice blasted by the woes, is illustrated in chapter 6 by members of the synagogue, and in this respect and others chapter 23 is indeed a negative supplement to the Sermon on the Mount. And yet there is no evidence that our author intended the reader to juxtapose the Sermon on the Mount and chapter 23. There are not even any redactional prods to lay the woes beside the beatitudes. There exist common themes, such as the need for mercy (5.7; 23.23) and inner purity (5.8; 23.25–6). But this does not suffice to make the case. The woes did not serve Matthew's community as paranaesis. Their import was not moral but rather social. The castigation of opponents contributed to the task of self-definition; the woes both clarified and justified the decision to follow Jesus Christ.

(vii) Christian history has demonstrated that, whoever the polemical objects originally were, and whatever they might have done, contemporary application of Mt 23 should target the church; for all the vices here attributed to the scribes and Pharisees have attached themselves to Christians, and in abundance. While Eastern Orthodox bishops have, despite 23.6, enthroned themselves at the fronts of churches, Pentecostal leaders have sat on raised stages during revival meetings; and in the Old American south the pews were often ranked according to social status. Christian leaders of all stripes have, against the spirit of 23.7–12, bestowed upon themselves honorifics, including 'father' and 'teacher' and 'bishop'; and of course many post-Constantine churches have gloried in pomp and circumstance, with leaders adorning themselves with costly raiment. Protestants have so strained at gnats as to splinter their denominations for every trivial matter under the sun. And what Christian body has been immune from losing focus on the weightier matters: justice, faith, mercy? In view of all this, commonsense and sound theology require that, even though this may be incongruent with the original function of the text, Matthew 23 should not encourage Christians to imagine that they are unlike others. Rather should the chapter stimulate self-examination. It is fitting that the polemic of Matthew 23 has, throughout sermonic history, been turned against the church itself.

LAMENT OVER JERUSALEM (23.34–9)

[34]Therefore I send to you prophets, sages, and scribes, some of whom you will kill and crucify, and some of whom you will flog in your synagogues and persecute from town to town, [35]so that upon you may come all the righteous blood shed on the earth, from the blood of righteous Abel to the blood of Zechariah son of Barachiah, whom you murdered between the sanctuary and the altar. [36]Amen I say to you, all this will come upon this generation. [37]O Jerusalem, Jerusalem, the city that kills the prophets and stones those who are sent to it! How often have I desired to gather your children together as a hen gathers her brood under her wings, and you would not! [38]Behold, your house is forsaken and desolate. [39]For I say to you, you will not see me again until you say, "Blessed is the one who comes in the name of the Lord."

Parallels: Lk 11.49–51; 13.34–5

This passage draws heavily upon 2 Chr 24:17–25:

Mt 23.34-9	2 Chr 24.17-25
'I send you prophets'	'he sent prophets among them', v. 19
'some of whom you will kill'	the stoning of Zechariah, vv. 20-2
'so that upon you may come all the righteous blood shed on the earth'/ 'all this will come upon this generation'	'May the Lord see and avenge!', v. 22; cf. Tg. 2 Chr 24.25: 'that the blood of the sons of Jehoiada the priest might be avenged'
'the blood of Zechariah'	'the blood of the son of the priest Jehoiada', that is, of Zechariah, v. 25
'whom you murdered between the sanctuary and the altar'	'stoned him to death in the court of the house of the Lord', v. 21
'stones those who are sent to it'	'stoned him to death', v. 21
judgement upon Jerusalem	Judah and Jerusalem delivered into the hands of the Syrians, vv. 23-4
'your house is forsaken'	'they forsook the house of the Lord', v. 18; 'because you have forsaken the Lord, he has forsaken you', v. 20 (cf. v. 24); *Midr. Num* 30.15 says that the murder of Zechariah caused the Shekinah to depart from the temple

Mt 23.34-9 is an updating of 2 Chr 24.17-22, 25: it moves the historic language of Chronicles to the eschatological time of the Jesus.

How does this affect interpretation? There is an implicit analogy. As it was in the days of Zechariah, so now is it in the days of Jesus. If in the past Jerusalem forsook the Lord so that the Lord forsook the city, so again has this happened: the rejection of Jesus means the rejection of Jerusalem. The house is abandoned, the divine presence withdrawn ('You will not see me again . . .'). In this way tragedy wears a familiar face – from one point of view it has all happened before – and Jesus' verdict, however dreadful, is made both more authoritative and more palatable through contemporary circumstances being akin to 2 Chr 24: there is scriptural precedent.

It may also be significant that 2 Chr 24 is not unremittingly negative. The chapter, after narrating the martyrdom of Zechariah, the conquest of Jerusalem, and the murder of king Joash, ends by speaking of 'the rebuilding of the house of God' (v. 27). This positive conclusion interests because while the majority of commentators have thought the 'You will not see me again until you say, "Blessed is the one who comes in the name of the Lord"'' to anticipate only condemnation, others have agreed with John Wesley, who found in our text the hope that someday the Jerusalemites will receive Jesus 'with joyful and thankful hearts'. Perhaps Wesley's interpretation is more credible when one sees that Mt 23.39 belongs to a complex that rewrites an OT text where there is restoration in the end.

34. The avowal of v. 30 ('we would not have shared in the blood of the prophets') is now contradicted. Salvation-history becomes damnation-history.

Therefore I send you prophets, sages, and scribes. Cf.10.16; 2 Chr 24.19; 36.15; Jer 7.25; 8.17; 25.4; 35.14–15; *Jub*. 1.12 ('I will send witnesses to them so that I may testify to them, but they will not listen and will kill the witnesses. They will persecute those who study the Law diligently'); Tg. on Isa 50.2 ('Why, when I sent my prophets, did they not repent?'). 'Prophets and sages and scribes' is not a chronological sequence moving from OT to NT times. Nor should one think only of Jesus' disciples and Christian charismatics. The three groups, which cannot be neatly distinguished, rather stand for the totality of those specially sent by God and Jesus. Thus Christian prophets and sages and scribes are included. Jesus sends prophets to those who honour only dead prophets (v. 29), sages to those whose wisdom is in name only (11.25), and scribes to those who have failed in their scribal duties (v. 3; etc.).

some of whom you will kill and crucify. Those sent by Jesus, who are elsewhere exhorted to be wise as serpents (10.16), here fall into the hands of serpents and suffer martyrdom. 'Crucify' adds a christological element by bringing the passion into view, although it is not impossible that Matthew also knew stories of the crucifixion of Christians. Jesus was God's messenger *par excellence*, and his suffering paradigmatic, an embodied prophecy of what others can expect.

some of whom you will flog in your synagogues and persecute from town to town. Cf. 10.17, 23. Flogging is a punishment also suffered by Jesus (cf. 20.19), so once more his fate is paradigmatic.

It goes without saying that the details of v. 34 are not a true-to-life record of the punishments typically endured by first-century Christian missionaires. We cannot infer actual events from polemical prophecies. Matthew, moreover, may have had Jesus in mind as much as later missionaries.

35. Threat now follows accusation, as in Amos 3.11; 4.11; 5.11; etc. Those persecuting Jesus and his followers – and so opposing God – participate in the sins of their ancestors and thereby unwittingly make their own the punishment stored up for these last.

blood appears three times in our verse and suggests the notion that God will avenge the innocent. It is particularly noteworthy that Gen 4.10 refers to the avenging of the blood of Abel. But the chief parallel to v. 35 lies in 27.24–6, where Pilate washes his hands of 'this man's blood' and the crowd responds, 'May his blood be upon us and upon our children'. By so speaking the crowd unwittingly assents to Jesus' dire prophecy.

on the earth translates a Greek expression that might mean 'on the land': that is, the land of Israel is a better translation. Cf. Num 35.33: 'Blood pollutes the land, and no expiation can be made for the land, for the blood that is shed in it, except by the blood of him who shed it.'

Why does the recompense due for the murders of all the righteous come down upon only one group? The question is often asked, especially as (i) the scribes and Pharisees had nothing to do with the murder of Zecharaiah and (ii) no Israelite had anything to do with Abel's murder. But the answer lies in v. 32: those who overflow the measure of allotted wrath are those upon whom that wrath will fall.

the blood of righteous Abel. Cf. Heb 11.4 (Abel as 'righteous', cf. 1 Jn 3.12); Josephus, *Ant.* 1.53 (Abel had respect for 'righteousness'); *Fg. Targ.* on Gen 4.10 ('the voice of the blood of the righteous multitudes that were to arise from Abel your brother cry out against you, before Me, from the earth').

the blood of Zechariah son of Barachiah has long puzzled interpreters. Zech 1.1 refers to its author as 'Zecharaiah, son of Berecchia'. There is, however, no biblical evidence of his death as a martyr; and, as Jerome observed, the temple was in ruins in his time. The one biblical martyr named Zechariah is the son of Jehoiada, a priest whose story appears near the end of Chronicles. Still other candidates have been forwarded, most often either the father of the Baptist (Lk 1.5–23) or the son of Baris (or Bariscaeus or Baruch) martyred in the temple during the Jewish war. There is also, among the more than thirty biblical Zechariahs, the Zechariah son of Jeberechiah of Isa 8.2, who is called a 'faithful witness'. Given, however, that Jewish tradition – which often merged two distinct persons (cf. Phineas and Elijah) – conflated the prophet Zecharaiah with the son of Jehoiada, and given that the death of the latter became the popular subject of legends, we may assume the same for our text. The passage refers to the murders of the righteous from Genesis 4 (the first murder in the Hebrew Bible) to 2 Chr 24 (the last murder in the Hebrew Bible); in other words, Abel and Zecharaiah are the first and last in a series. This is confirmed by four facts: the son of Jehoiada's murder was particularly heinous and his blood (mentioned in 2 Chr 24.25) became the subject of legend; the wicked deed took place 'in the court'; like Abel's death (Gen 4.10), that of Zechariah son of Jehoiada cried out for vengeance (2 Chr 24.22); and Mt 23.34–9 seems in its entirety to rest upon 2 Chr 24.

whom you murdered is odd: 'you' refers to the scribes and Pharisees, but Zechariah was killed long ago. Perhaps the notion of communal solidarity is implicit: by their own deeds the scribes and Pharisees assent to and so join in their ancestors' crimes. One might compare the common homiletical assertion that, through their sins, all Christians somehow share in the guilt of Christ's crucifixion.

between the sanctuary and the altar. 'Between the sanctuary and altar' (= altar of burnt offering) has a parallel in Ezek 8.16 and Joel 2.17 ('between the porch [of the holy place] and the altar'). The words interpret the 'in the court of the house of the Lord' of 2 Chr 24.21 to mean 'in the court [of the priests]'. Zechariah must have been a priest.

36. This verse may enlarge the prophetic condemnation beyond the scribes and Pharisees: 'this generation', which follows its corrupt leaders, is also corrupt. Perhaps, however, the point is just that judgement will fall now, in the days of 'this generation'. In either case the verse prepares for the lamentation over Jerusalem (v. 37) and anticipates the tribulations of the eschatological discourse.

all this will come upon this generation. 'This generation' refers to the contemporaries of Jesus and his followers. This is clearly the meaning throughout Matthew (11.16; 12.41–2, 45; 24.34). The evangelist likely saw a partial or initial fulfilment of 'all this' in the tragedy of AD 70.

37. The chapter concludes with a lament addressed directly to Jerusalem. The city shares in the sins of the scribes and Pharisees: it too has murdered God's messengers. Manifest is the constancy of Jesus' affection: despite its bloodstained history, he has ever loved Jerusalem.

O Jerusalem, Jerusalem, the city that kills the prophets and stones those who are sent to it! Cf. 21.35; also Neh 9.26; Jer 2.30. The double vocative here adds, as Clement of Alexandria saw, emphasis and pathos (cf. Acts 9.4), and the divine passive ('sent') distinguishes the speaker (Jesus) from the sender (God). For the killing of the prophets cf. 23.31, and for stoning note Jn 8.59 (Jesus); Acts 7.59 (Stephen); Heb 11.37 (OT heroes); *4 Baruch* 9 (Jeremiah); Josephus, *Ant.* 4.22 (Moses); *b. Sanh.* 43a (Jesus); *Exod. Rab.* on 6.13 (Moses). The Zechariah of 2 Chr 24.20–2 (cf. v. 35) was stoned, and this fact enhances narrative continuity. It has been observed that Jewish tradition does not place many executions of prophets in Jerusalem, so the present participles may mean 'ever ready to slay and stone'. This is probably correct, although in our Gospel 'all Jerusalem' has been complicit in the slaughter of infants (2.1–12), has sent Pharisees to oppose Jesus, and has been predicted as the place of the Messiah's execution (16.21; 20.17–18).

How often have I desired to gather your children together as a hen

gathers her brood under her wings, and you would not! Cf. Deut 32.11 ('like an eagle that stirs up its nest, that flutters over its young ... catching them'); Ruth 2.12; Ps 17.8 ('I hide me under the shadow of thy wings'); 36.7; 57.1; 61.5; 63.7; 64.4; 91.4. 'Everywhere in the prophets is this same image of the wings, and in the song of Moses and the Psalms, indicating his great protection and care' (Chrysostom). For Jerusalem as a 'mother' with 'children' (= Israel or, more likely, the capital's citizens, cf. Lk 19.44) see Gal 4.25; Bar 4.12 ('I am forsaken on account of the sins of my children'). The image of maternal protection proves that Jerusalem's failure is her own fault, not that of Jesus.

'How often' has struck many as awkward, for Matthew tells of only one visit to Jerusalem. Several explanations – none of which can be excluded – have been advanced. (i) While the word makes no sense in Matthew or Luke, it did when Jesus spoke it, for, as John's Gospel has it, he went up to Jerusalem on several occasions. (ii) The words were originally spoken by Wisdom (cf. Lk 11.49) and had to do with her repeated appeals. Similarly, if in Matthew Jesus = Wisdom, then Jesus need not be speaking about trips he has made to Jerusalem. (iii) 'Your children' embraces all of Israel so that Jesus' ministry outside Jerusalem is included. (iv) The meaning is: 'How often (when I was away in Galilee) did I long to come to Jerusalem and gather you all into my discipleship and protect you in the coming judgement; and now that I have come, you refuse to be gathered.' The text is about longing, not doing. (v) 'How often' makes sense only as a word of the risen Jesus: he has often sent missionaries to Israel. (vi) Jesus speaks on behalf of God or Wisdom: the 'I' is not Jesus but (as so often in the prophets) the divine word speaking through him. In this case 'how often' envisages Jerusalem's whole history.

38. Matthew concludes by referring to two events that are closely related in the next chapter: the destruction of Jerusalem (v. 38) and the *parousia* of the Son of man (v. 39). The one speaks of judgement, the other, as we shall see, of hope.

your house is forsaken and desolate envisages the destruction of AD 70. The present tense is an expression of prophetic certainty – a feature of NT prophecy generally. For related declarations see 1 Kgs 9.6–9; Isa 64.10–11; Jer 12.7; 22.5; Ezek 8.6; Tacitus, *Hist.* 5.13 ('the doors of the Holy Place [Jerusalem's temple] abruptly opened, a superhuman voice was heard to declare that the gods were leaving it'); *Gos. Phil.* 84.27–8 ('when the veil is rent and the things inside become visible, this house will be left, or rather will be destroyed'). These citations imply that (i) no particular OT text lies behind our passage but rather a far-flung way of speaking and (ii) when God deserts the house, it is left to enemies (*Ps. Sol.* 7.1).

Scholars have debated whether 'your house' – the pronoun itself implies that the house has already been abandoned – refers to the temple, to Jerusalem, or to 'the house of Israel'. In view of 21.13 ('my house') and 24.1–2, one thinks first of the temple, which is no longer God's house but, ironically, 'your house'. Yet one must add that Jewish texts do not always distinguish between the temple and the capital. Quite often the one implies the other and there are indiscriminate transitions from temple to city or *vice versa*, so that one may often speak of their identification.

Ps 118.26a, which is quoted in the next verse, is followed by this: 'We bless you from the house of the Lord'. This is part of the scriptural context for our line. Psalm 118 tells not only of worshippers blessing the one who comes in the name of the Lord but also of a blessing from the house of the Lord, from the temple. This explains why Jesus' assertion about the forsaken house is accompanied by another which concerns the eschatological future. Verse 38 implies that Jerusalem and its temple have fallen into sin and are headed for disaster. It follows that the temple in the capital cannot presently be, as it is in Ps 118.26, the source of any proper blessing. It likewise follows that those in the temple do not now bless Jesus, who will someday come as the Messiah. Thus we have here a consistent interpretation of Ps 118.26. 'Your house if forsaken' is the reason why there is presently no fulfilment of the prophetic Psalm, and why the exclamation, 'Blessed is he who comes in the name of the Lord,' belongs to eschatology. This is good reason to regard vv. 37–9 as a unit, which puts a question mark over any interpretation that requires us to divide them.

'Forsaken' was originally a reference to the departure of the Shekinah from the temple. That may still be true in Matthew, although many have thought of Jesus leaving the temple until he returns: he has abandoned the temple. Perhaps the distinction is without a difference, for Matthew identified Jesus with the Shekinah. In any case, 'desolate' directs thoughts to AD 70. Maybe Jesus' words would have gained confirmation for first-century readers from three subsequent events: Jesus' leaving of the temple (24.1–2); the rending of the veil (27.51); and the destruction of Jerusalem.

39. Jesus quotes Ps 118.26, which the crowd quoted at the entry into Jerusalem. The eschatological reference – 'he here speaks of the future day of his second coming' (Chrysostom) – makes for continuity with the following chapter.

you will not see me again until you say, 'Blessed is the one who comes in the name of the Lord.' 'You will not see' is, so to speak, the antithesis of the *parousia*. If the Son of man's resurrection means he will no longer be seen, the *parousia* is when he will be seen again: 24.30; 26.64 (cf. Acts 1.11). As Jn 16.16 puts it: 'A little while and you will see me no longer, and again a little while and you will see me'.

Interpreters have generally followed one of two paths. Either the verse has been construed as a declaration of unqualified judgement, or it has been thought to hold out hope of Israel's repentance and therefore salvation. The first view is difficult because 'blessed' does not connote fear and trembling. Further, Jewish and Christian texts teach that the Day of the Lord will see the wicked weep and wail. The second view is also problematic, for it would be jarring indeed for a straightforward promise of salvation to follow the declaration of judgement in v. 38. It seems best to adopt a third interpretation: 'until you say' signals a conditional sentence. The text means not that when the Messiah comes, his people will bless him, but rather that when his people bless him, the Messiah will come. While Israel's redemption may be, on the basis of both OT promises and 19.28, a firm hope, its date is contingent upon Israel's acceptance of Jesus.

* * * * *

(i) The scholarly consensus is that our passage records God's definite rejection of Israel. The text, however, does not plainly implicate Israel as a whole, only the leaders of Israel and Jerusalem. Where is the statement that the special relationship between God and Israel has been cancelled? Beyond that, v. 39 is best understood not as a pronouncement of condemnation but instead as a promise of redemption: the Messiah will come when the people repent; cf. Acts 3.19–20.

(ii) Verses 37–9 temper what has gone before. Without these verses the Jesus of chapter 23 would issue nothing but judgements, with no tinge of regret. But the evangelist did not wish to leave such an impression. Hence the conclusion discloses that the woes were uttered in sadness, that the indignation was righteous. When the threats give way to the image of Jesus as a mother hen lamenting her loss, the reader is reminded of the compassionate Son of 11.28–30. In this way the prophetic judgements are mingled with affection and Jesus becomes, like Jeremiah, a reluctant prophet.

THE END OF THE AGES (24.1–35)

24 [1]As Jesus went out of the temple and was going away, his disciples came to show him the buildings of the temple. [2]Responding, he asked them, 'Do you see all these? Amen I say to you, there will not be left here one stone upon another that will not be thrown down.' [3]As he was sitting on the

Mount of Olives, the disciples came to him privately, saying, 'Tell us, when will these things be, and what will be the sign of your *parousia* and of the end of the age?' ⁴And answering Jesus said to them, 'Take heed that no one lead you astray. ⁵For many will come in my name, saying, "I am the Messiah!" and they will lead many astray. ⁶And you will hear of wars and rumours of wars. Take care that you are not alarmed, for this must take place; but the end is not yet. ⁷For nation will rise against nation, and kingdom against kingdom, and there will be famines and earthquakes in various places. ⁸All this is but the beginning of the woes.

⁹'Then they will deliver you over to tribulation and will put you to death, and you will be hated by all nations on account of my name. ¹⁰Then many will be scandalized, and they will betray one another and hate one another. ¹¹And many false prophets will arise and lead many astray. ¹²And because of the increase of lawlessness, the love of many will grow cold. ¹³But the one who endures to the end will be saved. ¹⁴And this good news of the kingdom will be proclaimed throughout the world, as a testimony to all the nations; and then the end will come.

¹⁵'So when you see the abomination of desolation, spoken of by Daniel, standing in the holy place (let the reader understand), ¹⁶then let those in Judea flee to the hills. ¹⁷The one on the housetop should not go down to take what is in the house. ¹⁸The one in the field should not turn back to get a coat. ¹⁹Woe to those who are pregnant and to those who are nursing infants in those days! ²⁰Pray that your flight may not be in winter or on a Sabbath. ²¹For at that time there will be great suffering, such as has not been from the beginning of the world until now, no, and never will be. ²²And if those days had not been shortened, no one would be saved; but for the sake of the elect those days will be shortened. ²³Then if anyone says to you, "Behold! Here is the Messiah" or "There he is!", do not believe it. ²⁴For false messiahs and false prophets will appear and produce great signs and omens, to lead astray, if possible, even the elect. ²⁵Behold, I have told you beforehand. ²⁶So, if they say to you, "Behold! He is in the desert," do not go out. If they say, "Behold! He is in the inner rooms," do not believe it. ²⁷For as the lightning comes from the east and flashes as far as the west, so will be the coming of the Son of man. ²⁸Wherever the corpse is, there the vultures will gather.

²⁹'Immediately after the suffering of those days the sun will be darkened, and the moon will not give its light; the stars will fall from heaven, and the powers of heaven will be shaken. ³⁰Then the sign of the Son of man will appear in heaven, and then all the tribes of the earth will mourn, and they will see the Son of man coming on the clouds of heaven with power and great glory. ³¹And he will send out his angels with a loud trumpet call, and they will gather his elect from the four winds, from one end of heaven to the other.

³²'**From the fig tree learn its lesson. As soon as its branch becomes tender and puts forth its leaves, you know that summer is near.** ³³**So also, when you see all these things, you know that he is near, at the very gates.** ³⁴**Amen I say to you, this generation will not pass away until all these things have taken place.** ³⁵**Heaven and earth will pass away, but my words will not pass away.'**

Parallels: Mk 13.1–31; Lk 21.1–33

The first large portion of Jesus' eschatological testament, which begins as a dialogue but soon turns into a discourse, runs to v. 35 and contains several subsections. There is first an introductory scene in which Jesus predicts the temple's destruction (vv. 1–2). This in turn provokes the query concerning the timing of things to come, to which Jesus first responds with warnings and predictions about eschatological tribulation:

Vv. 3–8: the beginning of the woes
Vv. 9–14: the intensification of the woes
Vv. 15–28: the climax of the woes

These three sections become progressively longer and move from the world at large (vv. 3–8) to the church (vv. 9–14) to Judaea (vv. 15–28), a movement which implies that the end events are, as throughout the OT, focused in the holy land.

There follow vv. 29–35, which depict God's eschatological victory in the coming of the Son of man (vv. 29–31), continue with the parable of the fig tree (vv. 32–3), and end with two asseverations, the first about 'this generation' (v. 34), the second about Jesus' authoritative speech (v. 35):

I. Narrative introduction (1–2)
    A. Observation of disciples (1)
    B. Jesus' response: the destruction of the temple (2)
II. Things to come (3–36)
    A. Disciples' question (3)
    B. Jesus' answer (4–36)
        i) The period of tribulation (4–28)
            a. The beginning of the woes (4–8)
            b. The intensification of the woes (9–14)
            c. The climax of the woes (15–28)
                1. The abomination and flight (15–19)
                2. The terror of those days (20–2)
                3. Where? (23–8)

ii)   The *parousia* (29–35)
    a.   The coming of the Son of man (29–31)
    b.   A parable (32–3)
    c.   Two concluding asseverations (34–6)
       1.   'This generation will not pass away' (34)
       2.   'My words will not pass away' (35)

The large, esoteric section presents Jesus as seer of the eschatological future. This, however, is nothing new: throughout Matthew Jesus prophesies the last things. Yet even though chapters 24 and 25 in several particulars recapitulate earlier material – readers already know of false leaders (7.15–23); of the persecution of disciples (10.21–39); of the coming of the Son of man (16.27); and of the angelic harvest (13.49) – the result is not redundancy but clarification through augmentation.

Much of the traditional end-time scenario is untouched. There is, for example, no account of either the resurrection or the eternal state. Obviously Matthew 24 is not a detailed blueprint (cf. the chronological imprecision). Interest is elsewhere: (i) in supplying the true ending of the Messiah's story so that the whole can be rightly grasped; (ii) in foretelling and therefore making bearable Christian suffering; (iii) in nurturing hope by showing how a good future can issue from an evil present; and (iv) in encouraging battle against moral languor.

Beyond these generalities, the meaning of many individual verses is disputed, as is the meaning and reference of the whole, a situation largely due to the lack of any *direct* answer to the question in v. 2 about the temple, a lack inherited from Mark. One approach holds that much or most of Matthew 24 is fulfilled prophecy. According to some, vv. 3–35 have to do with the events surrounding the destruction of Jerusalem that occurred within Jesus' 'generation', and vv. 36ff. with the *parousia* whose date is unknown. Others see v. 32 as the point at which eschatology proper appears. Already Theophylact offered this sort of analysis, although he found the transition in v. 23. John Lightfoot, in *Horae Hebraicae*, even contended that the entire chapter concerns AD 70.

Against all this, the eschatological reference of vv. 6–13, 21–2, and 27–31 is scarcely to be doubted in view of (i) the many Jewish, Christian, and Matthean parallels, (ii) the dependence upon the eschatological prophecies of Daniel, and (iii) the absence of clear indications to the contrary.

A second opinion, which holds that chapter 24 is purely eschatological, is favoured by (i) the thoroughly eschatological nature of the language, (ii) the linguistic unity of the discourse, which argues against referring different sections to different events, and (iii) the 'immediately' of v. 29; for if Matthew wrote much after AD 70, he could not have thought the *parousia* would follow immediately upon the destruction of the temple, which in turn makes it unlikely that vv. 15ff. depict that destruction.

The chief objection to this approach – that if the discourse is purely eschatological, there is no direct answer to the question about the temple – falls to two observations: (i) the event was past and so the answer was known to all; and (ii) Matthew elsewhere leaves narrative ends dangling (see e.g. 14.3–12).

A third option urges that our text refers to both the destruction of Jerusalem and the *parousia,* and holds them in close chronological sequence; this implies Matthew was written not long after 70. Favouring this is the local nature of vv. 15ff. ('those in Judaea') and the 'immediately' of v. 29. Verse 34 – 'all these things' will come upon 'this generation' – can also be regarded as supportive. But most recent commentators have preferred a later date for our Gospel.

A fourth approach also thinks of both AD 70 *and* the end of the world. Unlike the third, however, it finds not a chronological sequence – first the destruction of the temple, then (soon) the end – but a single prophecy with two fulfilments. Already Ephrem the Syrian reported: 'It is said that he [Jesus] was speaking of the punishment in Jerusalem and at the same time referring to the end of this world.' According to some commentators, vv. 14–22 refer simultaneously to AD 70 and to the future. We are reminded of the Antiochean school's notion of *theoria*, according to which the OT can prophesy two things at once. That such an idea was not foreign to our text's age is clear from Jewish apocalypses such as 4 Ezra and *2 Baruch*, which use past events (e.g. Jerusalem's first destruction) as transparent ciphers for contemporary events (e.g. Jerusalem's second destruction).

The view of this commentary is that vv. 4ff. are a depiction of the entire post-Easter period, interpreted in terms of the messianic woes. This means that the discourse, which freely mixes experience with conventional themes, concerns the past, the present, and the future. What has happened will continue to happen and only get worse: 'the mystery of lawlessness is already at work' (2 Thess 2.7). Whether the fall of Jerusalem in AD 70 is directly referred to in vv 15ff. or is instead indirectly included in the tribulations of vv. 15ff. is uncertain. But if it is the former, AD 70 does not exhaust the significance of vv. 5ff., which plainly envisage eschatological events to come. So the answer to the disciples' two-part question in v. 3 is this: the temple will be destroyed during the tribulation of the latter days, which runs from the first advent to the second; and after that tribulation the end, whose date cannot be known, will come.

While it alludes to many OT texts, Matthew 24, like Mark 13, draws especially upon Daniel. The following parallels are more or less clear:

	Matthew 24	*Daniel*
temple destroyed	v. 3	9.26
time of the end	v. 3	12.6–7
rumours of war	v. 6	9.26; 11.44
persecution of saints	vv. 9–11	7.25; 11.33
abomination	v. 15	8.13; 9.27; 11.31; 12.11
time of tribulation	v. 21	12.1
Son of man on clouds	v. 30	7.13

While it is too much to say that Matthew 24 (or its main source) is a midrash upon Daniel, the clear allusions and the explicit citation of 'the prophet Daniel' (v. 15) are proof that, for Matthew, the end-time scenario will fulfil the words of Daniel and Jesus simultaneously.

The Destruction of the Temple (24.1–2)

For post-70 readers who find in Jesus' words a fulfilled prophecy, the placing of 24.1–2 at the head of the eschatological discourse serves to create confidence that the speaker can indeed see the future.

1. Jesus entered the temple area in 21.23, so the entirety of 21.23–23.39 has occurred there. The present change of scene brings a new, smaller audience but does not much alter the subject matter; cf. 13.1–2, 36.

Jesus went out of the temple and was going away. Most commentators see symbolic content in Jesus' departure: he abandons the temple, and so 'your house is forsaken' (23.38; cf. Ezek 11.23). Accordingly in the background is the theme of the deity forsaking his people. Observe also that Jesus is terminating his public ministry; cf. 23.39: 'from now on you will not see me'. With few exceptions he henceforth speaks only to disciples.

his disciples came to show him the buildings of the temple. Why the disciples show Jesus the temple is unstated. Is it because they find it incredible that he could utter judgement against such an important and proverbially magnificent structure with so many profound associations?

2. Jesus prophesies the end of the temple (cf. 26.61; 27.40). This is usually thought of as a fulfilled prophecy for readers, who know the events of AD 70. The declaration does not of itself question the legitimacy of the cult. Certainly other Jewish prophets foretold doom without attacking the Pentateuch. What we have here is not repudiation of a divinely founded institution but a tragic forecast by Jerusalem's king of a disaster fostered by human sin. The destruction of the temple is God's verdict upon the capital.

Amen I say to you. This redactional phrase recurs in v. 34 and so produces an *inclusio* for the first portion of the discourse.

there will not be left here one stone upon another that will not be thrown down. That a stone will not be left upon a stone expresses uttermost devastation and recalls Josephus, *Bell.* 7.1: 'Caesar ordered the whole city and the temple to be razed to the ground.' 'That will not be thrown down' is strictly unnecessary, but it reinforces the sense of devastation.

The Beginning of Woe (24.3–8)

3. This verse, which links the prophecy of the temple's destruction to the eschatological discourse proper, implies that the disciples do not know when the temple will be destroyed or when Jesus will return. But their question (cf. 18.1) assumes the reality of both events.

As he was sitting on the Mount of Olives, the disciples came to him privately, saying. Cf. v. 1 and the other introductions to major discourses; also Zech 14.4. On 'the Mount of Olives' (which will reappear in 26.30) and its eschatological associations see p. 343. Future events are often revealed on a mountain in ancient literature: Ezek 40–8; *Jub.* 1.1–4; 4 Ezra 4.5; *2 Bar.* 4; 13.1; *Apoc. Abr.* 21–3; *Sifre Deut.* § 357; *Tg. Ps.-Jn.* on Deut 34.1 etc. Because many of the relevant Jewish texts have to do with Moses, and because the reader of 24.3 is reminded of 5.1–2 and 15.29 (in all three Jesus sits on a mountain), places which feature a Moses typology, it is possible that the shadow of Moses falls here too.

when does not elicit a date.

what will be the sign of your *parousia* and of the end of the age? The clarifying and christological 'your *parousia*' – which takes up 23.39 and anticipates 24.30 – and the nearly synonymous 'the end of the age' apparently explicate 'these things'. Their addition puts the emphasis of what follows upon not the destruction of the temple but the last things.

The disciples' question seemingly presumes a close connexion between AD 70 and the end, especially as 'these things' implies that the event prophesied in v. 2 belongs to a complex of eschatological events. But whether the discourse itself confirms that connexion is a point of disagreement among interpreters.

'*Parousia*' (lit. 'presence') designated both the official arrival of a high-ranking person, especially a king or emperor (cf. *adventus*), as well as the manifestation of a hidden deity. The word came into

Judaism with reference to the entries of God into salvation-history and may, in pre-Christian times, have already been used of God's eschatological coming. In Matthew it means public 'arrival' (not 'return') and refers to the eschatological coming of the Son of man.

4. Take heed that no one lead you astray. Cf. 24.42–3; 2 Thess 2.3. The notion that people will be led astray (cf. 18.2–3; 22.29) in the latter days was common enough, and Matthew's readers would have known that some ironically identified Jesus himself as an eschatological deceiver; cf. 27.64. The exact nature of deception appears in the next verse (as well as in vv. 11 and 24). Here it is only taught that deception can be perceived and so avoided.

5. For many will come in my name. Cf. vv. 11 and 24 (the repetition underlines the importance of the theme). 'Come in my name' appears to mean 'come as the Messiah'. The first and second centuries saw quite a few famous false prophets who made eschatological claims. That any of them (before Bar Kochba) said, in so many words, 'I am Messiah', is undemonstrated by the sources. But several did identify themselves as the eschatological prophet like Moses, a figure Matthew equated with the Messiah. So for him the two things were one. Our verse is then about Jewish messianic deceivers and for Matthew was illustrated by past history.

they will lead many astray. Eagerness to believe will always lead to deception, especially if the alternative is waiting.

Verse 5 should be carefully compared with vv. 11 and 24. The resemblances may be set forth thus:

subject:	many (v. 5)
	many false prophets (v. 11)
	false Messiahs and false prophets (v. 24)
verb:	will come (v. 5)
	will arise (v. 11)
	will arise (v. 24)
action:	claim to be Messiah (v. 5)
	. . . . . . (v. 11)
	show great signs and wonders (v. 24)
result:	deceive many (v. 5)
	deceive many (v. 11)
	deceive the elect (v. 24)

The one constant is the concluding line on deception, which is therefore stressed most.

6. It is plain from this verse – and may have been something learned by the Matthean community through experience – that one must beware of hastily drawing eschatological conclusions.

And you will hear of wars and rumors of wars. Cf. Jer 51.46; Dan 9.26; 11.44; *2 Bar.* 48.34 ('there will be many tidings and not a few rumours'). Although the prophecy of war for the latter days (both as a sign of the end and evidence of divine judgement) was standard in Jewish and Christian eschatology, we should not forget the real conflicts of ancient Palestine, nor those in the larger world. Their bitter reality would have lent substance to Jesus' words.

Take care that you are not alarmed. Cf. 2 Thess 2.3: 'do not be quickly shaken in mind or alarmed . . . to the effect that the day of the Lord has come. Let no one deceive you . . .'

must reminds that, despite appearances, history is in God's hands.

the end means 'the end of the age'; cf. v. 3.

7. This verse explicates the previous verse.

For nation will rise against nation, and kingdom against kingdom. The language is biblical and the notion itself – that wars will herald the end – conventional.

and there will be famines and earthquakes in various places. Cf. *2 Bar.* 70.8, where war, earthquake, and famine all characterize the messianic woes. The chaos extends beyond society to nature itself. Many are the eschatological prophecies in which natural disasters such as famine (a consequence of war) and earthquakes fall upon a hapless world. So we have here another standard *topos*, yet one which Matthew's readers would have seen as partially fulfilled in known events (and which they would not have limited to Palestine).

8. The identification of preceding calamities as but 'the beginning of woes' not only cancels the claim of the messianic pretenders – the end is not yet – but makes the eschatological tribulation extend over time. The practical side of this theologoumenon is patient endurance.

All this is but the beginning of the woes. Dan 11.27 ('for the end is yet to be at the time appointed') may be in the background. 'Woes' is literally 'birth pangs', and frequently the new world was anthropomorphized as coming to birth in labour pains.

The Persecution of Disciples (24.9–14)

9. **Then they will deliver you over to tribulation.** Obviously 'you' = 'some of you (Christians)'. Not obvious is the subject: who are 'they'?

and will put you to death. Cf. 10.28; 21.35; 22.6. The prophecy reveals that the eschatological violence of vv. 6 and 7 will extend to Christians. Although there is no real evidence that Matthew's own community had known persecution unto death, it had previously heard stories of Nero's persecution and of occasional martyrdom (e.g. Stephen).

and you will be hated by all nations on account of my name. Cf. 10.22; Jn 15.18ff. It is precisely those who persecute the church who are the object of its mission (28.19). Is this an instance of 5.44 – love your enemies?

10. The upshot of external persecution is internal disorder. Hatred from outsiders will produce hatred among insiders.

Then many will be scandalized, and they will betray one another and hate one another. Cf. LXX Dan 7.25. As in 18.6, 'to be scandalized' refers to losing faith and falling away from God: one of the effects of the confusion and rebellion of the end-time.

11. And many false prophets will arise and lead many astray. Cf. Acts 20.29–30. This reminds one of vv. 4–5 (although here false Christian leaders may be in view) and foreshadows vv. 23–4, which are inspired by Deut 13.1–2.

12. Love and lawlessness are antithetical, for love fulfils the law.

And because of the increase of lawlessness, the love of many will grow cold. Cf. LXX, Theod. Dan 12.4 and *Did.* 16.3–4 ('love will be turned into hatred', 'for as wickedness increases, they will hate one another and persecute and betray'). 'Lawlessness,' which recurs in 7.23; 13.41; and 24.12, also characterizes their end in 2 Th 2.3 and *Did.* 16.4. One can ask whether 'love' is here love for God or for fellow human beings, especially other Christians. But in our Gospel the distinction is insignificant: to forsake God is to abandon one's neighbour.

13. 'Love endures all things' (1 Cor 13.7).

But the one who endures to the end will be saved. In 10.22 the persecution comes from outsiders; here insiders are the culprits – and only a remnant remains faithful.

14. The Christian mission belongs to eschatology. Indeed, the conjunction of vv. 13 and 14 produces the thought that those who endure the eschatological trial are precisely those who, whatever comes, remain faithful bearers of 'the gospel of the kingdom'.

And this good news of the kingdom will be proclaimed throughout the world, as a testimony to all the nations; and then the end will come. The untypically fulsome sentence – 'this' (cf. 26.13), 'of the kingdom' (cf. 4.23; 9.35), and 'throughout the world' are all strictly unnecessary: their absence would not change the meaning – sets forth the what ('the gospel of the kingdom'), the where ('the world'), the wherefore ('as a testimony to all the nations'), and the conclusion ('and then the end will come') of Christian proclamation.

'The gospel of the kingdom' (= 'the word of the kingdom', 13.19), which is both what Jesus preached and what is preached about him, will be heard throughout the world before the end comes: so prepare for the universal judgement (25.31–46). This idea, found only here in Matthew, reminds one of Rom 11.11–15, and it presupposes the well-attested notion that a lack of repentance hinders the consummation: it is Christian proclamation which will encourage such repentance and so hasten the end. One may also find here an explanation of the delay of the *parousia*: the end does not come until the missionary task is discharged. Perhaps one should see in this, as in v. 32, acknowledgement that the time of end cannot be known beforehand.

'And then the end will come' takes up the language of v. 6 and points ahead to the events recounted in vv. 29ff. In the background is the OT motif of the nations' end-time conversion to Yahweh. Here that conversion heralds the end.

The Climax of the Woes (24.15–28)

15. This verse is the closest the text comes to answering the question about the temple (v. 3).

So when you see the abomination of desolation, spoken of by Daniel, standing in the holy place. 'The abomination of desolation' is, as Matthew makes explicit, from the prophet Daniel, where it refers to the pagan altar and/or image of Olympian Zeus set up in the Jerusalem temple by Antiochus IV Epiphanes in 167 BC (9.27; 11.31; 12.11). Many have supposed that, in the tradition, the phrase was applied to the attempted desecration of Caligula in AD 40. Whether that is so or not, Luke seems to refer it to the destruction of the temple in AD 70 (21.20), and many commentators think this also the reference in Matthew. That is possible. But it is no less likely that our evangelist had in mind some future, eschatological defilement and destruction, and perhaps even activities of an anti-Christ: (i) 2 Thess 2.3–4 (which may depend upon the Jesus tradition) shows the early existence of such a tradition within Christianity; (ii) Mark's personifying 'standing' suggests such; and (iii) *Didache* 16 (which depends upon extra-synoptic tradition as well as Matthew) speaks of 'the world-deceiver' who makes himself out to be a son of God.

let the reader understand. 'The reader' can mean either the reader of Matthew (in this case the words are an editorial aside) or the reader of Daniel (in this case the comment is part of Jesus' speech). The latter is more likely. The parenthesis, whatever its original significance, suggests careful and maybe even an esoteric interpretation of the previous clause (cf. Rev 13.18; 17.9), or perhaps a new interpretation of the relevant passages in Daniel.

16. The 'abomination of desolation' sets off a series of frightful events about which practical advice is given: flee! As in 10.23, eschatological flight will be interrupted by the return of the Son of man (v. 29). Whether one is fleeing from evil or fleeing because God, in response to the abomination, is about to let loose wrath, is not stated.

to the hills means 'to where the caves (for hiding) are'. The temple and city have already fallen into enemy hands (v. 15) and so refuge must be taken elsewhere. The prototypical flight from wickedness was that of Lot and his wife from Sodom (Gen 19.15–22), and it may be in view here. That flight became, in Jewish eschatology, a type of the eschatological flight from wickedness in the final days; and Gen 19.17 contains the command: 'Flee to the hills'. As Lk 17.32 has it, 'Remember Lot's wife'.

Many have thought that our verse either prophesies or looks back to the flight of Jewish Christians to Pella shortly before the destruction of Jerusalem in AD 70. It is in any event possible that Matthew and his readers had that occurrence in mind (especially if some of them participated in it) – presuming that the tradition of a flight to Pella is historical. But this has been doubted.

17. This verse functions to stress that immediate and unencumbered flight is necessary: there is not even time to pack one's belongings. One is reminded of the privations of the disciples in chapter 10 and the haste of the exodus tradition (Exod 12.39).

The one on the housetop should not go down to take what is in the house. Cf. 1 Macc 2.28 ('he and his sons fled to the hills and left all that they had in the city'). Perhaps we find here reinforcement of Jesus' teaching about wealth: possessions cannot help in the truly important matters. They may even need to be forsaken.

Ancient Palestinians spent much time on their flat, clay roofs, which were used for dining, drying produce, conversation, and sleeping during the summer months. Maybe we are to think of trials overcoming leisure activities.

18. The one in the field must behave like the one on the roof: both, like Lot, must flee without turning back.

The one in the field should not turn back to get a coat. Cf. Gen 19.17. The reader can imagine either that the cloak is left in the house or beside the field. In either case time is too short to look for it.

19. To flee means to travel; but travel with infants or children is more difficult than unencumbered travel.

Woe to those who are pregnant and to those who are nursing infants in those days! The line, like several Jewish and most Christian texts to touch the issue, assumes that the messianic tribulation will see even the righteous and innocent suffer.

20. This verse hints that our section is not historical description but eschatological prophecy; for what would be the point of inserting an imperative to pray about a past event, that it not take place at a particular time?

winter was the rainy season and so brought floods and muddy roads (to hinder flight).

on a Sabbath has been variously explained. (i) Times will be hard because, on a Sabbath, gates will be shut and provisions unobtainable. (ii) Flight on a Sabbath will antagonize Jewish opponents and make Palestinian Christians immediately visible. (iii) The clause is a relic of pre-Matthean tradition. (iv) It is a deliberate literary anachronism descriptive of events surrounding AD 70 and says nothing about Matthew's contemporaries. (v) Some members of Matthew's community still observed the Sabbath; and, given the traditional travel restrictions, they would be both hesitant and unprepared for flight on the day of rest.

Option (v) is the best choice because elsewhere in Matthew the Sabbath remains in force. This does not mean that Matthew himself would have firmly opposed such flight, for he might have recognized circumstances which overrode the keeping of the Sabbath. But he nonetheless knew that among his readers were some who would be sorely tried to flee on a Sabbath.

21. For at that time there will be great suffering, such as has not been from the beginning of the world until now, no, and never will be. 'The great tribulation etc.' is from Dan 12.1. Cf. 1QM 1.11–12 ('And it shall be a time of tribulation ... of all its afflictions none shall be as this'); *T. Mos.* 8.1 ('and there will come upon them punishment and wrath such as has never happened to them from the creation until that time when he stirs up against them a king').

22. And if those days had not been shortened, no one would be saved. The past tense is prophetic: God has already decided the future. The line probably continues the adaption of Dan 12.1: 'at that time your people will be delivered'.

The notion that God, out of grace, will hasten the coming of salvation, either by cutting days short or altering the prescribed measure of eschatological suffering, is attested elsewhere. Texts for comparison include: Sir 36.8 ('Hasten the day, and remember the appointed time'); 4Q385 frag. 3 ('the days will hasten quickly, until [all the children of] men will say: Are not the days hastening on in order that the children of Israel may inherit [the land]? ... I will shorten the days and the year[s'); *LAB* 19.13 ('I will command the years and order the times and they will be shortened'); *2 Bar.* 20.1–2; 54.1; 83.1; 2 Esdr 2.13 ('pray that your days may be few, that they may be shortened'); *Barn.* 4.3 ('the Master has cut the seasons and the days short, that his

beloved might hasten and come'); *Apoc. Abr.* 29.13 ('the curtailing of
the age of impiety'); *Trimorphic Prot.* 44.16 ('the times are cut short
and the days have been shortened'). The Jesus tradition itself may
offer further examples: both 'thy kingdom come' and Lk 18.1–8 (the
unjust judge) have been construed to mean that God will respond to
prayers to hasten the end.

23. This and the following verses have often been taken to refer to
the anti-Christ, and Matthew may have thought in terms of such a
figure.

Then means 'during the time of tribulation', not 'after the days are
shortened'.

if anyone says to you. The unspecified 'anyone' reminds one of the
false prophet who promotes the beast in Revelation.

'Behold! Here is the Messiah' or 'There he is!', do not believe it. 'Do
not believe it' may here mean something like: 'Do not believe and
follow them.' Note that 'behold' appears four times in the next three
verses: the narrative is coming to its climax.

24. Unlike Jesus, who is reluctant to show signs and wonders (4.1–
11; 12.39; 16.1–4; 27.40) and often asks for quiet about his miracles
(e.g. 8.4; 9.30), his false imitators will work wonders for public display;
cf. Revelation 13.

**For false messiahs and false prophets will appear and produce great
signs and omens, to lead astray, if possible, even the elect.** Cf. 24.5, 11; 2
Thess 2.9; 2 Pet 2.1; 1 Jn 2.18; 4.1; Rev 13.3. The words are based upon
the instructions concerning false prophets in Deut 13.2 ('If a prophet
arises among you or a dreamer of dreams, and gives you a sign or a
wonder...') and 6 ('because he spoke to deceive you concerning the
Lord your God').

25. Behold, I have told you beforehand. Cf. Jn 16.1–4. The point is
threefold: (i) Jesus himself has made it plain that signs and wonders
are not of themselves guarantees of God's activity: incredulity has its
place (cf. 7.21–3); (ii) tribulation can be no surprise for it has been
predicted, and so must it be endured; and (iii) unlike the false
prophets, Jesus' prophecy is true. Note that whereas 'behold' is a way
for calling attention to something, here it is used in connection with
things one should not attend to.

26. More scepticism.

Verses 26–7 have to do with rumours of false Messiahs being here
or there. This makes for a happy contrast with vv. 23–5: one must
discount messianic reports because, when the Son of man comes, all
doubt will fly: his coming will not be secondhand rumour but the
indubitable object of observation.

'Behold! He is in the desert', do not go out. Cf. LXX Jer 4.11 ('a spirit of error in the wilderness'); 2 Thess 2.1–2. 'In the desert' was presumably a well-known haunt of messianic pretenders who sought to imitate the wilderness miracles of Moses.

If they say, 'Behold! He is in the inner rooms', do not believe it. Should we think of a political leader plotting national liberation while hiding from the Romans (cf. the Zealots), or of a hidden Messiah, or of a room within the temple?

27. Unlike his first advent, the Messiah's *parousia* will be of a sudden (cf. Ps 144.6), as unmistakable as a lightning flash. All doubt will vanish, and all false messiahs will be unmasked. No one will have to say, 'Look here, look there'.

For as the lightning comes from the east and flashes as far as the west, so will be the coming of the Son of man. Cf. Ps 97.4 ('His lightnings lighten the world'); Isa 62.1; Zech 9.14; Ep. Jer. 61 ('lightning, when it flashes, is widely seen'); 4Q246 2.1–2 ('their kingdom will be like the flashes that you saw'); 2 *Bar.* 53.9 (lightning 'lighted the whole earth'); and for lightning with a divine theophany or judgement Exod 19.16; Ps 18.14; 144.6. The early church's custom of praying and worshipping while facing the east, and the habit of turning to the east while dying, may derive from this verse and the belief that Jesus would come from that direction.

28. With this verse the review of tribulation ends.

Wherever the corpse is, there the vultures will gather. Cf. Job 9.26; LXX Job 15.23 ('He [the tyrant] is cut down as food for vultures, and he knows in himself that he will remain a carcass, and the dark day will terrify him'); 39.27, 30 ('Is it at your command that the eagle mounts up and makes his nest on high? ... and where the slain are, there is he'); Hab 1.8 ('they fly like an eagle swift to devour'); Cornutus, *Nat. deorum* 21 ('the birds [vultures] ... gather together wherever there are many corpses slain in war'); Seneca, *Ep.* 95.43 ('where the vulture is, expect a corpse'). Both the form ('where ... there') and content were conventional.

What is the meaning in Matthew? There are several possibilities, between which one cannot choose with confidence. (i) The coming of the Son of man will be as public and obvious as eagles or vultures circling over carrion. (ii) The eschatological tribulation will be concluded by vultures devouring the flesh of the wicked dead, as in Rev 19.17–18. (iii) The Son of man will descend when the world becomes rotten with evil, just as a vulture swoops down upon a rotting corpse. (iv) The body is Jesus, the eagles the disciples: the saints will mount as eagles to be gathered to the Son of man when he comes. (v) Some have equated the corpse with a spiritually dead Israel, the eagles with angels of judgement or the avenging Son of man or messiahs pretenders. (vi) Application to the destruction of the temple or Jerusalem might equate the eagles with the Roman standards which surrounded Jerusalem, the body with the wrecked capital or temple. (vii) Because of the verbal connexion with v. 31, where angels gather the saints, one might identify the eagles with angels. There is some evidence for angelic eagles, and Chrysostom equated the eagles with the heavenly host.

The *Parousia* of the Son of Man (24.29–31)

This paragraph, which ends the account of the tribulation and narrates the *parousia* in the traditional language of the OT theophany, so that Jesus' coming is the arrival of God's glory, lacks imperatives. The verbs are all descriptive futures.

29. Having, in v. 28, moved the mind's eye from earth to sky, the text now directs our gaze even higher. This imaginative raising of vision leaves distress behind and prepares for envisaging the good help that comes from heaven (v. 30).

Immediately after the suffering of those days. These words are reason either for dating Matthew shortly after AD 70 or for regarding vv. 15ff. as still wanting fulfilment.

the sun will be darkened, and the moon will not give its light; the stars will fall from heaven, and the powers of heaven will be shaken. Bengel: 'According to the course of nature, the sun and moon are eclipsed at different times: then, however, they will be troubled at once.' The prophecy – which shows that the matter of our Gospel is bound up with the meaning of the cosmos in its entirety – is largely a free conflation of Isa 13.10 ('For the stars of the heavens and their constellations will not give their light; the sun will be dark at its rising, and the moon will not give its light') and 34.4 ('all the host of heaven shall rot away, and the skies roll up like a scroll. All their host shall fall'). Related forecasts can be found throughout the OT, intertestamental and early Christian literature. In many instances the post-exilic texts may be read more or less literally, as perhaps here: the lawless behaviour of the heavenly bodies – and perhaps comets – is the sign that God has let them go and their time is up: a new world is coming; cf. 2 Pet 3.10, 12.

'The powers of heaven' may simply be a summarizing expression that includes the sun, the moon, and the stars. But one should not forget that the ancients identified the heavenly lights with living beings; so we could here think of the fall of evil beings, 'the spiritual forces of wickedness in the heavenly places' (Eph 6.12) or, alternatively, of the heavenly hosts who come down to do battle against evil.

The supernatural darkness of the consummation is richly symbolic. Not only does it belong to the correlation of beginning and end, but it is a sign of both divine judgement and mourning and becomes the velvet background for the Son of man's splendour (24.27, 30). Moreover, on the literary level it foreshadows the darkness of Jesus' death (27.45) while that darkness in turn presages the world's assize.

Perhaps the falling of the stars and the resultant darkness adds to the *Urzeit/Endzeit* correlation in more than one way. Jewish legend spoke of a falling of stars near the beginning of the world: the fall of Satan and his hosts was often depicted as a crash of stars from the sky; cf. Rev 12.4.

30. This verse and the next constitute the dramatic zenith of chapter 24. The coming of the Son of man – which takes place neither in desert nor inner room but is rather universally witnessed – is what vv. 3ff. introduce and that for which vv. 32ff. call one to look. When the Son of man finally appears, all will recognize what the church even now confesses: that he has all authority in heaven and earth (28.18).

Then the sign of the Son of man will appear in heaven. Cf. Rev 12.1 ('a great sign appeared in the heaven'), 3; 15.1. 'The sign of the Son of man' (an unparalleled expression) has been variously understood. (i) The genitive may be appositive: the sign which is the Son of man, or, more precisely, the Son of man's coming. (ii) The sign might be the cross, as often in the church fathers. (iii) It could be a great light. (iv) 'Sign' = Heb. *nēs*, 'ensign': the Son of man will raise an eschatological ensign, signalling muster for the eschatological battle.

Option (iv) is the most plausible understanding. In ancient Israel the horn of a ram was blown to rally the tribes for war. This act was accompanied by the raising of an ensign upon a hill. The ensign consisted of a wooden pole upon whose top crosspiece was an insigne, most often an animal. In later times, especially in Isaiah, the old custom was put to prophetic use: the Lord will raise an ensign and call for war (Isa 13.2–4), or the root of Jesse will 'stand as an ensign to the peoples' (Isa 11.10). The old tradition that the cross will accompany Jesus at his *parousia* has a straightforward explanation if 'sign' = *nēs*, for the *nēs* had a crossbar and would naturally have encouraged Christians to think of a cross.

and then all the tribes of the earth will mourn. Cf. *1 En.* 62.5 (where the wicked ruling class sees the Son of man). This combination of Zech 12.10 ('when they look upon me [v.l.: him] whom they have pierced, they shall mourn'), 12 ('the land shall mourn, each tribe by itself'), 14 ('and all the tribes that are left'), and perhaps 14.17 has no synoptic parallel. But Rev 1.7 also conflates Dan 7.13–14 and Zech 12.10, 12, and 14: 'Behold, he is coming with the clouds, and every eye will see

him, every one who pierced him; and all the tribes of the earth will
mourn on account of him.' Despite the striking agreements, the
Apocalypse does not seem to presuppose Matthew. Rather, a pre-
Matthean origin for both the christological exegesis of Zech 12.10–14
and the confluence with Daniel 7 is indicated. These things probably
belonged to Christian oral tradition.

The people mourn on earth because they see in heaven the sign of
the Son of man, which I have argued is the cross. But whether their
mourning is unto repentance (as in Zechariah) or (so most) despair is
not stated.

Matthew and his first readers presumably identified the pierced one
with the smitten shepherd of Zech 13.7; cf. 26.31. They may further
have remembered that the mourning of Zech 12.10 is 'as for a
beloved'; cf. 3.17; 12.18; 17.5.

and they will see the Son of man. Cf. Mt 16.27; 26.64; 1 Thess 4.16–
17; Rev 14.14. The whole line draws upon Dan 7.13–14, although there
may be some influence from Zech 12.10. While the Son of man's origin
and destination are not here stated, one naturally envisages a heavenly
figure descending to earth, somehow in the vision of all.

coming on the clouds of heaven does more than just recall Daniel 7
and other texts in which heavenly figures appear on clouds. In Exod
13.21–2, the Lord goes before Israel in a pillar of cloud, while in Exod
40.35–8 the cloud over the tabernacle is the glory of God. In these
texts, as in others, a cloud is the visible sign of the invisible presence of
God and so a regular element of the theophany. So the Son of man's
coming on the clouds marks the approach of God. This drawing near
of the divine presence must mean judgement for those who have set
themselves against God. In line with this, Dan 7.13 itself depends upon
Jer 4.13 ('he comes with the clouds'), where the arriving clouds
connote the swiftness of judgement. Perhaps the reader of Matthew
will also recall the eschatological promise that the cloud of divine
presence will someday return: Isa 4.5; 2 Macc 2.8.

power here means not 'miracle' but (as in 22.29) the divine 'power'
which overshadows the powers of all false prophets and messiahs.

great glory. With the heavenly lights darkened, the one light will be
the eschatological *doxa*.

31 The happy conclusion not only fails to mention God the Father
but, even more surprisingly, alludes neither to the judgement of the
wicked nor the resurrection of the dead.

And he will send out his angels with a loud trumpet call. The Son of
man's *parousia* will not only be seen by all: it will be heard by all. 'With
a great [= loud] trumpet blast', which may allude to Isa 27.13 ('in that
day a great trumpet will be blown'), has many parallels: 1 Cor 15.52

('at the last trumpet. For the trumpet will sound, and the dead will be raised'); 1 Thess 4.16 ('the Lord himself will descend from heaven ... with the sound of the trumpet of God'); *Did.* 16.6 ('a sign of a voice of a trumpet, and thirdly a resurrection of the dead'); *Apoc. Abr.* 31.1 ('I will sound the horn in the air, and I will send my chosen one ... and he will summon my people'); the *Shemoneh Esreh*, benediction 10 ('Sound the great sophar for our freedom; lift up the ensign to gather our exiles, and gather us from the four corners of the earth'); and *Gk. Apoc. Ezra* 4.36 ('After these things a trumpet, and the graves will be opened').

The sophar was a signalling device, not really a musical instrument. It sounded to announce the beginning of the Sabbath, to muster and direct armies, to frighten enemies, to greet the new moon, to warn of danger, to herald a king's coronation, and to mark sacred occasions (including temple activities). It was also an element in the OT theophany (Exod 19.16 etc.). In Isa 27.13 it calls for the Jewish exiles to return to the land, and in Joel 2.1 and Zeph 1.16 the sophar proclaims the Day of the Lord. These texts naturally led to association with the resurrection of the dead and so, in early Christianity, with Jesus' *parousia*.

The use of 'his angels' with reference to the Son of man not only enhances his authority: it also reminds one of Hebrews 1, which rejects an angel Christology. One might find the same idea implied here; for if the angels belong to the Son of man, or are at his disposal (cf. 26.53), then is he himself not above them?

and they will gather his elect from the four winds, from one end of heaven to the other. Cf. Isa 43.6; LXX Zech 2.6 ('For from the four corners of heaven I will gather you, says the Lord'); 1 Thess 4.17; Rev 7.1. The language, although it probably denotes a rapture to heaven, as in 1 Thess 4.17, derives from the Jewish hope that, in the latter days, God will ingather the Jews of the diaspora. Commentators usually assume that the elect must be the Christian faithful, and *Did.* 9.4 and 10.5 (prayers to gather the church from the ends of the earth) support this judgement. In view, however, of the strong Jewish background, it cannot be excluded that Matthew also thought of faithful Jews being gathered from the diaspora: 'all Israel will be saved' (Rom 11.26).

For angels accompanying Jesus at his *parousia* see 13.41; 16.27; 25.31; 2 Thess 1.7. In the biblical tradition angels often accompany a theophany, including a divine appearance for judgement (e.g. Deut 33.2; Ps 68.17). In the NT angels are helpers with the last judgement and appear at the end with Jesus.

The Parable of the Fig Tree (24.32–5)

This briefest of parables gives an illustration of one circumstance heralding another and then likens that illustration to the content of chapter 24: when 'all these things' – that is, the signs of vv. 5ff. (or perhaps especially those in 15ff.) – are seen, then the end, that is, the consummation described in vv. 29ff., must be near.

32. As soon as its branch becomes tender and puts forth its leaves, you know that summer is near. While most Palestinian trees are non-deciduous, the fig tree loses its leaves in the rainy winter, so that its branches become bare; but in the late spring it begins to bud, and then follows summer; cf. Cant 2.11–13.

33. The application may be compared with 4 Ezra 8.63–9.2: 'You have shown me now many of the signs which you will do in the last times but have not shown me when you will do them. He answered me and said, " . . when you see that a certain part of the predicted signs are past, then you will know that it is the very time when the Most High is about to visit the world . . .".'

all these things (cf. vv. 2, 3, 34) embraces all the signs and events leading up to the *parousia*.

you know that he is near, at the very gates. Cf. Isa 13.6 ('the day of the Lord is near'); Ezek 30.3 ('the day is near'); Joel 1.15; 2.1; Zeph 1.7, 14; Jas 5.9 ('the judge is standing at the doors'). Whether 'know' is an indicative (cf. v. 32) or an imperative cannot be decided.

The Time of the *Parousia* (24.34–6)

34. This takes us back to the question in v. 3.

this generation will not pass away until all these things have taken place. 'Generation' and 'all these things' have both been given several meanings and so there are the following explanations:

  (i)   'All these things' refers to the destruction of Jerusalem in AD 70, which came to pass within the 'generation' of Jesus' audience. In favour of this, v. 3's 'these things' does refer to the temple's destruction. Against it, the 'all these things' of vv. 8 and 33 naturally have a much wider reference.

  (ii) 'All these things' refers to the eschatological scenario as outlined in vv. 4–31 and declares that it shall come to pass before Jesus' 'generation' has gone. In favour of this is the imminent eschatological expectation of many early Christians (cf. esp. 10.23 and Mk 9.1) as well as Jn 21.20–3, which reflects the belief that Jesus would come before all his disciples had died.

(iii) Patristic opinion could identify the 'generation' with the church: the church, against which the gates of Hades will not prevail, will endure to the end.

(iv) Occasionally 'generation' is equated with the Jewish people or the human race in general. While the latter equation creates banality, the first perhaps fits the broader context: Jesus promises that the tribulation in Judaea (v. 16), however terrible, will not obliterate the chosen people (cf. Dan 12.1). But, given that our verse immediately trails the parable of the fig tree, surely the chronological sense of 'generation' is more natural.

(v) 'This generation' might be the generation that sees 'all these things', and from Matthew's perspective therefore perhaps some future generation.

(vi) 'This generation' could mean 'this kind', with qualitative sense. The point is perverse character, not chronology.

(vii) Maybe Matthew's presentation of the resurrection as an eschatological event means that the *parousia* has already in some sense taken place.

Interpretation (ii) seems best. 'Generation' plainly refers to Jesus' contemporaries in 11.16; 12.39, 41, 42, 45; 16.4; and 17.17 as well as in the close parallel in 23.36, and the placement of our verse after a prophecy of the *parousia* is suggestive. If it be objected that this makes for a false prophecy and raises the issue of 2 Pet 3.3–4, one can only reply that some of Jesus' contemporaries were perhaps still alive when Matthew wrote, so he did not have the problem we do.

35. If all of Jesus' predictions have not yet been fulfilled, their day will surely come ('heaven and earth will pass away'); in the meantime, Jesus' words abide.

Heaven and earth will pass away, but my words will not pass away. That the world will pass away (already stated in 5.18) was a common conviction (cf. v. 29); and ours is not the only text to contrast the passing of heaven and earth with something of greater endurance; cf. Isa 51.6. But here that something is Jesus' speech, which therefore sets him above Torah and makes his words like God's words (cf. Ps 119.89; Isa 40.8): they possess eternal authority. This is the presupposition of 7.24–7 and 28.20. In context, the assertion functions as do vv. 1–2: it confirms that Jesus can speak authoritatively even about the future, a subject beyond normal human reach.

* * * * *

(i) Matthew's last major discourse is the only discourse to treat eschatology exclusively. But each of the other major discourses (5–7,

10, 13, 18) concludes by turning to the last things. So the pattern of the individual discourses is the same as the pattern of the five taken together: the conclusion is eschatology every time. This reflects the conviction that the meaning of Matthew's story is determined not only by its literary ending but by the ending of history itself. The evangelist plainly believed that if history's conclusion is not christological, then christology itself becomes problematic.

(ii) Chapter 24 interprets the interim between the two advents as the time of messianic woe, a time characterized by an absent Lord. But 28.16–20 – which recalls our discourse in that it also features a mountain, refers to 'the end of the age', alludes to Dan 7.13, and proclaims the Gentile mission – depicts the time of the church as one of Jesus' consoling and all-powerful presence. The two contrasting pictures, these two different perspectives on the same period, reflect the paradox of Christian experience. Jesus is even now the present Lord who rules heaven and earth. He is also the absent master whose delay permits the powers of evil to inflict tribulation.

(iii) While most of 24.1–36 is description, much of it is paraenesis. Imperatives appear in vv. 4, 6, 16–18, 20, 23, 26, and 32. So the lesson in eschatology does not simply console: it also demands discernment and adherence to Jesus' commands. The eschatological imagination does not displace practical moral concern .

(iv) The passage links up with both chapter 23 and the passion narrative. Mt 23.29–39 is an indictment of the Jewish leaders and a declaration of the consequent divine abandonment; and the paragraph ends by referring to the second advent. Mt 24.1ff. continues the latter two themes. Indeed, the connexion is such that one might interpret the messianic woes as the result of the rejection of Jesus by his own. As for the connexion with 26–8, the themes of the temple's demise (v. 3), of 'handing over' to death (vv. 9, 10), of 'falling away' (v. 10), of the *parousia* (vv. 27, 30), and of heavenly darkness (v. 29) all reappear in the passion; see 26.31–5, 45–9, 64, 27.45, 51. Following several interpreters of Mark 13 it is not going too far to see in the end of Jesus either a foreshadowing of the end of all things or 'the beginning of the end-time'.

ESCHATOLOGICAL VIGILANCE (24.36–25.30)

[36]'But concerning that day and hour no one knows, neither the angels of heaven nor the Son, but only the Father.

[37]'For as the days of Noah were, so will be the coming of the Son of man. [38]For as in those days, before the flood, they were eating and drinking, marrying and giving in marriage, until the day Noah entered

the ark, ³⁹and they knew nothing until the flood came and took them all away, so too will be the coming of the Son of man.

⁴⁰'Then two will be in the field. One will be taken and one will be left. ⁴¹Two women will be grinding meal together. One will be taken and one will be left. ⁴²Keep awake, then, for you do not know on what day your Lord is coming.

⁴³'But know this, that if the owner of the house had known in what part of the night the thief was coming, he would have stayed awake and would not have let his house be broken into. ⁴⁴Therefore you also must be ready, for the Son of man comes in an hour you do not expect.

⁴⁵'Who then is the faithful and wise slave, whom his master has put in charge of his household, to give them their food in its season? ⁴⁶Blessed is that slave whom his master will find at work when he comes. ⁴⁷Amen I say to you, that he will put that one in charge of all his possessions. ⁴⁸But if that wicked slave says in his heart, "My master delays," ⁴⁹and begins to beat his fellow slaves, and eats and drinks with the drunkards, ⁵⁰the master of that slave will come on a day when he does not expect him and at an hour that he does not know. ⁵¹He will cut him in two and assign his portion with the hypocrites, where there will be weeping and gnashing of teeth.

25 ¹'Then the kingdom of heaven will be like ten bridesmaids, who took their lamps and went to meet the bridegroom. ²Five of them were foolish, and five were wise. ³For the foolish, taking their lamps, took no oil with them. ⁴But the wise took flasks of oil with their lamps. ⁵With the bridegroom being delayed, they all became drowsy and slept. ⁶But at midnight there was a shout, "Behold the bridegroom! Come out to meet him." ⁷Then all those bridesmaids got up and trimmed their lamps. ⁸The foolish said to the wise, "Give us some of your oil, for our lamps are going out." ⁹But the wise replied, "No, lest there not be enough for you and for us. Go rather to the dealers and buy some for yourselves." ¹⁰And with them going away to buy it, the bridegroom came, and those who were ready went with him into the wedding banquet; and the door was shut. ¹¹Later on, the other bridesmaids came also, saying, "Lord, lord, open to us." ¹²But he replied, "Amen I say to you, I do not know you." ¹³Keep awake, then, because you know neither the day nor the hour.

¹⁴'For it is as with a man going away on a journey, who called his slaves and entrusted his property to them. ¹⁵And to one he gave five talents, to another two, to another one, to each according to his ability. Then he went away. ¹⁶The one who had received the five talents went off and traded with them, and he made five more talents. ¹⁷Likewise, the one who had the two talents made two more talents. ¹⁸But the one who had received the one talent went off and dug a hole in the ground and

hid his master's money. [19]After a long time the master of those slaves came and settled accounts with them. [20]And the one who had received the five talents came forward, bringing five more talents, saying, "Master, you handed over to me five talents; see, I have made five more talents." [21]His master said to him, "Well done, good and trustworthy slave. Over a few things you have been faithful; over many things will I put you in charge. Enter into the joy of your master." [22]And the one with the two talents came forward, saying, "Master, you handed over to me two talents; see, I have made two more talents." [23]His master said to him, "Well done, good and trustworthy slave. Over a few things you have been faithful; over many things will I put you in charge. Enter into the joy of your master." [24]Then the one who had received the one talent also came forward, saying, "Master, I knew that you were a harsh man, reaping what you did not sow, and gathering where you did not scatter. [25]So I was afraid, and I went and hid your talent in the ground. See, you have what is yours." [26]But his master answered and said, "You evil and lazy slave! Did you not know that I reap where I did not sow, and gather where I did not scatter? [27]Then you ought to have invested my money with the bankers, and on my return I would have received what was my own with interest. [28]So take the talent from him, and give it to the one with the ten talents. [29]For to everyone who has, will more be given, and he will have an abundance; but from the one who has nothing, even what he has will be taken away. [30]As for this worthless slave, throw him into the outer darkness, where there will be weeping and gnashing of teeth".'

Parallels: Mk 13.32, 33–7; Lk 17.26–36; 12.35–46; 19.11–17

Verse 36 is the introduction. Its declaration of eschatological ignorance grounds the entire section: one must be ever prepared for what may come at any time. There follow as illustrations (i) a simile: as it was in the days of Noah, so shall it be at the Son of man's *parousia* (vv. 37–9); (ii) a description of the division caused by the coming of the Son of man plus an imperative: one will be taken, one left, so keep watch (vv. 40–2); and (iii) a parable and its application: the Son of man will come as unexpected as a thief, so be ready (vv. 43–4).

The sayings and similes of vv. 36–44 preface three long parables: the faithful and wise servant (24.45–51), the wise and foolish virgins (25.1–13), and the talents (vv. 14–30). All three concern the delay of the *parousia*, preparedness for the end, and recompense at the great assize; and in each the concluding emphasis is upon those who suffer punishment (24.50–1; 25.10–2, 24–30).

Declaration of Ignorance (24.36)

36. This verse, which is the first to suggest a real limitation to Jesus' knowledge, both brings to a close the previous section and introduces verses which unfold the practical implications of Jesus' eschatological utterances.

concerning that day and hour no one knows, neither the angels of heaven nor the Son, but only the Father. Cf. 11.27; the numerous Johannine contrasts between 'the Father' and 'the Son'; Acts 1.7; Rev 19.12; *Mek.* on Exod 16.32 ('No one knows when the kingdom of David will be restored to its former position', in a list of things 'hidden from people', things introduced with 'No one knows'). 'That day' is the OT's 'day of the Lord', which in the NT is the *parousia*; and 'that hour' is a further specification that is effectively synonymous. On God's knowledge of the end time see *Ps. Sol.* 17.21 ('in the time known to you, O God'); *2 Bar.* 21.8 ('You alone know the end of times'); 48.3 ('Only you know the length of the generations'); 54.1 ('the ends of the periods you alone know'); and for angelic ignorance cf. 1 Pet 1.12; *4 Ezra* 4.52.

Although Daniel 11–12; *T. Mos.* 10.12; and *Apoc. Abr.* 28 attempt to calculate the date of the end, Matthew's Jesus negates all such endeavours. If the angels and the Son, the leading characters in the eschatological scenario, do not know something, it must lie beyond all others. This does not contradict v. 34. Rather does the uncertainty of v. 36 interpret the certainty of the earlier verse: although the end will come upon 'this generation', its exact time cannot be fixed. The signs of vv. 5ff. do not constitute a timetable. They invite the vigilance of eschatological agnosticism.

Although Irenaeus could still take our saying at face value, older Christian theology often struggled with Jesus' declaration of ignorance. Luke omitted the saying, as did certain copyists of Matthew and Mark. Origen wondered whether Jesus was referring to the church of which he is the head. Ambrose attributed 'nor the Son' to an Arian interpolation. Athanasius suggested that Jesus only feigned ignorance. The Cappadocians thought that the Son did not know the date on his own but only through the Father; or, as Gregory Nazianzen put it: 'He knows as God and knows not as man'. Chrysostom, in a prize example of bad exegesis, simply denied that Jesus was ignorant of anything: 'neither is the Son ignorant of the day, but is even in full certainty thereof'. So too Cassiodorus, citing Jn 21.17 and contending that 'nor the Son' means that the Son did not make others know. But modern Christian theology, emphasizing with the creeds that Jesus was 'true man', has come to terms with our saying as an expression of *kenosis*.

The Comparison with Noah (24.37–9)

37. As it was in the beginning, so will it be in the end.

For as the days of Noah were, so will be the coming of the Son of man.
Cf. Isa 54.9–10. Noah's contemporaries – the rabbinic *dor-hammabûl*,
excluded from the world to come – were remembered as great sinners
who did not foresee God's wrath: Ecclus 16.7; 2 Macc 2.4; 2 Pet 2.5
etc. Sometimes the flood was a prototype of the last judgement or end
of the world: *1 Enoch* 1–16; 2 Pet 3.6–7; *2 En.* J 70.10. But our saying
goes its own way in focusing upon neither the sins of Noah's
generation nor his righteousness but rather upon the unexpected
nature of the cataclysm that overtook the world while people went
about their daily business unawares.

38. Verses 38–9 are a clarifying expansion of v. 37.

they were eating and drinking, marrying and giving in marriage. Cf.
Gen 6.4; Mt 24.49 ('eats and drinks' with pejorative sense). Following
as it does the dramatic narration in 24.3–28, our line implies that even
in the midst of the eschatological tribulation life will for many
continue as ever.

until the day Noah entered the ark. This borrows the language of
LXX Gen 7.7.

One Taken, One Left (24.40–2)

40–1. Two verses in perfect parallelism now supply two additional
illustrations of judgement unexpectedly falling upon people while they
go about their daily chores. The first illustration concerns two men
doing the same thing, the second two women doing the same thing.
The divergent fates show that God's sudden judgement annuls external
similarities; cf. 13.30.

One will be taken and one will be left. Why one is taken and one left
is unstated, but the surrounding verses supply the answer: one is
prepared, one not.

Two women will be grinding meal together. Grinding at a mill was
considered woman's or slave's work.

In vv. 40–1 one is taken and one is left. But are the righteous taken
to meet the Lord in the air? Or are the wicked removed by angels and
cast into fire? The former is more likely. (i) Often in Matthew, the verb
translated 'left' means 'abandon' or 'forsake'. (ii) The verb translated
'take' means 'take (to safety)' in 2.13, 14, 20, 21. (iii) The picture of
angels taking the saints to meet the Son of man was probably common
in early Christianity. (iv) In vv. 37–9 those 'taken' (into the ark) are
saved while those left behind perish.

42. Keep awake. Given ignorance of the *parousia*'s date, leisurely repentance is foolish. Fear of being caught off guard should motivate one to watch.

you do not know on what day your Lord is coming. This recalls the Aramaic, *Maranatha* (1 Cor 16.22).

The Thief (24.43–4)

This simple parable, which continues the twin themes of eschatological ignorance and vigilance, consists of a parabolic saying (v. 43) plus an application (v. 44).

43. The likening of the eschatological end to an unexpected thief is unattested in ancient Jewish sources.

if the owner of the house had known in what part of the night the thief was coming. Matthew's night setting for the *parousia* appears again in 25.6. One is reminded of Mk 13.35–6 and of the Jewish expectation (of uncertain date and origin) that the Messiah will return at night.

The metaphor of the thief, applied to the *parousia*, became very popular in the early church and is echoed in 1 Thess 5.2 (of the coming day of the Lord); 2 Pet 3.10 (also of the day of the Lord); Rev 3.3 ('If you will not awake, I will come like a thief, and you will not know at what hour I will come upon you'); and 16.15 ('I am coming like a thief! Blessed is the one who is awake'). The parable also appears in *Gos. Thom.* 21 and 103. These last two variants, which equate the robbers with hostile cosmic powers, may be independent of the synoptics, although the non-eschatological application is secondary. Later exegetes often refer the text to death (so e.g. Chrysostom).

his house be broken into. Here, as in 6.19–20, the image is of a thief breaking through the mud wall of a house.

44. Therefore you also must be ready. Cf. LXX Exod 19.15; 34.2. While physical sleep may be necessary, spiritual sleep is not. Indeed, it leads to death.

the Son of man comes in an hour you do not expect. Cf. vv. 36, 39, 42, 50; 25.13.

The Parable of the Servant (24.45–51)

This parable, which is a further example of the need for constant vigilance before an event whose time of arrival one does not know, falls into two parts. Verses 45–7 tell of a faithful and wise servant who carries out his duties in his master's absence and so is rewarded when the master returns. Verses 48–51 tell of a wicked servant who disobeys his master's instructions and so is punished when his master returns.

The meaning of the transparent allegory is congruent with the *agraphon* preserved in Justin Martyr and Clement of Alexandria: 'In whatsoever I find you, in this will I also judge you'.

Mt 24.45–51 may be particularly – although not exclusively – applicable to community leaders: (i) the 'servant' is set over 'fellow servants' to give them their food at the proper time; (ii) the similar 21.28–32 is directed at leaders (albeit Jewish leaders); and (iii) such an interpretation was common in the early church and has remained homiletically popular.

45. **Who then is the faithful and wise slave.** Cf. 25.2, 4, 8–9, 21; also 1 Cor 4.1–2. This servant appears to be modelled upon Joseph. Not only does Genesis tell us about a wise servant who was appointed over his lord's house and all his possessions and supplied food for Egypt, but according to Gen 39.16, the lord's wife kept Joseph's garment 'until his lord came'. Clearly Joseph faced temptation while his master was gone. Moreover, *T. Jos.* 3.5–6 has the patriarch say this, 'If my master was absent, I drank no wine; for three-day periods I would take no food but give it to the poor and the ill. I would awaken early and pray to the Lord, weeping over the Egyptian woman of Memphis because she annoyed me exceedingly and relentlessly.' This presupposes that Joseph sometimes carried out his supervisory duties while his lord was away: precisely the situation in Matthew, where we find the phrase, 'the master will come', which corresponds to 'the master came' in Gen 39.16.

whom his master has put in charge of his household, to give them their food in its season? Cf. Gen 39.4–5 (where Joseph's 'lord' makes him overseer of his house); Ps 104.27; 145.15. 'The Lord' obviously represents Jesus, the Son of man. 'Has put in charge' can allude to current ecclesiastical authorities. In any case, elevation of office means service to others: the higher the rank, the higher the responsibility.

Christian allegorizing has often given an ecclesiastical meaning to 'food'. Some have thought in terms of spiritual food, that is, the Scriptures.

46. Watching entails service to others.

Blessed is that slave whom his master will find at work when he comes. For Matthew, the *parousia* is envisaged, not death – although the delay of the former has understandably moved many interpreters to find an application to the latter.

47. The reward is more responsibility, not (as one might expect for a slave) freedom. But the former alone works on the allegorical level: one always remains God's servant.

Amen signals the close of the first half of the parable.

he will put that one in charge of all his possessions. Cf. 25.21, 23. The reward seems to be authority over all property, not just slaves.

48. The second half of the parable, which begins here, is longer than the first half. It passes beyond possible earthly circumstances (v. 51) and carries the emphasis.

says in his heart is a Hebrew idiom meaning 'thinks'. It often connotes self-deception.

My master delays. Cf. Exod 32.1. Here, as in 25.5 and 19, we have plain reference to the delay of the *parousia*. The disturbing conviction that certain divine prophecies had been delayed already appears in the OT: Ezek 12.22; Hab 2.3. The problem also existed for the Qumran sectarians, as 1QpHab 7.5ff testifies. For their part, early Christians sometimes wondered about the apparent delay of Jesus' *parousia*: 2 Pet 3.4. But there is no good reason to speak of a 'crisis' in connexion with this theme in Matthew.

In Hab 2.3 the notice of delay is followed by mention of two different sorts of people: the righteous and those without upright soul; cf. Ps 37.7, 12–13; 1QpHab 7.9–17 (where 'the men of truth' have hands which 'do not grow slack in the service of the truth, when the last end-time is drawn out for them'). Evidently the notion of divine delay was traditionally associated with the theme of right and wrong response to it.

49. The wicked servant passes his time as did the careless generation of Noah (v.38) and wrongly usurps the place of his master (from a slave's point of view, masters were precisely those who ate and drank and beat their servants).

and begins to beat his fellow slaves. Cf. Eccles 8.11; Mt 18.28; Lk 21.34; *Ahiqar* 3.2; 4.15 (where the wicked Nathan eats and drinks with dissolute people and beats Ahiqar's slaves and handmaidens). Contrast the admonitions against violence in the Sermon on the Mount.

eats and drinks with the drunkards. Cf. LXX Cant 5.1. For drunkenness within the church see 1 Cor 11.21; 2 Pet 2.13.

50. The rude awakening.

the master of that slave will come on a day when he does not expect him and at an hour that he does not know. Cf. 24.36 (with 'that day or hour'), 39, 42, 44; 25.13; Heb 10.37.

51. The conclusion breaks the parabolic form through its indirect reference to hell. More description is given to the punishment of the evil servant than to the reward of the wise servant.

He will cut him in two. Some have thought 'cut in two' inappropriate here, and modern versions sometimes paraphrase with the bland 'punish' (so RSV). Others have speculated that here the sense is (or at least was for Matthew's tradition) figurative: 'cut off from the community'. A few, finding the punishment cruel and out of proportion to the crime, have suggested that the shocking punishment is characteristic of Jesus' style. But the ancient sources warn that what offends us may have been all too commonplace in the Graeco-Roman world.

A connexion with the tradition of Judas' death, as recorded in Acts 1.18, seems remote. More plausible is a link with the famous story of *Ahiqar*. In addition to the parallel between v. 49 and Nathan's activities (see above), it was said that Nathan 'was torn and his belly burst asunder ... And his latter end was destruction, and he went to hell' (*Ahiqar* 8.38 Arabic). One suspects that the popular legend of Ahikar has coloured our text.

assign his portion means 'treat him as' or 'give him a share with'.

hypocrites is especially strong here because of the polemic of chapter 23, and shows that those within the church can share the fate of the outsiders just so harshly condemned.

where there will be weeping and gnashing of teeth. Cf. 8.12.

The Parable of the Wise and Foolish Virgins (25.1–13)

Mt 25.1–13 falls into four parts. After an elaborate prologue which sets the scene (vv. 1–5), a temporal marker ('in the middle of the night', v. 6) introduces the central narrative portion (vv. 6–10). A second temporal marker ('afterward', v. 11) then signals the brief and tragic denouement (vv. 11–12). All this is followed by an exhortation which recalls the chief theme of 24.37–51 (v. 13). In the first section the groom is expected, in the second section he comes, and in the third we learn of what happened after his arrival.

Matthew's text is plainly an allegory of the second coming. The ten virgins stand for the Christian community. The delay of the bridegroom (v. 5) is the delay of the *parousia*. The bridegroom's sudden appearance (v. 6) is Jesus' sudden return. The closing of the door upon the foolish virgins (v. 11) is the final judgement.

The parable and application teach three simple lessons, the first indicated by the behaviour of the bridegroom, the second by the behavior of the wise virgins, the third by the behavior of the foolish virgins. The bridegroom delays and comes at an unforeseen time, which circumstance entails yet again that no one knows the day or hour of the Son of man's *parousia*. The wise virgins, who stand for faithful disciples, reveal that religious prudence will gain eschatological reward. The foolish virgins, who stand for unfaithful disciples, reveal that religious failure will suffer eschatological punishment.

Related rabbinic parables appear in *b. Šabb.* 153a and *Eccles Rab.* on 9.8. Although late, these imply that the theme of preparedness was commonly given parabolic form. But the pertinent rabbinic parables all have to do with death, not the last judgement.

The parable is thoroughly assimilated to its present context: its major themes are all reflected in the surrounding material, as one can see in a glance at the following:

> Division into two groups: cf. 24.37–41, 45–51; 25.14–46
> Delay of the *parousia*: cf. 24.48; 25.14, 19
> Ignorance of the hour: cf. 24.36, 42, 44, 50
> Suddenness of the end: cf. 24.27–9, 39, 43–4, 50
> Necessity to watch: cf. 24.42, 43
> Requirement of prudence: cf. 24.45–51; 25.14–30

1. Then (cf. 24.40) refers back to 24.44 and 50, that is, to the Son of man's *parousia* (cf. v. 13).

the kingdom of heaven will be like ten bridesmaids interprets the parable as having to do with the kingdom of God and its attendant judgement. Implicit is the comparison of the kingdom of God with a wedding celebration; cf. 22.1–14. Whether we here translate 'virgins' or 'maidens' makes little difference, although Christian tradition has often used the passage to commend virginity. Did Matthew already know the tradition which depicted the church as a virgin or a group of virgins?

Ten often indicates fullness, completeness, perfection. Recall the ten commandments, the ten plagues, the ten percent tithe, and the rabbinic dictum that ten form a congregation.

who took their lamps and went to meet the bridegroom. Cf. Cant 3.11. This proleptic summary (cf. vv. 6ff.) seems to picture women going forth from the (groom's?) house to welcome him and his bride as they come from her parents' house. We unfortunately know very little about ancient Jewish wedding customs; but there are modern examples of bridegrooms being met and accompanied with torches.

The word traditionally translated 'lamps' usually refers not to clay or metal lamps (cf. 5.14; 6.22) or lanterns but, as in Ecclus 48.1 and Josephus, *Bell.* 6.16, to torches, that is, heavy sticks wrapped with oil-soaked rags. But the Greek must mean 'lamp' in Jud 10.22, and probably does in Acts 20.8. Moreover, Mt 25.7 may imply that the virgins' lights burned for hours, which suits lamps, not torches; and in Lk 12.35–6, which seems related to our parable, the lights are clearly indoor lamps. So some incline to think the same for our parable. But others give *lampas* its usual meaning: torches, not lamps, were used to light outdoor processions; and there are reports (albeit modern) of Palestinian girls dancing with torches at wedding processions. A decision is difficult.

2. This premature verdict, which greatly reduces the story's dramatic impact because it makes the ending no surprise, is like a thesis statement whose truth is demonstrated by the rest of the parable.

Five of them were foolish, and five were wise. 'Wise' and 'foolish' do not refer to intellectual capacities. It is rather that one group makes the right and prudent decision, the other the wrong and imprudent decision. This reminds one of 7.24–7, where response to the words of Jesus reveals one to be either wise or foolish.

The division of humanity into two classes, the wise and the foolish, was conventional among the Cynics and early Stoics. But the background here is thoroughly Jewish. Proverbs and the Jewish wisdom tradition often contrast the wise and foolish, who also appear in rabbinic parables.

Although exegetical history has sometimes identified the wise virgins with Gentiles and the foolish virgins with Jews, the parable has to do with faithful and unfaithful Christians.

3–4. These two verses begin to explain the summary characterization of v. 2. They relate an error that becomes patent in vv. 6–10 and whose consequences are outlined in vv. 11–13.

For the foolish, taking their lamps, took no oil with them. In view of 5.15–16 and the parallels with 7.24–7 and 22.11–14 (where the absence of a wedding garment must symbolize the absence of good deeds), one wonders whether Matthew did not identify the lamp (and/or its fuel) as a symbol of good works. Certainly the next parable, that of the talents, has to do with good deeds, and Jewish sources use both lamp and oil as metaphors of the law and virtue.

5. The prudent will expect delay.

With the bridegroom being delayed, they all became drowsy and slept. Cf. v. 19. The delay – left unexplained here and elsewhere – is the key to the story, for it reveals who is wise and who foolish. How much time passed is unsaid; but its great length is indicated by the notice of sleep.

In the preceding parable, the evil servant misbehaves because he expects delay. In this parable, the foolish err because they do not expect delay. The upshot is that Matthew enjoins the same responsible behaviour whether the end is thought of as near or far.

6. **But at midnight.** The notice may be either inexact ('in the middle of the night') or precise (cf. our 'midnight'). Should the voice recall the trumpet of 24.31? On the coming of the Son of man at night see 24.43.

there was a shout. Cf. 1 Thess 4.16. The speaker is unnamed. All that matters is the suddenness of the cry, or rather what it announces; cf. 24.27, 28, 37, 43.

7. **Then all those bridesmaids got up and trimmed their lamps.** If the reference were to torches, the Greek here translated 'trimmed their lamps' would indicate removal of charred cloth and dipping the torch again in oil. If the reference is to lamps, the expression refers to trimming the wicks and adding oil.

8. The foolish virgins expect the bridegroom to come when they are ready. Their folly is to act according to their own expectations. They do not recognize that the bridegroom might delay and come at an unexpected hour.

The foolish, who behave as a unit, will speak again in v. 11.

9. But the wise speak only here.

No, lest there not be enough for you and for us. Seemingly the lamps would go out early if the oil were shared. Although interpreters have wondered about the selfishness of the wise, nothing on that subject is here implied: the parable is not about the golden rule; its meaning lies elsewhere.

Go rather to the dealers and buy some for yourselves. The imperative – which is not ironic or reproachful – raises a question. Would shops have been open at such a late hour? But in a small, rural village maybe all would have been awake for the celebration, so commerce might have been possible.

10. The five foolish virgins leave just as the bridegroom arrives.

And with them going away to buy it, the bridegroom came. The movement in opposite directions foreshadows the tragic conclusion: the five foolish virgins will not be with the bridegroom.

those who were ready went with him into the wedding banquet. Cf. 24.44.

and the door was shut. Cf. Gen 7.16; Mt 24.33; Lk 13.25. The closed door is lost opportunity.

11. What follows is an allegorical depiction of the final judgement. Membership in the faithful community does not bring salvation.

Lord, lord reveals that the foolish virgins belong to the Christian community and that the bridegroom is the Son of man.

12. The curt response of the groom – he speaks only six words in the parable – seems excessively harsh.

Amen I say to you is out of place in a bridegroom's mouth, but not in the mouth of the Son of man.

I do not know you. Cf. 7.23; 26.74. Recall the rejected wedding guest in 22.11–14. Obviously, the mere wish to enter is not enough; other conditions must be met.

13. The editorial conclusion makes the application.

Keep awake, then, because you know neither the day nor the hour. Cf. Mk 13.35. The call to wakefulness – a conflation of 24.36, 42, and 50 – has been thought odd given that even the five wise virgins fall asleep (v. 5). But the Greek may mean only 'be prepared!' And in any case the imperative is addressed to the reader, not the foolish virgins. What wakefulness precisely consists in is here left unsaid, although it plainly involves looking to the future.

The Parable of the Hidden Talents (25.14–30)

This parable, which features triads and extensive parallelism, contains three main parts:

Scene I. The master entrusts property to slaves (vv. 14–15a)
A) The master calls slaves (14)
B) The master entrusts slaves with property (15a)
1. Five talents to one
2. Two talents to a second
3. One talent to a third

Scene II. The slaves carry out their business (vv. 15b–18)
A) The master departs (15b)
B) The actions of the slaves (16–18)
1. The making of five talents (16)
2. The making of two talents (17)
3. The burying of one talent (18)

Scene III. The master settles accounts (vv. 19–30)
A) The master returns (19)
B) The reckoning of accounts (20–30)
1. Reward for the one who made five talents (20–1)
2. Reward for the one who made two talents (22–3)
3. Punishment for the one who buried his talent (24–30)

That the three scenes and the entire story end by referring to the slothful slave shows where the emphasis lies, as does the extra space given to his punishment: the parable is more warning than encouragement. This does not, however, eliminate the positive elements in vv. 21 and 23 ('enter into the joy of your lord').

Whether or not one uses the word allegory, this parable, like the preceding, is filled with obvious symbols. The master is Jesus. His slaves represent the church, whose members have received various responsibilities. The master's departure is the departure of the earthly Jesus. The long time of the master's absence is the age of the church. His return is the *parousia* of the Son of man. The rewards given to the good slaves stand for heavenly rewards given to the faithful at the great assize, and their joy is that of the messianic banquet. The punishment of the evil slave represents those within the church who, through their sins of omission, condemn themselves to eschatological darkness.

Although most of the themes and motifs of 25.14–30 appear in the surrounding material, the passage is not otiose. Not only does repetition make for emphasis, but the notion that Christians have received gifts according to their ability (v. 15), and that it is what they make of those gifts which counts at the last judgement, is something new.

There is a parallel to our passage in *3 Bar.* 12–16, where three groups of angels bring before God and Michael the archangel baskets of flowers. These represent 'the merits of the righteous', whom the angels oversee. The first group has full baskets. The second group has baskets half full. The third group has empty baskets. Both the first and second groups of angels are given rewards for the righteous they represent. But the third group is instructed to punish those without merit. Perhaps the striking parallels are coincidence, or perhaps *3 Baruch* depends upon our parable, or perhaps the texts are variants of a common folk-motif.

There are also a few rabbinic parables of comparative value: *Mek.* on Exod 20.2 ('A king had appointed two administrators. One was appointed over the store of straw and the other was appointed over the treasure of silver and gold . . .'); *ARN* A 14 ('It is like a man with whom the king deposited a deposit. Every single day the man would weep and cry out and say: Woe unto me! When shall I be quit of this responsibility in peace?'); *b. Šabb.* 152b ('This [the returning of the soul to God] may be compared to a mortal king who distributed royal apparel to his servants. The wise among them folded it up and hid it away in a chest, whereas the fools among them went and did their work in them . . .'); *Cant. Rab.* 7.14.1 ('The rabbis compare it to a king who had an orchard which he handed over to a tenant. What did the tenant do? He filled some baskets with the fruit of the orchard and put them at the entrance of the orchard. When the king passed and saw the goodly show, he said, "All this fine fruit is at the entrance of the orchard; then what must be in the orchard itself"'; the subject is Israel's keeping of the Torah, as in *Mek.* on Exod 20.2). While none of these is directly related to Jesus' parable, they do probably indicate that the motifs of Mt 25.14–30 were traditionally at home in parables, perhaps especially in parables about Israel being entrusted with the Torah by God.

14. The implicit subject of this abbreviated introduction is the kingdom of God: the kingdom of God is or will be like ... (cf. 25.1).

For it is as with a man going away on a journey, who called his slaves

and entrusted his property to them. Cf. 24.45. The parable illustrates what it means to watch. That a wealthy businessman, before leaving on a commercial venture, entrusted *slaves* with so much money and responsibility may seem strange to us; but slaves did many things in the ancient world, and sometimes held high positions.

15–16. Although the master leaves his slaves with talents, we do not learn his instructions. Perhaps we are to think he leaves the possibilities up to them.

And to one he gave five talents, to another two, to another one. The talent was a very large sum of money that might have weighed between 50 and 75 lbs. Although reckonings vary, 5 talents = approx. 30,000 denarii; two talents = approx. 12,000 denarii; and 1 talent = approx. 6,000 denarii, with a denarius being the standard day's wage for a labourer (cf. 20.1–16). The very large sums, which reflect Matthew's oriental delight in large numbers, imply the greatness of God's gifts.

Exegetical tradition has equated talents with faith, the gifts of the Holy Spirit, and Jesus himself. But the parable implies that the gifts are various, so it makes little sense to be specific. We should rather think of God's gifts in general.

to each according to his ability. Cf. 16.27; Mk 13.34 ('each with his work'); Rom 12.3–8 ('the measure of faith which God has assigned him', 'gifts that differ according to the grace given to us'); Eph 4.7–8; 1 Pet 4.10 ('as each has received a gift, employ it for one another, as good stewards of God's varied grace').

Then he went away. The nobleman's absence stands for the post-Easter period: the Lord is gone but will come again.

he made five more talents. Although we are told that the slave gains five talents, we do not learn how.

17. the one who had the two talents made two more talents. Just as the first slave turns five into ten, so the second turns two into four. The doubling in both instances leads one to anticipate that the next slave will turn one talent into two.

18. But the one who had received the one talent went off and dug a hole in the ground and hid his master's money. Cf. *b. Bab. Me.* 42a ('Anyone who buried a pledge or a deposit immediately upon receipt of it, was free from liability'; 'money can only be guarded by placing it in the earth'). Burying money in the ground to hide it was reckoned good security against theft. See further 13.44; *b. Šabb.* 102b ('a poor man digs a hole to hide his small coin'). The third slave shows himself to be lazy because he makes no profit with what he has been given.

19. After a long time the master of those slaves came and settled accounts with them. Cf. 18.23; 24.48; 25.5. 'After a long time' clearly implies the delay of the *parousia*.

21. **His master said to him, 'Well done, good and trustworthy slave. Over a few things you have been faithful; over many things will I put you in charge.'** So too v. 23. Cf. 24.45, 47. Because 'over a little' means 'over a few talents', 'over much' might mean 'over many talents'.

Enter into the joy of your master. The words, which go beyond the parable itself to its religious application, suggest joy at the messianic banquet (cf. vv. 1–13; 26.29): disciple and master rejoice together.

22. This verse is parallel to v. 20, while v. 23 reproduces v. 21. That is, the first and second slaves say much the same thing, and the response of the master is identical. For all practical purposes the two faithful slaves play the same role. That the two servants gain the same reward shows that what matters is commitment, not a relative weighing of deeds. Recall the labourers in the vineyard (20.1–16).

24. Evidently the third slave expects to be commended for his caution; and perhaps Jesus' hearers and Matthew's readers would have thought him prudent. But the master regards him as slothful.

Master indicates that the speaker belongs to the church, a fact in any case clear from the broader context. We have here the same situation as in 7.21–3: the tongue says 'Master' but the deeds do not.

I knew that you were a harsh man, reaping what you did not sow, and gathering where you did not scatter. When the master repeats these words (v. 26) he omits 'you are a harsh man'. Cf. Mic 6.15 ('you shall sow but not reap'); Mt 12.30 ('the one who does not gather with me scatters').

The meaning of 'reaping (cf. 6.26; 25.26) where you did not sow' seems clear enough, and 'gathering where you did not scatter' must be synonymous. That is, it too is an agricultural metaphor: 'gathering crops where you did not scatter seed'.

25. Although nothing was said of the psychology of the first two slaves, we are here given a glimpse into the alleged motives of the third slave.

So I was afraid, and I went and hid your talent in the ground. See, you have what is yours. While the slave puts his failure down to fear, the master himself will offer a different diagnosis (v. 26).

26. The slave who hides his talent turns out to be as senseless as the one who hides a lamp under a bushel (5.15).

lazy is a statement about the man's actions rather than his beliefs, and clarifies his chief fault.

27. **Then you ought to have invested my money with the bankers, and on my return I would have received what was my own with interest.** The thought seems to be: you could at least have deposited my money with the bankers so that upon returning I might receive the interest.

28. To whom the following command is addressed we are not told. Allegorically they might be the angels.

29. This general maxim does not perfectly fit the parable, for the wicked slave is deprived not because he had little but because he did not multiply what he had.

For to everyone who has, will more be given, and he will have an abundance; but from the one who has nothing, even what he has will be taken away. Cf. Prov 9.9; Mt 13.12; Lk 12.48; *Gos. Thom.* 41 ('Whoever has in his hand, to him shall be given; and whoever does not have, from him shall be taken even the little which he has'); *b. Ber.* 55a ('The Holy One, blessed be He, gives wisdom only to one who already has wisdom'). The passives are divine: God is the implicit subject. In the present context, 'everyone who has' must mean 'everyone who has increased talents' while 'the one who has nothing' must mean 'the one who has not increased talents'.

30. **throw him into the outer darkness, where there will be weeping and gnashing of teeth.** Cf. 8.12; 13.42, 50; 22.13; 24.51; 25.30.

* * * * *

(i) If 24.4–36 is in part designed to quell uninformed eschatological enthusiasm, the intended effect is not apathy. This is why the paraenesis of 24.37ff. seeks to instill an appropriate eschatological fervour and vigilance. Ignorance concerning the date of the end (v. 36), although necessary, is dangerous, for it may lead to spiritual lethargy. But in Matthew it leads instead to moral preparation. For the *parousia* may come at any time (and will probably come sooner rather than later: v. 34). One must accordingly be ever prepared to give an account of oneself to the divine justice, from which there is no escape (25.31–46).

(ii) The rabbis taught that one should repent a day before one's death (e.g. *b. Šabb.* 153a). Of course, because one never knows when death will come, one must repent daily. In Matthew the *parousia* of the Son of man serves the same function as death for the rabbis: its unpredictable date demands constant preparation.

(iii) Mt 24.37–51 offers a collection of scenes from everyday life: people eating and drinking, people marrying and giving in marriage, two men in a field, two women at a mill, a man asleep in his house, a slave doing his duty, a slave not doing his duty. These images of day-to-day existence stand in stark contrast to the unusual and even surrealistic events depicted in vv. 4ff.: wars, famines, earthquakes, flight from the abomination of desolation, darkened luminaries, a sign in the firmament, the Son of man on the clouds of heaven. But the transition from the extraordinary to the ordinary well serves Matthew's paraenetic purpose. Those whose imaginations hold the terrors and hope of things to come still live in the often mundane present, and their eschatological expectation does not undo the fact that they must still work in the field and grind at the mill.

THE JUDGEMENT OF THE SON OF MAN (25.31–46)

[31]**When the Son of man comes in his glory, and all the angels with him, then he will sit on the throne of his glory.** [32]**And all the nations will be gathered before him, and he will separate them from each other, as the shepherd separates the sheep from the goats;** [33]**and he will put the sheep at his right hand and the goats at his left.** [34]**Then the king will say to those at his right hand, 'Come, you that are blessed by my Father, inherit the kingdom prepared for you from the foundation of the world.** [35]**For I was hungry and you gave me food. I was thirsty and you gave me something to drink. I was a stranger and you welcomed me.** [36]**I was naked and you gave me clothing. I was sick and you took care of me. I was in prison and you visited me.'** [37]**Then the righteous will answer him, 'Lord, when was it that we saw you hungry and gave you food, or thirsty and gave you something to drink?** [38]**And when was it that we saw you a stranger and welcomed you, or naked and gave you clothing?** [39]**And when was it that we saw you sick or in prison and visited you?'** [40]**And the king will answer them, 'Amen I say to you, just as you did it to one of the least of these my brothers, so you did it to me.'** [41]**Then he will say to those at his left hand, 'You that are accursed, depart from me into the eternal fire prepared for the devil and his angels.** [42]**For I was hungry and you did not give me food. I was thirsty and you gave me nothing to drink.** [43]**I was a stranger and you did not welcome me, naked and you did not clothe me, sick and in prison and you did not visit me.'** [44]**Then they too will answer, 'Lord, when was it that we saw you hungry or thirsty or a stranger or naked or sick or in prison and did not take care of you?'** [45]**Then he will answer them, 'Amen I say to you, just as you did not do it to one of the least of these, you did not do it to me.'** [46]**And these will go away into eternal punishment, but the righteous into eternal life.**

Parallels: none

Verses 31–3 set the scene for this poetic and dramatic climax, which is the final portion of the final major discourse. They are followed by the twin conversations in vv. 34–45, the first between the judge and those on his right, the second between the judge and those on his left. Each dialogue consists of (i) declaration of king; (ii) response of just/unjust; and (iii) justification of sentence, and each features on introductory and responsive 'then' (vv. 34, 37, 41, 44, 45) and concludes with a statement prefaced by the king's determinative 'Amen, I say to you'

(vv. 40, 45). The narrative ends with v. 46, a succinct summary which spells out the opposing fates of the two groups.

The most prominent structural feature is the fourfold repetition of affliction and alleviation (which repetition strengthens the memory):

The judge's first speech	Those on the right
hungry/gave me food	hungry and feed you
thirsty/gave me drink	or thirsty and gave you drink
stranger/welcomed me	stranger and welcomed you
naked/clothed me	or naked and clothed you
sick/visited me	sick
prison/came to me	in prison and came to you

The judge's second speech	Those on the left
hungry/gave me no food	hungry
thirsty/gave me no drink	or thirsty
stranger/did not welcome me	or stranger
naked/not clothed me	or naked
sick	or sick
and in prison/not visit me	or in prison/not served you

Abbreviation increases as the text moves forward. The judge's first speech recites six unfortunate states and six remedies. But his second speech, like the speech of those on the right, combines the last two acts of kindness. And in the final enumeration, which comes from the condemned, the acts of mercy are not detailed at all – a circumstance most appropriate rhetorically. They are rather summarized with one phrase, 'did not serve you.'

Although reminiscent of the earlier parables of separation (13.24–30, 36–43, 47–50), this is not a parable but a picture of the last judgement. Its special force derives in part from its climactic placement at the end of Jesus' public ministry and at the end of the eschatological discourse.

Mt 25.31–46 is in several ways a conventional judgement scene, as the table on p. 453 suggests. The dialogue between judge and judged (cf. 7.22–3; 25.11–12) is also conventional; see *1 En.* 63; Justin, *Dial.* 76; *1 Apol.* 16; and *Midr. Ps.* on 118.17, the last of which offers a particularly striking analogy: 'In the world to come it will be said to him, "What has your work been?" If he then says, "I have fed the hungry," it will be said to him, "That is the gate of Yahweh (Ps 118.20); you who have fed the hungry, enter in the same." If he says, "I have given the thirsty to drink," it will be said to him, "That is the gate of Yahweh; you who have given the thirsty to drink, enter in the

	Daniel	*1 Enoch*	*1 Enoch*	Rev	*2 Bar.*	*T. Abr.*	*Sib. Or.*
Enthronement of judge	7.9–10 (7.10)	62.2–3	90.20	20.11	(73.1)	11.4, 12.4	2.239–40
Presence of angels	7.10	62.11	90.21–2			11.5 12.1–18	2.242
Gathering of people		62.3		20.12	72.2		
Separation into two groups		62.5		20.12–15	72.2	11.1ff	2.252–4
Reward of righteous	7.18	62.8, 13–16	90.23–7	(20.15)	73.1–74.4		2.313–38
Punishment of wicked	7.26	62.10–12 63.1–12	90.28–36	20.15	72.6	11.11 13.12	2.249–51, 312

same.' If he says, "I have clothed the naked," it will be said to him, "That is the gate of Yahweh, you who have clothed the naked, enter in the same." And similarly he who has brought up the orphans, and he who has given alms, and he who has practised works of love.'

31. The introduction, which gives a when but not a where, makes vv. 31ff. an exposition of 24.29–31.

When the Son of man comes in his glory. Mt 16.27; 19.28; and 24.30 also link the Son of man with glory. Dan 7.14 already declares that glory will be given to the one like a son of man, and the notion reappears in the Similitudes of Enoch.

all the angels with him. This takes up LXX Zech 14.5, a verse also used in 27.51–3. Whereas here the verse is applied to the angels who come with the Son of man at the end, there it is applied to the saints whose resurrection accompanies that of Jesus.

then he will sit on the throne of his glory. The angels stand while the Son of man sits. Jewish tradition could place more than one throne in heaven. The judgement scene in Daniel 7 refers to 'thrones', and R. Akiba is purported to have taken this to mean one throne for God, another for David (*b. Hag.* 14a). When one adds that Psalm 110 appears to depict an enthronement alongside God; that heavenly angels sometimes have their own thrones; and that Matthew elsewhere refers to more than one eschatological throne (cf. 19.28; 20.21), probably the Son of man's throne is not God's throne.

The motif of a human figure judging others in the afterlife or in an eschatological context appears in more than one Jewish text. In *T. Abr.* 12.4–13.4, Abel sits upon a heavenly throne and judges 'the entire creation', including the 'righteous and sinners'. According to 11QMelch 2.13, Melchizedek 'will exact the vengeance of El's judgements'. In *2 Bar.* 72.2–6, God's Messiah 'shall summon all the nations, and some of them he will spare, and some of them he will slay'; cf. Isa 11.4. Related pictures appears in *Psalms of Solomon* 17 and 4Q246 col. 2; and Rev 20.4 probably foretells that the followers of Jesus will sit on thrones and have judgement committed to them. One also recalls 1 Cor 6.2 ('the saints will judge the world') and the possibility that the Son of man in the Similitudes of Enoch should be identified with an exalted Enoch.

32. The resurrection of the dead is presupposed.

And all the nations will be gathered before him. Cf. Isa 66.18 ('I am coming to gather all nations and tongues; and they shall come and shall see my glory'). 'Gather' is a shepherd's term otherwise used in eschatological contexts. 'All the nations' are (i) all non-Christians or (ii) all non-Jews who are not Christians or (iii) all humanity. Because the passage belongs to a long section which is full of paraenesis for believers, one expects here a solemn appeal to those within the church, which is not the case for (i) and (ii). Moreover, the probable identification of 'the least of these my brothers' in v. 40 (cf. v. 45) with the needy in general (see below) supports the universalist interpretation (iii).

Many, however, now identify 'the least' of vv. 40 and 45 with Christians and do not think this group included among 'the nations'. They endorse (i) or (ii). This interpretation implies that there are in Matthew two judgements: one for the church (cf. 24.45–25.30) and one for those outside the church (25.31–46). One can urge that this is a Christian mutation of the expectation that God will first judge Israel and then the nations: the church now takes the place of Israel.

This approach might imply that Matthew did not accept the notion, popular since Cyprian, that 'outside the church there is no salvation'. Rather did he hold the position stated in the *Apocalypse of Sedrach*: 'there are nations which have no law, yet fulfil the law; they are not baptized, but my divine Spirit enters them and they are converted to my baptism, and I receive them with my righteous ones in the bosom of Abraham.'

The context, however, does not explicitly teach two judgements, and there are problems with identifying 'the least' with Christians (see below). At the same time, 25.31–46 may very well imply that Matthew thought salvation possible for those outside the church. One is reminded of Karl Rahner's so-called 'anonymous Christian'.

he will separate them from each other, as the shepherd separates the sheep from the goats. The image is probably of a mixed flock of sheep and goats which, although herded together in the day (cf. Gen 30.32), are separated at night so that the latter can be kept warm. The sheep (which are more commercially valuable and typically white) represent, as in 18.12 and 26.31, the righteous (the biblical goat was commonly black). Probably the main idea is the ease with which the Son of man can tell which are the righteous and which are the wicked.

Sheep and goats typically belong together in a flock, and there is no pre-Christian evidence for goats as a symbol of evil. It follows that their permanent separation is unforeseen. So here as elsewhere eschatology brings surprise.

33. Unlike many scenes of eschatological judgement, this one offers little suspense: the judge immediately knows who belongs on the right and who belongs on the left; and no use is made of scales or books. Is the near omniscience of the king implied?

he will put the sheep at his right hand and the goats at his left. For other contrasts between right and left see 6.3; 20.21, 23; 27.38; 1 Kgs 22.19 ('I saw the Lord sitting on his throne, and all the host of heaven sitting beside him on his right hand and on his left'). The superiority of the right hand over the left, and the greater honour of the former (the seat of honour next to a king was on his right) is presupposed. Texts for comparison include Plato, *Rep.* 10.614c, where, in the afterlife, there are judges who send the just 'to the right and upwards through heaven' while 'the unjust they send down to the left'; Virgil, *Aen.* 6.540–4, in which the road to the afterlife splits and the fork on the right is 'our highway to Elysium' while that on the left 'leads down to godless Tartarus'; *T. Abr.* 12.12; 13.9, according to which the angel on the right of the throne of judgement records righteous deeds, the angel on the left sins; and *Midr. Rab.* on Cant 1.9, in which 1 Kgs 22.19 is interpreted to mean that the heavenly host on God's right defend while those on the left accuse.

34. Exposition now gives way to dialogue. The first speaker (the king) is also the teller of the parable (Jesus).

Then the king will say to those at his right hand. The shepherd, like Moses and David, is also a king. 'King' harks back to 2.2 and 21.5, recalls Jesus' status as the Son of David, and reinforces the irony which will come to expression in 27.11, 29, 37, and 42 (where Jesus' kingship is mocked or questioned). One is also reminded of 22.11–14, where a king passes eschatological judgement against one without a wedding garment. But if there the king represents God the Father, here Jesus is the king in the kingdom of God (cf. Col 1.13: 'the kingdom of his dear Son').

Come, you that are blessed by my Father. Cf. 20.23. The king's 'come' recalls the invitations in 11.28 and 22.4, while the blessing of the father reminds one of OT scenes of patriarchal blessing. Also in the background is the ancient link between blessing and inheritance (cf. the next clause): the divine blessing means inheritance of the land.

inherit the kingdom prepared for you from the foundation of the world. Cf. 5.5; 19.29. 'Prepared [by God] from the foundation of the world' implies that God's purpose does not change: it will be the same at the end as in the beginning.

35. The speaker – himself no foreigner to hunger and thirst and other hardships – offers not a list of afflictions experienced by missionaries but a list of mundane deeds of mercy.

Matthew's deeds of unobtrusive charity are sometimes joined in other texts:

	Feed the hungry	Give drink to the thirsty	Take in strangers	Clothe the naked	Visit the sick	Visit prisoners
Job 22.7	3	2		1		
Isa 58.7	1		2	3		
Ezek 18.7, 16	1			2		
T. Jos. 1.5–7	1				2	3
T. Jacob 2.23		1	2	4	3	
T. Jacob 7.24–5	2			1		
2 En. 9.1; 10.5; 42.8; 63.1	1			2		
Justin, 1 Apol. 67					1	2
Mek. on Exod 14.19	2	3		1		
b. Sota 14a				1	2	
Tg. Ps.-Jn. on Deut 34.6	3			1	2	
Eccles. Rab. on 11.1	2	3		1		

Obviously feeding the hungry and clothing the naked were frequently conjoined. Just as obviously, taking in strangers and visiting prisoners were less common imperatives. Perhaps the chief distinguishing feature of Matthew's list (which might be a development of Isa 58.7) is its poetic quality. It consists, as vv. 37–9 reveal, of three pairs: feeding the hungry and giving drink to the thirsty, taking in strangers and clothing the naked, and visiting the sick and imprisoned.

For I was hungry and you gave me food. Cf. 14.16; Ps 146.7; and recall that, on two previous occasions, Jesus himself feeds the hungry (14.13–21; 15.32–9). The 'for' generated much discussion after the Reformation. To Catholics such as Robert Bellarmine, it implied that meritorious works can help earn salvation. Protestants such as Calvin and John Piscator stressed that such works are a sign of salvation but do not earn it.

I was thirsty and you gave me something to drink. While in 10.42 those who give cold water know for whom they care, such is not the case here.

I was a stranger and you welcomed me. Because of Gen 18.1–8, Abraham was especially remembered as one who welcomed (and fed) strangers.

36. Chrysostom observed that the list of ministries does not include miracles: the sick and imprisoned are visited, not healed and set free. The implicit injunctions are 'easy'.

I was naked and you gave me clothing. Given Gen 3.21, this may be regarded as the imitation of God.

I was sick and you took care of me. This is another work of mercy which Jesus himself performs (8.14–17, etc.).

I was in prison and you visited me. Visitation of prisoners was not a standard item in Jewish lists of good works. Has early Christian experience or the memory of John the Baptist influenced the text?

37–9. The just, like the man without a wedding garment and the man who buried his talent, are surprised: it is not natural to identify the Son of man in glory with the destitute. In the language of 6.3, the left hand never knew what the right hand did.

Then the righteous will answer him. Cf. v. 44a. If the argument above is correct, 'the righteous' are not simply the followers of Jesus but include the righteous outside the church (a fact consistent with their not knowing that their service was to Christ). Recall the formulation in *t. Sanh.* 13.2: 'there must be righteous individuals among the heathen who have a share in the world to come.'

40. just as you did it to one of the least of these my brothers, so you did it to me. Who are 'the least of these my brethren'? The possibilities are as follows:

(i)   Everyone in need, whether Christian or not
(ii) All Christians/disciples
(iii) Christian missionaries/leaders

Both (ii) and (iii) gain support from 10.40–2; and the theme of how those outside the believing community have treated those within is quite at home in apocalyptic literature. Furthermore, in Matthew the non-biological 'brother' usually refers to Christians (cf. esp. 28.10); and 10.42–4; 11.11; 18.6, 10, and 14 might favour identifying 'the least' with believers. Yet the superlative 'least' appears here whereas 'little' (whose comparative, 'smaller', is used in 11.11; 13.32) is used in 10.42–4; 11.11; 18.6, 10, and 14. In addition, a more comprehensive, non-ecclesiological use of brother may appear in 5.22–4; 7.3–5. There are also further questions. Can we, even with 24.14 in mind, believe that Matthew thought 'all the nations' would have opportunity to succour needy Christians? Is not the identification of the needy with all in distress more consistent with the command to ignore distinctions between insiders and outsiders, and with Jesus' injunction to love even enemies? Is there anything in 25.31–46, taken by itself, which suggests that the needy are Christians? Does not 'the least of these' refer back to the immediately preceding narrative, not remarks on 'little ones' made chapters earlier? Why is 'brother' omitted in the parallel v. 45? If 'all the nations' be thought to include non-Christians, how likely is it that our text envisages them visiting Christians in prison? Are not the unfortunate circumstances of those who served in no way peculiarly Christian? If the least represent the king, as they would if they were Christian missionaries, how can people not know their identity? And how can people be judged by their response not to the proclamation of the least (assuming they are Christians) but instead to their condition? Suggestion (i) remains the best reading of the text. 'Blessed are the merciful for they shall obtain mercy' requires no qualification.

The motif (so important for Luther) of service to Jesus through service to others has fed the Christian moral imagination. One recalls chapter 53 of the Rule of St Benedict, the German folktale about Offerus, and much else, including the story told by Sulpicius Severus about St Martin of Tours: in winter the latter cut in two his coat (his only clothing) to share it with a beggar, after which Martin saw a vision of Christ dressed in half a cloak.

The concept goes back through our text to Prov 19.17: 'The one who is kind to the poor lends to the Lord, and he will repay him for his deed.' It was not altogether neglected by the Jewish tradition. What is new in Matthew is neither this idea nor the particular deeds of mercy, but the identification of the needy with Jesus the Son of man. This novel identification – another aspect of the messianic secret – is, however, left unexplained. Do we have here the real personal presence of the Son of man in the poor; or the identification of the world's king with his people; or – a possibility for those who identify 'the least' with Christians – another example of the Jewish principle that the one sent is as the sender? Or is the answer some combination of these?

41. Then he will say to those at his left hand. One surmises that those on the left have already overheard the conversation with those on the right, which fact must cause them grief.

42–3. Sins of omission, not commission, here lead to the ostracism known as hell.

44. Lord, when was it that we saw you hungry or thirsty or a stranger or naked or sick or in prison and did not take care of you? The confession of 'Lord' is either insincere (as in 7.21–3) or signals the eschatological recognition of the truth by all; cf. Phil 2.11. 'Serve' summarizes the content of the six works of mercy and shows them to be exemplary: they are all examples of service to Christ.

46. The king's address has ended. The conclusion is editorial comment.

And these will go away into eternal punishment, but the righteous into eternal life. 'Eternal punishment' appears only here in Matthew, 'eternal life' in 19.16 and 29. The line is based upon LXX Dan 12.2–3: 'And many of those who sleep in the dust of the earth shall rise, some to life everlasting, some to reproach, and some to dispersion and eternal shame.' The same verse also lies behind Jn 5.29. Happily there is no dwelling upon the fate of the wicked: the sort of sadism or delight in the punishment of others that one finds in Tertullian is absent. It is further interesting that Matthew's order is not that of Daniel: in Matthew the pericope ends on the happier note; contrast 24.48–51; 25.11–12, 24–30.

* * * * *

(i) The previous pericopae have enjoined readers to be faithful, to be prepared, and to invest talents. But exactly what these things mean or entail has not been explicit. Mt 25.31–46, however, makes all clear and so brings to a climax Matthew's eschatologically grounded paraenesis. The believer prepares for the *parousia* by living the imperative to love one's neighbours, especially the marginal. The chief moral imperative (7.12; 19.19; 22.39) is the law by which all are judged on the far side of history.

(ii) Given the abundant evils of history (well attested in both the teachings and fate of Jesus), one may wonder whether, in any final or lasting sense, good deeds have good consequences. Matthew, however, offers that beyond the injustice and disorder of this world is the order and justice of another, which fact guarantees that the actions – even ordinary actions – of human beings matter and have consequences: people are truly responsible. Moreover, faith that moral order and a happy ending will someday be wrought out of the chaos of human history enables the imagination of Matthew's reader to see what God has not yet done but will indeed do, and in this way succours those who live the Messiah's Torah.

(iii) Feeding the hungry and welcoming strangers and visiting the sick are mundane, unspectacular acts. In this sense 'virtue is not far from us, nor is it without ourselves, but it is within us, and is easy if only we are willing' (Anthony the Great). The Son of man does not demand supernatural feats but simple charity. The former can be more easily counterfeited than the latter; cf. 24.24. Charity is accordingly the true test of faith.

(iv) Mt 25.31–46 is christologically rich. Jesus is the Son of man of Daniel 7. Angels belong to him. And he is destined to be the king and judge of the world. The confluence of these powerful christological facts, which recapitulate so much that has come before, provides the immediate background for the passion narrative and lends to that narrative great irony. Those who condemn and pass judgement upon Jesus know not what they do. The one whom they mock as 'king of the Jews' is destined to become the king of the world. It is not his fate that is in their hands but their fate that is in his. It is, furthermore, striking that, as soon as he finishes recounting the judgement of the Son of man, Jesus declares: 'The Son of man will be handed over to be crucified' (26.2). Darkness (cf. 27.45) is about to envelope the glory of the Son of man.

INTRODUCTION TO THE PASSION NARRATIVE (26.1–5)

26 **¹And when Jesus had finished saying all these things, he said to his disciples, ²'You know that after two days the Passover is coming, and the Son of man will be handed over to be crucified.'**

³Then the chief priests and the elders of the people gathered in the palace of the high priest, who was named Caiaphas, ⁴and they took counsel to arrest Jesus by stealth and to kill him. ⁵But they said, 'Not during the festival, lest there be a riot among the people.'

Parallels: Mk 14.1–2; Lk 22.1–2; Jn 11.47–53

The prologue to the passion narrative contains two brief scenes. They are parallel in structure but antithetical in content. In the first Jesus is the subject and prophesies his dark future. In the second his enemies, the chief priests and elders, are the subjects, and they conspire against him.

1. Having spoken at length of the last things, it remains for Jesus to see them commence through his death and resurrection.

And when Jesus had finished saying all these things. On this formula see p. 115. It recalls Deut 31.1, 24; and 32.45 and so adds to Matthew's Moses typology. 'All', absent from the parallels in 7.28; 11.1; 13.53; and 19.1 (but cf. the passages in Deuteronomy), is used because Jesus' teaching ministry is nearly over: the word looks back over not just over chapters 24–5 or 23–5 but the entire Gospel. As Bengel put it: 'he had said all he had to say.'

he said to his disciples. The setting presumably remains the same as in 24.3.

2. The passion commences with a word of Jesus, who thereby sets events in motion. He is completely aware of what lies ahead and determined to face it. That his prophecy precedes the account of his opponents' plot (vv. 3–5) underlines his foreknowledge. He is more in charge than they are. This was not a 'death forced by the violence of an oppressor, which he could not escape, but rather ... death of his own will' (Calvin).

You know that after two days the Passover is coming. Jesus appears to be speaking on Wednesday (13 Nisan) about Friday (15 Nisan). 'You know' may be indicative: Jesus has said enough about his approaching passion that his disciples know what is coming (cf. 20.25; 22.16). One can, however, read the Greek as an imperative ('know you that'): Jesus is announcing the end of his ministry. That Jesus' saving death is associated with Passover is part of a new exodus typology: Passover, the time of the redemption from Egypt, becomes the time of the redemption wrought by Jesus.

'After two days' (cf. Hos 6.2) is unusual in its specificity. Some find a background in the Isaac traditions. Gen 22.4 puts the sacrifice of Isaac on the third day, a fact remembered in *Jub.* 18.3 and Josephus, *Ant.* 1.226. Moreover, in *Jubilees* the Aqedah occurs during Passover (17.15; 18.3), and in *LAB* 32.1–4 Isaac voluntarily offers himself as a sacrifice (32.3; cf. 4 Macc 16.20; Josephus, *Ant.* 1.232). When one adds that a parallel between Jesus and Isaac is explicit in *Barn.* 7.2 and probably implicit in Rom 8.32, and further that Mt 26.36 may allude to Gen 22.2–5, the proposal merits reflection.

and the Son of man will be delivered over to be crucified. On the passion predictions see pp. 272–73. This prophecy, whose content is the theme of the following two chapters, draws primarily upon 20.18–19 ('Son of man ... delivered ... crucified'). If 'and' stands under 'know', then the disciples are being reminded of what they already know. If 'and' is not dependent upon 'know', then Jesus is telling them something new: now is the time for the Son of man to suffer.

3. With the protagonist and his purposes introduced, his enemies and their scheme now appear. One thinks of Ps 2.2.

Then the chief priests and the elders of the people gathered. Cf. Jn 18.14. On the 'elders' see p. 272. They are linked with the chief priests also in 16.21; 21.23; 26.47; 27.1, 3, 12, 20, 41. The absence of the Pharisees, who play almost no part in the following story (see only 27.62), surprises; but they presumably played no part in Matthew's passion sources. Historically no doubt Jesus' opponents at the end belong to the temple aristocracy. The same fact explains the relative neglect of the scribes, who show up only twice (v. 57; 27.41).

Caiaphas. While Caiaphas is not named in the passion narratives of Mark or Luke, John names him more than once: 11.49; 18.13–14 (this makes him the son-in-law of Annas), 24, 28 (cf. Lk 3.2; Acts 4.6). He is also present in Josephus and perhaps rabbinic sources (*m. Parah* 3.5; cf. *t. Yeb.* 1.10). Little more is known about him than his dates as High Priest – approximately AD 18–36 – and his involvement with Jesus' death. But in 1990, in the so-called Peace Forest, south of Abu Tor, a burial cave was unearthed with several ossuaries, two of which have inscriptions with the name *Qp'* (= *Qapa'*). One of these, with elaborate decorations, contained the bones of several people, including those of a sixty-year-old man; and 'Joseph bar Caiaphas' (= Joseph of the family Caiaphas?) is inscribed on the box. Whether or not the remains are those of the NT Caiaphas, it does seem likely that at least his family tomb has been found.

4. The leaders betray the fact that their designs, which are borne of fear rather than a love of justice or truth, may not please the multitude.

they took counsel to arrest Jesus by stealth and to kill him. Cf. 2.7. The leaders' plans unfold what Jesus has already foreseen.

5. **Not during the festival.** Whereas Jesus, the victim of conspiracy, accurately knows that he will be arrested on Passover, that is – 'after two days' (v. 2) – those who arrange the conspiracy cannot anticipate the future: unlike Judas, they do not foresee the opportunity they will be given *during the feast*. (They also fail to see the truth about the crowds, who will not protect Jesus but rather turn upon him.)

lest there be a riot among the people. Cf. 27.24, where Pilate has to worry about a possible riot. One thinks of the friendly crowds in Matthew 21 – would they not oppose enemies of Jesus? cf. 22.46 – and of the unrest at festivals so often narrated by Josephus.

* * * * *

Matthew's passion narrative features two main characters. The first is Jesus, the second the collectivity composed of the Jewish leaders in Jerusalem. Both appear here, where they step into their roles. It is the Son of man's part to obey the will of God and so to suffer betrayal to crucifixion. It is his enemies' part to plot and scheme to bring about that same end. In one sense then the ends of the two parties are similar: both lead to the cross. In a much more important sense, however, the two ends are antithetical; for Jesus' aspiration is assimilated to the divine good will, whereas the object of the Jewish leaders is, in Matthew's view, born of human sin.

THE ANOINTING AT BETHANY (26.6–13)

⁶**While Jesus was in Bethany, in the house of Simon the leper, ⁷a woman came to him with an alabaster jar of very costly ointment; and as he sat at table, she poured it on his head. ⁸But the disciples, seeing what had happened, were angry and said, 'What is this waste for? ⁹For this (ointment) could have been sold for a large sum, and the money given to the poor.' ¹⁰But Jesus, knowing this, said to them, 'Why do you trouble the woman? For she has performed a good service for me. ¹¹For you always have the poor with you, but you will not always have me. ¹²For she, by pouring this ointment on my body, has prepared me for burial. ¹³Amen I say to you, wherever this good news is proclaimed in all the world, what she has done will indeed be told in remembrance of her.'**

Parallels: Mk 14.3–9; Lk 7.36–50; Jn 12.1–8

The paragraph offers both continuity and contrast with vv. 1–5. In continuity with vv. 1–2, Jesus' death is again plainly set forth and Jesus' foreknowledge underlined (v. 12). In contrast with vv. 3–5, the woman does not oppose Jesus but serves him. Her action is antithetical to that of the Jewish leaders.

6. The scene is set: we have moved from the courtyard or palace of the high priest, where evil plots are laid, to the residence of a leper, where kindness shows itself.

in Bethany. On 'Bethany' (cf. 21.17) see p. 353. Evidently Jesus has returned there after the day recounted in 21.18–26.2.

the house of Simon the leper. That Simon is 'the leper' makes him yet one more social outcast befriended by Jesus. 'The leper' serves to distinguish this Simon from the four other Simons in our Gospel. But this Simon – probably no more than a name for Matthew's community – plays no role in our text, which leaves unaddressed the questions later asked and answered by Christian legend: is he the father of Lazarus and Martha? Is the unnamed woman (cf. 15.22) his wife? And how is it that his leprosy is gone? (The informed reader knows that lepers did not act as dinner hosts, and also that people would not, through contact with a leper, enter a state of uncleanness immediately before the Passover. The fathers and later commentators regularly assume a healing by Jesus; cf. 8.1–4).

7. A woman, with motives unknown, impulsively performs an extravagant act which inevitably suggests Jesus' messianic status: he is the anointed one.

a woman came to him. We learn nothing of the woman save her action. But her positive act and the disciples' protest foreshadow what is to come: whereas faithful women follow Jesus to cross and tomb (27.55–6, 61; 28.1), the male disciples flee (26.56).

an alabaster jar of very costly ointment. The expensive item contrasts sharply with the low price Judas settles upon to betray Jesus (26.15). According to Pliny, *N.H.* 13.3, 'perfumes are best kept in alabaster vases,' and archaeology confirms that the stone, often imported from Egypt, was frequently made into handleless perfume flasks. The necks were typically long and thin.

she poured it on his head. Cf. Ignatius, *Eph.* 17.1 ('the Lord received ointment on his head, that he might breathe incorruption upon the church'). Because anointing was, at least in well-to-do circles, probably customary at feasts the reader may think that the woman affectionately anoints Jesus as part of a celebration (it is only Jesus' words which connect the act with burial). The use of 'head', however, makes one think of the OT narratives in which kings are anointed; see Exod 29.7; 1 Sam 10.1.

8. The disciples' negative response reflects a shortsighted utilitarianism, which concerns not the act itself but the waste. They thereby distance themselves from Jesus and so initiate his isolation – a motif which grows with the length of the passion narrative.

9. The disciples' denigration of a luxurious waste seems a fitting expression of piety and, especially following 25.31–46, in accord with Jesus' own concerns (cf. 11.5; 19.21).

For this (ointment) could have been sold for a large sum, and the money given to the poor. Our story is prefaced with the mention of Passover (v. 2). This might be relevant because it is often said (although the evidence is meagre) that the eve of Passover was a special time of charity.

10. Jesus, who until now has been passive and silent, responds, effectively impressing silence upon the disciples' objections.

knowing this. Does this imply knowledge of a hidden fact, as though the words the narrator has attributed to the disciples were whispered or said in their hearts? Is Jesus here psychic or omniscient?

The merit of the woman's good work, with its christological orientation, is not a general act of almsgiving without knowledge of its recipients but a personal act of devotion to Jesus. The situation is akin to 8.21–2, where allegiance to Jesus means leaving one's father unburied; here allegiance to Jesus means not being prudent with resources, even when they could benefit the poor.

11. As in 9.14–17, Jesus draws a distinction between the pre- and post-Easter periods, and views the former as a time of unique opportunity.

For you always have the poor with you. Cf. Deut 15.11: 'the poor will never cease out of the land.'

12. Jesus interprets the woman's action as a prophetic deed.

has prepared me for burial. Perfumes and ointments were often used to ready corpses for burial, and Matthew recounts no other anointing of Jesus' body; contrast Mk 16.1; Jn 19.39.

13. When Jesus declares that the woman 'will be held in honoured record throughout the whole world, the comparison is an indirect reproach to his disciples, that by consent of all races in foreign and extreme regions of the globe an action will be praised which the men of his own household condemned with such bitterness' (Calvin).

good news refers neither to Jesus' preaching (cf. 4.23; 9.25) nor to the First Gospel but to the good news about the Messiah – news which must include his story and so his passion. That the woman shall have a memorial in the church's proclamation moves the reader beyond the upcoming passion to the vindicating resurrection and the time of the church.

* * * * *

(i) The previous pericope, 26.3–5, illustrates one response to Jesus' mission, namely, opposition, a theme continued in vv. 14ff. Verses 6–13, on the other hand, illustrate two different responses: service, as evidenced in the unnamed woman, and misunderstanding, as evidenced in the disciples.

(ii) The anointing is a simple act of love. This is most fitting after 25.31–46, which attributes profound meaning to modest deeds of kindness. Our text, as in illustration, depicts an anonymous woman whose kind act unexpectedly becomes preparation for Messiah's burial.

THE BETRAYAL FOR MONEY (26.14–16)

¹⁴**Then one of the twelve, who was called Judas Iscariot, went to the chief priests ¹⁵and said, 'What will you give me if I betray him to you?' They paid him thirty pieces of silver. ¹⁶ And from that moment he began to look for an opportunity to betray him.**

Parallels: Mk 14.10–11; Lk 22.3–6; Jn 6.70–1; 13.2, 27

After the circumstantial introduction (v. 14), Judas asks the authorities a question which amounts to a bargain (v. 15a). Their payment of silver is the response to his overture: an agreement has been reached (v. 15b). Verse 16 then records the aftermath: thereafter Judas seeks an opportune time.

In contrast with the woman who anoints Jesus in the preceding pericope, Judas, 'one of the twelve', acts with treachery. While she unselfishly gives what she has, Judas seeks his own gain; and whereas her sacrifice is costly, Judas settles his bargain for a relatively paltry sum.

14–15. The narrative reverts to v. 5 (and it will be continued in 27.3ff.).

Judas Iscariot. On Judas and the obscure name, 'Iscariot', see p. 149. He has until now been named only once, in 10.4; but from here on out he is a major figure.

Judas goes not to the Romans but to the Jewish authorities, for it is the latter who must make the decision for or against Jesus, whose mission is to Israel.

went to the chief priests. Matthew, under the influence of Zech 11.12–13, emphasizes the notion of a business deal: Judas, with apparent eagerness, cooperates with Jesus' enemies and exchanges Jesus for monetary gain. Whereas Jesus has just expressed indifference to money, Judas now makes money his motive.

At the level of history, Judas' purposes remain as mysterious as his name, Iscariot. Was his determination to betray Jesus passionate and chronic or the impulse of a moment? Was it the product of revenge for some imagined slight? Or did it come from avarice or thwarted hopes or frustrated ambition or intense theological differences? Was Judas, out of misdirected idealism, seeking to force the eschatological scenario or to make Jesus play a messianic role different from the one he had adopted? Both Luke and John link Judas with Satan, a motif which in later Christian thought grows so much that he sometimes passes beyond the pale of humanity. On the lighter side, tradition has also offered that he was moved by his wife's nagging. The only certainty remains our ignorance.

If the historical facts are obscure, in Matthew at least the emphasis falls upon the payment: Judas – in complete antithesis to everything Jesus has taught – wants money. One cannot but think of 1 Tim 6.10. Judas nonetheless later returns the silver, so his avarice is not unbounded. Further, Matthew leaves much unexplained, and this circumstance enlarges the aura of mystery that hangs over the narrative.

They paid him thirty pieces of silver. These words, which anticipate 27.9, stand under the influence of Zech 11.12: 'And they weighed out as my wages thirty shekels of silver.' This OT text, which also lies beneath the story in 27.3–10, shows that the betrayal is in accord with what God has foreseen. Indeed, the apparent triumph of evil is mysteriously also the work of God, as in Gen 50.20: 'you meant evil against me, God meant it for good.' There might also be an allusion to Exod 21.32: Judas reckons Jesus worth no more than a slave. Whether that is so or not the amount is surely intended to be paltry, as it is in Zech 11.13, where 'the lordly price' is ironic.

The denomination of the thirty silver pieces is not given. If they are Tyrian shekels, as the use of Zech 11.12–3 implies, Judas gains the equivalent of about four months of minimum wage. That there is any allusion to the silver shekels for which Joseph's brothers sold him into slavery seems unlikely. For although *T. Gad* 2.3 says that the sum involved was *thirty* pieces of gold, and that the sale was made by Judas and Gad, members of a group of twelve, this may well be a Christian interpolation; and the other sources which have Joseph betrayed for thirty pieces of money and so assimilate the OT Judas to the NT Judas all appear to be later than Matthew.

But there is a possible intratextual link with 10.9, where Jesus commands his disciples to take no silver: Judas' desire for monetary gain shows him to be no true follower of Jesus. His actions, moreover, make him like the guards at the tomb, whose cowardice leads them to lie: they also take silver from the authorities (28.11–15).

16. And from that moment he began to look for an opportunity to betray him. The opportune time (cf. v. 18) is a moment and place in which concealment from the public eye can be secured (cf. v. 5). Judas must exercise a hunter's patience.

* * * * *

When Judas strikes his bargain over the time to arrest Jesus, the latter's freedom to speak and act is about to be taken from him. The circumstance imparts emphasis to what follows, for what Jesus does with time running out must take on special meaning. In other words, vv. 14–16 not only make the time before the arrest tense with anticipation, they also indicate that the narrative is about to depict Jesus' final free acts and in this way enlarge the significance of those acts.

THE LAST SUPPER (26.17–29)

[17]On the first day of Unleavened Bread, the disciples came to Jesus, saying, 'Where do you want us to make the preparations for you to eat the Passover?' [18]He said, 'Go into the city, to a certain man, and say to him, "The Teacher says, My time is near; I will keep the Passover at your house with my disciples."' [19]And the disciples did as Jesus directed them, and they prepared the Passover meal.

[20]When it became evening, he sat at table with the twelve; [21]and while they were eating, he said, 'Amen I say to you that one of you will betray me.' [22]And they, becoming greatly grieved, began to say to him one after another, 'Surely it is not I, Lord?' [23]He answered, 'The one who dipped his hand into the bowl with me will betray me. [24]The Son of man goes as it is written of him, but woe to that one by whom the Son of man is betrayed! It would have been better if that man had never been born.' [25]Judas, who betrayed him, answered and said, 'Surely it is not I, Rabbi?' He replied, 'You have said so.'

[26]While they were eating, Jesus, taking bread and uttering a blessing, broke it and gave it to the disciples and said, 'Take, eat; this is my body.' [27]And taking a cup and giving thanks he gave it to them, saying, 'Drink from it, all of you; [28]for this is my blood of the covenant, which is poured out for many for the forgiveness of sins. [29]I say to you, I will no longer drink of this fruit of the vine until that day when I drink it new with you in my Father's kingdom.'

Parallels: Mk 14.12–25; Lk 22.7–23; Jn 13.1, 21–30

Preparation for the Passover (26.17–19)

The juxtaposing of our passage with Judas' agreement to betray Jesus sets the preparation of Jesus beside that of Judas: if the betrayer seeks an 'opportune time' for betrayal, the Son of man makes ready for his crisis, which has come. In thus making ready Jesus acts with sovereign authority. He commands his disciples to 'go'. He tells them what to say. And, with knowledge of the future, he refers to himself as 'the teacher' who, instead of waiting for an invitation, gives orders to his host.

Whether the last supper was or was not a passover celebration is a vexed matter to which nothing can be contributed in this context.

Jn 13.1–4; 18.28; and 19.14 appear to assume it was not; and certain features in the synoptics themselves have been thought incongruent with Mt 26.17–19 par., and rather in harmony with John. But whatever the historical fact, Matthew's point of view is clear: the last supper was a passover seder.

17. The disciples' question offers a striking contrast with the question in v. 15: Judas asks how he can betray Jesus; the others ask how they can serve him.

19. a certain man seems studiously vague; it adds an aura of mystery to the scene.

My time is near; I will keep the Passover at your house with my disciples. Whether or not 'time' has here eschatological sense, the word tells us that the story is approaching its dramatic climax, the crucifixion. It is suggestive that Jesus celebrates the seder not with his family but with his followers. This reflects the replacement of his physical family by his spiritual family; cf. 12.46–50.

19. The disciples obey and become models of right response: they serve Jesus by doing his word.

And the disciples did as Jesus directed them. Matthew's construction is close to 1.24 and 21.6; see p. 18. But it also resembles Exod 12.28, which is probably here recalled. Not only are there other allusions to the exodus in the immediately context (see below), but Exod 12.28 directly follows Moses' instructions for passover.

The Foretelling of Betrayal (26.20–5)

This pericope, whose key word is 'betray' or 'hand over' (vv. 21, 23, 24, 25), offers an illustration of the parables of the wheat and the weeds and of the net: good and bad are side by side.

The setting of the scene (vv. 20–1a) introduces two parallel exchanges:

> Prophecy: Jesus predicts betrayal (21b)
> > Response: the disciples ask, 'Surely it is not I, Lord?' (22)
> > Identification: 'The one who dipped . . .' (23)

> Prophecy: Jesus again predicts his betrayal (24)
> > Response: Judas asks, 'Surely it is not I, Rabbi?' (25a)
> > Identification: 'You have said so' (25b)

The parallelism accentuates a progression which differentiates Judas from the others. Verses 21–3 focus on the disciples, who call Jesus 'Lord'. But the remark in v. 23 naturally leads to vv. 24–5, which focus on the betrayer, who calls Jesus 'rabbi'. So it natural that the second prophecy of betrayal (v. 24), unlike the first (v. 21), elaborates with a woe concerning Judas (v. 24).

20. When it became evening. The passover meal was eaten after sunset.

he sat at table with the twelve. Cf. Jn 13.23, 25. In rabbinic sources it is a ritual duty to recline at table at the passover meal.

21. Whether or not vv. 17–19 are supposed to display Jesus' foreknowledge of events, what follows certainly does.

while they were eating. The setting of table fellowship makes the betrayal all the more heinous; cf. Ps 41.9.

22. Although Jesus has before spoken of being handed over, only now does he indicate to the twelve that he will be handed over by one of them. Their immediate horror is natural and instinctive.

And they, becoming greatly grieved, began to say to him one after another. Compare Jn 13.22. If it is now the disciples' turn to be greatly grieved, it will be Jesus' turn soon enough (v. 37).

Surely it is not I, Lord? 'Lord' contrasts with 'rabbi', which Judas uses (v. 25).

23. It is unclear whether Jesus' remark denotes Judas (because only he dips his hand in the dish) or simply says again that the betrayer is one of the twelve (for all dip in the dish; in this case identification of the betrayer takes place only in v. 25). The latter, because it preserves the dramatic tension, seems the best guess. If so Calvin was right: 'Christ's reply does not relieve their anxiety nor point out the person of Judas, but only confirms what he had just said: that one of his friends that sat with him at table would betray him.'

The one who dipped his hand into the bowl with me will betray me. Cf. Jn 13.26. Perhaps we should think of the bowl in which the bitter herbs were dipped.

24. The Son of man goes. Cf. Lk 13.33. 'Goes' is a euphemism for dying.

as it is written of him, which has no particular passage in view, implies that evil does not take God or Jesus by surprise: it can only do what has already been foreseen. What follows indicates that 'it is written' does not contradict human responsibility: even when human beings are instruments of God they are accountable.

but woe to that one by whom the Son of man is betrayed! It would have been better if that man had never been born. These words are usually thought to seal Judas' eternal perdition; but see p. 503. They in any case seem appropriate as a general judgement upon all apostasy and betrayal.

25. This editorial addition, which makes Jesus' foreknowledge all the more precise and brings betrayer and betrayed face to face, makes for a climax. Its language is drawn from elsewhere; cf. especially vv. 22, 49, 64.

Judas, who betrayed him, answered and said, 'Surely it is not I, Rabbi?' The hypocritical question imitates v. 22. But whereas there the disciples call Jesus 'Lord', here Judas, as again in v. 49, calls him 'rabbi', an inadequate appellation.

Is Judas included in v. 22's 'one after another'? If he is then he now asks his question a second time and so is all the more guilty of hypocrisy. If not then he is evidently the last disciple to speak: he has remained silent until everybody else has spoken, surely a sign of reluctance.

You have said so. This is a qualified affirmation which reveals Jesus' foreknowledge as well as Judas' responsibility.

Jesus Observes His Last Passover (26.26–9)

The tragedy of the previous pericope is now interpreted as redemptive: the betrayed Jesus will become a sacrifice whose blood is poured out 'for the many'. In this way the suffering servant, who offers himself willingly, inaugurates a new covenant for the new community.

Matthew's version of the last supper is enriched by its links with other texts. Verses 26a and 27a strongly recall the two feeding stories of chapters 14 and 15: the last supper has been foreshadowed by the miraculous multiplications. Also, there might be a link with 'Give us this day our daily bread' – at least the interpreters down through the ages have in this way connected Lord's Prayer and Lord's Supper. As for the Old Testament, 'This is the blood of the covenant' takes up Exod 24.8 and makes the act of Jesus resemble an act of Moses. The reference to 'covenant' might also allude to Jer 31.31. 'For many' and 'poured out' likely advert to Isa 53.12, and so imply that Jesus in his death is the suffering servant of Isaiah.

Matthew's text recounts a past event, the last supper of Jesus with his disciples. But all commentators presume that Matthew's first readers saw in the last supper the foundation of the Lord's supper: 26.26–9 is an etiological cult narrative. While this is true enough, the text does not say this about itself. Jesus does not invite repetition of his actions; there is no 'Do this in remembrance of me'. The last supper is, then, an example of how the text gives its full meaning only to readers who bring to it extratextual knowledge, in this case of the Christian celebration of the eucharist.

26. Just as the food of the seder has traditionally been interpreted, so does Jesus now interpret the food before him.

While they were eating. Although the words and deeds that follow belong to a passover meal, no mention is made of the roasted lamb, the four cups, unleavened bread, the traditional interpretations of the rite, or other details unique to passover. Many have thought this a sign that, in the tradition, the meal was not a seder. But one could assume for the pre-Markan tradition what one assumes for Matthew: namely, that the particulars of passover did not need explanation because they could be assumed; what mattered were the distinctive actions and words of Jesus. One should also, however, seriously reckon (as most NT scholars have not) with the possibility that the seder service known to us from the *Mishnah* took much of its present shape after AD 70, so that one should not expect correspondence with the synoptic accounts.

Jesus, taking bread and uttering a blessing, broke it and gave it to the disciples. Jesus is the *paterfamilias* and so presides. The blessing is not specified but one thinks of the traditional formula, 'Blessed are you, O Lord our God, king of the universe, who brings forth bread from the earth.' Perhaps the breaking of the bread signifies the Messiah's broken body.

Take, eat. The command to eat, followed by 'this is my body', implies participation in the death of Jesus or its effects: just as those who partook of passover shared in the redemption from Egypt, so those who take and eat share in the benefits of Jesus' atoning death.

this is my body. While everything up to these words could be reckoned part of a conventional passover meal, 'This is my body' introduces something new. Bitter debate has accompanied their reading throughout the centuries. There is a natural tendency to think of 'blood' and 'body' as correlative: together they are the elements of sacrifice, or the two elements making up a person. But in Luke and Paul the two elements are separated by a meal; it was only the liturgy and the separation of the eucharist from the agape meal which made them adjacent. Moreover, 'body' can mean simply 'self', so 'This is my body' may originally have meant 'This is myself'. Perhaps it even does so in Matthew.

The orthodox identification of the elements with the body and blood of Jesus Christ has made much of 'this is': it is a verb of identification. But others have found here only figurative representation: the bread symbolizes Jesus or what will happen to him. This accords with the use of 'this is' in 13.19–23, 37–9 (where 'this is that' means 'this represents that') and Jesus' frequent use of metaphorical language. The truth is that one cannot build anything on 'this is' by itself; the words have a range of uses. It is, moreover, impossible to say precisely what Matthew believed about the elements: whether, for example, one should think of him as being closer to Luther than to Zwingli, or whether the categories from later theological debates –

transubstantiation, consubstantiation, vitalism, memorial rite – would even be relevant.

27. Unlike 1 Cor 11.25, there is no interval between the eating of the bread and the drinking of the cup; but because Matthew is narrating a passover meal such an interval should be assumed.

And taking a cup and giving thanks he gave it to them, saying. Note the extensive and presumably intended parallelism between vv. 26 and 27:

V. 26:   taking
   bread
     and
       blessing it
        gave it to the disciples
          saying
            eat
              this is my body

V. 27:   taking
   a cup
     and
       giving thanks
        gave it to them
          saying
            drink
              this is my blood

The blessing for wine ran: 'Blessed are you, O Lord our God, king of the universe, creator of the fruit of the vine.' Among those who think of passover there is disagreement as to whether we should identify the cup with the second or the third or the fourth cup of the seder. But again one should remember that the sources for passover (and the four cups) are from later times, so that it may be anachronistic to read the text passage through them.

28. That Jesus' blood is for the forgiveness of sins is congruent with salvation being the gift of God. But the main point seems to be that Jesus' sacrifice is the basis of a new covenant.

for this is my blood of the covenant. For wine associated with blood see Gen 49.11 ('the blood of grapes'); Deut 32.14; Isa 63.3, 6; Ecclus 39.26. Both this and the version in Mark and Matthew recall the covenant ratification on Sinai; Exod 24.8 reads: 'And Moses took the blood and threw it upon the people, and said, "Behold, the blood of the covenant which the Lord has made with you in accordance with all these words".' There is a typological relationship between the act of

Moses and the act of Jesus, a relationship consistent with and reinforced by the Moses typology present elsewhere in Matthew. As the first redeemer made a sacrifice for the people so that they might enter into a new covenant with God, so does the last redeemer inaugurate another covenant by offering his blood – that is, his life – for the forgiveness of sins.

Commentators have also been reminded of Jer 31.31–4. But the verbal links with that passage ('covenant', 'sins') are less obvious; and only Lk 22.20 and 1 Cor 11.25 explicitly refer to a 'new covenant'; cf. Jer 31.31. Furthermore, the notion of a new covenant was known apart from Jeremiah, and it has been argued that Jeremiah 31 did not influence the new covenant concept at Qumran. So this second allusion is uncertain. One might even wish to urge, given the possible allusion to Isa 53.12, that the notion of a new covenant comes from Deutero-Isaiah: 42.6; 49.8–10; 55.3.

which is poured out for many. 'Many' has comprehensive sense and 'poured out' clarifies 20.28: the 'ransom for many' is made through sacrificial blood. This last fact is emphasized by the use of 'poured out', a sacrificial word which connotes a violent death and, in connexion with passover, recalls the slaughtered paschal lamb. One should also probably, in view of Matthew's use elsewhere of Deutero-Isaiah, recall MT Isa 53.12: 'he poured out his life to death ... bore the sin of *many*.'

for the forgiveness of sins. There is no parallel in the other accounts of the last supper to this clause, which underlines that the death of Jesus is soteriological, a deliverance from slavery to sin; cf. Rom 11.26–7; Heb 10.16–19; 11.15. The result is partial exegesis of 1.21: Jesus saves his people from their sins by dying for them and so permits a new relationship with God.

It has been suggested that the addition of 'for the forgiveness of sins' reflects the influence of Jer 31.34. But the allusion to Exod 24.8 is much firmer than the allusion to Jer 31.34, and in Jewish tradition the Sinai offering becomes explicitly expiatory. The currency of this interpretation in the first century is guaranteed by Heb 9.19–22, where it is taken for granted that the blood Moses sprinkled was for the forgiveness of sins. Perhaps then the addition of 'unto the forgiveness of sins' reflects the influence of Exod 24.8.

Matthew's seeing in the last supper a parallel to Moses' sprinkling of blood at the Sinai covenant has a striking parallel in Heb 9.15–22, where the surpassing self-sacrifice of Jesus is compared with the sprinkling in Exod 24.6–8. Moreover, Heb 9.20 uses the phrase, 'This is the blood of the covenant which ...'. There is no 'this is' in Exod 24.8: the words rather come from the tradition of the Lord's supper.

So the writer of Hebrews was put in mind of this last when likening Jesus' mediation of a new covenant in blood to the inauguration of the old covenant through Moses' sprinkling of blood. This is what one finds also in the First Gospel.

29. Jesus' prophecy of abstinence is in effect another passion prediction: it foretells imminent death as well as resurrection and eschatological victory. Thus the Lord's Supper is not just commemorative but prophetic.

One wonders whether the sequence in Exod 24.8–11 does not underlie vv. 28–9. In Exodus the establishing of the covenant through blood is followed by eating and drinking and seeing God. In Matthew the proclamation of the eschatological covenant through blood prefaces the promise of the eschatological banquet. Already Isa 24.23–25.8 takes up the language of Exod 24.8–11 to prophesy the eschatological feast.

I will no longer drink of this fruit of the vine until that day when I drink it new with you in my Father's kingdom. Jesus' solemn proclamation of abstinence connects the last supper with the eschatological banquet: a broken fellowship will be renewed at what Revelation calls 'the marriage supper of the Lamb'. Many ecclesiastical commentators have instead thought of post-Easter fellowship – the meals of the post-resurrectional appearances or the Eucharist. But (i) wine and drinking wine were stock symbols for the age to come; (ii) elsewhere in Matthew the consummated kingdom is spoken of as a banquet; and (iii) the eschatological dimensions of the early Christian eucharist are manifest from Paul and the *Didache*.

* * * * *

(i) When read in the light of the practice of the community, 26.26–9 is a text with three tenses: it looks back to a foundational event of the past, prescribes a fundamental rite for the present, and prophesies a central event of the eschatological future. Regarding the past, the text tells us that Jesus established a new covenant through the sacrifice of his own blood. Concerning the present, Matthew's narrative of the last supper is instruction for the church's ongoing celebration of the Lord's supper, and it implies that participation in this rite is participation in the effects of Jesus' self-sacrifice. As for the future, the eschatological banquet is here interpreted as a restoration of the table fellowship broken by Jesus' death, which in turn suggests that table fellowship with the risen Lord is a foretaste of the consummation.

(ii) Mark and Luke make Jesus' last supper a passover seder. John 6 links the bread of the eucharist with the manna given to Israel during the exodus. In 1 Cor 10.1ff. participation in the Lord's supper is likened to drinking from the rock which followed Israel in the desert. And Heb 9.15–22 uses eucharistic language in retelling the story of Moses' covenantal sacrifice (see on v. 28). Clearly it was conventional in early Christian circles to view the last supper as part of a new exodus. It is no surprise then that Matthew's account, which has been foreshadowed by two stories in which Jesus seems to be like Moses, also suggests parallels between the last supper and the exodus narrative:

> Jesus celebrates the passover, vv. 17–18; cf. Exodus 12
> 'The disciples did as Jesus directed them', v. 19; cf. Exod 12.28
> 'This is my blood of the covenant', v. 28; cf. Exod 24.8
> 'For the forgiveness of sins', v. 28; cf. the targums on Exod 24.8

In Matthew the last redeemer is as the first: Jesus inaugurates a second exodus.

SCATTERING AND DENIAL FORESEEN (26.30–5)

[30] And having sung the hymn, they went out to the Mount of Olives. [31] Then Jesus said to them, 'All of you will be scandalized because of me this night. For it is written, "I will smite the shepherd, and the sheep of the flock will be scattered." [32] But after I am raised up, I will go ahead of you into Galilee.' [33] Peter said to him, 'Although all become scandalized because of you, I will never be scandalized.' [34] Jesus said to him, 'Amen I say to you that this very night, before the cock crows, you will deny me three times.' [35] Peter said to him, 'Even though I must die with you, I will not deny you.' And all the disciples said the same.

Parallels: Mk 14.26–31; Lk 22.31–4; Jn 13.36–8

Mt 26.30–5 is a prophetic view of impending events. From it we learn (i) the future of the disciples: they will fall away and be scattered but later gathered in Galilee to see Jesus; (ii) the future of Peter: he will deny his Lord three times before the cock crows; and (iii) the future of Jesus: he will be struck (= killed, cf. v. 35), but then raised from the dead. Despite the promise of resurrection in v. 32, the predominant feeling is one of gloom. When Jesus looks into the future he is like Jeremiah: his foreknowledge brings grief.

30. Jesus goes out; he does not hide himself, despite the danger.

sung the hymn. Because the last supper is in Matthew a passover meal, many have found here the custom of singing the second half of the great Hallel (Psalms 114/5–8) at Passover. But first-century Christian readers may also or instead have thought of Christian hymns sung with or after the Eucharist. On the Mount of Olives (cf. 24.3) see p. 343. Here there is an allusion to 2 Sam 15.30 where David, who has been plotted against by his trusted royal counsellor, Ahithophel (see p. 504), leaves Jerusalem and goes up 'the ascent of the Mount of Olives'. There the king weeps and prays for deliverance; cf. Gethsemane. That Matthew intends the parallelism follows from 27.3–10, where Judas is modelled on Ahithophel. Perhaps then it is more than coincidence that Ahithophel wants to overtake David at night (17.1; cf. Mt 26.31) with 12,000 men (17.1; cf. Mt 26.53) so that he can strike (cf. Mt 26.31) the king and make all the people with him (17.2; cf. Mt 26.18, 20, 38, 40, 51, 69, 71) flee (17.2; cf. Mt 26.56).

31. It is unclear whether the following conversation takes place on the Mount of Olives or on the way there. The prophecy in any case expands betrayal beyond Judas: all the disciples are implicated. As in 13.21, when persecution comes, the disciples fail.

All of you will be scandalized because of me this night. Cf. Jn 16.1, 32. The disciples will for a time abandon their discipleship: their flight is a loss of faith.

For it is written. The words belong to Jesus, not the narrator.

I will smite the shepherd, and the sheep of the flock will be scattered. The words depend upon an eschatological text, Zech 13.7: '"Awake, O sword, against my shepherd, against the man who is my associate," says the Lord of hosts. Strike the shepherd, that the sheep may be scattered; I will turn my hand against the little ones.'

32. This promise of restoration, which offers forgiveness in advance, envisages the scattering being undone.

But after I am raised up, I will go ahead of you into Galilee. In 28.7 and 10 an angel and the risen Jesus respectively repeat these words and leave no doubt that their fulfilment is in 28.16–20: on a mountain in Galilee the disciples see Jesus. 'Go ahead' probably continues the shepherd imagery (cf. Mic 2.12–13; Jn 10.4, 27); it refers less to spatial ('go before') or chronological ('to arrive before') priority as to leadership (cf. 2 Macc 10.1): not in Jerusalem but in 'Galilee of the Gentiles', where he first gathered his community, will Jesus reconstitute the flock that has been scattered and then inaugurate the world mission.

33. Peter, quitting the doubt of v. 22 for 'the intoxication of human self-confidence' (Calvin), not only contradicts his Lord (cf. 16.21–3) and the Scripture but makes himself out to be more loyal than his fellow disciples: Jesus cannot be talking about him. Instead of asking for Jesus' help in the coming crisis, he is confidently self-sufficient.

35. Even though I must die with you, I will not deny you. Cf. Jn 11.16; 13.37. Peter knows that death lies ahead for Jesus and maybe for himself also. The irony is two-fold: (i) Jesus will die 'with' others, but they will not be Peter and the disciples but two nameless criminals (27.38, 44); and (ii) earlier Peter strongly opposes the Messiah's suffering (16.21–3), so his present concession to the possibility betrays inconsistency.

And all the disciples said the same. The choir of disciples gives Peter company in his delusion. Although the disciples are sincere in their protest that they will not fall away, Jesus knows them better than they know themselves: their spirits are willing, their flesh is weak.

It is noteworthy that Jesus is not the last to speak. The closing instead relates the false bravado of Peter and the disciples. Jesus leaves persuasion to events.

* * * * *

Mt 26.30–5 is almost an outline of the remainder of the Gospel. It foretells that the disciples will forsake Jesus (26.56); that Peter will deny his Lord (26.69–75); that Jesus will be killed; that he will be raised from the dead (28.1–10); and that he will appear to his disciples in Galilee (28.16–20). Because the synopsis comes from Jesus himself, his foreknowledge is emphasized. Further, the citation of Zech 13.7 places all that follows under God's providence; and, because the OT context of Zech 13.7 is a little apocalypse, and because that apocalypse is cited or alluded to elsewhere in Matthew's passion, the prophecy from Scripture strongly hints that what follows is bound up with eschatology. It inaugurates the end, or at least foreshadows it.

JESUS IN GETHSEMANE (26.36–46)

[36]**Then Jesus went with them to a place called Gethsemane, and he said to his disciples, 'Sit here while I go there and pray.'** [37]**And taking Peter and the two sons of Zebedee, he began to grieve and to be troubled.** [38]**Then he said to them, 'I am deeply grieved, even unto death. Remain here and watch with me.'** [39]**And going a bit farther, he fell on his face, praying and saying, 'My Father, if it is possible, let this cup pass from me; yet not what I will but what you will.'** [40]**And he came to the disciples and found them sleeping. And he said to Peter, 'So, were you not able to watch with me one hour?** [41]**Watch and pray, so that you may not enter into the time of trial. The spirit indeed is willing, but the flesh is weak.'** [42]**Again for a second time he went away and prayed, saying, 'My Father, if it is not possible for this to pass unless I drink it, your will be done.'** [43]**And again coming he found them sleeping, for their eyes were heavy.** [44]**And leaving them again he went away and prayed for the third time, saying the same words.** [45]**Then he came to the disciples and said to them,**

'So are you still sleeping and taking your rest? Behold, the hour has come, and the Son of man is delivered into the hands of sinners. ⁴⁶Get up, let us be going. Behold, my betrayer has come near.'

Parallels: Mk 14.32–42; Lk 22.39–46; Jn 12.27; 18.1

The hour 'has come' (v. 45) when Jesus must drink 'this cup' (v. 39; cf. 20.22), when he must give his life as a ransom for many (20.28). Given his foreknowledge and his frequent passion predictions, one may wonder at his grief and apparent protest. But he does not so much struggle with God as with himself. And whatever the source of the upset – Matthew, unlike so many commentators through the ages, does not tell us – God's will is not questioned (vv. 39, 42). Resignation comes.

The whole of 26.36–46 is dominated by Jesus' speech. Four times he speaks to his disciples, and three times he prays:

36: 'and he said to his disciples'
38: 'Then he said to them'
40: 'And he said to Peter'
45: 'Then he came to the disciples and said to them'

39: 'praying and saying'
42: 'prayed, saying'
44: 'prayed ... saying'

The three parallel prayers exhibit a literary technique found elsewhere. While Jesus' first and second prayers are quoted, his third is just summarized ('saying the same words'). This recalls 20.1–16, wherein we hear the instructions given to the labourers hired at the early and the third hour but not the instructions given to those hired at the sixth and ninth hours. Of these last we are simply told: 'he [the householder] did the same.' Similar is 27.39–44, which quotes the mockery of two groups but says of a third: they 'also reviled him in the same way.' For an OT example of this method of recounting several parallel episodes see Josh 6.12–14.

36. The scene is set; Jesus comes to pray.
Then Jesus went with them to a place called Gethsemane. 'Gethsemane' was evidently the name of an olive orchard on the Mount of Olives. Only Matthew and Mark use the name. Lk 22.39 speaks only of the Mount of Olives, Jn 18.1 of a garden near the Kidron valley (whence 'garden of Gethsemane'). The precise location remains unknown. Traditional and modern proposals (e.g. the Grotto of the Agony) are guesses.

Sit here while I go there and pray. In the story of the binding of Isaac, Abraham says to his servants: 'Sit here ... I and the lad will go there ...' (Gen 22.5). Does Matthew's language suggest a parallel between Abraham's faith and Jesus' faith? Or between Isaac's sacrifice and Jesus' sacrifice? Both Abraham and Jesus take along three people, and both separate themselves from others for worship or prayer. The two episodes are set on a mountain, and each involves trial.

37. Jesus separates himself and Peter, James, and John from the rest of the disciples.

And taking Peter and the two sons of Zebedee, he began to grieve and to be troubled. Cf. 17.1; Jn 12.27; Heb 5.7. The presence of Peter and the two sons of Zebedee recollects 4.28–22 (the call stories); 17.1–8 (the transfiguration); and 20.20–8. In this last the sons of Zebedee are asked whether they can drink the cup Jesus is to drink. In Gethsemane they – as well as Peter, who also turns out to be guilty of false bravado (cf. v. 33) – prove they cannot.

38. Jesus speaks his heart to his own. The verse, which reminds one of the psalms of lament, functions as a sort of heading.

I am deeply grieved, even unto death. Cf. Jn 12.27; Heb 5.7–8. The words, which convey that Jesus' sorrow is so great as to feel fatal, seemingly conflate LXX Ps 41.6, 12 = 42.5 with Jon 4.9.

Remain here and watch with me. Cf. v. 36 ('sit here'). Pascal, in *Le mystère de Jésus*, aptly commented: 'Jesus seeks companionship and solace from men. It seems to me that this is unique in his whole life, but he finds none, for his disciples are asleep.' 'Watch', which embraces both physical and spiritual alertness – the former is the prerequisite for the latter – recalls the exhortations of 24.36–24.30 (see especially 24.42–3; 25.13); it probably adds an eschatological element to the passion narrative.

39. Although Jesus contemplates the possibility of not drinking 'this cup', his prayer reveals that he has set aside his own will. This does not mean he is a Stoic: he does not 'look unmoved on fortune good and bad' (Boethius).

My Father. Cf. v. 42; also 4Q372 1.16 (where Joseph calls God 'my Father'). The address in its context recalls the Lord's Prayer:

The Lord's Prayer	*Gethsemane*
'our Father'	'my Father'
'your will be done'	'your will be done'
'lead us not into the time of trial'	'not enter into the time of trial'

Jesus prays in the way he tells others to pray.

let this cup pass from me. What is the meaning of 'this cup'? In *T. Abr.* 16.11, the angel of death calls himself 'the bitter cup of death' (cf. 1.3). But in the OT, intertestamental literature, and the Apocalypse, 'cup' is most often used figuratively in texts about suffering, especially suffering God's wrath or judgement. In 20.22, moreover, the cup Jesus must drink is neither temptation nor death nor martyrdom but rather eschatological sorrow, which will be poured out first upon the people of God; cf. Jer 25.15–29. And so it is here: the crucifixion belongs to the messianic woes. It is uncertain whether there is also the thought of Jesus, on behalf of others, becoming the object of God's wrath for sin.

Although Jesus has plainly prophesied his fate he here recoils from it. This is not, however, an act of rebellion. Rather does the plea harmonize with the Jewish notion that God can, in response to prayer or repentance or sin, undergo a change of mind.

yet not what I will but what you will. Cf. Ps 40.8; 143.10; 1 Macc 3.58–60. Christian theology has often observed how Jesus seems to wrestle with himself, and so has found here substantiation for the doctrine of Christ's two natures. Compare John of Damascus, *De fid. orth.* 24: Jesus' words show that 'he did in truth possess two wills ... corresponding to his natures'. At the same time Orthodox theology has sometimes hesitated to accept the sincerity of Jesus' prayer and urged that he prayed not for himself but for others, or to show the weakness of the human nature he bore.

40. Not only does 'the only answer' to Jesus' prayer seem to be 'the hard answer of events', but the disobedient disciples – who promised so much (vv. 33–5) – sleep and so add to the hurt done by enemies.

And he came to the disciples and found them sleeping. 'Jesus seeks some comfort at least from his three dearest friends, and they sleep: he asks them to bear with him a while, and they abandon him with complete indifference, and with so little pity that it did not keep them awake even for a single moment. And so Jesus was abandoned ...' (Pascal).

And he said to Peter. Jesus addresses Peter as representative disciple.

41. **Watch and pray, so that you may not enter into the time of trial.** It is unclear whether 'so that' depends solely upon 'pray' and gives the content of prayer or whether it depends upon both verbs. In the latter case, 'so that' introduces the goal of watching and praying.

The spirit indeed is willing, but the flesh is weak. Cf. Ps 51.12 ('a willing spirit'); Rom 6.19 ('the weakness of your flesh'). The antithetical line sounds like a proverb; cf. Jn 6.63. It also has a Pauline ring; but the background is Jewish, and there is probably no thought of a Platonic dualism (soul against body). In the Dead Sea Scrolls 'flesh' can denote the morally lower nature of human beings, that aspect through which sin and darkness can corrupt human weakness, while 'spirit' can be that through which God's Spirit directs people (cf. 'heart'). Such are the likely meanings here.

42. Jesus prays again but as before yields to his lifelong fixation, the will of God.

if it is not possible for this to pass unless I drink it, your will be done. Cf. Isa 51.17–23 (where God takes 'the cup of his wrath' away from Israel); Heb 10.9. 'This' = 'cup'. This redactional prayer borrows the wording and themes of v. 39 and likewise draws upon the Lord's Prayer ('your will be done'). The citation of the Lord's Prayer makes Jesus embody his own instructions on prayer once more.

43. **for their eyes were heavy.** Cf. LXX Gen 48.10. Jesus does not even bother to wake the disciples; contrast Mark.

44. Jesus goes away for a third time.

And leaving them again he went away and prayed for the third time, saying the same words. In 2 Cor 12.8 Paul says that thrice he sought the Lord for the messenger of Satan to leave him. Threefold petitions also appear in 2 Kgs 1.9–16; Ps 55.17 (the three daily prayers; cf. Dan 6.10; Did. 8.3); and b. *Yoma* 87a ('one who asks pardon of his neighbour need do so no more than three times'). Asking for something three times expresses earnestness.

45. So are you still sleeping and taking your rest? Jesus is resigned to his followers' failure.

the hour has come. Cf. Jn 5.25; 12.23; 17.1; *T. Abr.* 20.2 ('there is one death that comes to the righteous, a death that has its set time').

delivered. As in 17.22, God probably stands behind the verb.

sinners. Because the term is so often used to refer to the lawless, to those outside the law, we might here think of Gentiles, that is, the Roman authorities. But in Matthew the Jewish authorities also break God's law. In any case the word reinforces Jesus' innocence: his fate is the work of sin on the part of others.

46. Jesus, seeing Judas approach, goes out to meet him; he does not retreat.

Get up, let us be going. Cf. Jn 14.30–1. Perhaps there are military connotations: 'Rise, let us meet the advancing enemy.'

* * * * *

(i) One can embrace death because one thinks it a good (so Plato's Socrates) or one can resist it because one thinks it an evil; cf. the legends about Abraham and Moses. Jesus does neither. Although he recoils from death, or at least crucifixion, his course is fixed by the will of God, and this overrides his reluctance over death, so there is no real resistance. For Jesus the issue is not death but submission to the divine will: 'Thy will be done.'

(ii) Many of the key words in 26.36–46 have eschatological associations. 'Watch' harks back to 24.42, 43, and 25.13, all verses about watching for the coming of the Son of man. 'Cup' is associated with eschatological judgement. 'The time of trial' envisages eschatological tribulation. 'Sleeping' recalls 25.5, where the foolish virgins sleep and so miss the messianic banquet. 'Has come' (in first position) echoes 3.2; 4.17; and 10.7 – all proclamations about the nearness of the kingdom. Finally, 'the hour' has eschatological sense in 24.36, 44, 50; and 25.13. The confluence of these loaded terms strongly implies that in Matthew the passion of Jesus is eschatological: it belongs to or foreshadows the messianic woes.

(iii) There are three sources of pathos in 26.36–46. First there is the innocence of the one who suffers: like Job he is not guilty. Second, Jesus seemingly acts against what he says elsewhere. While, for example, he has plainly prophesied crucifixion for himself and even rebuked Peter for proposing some other course, here he himself contemplates a route around suffering. Again, whereas he has foretold that his disciples will forsake him, here he asks them to stay with him. He seems at war with himself. Third, there is Jesus' isolation. Although he comes with his disciples he soon separates himself from them and casts his face to the ground. The physical circumstances are symbolic: Jesus is alone. Despite the threefold 'with' linking him to others, his followers, as though indifferent, abandon him for sleep. Moreover, if what Jesus asks of them goes unheard, we likewise hear nothing from heaven: it is as if Jesus' prayers go unanswered. Thus he becomes, as in 17.17, a solitary figure; and our narrative has its natural conclusion in the fleeing of the eleven.

(iv) Pascal famously found in our passage a parable on discipleship: 'Jesus is in agony until the end of the world; during that time there must be no sleeping.' This interpretation accords with the Matthean narrative. Jesus' calls to stay awake and watch are general imperatives: they apply to all. In line with this Jesus' behaviour is, as in Heb 5.7–8, exemplary; he is a model of faithful discipleship. Jesus stays awake to watch, he prays the Lord's Prayer, and he submits to the will of God.

THE ARREST OF JESUS (26.47–56)

[47]While he was yet speaking, Judas, one of the twelve, came, and with him was a a large crowd, with swords and clubs, from the chief priests and the elders of the people. [48]Now the betrayer had given them a sign, saying, 'Whomever I kiss is the one; arrest him.' [49]And immediately coming to Jesus he said, 'Greetings, Rabbi!', and he kissed him. [50]But Jesus said to him, 'Companion, do what you are here to do.' Then they

came and laid hands on Jesus and arrested him. [51]And behold, one of those with Jesus brought forth his hand and drew his sword and struck the slave of the high priest, cutting off his ear. [52]Then Jesus said to him, 'Return your sword to its place, for all who take the sword will die by the sword. [53]Or do you not think that I am able to call upon my Father, and that he will at once send me more than twelve legions of angels? [54]Yet how then would the scriptures be fulfilled, that thus it is necessary for things to transpire?' [55]At that hour Jesus said to the crowds, 'Have you come out with swords and clubs to arrest me as though I were a bandit? Day after day I sat in the temple teaching, and you did not arrest me. [56]But all this has happened, so that the scriptures of the prophets might be fulfilled.' Then all the disciples, deserting him, fled.

Parallels: Mk 14.43–52; Lk 22.47–53; Jn 18.2–12

The busy story of Jesus' arrest, which is unusually full of characters, pulls together several strands from earlier sections. The setting at night matches the intention of the Jewish leaders to take Jesus 'by stealth' and avoid a riot (v. 4; cf. v. 16). Judas' presence vindicates Jesus' foresight in vv. 21, 25, and 45. That the crowd is 'from the chief priests and the elders of the people' takes one back to vv. 3–5 and 14–16, and likewise to Jesus' passion predictions. Judas' use of 'rabbi' recalls v. 25 and here as there tells us that he is no authentic disciple of Jesus. 'They came up and laid hands on him' (v. 50) makes for a literal fulfilment of 17.22 ('into the hands of men'). Jesus' passivity and non-resistance harmonize with his decision in Gethsemane and his earlier moral instruction. The two references to Scripture (vv. 54, 56) resonate with the entirety of Matthew: all takes place 'that the Scriptures of the prophets might be fulfilled'. And the disciples' flight shows Jesus, not his disciples, to be the true prophet; cf. vv. 31–5.

The narrative conveys sorrow through irony. Judas is no stranger but 'one of the twelve' (v. 47). The crowd has swords and clubs (v. 47) while the man they seek resists not evil. Judas, the betrayer, kisses Jesus and greets him (v. 49). And Jesus' own disciples, instead of standing by him, forsake him and flee (v. 56). At the same time, the sorrow is balanced by Jesus' authority and the motif of fulfilment. The Messiah's fate is his own will: he decides not to ask for legions of angels (v. 53). His resolution is, moreover, determined by the voice of the prophets (vv. 54, 56), which is to say: Jesus' will is God's will.

The Kiss of Judas (26.47–50)

47. The sad scene is set and the hour of crisis (cf. 26.45) comes. Cf.

Ecclus 37.2 ('is it not a grief to the death when a companion and friend turns to enmity?').

one of the twelve adds pathos and recalls Jesus' prophecy in vv. 20–1: the betrayer is one of the twelve.

swords and clubs reappear in v. 55, where their irony is plain: weapons are superfluous, for Jesus, faithful to his word, eschews physical violence.

from the chief priests and the elders of the people. No Romans are yet mentioned.

48. A kiss marks Jesus as the man to arrest. Evidently his face is not known to his captors, and besides that it is dark. He is taken by people who do not know him.

Whomever I kiss is the one. We know little about ancient Jewish greetings. Some find nothing unusual in Judas' kiss: such was the standard salutation. But nowhere else does our Gospel depict a disciple kissing Jesus; and among Jews, kissing was probably rare in public and usually reserved for solemn or formal occasions, being typically a token of respect and reconciliation. So even if Judas' kiss is not effusive (an issue hard to decide) it is certainly hypocritical. Judas brings not affection but violence. Like Herod, who spoke to the magi of worship when his intention was murder, so Judas conceals his evil intentions behind a greeting and a kiss. Deceit is the handmaiden of the wicked.

49. 'Greetings, Rabbi!', and he kissed him. Cf. v. 25; Prov 27.6 ('profuse are the kisses of an enemy'). The greeting, like the kiss, is insincere and so ironic: Judas does not wish Jesus well. He is rather like those who mock Jesus in 27.29, and also like Joab who, in 2 Sam 20.9–10, kisses Amasa and then slays him.

50. Jesus now speaks – which is all he does in this scene. Otherwise he does nothing. He lets tragedy take him.

Companion, do what you are here to do. 'Jesus, remaining friendly to his betrayer, disregards the enmity of Judas and sees in him only God's will, which he loves; so much so that he calls him friend' (Pascal). The Greek translated by 'do what you are here to do' is difficult. If not the product of textual corruption or an intentional fragment, it can be taken in several different ways. It may be an ironic allusion to a toast like the one attested on a goblet from Syria: 'Enjoy yourself! for that's why you are here.'

laid hands on Jesus. 'To lay hands on' is a Septuagintal expression connoting hostility.

Eschewing Violence (26.51–4)

The pre-Easter Jesus instructs a disciple for the last time.

51. An unnamed disciple now meets sword (cf. v. 47) with sword. Against the spirit of 5.38–48, violence begets violence.

And behold. The introduction connotes surprise.

brought forth his hand and drew his sword. That a disciple of Jesus wears a sword is unexplained and unexpected in view of 5.34–58 and 10.10.

the slave of the high priest. Jn 18.10 names the servant Malchus.

52. The disciple is unaccountably not arrested, and the narrative continues with Jesus responding with words which have often been thought to imply pacifism. One has the impression – so much strengthened in John's version – that Jesus is really the one in charge; cf. Jn 10.18.

Then Jesus said to him. In Mark, Jesus fails to respond verbally to the cutting off of the slave's ear: the event has no commentary and no obvious meaning. In Matthew, the commentary becomes the whole point.

Return your sword to its place. The command recalls the Sermon on the Mount and its sayings about non-retaliation.

all who take the sword will die by the sword. The generalization – which goes beyond our episode to affirm that violence everywhere reproduces itself – is, as Rev 13.10 shows, a traditional line which owes its placement to our author. The words remind one both of Gen 9.6 ('Whoever sheds the blood of a person, by a person shall that one's blood be shed') and Tg. Isa. 50.11 ('Behold, all you that kindle a fire, that take a sword, go, fall into the fire you have kindled and on the sword you have taken. From my Memra you have this: you shall return to your destruction').

53. As in 4.6–7, so here too: Jesus refuses angelic help. The man who has come not to be served but to serve uses his supernatural powers only on behalf of others. The verse resolves the scandal of the Son's impotence – it is, in accordance with the resignation of Gethsemane, voluntary – and makes him a moral model: the pacifistic Messiah eschews holy war.

Or do you not think that I am able to call upon my Father, and that he will at once send me more than twelve legions of angels? This reveals Jesus' majesty and control and mocks the far from mortal sword thrust of the sole unnamed disciple. That angels are at Jesus' disposal is clear from 4.11; 13.41; 16.27; and 25.31.

Angels, popularly divided in Judaism into numbers and ranks, are sometimes warriors in the biblical tradition, where they can fight with or on behalf of the saints. Often they have swords. That the legions of angels which the Son can command – this is practical omnipotence – are twelve likely adverts to the twelve disciples (so already Jerome): Jesus, who has just rejected armed intervention by the twelve, and who long ago rejected angelic intervention (4.5–7), now rejects assistance from twelve legions of angels. Twelve disciples or twelve legions of angels, it makes no difference: Scripture must be fulfilled. Calvin rightly finds rebuke here: the disciple's foolishness is the more plain from the comparison, for as Jesus 'does not call upon angels to bring him aid, far less does he resort to inconsidered means, from which he cannot hope to benefit.'

54. Jesus' behaviour is justified not only by his own moral teaching but also by biblical prophecy, both of which are rooted in the same source: God's will.

Yet how then would the scriptures be fulfilled, that thus it is necessary for things to transpire? We should probably think neither of a particular text (e.g. Zech 13.7, cited in 26.31), nor of a series of texts (those cited throughout the passion narrative), but of the Scriptures in their entirety, conceived of as fulfilled in Jesus and his redemptive work.

Jesus Addresses the Crowd (26.55–6)

Having rebuked his own, Jesus now rebukes his enemies.

55. **to the crowds** refers back to v. 47 (not to a second crowd).

with swords and clubs comes from v. 47, so Jesus uses the editor's language to disclose to the crowd what has already been communicated to the disciples: violence is not the Son's way. It is striking that Jesus never returns to this thought when speaking with Caiaphas or Pilate; contrast Jn 18.20. This is his last defence.

as though I were a bandit? The irony is that, although Jesus will be executed between brigands (27.38), his opponents, with their swords and clubs, are more accurately characterized as such (21.13).

Day after day I sat in the temple teaching. Cf. 21.23ff.; Jn 18.20. Is there an allusion to 24.3? Or an emphasis on Jesus' passivity and lack of movement? Or do we have here simply another instance of the Matthean link between teaching and sitting? Some find in 'day after day' evidence for a gap in the synoptic record: Jesus does not teach day after day in either Matthew or Mark. But that may read into the words too much; perhaps Matthew tells of enough teaching in the temple to justify the phrase. One might also take the words to mean 'by day', and the context (arrest at night) makes this a plausible proposal (cf. Lk 21.37). In either case Jesus has taught openly.

you did not arrest me. The reader naturally supplies 'then': 'and you did not then arrest me'. Jesus is fully aware that his enemies feel compelled to take him by stealth.

56. Jesus cites the Scriptures and stands fast while the fearful disciples forsake him by running into the asylum of darkness. They illustrate how to lose one's life by saving it (16.25) and leave Jesus a solitary figure.

But all this has happened. It is doubtful that the phrase refers simply to the disciples' flight or to Judas' betrayal; the words rather refer to the entirety of our pericope as well as to the events which flow to and from it. The passion narrative in its entirety stands under v. 56. Jesus, whose life has heretofore been protected (2.4ff.; 12.14–15; 21.46), is no longer protected.

so that the scriptures of the prophets might be fulfilled. Cf. 1.22; 21.4. Whether the words belong to Jesus' speech or are editorial commentary is disputed. Some have imagined that a particular Scripture is in mind, but this seems unlikely; as in v. 54, no text is cited.

all the disciples, deserting him, fled. While the disciples had previously forsaken everything to follow Jesus (19.27), now they forsake him and so quit following him. Given the proximity to statements about prophetic fulfilment, 26.30–5 (where 'all' is used twice of the disciples) is surely in view: the disciples' cowardice fulfils Zech 13.7 and belies the earlier vows of allegiance. Fulfilment comes to Scripture and to Jesus' words, not to his followers' empty pledges.

The disciples' flight does not come when Jesus is seized but only after he speaks. Why? Chrysostom seems to get it right: 'Thenceforth they saw that escape was no longer possible, when he was giving himself up to them voluntarily, and saying, that this was done according to the Scriptures.'

* * * * *

(i) After Gethsemane there is nothing left for Jesus to do save passively endure what others do to him. But his inactivity is full of meaning. It is firstly the consequence and illustration of his own teaching, especially that in Matthew 5: Jesus lives his own speech. It is secondly the result of his belief in the prophets, who have foretold the Messiah's suffering and death. His passivity is conformity to his understanding of God's will. And it is thirdly the consequence of his own predictions, for throughout Matthew Jesus has foretold his being handed over into the hands of others.

(ii) In 26.47–56 the twelve are utter failures. One of them betrays Jesus. Another vainly takes up his sword to return evil for evil. And all finally forsake Jesus and flee. So as a group they augment Jesus' suffering. Not only is he forsaken and left alone, but his teaching seems without effect: tragically, betrayal, violence, and cowardice characterize those who have paid him most heed. And yet this failure is not the last fact but rather the introduction to the story of the resurrection, which for the disciples will mean reconciliation.

JESUS CONFESSES BEFORE THE SANHEDRIN (26.57–68)

[57]**Those who had arrested Jesus took him to Caiaphas the high priest, in whose house the scribes and the elders had gathered.** [58]**But Peter was following him from a distance, as far as the courtyard of the high priest; and going inside, he sat with the guards in order to see the end.**

[59]**Now the chief priests and the whole sanhedrin were looking for false testimony against Jesus so that they might put him to death.** [60]**Yet they found none, although many false witnesses came forward. Finally, two came forward** [61]**and said, 'This fellow said, "I am able to destroy the temple of God and to build it in three days".'** [62]**And standing up, the high priest stood and said, 'Have you no answer? What is it that these testify against you?'** [63]**Jesus, however, was silent. And the high priest said to him, 'I adjure you by the living God that you tell us if you are the Messiah, the Son of God.'** [64]**Jesus said to him, 'You have said so. But I say to you, from now on you will see the Son of man seated at the right hand of Power and coming on the clouds of heaven.'** [65]**Then the high priest tore his clothes and said, 'He has blasphemed! What need for witnesses is there anymore? Behold now, you have now heard his blasphemy.** [66]**What is your verdict?' They answered, 'He is guilty of death.'** [67]**Then they spat in his face and struck him, and some slapped him,** [68]**saying, 'Prophesy to us, you Messiah! Who is it who struck you?'**

Parallels: Mk 14.53–65; Lk 22.54–71; Jn 18.13–24

Matthew's Jesus is neither the victim of tragic, impersonal circumstances nor the casualty of the ordinary machinery of justice. He is rather done in by wicked people. Jesus' adversaries speak falsehoods (vv. 59–60), accuse him of blasphemy (v. 65), condemn him to death (v. 66), and viciously hit and mock him (vv. 67–8). In the midst of this sinful folly Jesus' identity becomes fully visible. He is the Son of God and Messiah who, in accordance with 2 Sam 7.14, builds the temple. He is the king of Ps 110.1, who sits at God's right hand. He is the suffering servant of Isa 50.6, whose face is spat upon. And he is the Son of man of Dan 7.14, who will come on the clouds of heaven. Like 16.13–20, the passage is a climactic confluence of the main christological streams which run throughout the text.

57. The main characters are introduced in this transitional scene, which recalls vv. 3–4. Common to both are 'arrest Jesus', 'Caiaphas', 'high priest(s)', 'elders', 'gather', and 'courtyard/hall'. The goals of the earlier hostile gathering – to arrest and kill Jesus – are coming to realization.

Verse 57 introduces vv. 59–68 whereas v. 58 introduces vv. 69–75:

Introduction to Jesus' confession, v. 57
  Introduction to Peter's denial, v. 58
Jesus' confession, vv. 59–68
  Peter's denial, vv. 69–75

the scribes and the elders had gathered. This recalls v. 3 and points ahead to 27.17, 27, 62, and 28.12: in all of these people 'gather' against Jesus.

58. This, a sort of parenthesis which prepares for vv. 69ff., invites the reader to keep Peter in mind throughout the following story. The upshot is contrast between faithful Lord and unfaithful servant. This contrast is all the more painful because Peter has already answered the high priest's question in the affirmative; he has confessed Jesus to be the Messiah and Son of the living God.

But Peter was following him from a distance, as far as the courtyard of the high priest. Evidently the trial takes place in the residence of the high priest.

he sat with the guards in order to see the end. On Peter sitting see p. 496. Here we learn Peter's motive: part of him hopes to live up to the promise of v. 35.

59. The verse is resumptive: those gathered in v. 57 begin to judge the one who will someday judge them.

Now the chief priests and the whole sanhedrin were looking for false testimony against Jesus so that they might put him to death. Whatever the historical facts may have been, Matthew, according to his polemical prejudices, implies that the sanhedrin, violating Torah, did not seek the truth. It rather wanted – as the rest of the Gospel might lead us to expect – only testimony to incriminate Jesus, that is, false testimony. It was as devious as the gathering of 2.3–4.

'The sanhedrin' (cf. 5.22; 10.17), known also as 'the gerousia' or 'boule', was the ruling council of the Jews. Made up of priests, elders, and scribes, it was recognized by the Romans as a self-governing body with judicial authority over Judaea under the leadership of the high priest. It met near or in the temple. The *Mishnah* assumes that the sanhedrin or Beth-Din, composed of seventy-one members, was primarily concerned with matters of religious law. But this conflicts with the more political institution Josephus depicts. For this and other reasons some have suggested the existence of two or more different bodies which may not even have had fixed memberships. But this judgement remains that of a minority. Especially disputed has been the issue raised by Jn 18.31: during Jesus' day, did the Jerusalem sanhedrin have the authority to carry out a death sentence? But the prudent guess seems to be that although exceptions were allowed for a few specific religious cases (profanation of the temple – as in Acts 21.27–31 – and maybe adultery), the Romans generally reserved the right to decide cases of life and death.

60–1. The witnesses accuse Jesus of predicting something (the raising of a new temple after three days) that, ironically, they themselves make possible.

two recalls Deut 19.15, a text already alluded to in 18.16: two witnesses are needed for legal testimony.

I am able to destroy the temple of God and to build it in three days. 'I am able' instead of 'I will' has been variously explained: Jesus did not in fact destroy the (Jerusalem) temple; 'I am able' mutes the hostility against the (Jerusalem) temple; the verb adds to Jesus' messianic majesty: he has extraordinary power. This last seems, in view of 8.2; 9.28; and especially 26.53, to be the best guess.

Matthew's omission of the Markan antithesis, temple made with hands/not made with hands, has engendered debate. Some find the simpler form likely to be more primitive. But there is a good motive for omission: a temple 'not made with hands' readily refers to the church, and so one might think of Jesus founding that institution only after Easter (or even after the destruction in AD 70). In Matthew, however, Jesus founds the church during his ministry.

In line with this it seems likely that our evangelist interpreted the saying attributed to Jesus neither as an ecclesiological statement nor an apocalyptic prophecy about the destruction and rebuilding of Jerusalem's temple, but as a passion prediction: 'I am able to destroy the temple of God' = 'I am able to lay down my life', and 'to build it in three days' = 'to rise from the dead in three days'. This is how the prophecy is interpreted in Jn 2.21, and 'in three days' inevitably recalls Jesus' other prophecies of his resurrection. Paul moreover shows us the possibility of speaking of the individual as temple (1 Cor 6.19). If this is the correct interpretation, then v. 61 adds irony. For while Jesus has spoken about himself, the authorities take him to be speaking about the buildings that make up the temple.

63. Jesus, however, was silent. Does silence in this context mean consent? The words probably allude to Isa 53.7 ('He did not open his mouth', quoted in Acts 8.32), and there are other links to Isaiah's suffering servant:

Isa 50.6 struck   Mt 26.67 struck
      50.6 face   26.67 face
      50.6 spitting   26.67 spat

I adjure you by the living God. Like Herod (14.7) and Peter (v. 72) but unlike Jesus, Caiaphas is friends with the oath. The high priest examines the matter on oath as though he were prepared to look into the matter properly and give way.

tell us if you are the Messiah, the Son of God. Why does the prophecy about the temple raise the issue of Jesus' status as Messiah and Son? Zech 6.12 predicts that 'the Branch' will 'build the temple of the Lord', and 2 Sam 7.13–14 – given messianic sense in both the Dead Sea Scrolls and the NT – foretells a royal figure who will build for God a house and be God's 'son'.

64. Confronted by the question of his own identity, silence would be the same thing as denial. So Jesus, speaking for the last time of the Son of man, makes a dramatic public confession. He goes beyond the high priest's question and in effect answers the question left unanswered in 22.45.

You have said so. This expression has already been used in v. 25, where an affirmative sense is demanded. The related expression in 27.11 is also positive: Pilate unwittingly speaks the truth; Jesus is the king of the Jews. And so it is here, as the context confirms. That those who hear Jesus' response call him 'Christ' (v. 68) shows how they have understood him to claim this (cf. 27.43); and, beyond that, one cannot imagine Matthew's Jesus denying or qualifying the Christian confession.

From now on you will see the Son of man seated at the right hand of Power and coming on the clouds of heaven. Cf. Ps 110.1; Dan 7.13–14; *1 En.* 62.5 ('when they see that Son of man sitting on the throne of glory'); *T. Benj.* 10.6 (Enoch, Seth, Abraham, Isaac, Jacob raised to the right hand); Mt 19.28; 24.30; 25.31; Jn 1.51 (another Son of man saying); and for sitting on a heavenly throne as the vindication of an individual see *T. Job.* 33.3–9; *Apoc. Elijah* 1.8. 'The Power' (cf. Ps 110.2?; *1 En.* 1:4) is a divine name in rabbinic sources.

Although the ultimate vindication of Jesus is the *parousia*, his reign already begins in his death, resurrection, and exaltation. So the sitting and coming might be not simultaneous but consecutive: the former could be a reference to exaltation soon after the trial (cf. esp. 28.18), the latter a reference to judgement in the more distant future.

Here Jesus is asked whether he is the Messiah and Son of God and answers in terms of the Son of man. Earlier, in 16.13ff., Jesus himself asks about the identity of the Son of man and the answer is 'the

Messiah, the Son of the living God'. Obviously the titles are closely related, a circumstance in need of no explanation, since early Christians identified Jesus with all three (cf. Lk 4.41). Nonetheless there was probably already a close relationship between the three appellations in some Jewish circles around the turn of the era. *1 En.* 48.10 and 52.4 seemingly presume the identification of Daniel's 'one like a son of man' with God's Messiah. And 4 Ezra 13 not only calls the Messiah 'Son' (vv. 32, 52) but identifies him as the figure in Daniel's vision (v. 3).

There has been some discussion over whether the image in our text is of the Son of man going *to* God – an ascension and enthronement – or coming to earth *from* God – the *parousia*. In support of the former one might observe that elsewhere in the NT Ps 110.1 is used to depict Jesus' enthronement at his ascension. Moreover, Dan 7.13 says that the one like a son of man 'came to' the Ancient of Days, and Matthew's redactional 'from now on' might be thought a pointer to the immediate future, which could therefore be Jesus' exaltation but not his *parousia*. On the other hand, Daniel 7 is a theophany which issues in the *earthly* rule of the one like a son of man (v. 14); and v. 22 speaks of the Ancient of Days coming (to earth) for judgement. Further, in Mk 14.62 = Mt 26.64, sitting is mentioned before coming, which means that the coming must be to earth, for Jesus must come to God before he can sit at God's side. But the decisive point is that everywhere else in our Gospel the coming of the Son of man and Dan 7.13–14 both refer to the *parousia*; and in 19.28 and 25.31 the sitting on a throne belongs not to the Son of man's present reign but to the eschatological future.

If the first point of 26.64 is Jesus' vindication, a second is Jesus' defeat of those who condemn him. The Son of man is a figure of judgement; and when he sits on his throne of judgement and comes to reckon accounts, the members of the council, who have denied Jesus, will be denied by him.

65. By declaring that the Son of God, who has spoken the truth, has blasphemed, the high priest himself is ironically guilty of blasphemy.

the high priest tore his clothes. To tear a garment signifies upset, anger, or mourning. Here, however, it is the high priest himself – could Matthew think of this as ironically foreshadowing the rending of the veil of the temple he serves? – who so acts, and Lev 21.10 prohibits him from rending the sacred vestments. Now when *m. Sanh.* 7.5 tells of judges who, as a symbolic, ritual act, rend their clothes in response to blasphemy, we should presumably think of other garments. But given Matthew's cynicism about the Jewish leaders – they do not practise Moses (23.3) – the reader wonders if the high priest violates the law.

He has blasphemed! In Lev 24.10–23, a blasphemer is to be stoned, so Jesus must be deserving of death; cf. v. 66. But Leviticus does not precisely define 'blasphemy'. The belief that by Jesus' day it involved pronouncing the divine name (so *m. Sanh.* 7.5) overlooks broader definitions found not only elsewhere in rabbinic literature but also throughout intertestamental literature and the NT. A fairer conclusion from the evidence is that 'blasphemy' was most commonly used for serious insults of God, or for wrongly claiming for oneself divine prerogatives. The seriousness of the crime appears not only from the regularity with which it is associated with other heinous sins but the severe punishment it brings at the last judgement or in the afterlife. Matthew unfortunately does not spell out exactly what the sanhedrin finds blasphemous; cf. the silence of 9.3. But Jn 10.36 has Jesus' claim to be the Son of God evoke the accusation of blasphemy, and this must be close to the sense in Matthew. The accusation of blasphemy is a response to Christology. Jesus, by claiming to be God's Son, to have a heavenly throne, and to be the exalted figure of Dan 7.13, insults the majesty of God.

What need for witnesses is there anymore? The question is rhetorical. Obviously Jesus' opponents, heretofore frustrated in their attempts to get him to incriminate himself (cf. 22.15), have finally gotten him to speak unambiguous words which can be used against him. Jesus has confirmed the testimony brought against him: he does claim to be the builder of the new temple, that is, the Davidic Messiah and Son of God.

66. Although the high priest, having decided for himself, now seeks the consent of the entire sanhedrin, the conclusion is foregone.

67–8. The scene ends with Jesus passively enduring violence and a ritual of dishonour. This makes him the exemplar of the teaching in 5.38–42.

Then they spat in his face. Cf. 27.30 (one of the parallels between the two trials).

some slapped him. Cf. Jn 18.22; 19.3. In 5.38–42, where Jesus exhorts disciples to eschew violence and not resist evil, he borrows language from LXX Isa 50.4–9, which also lies behind 26.67–8; cf. 27.30. So the OT text associated with turning the other cheek is also associated with the passion of Jesus. Furthermore, of the seven words shared by Mt 5.38–42 and Isa 50.4–9, two appear again in the passion narrative: 'strike' (26.67) and 'garment' (27.31, 35). Indeed, 'strike' appears only twice in Matthew, in 5.39 and 26.67; and in both an innocent person is struck – just as in 5.40; 27.31; and 35 an innocent person's clothes are taken. If then the language of Isa 50.4–9 is used in 5.38–42 to depict the behaviour Jesus demands, in 26.67–8 the language of Isa 50.4–9 describes a scene from Jesus' own life. The suffering servant is the model for the suffering Christian.

Prophesy to us, you Messiah! Who is it who struck you? Cf. the taunting with titles in 27.29 ('king of the Jews'), 40, 42–3; also Lk 7.39 ('if this man were a prophet he would have known . . .'). That Jesus is taunted to prophesy is perhaps a mocking response to the words he has just spoken: if he claims to predict the great thing, that is, his session at the right hand of God and his coming on the clouds of heaven, should he not be able to divine the little thing, who it is who strikes him? But the irony is that Jesus' opponents have themselves just reported a prophecy that shall be fulfilled directly – 'and to build it in three days' – and further that Jesus' prophecy to Peter (v. 34) is being fulfilled as they speak (vv. 69–75).

* * * * *

(i) Mt 26.57–68 is the natural outcome of Jesus' ministry. He has from the beginning been misunderstood, disbelieved, persecuted, and rejected. He has also consistently demanded passivity in the face of unjust treatment as well as loyalty to the truth. Thus the trial, its verdict, and Jesus' response are only expected.

(ii) The chief literary feature of 26.57–68 is its irony. The authorities pass judgement on the one who will some day pass judgement on them. They, by seeking false witnesses, and the high priest, by rending his robe, disobey Moses (see p. 493) whereas Jesus, by refusing an oath, lives by his messianic Torah. The authorities mock Jesus' claim to be the Davidic Messiah, the fulfilment of OT hopes, while their very actions bring to pass Jesus' prophecies about Isaiah's suffering servant. They accuse Jesus of blasphemy and yet it is they who blaspheme the Son of God. Lastly, those who accuse Jesus of saying that he will destroy the temple of God and in three days build another themselves help fulfil that prophecy; for by handing him over to Pilate they are creating the circumstance that makes it possible for the temple of his body to be raised in three days. So the sanhedrin has everything backwards. All it does is ironic. And it ignorantly acts against its own true interests. Evil knows not what it does.

PETER'S DENIAL (26.69–75)

[69]Peter sat outside in the courtyard. And a servant-girl came to him saying, 'You also were with Jesus, the Galilean'. [70]But he denied it before them all, saying, 'I do not know what you are talking about.' [71]When he went out to the porch, another servant-girl saw him, and she said to the bystanders, 'This man was with Jesus of Nazareth.' [72]Again

he denied it with an oath, 'I do not know the man.' [73]After a bit the bystanders came up and said to Peter, 'Truly you also are one of them, for your speech betrays you.' [74]Then he began to curse, and he swore an oath, 'I do not know the man!' And immediately the cock crowed. [75]And Peter remembered the word of Jesus which he had said, that 'Before the cock crows, you will deny me three times.' And going out, he wept bitterly.

Parallels: Mk 14.66–72; Lk 22.56–62; Jn 18.25–7

The first accusation is spoken to Peter by a maid, the second to bystanders by another maid, and the third to Peter by bystanders: things become more and more public. Further, the intensity of Peter's denials increases with the accusations: he first denies that he knows what is being said, then he denies with an oath that he knows Jesus, then he denies Jesus with both an oath and a curse. Peter's movements, which take him further and further away from Jesus, also add drama: he is in the courtyard, then he goes to the gateway, then he leaves altogether.

Earlier in this chapter Judas defects. Later the other disciples flee. Now Peter, retreating from his promise (v. 35), denies his Lord. This is the climax of the disciples' failure. The first to be called is now the last to fall away.

In its present context, 26.69–75 supplies irony by balancing vv. 67–8, where Jesus' prophetic powers are mocked. Although Jesus makes no appearance in our story, it shows that, so far from being a false prophet, he has predicted the events of the evening in detail. 'This very night, before the cock crows, you will deny me three times' (v. 34) comes to literal fulfilment precisely while Jesus is being reviled with 'Prophesy to us, you Messiah!' (v. 68).

Our story also balances the trial, where Jesus, like Peter, and not far away, faces three sets of accusers (false witnesses, v. 60, the two true witnesses, vv. 61–2, Caiaphas, vv. 63–6). Jesus is asked whether he is the Messiah, the Son of God. He, although heretofore reticent about his identity, fearlessly confesses that he is. But Peter, who earlier confessed Jesus to be the Messiah, the Son of God, no longer acknowledges his Lord: when confronted he becomes a coward. Jesus illustrates the good confession of 10.32, Peter the damning denial of 10.33.

69. The narrative picks up v. 58, which also has Peter sitting in the courtyard. Clearly Peter's trial occurs at the same time as Jesus' trial.

sat, which comes from v. 58, interests because the disciples sit in Gethsemane (v. 36); the guards (and evidently the high priest) sit at the trial (cf. vv. 58, 62); Pilate sits when interrogating Jesus (27.19); and the soldiers at the cross likewise sit (27.36). All this contrasts with earlier chapters, in which it is Jesus who sits, that is, takes the position of authority and rest (5.1; 13.2; 15.29; 21.7; 24.3; 25.31). But after the last supper he no longer sits or reclines. He instead stands (27.11), falls to ground (26.39), and hangs from a cross (27.35). His posture during the passion reflects his temporary renunciation of authority (cf. 26.53) and the lack of all comfort.

And a servant-girl came to him. Surely Peter's cowardice is enhanced by his accuser's status: she is only a female slave. As Bengel observes, 'the temptation was not great, in view of the questioner.'

70. What would happen to Peter if he admitted association with Jesus is unsaid. But plainly he is trying to save his life, which means he is risking losing it (16.25).

But he denied it. Peter, instead of confessing Jesus, denies him – like those who will be denied by Jesus at the last judgement; see 10.33. Yet Peter's reception of forgiveness after Easter annuls a literal interpretation: although Peter denies Jesus before others, Jesus will confess him before the Father in heaven.

I do not know what you are talking about. Peter, who earlier confessed Jesus to be the Messiah, the Son of the living God (16.13–20), evades the issue by professing ignorance: I do not know what you mean.

71. Unlike Jesus, who advances to meet his enemies (v. 46), Peter, to avoid more attention, retreats (cf. v. 75). But the apostle is still not ready to leave Jesus altogether: even his retreat is half-hearted.

with reminds one of Gethsemane, where 'with' appears several times. And as there so here: those physically 'with' Jesus are in another sense not 'with' him at all. The disciples are in Gethsemane, but they fall asleep and so leave Jesus alone; and in 26.69ff. Peter, although he has followed Jesus to the courtyard, denies that he has been with him. In effect he denies his discipleship and the meaning of all he has done since forsaking his livelihood (4.18–20).

72. Again he denied it with an oath, 'I do not know the man.' Cf. Mt 7.23; 25.12. This marks an advance over v. 70: there Peter denies, here he denies with an oath. On 'the man' Bengel commented: 'as if Peter did not even know the name of Jesus'.

'With an oath' recalls 5.33–7, where Jesus prohibits swearing. Is Peter not a little like Herod, whose vain oath (14.7) worked against him? Note that the introduction of (male) bystanders to hear Peter's oath satisfies the Torah's legal demand for two or more qualified witnesses (Num 35.30; Deut 17.6).

73. for your speech betrays you. Peter, like the Ephraimites who were made to say 'shibboleth' (Judg 12.5–6), is given away by his speech. Matthew does not help the reader understand exactly why Peter's accent betrays him. Certainly not all Galileans in Jerusalem for the feast are Jesus' followers. Probably the thought is that Peter is already suspected on other grounds of following Jesus. His accent is simply supporting evidence.

74. A cock crow is not usually a cause for reflection. Here, because of Jesus' prophecy, it becomes ominous.

Then he began to curse, and he swore an oath, 'I do not know the man!' Peter swears and curses; so this last denial is stronger than the first two. Does 'cursed', which one expects to be transitive, have an implicit object – 'cursed (him)'? Most have suggested that Peter curses himself or the bystanders. But the best guess is that Jesus is the object of the curse: just as persecuted Christians were later on asked to curse Jesus and so dissociate themselves from their religion, so Peter here curses Jesus in an attempt to prove he is not a disciple. If so, then Peter conciliates his accusers by taking their side: he is one with those who disbelieve.

Intent cannot always be judged when a thing is done once. But this is not true of something done thrice: repetition reflects resolution. This is why Peter's multiple denials are so damning.

the cock crowed is probably the sign that night is passing and day is coming, for 27.1 relates the advent of morning.

75. Peter does not 'see the end' (v. 58) but exits with remorse. His departure from the high priest's residence is departure from Jesus. As Chrysostom observes, 'and not even when reminded of his sin by Christ did he dare to weep openly, lest he should be betrayed by his tears ...'.

Before the cock crows, you will deny me three times. Matthew's phrase agrees precisely with v. 34.

And going out, he wept bitterly. It follows from v. 31 and 28.16 that Peter will be restored; the judgement of 10.33 will not be spoken against him. His bitter weeping is the beginning of his repentance.

* * * * *

Matthew's Gospel does not idealize Peter and the other disciples. Rather does it present them as completely human, as complex and inconstant creatures who resist easy caricature. While on the one hand they leave all to follow Jesus, on the other they forsake and deny him. And Peter, who confesses Jesus to be the Messiah, the Son of the living God, in the end denies that he knows him. Such contradictory behaviour should not surprise. The Bible of Matthew's community, the OT, does not free Noah or David or Solomon from their sins. Even

Moses is said to have disobeyed God when he struck the rock twice. We may assume that Matthew's readers interpreted the disciples' failures as they did the failures of OT heroes: God can use ordinary and even weak people for extraordinary purposes and, when they fall into sin, can grant them forgiveness. As Peter says in *Acts of Peter* 7.20: 'He who defended me also when I sinned and strengthened me with his greatness will also comfort you that you may love him.' Calvin got it right: 'Peter's fall ... brilliantly mirrors our own infirmity. His repentance in turn is a memorable demonstration for us of God's goodness and mercy. The story of one man contains teaching of general, and indeed prime, benefit for the whole Church; it teaches those who stand to take care and be cautious; it encourages the fallen to trust in pardon.'

JESUS DELIVERED TO PILATE (27.1–2)

¹When morning came, all the chief priests and the elders of the people took counsel together against Jesus in order to kill him. ²They bound him, led him away, and handed him over to Pilate the governor.

Parallels: Mk 15.1; Lk 23.1; Jn 18.28

In fulfilment of the prophecy in 20.18–19 ('and hand him over to the Gentiles'), the Jewish leaders deliver Jesus to Pilate, the official representative of Caesar.

1. When morning came creates an *inclusio* with v. 57: the day dawns with the Jewish leaders handing Jesus over to Pilate; it sets with Pilate handing Jesus' body over to Joseph of Arimathea.

all the chief priests and the elders of the people took counsel together against Jesus in order to kill him. Cf. 20.18–19; 26.59, 66; also Ps 2.2.

2. This verse, whose connexion with vv. 11ff. is interrupted by vv. 3–10 (the end of Judas), introduces the last named major character, Pontius Pilate.

They bound him reflects the outcome of Jesus' trial and makes him look like a criminal; cf. Mk 15.7. The deliverance to Pilate, unexplained by Matthew, probably assumes the fact, sometimes disputed but nonetheless probable, that (with few exceptions) the Jews did not have the authority to execute criminals (Jn 18.31): such was the responsibility of the prefect or procurator.

handed him over to Pilate the governor. 'The governor' makes Jesus an instance of his own prediction in 10.18 ('dragged before governors'). Perhaps, in view of what follows, 'Pilate the governor' is (like 'Herod the king') ironic: certainly Pilate does not take charge.

This is the first Matthean mention of Pontius Pilate, the prefect of Judaea AD 26–36/7. Although there were, according to Josephus, no significant confrontations between Jews and Romans between AD 6 and 26, Pilate's tenure saw several conflicts. In AD 26 he had army standards with offensive images – embossed figures of the emperor – brought into Jerusalem under the cover of night. Later he confiscated money from the temple treasury to build an aqueduct into Jerusalem and, when a crowd protested, had disguised soldiers club people. In AD 36 he ordered an attack on a Samaritan mob near Mount Gerizim (an action which led to his recall by the Syrian legate Vitellius). Lk 13.1 adds that Pilate once mingled the blood of Galileans with their sacrifices. These facts help explain why Pilate was remembered in Jewish tradition as brutal and greedy. If Philo's account of his violent death had survived, it would no doubt show the procurator getting his just deserts.

The Christian tradition, seemingly impelled to turn Pilate either into a saint or a devil, has displayed two contrasting pictures. In one (mostly Egyptian and Syrian) Pilate is, at the expense of the Jews, presented as an unwilling participant in the death of Jesus: he is innocent of Jesus' blood. Tertullian even makes him 'a Christian in his own convictions', and there are apocryphal letters which proclaim Pilate's dismay at Jesus' execution and make him a Christian martyr. Indeed, in the Coptic church Pilate has been canonized. In the other (mostly Western) picture Pilate bears full responsibility for the death of Jesus and so is presented as 'an unjust judge' (1 Pet 2.23 v.l.) – weak-willed at best, evil at worst. In the so-called *Death of Pilate,* for instance, he is forced to commit suicide, and his corpse becomes a home for demons.

The Markan picture, in which a hesitant governor, pressured by others, wrongly acts against his better judgement (15.10: 'he perceived that it was out of envy that the chief priests had delivered him up'), looks more like this second picture. The same is true of Matthew, who does not exculpate Rome. Not only is all the Markan material reproduced, but in our Gospel Pilate's wife is granted a dream which moves her to warn her husband not to have anything to do with Jesus – which dream the governor does not heed. Further, after Jesus is dead, Pilate cooperates with the Jewish authorities to appoint a guard for the tomb. So the declaration of his own innocence in v. 24 is ironic: despite his words Pilate is responsible. Washing his hands does not make them clean.

* * * * *

This short, transitional section recounts the end of the Jewish proceedings and the beginning of the Roman proceedings. The key word is the richly connotative 'deliver'. This same verb is also used when Judas hands Jesus over to the Jewish authorities (26.45, 47–56) and when Pilate hands Jesus over to be crucified (27.26). So there is a series of related actions:

> Judas delivers Jesus to the Jewish authorities
> The Jewish authorities deliver Jesus to Pilate
> Pilate delivers Jesus to be crucified

In each instance Jesus is the object of the action and suffers passively. Surely the informed reader recalls not only the passion predictions (17.22; 20.18–19; 26.2) but also the fate of the suffering servant of Isaiah (Isa 53.6, 12). Furthermore, 'deliver' aligns Jesus with the fate of John the Baptist (4.12) and the fate of Christians (10.17, 19, 21; 24.9–10). In this way the handing over of Jesus has both precursor and successor: it is foreshadowed in the end of John the Baptist and equally foreshadows what is to come for disciples.

JUDAS AND THE MONEY OF BETRAYAL (27.3–10)

[3]**Then Judas, his betrayer, seeing that Jesus was condemned, repented and took back the thirty pieces of silver to the chief priests and the elders,** [4]**saying, 'I have sinned, betraying innocent blood.' But they said, 'What is that to us? See to it yourself.'** [5]**Throwing the pieces of silver into the temple, he departed; and he went and hanged himself.** [6]**But the chief priests, taking the pieces of silver, said, 'It is not lawful to put them into the treasury, since they are the price of blood.'** [7]**After taking counsel together, they bought with them the potter's field as a place to bury strangers.** [8]**For this reason that field has been called the 'Field of Blood' to this day.** [9]**Then was fulfilled the word through Jeremiah the prophet, saying, 'And they took the thirty pieces of silver, the price of the one on whom a price had been set, on whom some of the people of Israel had set a price,** [10]**and they gave them for the potter's field, as the Lord commanded me.'**

Parallels: Acts 1.16–20

Mt 27.3–10's major theme is that Jesus' death and the events attending it are within the design of God as announced in Scripture; cf. vv. 9–10. Subsidiary themes include Jesus' innocence (Judas regrets betraying 'innocent blood') and the responsibility, despite disavowal, of the Jewish leaders (the blood money ends up in the temple, and the leaders take it). The very placement of the narrative furthers this last theme:

the story is prompted by the sanhedrin's condemnation of Jesus (and not, as it could have been, by sight of Jesus' crucifixion).

The relationship between 27.3–10 and the OT is extensive and complex. Here is a brief overview:

- 'Judas', v. 3: 'Judah' is mentioned in Zech 11.14 and Jer 18.11; 19.3, 7, 13; 32.11–14.
- 'thirty pieces of silver', v. 3: 'thirty shekels of silver' is the amount in Zech 11.12–13.
- 'the chief priests and the elders', v. 3: Jer 19.1 refers to 'the elders of the people and some of the senior priests.'
- 'innocent blood', v. 4: the phrase occurs in Jer 19.4.
- 'throwing the pieces of silver into the temple', v. 5: cf. Zech 11.13: 'I took the thirty shekels of silver and cast them into the house of the Lord.'
- 'he went out and hanged himself', v. 5: cf. 2 Sam 17.23: Ahithophel goes away and hangs himself.
- 'it is not lawful to put them [the silver pieces] into the treasury', v. 6: cf. Zech 11.13 in the Peshitta: 'and cast them into the treasury.'
- 'bought the potter's field', v. 7: 'to the potter' appears in MT Zech 11.13; Jer 18.1–12 contains the allegory of the potter; Jer 19.1 instructs the prophet to purchase a potter's earthen flask; Jer 32.6–15 recounts the prophet's purchase of a field with silver.
- 'to bury strangers in', v. 7: Jer 19.11 says that 'men will bury in Topheth.'
- 'and they took the thirty pieces of silver', v. 9: this reproduces Zech 11.13.
- 'the price of him on whom a price had been set', v. 9: cf. MT Zech 11.13.
- 'by some of the people of Israel', v. 9: this enlarges the 'by them' of Zech 11.13.
- 'and they gave them for the potter's field', v. 10: in Jer 32.6–15 silver buys the prophet a field; 'potter' is used in Zech 11.13 and Jer 18.1–12.
- 'as the Lord directed me', v. 10: this might refer to God telling Jeremiah and/or Zechariah to perform symbolic actions; but the phrase is pentateuchal.

Three other early Christian accounts of Judas' death exist: Acts 1.16–20 and two fragments assigned to Papias. Although very different from Matthew and each other, there are common items: (i) money from Judas purchases a property near Jerusalem (Matthew: the chief priests use the money of betrayal; Luke: Judas himself acquires the land); (ii) that property was known as 'the Field of Blood' (whereas in Matthew the name is associated with the innocent blood of Jesus, in Acts it derives from Judas' gruesome end); (iii) the fate of Judas fulfils Scripture (Matthew and Acts cite different OT texts); (iv) Judas comes to a bad end (Matthew: he hangs himself; Acts: he bursts open; Papias short version: a wagon runs over him).

3. The passage opens with Judas' response to the events narrated in vv. 1–2. Jesus is offstage.

Then is imprecise. It indicates neither exactly when Judas went to the priests nor when the priests (who are now with Pilate) bought the potter's field. Nor does the text clarify Judas' motive for repentance. Has Judas come to believe in the resurrection?

repented is difficult. The accounts in Acts and Papias have Judas die by the hand of heaven: there is no room for authentic repentance. This and the depiction of Judas as infamy embodied throughout much of church history have led most exegetes to interpret Matthew accordingly: Judas experiences regret but not repentance. He is an everlasting failure doomed for destruction.

It is, however, possible that Judas, who not only feels remorse but also confesses and returns his ill-gotten gain, makes authentic repentance. This would not only give 'to repent' its natural meaning and cohere with the praise of repentance in Judaism and Christianity (true repentance can be effective even if it comes at the last hour of life), but also do justice to Judas' words, which for Matthew declare the truth: 'I have sinned against innocent blood.' This seems a heartfelt confession. Judas' actions also show repentance. When the authorities refuse his money, he himself throws it into the temple, thus ridding himself of any profit; and when they do not reconsider his crime and try him anew for innocent blood, he executes the fitting sentence. It is worth noting that in 4 Macc 17.21 and *Gen. Rab.* on 27.27, suicide makes atonement.

the thirty pieces of silver alludes to Zech 11.12–13.

4. Judas, in the bright light of hindsight, confesses his sin: he is guilty, Jesus is innocent. The Jewish leaders respond with indifference: they have no remorse. What has happened has happened; it cannot be undone.

I have sinned, betraying innocent blood. The stress lies upon 'innocent blood', which betokens a heinous crime. Maybe Deut 27.25 ('Cursed be he who takes a bribe to slay the life of innocent blood') is in the background. But there is no allusion to Gen 4.11: the innocent blood of Jesus does not cry out for vengeance but instead makes atonement (26.28).

What is that to us? See to it yourself. The profession of indifference masks culpability. There is a parallel in v. 24. Pilate, as he washes his hands, declares: 'I am innocent of this man's blood; see to it yourselves.' The similarities are really differences. Whereas Judas declares his guilt for innocent blood, Pilate denies his; and while Pilate, seeking to avoid responsibility, tells others to 'see to it yourselves', this is what Judas, who acknowledges his responsibility, is told to do by others. The fallen disciple is a more sympathetic figure than the Roman governor.

5. Judas separates himself from the money of betrayal and then, as proof of his overwhelming remorse, hangs himself.

Throwing the pieces of silver into temple, he departed. If 'the temple' is the inner shrine (as usual in Matthew) then the meaning is that the sanctuary is defiled by the money of innocent blood; cf. 23.35. In any event the gesture places responsibility on the priests and implies that the money, which has bought Jesus' saving death, should be consecrated.

he went and hanged himself. Like 26.30 and 50, this draws upon the story of Ahithophel, who went out and hung himself (2 Sam 17.23; the LXX uses the same two verbs as Matthew). Judas is akin to the famous betrayer of king David. The correlation between the two traitors was traditional:

- Ahithophel betrays king David, 2 Samuel 15–17: Judas betrays Jesus, the Son of David, Mt 26 par.
- David, after being betrayed by Absalom and Ahithophel, crosses the Kidron, 2 Sam 15.23: Jesus, after Judas has left to betray him, crosses the Kidron, Jn 18.1.
- David prays on the Mount of Olives that God might 'turn the counsel of Ahithophel into foolishness', 2 Sam 15.31: Jesus prays on the Mount of Olives that God might let the hour and cup pass, Mt 26.36–46 par.; moreover, the language of Jesus' prayer echoes Ps 41.5 and 11, which Jewish tradition assigned to David and referred to the incident with Absalom and Ahithophel.
- While the king is 'weary and discouraged', Ahithophel plans to take David at night with twelve thousand men and make 'all the people that are with him flee', 2 Sam 17.1–2: after the agony of Gethsemane, Judas comes upon Jesus at night with a crowd with swords and clubs, and all the disciples flee, Mt 26.47–56 par.
- In Ps 41.9 (attributed to David), we read: 'Even my bosom friend in whom I trusted, who ate of my bread, has lifted his heel against me'; Jewish tradition referred this to Ahithophel, *b. Sanh.* 106b: Mk 14.18 alludes to Ps 41.10 in connexion with Judas while Jn 13.18 explicitly cites it in the same connexion.

- In 2 Sam 18.28 we read, concerning the failure of Absalom and Ahithophel: 'Blessed be the Lord your God who has delivered up the men who raised their hand against my lord the king': Jn 13.18 inserts language from 2 Sam 18.28 into its quotation of Ps 41.10.
- Ahithophel was known as a companion and friend of David, Ps 55.12–14; *m*. *'Abot* 6.3; *Tg*. on Ps 55.12–14: Judas is 'one of twelve' and Jesus calls him 'friend' or 'companion', Mk 14.10; Mt 26.50.

Because he cannot halt what he began, Judas now, if his repentance is heartfelt, seeks to make atonement through his own death, according to the law of life for life. His deed may stand under the divine 'must' of Scripture, but this does not annul human responsibility.

6. As the coins pass from Judas to the authorities so does the narrative.

the chief priests, taking the pieces of silver. Only the chief priests speak; the elders of v. 3 have disappeared. The verb not only anticipates the quotation in v. 9 but implicates the authorities: by taking the money they become contaminated by the guilt attached to it.

It is not lawful to put them into the treasury, since they are the price of blood. Cf. Deut 23.18 ('You shall not bring the hire of a harlot, or the wages of a dog, into the house of the Lord your God in payment for any vow, for both are an abomination to the Lord your God') and Acts 1.18. The professed concern with Torah is ironic because the leaders have shown no scruples in asking death for an innocent man; cf. 23.23. 'It is very obvious that the hypocrites, by pursuing the outward form, are making a gross mockery of God' (Calvin).

7. After taking counsel together, they bought with them the potter's field as a place to bury strangers. 'After taking counsel together' harks back to v. 1. 'The potter's field' – which Matthew presumably identified with the area of Jer 19.2 – anticipates the formal citation in v. 10 (Zech 11.3: 'to the potter'). Whether the definite articles direct attention to Scripture (that is, to the setting of Jer 19.1ff.) or to a place known to Matthew's audience is unclear; perhaps both are true at the same time. Regarding the 'place to bury strangers': even Jesus' enemies are mindful of charity.

8. This makes the story an aetiology.

For this reason that field has been called the 'Field of Blood' to this day. Cf. 28.15; Acts 1.19. There was evidently a 'Field of Blood' in first-century Jerusalem which was used for the charitable burial of foreigners. Presumably the origin of the name was forgotten or not known to all and Christians offered their own explanation. Although Eusebius located the site north of Jerusalem, Jerome put it on the south side of the Hinnom Valley. The traditional location is near the juncture of the Kidron and the Hinnom Valley, on the cliffs on the south side of the latter.

9. To the allusion to Zech 11.12 made with reference to Judas in 26.15, the evangelist now adds a formal citation – the last in his Gospel – of Zech 11.13, which has been prepared for by the vocabulary in vv. 3–8. There is also dependence upon lines from Jeremiah.

Then was fulfilled the word through Jeremiah the prophet. This introduces the last of Matthew's formula quotations. Although the words are mostly from Zechariah, Jeremiah is named. Why? Jeremiah 18–19 concerns a potter (18.2–6; 19.1), a purchase (19.1), the Valley of Hinnom (where the Field of Blood is traditionally located, 19.2), 'innocent blood' (19.4), and the renaming of a place for burial (19.6, 11); and Jer 32.6–15 tells of the purchase of a field with silver. Now it was common practice in Jewish texts to create conflated citations, and in early Christian circles such citations could be attributed to a single source. Mk 1.2 attributes Mal 3.1 + Isa 40.3 to Isaiah. Rom 9.27 assigns Hos 2.1 + Isa 10.22 to the same prophet. Mt 2.5–6 attributes to 'the prophet' a quotation from Mic 5.2 + 2 Sam 5.2 = 1 Chr 11.2, and 21.5 prefaces its conflation of Isa 62.11 and Zech 9.9 with 'the word through the prophet saying'. Mt 27.9–10 is one more example of this phenomenon. That Jeremiah is named rather than Zechariah (who is never assigned a quotation in the NT, despite several citations) may be due to the prominence of the former or to his reputation as the prophet of doom. The effect in any event is to prod one to read Zech 11.13 in the light of Jer 18.1ff. (the allegory of the potter) and 32.6–9 (Jeremiah's purchase of a field with silver).

And they took the thirty pieces of silver. This is close to LXX Zech 11.13. The subject is not 'I' (as in Zechariah) but, in accord with v. 6, 'they', that is, the priests.

the price of the one on whom a price had been set. This too corresponds to Zech 11.13. In this context the words are ironic: the Messiah, so far from being honoured, is worth only the price of a slave.

10. they gave them for the potter's field. This might be a free rendering of Zech 11.13: 'throw them to the potter ... and I cast them into the house of the Lord to the potter'. Cf. also the allegory of the potter in Jeremiah 18 and 19. Jeremiah seems at least the source for the 'field'; for although the field there is Anathoth, it is purchased with silver. Evidently Matthew knew that the 'Field of Blood' (v. 8) was also called the 'Potter's Field', or at least associated with potters.

as the Lord commanded me. This depends upon a LXX pentateuchal formula and may paraphrase Zech 11.3a: 'And the Lord said to me'. But as Zechariah 11 mentions no field, the words might refer to God's instructions to Jeremiah in Jeremiah 18–19 and/or 32.

* * * * *

Because 27.3–10 immediately follows the story of Peter's denial, one may ponder the similarities between Judas and Peter. Both are disciples of Jesus. Both are told by Jesus that they will betray or deny him (26.21; 26.34). Both are central characters in narratives where Jesus' predictions come true (26.69–75; 27.3–10). Both, in betraying or denying Jesus, fulfil OT prophecy (26.31; 27.9–10). Both 'go out' (26.75; 27.5). And both are overcome with remorse (26.75; 27.3–5). Whether the reader is to imagine that the parallelism extends to the restoration of Judas or instead highlights the contrast between effective repentance (Peter) and ineffective regret (Judas) is unclear.

JESUS BEFORE THE GOVERNOR (27.11–26)

[11]**Jesus stood before the governor. And the governor asked him, 'Are you the King of the Jews?' Jesus said, 'You say so.'** [12]**But when he was accused by the chief priests and elders, he answered nothing.** [13]**Then Pilate said to him, 'Do you not hear how many accusations they make against you?'** [14]**But he did reply at all to a single charge, so that the governor was greatly amazed.**

[15]**At the festival the governor was accustomed to release to the crowd a prisoner, whomever they wanted.** [16]**They had at that time a notorious prisoner named Jesus Barabbas.** [17]**So when they had gathered, Pilate said to them, 'Whom do you want me to release to you, Jesus Barabbas or Jesus the so-called Messiah?'** [18]**For he knew that it was because of jealousy they had handed him over.**

[19]**While he was sitting on the judgement seat, his wife sent word to him saying, 'Have nothing to do with that innocent man, for today I have suffered a great deal because of a dream about him.'**

[20]**The chief priests and the elders persuaded the crowds to ask for Barabbas but to have Jesus killed.** [21]**The governor answered and said to them, 'Which of the two do you want me to release for you?' And they said, 'Barabbas.'** [22]**Pilate said to them, 'What then should I do with Jesus the so-called Messiah?' They all said, 'Let him be crucified!'** [23]**But he asked, 'Why, what evil has he done?' But they shouted all the more, 'Let him be crucified!'** [24]**So when Pilate saw that he could do nothing, but rather that a riot was beginning, he took some water and washed his hands before the crowd, saying, 'I am innocent of this man's blood; see to**

it yourselves.' ²⁵And all the people answered, 'May his blood be upon us and upon our children!' ²⁶Then releasing Barabbas for them, he flogged Jesus and handed him over to be crucified.

Parallels: Mk 15.2–15; Lk 23.2–5, 17–25; Jn 18.29–40; 19.16

This passage, which returns to 27.1–2, is full of characters: Jesus, Pilate, the chief priests, the elders, Barabbas, Pilate's wife, and a crowd. The subject is the Roman trial of Jesus, the focal issue culpability for Jesus' execution. The main character, the governor, instead of conducting an objective inquiry and justly acting upon the outcome, rather gives cowardly heed to the Jewish leaders and the crowd they have agitated. The effect is to highlight not just the innocence of Jesus but also the fault of Rome's representative and especially the guilt of the chief priests and elders, who manipulate Pilate and stir up the crowd against the Messiah.

Although Matthew enhances the guilt of the Jewish authorities, the text does not excuse the Romans. Certainly both Luke and John go far to reduce Rome's responsibility. Matthew, however, does not so obviously tend in this direction. He certainly does not make Pilate a Christian. The governor allows injustice to prevail, and his underlings torture Jesus: vv. 27–31. Surely Pilate stands condemned by our Gospel's harsh words about those who do not act in accord with their words or convictions: he is a hypocrite.

Jesus Interrogated (27.11–14)

For a second time Jesus is interrogated. In many respects matters are as they were at the first trial. The chief priest(s) and elders are present both times (26.57; 27.12, 20). On both occasions he is called 'the Messiah' by others (26.63; 27.17, 22). In both episodes he is silent before his accusers (26.62–3; 27.11–14). In both he nonetheless says to his interrogator, 'You have said so' (26.64; 27.11). Both trials end with a judgement of death (26.66; 27.24–6). And both are followed by scenes of mockery (26.67; 27.27–31). The correlations convey futility: the new trial corrects nothing of the first. Roman justice does no better than the sanhedrin.

11. Jesus now has the opportunity to defend himself before the Roman representative.

Jesus stood before the governor. This is an editorial transition necessitated by the interruption of vv. 3–10. That Jesus now appears before 'the governor' makes him like the persecuted disciples of 10.18.

And the governor asked him. What follows is unprepared for, in that we have not been informed that the Jewish leaders told Pilate anything. Certainly the accusation of 'blasphemy' (26.65) would not impress him. But given the question that the governor asks ('Are you the King of the Jews?'), the reader assumes that Pilate has learned of Jesus' claim to kingship (26.64).

Are you the King of the Jews? The pronoun, in first position in the Greek, is emphatic: Are *you* the king? 'The King of the Jews' (always spoken by Gentiles, who use 'king' and 'Jews' instead of 'Messiah' and 'Israel') reappears in vv. 29 and 37, and so marks a theme of the chapter (cf. v. 42, 'king of Israel'). Here the words convey that Jesus' claim to be the Messiah (cf. 26.64) involves kingship (cf. 21.5; 25.34, 40) and so means political sedition: there can be no king but Caesar (cf. Jn 19.12, 15).

You say so. Cf. 26.25; 26.64. The words seem ambiguous and yet in fact mark courageous agreement: Pilate has unwittingly spoken the truth and Jesus does not deny it. It is thus odd that, to judge from his response, Pilate does not take the treasonous affirmation to be a threat to Rome. Evidently Pilate views Jesus with incredulous contempt: he is too impotent to be dangerous.

12. The chief priests and elders accuse Jesus anew. The content of their accusation is not detailed; contrast Lk 23.2. Jesus responds with silence, and he will not speak again until he cries out in death, v. 46. It is long past the point where words can serve any good purpose.

But when he was accused by the chief priests and elders, he answered nothing. Jesus' silence will make for repetition (Jesus will again answer nothing in v. 14) and so underlines the theme of silent passivity; cf. 12.19; 26.63. This is turn reminds us that Jesus is the suffering servant (Isa 42.2; 53.7; Acts 8.32) and akin to others who suffered unjustly; cf. Ps 38.13–15; 39.9. The reader may also recall Jesus' earlier teaching on and demonstrations of meekness (5.5, 38–48; 11.29; 21.5).

14. Here we enter Pilate's thoughts: he does not take Jesus' silence as a sign of guilt but as a cause for wonder.

the governor was greatly amazed. Cf. Isa 52.15: 'so shall he startle many nations; kings shall shut their mouths because of him.' Bengel correctly diagnosed Pilate's wonder: 'no one is wont to be silent when his life is at stake.' To which one may add that Roman law may have presumed that those who do not defend themselves are guilty.

Jesus Barabbas or Jesus Messiah (27.15–23)

Because Pilate believes Jesus unworthy of death, he schemes to set him free by offering an amnesty. The ploy fails.

Although we know that a Roman governor could release a prisoner in order to curry favour, there is no certain evidence for an annual custom of release during Passover or any other festival. But there are analogies which lend our scene historical verisimilitude, and it is possible that the synoptics preserve the memory of a short-lived local custom – perhaps one of Pilate's invention – or that they wrongly present an occasional affair as an annual ritual.

15. Here we begin to learn that Pilate's title is ironic: the governor leaves the governing to others.

16. They had at that time a notorious prisoner named Jesus Barabbas. The name, 'Jesus Barabbas', heightens the drama: the crowd must choose between two men named 'Jesus'. 'Barabbas', a political insurrectionist (cf. Mark's 'rebel'), is known only from the NT and sources dependent upon it. The name itself is Aramaic and probably means 'Son of Abba'. Abba (= 'father') was a popular name in the Talmudic period; but it, like 'Barabbas', is attested in the pre-Christian period. One must wonder, given the first name 'Jesus' as well as the likely etymology of 'Barabbas' and Matthew's interest in the meaning of names (cf. 1.21; 16.17), whether we do not here have profound irony. The two prisoners named 'Jesus' are both 'son of the Father'.

17. Pilate vainly attempts to free Jesus by hoping the crowd will want him and not Barabbas freed.

Whom do you want me to release to you, Jesus Barabbas or Jesus the so-called Messiah? The crowd is confronted by the same choice that the Christian mission constrains: one is either for Jesus or against him.

If Matthew wrote after AD 70, the choice between Barabbas the insurrectionist (which Matthew and his readers would have associated with Zealots) and the meek Christian Messiah, who called for love of enemies, would have been full of meaning. The choice would symbolize the contrast between political rebellion and passive waiting for the kingdom of God. Further, given the upshot of AD 70, Christian readers would surely have felt their teacher vindicated.

18. The real motive for handing Jesus over is here uncovered: not offence at blasphemy but desire for power over the populace. The leaders of Jerusalem were, so Matthew implies, threatened when significant numbers gave heed to Jesus instead of them; cf. 21.15, 33–41. Their envy came from their thirst for power.

For he knew that it was because of jealousy they had handed him over. The aside shows the narrator's omniscience: he can tell us what Pilate thought.

19. If the temple hierarchy has, out of envy, prosecuted Jesus, Pilate's wife now, moved by a dream, steps forward as his advocate. As in 15.21–8, it is a non-Jewish woman who recognizes the truth about Jesus.

While he was sitting on the judgement seat. That Pilate sits as judge is ironic: Jesus, the one who now stands, is the rightful occupant of the judgement seat (25.31).

his wife sent word to him saying, 'Have nothing to do with that innocent man, for today I have suffered a great deal because of a dream about him.' Without parallel in Mark, Luke, or John, this interlude introduces a new character, who exits as soon as she enters. The explanation for the woman's counsel is that she has been warned (by God) in a dream and accordingly suffered much. This makes her resemble Joseph (1.20; 2.13, 19, 22) and the magi (2.12), earlier characters to whom God sent dreams of revelation.

That the message to Pilate comes indirectly through another's dream is congruent with other stories in which God does not deign to speak directly to pagan rulers. See Genesis 37–41 (Pharaoh); Daniel 1–6 (Nebuchadnezzar); and Josephus, *Ant.* 17.345–8; *Bell.* 2.111–13 (Archelaus). Here, however, Pilate is not even worthy of receiving a dream needing interpretation: the dream meant for him is given to another. But why Pilate's wife? Pagan temples often had female dream interpreters, so perhaps women were thought particularly adept at deciphering dreams. Or do we instead have the universal motif of the wife whose wise advice is ignored by her foolish husband? The introduction of Pilate's wife in any event adds one more character who knows that Jesus should not be crucified.

Although pious legend has appropriately made up the lack, our text says next to nothing about Pilate's wife. Did Matthew's church remember her as a god-fearer or a Christian (so Origen)? One might also ask whether she furthers a typology. Jesus is like the patriarch Joseph in that the two are, out of 'envy' (Gen 37.11), sold for 'thirty pieces' of money by a Judas who belongs to a group of 'twelve'. And in *T. Jos.* 14.1 and 5, Potiphar's wife (although for admittedly different motives than Pilate's wife) implores her husband to set Joseph free: 'Your sentence is unjust, for you have punished as a wrongdoer someone who, though a freeman, was stolen ... It is not proper for Egyptians to take away what belongs to others before the evidence has been presented.'

20. For the first time, the chief priests and elders master the popular heart and so command the anonymous majority: the blind lead the blind (15.14). Soon leaders and followers will act together.

The chief priests and the elders persuaded the crowds to ask for Barabbas but to have Jesus killed. The crowds which cry out against Jesus have undergone a reversal of sentiment, for once they welcomed him (21.9). The crowd's fickle metamorphosis – they are no more consistent than the disciples – serves to emphasize the wickedness of the Jewish leaders, for they are responsible for the new hostility.

21–2. And they said, 'Barabbas.' To Matthew's faithful readers the choice must appear inexplicable, an instance of the madness of crowds.

23. Because he has heard his wife's dream, because he knows that Jesus has been handed over out of envy, and because he has interviewed Jesus and found him innocent, Pilate knows that Jesus is not deserving of death. This is why he asks the crowd, 'Why, what evil has he done?' The query – which shows that no cause for death has appeared – is Pilate's feeble attempt to alter sentiment.

The Handwashing (27.24–6)

24. The point is neither Pilate's exoneration nor disobedience to his wife's warning – as though Matthew extols the governor's cowardice. Pilate's 'see to it yourselves' no more excuses him than 'see to it yourselves' excuses the chief priests and elders (27.4). He is rather the antithesis of Joseph, Mary's husband; for if the latter is just and obeys divinely sent dreams, Pilate, who knows that Jesus is just, does not obey the warning that has come to him through his wife's dream – a warning he should not need in the first place were he a just judge. The ineffectual Pilate, having ceded justice to mob rule, remains, despite his handwashing, responsible.

he took some water and washed his hands before the crowd. Cf. Deut 21.1–9 (ritual expiation of murder through the washing of hands over a dead heifer and the confession: 'Our hands did not shed this blood ... set not the guilt of innocent blood in the midst of your people Israel'); Ps 26.6 ('I wash my hands in innocence and go about thy altar, O Lord'); 73.13 ('washed my hands in innocence'); Aristeas, *Ep.* 305–6 (the Jews wash their hands to show they have done no evil). Many commentators suspect that Deut 21.1–9 in particular lies in the background. If so, there is more irony, for the OT text is about Israel not contracting blood guilt.

Pilate is more concerned to deny his own responsibility than he is to do the just thing with an innocent man; so instead of freeing 'the king of the Jews' he washes his hands. His act, which acknowledges that Jesus is about to be murdered, is hypocritical; he is no more free of responsibility than was Adam when he complained about Eve's advice.

I am innocent of this man's blood. The declaration is plainly against the facts.

see to it yourselves. This is what the authorities say to Judas in v. 4 and so belongs to the parallels between them and Pilate. Here the imperative is disingenuous, for Pilate, through his inefficacious actions, has himself seen to Jesus' execution.

25. May his blood be upon us and upon our children! This climactic sentence is not a self-curse but a declaration of responsibility: we acknowledge our involvement if the governor will not. The words are an ironic prophecy (cf. Jn 11.50); for surely Matthew, like so many of the church fathers after him and most modern exegetes, related the cry to the fall of Jerusalem in AD 70; cf. 23.35. This accords with the Jewish habit of associating disaster with sin – even (despite Jer 31.29–30) the disaster of one generation for the sin of another. 'And our children' accordingly carries literal sense. We have here an aetiology, an explanation in terms of collective guilt for the destruction of the capital.

The exegete must distinguish between the original intention of verses and their effects, especially here. Mt 27.25 does not refer to all Israel (neither Jewish Christians nor the Jewish diaspora are represented by the crowd); nor (against Origen and so many after him) should we find here a curse for all time. Nor is the verse an explanation for God's supposed abandonment of Jews or of the supposed end of the Jewish mission. The troubling passage instead functioned for Matthew's first audience as an explanation of the tribulations of Jerusalem and its environs during the Jewish war. For us it can only function as an opportunity for Christians to repent of past wrongs done to Jews.

26. he flogged Jesus and handed him over to be crucified. Mt 10.17 prophesies that missionaries will be flogged, so once more the story of Jesus, the exemplar in suffering, makes his speech come to life. The 'scourging', perhaps intended to recall Isa 53.5 ('by his stripes we are healed'), is not described but only referred to: the grisly particulars are not given. The Roman act of *flagellum*, of tying non-Romans and slaves to a post and then whipping them with knotted leather straps (which sometimes held pieces of metal and/or bone), often preceded crucifixion. And sometimes prisoners were whipped on the way to crucifixion. The horrendous punishment (not humanely limited to forty stripes as in Jewish law) was so severe that it could expose bone and be by itself fatal; so it must have shortened the time spent on a cross. In Jesus' case, he appears to be half dead before he gets to Golgotha, which is why another is compelled to carry his cross and why he expires so soon.

* * * * *

(i) Mt 27.11–26 concerns responsibility for Jesus' death. Blame is attached to three parties: the Jewish leaders, the Jerusalem crowds, and the Roman governor. But if all three are culpable they are not equally culpable. Pilate only responds. He does not initiate: his actions are only the consequences of acquiescence to others. It is not dissimilar with the crowds, which have otherwise had some positive feeling for Jesus; cf. 21.46. Their apparent change of heart comes under outside pressure: 'the chief priests and elders persuaded the people to ask for Barabbas and destroy Jesus.' So the most blame lies with the Jewish leaders, those who slander Jesus before Pilate and stir up the crowds.

(ii) If the main theological theme of 27.26 is responsibility, the literary method is irony. Things are upside down, and words have unintended meaning. The judge of the world, instead of sitting upon his judgement seat, stands before the judgement seat of a lesser. The governor does not govern. While the religious leaders of Judaism rail against God's anointed, the truth is revealed to a pagan. The crowds prefer to free a criminal instead of a just man they once acclaimed. The criminal is named 'Jesus, Son of the Father'. Pilate declares his lack of responsibility in word and deed when he is in fact in charge of the proceedings and their outcome. And the crowd willingly accepts responsibility in words which unwittingly prophesy tragedy for itself. As throughout the Gospel things are not what they seem, and God's will works itself out in unexpected circumstances.

(iii) The report of Jesus before the governor moves the drama forward by accounting for what is to happen next, the crucifixion. But the story equally moves the reader backwards – back to the the trial before the sanhedrin and to the infancy narrative. Consider these echoes:

27.11–26 and 2.1–18

'the king of the Jews' (2.2; 27.11)
'the chief priests' (2.4; 27.12, 20)
'Messiah' (2.2; 27.17, 22)
'all Jerusalem', 'all the people' (2.3; 27.25)
warning to Gentiles in a dream (2.12; 27.19)
plot to kill Jesus (2.13–18; 27.15–26)
suffering of Jewish children (2.16–18; 27.25)

27.11–26 and 26.57–68

the chief priest(s) and elders (26.57; 27.12, 20)
people testify against Jesus (26.62; 27.13)
Jesus is called by others 'the Messiah' (26.63; 27.17, 22)
Jesus is silent (26.62–3; 27.11–14)
Jesus says to his interrogator, 'You have said so' (26.64; 27.11)
Jesus is deemed worthy of death (26.66; 27.24–6)
scenes of mockery (26.67; 27.27–31)

These parallels give Matthew a handsome unity. They also, by creating in the reader a sense of *deja vu*, breed a familiarity which enhances understanding. Repetition imparts importance: what matters is repeated. So the themes and motifs in 27.11–26 which we have met before – the enigmatic passivity of the innocent Messiah, the negative characterization of the hostile Jewish leaders, the rejection of Jesus by so many in Israel and its tragic consequences, and the possibility of salvation for the Gentiles – may all be reckoned among Matthew's major theological interests in composing his Gospel.

THE ROMAN MOCKERY (27.27–31)

[27]**Then the soldiers of the governor took Jesus into the governor's headquarters, and they gathered all the cohort around him.** [28]**Stripping him, they put a scarlet cloak on him;** [29]**and after twisting some thorns into a crown, they put it on his head, and a reed in his right hand; and kneeling before him they mocked him, saying, 'Hail, King of the Jews!'** [30]**And spitting on him, they took the reed and struck his head.** [31]**And when they had mocked him, they stripped him of the cloak and put his own clothes back on him. Then they led him away to be to crucified.**

Parallels: Mk 15.16–20; Jn 19.2–3

This scene, uncharacteristically full of vivid details, partially fulfils the third passion prediction: 'and deliver him to the Gentiles to be mocked and scourged' (20.19), as well as Isa 50.6 ('I gave my back to smiters ... I hid not my face from shame and spitting'). It also in several particulars repeats the conclusion of the trial before Caiaphas: 'Then they spat in his face and struck him, and some slapped him, saying, "Prophesy to us, you Messiah! Who is it that struck you?"' (26.67).

'Every king is proclaimed by soldiers' (Cyril of Jerusalem). But when the Roman soldiers, acting evidently not on order but on their own, give Jesus, who in this paragraph is an utterly passive object, a robe, a crown, and a sceptre and then hail him king they are making fun of him for their own amusement: their homage is pretended. Yet the truth is that the seemingly hapless criminal before them is indeed a king and will shortly wield all authority in heaven and earth (28.18). In this way the irony of the Roman burlesque is itself ironic, and the scene continues the message of 27.11–26: things are the opposite of what they seem to be. Jesus is in truth what he is mocked for being. As Cyril of Jerusalem wrote: the soldiers 'put on him a purple robe. They did it in mockery, but it was a prophetic act; for he was truly a king.'

Even if they did it in scorn, they still did it, and this was a symbol of his royal dignity.'

27. The scene changes and new characters are introduced – an entire Roman battalion (some of whose members will, at the cross, undergo a conversion of sorts). Evidently the setting is the courtyard within the praetorium.

into the governor's headquarters. The governor's headquarters, or *praetorium* (cf. 28.12), was the official residence of a provincial governor; cf. Acts 23.35. Pilate usually resided in Caesarea Maritima and stayed in Jerusalem only in times of potential unrest, and so was there for the great feasts. There is disagreement whether the *praetorium* of our passage should be located in the Tower of Antonia (at the northwest corner of the outer temple), or the old Hasmonean palace, or in Herod's palace in the Upper City.

they gathered all the cohort around him. 'Cohort' – presumably the 'all' is hyperbole – translates the technical military term, *cohors*; cf. Jn 18.3, 12 (of the soldiers at the arrest). The 'cohort' – there was one in Jerusalem during times of peace – was a tenth of a Roman legion, that is, between six hundred and a thousand men. Most would not be legionaries from Italy but non-Jewish Syro-Palestine auxiliaries.

28. Soldiers did sometimes entertain themselves by devising varied torments for victims of crucifixion. The satiric enthronement that follows strangely foreshadows the real enthronement declared in 28.18, where Jesus will be worshipped sincerely.

they put a scarlet cloak robe on him. 'Cloak' refers to a soldier's garb. This probably explains the substitution of 'scarlet' for Mark's 'purple'. For whereas purple was expensive and so firmly associated with wealth and royalty, scarlet was the colour of the Roman soldier's cloak: thus Jesus is dressed as a Roman soldier. It is historically more plausible that, if Roman soldiers did mock Jesus, a red cloak was to hand; and perhaps Matthew or his oral tradition knew this. In any case, the context requires that the 'robe', whether scarlet or purple, serve as a mock royal garb; and for this scarlet is only a little less appropriate than purple, for it too could be a sign of wealth and luxury.

29. Instead of weeping at the injustice, the soldiers, perversely displaying the sickness of human nature, add to it.

twisting some thorns into a crown. The crown of thorns does duty for the royal wreath or diadem; and perhaps the thorns simulate the light rays supposed to emanate from the heads of divinities, rays represented by the points on the royal diadems of, among others, Ptolemaic and Seleucid rulers and Augustus and Tiberius. Whether the thorny crown is just for scorn or also (as in most Christian tradition) causes pain is not stated; but the context – Jesus is not tortured until v. 30 – argues for the former.

a reed in his right hand. A king's rod should be a 'glorious staff' (Jer 48.17), a symbol of might; but Jesus has a sham sceptre. 'Reed' has been brought forward from Mk 15.19, where it strikes Jesus on the head but is not put in his hand.

kneeling before him they mocked him. The image is of men kneeling, as before a king. 'Mocked', which summarizes the scene and so is repeated in v. 31, harks back to the passion prediction in 20.19 ('and deliver him to the Gentiles to be mocked') and points ahead to the crucifixion (where the Jewish leaders mock Jesus in v. 41).

There are two other Matthean scenes which feature Gentiles bowing before Jesus: 2.11 and 15.22. Given that the former associates *proskynesis* with the title, 'the king of the Jews', and has Jesus being given royal gifts, one might divine a connexion: if at the beginning of the Gospel Gentiles reverently bow down before the king of the Jews and offer him treasures, at the end Gentiles mockingly bow down before Jesus, hail him as 'king of the Jews', and give him bogus signs of kingship: robe, reed, staff. The one scene is a burlesque of the other.

Hail, King of the Jews! First-century readers would have been put in mind of the Roman acclamation, 'Ave, Caesar'.

30. Psychological mockery gives way to crude physical abuse.

And spitting on him. 'Spitting' – an act of great contempt (cf. Job 30.10 and the ancient baptismal rite of spitting upon the devil) – also describes the mocking after the first trial (26.67) and strongly recalls LXX Isa 50.6, a text alluded to clearly in 5.39.

31. Jesus' clothes are returned to him (only to be taken away again in v. 35), and the pericope, like 27.11–26, ends with a notice of crucifixion.

* * * * *

(i) Matthew's earthly Jesus is a king. But he is not a potentate. He rules from a cross instead of a throne; he is not served but serves, and gives his life for others. By passively enduring abuse and torment for the greater good, he is the perfect illustration of strength out of weakness, of foolishness shaming the wise. In his character passivity becomes a manifestation of love. As Paul wrote, 'love is longsuffering', or, as the King James Version has it, love beareth all things and endureth all things. Even when evil has run riot, Matthew's Jesus – who could call legions of angels to make all right but does not – chooses both to endure and to endure in silence.

(ii) Interpreters tend to make Jews who act against Jesus representative of Judaism as a whole and to make Gentiles who believe in him or treat him kindly (e.g. the magi and Pilate's wife) symbolize Gentile acceptance of the Gospel. But our passage, which gives much space to Gentiles torturing Jesus, calls this common reading strategy into question. Obviously the Gentile soldiers do not stand for all Gentiles, so why assume that Jewish opponents must stand for all Jews? The truth is that if among the Jews are the Pharisees, the chief priests, and Judas, also among them are Jesus, Peter, the pious women from Galilee, and Joseph of Arimathea. And if among the Gentiles there are the magi and the centurion, there are also among them Pilate and the soldiers who torment Jesus. Participation in the people of God is not an ethnic issue but a matter of faith.

THE CRUCIFIXION (27.32–56)

[32]As they went out, they found a man from Cyrene named Simon. They compelled this man to carry his cross. [33]And coming to a place called Golgotha, which means Place of a Skull, [34]they offered him wine mixed with gall to drink; but when he tasted it, he would not drink it. [35]Crucifying him, they divided his clothes among themselves by casting lots; [36]and sitting down they kept watch over him there. [37]And above his head they put the charge against him, which read, 'This is Jesus, the King of the Jews.' [38]Then two bandits were crucified with him, one on his right and one on his left.

[39] The passers-by blasphemed him, shaking their heads [40]and saying, 'The one who would tear down the temple and build it in three days, save yourself, if you are the Son of God, and come down from the cross.' [41]Likewise also the chief priests, along with the scribes and elders, mocked him and said, [42]'He saved others; he cannot save himself. He is the king of Israel; let him come down now from the cross, and we will believe in him. [43] He trusts in God; let God deliver him now, if he wants to; for he said, "I am the Son of God."' [44]In the same way, the bandits who were crucified with him likewise reproached him.

[45]There was from the sixth hour a darkness upon all the land until three in the afternoon. [46]And about three o'clock Jesus cried out with a loud voice, 'Eli, Eli, lema sabachthani?' that is, 'My God, my God, why have you forsaken me?' [47]When some of the bystanders heard it, they said, 'This man is calling for Elijah.' [48]And immediately one of them ran and got a sponge, filled it with sour wine, put it on a stick, and gave it to him to drink. [49]But the others said, 'Leave off; let us see whether Elijah will come to save him.' [50]But Jesus, again crying out with a loud voice, gave up his spirit. [51]And behold, the veil of the temple was torn in two, from top to bottom. The earth shook, and the rocks were split. [52]And the tombs were opened, and many bodies of the saints who had fallen asleep

were raised, [53]and going forth from the tombs [[after his resurrection]] they entered the holy city and appeared to many. [54]When the centurion and those keeping watch over Jesus with him saw the earthquake and what took place, they were exceedingly afraid and said, 'Truly this man was God's Son!'

[55]Many women were also there, looking on from a distance, who had followed Jesus from Galilee and to serve him. [56]Among them were Mary Magdalene, and Mary the mother of James and Joseph, and the mother of the sons of Zebedee.

Parallels: Mk 15.20–41; Lk 23.26–49; Jn 19.17–30

This haunting scene depicts Jesus as the suffering righteous one akin to the figures in Psalm 22; Isaiah 53; and Wisdom 2; and perhaps its outstanding feature is its scriptural language. Although the OT is not formally introduced, its presence is recurrent:

> 34: wine mingled with gall: allusion to Ps 69.21
> 35: division of garments: borrowing from Ps 22.18
> 38: death between robbers: possible allusion to Isa 53.12
> 39: passers-by wag their heads: cf. Ps 22.7; Lam 2.15
> 39–40: mockery: borrowing from Ps 22.7; cf. 109.25
> 43: mockery: borrowing from Ps 22.9
> 44: mockery: possible borrowing from Ps 22.7 or 69.9
> 45: darkness at noon: allusion to Amos 8.9
> 46: cry from the cross: borrowing from Ps 22.1
> 48: vinegar to drink: allusion to Ps 69.21
> 51–3: earthquake and resurrection: use of Ezek 37; Zech 14.4–5

Scripturally literate readers will come away with two convictions: the death of Jesus fulfils several eschatological prophecies (Ezekiel 37; Amos 8.9; Zech 14.4–5) as well as Psalms 22 and 69 (both Davidic laments).

There are also striking parallels with Wisd 2.10–20, which records the speech of the ungodly who oppress 'the righteous poor man':

> Wisd 2.13: 'he calls himself a child of the Lord'
> Wisd 2.16: 'boasts that God is his Father'
> Mt 27.40: 'if you are the Son of God'
> Mt 27.43: 'he said, "I am the Son of God"'

> Wisd 2.17: 'let us test what will happen at the end of his life'
> Mt 27.49: 'let us see whether Elijah will come to save him'

> Wisd 2.18: 'for if the righteous man is God's son, he will help him, and will deliver him from the hand of his adversaries'

Mt 27.43: 'He trusts in God; let God deliver him now, if he
wants to; for he said, "I am the Son of God"'

Wisd 2.19: 'let us test him with insult and torture'
Mt 27.39–44: 'blasphemed', 'mocked', 'reproved'

Wisd 2.10 'Let us condemn him to a shameful death,
for, according to what he says, he will be protected'
Mt 27.43: 'He trusts in God; let God deliver him now, if he
wants to'

These parallels may, but need not, show direct literary dependence
upon Wisdom (which itself draws upon both Isaiah 52–3 and Psalm
22). Use of a common tradition or collection of motifs is also possible.

The Crucifixion (27.32–8)

32. As it was custom to carry one's crossbeam or *patibulum*, this
transitional verse implies that the scourging (v. 26) left Jesus so
weakened that another had to be coerced to carry his cross.

**As they went out, they found a man from Cyrene named Simon. They
compelled this man to carry his cross.** Cf. 16.24. On a first-century AD
ossuary inscription from the Kidron Valley, published in 1967,
'Alexander son of Simon' appears in Greek on the front and back,
and on the lid in Hebrew is 'Alexander QRNYT'. QRNYT could
mean 'the Cyrenian', and there appear to be other Cyrenians in nearby
ossuaries. So we are faced with the tantalizing possibility that the
ossuary contained the bones of the son of the man who carried Jesus'
cross.

33. **And coming to a place called Golgotha.** 'Golgotha' means 'skull'
(not, as Matthew seems to say, 'place of the skull'). Why the place
(probably a well-known site for executions near crossroads) was
named 'Golgotha' is unknown. Was it because it in some way
resembled a skull? Or because it was a place of execution? Of the two
competing sites, 'Gordon's Calvary' and the vicinity of the Church of
the Holy Sepulchre, the former now seems a poor choice while the
latter could be correct.

Place of a Skull. Only here does Matthew explain a topographical
name. Why is unclear. There is no hint of a connexion with Adam's
skull or Christ as the 'head' of the church, or any other theological
theme. So one might urge the satisfaction of simple curiosity. It is
possible, however, that 'Golgotha' has been retained precisely in order
to be translated: the word 'skull' connotes death and so fittingly adds
to the narrative's dark atmosphere.

34. Only here and in vv. 46 and 50 does Jesus do anything while on his cross. We hear nothing of his faith and courage. The focus is on the responses of others.

they offered him wine mixed with gall to drink. 'Gall' is an allusion to LXX Ps 69.22 ('They gave gall for my bread, and for my thirst they gave me vinegar to drink') – a text alluded to again in v. 48. According to *b. Sanh.* 43a, 'when one is led out to execution he is given a goblet of wine containing a grain of frankincense, in order to benumb his senses, for it is written, "Give strong drink unto him that is ready to perish, and wine unto the bitter in soul"' (Prov 31.6). While this probably does illumine our text, Jesus is not given wine with frankincense but wine with gall. This, the context, and the allusion to Ps 69.22 indicate that the anodyne is offered not out of compassion (as seemingly in Mark) but mockery. Perhaps indeed we should imagine that the drink is an invitation to commit suicide.

but when he tasted it, he would not drink it. Why does Jesus not drink? One common answer, that the refusal accords with the vow of abstinence in 26.29, does not harmonize with 'tasted'. More likely Jesus, having tasted the drink, recognizes either that it is more malicious mockery or that it is a shortcut to death. In any case he endures his torture in full consciousness.

35. Crucifying him. The crucifixion itself is mentioned only in passing. On the matter of what sort of cross was used to crucify Jesus and how he was fastened upon it Matthew is mute. This betrays more than a lack of morbid curiosity. The dearth of details bespeaks a positive distaste for this most barbarous of ancient tortures. Matthew's silence reflects an aesthetic revulsion shared by ancient writers in general.

Archaeologists have recovered in Jerusalem the bones of a certain first-century Jew, Jehouanan. Originally it was thought that marks on his wrists were from nails. This is no longer clear, however; he may have been tied up with rope. In any case, the ancient sources indicate that there was no one way to crucify people: Roman soldiers in fact seem to have morbidly enjoyed affixing the crucified onto crosses in a variety of ways.

they divided his clothes among themselves by casting lots. Matthew's notice – which simply records common custom: executioners were entitled to a victim's garments – contributes two things, the first being the shame of nudity, the second being scriptural fulfilment, for the language is from LXX Ps 22.19.

36. and sitting down they kept watch over him there. The guards, like Pilate, sit. Their posture of ease contrasts with Jesus' agony.

37. Jesus is condemned as 'the king of the Jews'. This Roman mocking of both Jesus and Judaism (cf. Jn 19.21) is for the Christian reader a confession of faith and reminds one of the early Christian version of Ps 96.10: 'The Lord reigns from the wood.'

And above his head they put the charge against him. A résumé of charges, written on a tablet, was sometimes either hung around the neck of one condemned to crucifixion or paraded on a sign before him as he was marched to the site of execution. But we know of no evidence that the résumé was then fastened to the cross as a sort of ridiculing epitaph. Perhaps the singularity of the *titulus* being so displayed was the cause of its being remembered.

38. The two robbers who will revile Jesus in v. 44 are here introduced. Their presence adds to his indignity.

Then two bandits were crucified with him. One is reminded of Isa 53.12: 'was numbered with the transgressors'. That the two criminals are 'robbers', perhaps insurrectionists, creates an ironic link with 26.55: 'Have you come out as against a robber?' Although Jesus is no criminal, he is arrested as one and dies as one.

one on his right and one on his left. Being at his right and left, the bandits are where James and John professedly wanted to be (20.20–3). Jesus' right and left are not, however, now positions of honour.

Mocking the Crucified (27.39–44)

In vv. 27–31 there is a sham coronation: Jesus is given robe, crown, and sceptre and hailed king. Then in vv. 32–8 the cross of 'the king of the Jews' substitutes for a throne. Verses 38–44 continue the royal burlesque by recording the cry of the people before their king: instead of laud there is mockery.

Verses 39–44 build upon the trial narrative, and the mockery at the cross recapitulates the charges thought to make Jesus worthy of death:

Jesus said to blaspheme, 26.65	Jesus is blasphemed, 27.39
witnesses say Jesus threatened to tear down the temple and build it in three days, 26.61	passers-by address Jesus as he who threatened to tear down the temple and build it in three days, 27.40
'Are you the Messiah, the Son of God?', 26.63	'If you are the Son of God', 27.40
Caiaphas the high priest the scribes the elders, 26.57	the chief priests the scribes the elders, 27.41
'the Messiah', 26.63	'the king of Israel', 27.42

39–40. The first words spoken come from hostile passers-by. They are kin to the crowds who call for the release of Barabbas and the crucifixion of Jesus.

Passers-by. Cf. Lam 2.15 ('All who pass along the way clap their hands at you; they hiss and wag their heads'). While crucifixion was sometimes performed at the scene of a crime, it was also common to set up crosses on busy streets as an aid to deterrence.

blasphemed him, shaking their heads. 'Blasphemed him' has the informal sense of 'derided him'. 'Wagging their heads' is an allusion to Ps 22.7: 'All who see me mock me; they make mouths at me, they wag their heads.'

The one who would tear down the temple and build it in three days. This takes up the accusation at the trial, 26.61. Here the charge may be laden with irony. For the text may assume that the rejection of Jesus led to Jerusalem's misfortunes in AD 70; if so, it follows that those mocking Jesus as he who would take down the temple are themselves responsible for the temple's destruction.

save yourself, if you are the Son of God, and come down from the cross. 'If you are the Son of God' summons memory of the temptation narrative. There Jesus undergoes three temptations, just as here there are three mockeries; and there the devil twice prefaces his speech with 'If you are the Son of God' (4.3, 6). Now throughout Matthew Jesus' divine sonship takes up two OT models. On the one hand, God's Son is the enthroned king, victorious over his enemies; on the other, God's Son is true Israel, called to a life of humble obedience and service. Those who mock the crucified are like the devil in that they set these two concepts over against each other and propose a path without affliction. But Jesus refuses to sunder the two concepts of sonship; he refuses to reign without the suffering of obedience. He rather eschews self-serving acts of power and lets God save him in God's own time. Sonship does not mean leaving the cross but staying on it.

Throughout vv. 39–44 the jeering parties unwittingly speak the truth. Jesus *is* the Son of God (vv. 40, 43). The destruction of the temple (vv. 40) – which will almost immediately be foreshadowed by the veil rending – is a consequence of the rejection of his ministry. Jesus does save others (vv. 40, 42). He is the king of Israel (v. 42). He does trust in God (v. 43). And if he does not come down from the cross and save himself (vv. 40, 42), he does, in God's good time, overcome death. The ridicule, despite its source, discloses the truth.

41. Representatives of the sanhedrin, imitating the passers-by, join the taunting. They use the third person, talking to each other instead of to Jesus. He no longer has even the dignity of being directly addressed.

42. This is, like 12.38 and 16.1, one more vain demand for a sign. But only the sign of Jonah is to be given, and it requires that the Son of man first die. Jesus, who by hanging on the cross is simply being faithful to his own teaching (cf. esp. 10.38–9; 16.24–5), cannot save himself because he must, through death, save others (20.20). He finds his kingship by losing it.

He saved others; he cannot save himself. The leaders' words go even further than those of the passers-by: the latter challenged Jesus to save himself; the authorities are sure he cannot. Although intended as sarcasm (cf. v. 40), readers who believe know that Jesus has the ability to free himself (26.53), and further that Jesus' mission is to save others (1.21), that he has already delivered people from disease (cf. 9.21–2) and physical danger (8.25; 14.30), and that in hanging upon the cross he is redeeming the world (20.28; 26.28).

He is the king of Israel. Cf. the inscription on the cross. Jews say 'king of Israel' (only here in Matthew), not 'king of the Jews'.

let him now come down from the cross. Cf. v. 40. Calvin commented: 'As Christ did not at once tear himself away from death, they reproach him with impotence. This is too much the way of the wicked at all times, to measure God's power by present appearances, thinking that what He does not do He cannot do ... It is contrary to the nature of faith to insist on the adverb "now".'

and we will believe in him. The assertion, which takes up Christian confessional language (cf. Acts 11.17; 16.31; 1 Tim 1.16), is of course false. Even the resurrection does not dissuade the authorities from their chosen course (28.11–15; cf. Lk 16.31).

43. This redactional insertion, which reverts to the Psalm already alluded to in vv. 35 and 39–40, offers the last of three challenges:

    40: save yourself
    40, 42: come down from the cross
    43: let God save him

The three challenges are in truth one: avoid crucifixion.

He trusts in God; let God deliver him now, if he wants to. Cf. Judg 10.14 ('cry to the gods whom you have chosen; let them deliver you in the time of your distress'). The words reflect Ps 22.8: 'Commit your cause to the Lord; let him deliver – let him rescue the one in whom he delights!'

for he said, 'I am the Son of God.' This harks back to v. 40, which in turn depends upon 26.63. There might also be an allusion to Wisd 2.16 ('boasts that God is his father') or 18 ('For if the righteous man is God's son, he will help him, and will deliver him from the hand of his adversaries').

44. Matthew knows nothing of Luke's repentant robber. Rather, the reviling comes to a climax as both convicted criminals castigate Jesus: even those suffering his fate mock him.

The Death of Jesus (27.45–50)

45. Matthew generally shows little concern for chronological specification. Most of his pericopae are strung together with no account of the interval between them: we are simply left with the impression of great lapses of time. But 21.1–28.15 squeezes many events into a few days. This retards the narrative tempo as the book moves to its climax. Then time slows even further as hours begin to be counted: 'from the sixth hour ... until the ninth hour.' The effect, when united with the portentous darkness, is to grind all to a halt, and (to borrow from Wordsworth) one feels 'Weight and power, Power growing under weight'.

There was from the sixth hour a darkness upon all the land until three in the afternoon. Cf. Amos 8.9: 'On that day, says the Lord God, I will make the sun go down at noon, and darken the earth in broad daylight ... I will make it like the mourning for an only son.' The commentary on 24.30 documents several associations of darkness. They are not exclusive of one another but rather together contribute to interpretation: Jesus' death recalls the creation narrative (Gen 1.2) and presages the eschatological consummation (cf. 24.29); it is an omen of divine displeasure or judgement, a sign of cosmic significance, and a token of Nature's sympathy and mourning; and it makes Jesus resemble other famous individuals – including rabbis – whose deaths induced supernatural dusk.

Verse 45 says that there was darkness for three hours. No other circumstance for the interval between noon and 3 p.m. – typically the brightest time of day – is noted. But that the darkness is accompanied by silence is implied by v. 46, where speech terminates the period. So the darkness is silent, and although time advances, nothing happens: the narrative stops. Such narrative stillness is a common literary device. The effect is to isolate and so magnify a single circumstance: all attention is directed to one thing. Cf. *LAB* 19.16, where the angels cease their songs when Moses dies.

46. The crucified finally speaks. When he does, it is not to human beings but to God.

Eli, Eli, lema sabachthani? This is from Ps 22.2. Because a translation follows, one may ask why the Aramaic is given at all. The answer is twofold: (i) the words were Jesus' last and therefore deemed especially important; and (ii) without them the misunderstanding about Elijah would be unintelligible.

My God, my God, why have you forsaken me? Christian sensibility has often been reluctant to imagine that Jesus breathed his last with a cry of dereliction. Many have thought that he did not recite only the first verse of the psalm but continued with the rest. Maybe the rest of the psalm, repeated in a weak voice, was lost in the noise of the moment. Others have supposed that, whatever be the truth regarding Jesus himself, our evangelist and his first readers would have understood the quotation of Psalm 22.2 to be like a Jewish midrash, in which the first part of a verse is quoted and the rest assumed; and as Psalm 22 moves on from complaint to faith and praise, so should Jesus' words imply the same.

This interpretation dulls the impact of our verse, which is the culmination of a Matthean theme. Jesus is first abandoned by his own home (13.53–8), then by his disciples (26.56, 69–75), then by the crowds (27.15–26). The climax of this progressing desertion is the experience, following three hours of divine darkness and silence, of felt abandonment by God (who is here no longer addressed as 'Father'). This does not express a loss of faith – certainly the soldiers who soon confess Jesus Son of God have witnessed no such loss – but is instead a cry of pain in a circumstance (unparalleled elsewhere in the narrative) in which God does not seem to be God. And yet the truth, apparent from what follows, is that God has not forsaken Jesus. The experience of abandonment, although overwhelmingly real, is not the final fact. Vindication follows.

This man is calling for Elijah. The bystanders misunderstand 'My God' and instead hear 'Elijah'. This then becomes the opportunity to mock Jesus again. They joke either that the prophet – who did not die but ascended to heaven – will come to Jesus' personal aid, or perhaps that he will set certain eschatological events in motion. The (deliberate?) misinterpretation is ironic, because while the people wait to see if Elijah will come (v. 49), readers know that Elijah himself has borne testimony to Jesus (17.3) and further that John the Baptist, in the role of Elijah, has both ministered to Jesus and confessed him Messiah (3.11–17; 11.1–19)

48. Why the misunderstanding about Elijah should lead someone to give Jesus a drink is not said. Are we to surmise that Jesus' words are indistinct because of his condition and that the onlookers want to hear more of what he might say?

And immediately one of them ran and got a sponge. This refers back to v. 47 and so implies that the person is a Jewish by-stander, not a Roman soldier.

filled it with sour wine. 'Sour wine' creates an allusion to Ps 69.22 and so seemingly furthers the mocking or torment, in which case one can think either of its bitter taste (cf. Prov 10.26) or of it prolonging Jesus' life and so protracting his pain. Certainly an act of kindness does not suit the context, which, before v. 54, is one of unremitting hostility. The text probably assumes knowledge of Psalm 69 and the 'prophecy' that the wine was mixed with poison or gall.

put it on a stick, and gave it to him to drink. Cf. Ps 69.21: 'They gave me poison for food, and for my thirst they gave me vinegar to drink.'

50. The end comes with an inarticulate and uninterpreted cry. This is startling. People do not usually die with a shout, much less those who have been beaten and tortured. Is this then a hint of triumph? Or of Jesus' power even in death?

But Jesus, again crying out with a loud voice. Cf. v. 46. Perhaps pertinent are texts in which a scream is the response to unjust affliction: Gen 4.10; Exod 3.7; Rev 6.9–11; *T. Job* 19.4. In each of these instances God soon responds.

gave up his spirit. Matthew emphasizes the voluntary nature of Jesus' death (a theme so important in John and the Fathers): he returns his life or spirit (not the Holy Spirit) to the God who gave it.

Signs and Wonders (27.51–4)

This passage, which makes plain the eschatological meaning of the crucifixion, and which breathlessly moves the reader to the climax in v. 54, features parataxis, divine passives, and extensive parallelism:

And	the veil	was rent
and	the earth	was shaken
and	the rocks	were rent
and	the tombs	were opened
and	many bodies	were raised

Ezekiel 37, which was commonly read as a prophecy of eschatological resurrection, informs vv. 51b–3. There is a close resemblance between v. 52 and LXX Ezek 37.12, and there is an earthquake in Ezekiel 37. Matthew, however, does not mention bones – surely odd if that OT text is the exclusive background. There is even more influence from LXX Zech 14.4–5, which was also thought by the ancients to prophesy the resurrection. In both Matthew and Zechariah: (i) a resurrection of the dead (so the ancient interpretation) takes place immediately outside Jerusalem (contrast Ezekiel 37, where the resurrection is in the Diaspora); (ii) there is an earthquake; (iii) the Greek verb 'to split' is used in the passive, in connexion with a mountain (Zechariah) or rocks (Matthew); and (iv) the resurrected are called 'the holy ones'.

51. God, who has, for several chapters, seemingly remained aloof, now vindicates Jesus with a shower of astounding miracles. Nature speaks again, loudly; cf. v. 45.

And behold, the veil of the temple was torn in two, from top to bottom. Commentators have long debated the significance of 'the veil of the temple'. Is it the inner veil that covered the Holy of Holies or the outer curtain that separated the sanctuary from the forecourt? If it is the latter, then the rending must foreshadow or symbolize or inaugurate the destruction of the temple in AD 70, and thereby vindicate Jesus' prophecy against the place (24.2). Further, it is most appropriate that, immediately after people mock Jesus for his prophecy about the temple (v. 40), his words should be vindicated.

Other commentators take 'veil' to be the inner veil before the Holy of Holies and conclude that v. 51a signifies that the death of Christ makes the sacrificial system obsolete and that Gentiles – that is, those outside the cult – now have benefits heretofore effected only for Jews by the temple service. Appeal is made to Heb 6.9; 9.1–28; 10.19–22. The ancient tradition of the release of the Holy Spirit from confinement in the temple and going forth into all the world can be associated with this understanding.

The interpretation which relates the rending of the (outer) veil to the destruction of AD 70 is to be preferred. (i) The context refers to Jesus' prophecy of destruction (v. 40). (ii) The other signs surrounding the cross have an eschatological background, and there are Jewish texts which announce that the old temple will not continue into the new age. (iii) All the other portents around the cross are public, and if the rending is too – do not the guards see it? – then the veil must be generally visible, which excludes the inner veil. (iv) Matthew's Greek has great force and unquestioningly depicts a miracle if referred to a curtain eighty feet high. The effect is less dramatic if the words concern the much smaller inner veil.

According to Josephus, a Babylonian curtain, embroidered with blue, scarlet, linen thread, and purple hung before the main entrance of the sanctuary at the back of the vestibule, and 'worked into the tapestry was the whole vista of the heavens'. If this is the curtain of v. 51a, the picture is of the heavens splitting, something which occurs in the OT and came to be a common item of eschatological expectation.

The earth shook. Cf. 24.7; 28.2; Zech 14.5. Earthquakes – which ancients typically viewed not as whims of nature but as responses to human wickedness – are sometimes linked with the advent of a supernatural being; with judgement; with the deaths of great persons; and with tragedy in general.

and the rocks were split. This line elaborates on one of the effects of the earthquake: fissures appeared.

52. Jesus' death is a resurrecting death: the dead are revived by his dying. As he passes from life to death they pass from death to life.

And the tombs were opened. This draws upon LXX Ezek 37.12–13; see above.

and many bodies of the saints who had fallen asleep were raised. 'Sleep' was a common metaphor for death, which does not of itself imply an unconscious interim state. 'The holy ones' (cf. LXX Zech 14.4–5) is a designation not of angels but of saints. One should think of pious Jews from ancient times. Although the 'many' came to be commonly equated with all the redeemed of pre-Christian times, the text does not support this notion. We seem rather to have a local phenomenon, the primary purpose of which is testimony to Jesus in and around Jerusalem.

The text ignores a question so many have asked: what happened to the saints? Did they ascend to heaven with Jesus? Or did they (like Lazarus) return to earthly life (so *Acts of Pilate* 17.1: Simeon came to life only to die later; cf. Theophylact, who also records the opinion that some of those resurrected are, a thousand years later, yet alive).

53. The 'saints', as representatives of the Jewish past, add their testimony to Jesus, which confirms the Christian present.

and going forth from the tombs. Cf. Ezek 37.12: 'and I will bring you forth out of your tombs.'

[[after his resurrection]]. Although the phrase appears in all mss. and versions, it is absent from the Diatessaron, from Eg. Pap. 3 frag. 1 recto, and from the Palestinian Syriac Lectionary. It is likely a later gloss, presumably added to reserve to Jesus the honour of being the very first to rise from the dead; cf. Col 1.18; Rev 1.5. As it stands, one could infer that while the rocks split and the graves open when Jesus dies, the holy ones remain in their tombs until Easter: odd indeed. Further, how could Matthew write in v. 54 that the centurion and those with him 'saw the earthquake and what took place' if 'what took place' includes events of a later date?

they entered the holy city. 'The holy city' is here ironic.

54. The soldiers, who are set up as witnesses in v. 36, take up the title used to ridicule Jesus in vv. 40 and 43 and make it a sincere confession.

When the centurion and those keeping watch over Jesus with him. 'Those ... with him' reminds one of the guard that earlier mocked Jesus (vv. 27–36), as does 'keeping watch', which harks back in particular to v. 36 ('they kept watch over him'). This makes the confession all the more forceful: it represents a fundamental reformation of opinion. Weight is also added to the confession by the status of the high rank of the Roman centurion, who reminds one of the believing centurion in 8.5–12.

saw the earthquake and what took place. The soldiers see the earthquake and the events it inaugurates. More likely than not they also see the veil; see above.

Truly this man was the Son of God! Although there is no definite article before 'son of God', and although the soldiers are pagans, the meaning is not 'a son of God' (= 'a divine being') but '(the) Son of God'. The Roman soldiers are so overcome that they utter the full Christian confession (cf. 3.17; 14.33; 16.16; 17.5).

This is the third occasion on which the themes of Jesus as Son of God and the destruction of the temple have appeared in close connexion: 26.61–4; 27.40, 51–4. In the first Jesus is accused of threatening the temple and asked if he is God's Son. In the second he is mocked for claiming divine sonship and for being able to tear down the temple. In the third the temple's destruction begins and Jesus is confessed Son of God. The sequence reflects Jesus' status as the messianic Son of David according to 2 Samuel 7, where it is promised that David's son will be God's son and that he will build a house (temple) in God's name.

Many commentators see the soldiers as representatives of the Gentiles, who are now, after the death of Jesus, welcomed into the people of God. This seems likely, on the condition that this interpretation is not, as so often, taken to imply that God has rejected Israel.

The Faithful Witnesses (27.55–6)

When Jesus comes into Jerusalem he is accompanied by disciples and hailed by crowds. But the crowds soon turn hostile and the disciples forsake him and flee. And now, at the end, only several women from Galilee – whose relative unimportance for Matthew is communicated by their absence until now from the story – are left. Moreover, we do not read that they comfort or serve him. On the contrary, they, unlike the confessing soldiers, only look on 'from afar'. Their helpless presence only accentuates Jesus' loneliness.

In these anti-climactic verses, Matthew refers to many women, three of whom he names: Mary Magdalene, Mary the mother of James and Joseph, and the mother of the sons of Zebedee. In v. 61, in connexion with the burial, he names as witnesses Mary Magdalene and 'the other

Mary' (= Mary the mother of James and Joseph). And in 28.1ff. the two Marys again appear, this time as witnesses to the empty tomb and the resurrected Jesus. So the women lend both credibility and continuity to the story by serving as eye-witnesses to the confessional triad: Jesus died, was buried, was raised.

55. This is the first mention of the women followers of Jesus.

Many women were also there, looking on from a distance. Cf. v. 61. Is there an allusion to Ps 38.11 ('My friends and companions stand aloof from my affliction')?

who had followed Jesus from Galilee and to serve him. Cf. 8.15 (Peter's Galilean mother-in-law 'serves' Jesus); Lk 8.1–3.

56. Mary Magdalene. In Eastern Christianity, Mary Magdalene is, despite the tradition that seven demons dwelt within her (Lk 8.2), 'isapostolos', that is, equal to the apostles. Only in the West is she conflated with the sister of Lazarus (Mary of Bethany) and the woman of Lk 7.36ff. In some legends she is the travelling companion of St John the evangelist, whom she marries at the wedding at Cana.

Mary the mother of James and Joseph. This Mary has often been equated with the Mary of Jn 19.25, that is, Mary of Cl(e)opas. But she has also often been identified as Jesus' mother, for in 13.55 Jesus' brothers include a 'James' and a 'Joseph'; and John's Gospel (preserving tradition?) has Jesus' mother at the crucifixion. It is, however, odd that Jesus' mother would be identified by something other than her relationship to her son Jesus, or that the woman of chapters 1–2 would be called 'the other Mary' in v. 61 and 28.1. Further, 'James' and 'Joseph' were common names, so a first-century reader could easily suppose that two different women had sons with those names.

the mother of the sons of Zebedee. The third woman named in Mk 15.40 is 'Salome'. Did Matthew's tradition identify Salome as the mother of the sons of Zebedee? It is also possible that Matthew simply substituted a character from his story for another he knew nothing about. In either case the reader is taken back to 20.20 and the woman's request for James and John. Here she learns the true meaning of being on Jesus' left and right. Her presence also serves as a foil for her sons' cowardly absence.

* * * * *

(i) Matthew does not recount the glorious death of a martyr. Of Jesus' heroic valour and faith we hear nothing. Verses 32–50 do not encourage or inspire but rather depict human sin and its frightening freedom in the unfathomable divine silence. There is terror in this text. The mocking and torture of the innocent and righteous Son of God are not intended to make but to shatter sense, to portray the depths of irrational human depravity. And the patient endurance of God, which goes on for so long that the Son himself screams out feelings of abandonment, powerfully conveys the frightening mystery of God's seeming inactivity in the world. Verses 32–50 are the divine absence, a sort of deistic interlude, a portrait (in Luther's phrase) of *Deus absconditus in passionibus*. They are akin to portions of Job, and like the speech out of the whirlwind they can evoke what Rudolf Otto called the *mysterium tremendum*. 'You are a God who hides yourself, O God of Israel, the Saviour' (Isa 45.15).

(ii) While vv. 32–50 are seemingly devoid of supernatural activity, vv. 51ff. offer an explosion of the supernatural. One cannot but recall the habit of world mythology and literature to encircle the ends of great figures with extraordinary events. Trees bloomed out of season and powder fell from the sky when Buddha slipped away. The heavens shook when Moses was taken to God. As Francis of Assisi left the body, larks, otherwise only heralds of dawn, sang at night. And when Milarepa, the Tibetan yogi, died, comets flashed, flowers floated to earth, and strange sounds were heard. These parallels show that vv. 51ff. are in one important respect conventional.

At the same time, the Matthean signs have their own special meaning. First, most of them, and perhaps all of them, are eschatological in nature. It follows that the Day of the Lord dawns on Golgotha: the divine judgement descends, and the first fruits of the resurrection are gathered. The end of Jesus is the end of the world in miniature.

Second, the miracles come only *after* Jesus dies. Before then the Son's passivity is matched by God's passivity – so much so that the bystanders can jeer and proclaim God's indifference. But the preternatural events which follow death refute the mockers: their calls for a sign are more than answered. God does indeed fight for the one who has not fought for himself. The mystery is only why God is tardy, why torment and death must come first. Whatever the answer to that eternal question might be, the sequence itself cannot surprise. For that same sequence is near the heart of Jesus' own preaching, in which, again and again, tribulation and suffering precede vindication and victory (e.g. 5.10–12; 10.17–23; 24.4–34). Yet again Jesus' life is illustrated by his speech.

(iii) The passion and resurrection constitute the narrative climax of Matthew's story. In many ways the entire narrative leans forward, so to speak, to its end, especially to 27.32ff., so that the reader of earlier sections is never far from thinking of what is to come. Already in chapter 2 the chief priests and scribes conspire with secular authority to kill 'the king of the Jews', so that the end is foreshadowed in the beginning. Again, in chapter 14 the story of John the Baptist's demise is told in such a way as to anticipate Jesus' cruel fate. Mt 5.38–42; 10.17–23; 17.1–8; and 20.21 also foreshadow the ending. Additional preparation for the passion narrative emerges from the conflict stories: the growing strife between Jesus and the Jewish religious establishment inexorably leads to the trial, which in turn leads to the appearance before Pilate and Jesus' execution. Then there are the passion predictions, both explicit and implicit. These regularly move the reader from present narrative time to future narrative time, to the crucifixion in chapter 27. So too do the sayings about taking up one's cross and the interpretation of Jesus' death in 20.28.

(iv) Whether due to authorial design or not, the crucifixion narrative nicely balances the infancy narrative. In both chapters 2 and 27 Jesus is called 'the king of the Jews', he is passive, and people seek to kill him. Further, whereas in chapter 2 Jesus' birth is signalled by a light in the sky, in chapter 27 his death is accompanied by a heavenly darkness. And if, after Jesus' birth, Gentile foreigners, who otherwise play no role in the story, testify to his messianic status and worship him, after he dies Roman soldiers, who appear only in the crucifixion narrative, attest that Jesus is Son of God.

(v) There is striking resemblance between vv. 51ff. and 28.1ff:

The death of Jesus	*The resurrection of Jesus*
'and behold'	'and behold'
an earthquake	an earthquake
opening of tombs	opening of tomb
resurrection	resurrection
those guarding Jesus fear	those guarding Jesus fear
witnesses go to the holy city	witnesses go to the city
women witnesses (including two Marys)	women witnesses (including two Marys)

The resurrection of the saints foreshadows the resurrection of Jesus.

THE BURIAL OF JESUS AND THE GUARD AT THE TOMB
(27.57–66)

[57]**When it became evening, there came a rich man of Arimathea, named Joseph, who was also a disciple of Jesus.** [58]**Going to Pilate, he asked for the body of Jesus. Then Pilate ordered it to be given to him.** [59]**Taking the body, Joseph wrapped it in a clean linen cloth,** [60]**and he laid it in his own new tomb, which he had hewn in the rock. He then rolled a great stone**

before the door of the tomb and went away. [61]Mary Magdalene and the other Mary were there, sitting opposite the tomb.

[62]On the next day, which is the one after the day of Preparation, the chief priests and the Pharisees were gathered before Pilate [63]and said, 'Lord, we remember what that impostor said while he was still alive, "After three days I will rise again." [64]So command the tomb to be made secure until the third day, lest his disciples come and steal him away and say to the people, "He has been raised from the dead," and the last deception would be worse than the first.' [65]Pilate said to them, 'You have a guard of soldiers. Go and make it as secure as you can.' [66]So going with the guard they made the tomb secure by sealing the stone.

Parallels: Mk 15.42–7; Lk 23.50–6; Jn 19.38–42

The chief purpose of 27.55–66 is to prepare for the next section: the stories about the burial and the guard set the stage for 28.1ff. The tomb that is filled here is emptied there. The stone that is here rolled before the door of the tomb is there rolled away. The guard that secures the sepulchre here proves ineffective there. The leaders who here worry that the disciples will come and steal Jesus' body there put out the lie that just such a thing has happened. And the women who now see all later become witnesses to the empty tomb and the risen Lord.

The Burial of Jesus (27.57–61)

A corpse can be either disposed of dishonourably or given an honourable burial. In view of how Jesus has been treated throughout the passion narrative, one would anticipate for him the former treatment. But thanks to Joseph of Arimathea's unexpected and reverent intervention, Jesus is properly buried. Further, like the kings of Israel, he is buried near Jerusalem (1 Kgs 15.8, 24; etc.).

57. When it became evening alludes to Deut 21.23 ('his corpse must not remain all night upon the tree; you will bury him that same day') and continues a series of chronological notices:

27.1	morning
27.45	from the sixth to ninth hour
27.46	around the ninth hour
27.57	evening

there came a rich man. Many have recalled Isa 53.9: 'And they made his grave with the wicked, and with a rich man in his death.' The problem is that 'and they made his grave with the wicked' has nothing to do with Matthew's text. Further, the LXX has: 'I will give the wicked for his burial and the rich for his death.' The targum is also far from Matthew. It is nonetheless possible that the evangelist, who quotes Isa 53.4 in 8.17, had in mind the Hebrew and that he ignored the context of 'and with a rich man in his death' (recall the very loose use of Scripture in vv. 9–10).

of Arimathea. Although Arimathea was not in Galilee, we know little else about it. Ancient writers and modern scholars have identified it with several sites.

named Joseph. Although we know nothing of Joseph of Arimathea beside the few facts that can be gleaned from the canonical Gospels, Christian tradition has delighted to expand his biography. The *Gospel of Nicodemus* has him establish the Christian community at Lydda, and late legends have him going to Britain and founding the first English church.

who was also a disciple of Jesus. Mk 15.42 tells us that Joseph was 'a respected council [= sanhedrin] member' and 'was himself also awaiting the kingdom of God'. The last phrase may imply that Joseph, who buried Jesus, became a follower of Jesus – but only after the resurrection. Matthew, however, bypasses all ambiguity and thereby produces one more parallel between John and Jesus, for the former was buried by his disciples (14.12). The promotion of Joseph to pre-Easter discipleship makes it impossible that he voted to condemn Jesus and may explain why Mark's 'a respected council member' is dropped, an omission which sustains Matthew's consistently grim portrait of the Jewish leaders.

That Joseph is rich and a disciple proves that, although it is easier for a camel to go through the eye of a needle than for a rich man to enter the kingdom of God, with God all things are possible (19.23–6). Joseph does better than the rich young ruler (19.16–30).

58. Unlike Moses, who was, according to tradition, buried by God or angels in a place 'no one knows to this day' (Deut 34.6), Jesus is buried by a man while others look on.

59. Nothing is said of washing or anointing; cf. 26.12; contrast John.

Taking the body, Joseph wrapped it in a clean linen cloth. By laying Jesus in a linen winding sheet, Joseph is following custom. The kindness covers Jesus' nudity (v. 35).

60. Joseph, like so many other Matthean characters, disappears as suddenly as he appears.

and he laid it in his own new tomb. The tomb's newness (which may foreshadow the newness that is to come forth from it) and its belonging to Joseph may reinforce an allusion to Isa 53.9.

He then rolled a great stone before the door of the tomb and went away. Jerusalemites buried their dead outside their city, often in caves intended to hold multiple corpses; such caves were cut into the soft limestone rock. Archaeology confirms that often a body was placed on a shelf (cf. Jn 20.5–6) or recess, and further that a rounded stone or disc (like an upright millstone) was rolled in the groove before the entrance. This stone kept out animals and, when heavy enough, discouraged theft.

That the rock is 'large' means that the tomb itself is large and impressive. The way is prepared for 28.2, where the angel rolls back the rock and so shows supernatural strength.

61. Mary Magdalene. On Mary Magdalene see p. 531.

and the other Mary. This refers back to v. 56, so she should be equated not with Jesus' mother but with the mother of James and Joseph.

Verse 55 tells us that 'many women' were at the cross. Here, however, only two are named. If only two are present, not only have the disciples fled, but by this point even most of the women have abandoned Jesus.

sitting opposite the tomb. The women's posture reminds one of the soldiers, who in v. 36 sit and guard Jesus. But the main point is that they know that he has died and been buried, so their testimony to his rising is all the stronger.

The Guard at the Tomb (27.62–6)

This paragraph is apologetics and polemic at the same time. It refutes the criticism of 28.15: that is, it rebuts Jewish slander against the disciples by showing that they could not have stolen Jesus' body – there was a guard and in any case Jesus' followers were nowhere around – and so reinforces belief in the resurrection.

One can imagine an exchange between Matthew and critical Jews. Matthew: Jesus rose from the dead and his tomb was empty (28.6). Opponent: maybe Jesus never died. Matthew: a Roman guard 'kept watch over him'; surely he was dead before his body was released (27.36). Opponent: there must have been a mix-up in tombs. Matthew: women saw where Jesus was buried (27.61). Opponent: the disciples, seeking to confirm Jesus' prophecy of his resurrection after three days, stole the body. Matthew: the disciples had fled; they were nowhere near (26.56). Opponent: then someone else stole the body. Matthew: a large stone was rolled before the tomb; it was sealed; and Roman soldiers kept watch (28.62–6). Opponent: the soldiers fell asleep. Matthew: they were bribed to say that (28.12–15).

62–3. This is the only mention of the Pharisees in the synoptic passion narratives.

after the day of Preparation. 'The day of preparation' is Friday, when all was readied for the Sabbath. So 'after the (day of) preparation' is a roundabout way of saying the Sabbath, or Saturday.

the chief priests and the Pharisees were gathered before Pilate. Only here and in 21.45 are the chief priests and Pharisees brought together. One is reminded of 2.4, where the chief priests and scribes gather to Herod in the cause against Jesus.

Lord. For the Jewish leaders not Jesus but Pilate is 'lord'; cf. Jn 19.15.

we remember what that impostor said while he was still alive, 'After three days I will rise again.' Cf. v. 40. This is the one exception to Matthew's preference for 'on the third day' instead of 'after the third day'. If taken literally, it stands in tension with v. 64 ('secure until the third day'). Perhaps 'three days' here means, as so often in Jewish texts, 'a few days'. One might also surmise that the chief priests and Pharisees misrepresent Jesus' words – they are false witnesses – or guess that they are harking back to 12.38–42, where Jesus tells the Pharisees that, like Jonah, the Son of man will be three days and nights in the earth.

The Jewish leaders, being self-deceived, deceive others. While they call Jesus a deceiver, it is he who warns against deception: 24.4, 5, 11, 24. Further, in their attempt to persuade Pilate, the chief priests and Pharisees recall a prophecy of Jesus whose truth will soon be dramatically demonstrated.

64. The authorities worry about an eventuality which they will later claim, against the facts, happened.

lest his disciples come and steal him away. Tomb robbery was common.

and say to the people. This reflects missionary competition in Matthew's world: two groups have two different stories for 'the people'.

the last deception would be worse than the first. This sounds proverbial; cf. 2 Sam 13.16; Mt 12.45; Lk 11.26; 2 Pet 2.20; Jn 5.14. The first fraud is Jesus' teaching about himself, the last proclamation of his vindication by resurrection. The irony is that the speakers here indict themselves: their last deception – repudiation of the resurrection in the face of overwhelming facts – will be worse than their first – misleading the crowds about the pre-Easter Jesus; cf. 12.45.

65. You have a guard of soldiers. Cf. 28.11. The soldiers must be Roman. But some, taking the meaning to be not 'You have a guard' but 'You have (your own) guard (and can see to it yourselves)', think of a Jewish guard, specifically the temple police. Against this, in 28.13 the governor's soldiers are identified with the same word used in 27.27, where the soldiers are undoubtedly Romans. Moreover, why do the Jewish leaders need to ask permission of Pilate if they have their own guard to command? And does not 28.14 assume that the soldiers are Pilate's?

66. So going with the guard they made the tomb secure by sealing the stone. Cf. Josh 10.18 ('Roll large stones against the mouth of the cave, and set strong men by it to guard them'); Dan 6.17 ('a stone was brought and laid upon the mouth of the den, and the king sealed it with his own signet and with the signet of his Lords'); *Apoc. Mos.* 42.1 ('God made a triangular seal and sealed the tomb in order that no one might do anything to him for six days'); *Gos. Pet.* 8.32–3 (after rolling a large stone in place the elders and scribes and soldiers mark the tomb with 'seven wax seals', cf. 9.34); *Gos. Naz.* frag. 22 ('And he delivered to them armed men that they might sit over against the cave and guard it day and night'). Is the picture of a (wax?) seal securing the stone so that any tampering will be detected? Or are we to imagine a cord around the stone disc that is attached to the face of the rock tomb by sealing-clay?

* * * * *

(i) Richard Crashaw penned these words:

> How Life and Death in Thee
>   Agree!
> Thou had'st a virgin wombe
>   And Tombe
> A Joseph did betroth
>   Them both.

Although Matthew nowhere hints at a parallel between the new tomb and Mary's virgin womb, there are other similarities between 27.57–66 and the Gospel's opening. Both sections tell of the pious actions of a Joseph on behalf of a helpless Jesus. Neither Joseph says anything. And in both instances Jewish leaders gather to the secular authority to oppose Jesus and his cause. These agreements produce aesthetic satisfaction: beginning and end mirror each other. They also teach a theological lesson: despite all that happens between the birth and death of Jesus, unbelief stands fast, hostility endures. The wicked stay set in their ways.

(ii) Ps 2.1 asks, 'Why do the nations conspire, and the peoples plot in vain?' The theme of human impotence versus divine power runs throughout the Bible, and it is part and parcel of 27.62–6. Jesus' opponents take every precaution to prevent proclamation of the resurrection: they seal the stone and set a guard. But their efforts are futile: the one 'who sits in the heavens laughs'. Human beings cannot oppose earthquakes and angels and the power of God.

EMPTY TOMB AND RISEN LORD (28.1–15)

28 **[1]After the Sabbath, with the dawning of the first day of the week, Mary Magdalene and the other Mary went to see the tomb. [2]And behold, there was a great earthquake. For an angel of the Lord, descending from heaven, came and rolled away the stone and sat upon it. [3]His appearance was as lightning, and his clothing white as snow. [4]For fear of him the guards shook and became like dead men. [5]The angel said to the women, 'Fear not, for I know that you seek Jesus who was crucified. [6]He is not here, for he has been raised, just as he said. Come, see the place where he lay. [7]And go quickly and tell his disciples that "He has been raised from the dead, and indeed does ahead of you to Galilee, where you will see him." Behold, I have told you.' [8]And leaving the tomb quickly with fear and great joy, they ran to tell his disciples.**

[9]And behold, Jesus met them and said, 'Greetings!' And coming to him they took hold of his feet and worshipped him. [10]Then Jesus said to them, 'Fear not. Go and tell my brothers to go to Galilee, and there they will see me.'

[11]While they were going, behold, some of the guard went into the city and told the chief priests all that had happened. [12]After the priests had assembled with the elders, they devised a plan to give a large sum of money to the soldiers, [13]saying, 'Assert this, that "His disciples came by night and stole him away while we were asleep." [14]And if this comes to the governor's ears, we will satisfy him and keep you out of trouble.' [15]So they took the money and did as they were directed. And this story is still told among the Jews to this day.

Parallels: Mk 16.1–8, 9–11; Lk 24.1–12; Jn 20.1–18

The first two paragraphs are united by the similarity between the words of Jesus and those of the angel:

5–7:   Do not fear
        Go quickly and tell his disciples
            he goes ahead of you to Galilee
                where you will see him.

10:   Do not fear
        Go and tell my brothers

> to go to Galilee
> there they will see me.

The repetition makes for emphasis. An additional unifying feature is the artistic correlation between the women and the guards. Both groups gather at Jesus' tomb (vv. 1, 4). Both see an angel (vv. 2–5). Both feel fear (vv. 4, 8). Both leave the tomb in order to tell others what has happened. And both are told by others what they should say (vv. 7, 10, 13–14). The difference lies in this: that while the women will tell the truth to the disciples, the guards will tell a lie about the disciples.

The Opened and Empty Tomb (28.1–8)

This angelophany mirrors the angelic appearance to Joseph in chapter 1:

Chapter 28		Chapter 1
28.1	Introduction of recipients	1.18–20
28.2–3	Appearance of angel	1.20
28.5	Word of consolation	1.20
28.5–6a	Revelation	1.20
28.6b-7	Command	1.21
28.8	Obedient response	1.24–5

Once more, the end is like the beginning.

1. After the Sabbath, with the dawning of the first day of the week. 'Dawning' could have the sense it seems to have in Lk 23.54 and *Gos. Pet.* 2.5; 9.35: the night was dawning. On this interpretation, the events described would take place at the end of the Sabbath, at sunset. Would it make sense, however, for the women to go out 'to see' the tomb if darkness were settling? It is better to envisage the women, having observed the Sabbath and waited until the following dawn, setting forth to visit the tomb on the first day of the week. Mark, Luke, and John all place the visit at Sunday dawn, so this circumstance was probably part of Christian tradition.

Mary Magdalene and the other Mary. The two Marys become witnesses to Jesus' resurrection as they were earlier witnesses to his death and burial; see 27.55, 61.

went to see the tomb is unexplained. Mark's explanation – it is to anoint Jesus (Mk 16.1) – is missing. Did Matthew believe that 26.12 (where Jesus is anointed) stood in tension with Mark's account? Or did he believe that Joseph of Arimathea had already completed the burial rites? Or did he suppose that the introduction of guards makes Mark's explanation implausible? Or did he think that too much time had passed for anointing to make sense? Or was visitation of the newly entombed already in the first century an established part of Jewish burial custom? *Sem.* 8.1 records the habit of visiting graves 'until the third day' (cf. Jn 11.17, 39) in order to prevent premature burial.

2. The women find not Jesus but an angel.

And behold, there was a great earthquake. The '*great* earthquake' moves the '*great* stone' (27.60). Mt 24.7 prophesies eschatological earthquakes (cf. their frequency in Revelation), and 27.51–3 records the earthquake that accompanied Jesus' death, in fulfilment of Zech 14.4–5. The present earthquake also probably has eschatological content: Jesus' resurrection is an end-time event.

Commentators are divided over whether the women witness the descent of the angel and its consequences or only come along later. Given the introduction of the women before v. 2, it may be best to think of them seeing everything.

For an angel of the Lord, descending from heaven, came and rolled away the stone and sat on it. Only Matthew's narrative clearly explains how the stone before the tomb was removed. Is the angel the same one that appeared at the beginning of our story (1.20)? In any case, angels, although often spoken of by Jesus, appear only twice as actors on the Matthean stage, and on both occasions they say, 'Do not fear'.

The stone which Joseph rolled before the tomb and which the guard subsequently sealed is now rolled back by a divine messenger, who sits upon it, an elevated posture of triumph. Whether the stone is rolled back in order to let others look in or to let Jesus out is not said. The former is more likely given that Jesus evidently has risen before the women arrive.

3. His appearance was like lightning, and his clothing white as snow. The angel's appearance recalls that of the transfigured Jesus (17.2; cf. Dan 10.6), and the description of the garment draws upon the theophany of Dan 7.9.

4. The earthquake shakes the guards, the last nameless walk-ons. Ironically they, not Jesus, are the dead ones. This makes for a contrast with 27.54, where the guards who experience an earthquake and other wonders fear and come to faith. Here the guards who experience an earthquake and other wonders fear but do not come to faith.

For fear of him the guards shook and became like dead men. Cf. 14.26; 27.54; Dan 10.7. The first few words are a variation of the old formula, 'fear and trembling' (as in Gen 9.2; 1 Cor 2.3 etc.); the expression connotes terror, not reverence. The response of the Roman guards to the angel has many parallels, for in the biblical tradition fear is what people typically feel in the presence of an otherworldly being.

5. The angel proclaims the Christian message in terms that recall the primitive confession in 1 Cor 15.3–5: Jesus has been crucified, buried, and raised from the dead.

Do not fear. Cf. 1.20. Although we have heard only of the guards' fear, the angel addresses the women (whose fear is not mentioned until v. 8). Calvin wrote: 'Soldiers, accustomed to tumult, were terrified and so struck with panic that they fell down half-dead: no power raised them from the ground; but in the like alarm of the women, a comfort soon came to restore their spirits.'

6. The angel interprets the empty tomb ('he has been raised') and then offers supporting evidence ('see the place where he lay'). Jesus has, in the language of 22.30 (and in refutation of Sadducean belief), entered into 'the resurrection' and become 'like the angels'. He has experienced the end of history.

He is not here, for he has been raised, just as he said. 'As he said' harks back to the passion predictions and proves Jesus a true prophet.

Come, see the place where he lay. The angel invites the testimony of sight to confirm the testimony of speech.

7. And go quickly and tell his disciples. The omission of Peter, given his prominence in Matthew, has puzzled many. But the deletion corresponds to 28.16–20, where Peter is just one of a group.

he has been raised from the dead. Cf. 14.2; 17.9; 27.64. The confessional language makes Jesus 'the first fruits of those who have fallen asleep' (1 Cor 15.20).

and behold, he goes ahead of you to Galilee, where you will see him. Readers will remember the prophecy of 26.32, which is fulfilled in 28.16: the disciples meet Jesus in Galilee.

8. And leaving the tomb quickly with fear and great joy, they ran to tell his disciples. Cf. 2.10 ('great joy'); 8.33. In Mk 16.8 the women fear and say nothing. Here they experience great joy and, in obedience to the angel, tell the disciples. Although afraid because they have encountered a profound mystery, they nonetheless rejoice because of the message given to them.

The First Appearance (28.9–10)

This short Christophany sets forth the proper response to the risen Lord – worship – and, because Jesus' words about Galilee repeat those of the angel, throws additional emphasis upon the climax to come.

9. The women, upon seeing Jesus and hearing him speak,

immediately recognize him (contrast Lk 24.16; Jn 20.14) and bow before him. No mention is made of doubt; contrast 28.17.

And behold, Jesus met them and said, 'Greetings!' The standard Hellenistic greeting (cf. 26.49; 27.29) may here have the sense 'good morning' or 'rejoice'; cf. v. 8; Phil 4.4.

And coming to him, they took hold of his feet and worshipped him. The taking hold of Jesus' feet (cf. Jn 20.17) is unexplained. The parallels indicate that it may be an act of supplication. But throughout worldwide folklore ghosts often have no feet. If the text presupposes this idea, then the grasping of feet indicates that Jesus is not a spirit – precisely the same thought found in Lk 24.37–43.

10. Jesus becomes, after the angel, the second witness to the resurrection; cf. Deut 19.15.

Then Jesus said to them, 'Fear not.' The imperative answers to v. 8 and repeats the angel's consolation in v. 5.

Go and tell my brothers to go to Galilee, and there they will see me. This repeats the angelic message of v. 7. 'Brothers' – the 'eleven' of v. 16 – connotes Jesus' forgiveness of his own.

The Bribing of the Guard (28.11–15)

This episode, without canonical parallel, harks back to 27.62–6 and 28.2–4 and derives from the same source. Its purpose is transparently apologetical. Evidently the Jewish opponents of Matthean Christianity did not dispute the historicity of the empty tomb but rather assigned its cause to theft in the cause of piety. Our story answers that slander in kind: the rumour of theft was a self-serving lie fortified by money.

11. Like the women, the guards go and tell others about the resurrection of Jesus.

While they were going. This refers to the women; cf. v. 7.

some of the guard went into the city and told the chief priests all that had happened. Cf. 27.53, where the saints who have been brought to life go 'into the city' to testify to Jesus; here the guards who became as dead go 'into the city' to tell what has happened. 'Told the chief priests all that had happened' underlines the willful unbelief of the leaders, for surely they should ponder the guard's story of a supernatural visitation. But unlike the soldiers who, upon seeing what has happened, confess Jesus to be God's Son (27.54), these individuals choose to deceive others. Their blindness continues.

12. In an ironic twist, the guards, not the disciples, forsake truth.

After the priests had assembled with the elders, they devised a plan to give a large sum of money to the soldiers. This is the second time the chief priests purchase opposition to Jesus and his cause. The story of

Judas, recalled here through common vocabulary, marked the first (26.14–16). So the resurrection has not changed them at all. Cf. Lk 16.31: 'Neither will they be convinced if some one should rise from the dead.' The boast of 27.42 – 'Let him come down now from the cross and we will believe in him' – was empty.

13. Whereas the women are told by Jesus and the angel to proclaim the truth, the guards, being subjects of mammon, are persuaded by the money of the chief priests and elders to spread lies.

Assert this, that 'His disciples came by night and stole him away while we were asleep.' Readers know that the guards were not sleeping. But even if it were otherwise their testimony would be self-incriminating: what is the value of a slumbering witness? Chrysostom catches the narrative's intent: 'Due to the clearness and conspicuousness of the truth, they are not even able to make up a falsehood ...'.

15. The leaders feared that 'this last deception would be worse than the first' (27.64); but they in truth are the purveyors of deception.

So they took the money and did as they were directed. Cf. the formulas of fulfilment in 1.24–5; 21.6–7; 26.19; also 26.15. The soldiers are like Judas, who also took silver.

And this story is still told among the Jews to this day. 'The story' (literally 'word' in the Greek) that the authorities hand to the guards is the antithesis of both 'the word of the kingdom' (13.19) and the proclamation commanded in 28.19–20. 'Until this day' (cf. 11.23), a standard formula in OT aetiologies, lends a biblical aura to the passage and posits a substantial passing of time between Jesus' death and our Gospel.

* * * * *

(i) Mt 28.1ff. is the necessary ending to Matthew's story. Without the resurrection Jesus' words are vacant and his opponents exonerated. With it, Jesus is vindicated, his cause and authority confirmed, and his opponents disgraced. The empty tomb is a trophy; it stands for the victory of God and the defeat of Jesus' opponents.

(ii) The earthquake, the angelic descent, and the resurrection from the tomb together make the vindication of Jesus an eschatological event. When the Messiah enters into suffering and death and then is raised to new life amidst signs and wonders, he plays out in his own life the eschatological scenario. The end of Jesus is the end of the world in miniature.

(iii) The resurrection – the full meaning of which only becomes apparent in 28.16–20 – makes Jesus himself an illustration of his own teaching. He is, like the prophets before him, wrongly persecuted because of his loyalty to God, and he gains great reward in heaven. He finds his life after losing it. He is the servant who becomes great, the last who becomes first.

(iv) There are several happy parallels between chapter 2 and 28.1–15. In the former, Gentile magi inform Herod and the Jewish leaders in Jerusalem, including the chief priests, of events surrounding the advent of the Messiah. In the latter, Gentile soldiers announce to the chief priests of Jerusalem the events surrounding the resurrection of the Messiah. In the former, the king opposes the infant Messiah and tries to kill him. In the latter, the leaders seek to prevent a staged resurrection by setting a guard at the tomb and, when that fails, by promulgating a false rumour. In the former, the faithful magi worship Jesus and rejoice with great joy. In the latter, the faithful women worship Jesus and go on their way with great joy.

THE CONCLUDING COMMISSION (28.16–20)

[16]**The eleven disciples went to Galilee, to the mountain to which Jesus had directed them.** [17]**And seeing him, they worshipped. But some doubted.** [18]**And Jesus came and spoke to them, saying, 'All authority in heaven and on earth has been given to me.** [19]**So go and make disciples of all nations, baptizing them in the name of the Father and of the Son and of the Holy Spirit,** [20]**teaching them to observe all that I have commanded you. And behold, I am with you all the days, unto the end of the age.'**

Parallels: Mk 16.14–18

The resurrection marks the end of Jesus' earthly time and inaugurates the time of the post-Easter church. In accord with this our pericope (i) looks back to summarize Jesus' ministry as a whole ('all I have commanded you') and (ii) looks forward to the time of the church to outline a sort of programme. So 28.16–20 relates two periods which, although different, have the same Lord and so the same mission.

One expects much from an ending, and in this Matthew meets expectations. If Philo could affirm that Deuteronomy's conclusion 'stands to the whole law-book as the head to the living creature', this is equally true of 28.16–20, which has been called 'the key' to the Gospel, and even something like a table of contents placed at the end.

In addition to the allusion to Dan 7.13–14 in v. 18 (see below), 28.16–20 evokes Moses. Just as the law-giver, at the close of his life, commissioned Joshua both to go into the land peopled by foreign nations and to observe all the commandments in the law, and then further promised his successor God's abiding presence, so similarly Jesus: at the end of his earthly ministry he tells his disciples to go into all the world and to teach the observance of all the commandments of the new Moses, and then further promises his assisting presence.

16. In fulfilment of vv. 7 and 10, the obedient disciples are now in Galilee.

The eleven disciples went to Galilee. No time is specified. 'The eleven' – the 'brothers' of v. 10, whose forgiveness for their flight and denial is implicit – reflects Matthew's precision: in accord with 27.3–10 Judas has been subtracted.

to the mountain to which Jesus had directed them is the most likely translation. But the meaning could also be: 'where Jesus commanded them', which would be a plain reference to 5.1.

17. And seeing him, they worshipped. The form and nature of Jesus' resurrected body are not described at all, nor do we learn whether the appearance was from heaven (cf. Acts 9.3–5) or on earth (as in 28.9–11; Luke 24; John 20–1). The omissions are less surprising given the nearly exclusive emphasis upon Jesus' words.

But some doubted is unexplained. Seeing, some do not see – which leaves readers with many questions. But failure to recognize Jesus (cf. 14.26) does appear elsewhere in the resurrection traditions (Mk 16.11, 13–14; Lk 24.13–35; Jn 20.14; 21.4) and has precedent in Jewish literature: Gen 42.8 (Joseph's brothers do not recognize him); *LAB* 12.1 (the people do not recognize Moses when he descends Sinai); *LAB* 61.9 (Saul and others fail to recognize David); *T. Abr.* 2 (Abraham fails to recognize the archangel Michael, whom he entertained once before).

18. Jesus already exercises his lordship.

All authority in heaven and on earth has been given to me. Cf. 4.8–9 (where Jesus refuses Satan's offer of world rule); 9.8; 11.27; 13.37–43 (where the Son of man rules over the cosmos). The Son of man, who was once handed over to the authority of others, now has authority over everyone. The sense is not that Jesus has the ability to do all things but that he is the ruler of all. Most modern commentators correctly detect an allusion to LXX Dan 7.13–14. The resurrected Lord has fulfilled or proleptically realized the promise of the Son of man's vindication (26.64).

Mt 28.18 implies the same conviction that is expressed in several of the NT christological hymns: namely, that through the resurrection Jesus is exalted and enthroned and made Lord of the cosmos. In other words, God has entrusted to to him all authority. See Eph 1.20–3; Phil 2.6–11; Col 1.15–20; 1 Pet 3.18–22.

19. The prophecy that in Abraham all the families of the earth will be blessed (Gen 12.3) comes to fulfilment in the mission of the church.

So go and make disciples of all nations. The resurrection marks the end of the exclusive focus on Israel. The Jewish mission now gives way to the world mission. But does that world mission exclude or include the Jews? Surely the latter. 'Nations' in Matthew certainly can mean those outside Israel (4.15; 6.32; 10.5–6, 18; 15.24; 20.19). But it can also have comprehensive meaning (24.9, 14; 25.32). When this last is the case the qualifier 'all' is used, and because 'all' appears in 28.19, here too the expression presumably has universal sense. Inclusion of the Jews certainly harmonizes with the universalism of the rest of the passage.

baptizing them in the name of the Father and of the Son and of the Holy Spirit. Cf. Mk 16.16 and the baptismal language of Lk 24.47. Perhaps the commandment, which supplies an aetiology of Christian baptism, should be interpreted in the light of 3.13–17: undergoing baptism is part of the imitation of Christ.

Regarding 'in the name of the Father' etc., it is possible that the one divine name – the revealed name of power (Exod 3.13–15; Prov 18.10; *Jub.* 36.7) – is shared by the Father with Jesus and the Spirit. Some early texts speak of the Father giving his name to Jesus (Jn 17.11; Phil 2.9).

20. Jesus – who as the exalted Lord remains teacher – has the last word. What happened subsequently is not narrated and could only be anticlimactic.

teaching them to observe all that I have commanded you. By teaching what Jesus taught, the church becomes an extension of his ministry.

Verse 20 interprets Jesus as the authoritative bringer of revelation: he brings the new law. The reference is not to one command or to the Sermon on the Mount but to all of Jesus' teaching: not just imperatives, but also proverbs, blessings, parables, and prophecies. Beyond that, more than verbal revelation is involved, for such revelation cannot be separated from Jesus' life, which is itself a command. 'I have commanded' accordingly unifies word and deed and so recalls the entire book: everything is in view. The earthly ministry as a whole is an imperative.

Concerning the order of the verbs in vv. 19–20, perhaps one first hears the call to discipleship, then enters the community through baptism, and finally learns instruction with a view towards obedience. In this case 'make disciples' could refer to pre-baptismal instruction. But it is better to regard 'make disciples' not as the first in a series but as a general imperative which is filled out (although not exhausted) by what follows: baptism and instruction in obedience belong to discipleship.

And behold, I am with you all the days, unto the end of the age. The solemn 'I am with you' recalls 1.23 and 18.20 as well as many biblical and extra-biblical texts about God being 'with' the saints. Here the dominant sense may not be so much that of divine presence as of divine assistance.

That Jesus does not ascend (contrast Acts 1) is a fitting sign of his eternal presence: the risen Lord remains with his people.

* * * * *

(i) From the literary point of view, 28.16–20 satisfyingly completes the Gospel: one could hardly improve upon it. Nothing is superfluous, yet seemingly nothing more could be added without spoiling the effect. The grand dénouement, so consonant with the spirit of the whole Gospel because so full of resonances with earlier passages, is, despite its terseness, almost a compendium of Matthean theology:

- 'Galilee' fulfils the prophecies in 26.32 and 28.7 and with 4.12 creates a literary arch that spans the Gospel.
- 'Mountain' recalls other mountain scenes, especially 4.8 (where Jesus refuses to accept from Satan what he will later accept from the Father) and (perhaps) 5.1; see above.
- 'They worshipped him. But some doubted' recalls 14.31–3.
- 'All authority in heaven and on earth has been given to me' echoes 11.27 as well as a prophecy (Dan 7.13–14) which Jesus has elsewhere applied to himself (24.30; 26.64); it further brings to completion the theme of Jesus' kingship (1.1 etc.).
- 'Make disciples' reminds one of 13.52 (cf. 27.57) as well as the call stories in chapters 4, 8, and 9.
- 'All the nations' terminates the prohibition of 10.5–6 (cf. 15.24) and announces the realization of the promise made to Abraham; cf. 1.1; also Gen 12.3; 18.18; 22.18.
- 'The Father, the Son, and the Holy Spirit' in connexion with baptism reminds one of chapter 3, where the Son is baptized, the Father speaks, and the Spirit descends.
- 'Teaching' sends one back to the five major discourses and the instructions given to missionaries in chapter 10.
- 'All that I have commanded you' is a sweeping retrospective of all Jesus has said and done.
- 'I am with you always' forms an *inclusio* with 1.23 and is similar to 18.20.
- 'The end of the age' is a phrase used earlier (13.39, 40, 49; 24.3); it puts one in mind of Jesus' teachings about the end, and relates Jesus to all of subsequent church history.

Mt 28.16–20 also happily reflects the author's penchant for trumpeting scriptural fulfilment and underlining continuity with

Israel's sacred history. The allusion to Dan 7.14 wraps up the plot in splendid fashion through an overwhelming depiction of the Son of man's triumphant victory and consequent authority: Scripture is fulfilled and the word of Jesus (24.30; 26.64) vindicated. And the implicit comparison of Jesus with Moses and of the eleven with Joshua reactivates once more the Moses typology. This forges still additional links with the chapters leading to the climax and simultaneously signals, for one last time, the organic unity between the new text (Matthew) and the old text (the Old Testament).

(ii) Mt 28.16–20 expresses the meaning of Jesus' resurrection for Matthew. The resurrection is the exaltation of Jesus as Lord of all so that his cause is now universal: 'All authority in heaven and on earth has been given to me. So go and make disciples of all nations.' The resurrection marks the end of an old time and the beginning of a new time: 'baptizing them in the name of the Father, the Son, and the Holy Spirit.' The resurrection is the vindication of the earthly Jesus, whose words and deeds must be call and command: 'Teaching them to observe all that I have commanded you.' And the resurrection is the act by which Jesus becomes the ever present help of his followers: 'I am with you always.'

(iii) Mt 28.16–20 offers a christological concentration. Verse 19 calls Jesus 'the Son'. The allusion to Dan 7.13–14 confirms Jesus' status as 'Son of man'. The statement of exaltation and authority suggests the title 'Lord'. 'All that I have commanded you' presents Jesus as the authoritative teacher (cf. 23.10). The mission to 'all the nations' reminds that Jesus is the Son of Abraham (1.1). And in v. 20 Jesus is 'Emmanuel', 'God with us' (1.23).

(iv) The climax and crown of Matthew's Gospel is profoundly apt in that it invites the reader to enter the story: 28.16–20 is an open-ended ending. Not only does v. 20a underline that the particular man, Jesus, has universal significance, but 'I am with you always' reveals that he is always with his people. The result is that the believing audience and the ever-living Son of God become intimate. The Jesus who commands difficult obedience is at the same time the ever-graceful divine presence.